CCIE Fundamentals
Network Design and Case Studies
Second Edition

Cisco Systems, Inc.

Cisco Press

Cisco Press
201 West 103rd Street
Indianapolis, IN 46290 USA

CCIE Fundamentals
Network Design and Case Studies
Second Edition

Cisco Systems, Inc.

Copyright © 2002 Cisco Systems, Inc.

Published by:
Cisco Press
201 West 103rd Street
Indianapolis, IN 46290 USA

Printed in the United States of America 3 4 5 6 7 8 9 0

Third Printing   July 2001

Library of Congress Cataloging-in-Publication Number: 99-61713

ISBN: 1-57870-167-8

Warning and Disclaimer

This book is designed to provide information about network design. Every effort has been made to make this book as complete and as accurate as possible, but no warranty or fitness is implied.

The information is provided on an "as is" basis. The authors, Cisco Press, and Cisco Systems, Inc., shall have neither liability nor responsibility to any person or entity with respect to any loss or damages arising from the information contained in this book or from the use of the discs or programs that may accompany it.

The opinions expressed in this book belong to the authors and are not necessarily those of Cisco Systems, Inc.

Trademark Acknowledgments

All terms mentioned in this book that are known to be trademarks or service marks have been appropriately capitalized. Cisco Press or Cisco Systems, Inc., cannot attest to the accuracy of this information. Use of a term in this book should not be regarded as affecting the validity of any trademark or service mark.

Feedback Information

At Cisco Press, our goal is to create in-depth technical books of the highest quality and value. Each book is crafted with care and precision, undergoing rigorous development that involves the unique expertise of members from the professional technical community.

Readers' feedback is a natural continuation of this process. If you have any comments regarding how we could improve the quality of this book, or otherwise alter it to better suit your needs, you can contact us through e-mail at feedback@ciscopress.com. Please make sure to include the book title and ISBN in your message.

We greatly appreciate your assistance.

Publisher   John Wait

Editor-in-Chief	John Kane
Cisco Systems Management	Michael Hakkert
	Tom Geitner
	William Warren
Managing Editor	Patrick Kanouse
Senior Acquisitions Editor	Brett Bartow
Development Editor	Andrew Cupp
Project Editor	Dayna Isley
Copy Editor	Keith Cline
Technical Editors	Anthony Bruno, CCIE
	Chris Shaker
	Don Slice, CCIE
Team Coordinator	Amy Lewis
Book Designer	Regina Rexrode
Cover Designer	Louisa Klucznik
Proofreader	Lisa Stumpf
Compositor	Steve Gifford
Indexer	Craig Small

CISCO SYSTEMS

Corporate Headquarters
Cisco Systems, Inc.
170 West Tasman Drive
San Jose, CA 95134-1706
USA
http://www.cisco.com
Tel: 408 526-4000
    800 553-NETS (6387)
Fax: 408 526-4100

European Headquarters
Cisco Systems Europe s.a.r.l.
Parc Evolic, Batiment L1/L2
16 Avenue du Quebec
Villebon, BP 706
91961 Courtaboeuf Cedex
France
http://www-europe.cisco.com
Tel: 33 1 69 18 61 00
Fax: 33 1 69 28 83 26

**Americas
Headquarters**
Cisco Systems, Inc.
170 West Tasman Drive
San Jose, CA 95134-1706
USA
http://www.cisco.com
Tel: 408 526-7660
Fax: 408 527-0883

Asia Headquarters
Nihon Cisco Systems K.K.
Fuji Building, 9th Floor
3-2-3 Marunouchi
Chiyoda-ku, Tokyo 100
Japan
http://www.cisco.com
Tel: 81 3 5219 6250
Fax: 81 3 5219 6001

Cisco Systems has more than 200 offices in the following countries. Addresses, phone numbers, and fax numbers are listed on the Cisco Connection Online Web site at http://www.cisco.com/offices.

Argentina • Australia • Austria • Belgium • Brazil • Canada • Chile • China • Colombia • Costa Rica • Croatia • Czech Republic • Denmark • Dubai, UAE Finland • France • Germany • Greece • Hong Kong • Hungary • India • Indonesia • Ireland • Israel • Italy • Japan • Korea • Luxembourg • Malaysia Mexico • The Netherlands • New Zealand • Norway • Peru • Philippines • Poland • Portugal • Puerto Rico • Romania • Russia • Saudi Arabia • Singapore Slovakia • Slovenia • South Africa • Spain • Sweden • Switzerland • Taiwan • Thailand • Turkey • Ukraine • United Kingdom • United States • Venezuela

About the Contributors

Atif Khan: Edited Chapters 1, 2, 3, 4

Atif Khan, CCIE #1063, is a Network Design Consulting Engineer for Cisco Systems, Inc. He is a senior member of the team providing network design assistance, review, validation, and implementation strategies to Cisco customers. Atif has extensive experience with routing protocols (such as BGP, OSPF, IS-IS, and EIGRP), WAN technologies, and ISP features and products. He has developed and delivered several presentations on such topics as QoS, OSPF Routing Protocol, BGP, and selecting an IP Routing Protocol.

Ronald W. McCarty, Jr.: Edited Chapter 5

Ronald W. McCarty, Jr., is a Network Engineer and Project Manager at Software Spectrum Incorporated. His responsibilities include designing and implementing network solutions to support Software Spectrum's growing global network. Prior to Software Spectrum, Ronald worked at FreiNet GmbH, an ISP in Freiburg, Germany, where he planned and implemented edge networks and Internet services. He received his bachelor's degree in Computer Information Systems from the University of Maryland's international campus at Schwaebisch Gmuend, Germany. Ronald has published articles on the RADIUS protocol, packet filtering with Cisco routers, IP security, and intrusion detection.

Christopher J. Beveridge: Edited Chapter 6

Christopher J. Beveridge is a Consulting Engineer with Cisco Systems, Inc., focusing on ATM WAN systems. Over the past five years, Chris has served in various operations, training, systems engineering, and consulting roles within Cisco/StrataCom. Chris was also the original course developer and trainer for Cisco's BPX ATM WAN switch. For two years, Chris was the senior applications engineer at StrataCom responsible for BT/MCI/Concert's CFRS Frame Relay network based on Cisco/StrataCom IPX/IGX/BPX/AXIS switching platforms. Chris currently serves on the Multiservice Switching Forum working on media control protocols.

Nicole Park: Edited Chapters 7, 8

Nicole Park is a Network Consulting Engineer in the Design and Consulting Team at Cisco Systems, Inc. Before joining Cisco, Nicole was a Senior Technical Support Engineer at 3Com and a Systems Engineer and Instructor for IBM.

George Sackett and Nancy Sackett: Wrote Chapter 9

George Sackett is Managing Director at NetworkX Corporation, a Cisco Professional Services Partner specializing in merging legacy systems and networks to all-service networks. Mr. Sackett has 17 years experience in the networking arena and has previously authored and co-authored several books on networking. He has a master's degree in Management of Technology from Polytechnic University.

Nancy Sackett is Director of Operations at NetworX Corporation. She has 14 years experience in the field of telecommunications, concentrating in large-scale global enterprise networks. Ms. Sackett has been responsible for international telecommunications operations along with strategic and tactical network planning.

Salman Asad: Edited Chapters 10, 11, 19, 20, 21

Salman Asad, CCIE #2240, is a Network Consulting Engineer at Cisco Systems, Inc. During his tenure at Cisco, Salman has specialized in the design of large-scale strategic networks. Previously, he worked on complex routing protocols, dialup access technologies, and security protocols, and he has given numerous technical presentations and training sessions on these subjects. Salman has a bachelor's degree and a master's degree in electrical engineering. Salman's contributions to the CCIE program include helping write the written exam for CCIE and also proctoring the CCIE lab.

Christophe Paggen: Edited Chapter 12

Christophe Paggen is a Cisco Certified Network Expert (CCIE #2659) and a Network Consultant with the NSA Design Team at Cisco Systems, Inc. He has led several design reviews involving multilayer switching technologies and provided training on new products, such as the Catalyst 4000, Catalyst 6x00, and Gigabit Ethernet. He is the multilayer switching virtual team leader for the Network Supported Accounts group. Previously, Christophe provided dedicated support to a major large-scale IP network running a mix of technologies ranging from 10BaseT Ethernet to OC-12 ATM, OSPF and BGP, IP multicast, QoS, and Layer 2/Layer 3 switching.

Beau Williamson: Wrote Chapter 13

Beau Williamson is a Consulting Engineer in the Office of the CTO at Cisco Systems, Inc. His area of expertise is general IP networking and he is currently focused on the area of IP multicast. He received his bachelor's degree in Mathematics (with a specialty in Computer Science) from the University of Texas (Dallas) in 1984 and has been working in the computer and networking technology fields for well over 20 years. He is frequently called on by Cisco customers and internal Cisco engineers around the world to provide consulting services on the design, implementation, and debugging of IP multicast networks. Beau is also the author and developer of Cisco's internal IP multicast training class and frequent presenter on topics related to IP multicasting at Cisco Networkers and CCIE conferences both at home and abroad. He lives in the Dallas, Texas area with his wife and son. When not working on IP multicast, he enjoys a wide range of hobbies including amateur radio, golf, woodworking, and flying his own plane.

Paul Della Maggiora, et al.: Wrote Chapter 14

Gerard Berthet is an Independent Consultant in network and system management.

Paul Della Maggiora, CCIE #1522, is a Product Manager for Cisco Systems' network-management products. For the past eight years, he has helped customers with the management of their LANs. He has participated in network-management product development as well as numerous network designs. Paul also led the team that designed the CCIE recertification test in network management.

Chris Elliot, CCIE #2013, has over 20 years experience in the networking industry, starting with the ARPAnet. For the past eight years, Chris has concentrated on network-management systems. He has written SNMP polling and analysis systems and has been involved in all aspects of network management. Chris is currently an Internetwork Support Engineer in Network Management Systems at Cisco and is a member of the team writing the CCIE recertification exam in network management. He has been a Networld+Interop InteropNet Network Operations Center Team Member since 1993.

Mark Marsula has worked in the networking field since 1984. At Cisco Systems, Inc., he has worked in the Research Triangle Park Technical Assistance Center (TAC) since 1995 as a Customer Support Engineer, an Escalation Engineer, and currently as a Manager. He earned his CCIE certification (#1491) in 1995 and completed the LAN/ATM recertification in 1998.

Rob Pavone, CCIE #1265, is a Network Auditor for Cisco Systems, Inc., within the NSA Customer Advocacy support organization. He has been working at Cisco for 5 years and has 10 years experience in the data communication industry. Rob graduated from the University of Cincinnati, cum laude, with an associate degree in Electrical Engineering Technology in 1988.

Kent Phelps, CCIE #2149, has more than 15 years experience in information systems and communication networks. He has worked extensively with each layer from the physical to the application layer. For the past five years, he has concentrated in network management and analysis from a practical perspective. Kent is an Internetwork Support Engineer in Network Management Systems at Cisco, where he has worked closely with network engineers and end users, finding solutions to monitor and manage their networks. He is a member of the team that is writing the CCIE recertification exam for network management, and he has been a Networld+Interop InteropNet Network Operations Center Team Member since 1993.

Johnnie Salim is currently a Senior Network Consulting Engineer with Cisco Systems, Inc., focusing in network-management design for enterprises and service providers. He joined Cisco Systems in 1993 and is currently with the Network Supported Accounts (NSA) organization within Cisco. Johnnie completed his master's degree in Computer Science at Purdue University in 1992 and achieved CCIE certification in 1994.

David Stiff has been a Product Marketing Engineer in the networking industry for seven years. He has spent the past four years working on network-management systems (in particular, managing switched networks). David has a bachelor of science degree in Mathematics and a bachelor of arts degree in Geography from the University of California, Santa Barbara. When not using SNMP to make the world a better place, he enjoys outdoor activities such as hiking, skiing, and mountain biking.

Jim Thompson has been with the Network Supported Accounts (NSA) group as a Network Consulting Engineer since joining Cisco two years ago, supporting a large manufacturing company and a large government agency. Currently, he is working as a High-Availability Network Consultant in the NSA HA Services program. Before joining Cisco, Jim spent 20 years in the U.S. Army, doing both telecommunications and data networking. Since leaving the military, he has worked for Logicon, doing military and communications simulation studies, and for HP, doing network support engineering.

Vijay Bollapragada, CCIE #1606, is an Internetworking Engineer with the ISP Team at Cisco. He works closely with ISP customers to design future core Internet routing architectures are resolve complex software and hardware problems with Cisco equipment. He has extensive experience with Cisco routers and LAN and ATM switches. Vijay is an adjunct professor in Duke University's Electrical Engineering Department, and he also teaches Cisco engineers and customers several courses he has developed, including: Cisco Router Architecture, IP Multicast, Internet Quality of Service, and Internet Routing Architectures.

Curtis Murphy, CCIE #1521, has worked in the networking industry since 1989 and at Cisco since 1994. While at Cisco, he has worked both as a network troubleshooter in the Technical Assistance Center and as a software engineer in IOS Software Development for mid-range and high-end routers. He is currently working in Cisco's Customer Advocacy organization as a serviceability design

Engineer specializing in IOS products.

Russ White: Wrote Chapter 15

Russ White, CCIE #2635, is an Escalation Engineer focusing on routing protocols and the architecture that supports Cisco engineers worldwide. Russ is well-known within Cisco for his knowledge of EIGRP, BGP, and other IP routing issues.

Anthony Bruno: Edited Chapters 16, 17

Anthony Bruno is a Senior Network Systems Consultant for International Network Services (INS). His network certifications include CCIE #2738, Microsoft MCSE, Bay Networks CRS, Certified Network Expert (CNX) Ethernet, Certified Network Professional, Checkpoint CCSE, and CCNA-WAN. He has been responsible for several major network deployments and mergers at different clients, including one network of more than 1500 routers using BGP, OSPF, EIGRP, IS-IS, and RIP. He has extensive experience with Internet infrastructure design and implementation, including multi-homed ISP configuration. Anthony is also responsible for mentoring other engineers and teaching the design and configuration of such topics as OSPF, Gigabit Ethernet, Frame Relay, and DLSw. He completed his master's degree in Electrical Engineering from the University of Missouri-Rolla and his bachelor's degree in Electrical Engineering from the University of Puerto Rico-Mayaguez.

Himanshu Desai: Wrote Chapter 18

Himanshu Desai, CCIE #1320, is a Project/Consulting Engineer for service provider accounts at Cisco Systems, Inc. He currently leads a team of eight engineers that provides advanced design, implementation, and support services to Sprint. Himanshu has several years of experience helping large organizations define their network requirements, design their networks, and validate their configurations. He has given network-design presentations at Internet seminars worldwide and trained other employees on internetwork protocols and system architecture, multiprotocols, diagnostics, and long-term problem resolution. His paper, "Designing, Configuring, and Troubleshooting Multiprotocols over ATM," has been used by thousands of Cisco customers.

Thomas M. Thomas II: Edited Chapter 22

Thomas M. Thomas II is President and CEO of NetCerts, a virtual community for networkers who desire to learn and practice their networking skills. NetCerts empowers its members so that they can obtain their Cisco certifications by offering technical questions and networking labs relating directly to certification. NetCerts provides an Internet portal service and a variety of other resources for every visitor as well. Tom has been a Course Designer in Cisco Systems' Worldwide Training Division and a Senior Network Engineer and Group Leader of the Advanced Systems Solutions Engineering Team for MCI's Managed Network Services. He has extensive experience in network support and design consulting. He is a member of the OSPF Working Group and author of the Cisco Press publication *OSPF Network Design Solutions*. He is also a contributor to Cisco's Managing Cisco Network Security course.

About the Technical Reviewers

Anthony Bruno, CCIE #2738, listed already as a contributor, was also the lead technical reviewer of the book.

Chris Shaker joined Cisco Systems, Inc., in February 1989. Since then, he has obtained extensive experience with Cisco IOS software development. He was the main software developer to port IOS and Cisco's ROM monitor to their first low-end router, the IGS. He wrote the low-end fast-switching code for IP, DECnet, Frame Relay switching, and so on. He also wrote device drivers for Cisco's low-end and mid-range Ethernet, Serial, Token Ring, and FDDI interfaces and did the software for Cisco's IGS/TR. Chris implemented IOS changes for Chipcom, Cabletron, and Synoptics versions of the IGS and was part of the Cisco 3000, 4000, and initial 4500 teams. He was the primary fast-switching coder for the C7500 (RSP) product family and wrote new ATM fast-switching code for the RSP. Chris is currently developing software for new hardware upgrades to the C7500 product family.

Don Slice, CCIE #1929, is currently an Escalation Engineer at Cisco Systems, Inc., in Research Triangle Park, North Carolina. He is an acknowledged expert in EIGRP and other IP routing issues and is well known for his knowledge of DECnet and CLNS/ISIS routing. Don provides escalation support for routing-protocol issues to the Technical Assistance Center and Network Supported Accounts team.

Contents at a Glance

Contents

Foreword

In today's networking environment, protocols and services are being added constantly, making it more and more complex to design and implement large-scale networks. The demands for organizations and individuals to maintain and optimally run these networks requires networking expertise.

The Cisco Certified Internetwork Expert (CCIE) program has been in the forefront in providing the expertise for the design and implementation of large-scale networks. The basic criteria to design and implement a large-scale network is to have an in-depth knowledge of networking protocols and services transported.

CCIE Fundamentals: Network Design and Case Studies, Second Edition is an excellent CCIE preparation tool that covers in-depth analysis of IP, IBM, IPX, and ISDN protocols. An understanding of all these protocols is required to pass the CCIE exam. The best part about this book is that it covers issues such as convergence, route selection, topologies, and design issues. The case studies take these concepts a step further by providing configuration examples.

Please check the CCIE Web page at www.cisco.com/go/ccie for updates to the CCIE program, and check the Cisco Press Web site at www.ciscopress.com for future Cisco Press books.

Imran Qureshi
CCIE Program Manager
Cisco Systems, Inc.
July 1999

Preface

About This Book

This is the second edition of *CCIE Fundamentals: Network Design and Case Studies*, originally published in May 1998. Along with new content developed by Cisco Press authors, this publication is derived from two existing publications created by Cisco Systems: *Internetwork Design Guide* and *Internetworking Case Studies*. These publications evolved over the course of several years to provide a comprehensive collection of configuration scenarios and design recommendations tailored to the needs of the experienced internetworking specialist. Cisco Press has culled material from these publications to provide a primer covering many of the technologies and typical implementations encountered by professionals preparing for Cisco Certified Internetwork Expert (CCIE) candidacy.

Although the material provided in this publication was not developed with the specific intent of helping professionals achieve CCIE status, it has been used as a foundation guide by many CCIE candidates. It is one in a series of books that Cisco Press is delivering to prepare IS professionals who are working toward CCIE program completion.

Author Acknowledgments

The original Cisco publications, *Internetwork Design Guide* and *Internetworking Case Studies*, were developed over a period of several years by Andrea Cheek, H. Kim Lew, and Kathleen Wallace. Paula Delay, Donna Kidder, and Diantha Pinner integrated new material into the *Internetwork Design Guide* in the most recent update. An array of subject-matter experts and editors contributed to the development of the two source publications during their parallel evolution toward this combined product. Contributors included Rick Fairweather, Bill Kelly, Bill Miskovetz, Morgan Littlewood, Jeff Baher, Jim Grubb, Terri Quinn-Andry, Steve Spanier, Bob Deutsch, Paulina Knibbe, Adrien Fournier, Kris Thompson, Stuart Hamilton, Phil Byrnes, Bruce Pinsky, Won Lee, George Murickan, Dianna Johansen, and Betsy Fitch. This material was originally assembled to help Cisco network implementers build scalable, reliable, and secure networks. It is with this same intent that Cisco Press brings the combined publication *CCIE Fundamentals: Network Design and Case Studies*, Second Edition to the general networking community.

Document Objectives

The objective of this publication is to help you identify and implement practical networking strategies that are flexible enough to fit a variety of situations and that can also scale as your network requirements change.

Part I, "Network Design," provides a set of general guidelines for planning networks and specific suggestions for several key networking implementations. Part I focuses on identifying the essential technologies and appropriate implementations for specific environments.

Part II, "Network Case Studies," provides practical examples illustrating how you can implement Cisco Systems software features. Case studies address implementation concerns and show how to apply features. Detailed configuration file examples and network diagrams are included.

Part III, "Appendixes," offers nine appendixes as additional reference material that supplements the chapters in the book.

This collection of design tips and configuration examples is by no means the final word in network design. Do not try to use this as a step-by-step handbook for designing every facet of your network. Instead, use this publication as a reference to help you identify features and capabilities of routers and switches that meet specific networking requirements.

Audience

The design guide portion of this publication is intended to support the network administrator who designs and implements router- or switched-based networks. The case study portion of the publication is designed for a similar audience, but focuses on showing practical examples of how to apply Cisco features to meet networking needs. Readers should know how to configure a Cisco router and should be familiar with the protocols and media that their routers have been configured to support.

Document Conventions

This publication uses a number of conventions. Command syntax descriptions use these conventions:

- Commands and keywords are in **boldface** font.
- Variable arguments for which you supply values are in *italic* font.
- Elements in square brackets ([ ]) are optional.
- Alternative keywords are separated by vertical bars (|).

Examples use these conventions:

- Examples that contain system prompts denote interactive sessions, indicating that the user enters commands at the prompt. The system prompt indicates the current command mode. For example, the prompt router(config)# indicates global configuration mode.
- Terminal sessions, configurations, and information the system displays are in `screen` font.
- User input display commands are in **`boldface`** `screen` font.
- Modified configurations show new commands in **`boldface`** `screen` font.
- Exclamation points (!) at the beginning of a line indicate a comment line.

CCIE Program and Cisco Press

Cisco's efforts to facilitate the creation of competent network operations center (NOC) and information systems (IS) staff is exemplified in its CCIE program. To support these efforts, Cisco Press works closely with CCIE program management to create information products that help build the knowledge and expertise of NOC and IS professionals supporting Cisco-based networks. As of this writing, there are three CCIE program certifications:

- WAN Switching
- ISP
- Routing and Switching

It is likely that as the networking landscape evolves, the program will evolve to meet the changing needs of networking professionals. It is the intent of Cisco Press to coordinate its efforts to synchronize with changes in the CCIE program. The brief discussions that follow provide an overview of the CCIE program and lab tests and a summary of plans for additional products from Cisco Press that are intended to support CCIE programs.

You can obtain details about the CCIE program directly from Cisco's World Wide Web presence at www.cisco.com/go/ccie.

CCIE Program Description

In becoming the definitive network certification program for Cisco network professionals, the CCIE program provides the following:

- A definition of "expert-level" technical knowledge and skill
- State-of-the-art methods to evaluate this knowledge and skill
- Enhanced services targeting the needs of these "best-in-class" engineers

Achieving CCIE status denotes proficiency in supporting diverse networks that use routing, bridging, and switching technologies. By passing Cisco's rigorous assessment process, your organization or customers will know that you have passed strict testing and hands-on skill evaluations.

The Cisco Certified Internetwork Expert program certifies individuals, not companies. If you move to another company, your status remains with you as long as you adhere to the program requirements and maintain your certification.

CCIE Certification Laboratory

Networking experts agree that written evaluations alone cannot adequately measure an individual's ability to design, implement, or solve problems in a dynamic network.

Proper evaluation of these skills must include hands-on execution that is observed and quantified by a networking expert. Cisco has taken this concept to heart by creating the CCIE Certification Lab. Candidates are required to demonstrate competency by

- Building, configuring, and testing complex networks to provided specifications
- Diagnosing and resolving media, transport, and session problems
- Isolating application layer problems
- Using packet/frame analysis and Cisco debugging tools
- Documenting and reporting the problem-solving processes used

Candidates are evaluated individually by a senior CCIE networking engineer acting as the lab administrator. Cisco's intent is to make the CCIE Certification Lab as realistic as possible. The lab assessment is currently two full days in length and includes homework.

The CCIE candidate is presented with a complex design to implement from the physical layer through logical configuration. Candidates are not required to configure any end-user systems, but are responsible for any device residing in the network, including hubs, MAUs, DSU/CSU, and so on. Network specifics, point values, and testing criteria used to assess correctness of the individual configurations are provided.

Upon completion of the implementation, the lab engineer will insert faults in the candidate's network. The candidate must recognize, isolate, document, and resolve each fault. Additionally, the candidate will be required to outline the proper reporting procedures when dealing with the Cisco TAC.

Each configuration scenario and problem has pre-assigned point values. The candidate will strive to gain a minimum aggregate of 80% to pass.

Cisco Press CCIE Series

In close coordination with the Cisco CCIE program team, Cisco Press is creating a series of preparation materials aimed at providing up-to-date, accurate information on technologies addressed in the CCIE program. Two basic sets of materials will be developed for distribution via Cisco Press:

- **CCIE Professional Development Series**

  Based on CCIE program guidelines from Cisco. This series will be presented as a set of technology-specific volumes.

- **Cisco Certification Courseware Series**

  Based on the Cisco-developed Introduction to Cisco Router Configuration (ICRC), Advanced Cisco Router Configuration (ACRC), and other key implementation-oriented courses, this series will present course material provided in recommended Cisco-developed, instructor-led classes.

Disclaimer

Cisco Systems and Cisco Press make no claims that individual readers will pass any part of CCIE Qualification (Sylvan) tests or CCIE labs. Material presented in Cisco Press publications is not intended to be construed as a replacement for either recommended in-class training or the recommended two years of internetworking field experience. All material is offered as is. Cisco Systems and Cisco Press make no claims as to the effectiveness of information presented.

Network Design

CHAPTER 1

Introduction

Edited by Atif Khan

Networking—the communication between two or more networks—encompasses every aspect of connecting computers together. Networks have grown to support vastly disparate end-system communication requirements. A network requires many protocols and features to permit scalability and manageability without constant manual intervention. Large networks can consist of the following three distinct components:

- Campus networks, which consist of locally connected users in a building or group of buildings
- Wide-area networks (WANs), which connect campuses
- Remote connections, which link branch offices and single users (mobile users and telecommuters) to a local campus or the Internet

Figure 1-1 provides an example of a typical enterprise network.

Figure 1-1   *Example of a Typical Enterprise Network*

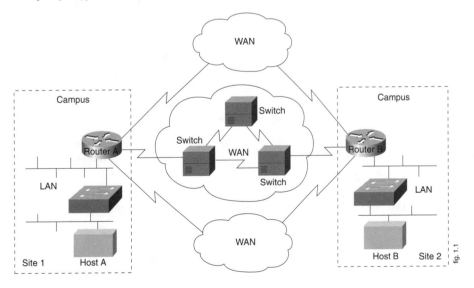

Designing a network can be a challenging task. To design reliable, scalable networks, network designers must realize that each of the three major components of a network has distinct design requirements. A network that consists of only 50 meshed routing nodes can pose complex problems that lead to unpredictable results. Attempting to optimize networks that feature thousands of nodes can pose even more complex problems.

Despite improvements in equipment performance and media capabilities, network design is becoming more difficult. The trend is toward increasingly complex environments involving multiple media, multiple protocols, and interconnection to networks outside any single organization's dominion of control. Carefully designing networks can reduce the hardships associated with growth as a networking environment evolves.

This chapter provides an overview of the technologies available today to design networks. Discussions are divided into the following general topics:

- Designing campus networks
- Designing WANs
- Utilizing remote connection design
- Providing integrated solutions
- Determining your networking requirements

Designing Campus Networks

A *campus network* is a building or group of buildings all connected into one enterprise network that consists of many local-area networks (LANs). A campus is generally a portion of a company (or the whole company) that is constrained to a fixed geographic area, as shown in Figure 1-2.

The distinct characteristic of a campus environment is that the company that owns the campus network usually owns the physical wires deployed in the campus. The campus network topology is primarily LAN technology connecting all the end systems within the building. Campus networks generally use LAN technologies, such as Ethernet, Token Ring, Fiber Distributed Data Interface (FDDI), Fast Ethernet, Gigabit Ethernet, and Asynchronous Transfer Mode (ATM).

A large campus with groups of buildings can also use WAN technology to connect the buildings. Although the wiring and protocols of a campus might be based on WAN technology, they do not share the WAN constraint of the high cost of bandwidth. After the wire is installed, bandwidth is inexpensive because the company owns the wires and there is no recurring cost to a service provider. However, upgrading the physical wiring can be expensive.

Figure 1-2   *Example of a Campus Network*

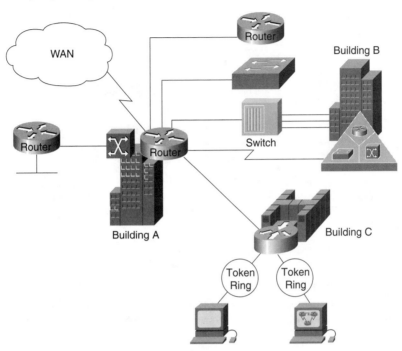

Consequently, network designers generally deploy a campus design optimized for the fastest functional architecture that runs on the existing physical wire. They might also upgrade wiring to meet the requirements of emerging applications. For example, higher-speed technologies—such as Fast Ethernet, Gigabit Ethernet, and ATM as a backbone architecture—and Layer 2 switching provide dedicated bandwidth to the desktop.

Trends in Campus Design

In the past, network designers had only a limited number of hardware options—routers or hubs—when purchasing a technology for their campus networks. Consequently, it was rare to make a hardware design mistake. Hubs were for wiring closets, and routers were for the data-center or main telecommunications operations.

Recently, local-area networking has been revolutionized by the exploding use of LAN switching at Layer 2 (the data link layer) to increase performance and to provide more bandwidth to meet new data networking applications. LAN switches provide this performance benefit by increasing bandwidth and throughput for workgroups and local servers. Network designers are deploying LAN switches out toward the network's edge in wiring closets. As Figure 1-3 shows, these switches are usually installed to replace shared concentrator hubs and give higher-bandwidth connections to the end user.

Figure 1-3 *Example of Trends in Campus Design*

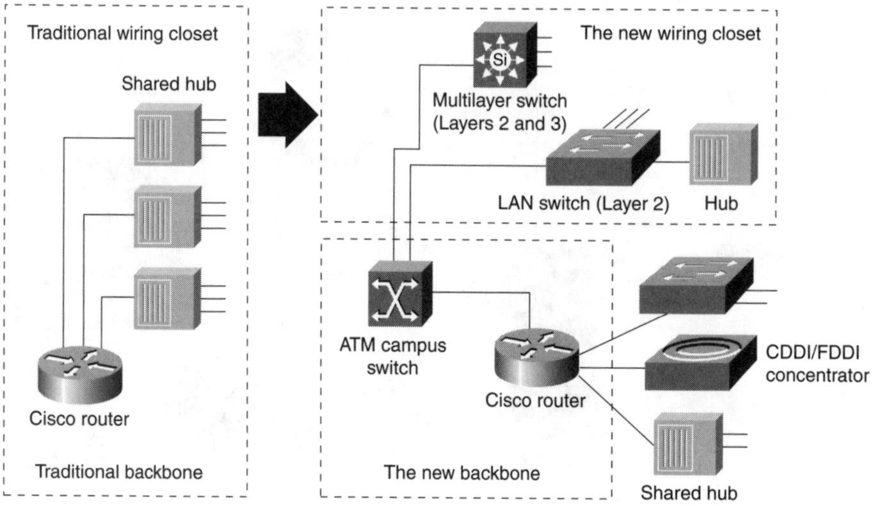

Layer 3 networking is required in the network to interconnect the switched workgroups and to provide services that include security, quality of service (QoS), and traffic management. Routing integrates these switched networks, and provides the security, stability, and control needed to build functional and scalable networks.

Traditionally, Layer 2 switching has been provided by LAN switches, and Layer 3 networking has been provided by routers. Increasingly, these two networking functions are being integrated into common platforms. Multilayer switches that provide Layer 2 and 3 functionality, for example, are now appearing in the marketplace.

With the advent of such technologies as Layer 3 switching, LAN switching, and virtual LANs (VLANs), building campus networks is becoming more complex than in the past. Table 1-1 summarizes the various LAN technologies required to build successful campus networks. Cisco Systems offers product solutions in all these technologies.

Table 1-1 *Summary of LAN Technologies*

LAN Technology	Typical Uses
Routing technologies	Routing is a key technology for connecting LANs in a campus network. It can be either Layer 3 switching or more traditional routing with Layer 3 switching and additional router features.
Gigabit Ethernet	Gigabit Ethernet builds on top of the Ethernet protocol but increases speed tenfold over Fast Ethernet to 1000 Mbps, or 1 Gbps. Gigabit Ethernet provides high-bandwidth capacity for backbone designs while providing backward compatibility for installed media.

Table 1-1   *Summary of LAN Technologies (Continued)*

LAN Technology	Typical Uses
LAN switching technologies—Ethernet switching	Ethernet switching provides Layer 2 switching and offers dedicated Ethernet segments for each connection. This is the base fabric of the network.
LAN switching technologies—Token Ring switching	Token Ring switching offers the same functionality as Ethernet switching but uses Token Ring technology. You can use a Token Ring switch as either a transparent bridge or as a source-route bridge.
ATM switching technologies	ATM switching offers high-speed switching technology for voice, video, and data. Its operation is similar to LAN switching technologies for data operations. ATM, however, offers high-bandwidth capacity.

Network designers are now designing campus networks by purchasing separate equipment types (for example, routers, Ethernet switches, and ATM switches) and then linking them. Although individual purchase decisions might seem harmless, network designers must not forget that this separate equipment still works together to form a network.

It is possible to separate these technologies and build thoughtful designs using each new technology, but network designers must consider the overall integration of the network. If this overall integration is not considered, the result can be networks that have a much higher risk of network outages, downtime, and congestion than ever before.

Designing WANs

WAN communication occurs between geographically separated areas. In enterprise networks, WANs connect campuses. When a local end station wants to communicate with a remote end station (an end station located at a different site), information must be sent over one or more WAN links. Routers within enterprise networks represent the LAN/WAN junction points of a network. These routers determine the most appropriate path through the network for the required data streams.

WAN links are connected by switches, which are devices that relay information through the WAN and dictate the service provided by the WAN. WAN communication is often called a *service* because the network provider often charges users for the services provided by the WAN (called *tariffs*). WAN services are provided through the following three primary switching technologies:

- Circuit switching
- Packet switching
- Cell switching

Each switching technique has advantages and disadvantages. For example, *circuit-switched* networks offer users dedicated bandwidth that cannot be infringed upon by other users. In contrast, *packet-switched* networks have traditionally offered more flexibility and used network bandwidth more efficiently than circuit-switched networks. *Cell switching*, however, combines some aspects of circuit and packet switching to produce networks with low latency and high throughput. Cell switching is rapidly gaining in popularity. ATM is currently the most prominent cell-switched technology. For more information on switching technology for WANs and LANs, see Chapter 2, "Network Design Basics."

Trends in WAN Design

Traditionally, WAN communication has been characterized by relatively low throughput, high delay, and high error rates. WAN connections are mostly characterized by the cost of renting media (wire) from a service provider to connect two or more campuses together. Because the WAN infrastructure is often rented from a service provider, WAN network designs must optimize the cost of bandwidth and bandwidth efficiency. For example, all technologies and features used to connect campuses over a WAN are developed to meet the following design requirements:

- Optimize WAN bandwidth
- Minimize the tariff cost
- Maximize the effective service to the end users

Recently, traditional shared-media networks are being overtaxed because of the following new network requirements:

- Necessity to connect to remote sites
- Growing need for users to have remote access to their networks
- Explosive growth of the corporate intranets
- Increased use of enterprise servers

Network designers are turning to WAN technology to support these new requirements. WAN connections generally handle mission-critical information and are optimized for price/performance bandwidth. The routers connecting the campuses, for example, generally apply traffic optimization, multiple paths for redundancy, dial backup for disaster recovery, and QoS for critical applications.

Table 1-2 summarizes the various WAN technologies that support such large-scale network requirements.

Table 1-2 *Summary of WAN Technologies*

WAN Technology	Typical Uses
Asymmetric Digital Subscriber Line	A new modem technology. Converts existing twisted-pair telephone lines into access paths for multimedia and high-speed data communications. ADSL transmits more than 6 Mbps to a subscriber, and as much as 640 kbps more in both directions.
Analog modem	Analog modems can be used by telecommuters and mobile users who access the network less than 2 hours per day, or for backup for another type of link.
Leased line	Leased lines can be used for Point-to-Point Protocol (PPP) networks and hub-and-spoke topologies, or for backup for another type of link.
Integrated Services Digital Network (ISDN)	ISDN can be used for cost-effective remote access to corporate networks. It provides support for voice and video as well as a backup for another type of link.
Frame Relay	Frame Relay provides a cost-effective, high-speed, low-latency mesh topology between remote sites. It can be used in both private and carrier-provided networks.
Switched Multimegabit Data Service (SMDS)	SMDS provides high-speed, high-performance connections across public data networks. It can also be deployed in metropolitan-area networks (MANs).
X.25	X.25 can provide a reliable WAN circuit or backbone. It also provides support for legacy applications.
WAN ATM	WAN ATM can be used to accelerate bandwidth requirements. It also provides support for multiple QoS classes for differing application requirements for delay and loss.

Utilizing Remote Connection Design

Remote connections link single users (mobile users and/or telecommuters) and branch offices to a local campus or the Internet. Typically, a remote site is a small site that has few users and therefore needs a smaller-size WAN connection. The remote requirements of a network, however, usually involve a large number of remote single users or sites, which causes the aggregate WAN charge to be exaggerated.

Because there are so many remote single users or sites, the aggregate WAN bandwidth cost is proportionally more important in remote connections than in WAN connections. Given that the three-year cost of a network is nonequipment expenses, the WAN media rental charge from a service provider is the largest cost component of a remote network. Unlike WAN connections, smaller sites or single users seldom need to connect 24 hours a day.

Consequently, network designers typically choose between dialup and dedicated WAN options for remote connections. Remote connections generally run at speeds of 128 kbps or lower. A network designer might also employ bridges in a remote site for their ease of implementation, simple topology, and low traffic requirements.

Trends in Remote Connections

Today, there is a large selection of remote WAN media that includes the following:

- Analog modem
- Asymmetric Digital Subscriber Line
- Leased line
- Frame Relay
- X.25
- ISDN

Remote connections also optimize for the appropriate WAN option to provide cost-effective bandwidth, minimize dialup tariff costs, and maximize effective service to users.

Trends in LAN/WAN Integration

Today, 90% of computing power resides on desktops, and that power is growing exponentially. Distributed applications are increasingly bandwidth-hungry, and the emergence of the Internet is driving many LAN architectures to the limit. Voice communications have increased significantly, with more reliance on centralized voice-mail systems for verbal communications. The network is the critical tool for information flow. Networks are being pressured to cost less, yet support the emerging applications and higher number of users with increased performance.

To date, local- and wide-area communications have remained logically separate. In the LAN, bandwidth is free, and connectivity is limited only by hardware and implementation costs. The LAN has carried data only. In the WAN, bandwidth has been the overriding cost, and such delay-sensitive traffic as voice has remained separate from data. New applications and the economics of supporting them, however, are forcing these conventions to change.

The Internet is the first source of multimedia to the desktop and immediately breaks the rules. Such Internet applications as voice and real-time video require better, more predictable LAN and WAN performance. These multimedia applications are fast becoming an essential part of the business productivity toolkit. As companies begin to consider

implementing new intranet-based, bandwidth- intensive multimedia applications over IP —
video training, videoconferencing, and voice, for example—the impact of these
applications on the existing networking infrastructure is a serious concern. If a company
has relied on its corporate network for business-critical SNA traffic, for example, and it
wants to bring a new video training application online, the network must be able to provide
guaranteed QoS that delivers the multimedia traffic but does not allow it to interfere with
the business-critical traffic. ATM has emerged as one of the technologies for integrating
LANs and WANs. The QoS features of ATM can support any traffic type in separate or
mixed streams (either delay-sensitive traffic or non-delay-sensitive traffic), as shown in
Figure 1-4.

ATM can also scale from low to high speeds. It has been adopted by all the industry's
equipment vendors, from LAN to private branch exchange (PBX).

Figure 1-4   *ATM Support of Various Traffic Types*

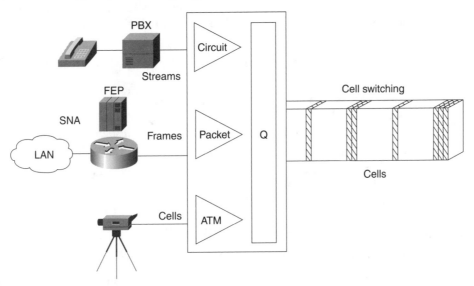

Providing Integrated Solutions

The trend in networking is to provide network designers greater flexibility in solving
multiple networking problems without creating multiple networks or writing off existing
data-communication investments. Routers might be relied on to provide a reliable, secure
network and act as a barrier against inadvertent broadcast storms in the local networks.
Switches (which can be divided into two main categories: LAN switches and WAN
switches) can be deployed at the workgroup, campus backbone, or WAN level. Remote
sites might use low-end routers for connection to the WAN.

Underlying and integrating all Cisco products is the Cisco Internetworking Operating System (Cisco IOS) software. The Cisco IOS software enables disparate groups, diverse devices, and multiple protocols to all be integrated into a highly reliable and scalable network. Cisco IOS software also supports this network with advanced security, quality of service, and traffic services.

Determining Your Networking Requirements

Designing a network can be a challenging task. Your first step is to understand your networking requirements. The rest of this chapter explains how to determine these requirements. After you have identified these requirements, refer to Chapter 2 for information on selecting network capability and reliability options that meet these requirements.

Networking devices must reflect the goals, characteristics, and policies of the organizations in which they operate. Two primary goals drive networking design and implementation:

- **Application availability**—Networks carry application information between computers. If the applications are not available to network users, the network is not doing its job.

- **Cost of ownership**—Information system (IS) budgets today often run in the millions of dollars. As large organizations increasingly rely on electronic data for managing business activities, the associated costs of computing resources will continue to rise.

A well-designed network can help balance these objectives. When properly implemented, the network infrastructure can optimize application availability and allow the cost-effective use of existing network resources.

The Design Problem: Optimizing Availability and Cost

In general, the network design problem consists of the following three general elements:

- **Environmental givens**—Environmental givens include the location of hosts, servers, terminals, and other end nodes; the projected traffic for the environment; and the projected costs for delivering different service levels.

- **Performance constraints**—Performance constraints consist of network reliability, traffic throughput, and host/client computer speeds (for example, network interface cards and hard drive access speeds).

- **Networking variables**—Networking variables include the network topology, line capacities, and packet-flow assignments.

The goal is to minimize cost based on these elements while delivering service that does not compromise established availability requirements. You face two primary concerns: availability and cost. These issues are essentially at odds. Any increase in availability must generally be reflected as an increase in cost. As a result, you must weigh the relative importance of resource availability and overall cost carefully.

As Figure 1-5 shows, designing your network is an iterative activity. The discussions that follow outline several areas that you should carefully consider when planning your networking implementation.

Figure 1-5   *General Network Design Process*

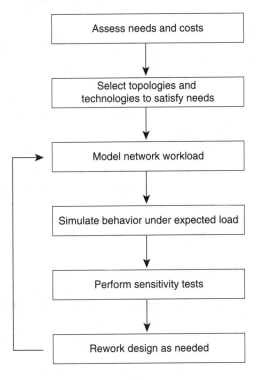

Assessing User Requirements

In general, users primarily want application availability in their networks. The chief components of application availability are *response time*, *throughput*, and *reliability*:

- Response time is the time between entry of a command or keystroke and the host system's execution of the command or delivery of a response. User satisfaction about response time is generally considered to be a monotonic function up to some limit, at which point user satisfaction falls off to nearly zero. Applications in which fast response time is considered critical include interactive online services, such as automated tellers and point-of-sale machines.

- Applications that put high-volume traffic onto the network have more effect on throughput than end-to-end connections. Throughput-intensive applications generally involve file-transfer activities. However, throughput-intensive applications also usually have low response-time requirements. Indeed, they can often be scheduled at times when response-time–sensitive traffic is low (for example, after normal work hours).

- Although reliability is always important, some applications have genuine requirements that exceed typical needs. Organizations that require nearly 100% uptime conduct all activities online or over the telephone. Financial services, securities exchanges, and emergency/police/military operations are a few examples. These situations imply a requirement for a high level of hardware and topological redundancy. Determining the cost of any downtime is essential in determining the relative importance of reliability to your network.

You can assess user requirements in a number of ways. The more involved your users are in the process, the more likely that your evaluation will be accurate. In general, you can use the following methods to obtain this information:

- **User community profiles**—Outline what different user groups require. This is the first step in determining network requirements. Although many users have roughly the same requirements for an electronic mail system, engineering groups using X Windows terminals and Sun workstations in an NFS environment have different needs than PC users sharing print servers in a finance department.

- **Interviews, focus groups, and surveys**—Build a baseline for implementing a network. Understand that some groups might require access to common servers. Others might want to allow external access to specific internal computing resources. Certain organizations might require IS support systems to be managed in a particular way according to some external standard. The least formal method of obtaining information is to conduct interviews with key user groups. Focus groups can also be used to gather information and generate discussion among different organizations with similar (or dissimilar) interests. Finally, formal surveys can be used to get a statistically valid reading of user sentiment regarding a particular service level or proposed networking architecture.

- **Human factors tests**—The most expensive, time-consuming, and possibly revealing method is to conduct a test involving representative users in a lab environment. This is most applicable when evaluating response-time requirements. You might set up working systems and have users perform normal remote host activities from the lab network, for example. By evaluating user reactions to variations in host responsiveness, you can create benchmark thresholds for acceptable performance.

Assessing Proprietary and Nonproprietary Solutions

Compatibility, conformance, and interoperability are related to the problem of balancing proprietary functionality and open networking flexibility. As a network designer, you might be forced to choose between implementing a multivendor environment and implementing a specific, proprietary capability. For example, the *Interior Gateway Routing Protocol* (IGRP) provides many useful capabilities, such as a number of features designed to enhance its stability. These include holddowns, split horizons, and poison reverse updates.

The negative side is that IGRP is a proprietary routing protocol. In contrast, the integrated *Intermediate System-to-Intermediate System* (IS-IS) protocol is an open networking alternative that also provides a fast converging routing environment; however, implementing an open routing protocol can potentially result in greater multivendor configuration complexity.

The decisions that you make have far-ranging effects on your overall network design. Assume that you decide to implement integrated IS-IS rather than IGRP. In doing this, you gain a measure of interoperability; however, you lose some functionality. For instance, you cannot load balance traffic over unequal parallel paths. Similarly, some modems provide a high level of proprietary diagnostic capabilities but require that all modems throughout a network be of the same vendor type to fully exploit proprietary diagnostics.

Previous networking investments and expectations for future requirements have considerable influence over your choice of implementations. You need to consider installed networking equipment; applications running (or to be run) on the network; traffic patterns; physical location of sites, hosts, and users; rate of growth of the user community; and both physical and logical network layout.

Assessing Costs

The network is a strategic element in your overall information system design. As such, the cost of your network is much more than the sum of your equipment purchase orders. View it as a total-cost-of-ownership issue. You must consider the entire life cycle of your networking environment. A brief list of costs associated with networks follows:

- **Equipment hardware and software costs**—Consider what is really being bought when you purchase your systems; costs should include initial purchase and installation, maintenance, and projected upgrade costs.

- **Performance trade-off costs**—Consider the cost of going from a 5-second response time to a half-second response time. Such improvements can cost quite a bit in terms of media selection, network interfaces, networking nodes, modems, and WAN services.

- **Installation costs**—Installing a site's physical cable plant can be the most expensive element of a large network. The costs include installation labor, site modification, fees associated with local code conformance, and costs incurred to ensure compliance with environmental restrictions (such as asbestos removal). Other important elements in keeping your costs to a minimum include developing a well-planned wiring-closet layout and implementing color-code conventions for cable runs.

- **Expansion costs**—Calculate the cost of ripping out all thick Ethernet, adding additional functionality, or moving to a new location. Projecting your future requirements and accounting for future needs saves time and money.

- **Support costs**—Complicated networks cost more to monitor, configure, and maintain. Your network should be no more complicated than necessary. Costs include training, direct labor (network managers and administrators), sparing, and replacement costs. Additional costs that should be considered are out-of-band management, SNMP management stations, and power.

- **Cost of downtime**—Evaluate the cost of every minute that a user is unable to access a file server or a centralized database. If this cost is high, you must attribute a high cost to downtime. If the cost is high enough, fully redundant networks might be your best option.

- **Opportunity costs**—Every choice you make has an opposing alternative option. Whether that option is a specific hardware platform, topology solution, level of redundancy, or system integration alternative, there are always options. Opportunity costs are the costs of *not* picking one of those options. The opportunity costs of not switching to newer technologies and topologies might be lost competitive advantage, lower productivity, and slower overall performance. Any effort to integrate opportunity costs into your analysis can help make accurate comparisons at the beginning of your project.

- **Sunken costs**—Your investment in existing cable plant, routers, concentrators, switches, hosts, and other equipment and software is your sunken costs. If the sunken costs are high, you might need to modify your networks so that your existing network can continue to be utilized. Although comparatively low incremental costs might appear to be more attractive than significant redesign costs, your organization might pay more in the long run by not upgrading systems. Too much reliance on sunken costs can cost your organization sales and market share when calculating the cost of network modifications and additions.

Estimating Traffic: Workload Modeling

Empirical *workload modeling* consists of implementing a working network and then monitoring traffic for a given number of users, applications, and network topology. Try to characterize activity throughout a normal workday in terms of the type of traffic passed, level of traffic, response time of hosts, time to execute file transfers, and so on. You can also observe utilization on existing network equipment over the test period.

If the tested network's characteristics are similar to a prospective network, you can try extrapolating to the prospective network's number of users, applications, and topology.

This is a best-guess approach to traffic estimation given the unavailability of tools to characterize detailed traffic behavior.

In addition to passive monitoring of an existing network, you can measure activity and traffic generated by a known number of users attached to a representative test network and then extrapolate findings to your anticipated population.

One problem with modeling workloads on networks is that it is difficult to accurately pinpoint traffic load and network device performance as functions of the number of users, type of application, and geographical location. This is especially true without a real network in place. Consider the following factors that influence the dynamics of the network:

- **The time-dependent nature of network access**—Peak periods can vary; measurements must reflect a range of observations that includes peak demand.

- **Differences associated with type of traffic**—Routed and bridged traffic place different demands on network devices and protocols; some protocols are sensitive to dropped packets; some application types require more bandwidth.

- **The random (nondeterministic) nature of network traffic**—Exact arrival time and specific effects of traffic are unpredictable.

Sensitivity Testing

From a practical point of view, sensitivity testing involves breaking stable links and observing what happens. When working with a test network, this is relatively easy. Disturb the network by removing an active interface, and monitor how the change is handled by the network: how traffic is rerouted, the speed of convergence, whether any connectivity is lost, and whether problems arise in handling specific types of traffic. You can also change the level of traffic on a network to determine the effects on the network when traffic levels approach media saturation. This empirical testing is a type of regression testing: A series of specific modifications (tests) is repeated on different versions of network configurations. By monitoring the effects of the design variations, you can characterize the relative resilience of the design.

NOTE   Using a computer to model sensitivity tests is beyond the scope of this book. A useful source for more information about computer-based network design and simulation is A.S. Tannenbaum's *Computer Networks* (Prentice Hall, 1996).

Summary

After you have determined your network requirements, you must identify and then select the specific capability that fits your computing environment. For basic information on the different types of networking devices, along with a description of a hierarchical approach to networking, refer to Chapter 2.

Chapters 2–13 of this book are technology chapters that present detailed discussions about specific implementations of large-scale networks in the following environments:

- Large-scale Internet Protocol (IP) networks
  - — Enhanced Interior Gateway Routing Protocol (IGRP) design
  - — Open Shortest Path First (OSPF) design
- IBM System Network Architecture (SNA) networks
  - — Source-route bridging (SRB) design
  - — Synchronous Data Link Control (SDLC) and serial tunnel (STUN), SDLC Logical Link Control type 2 (SDLLC), and Qualified Logical Link Control (QLLC) design
  - — Advanced Peer-to-Peer Networking (APPN) and data-link switching (DLSw) design
- ATM networks
- Packet service networks
  - — Frame Relay design
- Dial-on-demand routing (DDR) networks
- ISDN networks

In addition to these technology chapters, there are chapters on designing switched LAN networks, campus LANs, and networks for multimedia applications. The last 10 chapters of this book include case studies relating to the concepts learned in the previous chapters.

CHAPTER 2

Network Design Basics

Edited by Atif Khan

Designing a network can be a challenging task. A network that consists of only 50 meshed routing nodes can pose complex problems that lead to unpredictable results. Attempting to optimize networks that feature thousands of nodes can pose even more complex problems.

Despite improvements in equipment performance and media capabilities, network design is becoming more difficult. The trend is toward increasingly complex environments involving multiple media, multiple protocols, and interconnection to networks outside any single organization's dominion of control. Carefully designing networks can reduce the hardships associated with growth as a networking environment evolves.

This chapter provides an overview of planning and design guidelines. Discussions are divided into the following general topics:

- Understanding Basic Networking Concepts
- Identifying and Selecting Networking Capabilities
- Identifying and Selecting Networking Devices

Understanding Basic Networking Concepts

This section covers the following basic networking concepts:

- Overview of Networking Devices
- Switching Overview

Overview of Networking Devices

Network designers faced with designing a network have four basic types of networking devices available to them:

- Hubs (concentrators)
- Bridges
- Switches
- Routers

Table 2-1 summarizes these four networking devices.

Table 2-1 *Summary of Networking Devices*

Device	Description
Hubs (concentrators)	Hubs (concentrators) are used to connect multiple users to a single physical device, which connects to the network. Hubs (concentrators) act as repeaters by regenerating the signal as it passes through them.
Bridges	Bridges are used to logically separate network segments within the same network. They operate at the OSI data link layer (Layer 2) and are independent of higher-layer protocols.
Switches	Switches are similar to bridges but usually have more ports. Switches provide a unique network segment on each port, thereby separating collision domains. Today, network designers are replacing hubs in their wiring closets with switches to increase their network performance and bandwidth while protecting their existing wiring investments.
Routers	Routers separate broadcast domains and are used to connect different networks. Routers direct network traffic based on the destination network layer address (Layer 3) rather than the workstation data link layer or MAC address. Routers are protocol-dependent.

Data communications experts generally agree that network designers are moving away from bridges and concentrators and are primarily using switches and routers to build networks. Consequently, this chapter focuses primarily on the role of switches and routers in network design.

Switching Overview

Today in data communications, all switching and routing equipment performs two basic operations:

- **Switching data frames**—This is generally a store-and-forward operation in which a frame arrives on an input medium and is transmitted to an output medium.
- **Maintenance of switching operations**—In this operation, switches build and maintain switching tables and search for loops. Routers build and maintain both routing tables and service tables.

There are two methods of switching data frames: Layer 2 and Layer 3 switching.

Layer 2 and Layer 3 Switching

Switching is the process of taking an incoming frame from one interface and delivering it out through another interface. Routers use Layer 3 switching to route a packet, and switches (Layer 2 switches) use Layer 2 switching to forward frames.

The difference between Layer 2 and Layer 3 switching is the type of information inside the frame that is used to determine the correct output interface. With Layer 2 switching, frames are switched based on MAC address information. With Layer 3 switching, frames are switched based on network-layer information.

Layer 2 switching does not look inside a packet for network-layer information as does Layer 3 switching. Layer 2 switching is performed by looking at a destination MAC address within a frame. It looks at the frame's destination address and sends it to the appropriate interface if it knows the destination address location. Layer 2 switching builds and maintains a switching table that keeps track of which MAC addresses belong to each port or interface.

If the Layer 2 switch does not know where to send the frame, it broadcasts the frame out all its ports to the network to learn the correct destination. When the frame's reply is returned, the switch learns the location of the new address and adds the information to the switching table.

Layer 2 addresses are determined by the manufacturer of the data communications equipment used. They are unique addresses that are derived in two parts: the manufacturing (MFG) code and the unique identifier. The MFG code is assigned to each vendor by the IEEE. The vendor assigns a unique identifier to each board it produces. Except for Systems Network Architecture (SNA) networks, users have little or no control over Layer 2 addressing because Layer 2 addresses are fixed with a device, whereas Layer 3 addresses can be changed. In addition, Layer 2 addresses assume a flat address space with universally unique addresses.

Layer 3 switching operates at the network layer. It examines packet information and forwards packets based on their network-layer destination addresses. Layer 3 switching also supports router functionality.

For the most part, Layer 3 addresses are determined by the network administrator, who installs a hierarchy on the network. Protocols such as IP, IPX, and AppleTalk use Layer 3 addressing. By creating Layer 3 addresses, a network administrator creates local areas that act as single addressing units (similar to streets, cities, states, and countries) and assigns a number to each local entity. If users move to another building, their end stations obtain new Layer 3 addresses, but their Layer 2 addresses remain the same.

Because routers operate at Layer 3 of the OSI model, they can adhere to and formulate a hierarchical addressing structure. Therefore, a routed network can tie a logical addressing structure to a physical infrastructure, for example, through TCP/IP subnets or IPX networks for each segment. Traffic flow in a switched (flat) network is therefore inherently different from traffic flow in a routed (hierarchical) network. Hierarchical networks offer more flexible traffic flow than flat networks because they can use the network hierarchy to determine optimal paths and contain broadcast domains.

Implications of Layer 2 and Layer 3 Switching

The increasing power of desktop processors and the requirements of client/server and multimedia applications have driven the need for greater bandwidth in traditional shared-media environments. These requirements are prompting network designers to replace hubs in wiring closets with switches.

Although Layer 2 switches use microsegmentation to satisfy the demands for more bandwidth and increased performance, network designers are now faced with increasing demands for intersubnet communication. For example, every time a user accesses servers and other resources, which are located on different subnets, the traffic must go through a Layer 3 device. Figure 2-1 shows the route of intersubnet traffic with Layer 2 switches and Layer 3 switches.

Figure 2-1 *Flow of Intersubnet Traffic with Layer 2 Switches and Routers*

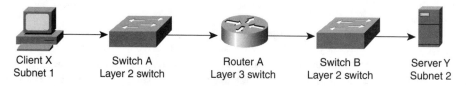

| Client X | Switch A | Router A | Switch B | Server Y |
| Subnet 1 | Layer 2 switch | Layer 3 switch | Layer 2 switch | Subnet 2 |

As Figure 2-1 shows, for Client X to communicate with Server Y, which is on another subnet, it must traverse through the following route: first through Switch A (a Layer 2 switch), and then through Router A (a Layer 3 switch), and finally through Switch B (a Layer 2 switch). Potentially there is a tremendous bottleneck, which can threaten network performance, because the intersubnet traffic must pass from one network to another.

To relieve this bottleneck, network designers can add Layer 3 capabilities throughout the network. They implement Layer 3 switching on edge devices to alleviate the burden on centralized routers. Figure 2-2 illustrates how deploying Layer 3 switching throughout the network allows Client X to directly communicate with Server Y without passing through Router A.

Figure 2-2   *Flow of Intersubnet Traffic with Layer 3 Switches*

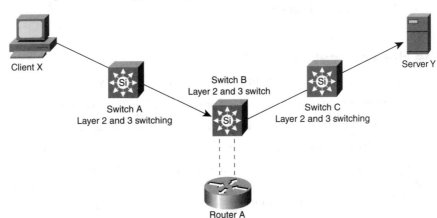

Identifying and Selecting Networking Capabilities

After you understand your networking requirements, you must identify and then select the specific capabilities that fit your computing environment. The following discussions provide a starting point for making these decisions:

- Identifying and Selecting a Networking Model
- Choosing Networking Reliability Options

Identifying and Selecting a Networking Model

Hierarchical models for network design enable you to design networks in layers. To understand the importance of layering, consider the Open System Interconnection (OSI) reference model, which is a layered model for understanding and implementing computer communications. By using layers, the OSI model simplifies the task required for two computers to communicate. Hierarchical models for network design also use layers to simplify the task required for networking. Each layer can be focused on specific functions, thereby enabling the networking designer to choose the right systems and features for the layer.

Using a hierarchical design can facilitate changes. Modularity in network design enables you to create design elements that can be replicated as the network grows. As each element in the network design requires change, the cost and complexity of making the upgrade is constrained to a small subset of the overall network. In large flat or meshed network architectures, changes tend to impact a large number of systems. Improved fault isolation is also facilitated by modular structuring of the network into small, easy-to-understand elements. Network managers can easily understand the transition points in the network, which helps identify failure points.

Using the Hierarchical Design Model

A hierarchical network design includes the following three layers:

- The backbone (core) layer, which provides optimal transport between sites
- The distribution layer, which provides policy-based connectivity
- The local-access layer, which provides workgroup/user access to the network

Figure 2-3 shows a high-level view of the various aspects of a hierarchical network design. A hierarchical network design presents three layers—core, distribution, and access—with each layer providing different functionality.

Figure 2-3   *Hierarchical Network Design Model*

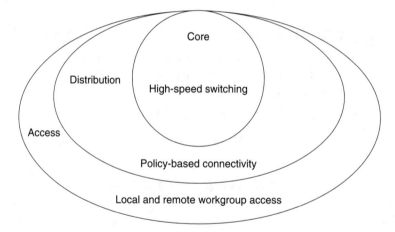

Function of the Core Layer

The core layer is a high-speed switching backbone and should be designed to switch packets as fast as possible. This layer of the network should not perform any packet manipulation, such as access lists and filtering, that would slow down the switching of packets.

Function of the Distribution Layer

The distribution layer of the network is the demarcation point between the access and core layers and helps to define and differentiate the core. The purpose of this layer is to provide boundary definition and is the place at which packet manipulation can take place. In the campus environment, the distribution layer can include several functions, such as the following:

- Address or area aggregation
- Departmental or workgroup access
- Broadcast/multicast domain definition
- Virtual LAN (VLAN) routing
- Any media transitions that need to occur
- Security

In the non-campus environment, the distribution layer can be a redistribution point between routing domains or the demarcation between static and dynamic routing protocols. It can also be the point at which remote sites access the corporate network. The distribution layer can be summarized as the layer that provides policy-based connectivity.

Function of the Access Layer

The access layer is the point at which local end users are allowed into the network. This layer may also use access lists or filters to further optimize the needs of a particular set of users. In the campus environment, access-layer functions can include the following:

- Shared bandwidth
- Switched bandwidth
- MAC layer filtering
- Microsegmentation

In the non-campus environment, the access layer can give remote sites access to the corporate network via some wide-area technology, such as Frame Relay, ISDN, or leased lines.

It is sometimes mistakenly thought that the three layers (core, distribution, and access) must exist in clear and distinct physical entities, but this does not have to be the case. The layers are defined to aid successful network design and to represent functionality that must exist in a network. The instantiation of each layer can be in distinct routers or switches, can be represented by a physical medium, can be combined in a single device, or can be omitted altogether. The way the layers are implemented depends on the needs of the network being designed. Note, however, that for a network to function optimally, hierarchy must be maintained.

The discussions that follow outline the capabilities and services associated with backbone, distribution, and local-access networking services.

Evaluating Backbone Services

This section addresses networking features that support backbone services. The following topics are discussed:

- Path Optimization
- Traffic Prioritization
- Load Balancing
- Alternative Paths
- Switched Access
- Encapsulation (Tunneling)

Path Optimization

One of the primary advantages of a router is its capability to help you implement a logical environment in which optimal paths for traffic are automatically selected. Routers rely on routing protocols that are associated with the various network layer protocols to accomplish this automated path optimization.

Depending on the network protocols implemented, routers enable you to implement routing environments that suit your specific requirements. In an IP network, for example, Cisco routers can support all widely implemented routing protocols, including Open Shortest Path First (OSPF), RIP, IGRP, EIGRP, IS-IS, Border Gateway Protocol (BGP), and Exterior Gateway Protocol (EGP). Key built-in capabilities that promote path optimization include rapid and controllable route convergence and tunable routing metrics and timers.

Convergence is the process of agreement, by all routers, on optimal routes. When a network event causes routes to either halt operation or become available, routers distribute routing-update messages. Routing-update messages permeate networks, stimulating recalculation of optimal routes and eventually causing all routers to agree on these routes. Routing algorithms that converge slowly can cause routing loops or network outages.

Many different metrics are used in routing algorithms. Some sophisticated routing algorithms base route selection on a combination of multiple metrics, resulting in the calculation of a single hybrid metric. EIGRP uses one of the most sophisticated distance vector routing algorithms. It combines values for bandwidth, load, and delay to create a composite metric value. Link-state routing protocols, such as OSPF and IS-IS, employ a metric that represents the cost associated with a given path.

Traffic Prioritization

Although some network protocols can prioritize internal homogeneous traffic, the router prioritizes the heterogeneous traffic flows. Such traffic prioritization enables policy-based routing and ensures that protocols carrying mission-critical data take precedence over less important traffic.

Priority Queuing

Priority queuing enables the network administrator to prioritize traffic. Traffic can be classified according to various criteria, including protocol and subprotocol type, and then queued on one of four output queues (high, medium, normal, or low priority). For IP traffic, additional fine-tuning is possible. Priority queuing is most useful on low-speed serial links. Figure 2-4 shows how priority queuing can be used to segregate traffic by priority level, speeding the transit of certain packets through the network.

Figure 2-4   *Priority Queuing*

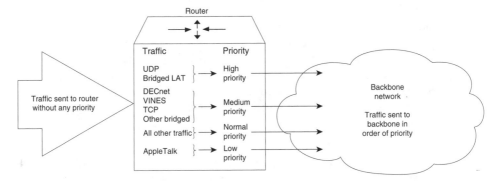

You can also use intraprotocol traffic prioritization techniques to enhance network performance. IP's type of service (ToS) feature and prioritization of IBM logical units (LUs) are intraprotocol prioritization techniques that can be implemented to improve traffic handling over routers. Figure 2-5 illustrates LU prioritization.

Figure 2-5   *LU Prioritization Implementation*

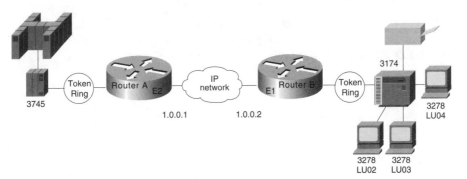

In Figure 2-5, the IBM mainframe is channel-attached to a 3745 communications controller, which is connected to a 3174 cluster controller via remote source-route bridging (RSRB). Multiple 3270 terminals and printers, each with a unique local LU address, are attached to the 3174. By applying LU address prioritization, you can assign a priority to each LU associated with a terminal or printer; that is, certain users can have terminals that have better response time than others, and printers can have lowest priority. This function increases application availability for those users running extremely important applications.

Finally, most routed protocols (such as AppleTalk, IPX, and DECnet) employ a cost-based routing protocol to assess the relative merit of the different routes to a destination. By tuning associated parameters, you can force particular kinds of traffic to take particular routes, thereby performing a type of manual traffic prioritization.

Custom Queuing

Priority queuing introduces a fairness problem in that packets classified to lower priority queues might not get serviced in a timely manner, or at all. Custom queuing is designed to address this problem. Custom queuing allows more granularity than priority queuing. In fact, this feature is commonly used in the networking environment, in which multiple higher-layer protocols are supported. Custom queuing reserves bandwidth for a specific protocol, thus allowing mission-critical traffic to receive a guaranteed minimum amount of bandwidth at any time.

The intent is to reserve bandwidth for a particular type of traffic. In Figure 2-6, for example, SNA has 40% of the bandwidth reserved using custom queuing, TCP/IP 20%, NetBIOS 20%, and the remaining protocols 20%. The APPN protocol itself has the concept of class of service (CoS), which determines the transmission priority for every message. APPN prioritizes the traffic before sending it to the DLC transmission queue.

Custom queuing prioritizes multiprotocol traffic. A maximum of 16 queues can be built with custom queuing. Each queue is serviced sequentially until the number of bytes sent exceeds the configurable byte count or the queue is empty. One important function of custom queuing is that if SNA traffic uses only 20% of the link, the remaining 20% allocated to SNA can be shared by the other traffic.

Custom queuing is designed for environments that want to ensure a minimum level of service for all protocols. In today's multiprotocol network environment, this important feature allows protocols of different characteristics to share the media.

Figure 2-6   *Custom Queuing*

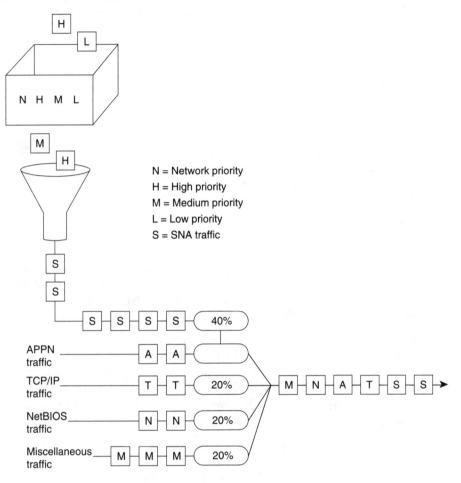

N = Network priority
H = High priority
M = Medium priority
L = Low priority
S = SNA traffic

APPN traffic

TCP/IP traffic

NetBIOS traffic

Miscellaneous traffic

Weighted Fair Queuing

Weighted fair queuing is a traffic priority management algorithm that uses the time-division multiplexing (TDM) model to divide the available bandwidth among clients that share the same interface. In time-division multiplexing, each client is allocated a time slice in a round-robin fashion. In weighted fair queuing, the bandwidth is distributed evenly among clients so that each client gets a fair share if each one has the same weight. You can assign a different set of weights—for example, through ToS—so that more bandwidth is allocated.

If every client is allocated the same bandwidth independent of the arrival rates, the low-volume traffic has effective priority over high-volume traffic. The use of weighting allows time-delay–sensitive traffic to obtain additional bandwidth, and thus consistent response time is guaranteed under heavy traffic. There are different types of data streams converging on a wire, as shown in Figure 2-7.

Figure 2-7 *Weighted Fair Queuing*

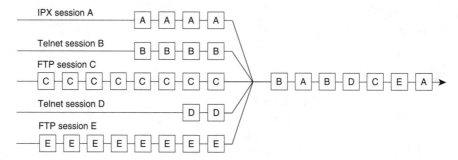

Both C and E are FTP sessions, and they are high-volume traffic. A, B, and D are interactive sessions, and they are low-volume traffic. Every session in this case is termed a *conversation*. If each conversation is serviced in a cyclic manner and gets a slot regardless of its arrival rate, the FTP sessions do not monopolize the bandwidth. Round-trip delays for the interactive traffic, therefore, become predictable.

Weighted fair queuing provides an algorithm to identify data streams dynamically using an interface and sorts them into separate logical queues. The algorithm uses various discriminators based on whatever network layer protocol information is available and sorts among them. For IP traffic, for example, the discriminators are source and destination address, protocol type, socket numbers, and ToS. This is how the two Telnet sessions (Sessions B and D) are assigned to different logical queues, as shown in Figure 2-7.

Ideally, the algorithm would classify every conversation that is sharing the wire so that each conversation receives its fair share of the bandwidth. Unfortunately, with such protocols as SNA, you cannot distinguish one SNA session from another. In DLSw+, for example, SNA traffic is multiplexed onto a single TCP session. Similarly in APPN, SNA sessions are multiplexed onto a single LLC2 session.

The weighted fair queuing algorithm treats these sessions as a single conversation. If you have many TCP sessions, the TCP sessions get the majority of the bandwidth, and the SNA traffic gets the minimum. For this reason, this algorithm is not recommended for SNA using DLSw+ TCP/IP encapsulation and APPN.

Weighted fair queuing, however, has many advantages over priority queuing and custom queuing. Priority queuing and custom queuing require the installation of access lists; the bandwidth has to be pre-allocated, and priorities have to be predefined. This is clearly a burden. Sometimes, network administrators cannot identify and prioritize network traffic in real time. Weighted fair queuing sorts among individual traffic streams without the administrative burden associated with the other two types of queuing.

Load Balancing

The easiest way to add bandwidth in a backbone network is to implement additional links. Routers provide built-in load balancing for multiple links and paths. You can use up to four paths to a destination network. In some cases, the paths need not be of equal cost.

Within IP, routers provide load balancing on both a per-packet and a per-destination basis. For per-destination load balancing, each router uses its route cache to determine the output interface. If IGRP or EIGRP routing is used, unequal-cost load balancing is possible. The router uses metrics to determine which paths the packets will take; the amount of load balancing can be adjusted by the user.

Load balancing bridged traffic over serial lines is also supported. Serial lines can be assigned to circuit groups. If one of the serial links in the circuit group is in the spanning tree for a network, any of the serial links in the circuit group can be used for load balancing. Data ordering problems are avoided by assigning each destination to a serial link. Reassignment is done dynamically if interfaces go down or come up.

Alternative Paths

Many network backbones carry mission-critical information. Organizations running such backbones are usually interested in protecting the integrity of this information at virtually any cost. Routers must offer sufficient reliability so that they are not the weak link in the network chain. The key is to provide alternative paths that can come online whenever link failures occur along active networks.

End-to-end reliability is not ensured just by making the backbone fault-tolerant. If communication on a local segment within any building is disrupted for any reason, that information will not reach the backbone. End-to-end reliability is possible only when redundancy is employed throughout the network. Because this is usually cost-prohibitive, most companies prefer to employ redundant paths only on those segments that carry mission-critical information.

What does it take to make the backbone reliable? Routers hold the key to reliable networking. Depending on the definition of reliability, this can mean duplicating every major system on each router and possibly every component. Hardware component duplication is not the entire solution, however, because extra circuitry is necessary to link the duplicate components to allow them to communicate. This solution is usually very expensive, but more importantly, it does not completely address the problem. Even assuming all routers in your network are completely reliable systems, link problems between nodes within a backbone can still defeat a redundant hardware solution.

To really address the problem of network reliability, links must be redundant. Further, it is not enough to duplicate all links. Dual links must terminate at multiple routers unless all backbone routers are completely fault-tolerant (no single points of failure). Otherwise, backbone routers that are not fault-tolerant become single points of failure. The inevitable conclusion is that a completely redundant router is not the most effective solution to the reliability problem because it is expensive and still does not address link reliability.

Most network designers do not implement a completely redundant network. Instead, network designers implement partially redundant networks. The section "Choosing Networking Reliability Options" later in this chapter addresses several hypothetical networks that represent commonly implemented points along the reliability continuum.

Switched Access

Switched access provides the capability to enable a WAN link on an as-needed basis via automated router controls. One model for a reliable backbone consists of dual dedicated links and one switched link for idle hot backup. Under normal operational conditions, you can load-balance over the dual links, but the switched link is not operational until one of the dedicated links fails.

Traditionally, WAN connections over the Public Switched Telephone Network (PSTN) have used dedicated lines. This can be very expensive when an application requires only low-volume, periodic connections. To reduce the need for dedicated circuits, a feature called dial-on-demand routing (DDR) is available. Figure 2-8 illustrates a DDR connection.

Figure 2-8   *The Dial-on-Demand Routing Environment*

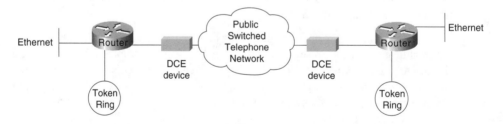

Using DDR, low-volume, periodic network connections can be made over the PSTN. A router activates the DDR feature when it receives a bridged or routed IP packet destined for a location on the other side of the dialup line. After the router dials the destination phone number and establishes the connection, packets of any supported protocol can be transmitted. When the transmission is complete, the line is automatically disconnected. By terminating unneeded connections, DDR reduces cost of ownership.

Encapsulation (Tunneling)

Encapsulation takes packets or frames from one network system and places them inside frames from another network system. This method is sometimes called *tunneling*. Tunneling provides a means for encapsulating packets inside a routable protocol via virtual interfaces. Synchronous Data Link Control (SDLC) transport is also an encapsulation of packets in a routable protocol. In addition, transport provides enhancements to tunneling, such as local data link layer termination, broadcast avoidance, media conversion, and other scalability optimizations.

Cisco routers support the following encapsulation and tunneling techniques:

- The IBM technology feature set provides these methods:
  - Serial tunnel (STUN) or Synchronous Data Link Control (SDLC) Transport
  - SRB with direct encapsulation
  - SRB with Fast-Sequenced Transport (FST) encapsulation
  - SRB with Transmission Control Protocol/Internet Protocol (TCP/IP) encapsulation
  - Data-link switching plus (DLSw+) with direct encapsulation
  - DLSw+ with TCP/IP encapsulation
  - DLSw+ with Fast-Sequenced Transport/Internet Protocol (FST/IP) encapsulation
  - DLSw+ with DLSw lite (Logical Link Control, type 2 [LLC2]) encapsulation

- Generic routing encapsulation (GRE)

  Cisco supports encapsulating Novell Internetwork Packet Exchange (IPX), Internet Protocol (IP), Connectionless Network Protocol (CLNP), AppleTalk, DECnet Phase IV, Xerox Network Systems (XNS), Banyan Virtual Network System (VINES), and Apollo packets for transport over IP.

- Single-protocol tunneling techniques: Cayman (AppleTalk over IP), AURP (AppleTalk over IP), EON (CLNP over IP), and NOS (IP over IP)

The following discussion focuses on IBM encapsulations and the multiprotocol GRE tunneling feature.

IBM Features

STUN allows two devices that are normally connected by a direct serial link, using protocols compliant with SDLC or High-level Data Link Control (HDLC), to be connected through one or more routers. The routers can be connected via a multiprotocol network of arbitrary topology. STUN allows integration of System Network Architecture (SNA) networks and non-SNA networks using routers and existing network links. Transport across the multiprotocol network that connects the routers can use TCP/IP. This type of transport offers reliability and intelligent routing via any supported IP routing protocol. Figure 2-9 shows a STUN configuration.

Figure 2-9   *STUN Configuration*

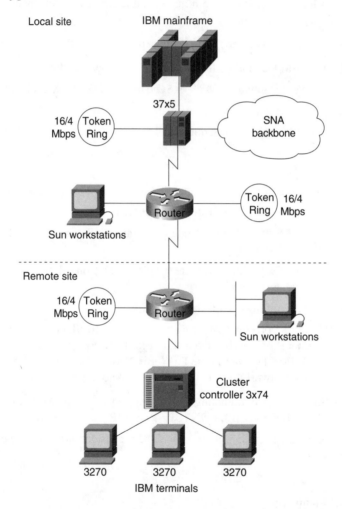

SDLC Transport is a variation of STUN that allows sessions using SDLC protocols and TCP/IP encapsulation to be locally terminated. SDLC Transport permits participation in SDLC windowing and retransmission activities.

When connecting remote devices that use SRB over a slow-speed serial link, most network designers choose RSRB with direct HDLC encapsulation. In this case, SRB frames are encapsulated in an HDLC-compliant header. This solution adds little overhead, preserving valuable serial-link bandwidth. Direct HDLC encapsulation is not restricted to serial links (it can also be used over Ethernet, Token Ring, and FDDI links), but it is most useful in situations in which additional control overhead on the encapsulating network is not tolerable.

When more overhead can be tolerated, frame sequencing is important, but if extremely reliable delivery is not needed, SRB packets can be sent over serial, Token Ring, Ethernet, and FDDI networks using FST encapsulation. FST is similar to TCP in that it provides packet sequencing. Unlike TCP, however, FST does not provide packet-delivery acknowledgment.

For extremely reliable delivery in environments in which moderate overhead can be tolerated, you can choose to encapsulate SRB frames in TCP/IP packets. This solution is not only reliable, it can also take advantage of routing features that include handling via routing protocols, packet filtering, and multipath routing.

Generic Routing Encapsulation (GRE)

Cisco's generic routing encapsulation (GRE) multiprotocol carrier protocol encapsulates IP, CLNP, IPX, AppleTalk, DECnet Phase IV, XNS, VINES, and Apollo packets inside IP tunnels. With GRE tunneling, a Cisco router at each site encapsulates protocol-specific packets in an IP header, creating a virtual point-to-point link to Cisco routers at other ends of an IP cloud, where the IP header is stripped off. By connecting multiprotocol subnetworks in a single-protocol backbone environment, IP tunneling allows network expansion across a single-protocol backbone environment. GRE tunneling involves three types of protocols:

- **Passenger**—The protocol is encapsulated (IP, CLNP, IPX, AppleTalk, DECnet Phase IV, XNS, VINES, and Apollo).
- **Carrier**—GRE protocol provides carrier services.
- **Transport**—IP carries the encapsulated protocol.

GRE tunneling allows desktop protocols to take advantage of the enhanced route-selection capabilities of IP. Many local-area network (LAN) protocols, including AppleTalk and Novell IPX, are optimized for local use. They have limited route selection metrics and hop count limitations. In contrast, IP routing protocols allow more flexible route selection and scale better over large networks. Figure 2-10 illustrates GRE tunneling across a single IP backbone between sites. Regardless of how many routers and paths may be associated with the IP cloud, the tunnel is seen as a single hop.

Figure 2-10 *Using a Single Protocol Backbone*

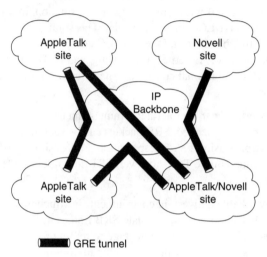

GRE provides key capabilities that other encapsulation protocols lack: sequencing and the capability to carry tunneled data at high speeds. Some higher-level protocols require that packets be delivered in correct order. The GRE sequencing option provides this capability. GRE also has an optional key feature that enables you to avoid configuration errors by requiring the same key to be entered at each tunnel endpoint before the tunneled data is processed. IP tunneling also enables network designers to implement policies, such as which types of traffic can use which routes or assignment of priority or security levels to particular traffic. Capabilities like these are lacking in many native LAN protocols.

IP tunneling provides communication between subnetworks that have invalid or discontiguous network addresses. With tunneling, virtual network addresses are assigned to subnetworks, making discontiguous subnetworks reachable. Figure 2-11 illustrates that with GRE tunneling, it is possible for the two subnetworks of network 131.108.0.0 to talk to each other even though they are separated by another network.

Figure 2-11 *Connecting Discontiguous Networks with Tunnels*

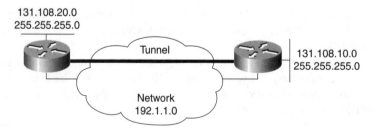

Because encapsulation requires handling of the packets, it is generally faster to route protocols natively than to use tunnels. Tunneled traffic is switched at approximately half the typical process switching rates. This means approximately 1,000 packets per second (pps) aggregate for each router. Tunneling is CPU-intensive, and as such, should be turned on cautiously. Routing updates, SAP updates, and other administrative traffic may be sent over each tunnel interface. It is easy to saturate a physical link with routing information if several tunnels are configured over it. Performance depends on the passenger protocol, broadcasts, routing updates, and bandwidth of the physical interfaces. It is also difficult to debug the physical link if problems occur. This problem can be mitigated in several ways. In IPX environments, route filters and SAP filters cut down on the size of the updates that travel over tunnels. In AppleTalk networks, keeping zones small and using route filters can limit excess bandwidth requirements.

Tunneling can disguise the nature of a link, making it look slower, faster, or more or less costly than it may actually be. This can cause unexpected or undesirable route selection. Routing protocols that make decisions based only on hop count usually prefer a tunnel to a real interface. This may not always be the best routing decision, because an IP cloud can comprise several different media with very disparate qualities; for example, traffic may be forwarded across both 100-Mbps Ethernet lines and 9.6-kbps serial lines. When using tunneling, pay attention to the media over which virtual tunnel traffic passes and the metrics used by each protocol.

If a network has sites that use protocol-based packet filters as part of a firewall security scheme, be aware that because tunnels encapsulate unchecked passenger protocols, you must establish filtering on the firewall router so that only authorized tunnels are allowed to pass. If tunnels are accepted from unsecured networks, it is a good idea to establish filtering at the tunnel destination or to place the tunnel destination outside the secure area of your network so that the current firewall scheme will remain secure.

When tunneling IP over IP, you must be careful to avoid inadvertently configuring a recursive routing loop. A routing loop occurs when the passenger protocol and the transport protocol are identical. The routing loop occurs because the best path to the tunnel destination is via the tunnel interface. A routing loop can occur when tunneling IP over IP, as follows:

1 The packet is placed in the output queue of the tunnel interface.

2 The tunnel interface includes a GRE header and enqueues the packet to the transport protocol (IP) for the destination address of the tunnel interface.

3 IP looks up the route to the tunnel destination address and learns that the path is the tunnel interface.

4 Once again, the packet is placed in the output queue of the tunnel interface, as described in Step 1 (hence, the routing loop).

When a router detects a recursive routing loop, it shuts down the tunnel interface for 1 to 2 minutes and issues a warning message before it goes into the recursive loop. Another indication that a recursive route loop has been detected is if the tunnel interface is up and the line protocol is down.

To avoid recursive loops, keep passenger and transport routing information in separate locations by implementing the following procedures:

- Use separate routing protocol identifiers (for example, IGRP 1 and IGRP 2).
- Use different routing protocols.
- Assign the tunnel interface a very low bandwidth so that routing protocols, such as IGRP, will recognize a very high metric for the tunnel interface and will, therefore, choose the correct next hop (that is, choose the best physical interface rather than the tunnel).
- Keep the two IP address ranges distinct; that is, use a major address for your tunnel network that is different from your actual IP network. Keeping the address ranges distinct also aids in debugging because it is easy to identify an address as the tunnel network rather than the physical network and vice versa.

Evaluating Distribution Services

This section addresses networking features that support distribution services. The following topics are discussed:

- Backbone Bandwidth Management
- Area and Service Filtering
- Policy-Based Distribution
- Gateway Service
- Interprotocol Route Redistribution
- Media Translation

Backbone Bandwidth Management

To optimize backbone network operations, routers offer several performance-tuning features. Examples include priority queuing, routing protocol metrics, and local-session termination.

You can adjust the output queue length on priority queues. If a priority queue overflows, excess packets are discarded and quench messages that halt packet flow are sent, if appropriate, for that protocol. You can also adjust routing metrics to increase control over the paths that the traffic takes through the network.

Local-session termination allows routers to act as proxies for remote systems that represent session endpoints. (A *proxy* is a device that acts on behalf of another device.) Figure 2-12 illustrates an example of local-session termination in an IBM environment.

Figure 2-12 *Local-Session Termination Over Multiprotocol Backbone*

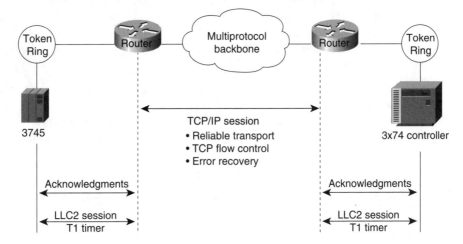

In Figure 2-12, the routers locally terminate Logical Link Control, type 2 (LLC2) data-link control sessions. Instead of end-to-end sessions, during which all session control information is passed over the multiprotocol backbone, the routers take responsibility for acknowledging packets that come from hosts on directly attached LANs. Local acknowledgment saves WAN bandwidth (and, therefore, WAN utilization costs), solves session timeout problems, and provides faster response to users.

Area and Service Filtering

Traffic filters based on *area* or *service* type are the primary distribution service tools used to provide policy-based access control into backbone services. Both area and service filtering are implemented using *access lists*. An access list is a sequence of statements, each of which either permits or denies certain conditions or addresses. Access lists can be used to permit or deny messages from particular network nodes and messages sent using particular protocols and services.

Area or network access filters are used to enforce the selective transmission of traffic based on network address. You can apply these on incoming or outgoing ports. Service filters use access lists applied to protocols (such as IP's UDP), applications such as the Simple Mail Transfer Protocol (SMTP), and specific protocols.

Suppose you have a network connected to the Internet, and you want any host on an Ethernet to be able to form TCP connections to any host on the Internet. However, you do not want Internet hosts to be able to form TCP connections to hosts on the Ethernet except to the SMTP port of a dedicated mail host.

SMTP uses TCP port 25 on one end of the connection and a random port number on the other end. The same two port numbers are used throughout the life of the connection. Mail packets coming in from the Internet will have a destination port of 25. Outbound packets will have the port numbers reversed. The fact that the secure system behind the router always accepts mail connections on port 25 is what makes it possible to separately control incoming and outgoing services. The access list can be configured on either the outbound or inbound interface.

In the following example, the Ethernet network is a Class B network with the address 128.88.0.0, and the mail host's address is 128.88.1.2. The keyword **established** is used only for the TCP protocol to indicate an established connection. A match occurs if the TCP datagram has the ACK or RST bits set, which indicate that the packet belongs to an existing connection.

```
access-list 102 permit tcp 0.0.0.0 255.255.255.255 128.88.0.0 0.0.255.255
  established
access-list 102 permit tcp 0.0.0.0 255.255.255.255 128.88.1.2 0.0.0.0 eq 25
interface ethernet 0
ip access-group 102
```

Policy-Based Distribution

Policy-based distribution is based on the premise that different departments within a common organization might have different policies regarding traffic dispersion through the organization-wide network. Policy-based distribution aims to meet the differing requirements without compromising performance and information integrity.

A *policy* within this networking context is a rule or set of rules that governs end-to-end distribution of traffic to (and subsequently through) a backbone network. One department might send traffic representing three different protocols to the backbone, but it might want to expedite one particular protocol's transit through the backbone because it carries mission-critical application information. To minimize already excessive internal traffic, another department might want to exclude all backbone traffic except electronic mail and one key custom application from entering its network segment.

These examples reflect policies specific to a single department. However, policies can reflect overall organizational goals. An organization might want to regulate backbone traffic to a maximum of 10% average bandwidth during the workday, for example, and 1-minute peaks of 30% utilization. Another corporate policy might be to ensure that communication between two remote departments can freely occur, despite differences in technology.

Different policies frequently require different workgroup and department technologies. Therefore, support for policy-based distribution implies support for the wide range of technologies currently used to implement these policies. This in turn enables you to implement solutions that support a wide range of policies, which helps to increase organizational flexibility and application availability.

In addition to support for networking technologies, there must be a means to both keep separate and integrate these technologies, as appropriate. The different technologies should be able to coexist or combine intelligently, as the situation warrants.

Consider the situation depicted in Figure 2-13. Assume that a corporate policy limits unnecessary backbone traffic. One way to do this is to restrict the transmission of Service Advertisement Protocol (SAP) messages. SAP messages allow NetWare servers to advertise services to clients. The organization might have another policy stating that all NetWare services should be provided locally. If this is the case, there should be no reason for services to be advertised remotely. SAP filters prevent SAP traffic from leaving a router interface, thereby fulfilling this policy.

Figure 2-13 *Policy-Based Distribution: SAP Filtering*

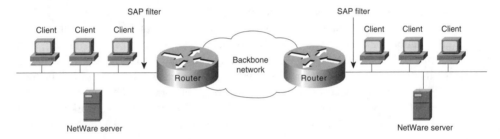

Gateway Service

Protocol gateway capabilities are part of each router's standard software. For example, DECnet is currently in Phase V. DECnet Phase V addresses are different from DECnet Phase IV addresses. For those networks that require both types of hosts to coexist, two-way Phase IV/Phase V translation conforms to Digital-specified guidelines. The routers interoperate with Digital routers, and Digital hosts do not differentiate between the different devices.

The connection of multiple independent DECnet networks can lead to addressing problems. Nothing precludes two independent DECnet administrators from assigning node address 10 to one of the nodes in their respective networks. When the two networks are connected at some later time, conflicts result. DECnet address translation gateways (ATGs) address this problem. The ATG solution provides router-based translation between addresses in two different DECnet networks connected by a router. Figure 2-14 illustrates an example of this operation.

Figure 2-14 *Sample DECnet ATG Implementation*

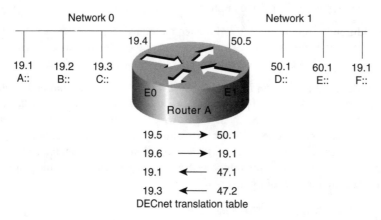

In Network 0, the router is configured at address 19.4 and is a Level 1 router. In Network 1, the router is configured at address 50.5 and is an area router. At this point, no routing information is exchanged between the two networks. The router maintains a separate routing table for each network. By establishing a translation map, packets in Network 0 sent to address 19.5 will be routed to Network 1, and the destination address will be translated to 50.1. Similarly, packets sent to address 19.6 in Network 0 will be routed to Network 1 as 19.1; packets sent to address 47.1 in Network 1 will be routed to Network 0 as 19.1; and packets sent to 47.2 in Network 1 will be sent to Network 0 as 19.3.

AppleTalk is another protocol with multiple revisions, each with somewhat different addressing characteristics. AppleTalk Phase 1 addresses are simple local forms; AppleTalk Phase 2 uses extended (multinetwork) addressing. Normally, information sent from a Phase 2 node cannot be understood by a Phase 1 node if Phase 2 extended addressing is used. Routers support routing between Phase 1 and Phase 2 nodes on the same cable by using transitional routing.

You can accomplish transitional routing by attaching two router ports to the same physical cable. Configure one port to support nonextended AppleTalk and the other to support extended AppleTalk. Both ports must have unique network numbers. Packets are translated and sent out the other port as necessary.

Interprotocol Route Redistribution

The preceding section, "Gateway Service," discussed how *routed* protocol gateways (such as one that translates between AppleTalk Phase 1 and Phase 2) allow two end nodes with different implementations to communicate. Routers can also act as gateways for *routing* protocols. Information derived from one routing protocol, such as the IGRP, can be passed to, and used by, another routing protocol, such as RIP. This is useful when running multiple routing protocols in the same network.

Routing information can be exchanged between any supported IP routing protocols. These include RIP, IGRP, OSPF, EIGRP, ISIS, EGP, and BGP. Similarly, route redistribution is supported by ISO CLNS for route redistribution between ISO IGRP and IS-IS. Static route information can also be redistributed. Defaults can be assigned so that one routing protocol can use the same metric for all redistributed routes, thereby simplifying the routing redistribution mechanism.

Media Translation

Media translation techniques translate frames from one network system into frames of another. Such translations are rarely 100% effective, because one system might have attributes with no corollary to the other. Token Ring networks support a built-in priority and reservation system, for example, whereas Ethernet networks do not. Translations between Token Ring and Ethernet networks must somehow account for this discrepancy. It is possible for two vendors to make different decisions about how this discrepancy will be handled, which can prevent multivendor interoperation.

For those situations in which communication between end stations on different media is required, routers can translate between Ethernet and Token Ring frames. For direct bridging between Ethernet and Token Ring environments, use either source-route translational bridging or source-route transparent bridging (SRT). Source-route translational bridging translates between Token Ring and Ethernet frame formats; SRT allows routers to use both SRB and the transparent bridging algorithm used in standard Ethernet bridging.

When bridging from the SRB domain to the transparent bridging domain, the SRB fields of the frames are removed. RIFs are cached for use by subsequent return traffic. When bridging in the opposite direction, the router checks the packet to determine whether it has a multicast, broadcast, or unicast destination. If it has a multicast or broadcast destination, the packet is sent as a spanning-tree explorer. If it has a unicast destination, the router looks up the path to the destination in the RIF cache. If a path is found, it will be used; otherwise, the router will send the packet as a spanning-tree explorer. Figure 2-15 shows a simple example of this topology.

Figure 2-15 *Source-Route Translational Bridging Topology*

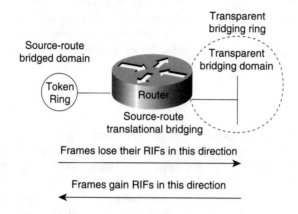

Routers support SRT through implementation of both transparent bridging and SRB algorithms on each SRT interface. If an interface notes the presence of a RIF field, it uses the SRB algorithm; if not, it uses the transparent bridging algorithm.

Translation between serial links running the SDLC protocol and Token Rings running LLC2 is also available. This is referred to as SDLLC frame translation. SDLLC frame translation allows connections between serial lines and Token Rings. This is useful for consolidating traditionally disparate SNA/SDLC networks into a LAN-based, multiprotocol, multimedia backbone network. Using SDLLC, routers terminate SDLC sessions, translate SDLC frames to LLC2 frames, and then forward the LLC2 frames using RSRB over a point-to-point or IP network. Because a router-based IP network can use arbitrary media, such as FDDI, Frame Relay, X.25, or leased lines, routers support SDLLC over all such media through IP encapsulation.

Figure 2-16 shows a complex SDLLC configuration.

Figure 2-16 *Complex SDLLC Configuration*

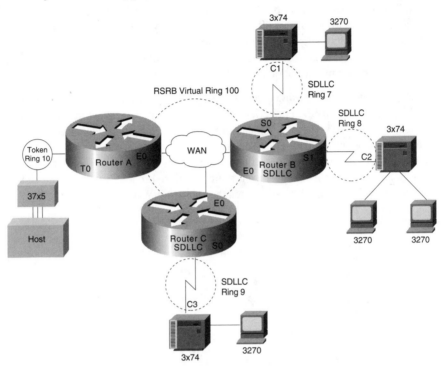

Evaluating Local-Access Services

The following discussion addresses networking features that support local-access services. Local-access service topics outlined here include the following:

- Value-Added Network Addressing
- Network Segmentation
- Broadcast and Multicast Capabilities
- Naming, Proxy, and Local Cache Capabilities
- Media Access Security
- Router Discovery

Value-Added Network Addressing

Address schemes for LAN-based networks, such as NetWare and others, do not always adapt perfectly to use over multisegment LANs or WANs. One tool routers implement to ensure operation of such protocols is protocol-specific *helper addressing*. Helper addressing is a mechanism to assist the movement of specific traffic through a network when that traffic might not otherwise transit the network.

The use of helper addressing is best illustrated with an example. Consider the use of helper addresses in Novell IPX networks. Novell clients send broadcast messages when looking for a server. If the server is not local, broadcast traffic must be sent through routers. Helper addresses and access lists can be used together to allow broadcasts from certain nodes on one network to be directed specifically to certain servers on another network. Multiple helper addresses on each interface are supported, so broadcast packets can be forwarded to multiple hosts. Figure 2-17 illustrates the use of NetWare-based helper addressing.

Figure 2-17   *Sample Network Map Illustrating Helper Address Broadcast Control*

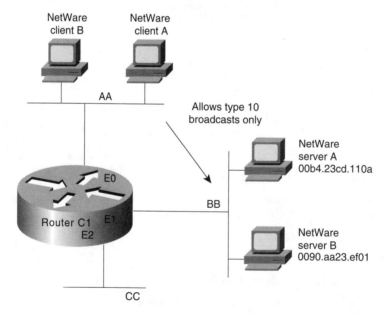

NetWare clients on Network AA are allowed to broadcast to any server on Network BB. An applicable access list would specify that broadcasts of type 10 will be permitted from all nodes on Network AA. A configuration-specified helper address identifies the addresses on Network BB to which these broadcasts are directed. No other nodes on Network BB receive the broadcasts. No other broadcasts other than type 10 broadcasts are routed.

Any downstream networks beyond Network AA (for example, some Network AA1) are not allowed to broadcast to Network BB through Router C1, unless the routers partitioning

Networks AA and AA1 are configured to forward broadcasts with a series of configuration entries. These entries must be applied to the input interfaces and be set to forward broadcasts between directly connected networks. In this way, traffic is passed along in a directed manner from network to network.

Network Segmentation

The splitting of networks into more manageable pieces is an essential role played by local-access routers. In particular, local-access routers implement local policies and limit unnecessary traffic. Examples of capabilities that enable network designers to use local-access routers to segment networks include IP subnets, DECnet area addressing, and AppleTalk zones.

You can use local-access routers to implement local policies by placing the routers in strategic locations and by configuring specific segmenting policies. For example, you can set up a series of LAN segments with different subnet addresses; routers would be configured with suitable interface addresses and subnet masks. In general, traffic on a given segment is limited to local broadcasts, traffic intended for a specific end station on that segment, or traffic intended for another specific router. By distributing hosts and clients carefully, you can use this simple method of dividing up a network to reduce overall network congestion.

Broadcast and Multicast Capabilities

Many protocols use *broadcast* and *multicast* capabilities. Broadcasts are messages sent out to all network destinations. Multicasts are messages sent to a specific subset of network destinations. Routers inherently reduce broadcast proliferation by default. Routers can be configured to relay broadcast traffic, however, if necessary. Under certain circumstances, passing along broadcast information is desirable and possibly necessary. The key is controlling broadcasts and multicasts using routers.

In the IP world, as with many other technologies, broadcast requests are very common. Unless broadcasts are controlled, network bandwidth can be seriously reduced. Routers offer various broadcast-limiting functions that reduce network traffic and minimize broadcast storms. Directed broadcasting, for example, allows for broadcasts to a specific network or a series of networks, rather than to the entire network. When flooded broadcasts (broadcasts sent through the entire network) are necessary, Cisco routers support a technique by which these broadcasts are sent over a spanning tree of the network. The spanning tree ensures complete coverage without excessive traffic because only one packet is sent over each network segment.

As discussed previously in the section titled "Value-Added Network Addressing," broadcast assistance is accommodated with the helper address mechanisms. You can allow a router or series of routers to relay broadcasts that would otherwise be blocked by using helper addresses. You can permit retransmission of SAP broadcasts using helper addresses, for example, and thereby notify clients on different network segments of certain NetWare services available from specific remote servers.

The Cisco IP multicast feature allows IP traffic to be propagated from one source to any number of destinations. Instead of sending one packet to each destination, one packet is sent to a multicast group identified by a single IP destination group address. IP multicast provides excellent support for such applications as video and audio conferencing, resource discovery, and stock-market traffic distribution.

For full support of IP multicast, IP hosts must run the Internet Group Management Protocol (IGMP). IGMP is used by IP hosts to report their multicast group memberships to an immediately neighboring multicast router. The membership of a multicast group is dynamic. Multicast routers send IGMP query messages on their attached local networks. Host members of a multicast group respond to a query by sending IGMP reports for multicast groups to which they belong. Reports sent by the first host in a multicast group suppress the sending of identical reports from other hosts of the same group.

The multicast router attached to the local network takes responsibility for forwarding multicast datagrams from one multicast group to all other networks that have members in the group. Routers build multicast group distribution trees (routing tables) so that multicast packets have loop-free paths to all multicast group members so that multicast packets are not duplicated. If no reports are received from a multicast group after a set number of IGMP queries, the multicast routers assume that the group has no local members and stop forwarding multicasts intended for that group.

Cisco routers also support Protocol Independent Multicast (PIM).

Naming, Proxy, and Local Cache Capabilities

Three key router capabilities help reduce network traffic and promote efficient networking operation: name service support, proxy services, and local caching of network information.

Network applications and connection services provided over segmented networks require a rational way to resolve names to addresses. Various facilities accommodate this requirement. Any router you select must support the name services implemented for different end-system environments. Examples of supported name services include NetBIOS, IP's Domain Name System (DNS) and IEN-116, and AppleTalk Name Binding Protocol (NBP).

A router can also act as a proxy for a name server. The router's support of NetBIOS name caching is one example of this kind of capability. NetBIOS name caching allows the router to maintain a cache of NetBIOS names, which avoids the overhead of transmitting all the broadcasts between client and server NetBIOS PCs (IBM PCs or PS/2s) in an SRB environment. When NetBIOS name caching is enabled, the router does the following:

- Notices when any host sends a series of duplicate query frames and limits retransmission to one frame per period. The time period is a configuration parameter.
- Keeps a cache of mappings between NetBIOS server and client names and their MAC addresses. As a result, broadcast requests sent by clients to find servers (and by servers in response to their clients) can be sent directly to their destinations, rather than being broadcast across the entire bridged network.

When NetBIOS name caching is enabled and default parameters are set on the router, the NetBIOS name server, and the NetBIOS name client, approximately 20 broadcast packets per logon are kept on the local ring where they are generated.

In most cases, the NetBIOS name cache is best used when large amounts of NetBIOS broadcast traffic might create bottlenecks on a WAN that connects local networks to distant locations.

The router can also save bandwidth (or handle nonconforming name resolution protocols) by using a variety of other proxy facilities. By using routers to act on behalf of other devices to perform various functions, you can more easily scale networks. Instead of being forced to add bandwidth when a new workgroup is added to a location, you can use a router to manage address resolution and control message services. Examples of this kind of capability include the proxy explorer feature of SRB and the proxy polling feature of STUN implementations.

Sometimes portions of networks cannot participate in routing activity or do not implement software that conforms to generally implemented address-resolution protocols. Proxy implementations on routers enable network designers to support these networks or hosts without reconfiguring a network. Examples of these kinds of capabilities include proxy ARP address resolution for IP networks and NBP proxy in AppleTalk networks.

Local caches store previously learned information about the network so that new information requests do not need to be issued each time the same piece of information is desired. A router's ARP cache stores physical address and network address mappings so that it does not need to broadcast ARP requests more than once within a given time period for the same address. Address caches are maintained for many other protocols as well, including DECnet, Novell IPX, and SRB, where RIF information is cached.

Media Access Security

If all corporate information is readily available to all employees, security violations and inappropriate file access can occur. To prevent this, routers must do the following:

- Keep local traffic from inappropriately reaching the backbone
- Keep backbone traffic from exiting the backbone into an inappropriate department or workgroup network

These two functions require packet filtering. Packet-filtering capabilities should be tailored to support a variety of corporate policies. Packet-filtering methods can reduce traffic levels on a network, thereby allowing a company to continue using its current technology rather than investing in more network hardware. In addition, packet filters can improve security by keeping unauthorized users from accessing information and can minimize network problems caused by excessive congestion.

Routers support many filtering schemes designed to provide control over network traffic that reaches the backbone. Perhaps the most powerful of these filtering mechanisms is the access list. Each of the following possible local-access services can be provided through access lists:

- You have an Ethernet-to-Internet routing network and you want any host on the Ethernet to be able to form TCP connections to any host on the Internet. You do not want Internet hosts to be able to form TCP connections into the Ethernet, however, except to the SMTP port of a dedicated mail host.

- You want to advertise only one network through a RIP routing process.

- You want to prevent packets that originated on any Sun workstation from being bridged on a particular Ethernet segment.

- You want to keep a particular protocol based on Novell IPX from establishing a connection between a source network or source-port combination and a destination network or destination-port combination.

Access lists logically prevent certain packets from traversing a particular router interface, thereby providing a general tool for implementing network security. In addition to this method, several specific security systems already exist to help increase network security. For example, the U.S. government has specified the use of an optional field within the IP packet header to implement a hierarchical packet security system called the Internet Protocol Security Option (IPSO).

IPSO support on routers addresses both the basic and extended security options described in a draft of the IPSO circulated by the Defense Communications Agency. This draft document is an early version of Request for Comments (RFC) 1108. IPSO defines security levels (for example, TOP SECRET, SECRET, and others) on a per-interface basis and accepts or rejects messages based on whether they include adequate authorization.

Some security systems are designed to keep remote users from accessing the network unless they have adequate authorization. For example, the Terminal Access Controller Access Control System (TACACS) is a means of protecting modem access into a network. The Defense Data Network (DDN) developed TACACS to control access to its TAC terminal servers.

The router's TACACS support is patterned after the DDN application. When a user attempts to start an EXEC command interpreter on a password-protected line, TACACS prompts for a password. If the user fails to enter the correct password, access is denied. Router administrators can control various TACACS parameters, such as the number of retries allowed, the timeout interval, and the enabling of TACACS accounting.

The Challenge Handshake Authentication Protocol (CHAP) is another way to keep unauthorized remote users from accessing a network. It is also commonly used to control router-to-router communications. When CHAP is enabled, a remote device (for example, a PC, workstation, router, or communication server) attempting to connect to a local router is challenged to provide an appropriate response. If the correct response is not provided, network access is denied.

CHAP is becoming popular because it does not require a secret password to be sent over the network. CHAP is supported on all router serial lines using Point-to-Point Protocol (PPP) encapsulation.

Router Discovery

Hosts must be able to locate routers when they need access to devices external to the local network. When more than one router is attached to a host's local segment, the host must be able to locate the router that represents the optimal path to the destination. This process of finding routers is called *router discovery*.

The following are router-discovery protocols:

- **End System-to-Intermediate System (ES-IS)**—This protocol is defined by the ISO OSI protocol suite. It is dedicated to the exchange of information between intermediate systems (routers) and end systems (hosts). ESs send "ES hello" messages to all ISs on the local subnetwork. In turn, "IS hello" messages are sent from all ISs to all ESs on the local subnetwork. Both types of messages convey the subnetwork and network layer addresses of the systems that generate them. Using this protocol, end systems and intermediate systems can locate one another.

- **ICMP Router Discovery Protocol (IRDP)**—Although the issue is currently under study, there is currently no single standardized manner for end stations to locate routers in the IP world. In many cases, stations are just configured manually with the address of a local router. However, RFC 1256 outlines a router-discovery protocol using the Internet Control Message Protocol (ICMP). This protocol is commonly referred to as IRDP.

- **Proxy Address Resolution Protocol (ARP)**—ARP uses broadcast messages to determine the MAC-layer address that corresponds to a particular network address. ARP is sufficiently generic to allow use of IP with virtually any type of underlying media-access mechanism. A router that has proxy ARP enabled responds to ARP requests for those hosts for which it has a route, which allows hosts to assume that all other hosts are actually on their network.

- **RIP**—RIP is a routing protocol commonly available on IP hosts. Many hosts use RIP to find the address of the routers on a LAN or, when there are multiple routers, to pick the best router to use for a given network address.

Cisco routers support all the router-discovery protocols listed. You can choose the router-discovery mechanism that works best in your particular environment.

Choosing Networking Reliability Options

One of the first concerns of most network designers is to determine the required level of application availability. In general, this key consideration is balanced against implementation cost. For most organizations, the cost of making a network completely fault-tolerant is prohibitive. Determining the appropriate level of fault tolerance to be included in a network and where redundancy should be used is not trivial.

The nonredundant network design in Figure 2-18 illustrates the considerations involved with increasing levels of network fault tolerance.

Figure 2-18   *Typical Nonredundant Network Design*

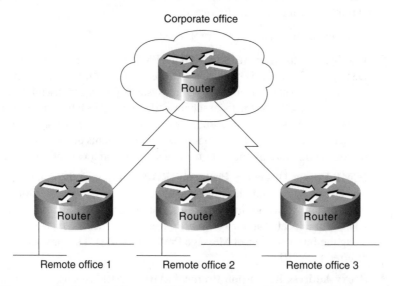

The network shown in Figure 2-18 has two levels of hierarchy: a corporate office and remote offices. Assume the corporate office has eight Ethernet segments, to which approximately 400 users (an average of 50 per segment) are connected. Each Ethernet segment is connected to a router. In the remote offices, two Ethernet segments are connected to the corporate office through a router. The router in each remote office is connected to the router in the corporate office through a T1 link.

The following sections address various approaches to creating redundant networks, provide some context for each approach, and contrast their relative merits and drawbacks. The following four sections are provided:

- Redundant Links Versus Meshed Topologies
- Redundant Power Systems
- Fault-Tolerant Media Implementations
- Backup Hardware

Redundant Links Versus Meshed Topologies

Typically, WAN links are the least reliable components in a network, usually because of problems in the local loop. In addition to being relatively unreliable, these links are often an order of magnitude slower than the LANs they connect. Because they are capable of connecting geographically diverse sites, however, WAN links often make up the backbone network, and are therefore critical to corporate operations. The combination of potentially suspect reliability, lack of speed, and high importance makes the WAN link a good candidate for redundancy.

As a first step in making the example network more fault-tolerant, you might add a WAN link between each remote office and the corporate office. This results in the topology shown in Figure 2-19. The new topology has several advantages. First, it provides a backup link that can be used if a primary link connecting any remote office and the corporate office fails. Second, if the routers support load balancing, link bandwidth has now been increased, lowering response times for users and increasing application availability.

Figure 2-19 *Network with Dual Links to Remote Offices*

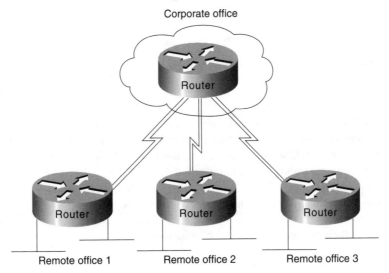

Load balancing in transparent bridging and IGRP environments is another tool for increasing fault tolerance. Routers also support load balancing on either a per-packet or per-destination basis in all IP environments. Per-packet load balancing is recommended if the WAN links are relatively slow (for example, less than 56 kbps). If WAN links are faster than 56 kbps, enabling fast switching on the routers is recommended. When fast switching is enabled, load balancing occurs on a per-destination basis.

Routers can automatically compensate for failed WAN links through routing algorithms of protocols, such as IGRP, EIGRP, OSPF, and IS-IS. If one link fails, the routing software recalculates the routing algorithm and begins sending all traffic through another link. This allows applications to proceed in the face of WAN link failure, improving application availability.

The primary disadvantage of duplicating WAN links to each remote office is cost. In the example outlined in Figure 2-19, three new WAN links are required. In large star networks with more remote offices, 10 or 20 new WAN links might be needed, as well as new equipment (including new WAN router interfaces). A lower-cost alternative that is becoming increasingly popular links the remote offices using a meshed topology, as shown in Figure 2-20.

Figure 2-20   *Evolution from a Star to a Meshed Topology*

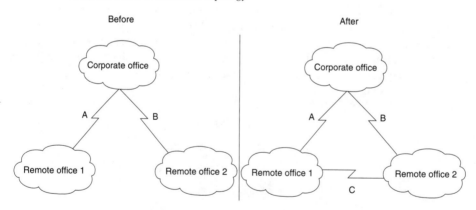

In the "before" portion of Figure 2-20, any failure associated with either Link A or B blocks access to a remote site. The failure might involve the link connection equipment, such as a data service unit (DSU) or a channel service unit (CSU), the router (either the entire router or a single router port), or the link itself. Adding Link C as shown in the "after" portion of the figure offsets the effect of a failure in any single link. If Link A or B fails, the affected remote site can still access the corporate office through Link C and the other site's link to the corporate office. Note also that if Link C fails, the two remote sites can communicate through their connections to the corporate office.

A meshed topology has three distinct advantages over a redundant star topology:

- A meshed topology is usually slightly less expensive (at least by the cost of one WAN link).
- A meshed topology provides more direct (and potentially faster) communication between remote sites, which translates to greater application availability. This can be useful if direct traffic volumes between remote sites are relatively high.
- A meshed topology promotes distributed operation, preventing bottlenecks on the corporate router and further increasing application availability.

A redundant star is a reasonable solution under the following conditions:

- Relatively little traffic must travel between remote offices.
- Traffic moving between corporate and remote offices is delay-sensitive and mission-critical. The delay and potential reliability problems associated with making an extra hop when a link between a remote office and the corporate office fails might not be tolerable.

Redundant Power Systems

Power faults are common in large-scale networks. Because they can strike across a very local or a very wide scale, power faults are difficult to preempt. Simple power problems include dislodged power cords, tripped circuit breakers, and local power-supply failures. More extensive power problems include large-scale outages caused by natural phenomena (such as lightning strikes) or brown-outs. Each organization must assess its needs and the probability of each type of power outage before determining which preventative actions to take.

You can take many precautions to try to ensure that problems, such as dislodged power cords, do not occur frequently. These fall outside the scope of this book and will not be discussed here. This chapter focuses on issues addressable by networking devices.

From the standpoint of networking devices, dual power systems can prevent otherwise debilitating failures. Imagine a situation where the so-called *backbone-in-a-box* configuration is being used. This configuration calls for the connection of many networks to a router being used as a *connectivity hub*. Benefits include a high-speed backbone (essentially the router's backplane) and cost efficiency (less media). Unfortunately, if the router's power system becomes faulty, each network connected to that router loses its capability to communicate with all other networks connected to that router.

Some backbone-in-a-box routers can address this requirement by providing redundant power systems. In addition, many sites connect one power system to the local power grid and the other to an uninterruptible power supply. If router power fails, the router can continue to provide connectivity to each connected network.

General power outages are usually more common than failures in a router's power system. Consider the effect of a site-wide power failure on redundant star and meshed topologies. If the power fails in the corporate office, the organization might be seriously inconvenienced. Key network applications are likely to be placed at a centralized, corporate location. The organization could easily lose revenue for every minute its network is down. The meshed network configuration is superior in this case because links between the remote offices would still be able to communicate with each other.

If power fails at a remote site, all connections to that remote site will be terminated unless otherwise protected. Neither the redundant star nor the meshed topology is superior. In both cases, all other remote offices will still be able to communicate with the corporate office. Generally, power failures in a remote office are more serious when network services are widely distributed.

To protect against local and site-wide power outages, some companies have negotiated an arrangement with local power companies to use multiple power grids within their organization. Failure within one power grid will not affect the network if all critical components have access to multiple power grids. Unfortunately, this arrangement is very expensive and should only be considered by companies with substantial resources, extremely mission-critical operations, and a relatively high likelihood of power failures.

The effect of highly localized power failures can be minimized with prudent network planning. Wherever possible, redundant components should use power supplied by different circuits. Further, these redundant components should not be physically co-located. If redundant routers are employed for all stations on a given floor, for example, these routers can be physically stationed in wiring closets on different floors. This prevents local wiring-closet power problems from affecting the capability of all stations on a given floor to communicate. Figure 2-21 shows such a configuration.

For some organizations, the need for fault tolerance is so great that potential power failures are protected against with a duplicate corporate data center. Organizations with these requirements often locate a redundant data center in another city, or in a part of the same city that is some distance from the primary data center. All backend services are duplicated, and transactions coming in from remote offices are sent to both data centers. This configuration requires duplicate WAN links from all remote offices, duplicate network hardware, duplicate servers and server resources, and leasing another building. Because this approach is so costly, it is typically the last step taken by companies desiring the ultimate in fault tolerance.

Partial duplication of the data center is also a possibility. Several key servers and links to those servers can be duplicated. This is a common compromise to the problem presented by power failures.

Figure 2-21 *Redundant Components on Different Floors*

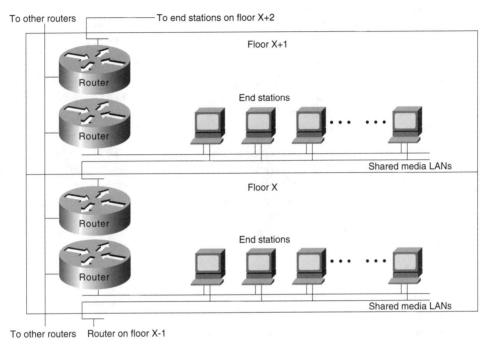

Fault-Tolerant Media Implementations

Media failure is another possible network fault. Included in this category are all problems associated with the medium and its link to each individual end station. Under this definition, media components include network interface controller failures, lobe or attachment unit interface (AUI) cable failures, transceiver failures, hub failures, and all failures associated with media components (for example, the cable itself, terminators, and other parts). Many media failures are caused by operator negligence and cannot easily be eliminated.

One way to reduce the havoc caused by failed media is to divide existing media into smaller segments and support each segment with different hardware. This minimizes the effect of a failure on a particular segment. If you have 100 stations attached to a single switch, for example, move some of them to other switches. This reduces the effect of a hub failure and of certain subnetwork failures. If you place a networking device (such as a router) between segments, you protect against additional problems and cut subnetwork traffic.

As shown in Figure 2-21, redundancy can be employed to help minimize media failures. Each station in this figure is attached to two different media segments. NICs, hub ports, and interface cables are all redundant. This approach doubles the cost of network connectivity for each end station as well as the port usage on all networking devices, and is therefore only recommended in situations where complete redundancy is required. It also assumes that end-station software, including both the network and the application subsystems, can handle and effectively use the redundant components. The application software or the networking software or both must be able to detect network failures and initiate use of the other network.

Certain media-access protocols have some fault-tolerant features built in. Token Ring multistation access units (MAUs) can detect certain media connection failures and bypass the failure internally. FDDI dual rings can wrap traffic onto the backup ring to avoid portions of the network with problems.

From a router's standpoint, many media failures can be bypassed as long as alternative paths are available. Using various hardware-detection techniques, routers can sense certain media-level problems. If routing updates or routing keepalive messages have not been received from devices that would normally be reached through a particular router port, the router will soon declare that route down and will look for alternative routes. Meshed networks provide these alternative paths, allowing the router to compensate for media failures.

Backup Hardware

Like all complex devices, routers, switches, and other networking devices develop hardware problems. When serious failures occur, the use of dual devices can effectively reduce the adverse effects of a hardware failure. After a failure, discovery protocols help end stations choose new paths with which to communicate across the network. If each network connected to the failed device has an alternative path out of the local area, complete connectivity will still be possible.

When backup routers are used, for example, routing metrics can be set to ensure that the backup routers will not be used unless the primary routers are not functioning. Switchover is automatic and rapid. Consider the situation shown in Figure 2-22, for example. In this network, dual routers are used at all sites with dual WAN links. If Router R1 fails, the routers on FDDI 1 will detect the failure by the absence of messages from Router R1. Using any of several dynamic routing protocols, Router A, Router B, and Router C will designate Router R3 as the new next hop on the way to remote resources accessible via Router R4.

To provide redundancy, many networks are designed with multiple routers connecting particular LANs. In the past, the effectiveness of this design was limited by the speed at which the hosts on those LANs detected a topology update and changed routers. In particular, IP hosts tend to be configured with a default gateway or configured to use proxy ARP to find a router on their LAN. Convincing an IP host to change its router usually required manual intervention to clear the ARP cache or to change the default gateway.

The Hot Standby Router Protocol (HSRP) is a solution that allows network topology changes to be transparent to the host. HSRP typically allows hosts to reroute in approximately 10 seconds. HSRP is supported on Ethernet, Token Ring, FDDI, Fast Ethernet, and ATM.

Figure 2-22 *Redundant FDDI Router Configuration*

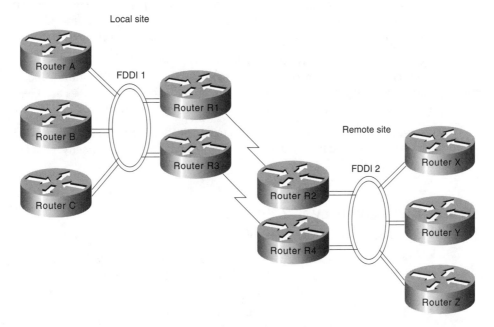

An HSRP group can be defined on each LAN. All members of the group know the standby IP address and the standby MAC address. One member of the group is elected the leader. The lead router services all packets sent to the HSRP group address. The other routers monitor the leader and act as HSRP routers. If the lead router becomes unavailable, the HSRP router elects a new leader, which inherits the HSRP MAC address and IP address.

High-end routers (Cisco 4500, 7000, and 7500 families) can support multiple MAC addresses on the same Ethernet or FDDI interface, allowing the routers to simultaneously handle traffic that is sent to both the standby MAC address and the private MAC address. The commands for enabling HSRP and configuring an HSRP group are **standby ip** and **standby group**.

Identifying and Selecting Networking Devices

Network designers have four basic types of networking devices available to them:

- Hubs (concentrators)
- Bridges

- Switches

- Routers

For a summary of these four networking devices, see Table 2-1 earlier in this chapter. Data communications experts generally agree that network designers are moving away from bridges and primarily using switches and routers to build networks. Consequently, this section focuses on the role of switches and routers in designing networks.

Switches can be functionally divided into two main groups: Layer 2 switches and multilayer switches that provide Layer 2 and Layer 3 switching capabilities. Today, network designers are replacing hubs in their wiring closets with switches to increase their network performance and protect their existing wiring investments.

Routers segment network traffic based on the destination network layer address (Layer 3) rather than the workstation data link layer or MAC address. Consequently, routers are protocol-dependent.

Benefits of Switches (Layer 2 Services)

An individual Layer 2 switch might offer some or all of the following benefits:

- **Bandwidth**—LAN switches provide excellent performance for individual users by allocating dedicated bandwidth to each switch port. Each switch port represents a different network segment. This technique is known as *microsegmenting*.

- **VLANs**—LAN switches can group individual ports into switched logical workgroups called VLANs, thereby restricting the broadcast domain to designated VLAN member ports. VLANs are also known as switched domains and autonomous switching domains. Communication between VLANs requires a router.

- **Automated packet recognition and translation**—This capability allows the switch to translate frame formats automatically, such as Ethernet MAC to FDDI SNAP.

Benefits of Routers (Layer 3 Services)

Because routers use Layer 3 addresses, which typically have structure, routers can use techniques (such as address summarization) to build networks that maintain performance and responsiveness as they grow in size. By imposing structure (usually hierarchical) on a network, routers can effectively use redundant paths and determine optimal routes even in a dynamically changing network.

Routers are necessary to ensure scalability as the network grows and expands. They provide the following capabilities that are vital in network designs:

- Broadcast and multicast control

- Broadcast segmentation

- Security
- Quality of service (QoS)
- Multimedia

Backbone Routing Options

In an ideal world, the perfect enterprise-wide network would feature a single, bullet-proof network protocol capable of transporting all manner of data communications seamlessly, error-free, and with sufficient resilience to accommodate any unforeseen connectivity disruption. In the real world, however, there are many protocols with varying levels of resilience.

In designing a backbone for your organization, you might consider several options. These options are typically split into the following two primary categories:

- Multiprotocol Routing Backbone
- Single-Protocol Backbone

The following discussions outline the characteristics and properties of these two strategies.

Multiprotocol Routing Backbone

When multiple network layer protocols are routed throughout a common backbone without encapsulation (also referred to as *native* mode routing), the environment is referred to as a multiprotocol routing backbone. A multiprotocol backbone environment can adopt one of two routing strategies, or both, depending on the routed protocol involved. The two strategies are generally referred to as the following:

- **Integrated routing**—Integrated routing involves the use of a single routing protocol (for example, a link-state protocol) that determines the least cost path for different routed protocols.

- **Ships in the night**—The ships-in-the-night approach involves the use of a different routing protocol for each network protocol. Some large-scale networks might feature multiple protocols, for example, in which Novell IPX traffic is routed using a proprietary version of the Routing Information Protocol (RIP), IP is routed with IGRP, and DECnet Phase V traffic is routed via ISO CLNS-compliant IS-IS.

Each of these network layer protocols is routed independently, with separate routing processes handling their traffic and separate paths calculated. Mixing routers within a network that supports different combinations of multiple protocols can create a confusing situation, particularly for integrated routing. In general, integrated routing is easier to manage if all the routers attached to the integrated routing backbone support the same integrated routing scheme. Routes for other protocols can be calculated separately. As an alternative, you can use encapsulation to transmit traffic over routers that do not support a particular protocol.

Single-Protocol Backbone

With a single-protocol backbone, all routers are assumed to support a single routing protocol for a single network protocol. In this kind of routing environment, all other routing protocols are ignored. If multiple protocols are to be passed over the network, unsupported protocols must be encapsulated within the supported protocol; otherwise, they will be ignored by the routing nodes.

Why implement a single-protocol backbone? If relatively few other protocols are supported at a limited number of isolated locations, it is reasonable to implement a single-protocol backbone. However, encapsulation does add overhead to traffic on the network. If multiple protocols are supported widely throughout a large network, a multiprotocol backbone approach is likely to work better.

In general, you should support all the network layer protocols in a network with a native routing solution and implement as few network layer protocols as possible.

Types of Switches

Switches can be categorized as follows:

- **LAN switches**—The switches within this category can be further divided into Layer 2 switches and multilayer switches.
- **ATM switches**—ATM switching and ATM routers offer greater backbone bandwidth required by high-throughput data services.

Network managers are adding LAN switches to their wiring closets to augment bandwidth and reduce congestion in existing shared-media hubs while using new backbone technologies, such as Fast Ethernet and ATM.

LAN Switches

Today's cost-effective, high-performance LAN switches offer network managers the following benefits:

- Superior microsegmentation
- Increased aggregate data forwarding
- Increased bandwidth across the corporate backbone

LAN switches address end users' bandwidth needs for wiring-closet applications. By deploying switches rather than traditional shared hubs, network designers can increase performance and leverage the current investments in existing LAN media and adapters.

These switches also offer functionality not previously available, such as VLANs, that provide the flexibility to use software to move, add, and change users across the network.

LAN switches are also suited to provide segment switching and scalable bandwidth within network data centers by delivering switched links to interconnect existing hubs in wiring closets, LAN switches, and server farms. Cisco provides the Catalyst family of multilayer switches for connecting multiple wiring-closet switches or shared hubs into a backbone configuration.

ATM Switches

Even though all ATM switches perform cell relay, ATM switches differ markedly in the following capabilities:

- Variety of interfaces and services that are supported
- Redundancy
- Depth of ATM networking software
- Sophistication of traffic-management mechanism

Just as there are routers and LAN switches available at various price/performance points with different levels of functionality, ATM switches can be segmented into the following four distinct types that reflect the needs of particular applications and markets:

- Workgroup ATM switches
- Campus ATM switches
- Enterprise ATM switches
- Multiservice access switches

Cisco offers a complete range of ATM switches.

Workgroup and Campus ATM Switches

Workgroup ATM switches have Ethernet switch ports and an ATM uplink to connect to a campus ATM switch. An example of a workgroup ATM switch is the Cisco Catalyst 5000.

Campus ATM switches are generally used for small-scale ATM backbones (for example, to link ATM routers or LAN switches). This use of ATM switches can alleviate current backbone congestion and enable the deployment of such new services as VLANs. Campus switches need to support a wide variety of both local backbone and WAN types but be price/performance-optimized for the local backbone function. In this class of switches, ATM routing capabilities that allow multiple switches to be tied together is very important. Congestion control mechanisms for optimizing backbone performance is also important. The LightStream 1010 family of ATM switches is an example of a campus ATM switch.

For more information on deploying workgroup and campus ATM switches in your network, see Chapter 12, "Designing Switched LAN Networks."

Enterprise ATM Switches

Enterprise ATM switches are sophisticated multiservice devices designed to form the core backbones of large enterprise networks. They are intended to complement the role played by today's high-end multiprotocol routers. Enterprise ATM switches are used to interconnect campus ATM switches. Enterprise-class switches, however, cannot only act as ATM backbones, but can also serve as the single point of integration for all the disparate services and technology found in enterprise backbones today. By integrating all these services onto a common platform and a common ATM transport infrastructure, network designers can gain greater manageability and eliminate the need for multiple overlay networks.

Cisco's BPX/IGX is a powerful broadband ATM switch designed to meet the demanding, high-traffic needs of a large private enterprise or public service provider. For more information on deploying enterprise ATM switches in your network, see Chapter 5, "Designing ATM Networks."

Multiservice Access Switches

Beyond private networks, ATM platforms will also be widely deployed by service providers both as customer premises equipment (CPE) and within public networks. Such equipment will be used to support multiple MAN and WAN services—for example, Frame Relay switching, LAN interconnect, or public ATM services—on a common ATM infrastructure. Enterprise ATM switches will often be used in these public network applications because of their emphasis on high availability and redundancy, their support of multiple interfaces, and their capability to integrate voice and data.

Switches and Routers Compared

To highlight the differences between switches and routers, the following sections examine the different roles of these devices in the following situations:

- Implementation of VLANs
- Implementation of switched networks

Role of Switches and Routers in VLANs

VLANs address the following two problems:

- Scalability issues of a flat network topology

- Simplification of network management by facilitating network reconfigurations (moves and changes)

A VLAN consists of a single broadcast domain and solves the scalability problems of large flat networks by breaking a single broadcast domain into several smaller broadcast domains or VLANs. Virtual LANs offer easier moves and changes in a network design than traditional networks. LAN switches can be used to segment networks into logically defined virtual workgroups. This logical segmentation, commonly referred to as VLAN communication, offers a fundamental change in how LANs are designed, administered, and managed. Although logical segmentation provides substantial benefits in LAN administration, security, and management of network broadcast across the enterprise, network designers should consider many components of VLAN solutions prior to large-scale VLAN deployment.

Switches and routers each play an important role in VLAN design. Switches are the core device that controls individual VLANs, while routers provide interVLAN communication, as shown in Figure 2-23.

Figure 2-23 *Role of Switches and Routers in VLANs*

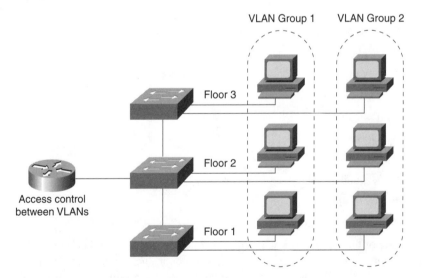

Switches remove the physical constraints imposed by a shared-hub architecture because they logically group users and ports across the enterprise. As a replacement for shared hubs, switches remove the physical barriers imposed within each wiring closet. Additionally, the role of the router evolves beyond the more traditional role of firewalls and broadcast suppression to policy-based control, broadcast management, and route processing and distribution. Equally as important, routers remain vital for switched architectures configured as VLANs because they provide the communication between VLANs. Routers also provide VLAN access to shared resources, such as servers and hosts. For more information on deploying VLANs, see Chapter 12.

Examples of Campus Switched Network Designs

A successful campus switched networking solution must combine the benefits of both routers and switches in every part of the network, as well as offer a flexible evolution path from shared-media networking to switched networks.

For example, incorporating switches in campus network designs will generally result in the following benefits:

- High bandwidth
- Improved performance
- Low cost
- Easy configuration

If you need advanced networking services, however, routers are necessary. Routers offer the following services:

- Broadcast firewalling
- Hierarchical addressing
- Communication between dissimilar LANs
- Fast convergence
- Policy routing
- QoS routing
- Security
- Redundancy and load balancing
- Traffic-flow management
- Multimedia group membership

Some of these router services will be offered by switches in the future. For example, support for multimedia often requires a protocol, such as Internet Group Management Protocol (IGMP), that allows workstations to join a group that receives multimedia multicast packets. Cisco allows switches to participate in this process by using the Cisco Group Management Protocol (CGMP). CGMP-enabled switches communicate with the router to determine whether any of their attached users are part of a multicast group.

Switching and bridging sometimes can result in non-optimal routing of packets. This is because every packet must go through the root bridge of the spanning tree. When routers are used, the routing of packets can be controlled and designed for optimal paths. Cisco now provides support for improved routing and redundancy in switched environments by supporting one instance of the spanning tree per VLAN.

The following figures illustrate how network designers can use switches and routers to evolve their shared-media networks to switching networks. Typically, this evolution to a campus switched network architecture will extend over four phases.

Phase 1 is the microsegmentation phase, in which network designers retain their hubs and routers but insert a LAN switch to enhance performance. Figure 2-24 shows an example of how a LAN switch can be used to segment a network.

Figure 2-24 *Using Switches for Microsegmentation*

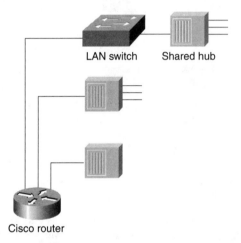

LAN switch   Shared hub

Cisco router

Phase 2 is the addition of high-speed backbone technology and routing between switches. LAN switches perform switch processing and provide dedicated bandwidth to the desktop and to shared-media hubs. Backbone routers are attached to either Fast Ethernet or ATM switches. The increase in backbone bandwidth matches the increased bandwidth in the wiring closet. Figure 2-25 shows an example of how you can add high-speed backbone technology and routing between existing switches in your network.

Figure 2-25 *Adding High-Speed Backbone Technology and Routing Between Switches*

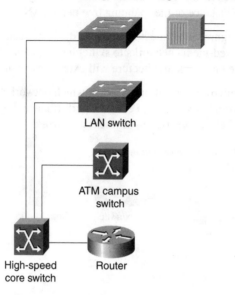

In Phase 3, routers are distributed between the LAN switches in the wiring closet and the high-speed core switch. The network backbone is now strictly a high-speed transport mechanism with all other devices, such as the distributed routers, at the periphery. Figure 2-26 illustrates such a network.

Phase 4 is the final phase—the endpoint. It involves end-to-end switching with integral VLANs and multilayer switching capability. By this point, Layer 2 and Layer 3 integrated switching is distributed across the network and is connected to the high-speed core. Figure 2-27 shows an example of this final phase.

Figure 2-26   *Distributing Routers Between High-Speed Core and LAN Switches*

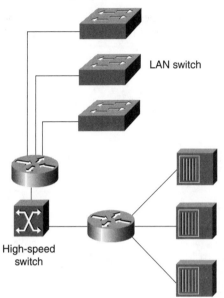

Figure 2-27   *End-to-End Switching with VLAN and Multilayer Switching Capability*

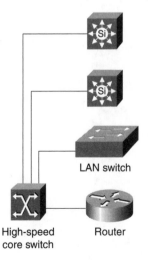

Summary

Now that the basic networking devices and general design principles have been examined, the remaining chapters in this part focus on the different technologies available when designing a network.

CHAPTER 3

Designing Large-Scale IP Networks with Interior Gateway Protocols

Edited by Atif Khan

This chapter focuses on the following design implications of the Enhanced Interior Gateway Routing Protocol (EIGRP), Open Shortest Path First (OSPF) Protocols, and On-Demand Routing (ODR):

- Network Topology
- Addressing and Route Summarization
- Route Selection
- Convergence
- Network Scalability
- Security

EIGRP and OSPF are routing protocols for the Internet Protocol (IP). An introductory discussion outlines general routing protocol issues; subsequent discussions focus on design guidelines for the specific IP protocols.

Implementing Routing Protocols

The following discussion provides an overview of the key decisions you must make when selecting and deploying routing protocols. This discussion lays the foundation for subsequent discussions regarding specific routing protocols.

Network Topology

The physical topology of a network is described by the complete set of routers and the networks that connect them. Different routing protocols learn topology information in different ways. Some protocols require hierarchy and some do not. Networks require hierarchy in order to be scalable. Those protocols that do not require hierarchy should be designed with some level of hierarchy; otherwise, they are not scalable.

Some protocols require the creation of an explicit hierarchical topology through the establishment of a backbone and logical areas. The OSPF and Intermediate

System–to–Intermediate System (IS-IS) protocols are examples of routing protocols that use a hierarchical structure. A general hierarchical network scheme is illustrated in Figure 3-1. The explicit topology in a hierarchical scheme takes precedence over the topology created through addressing.

Figure 3-1   *Hierarchical Network*

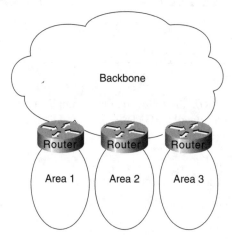

With any routing protocol, the addressing topology should be assigned to reflect the hierarchy. There are two recommended ways to assign addresses in a hierarchical network. The simplest way is to give each area (including the backbone) a unique network address. An alternative is to assign address ranges to each area.

Areas are logical collections of contiguous networks and hosts. Areas also include all the routers having interfaces on any one of the included networks. Each area runs a separate copy of the basic routing algorithm. Therefore, each area has its own topological database.

Addressing and Route Summarization

Route-summarization procedures condense routing information. Without summarization, each router in a network must retain a route to every subnet in the network. With summarization, routers can reduce some sets of routes to a single advertisement, reducing both the load on the router and the perceived complexity of the network. The importance of route summarization increases with network size.

Figure 3-2 illustrates an example of route summarization. In this environment, Router R2 maintains one route for all destination networks beginning with B, and Router R4 maintains one route for all destination networks beginning with A. This is the essence of route summarization. Router R1 tracks all routes because it exists on the boundary between A and B.

Figure 3-2   *Route Summarization Example*

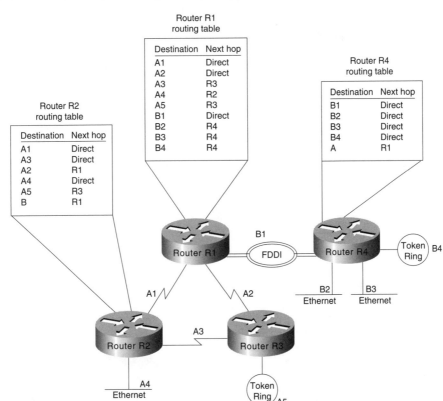

The reduction in route propagation and routing information overhead can be significant. Figure 3-3 illustrates the potential savings. The vertical axis of Figure 3-3 shows the number of routing table entries. The horizontal axis measures the number of subnets. Without summarization, each router in a network with 1,000 subnets must contain 1,000 routes. With summarization, the picture changes considerably. If you assume a Class B network with eight bits of subnet address space, each router needs to know all the routes for each subnet in its network number (250 routes, assuming that 1,000 subnets fall into four major networks of 250 routers each) plus one route for each of the other networks (three), for a total of 253 routes. This represents a nearly 75% reduction in the size of the routing table.

The preceding example shows the simplest type of route summarization: collapsing all the subnet routes into a single network route. Some routing protocols also support route summarization at any bit boundary (rather than just at major network number boundaries) in a network address. A routing protocol can summarize on a bit boundary only if it supports variable-length subnet masks (VLSMs).

Some routing protocols summarize automatically. Other routing protocols require manual configuration to support route summarization. Figure 3-3 illustrates route summarization.

Figure 3-3 *Route Summarization Benefits*

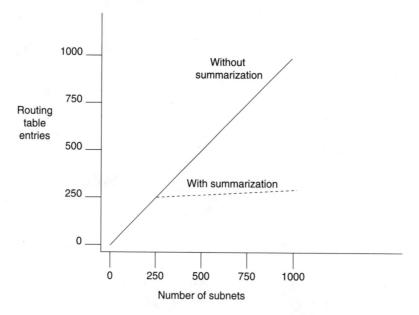

Route Selection

Route selection is trivial when only a single path to the destination exists. If any part of that path should fail, however, there is no way to recover. Therefore, most networks are designed with multiple paths so that there are alternatives in case a failure occurs.

Routing protocols compare route metrics to select the best route from a group of possible routes. Route metrics are computed by assigning a characteristic or set of characteristics to each physical network. The metric for the route is an aggregation of the characteristics of each physical network in the route. Figure 3-4 shows a typical meshed network with metrics assigned to each link, and the best route from source to destination identified.

Routing protocols use different techniques for assigning metrics to individual networks. Further, each routing protocol forms a metric aggregation in a different way. Most routing protocols can use multiple paths if the paths have an equal cost. Some routing protocols can even use multiple paths when paths have an unequal cost. In either case, load balancing can improve overall allocation of network bandwidth.

Figure 3-4   *Routing Metrics and Route Selection*

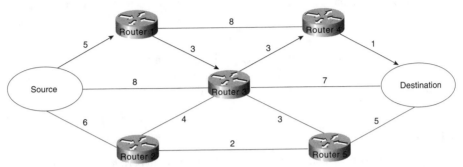

When multiple paths are used, there are several ways to distribute the packets. The two most common mechanisms are *per-packet load balancing* and *per-destination load balancing*. Per-packet load balancing distributes the packets across the possible routes in a manner proportional to the route metrics. With equal-cost routes, this is equivalent to a round-robin scheme. One packet or destination (depending on switching mode) is distributed to each possible path. Per-destination load balancing distributes packets across the possible routes based on destination. Each new destination is assigned the next available route. This technique tends to preserve packet order.

NOTE   Most TCP implementations can accommodate out-of-order packets. However, out-of-order packets may cause performance degradation.

When fast-switching is enabled on a router (default condition), route selection is done on a per-destination basis. When fast-switching is disabled, route selection is done on a per-packet basis. For line speeds of 56 kbps and faster, fast-switching is recommended.

Convergence

When *network* topology changes, network traffic must reroute quickly. The phrase "convergence time" describes the time it takes a router to start using a new route after a topology changes. Routers must do three things after a topology changes:

- Detect the change
- Select a new route
- Propagate the changed route information

Some changes are immediately detectable. For example, serial line failures that involve carrier loss are immediately detectable by a router. Other failures are harder to detect. If a serial line becomes unreliable but the carrier is not lost, for example, the unreliable link is not immediately detectable. In addition, some media (Ethernet, for example) do not provide physical indications such as carrier loss. When a router is reset, other routers do not detect this immediately. In general, failure detection depends on the media involved and the routing protocol used.

After a failure has been detected, the routing protocol must select a new route. The mechanisms used to do this are protocol-dependent. All routing protocols must propagate the changed route. The mechanisms used to do this are also protocol-dependent.

Network Scalability

The capability to extend your network is determined, in part, by the scaling characteristics of the routing protocols used and the quality of the network design.

Network scalability is limited by two factors: operational issues and technical issues. Typically, operational issues are more significant than technical issues. Operational scaling concerns encourage the use of large areas or protocols that do not require hierarchical structures. When hierarchical protocols are required, technical scaling concerns promote the use of areas whose size is based on available resources, such as CPU, memory, and so on. Finding the right balance is the art of network design.

From a technical standpoint, routing protocols scale well if their resource use grows less than linearly with the growth of the network. Three critical resources are used by routing protocols: memory, central processing unit (CPU), and bandwidth.

Memory

Routing protocols use memory to store routing tables and topology information. Route summarization cuts memory consumption for all routing protocols. Keeping areas small reduces the memory consumption for hierarchical routing protocols.

CPU

CPU usage is protocol-dependent. Routing protocols use CPU cycles to calculate routes. Keeping routing information small by using summarization reduces CPU requirements by reducing the effect of a topology change and by decreasing the number of routes that must be recomputed after a topology change.

Bandwidth

Bandwidth usage is also protocol-dependent. Three key issues determine the amount of bandwidth a routing protocol consumes:

- **When routing information is sent**—Periodic updates are sent at regular intervals. Flash updates are sent only when a change occurs.

- **What routing information is sent**—Complete updates contain all routing information. Partial updates contain only changed information.

- **Where routing information is sent**—Flooded updates are sent to all routers. Bounded updates are sent only to routers affected by a change.

NOTE   These three issues also affect CPU usage.

Distance-vector protocols, such as Routing Information Protocol (RIP) and Interior Gateway Routing Protocol (IGRP), broadcast their complete routing table periodically, regardless of whether the routing table has changed. This periodic advertisement varies from every 30 seconds for RIP, to every 90 seconds for IGRP. When the network is stable, distance-vector protocols behave well, but, waste bandwidth because of the periodic sending of routing table updates, even when no change has occurred. When a failure occurs in the network, distance-vector protocols do not add excessive load to the network, but they take a long time to reconverge to an alternative path or to flush a bad path from the network.

Link-state routing protocols, such as Open Shortest Path First (OSPF), Intermediate System–to–Intermediate System (IS-IS), and NetWare Link Services Protocol (NLSP), were designed to address the limitations of distance-vector routing protocols (slow convergence and unnecessary bandwidth usage). Link-state protocols are more complex than distance-vector protocols, and use more CPU and memory. The additional overhead (in the form of memory utilization and CPU utilization) dictates the number of neighbors that a router can support and the number of routers that can be in an area. These numbers vary from network to network, and depend on variables such as CPU power, memory, number of routes, and link stability.

When the network is stable, link-state protocols minimize bandwidth usage by sending updates only when a change occurs. A hello mechanism ascertains reachability of neighbors. When a failure occurs in the network, link-state protocols flood link-state advertisements (LSAs) throughout an area. LSAs cause every router within the failed area to recalculate routes. The fact that LSAs need to be flooded throughout the area in failure mode and the fact that all routers recalculate routing tables dictate the number of routers that can be in an area.

EIGRP is an advanced distance-vector protocol that has some of the properties of link-state protocols. EIGRP addresses the limitations of conventional distance-vector routing protocols (slow convergence and high bandwidth consumption in a steady-state network). When the network is stable, EIGRP sends updates only when a change in the network occurs. Like link-state protocols, EIGRP uses a hello mechanism to determine the reachability of neighbors. When a failure occurs in the network, EIGRP looks for new successors when there is no feasible successor present in the topology table by sending messages to its neighbors. The search for new successors can be aggressive in terms of the traffic it generates (updates, queries, and replies) to achieve convergence. This behavior constrains the number of possible neighbors.

In WANs, consideration of bandwidth is especially critical. Frame Relay, for example, which statistically multiplexes many logical data connections (virtual circuits) over a single physical link, allows the creation of networks that share bandwidth. Public Frame Relay networks use bandwidth sharing at all levels within the network. That is, bandwidth sharing may occur within the Frame Relay network of Corporation X, as well as between the networks of Corporation X and Corporation Y.

Two factors have a substantial effect on the design of public Frame Relay networks:

- Users are charged for each permanent virtual circuit (PVC), which encourages network designers to minimize the number of PVCs.

- Public carrier networks sometimes provide incentives to avoid the use of committed information rate (CIR) circuits. Although service providers try to ensure sufficient bandwidth, packets can be dropped.

Overall, WANs can lose packets due to a lack of bandwidth. For Frame Relay networks, this possibility is compounded because Frame Relay does not have a broadcast-replication facility; so for every broadcast packet sent out a Frame Relay interface, the router must replicate it for each PVC on the interface. This requirement limits the number of PVCs that a router can handle effectively.

In addition to bandwidth, network designers must consider the size of routing tables that need to be propagated. Clearly, the design considerations for an interface with 50 neighbors and 100 routes to propagate differ significantly from the considerations for an interface with 50 neighbors and 10,000 routes to propagate.

Security

Controlling access to network resources is a primary concern. Some routing protocols provide techniques that can be used as part of a security strategy. With some routing protocols, you can insert a filter on the routes being advertised so that certain routes are not advertised in some parts of the network.

Some routing protocols can authenticate routers that run the same protocol. Authentication mechanisms are protocol-specific and generally weak. In spite of this, it is worthwhile to take advantage of the techniques that exist. Authentication can increase network stability by preventing unauthorized routers or hosts from participating in the routing protocol, whether those devices are attempting to participate accidentally or deliberately.

EIGRP Network Design Guidelines

The Enhanced Interior Gateway Routing Protocol (EIGRP) is a routing protocol developed by Cisco Systems, and introduced with Software Release 9.21 and Cisco Internetworking Operating System (Cisco IOS) Software Release 10.0. EIGRP combines the advantages of distance-vector protocols, such as IGRP, with the advantages of link-state protocols, such as Open Shortest Path First (OSPF). EIGRP uses the Diffusing Update Algorithm (DUAL) to achieve convergence quickly.

EIGRP includes support for IP, Novell NetWare, and AppleTalk. The discussion on EIGRP covers the following topics:

- EIGRP Network Topology
- EIGRP Addressing
- EIGRP Route Summarization
- EIGRP Route Selection
- EIGRP Convergence
- EIGRP Network Scalability
- EIGRP Security

NOTE   Although this section is applicable to IP, IPX, and AppleTalk EIGRP, IP issues are highlighted here. For case studies on how to integrate EIGRP into IP, IPX, and AppleTalk networks, including detailed configuration examples and protocol-specific issues, see Chapter 17, "Configuring EIGRP for Novell and AppleTalk Networks."

EIGRP Network Topology

EIGRP can use a nonhierarchical (or flat) topology. To design a scalable network, it is important to have hierarchy. EIGRP automatically summarizes subnet routes of directly connected networks at a network number boundary. For more information, see the section titled "EIGRP Route Summarization," later in this chapter.

EIGRP Addressing

The first step in designing an EIGRP network is to decide how to address the network. In many cases, a company is assigned a single NIC address (such as a Class B network address) to be allocated in a corporate network. Bit-wise subnetting and variable-length subnetwork masks (VLSMs) can be used in combination to save address space. EIGRP for IP supports the use of VLSMs.

Consider a hypothetical network in which a Class B address is divided into subnetworks, and contiguous groups of these subnetworks are summarized by Enhanced IGRP. The Class B network 156.77.0.0 might be subdivided as illustrated in Figure 3-5.

Figure 3-5 *Variable-Length Subnet Masks (VLSMs) and Route Summarization Boundaries*

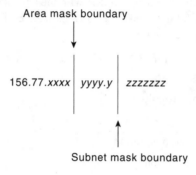

In Figure 3-5, the letters *x*, *y*, and *z* represent bits of the last two octets of the Class B network, as follows:

- The four *x* bits represent the route summarization boundary.
- The five *y* bits represent up to 32 subnets per summary route.
- The seven *z* bits allow for 126 (128 − 2) hosts per subnet.

Appendix A, "Subnetting an IP Address Space," provides a complete example illustrating assignment for the Class B address 150.100.0.0.

EIGRP Route Summarization

With Enhanced IGRP, subnet routes of directly connected networks are automatically summarized at network number boundaries. In addition, a network administrator can configure route summarization at any interface with any bit boundary, allowing ranges of networks to be summarized arbitrarily.

EIGRP Route Selection

Routing protocols compare route metrics to select the best route from a group of possible routes. The following factors are important to understand when designing an EIGRP network. EIGRP uses the same vector of metrics as IGRP. Separate metric values are assigned for bandwidth, delay, reliability, and load. By default, EIGRP computes the metric for a route by using the minimum bandwidth of each hop in the path and adding a media-specific delay for each hop. The metrics used by EIGRP are as follows:

- **Bandwidth**—Bandwidth is deduced from the interface type. Bandwidth can be modified with the **bandwidth** command.

- **Delay**—Each media type has a propagation delay associated with it. Delay can be modified with the **delay** command.

- **Reliability**—Reliability is dynamically computed as a rolling weighted average over five seconds.

- **Load**—Load is dynamically computed as a rolling weighted average over five seconds.

When EIGRP summarizes a group of routes, it uses the metric of the best route in the summary as the metric for the summary.

EIGRP Convergence

EIGRP implements a convergence algorithm known as DUAL (Diffusing Update Algorithm). DUAL uses two techniques that allow EIGRP to converge very quickly. First, each EIGRP router builds an EIGRP topology table by receiving its neighbors' routing tables. This allows the router to use a new route to a destination instantly if another feasible route is known. If no feasible route is known based on the routing information previously learned from its neighbors, a router running EIGRP becomes active for that destination and sends a query to each of its neighbors, asking for an alternative route to the destination. These queries propagate until an alternative route is found. Routers that are not affected by a topology change remain passive, and do not need to be involved in the query and response.

A router using EIGRP receives full routing tables from its neighbors when it first communicates with the neighbors. Thereafter, only changes to the routing tables are sent, and only to routers affected by the change. A successor is a neighboring router currently being used for packet forwarding, provides the least cost route to the destination, and is not part of a routing loop. When a route to a destination is lost through the successor, the feasible successor, if present for that route, becomes the successor. Feasible successors provide the next least cost path without introducing routing loops.

The routing table keeps a list of the computed costs of reaching networks. The topology table keeps a list of routes advertised by neighbors. For each network, the router keeps the real cost of getting to that network and also keeps the advertised cost from its neighbor. In the event of a failure, convergence is instant if a feasible successor can be found. A neighbor is a feasible successor if it meets the feasibility condition set by DUAL. DUAL finds feasible successors by performing the following computations:

- Determines membership of V_1. V_1 is the set of all neighbors whose advertised distance to network x is less than FD. (FD is the feasible distance and is defined as the best metric during an active-to-passive transition.)

- Calculates D_{min}. D_{min} is the minimum computed cost to network x.

- Determines membership of V_2. V_2 is the set of neighbors in V_1 whose computed cost to network x equals D_{min}.

The feasibility condition is met when V^2 has one or more members. Figure 3-6 illustrates the concept of feasible successors. Consider Router A's topology table entries for Network 7. Router B is the *successor* with a computed cost of 31 to reach Network 7, compared to the computed costs of Router D (230) and Router H (40).

Figure 3-6   *DUAL Feasible Successor*

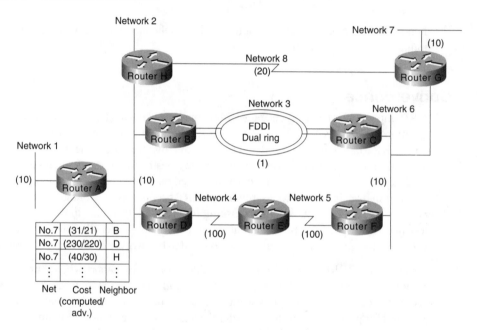

If Router B becomes unavailable, Router A will go through the following three-step process to find a feasible successor for Network 7:

1 Determining which neighbors have an advertised distance to Network 7 that is less than Router A's feasible distance (FD) to Network 7. The FD is 31, and Router H meets this condition. Therefore, Router H is a member of V_1.

2 Calculating the minimum computed cost to Network 7. Router H provides a cost of 40, and Router D provides a cost of 230. D_{min} is, therefore, 40.

3 Determining the set of neighbors in V1 whose computed cost to Network 7 equals D_{min} (40). Router H meets this condition.

The feasible successor is Router H, which provides a least cost route of 40 from Router A to Network 7. If Router H now also becomes unavailable, Router A performs the following computations:

1 Determines which neighbors have an advertised distance to Network 7 that is less than the FD for Network 7. Because both Router B and H have become unavailable, only Router D remains. The advertised cost of Router D to Network 7 is 220, however, which is greater than Router A's FD (31) to Network 7. Router D, therefore, cannot be a member of V_1. The FD remains at 31—the FD can only change during an active-to-passive transition, and this did not occur. There was no transition to active state for Network 7; this is known as a local computation.

2 Because there are no members of V_1, there can be no feasible successors. Router A, therefore, transitions from passive to active state for Network 7 and queries its neighbors about Network 7. There was a transition to active; this is known as a diffusing computation.

NOTE   For more details on EIGRP convergence, see Appendix H, "References and Recommended Reading," for a list of reference papers and materials.

The following example and graphics further illustrate how EIGRP supports virtually instantaneous convergence in a changing network environment. In Figure 3-7, all routers can access one another and Network N. The computed cost to reach other routers and Network N is shown. For example, the cost from Router E to Router B is 10. The cost from Router E to Network N is 25 (cumulative of 10 + 10 + 5 = 25).

Figure 3-7   *DUAL Example (Part 1): Initial Network Connectivity*

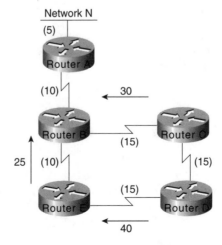

In Figure 3-8, the connection between Router B and Router E fails. Router E sends a multicast query to all of its neighbors and puts Network N into an active state.

Figure 3-8 *DUAL Example (Part 2): Sending Queries*

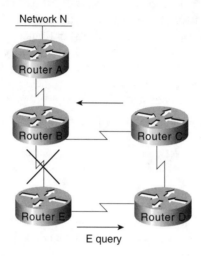

Next, as illustrated in Figure 3-9, Router D determines that it has a feasible successor. It changes its successor from Router E to Router C and sends a reply to Router E.

Figure 3-9 *DUAL Example (Part 3): Switching to a Feasible Successor*

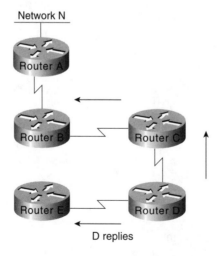

In Figure 3-10, Router E has received replies from all neighbors and therefore brings Network N out of active state. Router E puts Network N into its routing table at a distance of 60.

Figure 3-10 *Flow of Intersubnet Traffic with Layer 3 Switches*

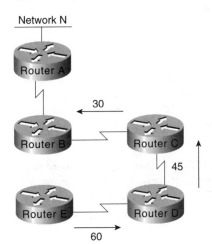

| NOTE | Router A, Router B, and Router C were not involved in route recomputation. Router D recomputed its path to Network N without first needing to learn new routing information from its downstream neighbors. |

EIGRP Network Scalability

Network scalability is limited by two factors: operational issues and technical issues. Operationally, EIGRP provides easy configuration. Technically, EIGRP uses resources at less than a linear rate with the growth of a network, if properly designed. Hierarchy, both physical and logical, is the key to designing a scalable EIGRP network.

Memory

A router running EIGRP stores routes advertised by neighbors so that it can adapt quickly to alternative routes. The more neighbors a router has, the more memory a router uses. EIGRP automatic route aggregation bounds the routing table growth naturally. Additional bounding is possible with manual route aggregation.

CPU

EIGRP uses the DUAL algorithm to provide fast convergence. DUAL recomputes only routes affected by a topology change. DUAL is not computationally complex, but utilization of the CPU depends on the stability of the network, query boundaries, and reliability of the links.

Bandwidth

EIGRP uses partial updates. Partial updates are generated only when a change occurs; only the changed information is sent, and this changed information is sent only to the routers affected. Because of this, EIGRP is efficient in its usage of bandwidth. Some additional bandwidth is used by EIGRP's Hello protocol to maintain adjacencies between neighboring routers.

To create a scalable EIGRP network, you should implement route summarization. To create an environment capable of supporting route summarization, you must implement an effective hierarchical addressing scheme. The addressing structure that you implement can have a profound impact on the performance and scalability of your EIGRP network.

EIGRP Security

EIGRP is available only on Cisco routers. This prevents accidental or malicious routing disruption caused by hosts in a network. In addition, route filters can be set up on any interface to prevent learning or propagating routing information inappropriately.

OSPF Network Design Guidelines

OSPF is an IGP developed for use in IP-based networks. As an IGP, OSPF distributes routing information between routers belonging to a single autonomous system (AS). An AS is a group of routers exchanging routing information via a common routing protocol. The OSPF protocol is based on shortest-path-first (SPF), or link-state, technology.

The OSPF protocol was developed by the OSPF working group of the Internet Engineering Task Force (IETF). It was designed expressly for the IP environment, including explicit support for IP subnetting and the tagging of externally derived routing information. OSPF Version 2 is documented in Request for Comments (RFC) 1247.

Whether you are building an OSPF network from the ground up or converting your network to OSPF, the following design guidelines provide a foundation from which you can construct a reliable, scalable OSPF-based environment.

Two design activities are critically important to a successful OSPF implementation:

- Definition of area boundaries
- Address assignment

Ensuring that these activities are properly planned and executed will make all the difference in your OSPF implementation. Each is addressed in more detail in the discussions that follow. These discussions are divided into nine sections:

- OSPF Network Topology
- OSPF Addressing and Route Summarization
- OSPF Route Selection
- OSPF Convergence
- OSPF Network Scalability
- OSPF Security
- OSPF NSSA (Not-So-Stubby Area) Capabilities
- OSPF On-Demand Circuit Protocol Issues
- OSPF Over Nonbroadcast Networks

NOTE   For a detailed case study on how to set up and configure OSPF redistribution, see Chapter 16, "EIGRP and OSPF Redistribution."

OSPF Network Topology

OSPF works best in a hierarchical routing environment. The first and most important decision when designing an OSPF network is to determine which routers and links are to be included in the backbone, and which are to be included in each area. You should consider several important guidelines when designing an OSPF topology:

- **The number of routers in an area**—OSPF uses a CPU-intensive algorithm. The number of calculations that must be performed given *n* link-state packets is proportional to *n log n*. As a result, the larger and more unstable the area, the greater the likelihood for performance problems associated with routing-protocol recalculation. The size of an area depends on the router CPU, memory, and number of links in an area.

- **The number of neighbors for any one router**—OSPF floods all link-state changes to all routers in an area. Routers with many neighbors have the most work to do when link-state changes occur. Number of neighbors per router depends on router CPU, number of links in an area, CPU of the neighboring routers, and bandwidth of link to neighbors.

- **The number of areas supported by any one router**—A router must run the link-state algorithm for each link-state change that occurs for every area in which the router resides. Every Area Border Router is in at least two areas (the backbone and one area).

- **Designated router selection**—In general, the designated router and backup designated router on a local-area network (LAN) are adjacent to all neighbors. They have the responsibility of generating flooding LSAs of adjacent routes, as well as generating network link states on behalf of the network. It is a good idea to select routers that are not already heavily loaded with CPU-intensive activities to be the designated router and backup designated router.

The discussions that follow address topology issues specifically related to the backbone and the areas.

Backbone Considerations

Stability and *redundancy* are the most important criteria for the backbone. Stability is increased by keeping the size of the backbone reasonable. The size of the backbone must be reasonable because each router in the backbone needs to recompute its routes after every link-state change. Keeping the backbone small reduces the likelihood of a change and reduces the amount of CPU cycles required to recompute routes. Redundancy is important in the backbone to prevent partition when a link fails. Good backbones are designed so that no single link failure can cause a partition.

OSPF backbones must be contiguous. OSPF includes the use of virtual links. A virtual link creates a path between two Area Border Routers (an *Area Border Router* is a router that connects an area to the backbone) that are not directly connected. A virtual link can be used to heal a partitioned backbone. It is not a good idea, however, to design an OSPF network to require the use of virtual links. The stability of a virtual link is determined by the stability of the underlying area. This dependency can make troubleshooting more difficult. In addition, virtual links cannot run across stub areas. See the section titled "Backbone-to-Area Route Advertisement," later in this chapter for a detailed discussion of stub areas.

Avoid placing hosts (such as workstations, file servers, or other shared resources) in the backbone area. Keeping hosts out of the backbone area simplifies network expansion and creates a more stable environment.

Area Considerations

Individual areas should be contiguous. An area can be partitioned, but it is not recommended. In this context, a contiguous area is one in which a continuous path can be traced from any router in an area to any other router in the same area. This does not mean that all routers must share common network media. The two most critical aspects of area design follow:

- Determining how the area is addressed
- Determining how the area is connected to the backbone

Areas should have a contiguous set of network or subnet addresses. Without a contiguous address space, it is not possible to implement route summarization. The routers that connect an area to the backbone are called Area Border Routers. Areas can have a single Area Border Router or they can have multiple Area Border Routers. In general, it is desirable to have more than one Area Border Router per area to minimize the chance of the area becoming disconnected from the backbone.

When creating large-scale OSPF networks, the definition of areas and assignment of resources within areas must be done with a pragmatic view of your network. The following are general rules that help ensure that your network remains flexible and provides the kind of performance needed to deliver reliable resource access:

- **Consider physical proximity when defining areas**—If a particular location is densely connected, create an area specifically for nodes at that location.

- **Reduce the maximum size of areas if links are unstable**—If your network includes unstable links, consider implementing smaller areas to reduce the effects of route flapping. Whenever a route is lost or comes online, each affected area must converge on a new topology. The Dykstra algorithm will run on all the affected routers. By segmenting your network into smaller areas, you can isolate unstable links and deliver more reliable overall service.

OSPF Addressing and Route Summarization

Address assignment and route summarization are inextricably linked when designing OSPF networks. To create a scalable OSPF network, you should implement route summarization. To create an environment capable of supporting route summarization, you must implement an effective hierarchical addressing scheme. The addressing structure that you implement can have a profound impact on the performance and scalability of your OSPF network. The following sections discuss OSPF route summarization and three addressing options:

- Separate network numbers for each area

- Network Information Center (NIC)–authorized address areas created using bit-wise subnetting and VLSM

- Private addressing, with a *demilitarized zone* (DMZ) buffer to the official Internet world

NOTE	You should keep your addressing scheme as simple as possible, but be wary of oversimplifying your address-assignment scheme. Although simplicity in addressing saves time later when operating and troubleshooting your network, taking shortcuts can have certain severe consequences. In building a scalable addressing environment, use a structured approach. If necessary, use bit-wise subnetting—but make sure that route summarization can be accomplished at the Area Border Routers.

OSPF Route Summarization

Route summarization is extremely desirable for a reliable and scalable OSPF network. The effectiveness of route summarization, and your OSPF implementation in general, hinge on the addressing scheme that you adopt. Summarization in an OSPF network occurs between each area and the backbone area. Summarization must be configured manually in OSPF. When planning your OSPF network, consider the following issues:

- Be sure that your network addressing scheme is configured so that the range of subnets assigned within an area is contiguous.

- Create an address space that will permit you to split areas easily as your network grows. If possible, assign subnets according to simple octet boundaries. If you cannot assign addresses in an easy-to-remember and easy-to-divide manner, be sure to have a thoroughly defined addressing structure. If you know how your entire address space is assigned (or will be assigned), you can plan more effectively for changes.

- Plan ahead for the addition of new routers to your OSPF environment. Be sure that new routers are inserted appropriately as area, backbone, or border routers. Because the addition of new routers creates a new topology, inserting new routers can cause unexpected routing changes (and possibly performance changes) when your OSPF topology is recomputed.

Separate Address Structures for Each Area

One of the simplest ways to allocate addresses in OSPF is to assign a separate network number for each area. With this scheme, you create a backbone and multiple areas, and assign a separate IP network number to each area. Figure 3-11 illustrates this kind of area allocation.

Figure 3-11 *Assignment of NIC Addresses Example*

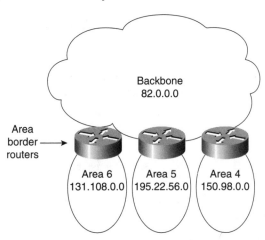

The following are the basic steps for creating such a network:

Step 1   Define your structure (identify areas and allocate nodes to areas).

Step 2   Assign addresses to networks, subnets, and end stations.

In the network illustrated in Figure 3-11, each area has its own unique address. These can be Class A (the backbone in Figure 3-11), Class B (Areas 4 and 6), or Class C (Area 5). The following are some benefits of assigning separate address structures to each area:

- Address assignment is relatively easy to remember.
- Configuration of routers is relatively easy and mistakes are less likely.
- Network operations are streamlined because each area has a simple, unique network number.

In the example illustrated in Figure 3-11, the route-summarization configuration at the Area Border Routers is greatly simplified. Routes from Area 4 injecting into the backbone can be summarized as follows: *All routes starting with 150.98 are found in Area 4.*

The main drawback of this approach to address assignment is that it wastes address space. If you decide to adopt this approach, be sure that Area Border Routers are configured to do route summarization. Summarization must be explicitly set.

Bit-Wise Subnetting and VLSM

Bit-wise subnetting and variable-length subnetwork masks (VLSMs) can be used in combination to save address space. Consider a hypothetical network in which a Class B address is subdivided using an area mask and distributed among 16 areas. The Class B network, 156.77.0.0, might be subdivided as illustrated in Figure 3-12.

Figure 3-12 *Areas and Subnet Masking*

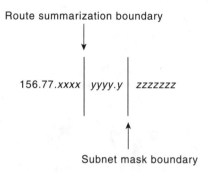

In Figure 3-12, the letters x, y, and z represent bits of the last two octets of the Class B network, as follows:

- The four x bits are used to identify 16 areas.
- The five y bits represent up to 32 subnets per area.
- The seven z bits allow for 126 (128 − 2) hosts per subnet.

Appendix A, "Subnetting an IP Address Space," provides a complete example illustrating assignment for the Class B address 150.100.0.0. It illustrates both the concept of area masks and the breakdown of large subnets into smaller ones using VLSMs.

Private Addressing

Private addressing is another option often cited as simpler than developing an area scheme using bit-wise subnetting. Although private address schemes provide an excellent level of flexibility and do not limit the growth of your OSPF network, they have certain disadvantages. Developing a large-scale network of privately addressed IP nodes limits total access to the Internet, for instance, and mandates the implementation of what is referred to as a *demilitarized zone* (DMZ). If you need to connect to the Internet, Figure 3-13 illustrates the way in which a DMZ provides a buffer of valid NIC nodes between a privately addressed network and the Internet.

Figure 3-13 *Connecting to the Internet from a Privately Addressed Network*

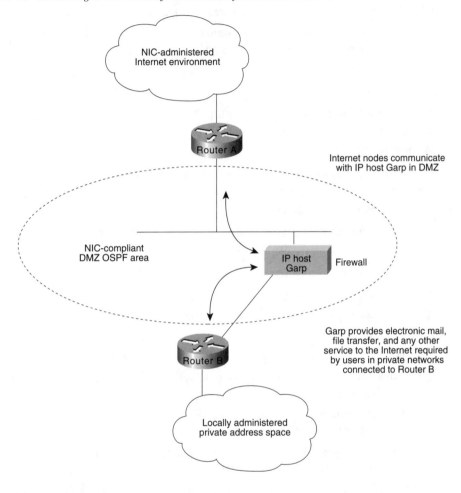

NOTE   For a case study on network security, including information on how to set up firewall routers and communication servers, see Chapter 22, "Increasing Security in IP Networks."

Route Summarization Techniques

Route summarization is particularly important in an OSPF environment because it increases the stability of the network. If route summarization is being used, routes within an area that change do not need to be changed in the backbone or in other areas. Route summarization addresses two important questions of route-information distribution:

- What information does the backbone need to know about each area? The answer to this question focuses attention on area-to-backbone routing information.

- What information does each area need to know about the backbone and other areas? The answer to this question focuses attention on backbone-to-area routing information.

Area-to-Backbone Route Advertisement

There are several key considerations when setting up your OSPF areas for proper summarization:

- OSPF route summarization occurs in the Area Border Routers.

- OSPF supports VLSM, so it is possible to summarize on any bit boundary in a network or subnet address.

- OSPF requires manual summarization. As you design the areas, you need to determine summarization at each area border router.

Backbone-to-Area Route Advertisement

There are four potential types of routing information in an area:

- **Default**—If an explicit route cannot be found for a given IP network or subnetwork, the router will forward the packet to the destination specified in the default route.

- **Intra-area routes**—Explicit network or subnet routes must be carried for all networks or subnets inside an area.

- **Interarea routes**—Areas may carry explicit network or subnet routes for networks or subnets that are in this AS but not in this area.

- **External routes**—When different ASs exchange routing information, the routes they exchange are referred to as external routes.

In general, it is desirable to restrict routing information in any area to the minimal set that the area needs. There are three types of areas, and they are defined in accordance with the routing information used in them:

- **Nonstub areas**—Nonstub areas carry a default route, static routes, intra-area routes, interarea routes, and external routes. An area must be a nonstub area when it contains a router that uses both OSPF and any other protocol, such as the Routing Information Protocol (RIP). Such a router is known as an autonomous system border router (ASBR). An area must also be a nonstub area when a virtual link is configured across the area. Nonstub areas are the most resource-intensive type of area.

- **Stub areas**—Stub areas carry a default route, intra-area routes, and interarea routes, but they do not carry external routes. See "Controlling Interarea Traffic," later in this chapter, for a detailed discussion of the design trade-offs in areas with multiple Area Border Routers. There are two restrictions on the use of stub areas: Virtual links cannot be configured across them, and they cannot contain an ASBR.

- **Stub areas without summaries**—Software Releases 9.1(11), 9.21(2), and 10.0(1) and later support stub areas without summaries, enabling you to create areas that carry only a default route and intra-area routes. Stub areas without summaries do not carry interarea routes or external routes. This type of area is recommended for simple configurations, in which a single router connects an area to the backbone. This kind of an area is also known as a totally stubby area.

Table 3-1 shows the different types of areas, according to the routing information that they use.

Table 3-1   *Routing Information Used in OSPF Areas*

Area Type	Default Route	Intra-area Routes	Interarea Routes	External Routes
Nonstub	Yes	Yes	Yes	Yes
Stub	Yes	Yes	Yes	No
Stub without summaries	Yes	Yes	No	No

NOTE   Stub areas are configured using the **area** *area-id* **stub** router configuration command. Routes are summarized using the **area** *area-id* **range** *address mask* router configuration command. Refer to your *Router Products Configuration Guide* and *Router Products Command Reference* publications for more information regarding the use of these commands.

OSPF Route Selection

When designing an OSPF network for efficient route selection, consider three important topics:

- Tuning OSPF Metrics
- Controlling Interarea Traffic
- Load Balancing in OSPF Networks

Tuning OSPF Metrics

The default value for OSPF metrics is based on bandwidth. The following characteristics show how OSPF metrics are generated:

- Each link is given a metric value based on its bandwidth. The metric for a specific link is the inverse of the bandwidth for that link. The metric for a route is the sum of the metrics for all the links in the route.

- When route summarization is enabled, OSPF uses the metric of the worst route in the summary.

- There are two forms of external metrics: type 1 and type 2. Using an external type 1 metric results in routes adding the internal OSPF metric to the external route metric. External type 2 metrics do not add the internal metric to external routes. The external type 1 metric is generally preferred. If you have more than one external connection, either metric can affect the way multiple paths are used.

Controlling Interarea Traffic

When an area has only a single Area Border Router, all traffic that does not belong in the area will be sent to the Area Border Router. In areas that have multiple Area Border Routers, two choices are available for traffic that needs to leave the area:

- Use the Area Border Router closest to the originator of the traffic. (Traffic leaves the area as soon as possible.)

- Use the Area Border Router closest to the destination of the traffic. (Traffic leaves the area as late as possible.)

If the Area Border Routers inject only the default route, the traffic goes to the Area Border Router closest to the source of the traffic. Generally, this behavior is desirable because the backbone typically has higher bandwidth lines available. If you want the traffic to use the Area Border Router nearest the destination (so that traffic leaves the area as late as possible), however, the Area Border Routers should inject summaries into the area instead of just injecting the default route.

Most network designers prefer to avoid asymmetric routing (that is, using a different path for packets going from A to B than for those packets going from B to A). It is important to understand how routing occurs between areas to avoid asymmetric routing.

Load Balancing in OSPF Networks

To prevent a partitioned network, network topologies are typically designed to provide redundant routes. Redundancy is also useful to provide additional bandwidth for high-traffic areas. If equal-cost paths between nodes exist, Cisco routers automatically load balance in an OSPF environment.

Cisco routers can use up to four equal-cost paths for a given destination. Packets might be distributed either on a per-destination (when fast-switching or better) or a per-packet basis. Per-destination load balancing is the default behavior.

OSPF Convergence

One of the most attractive features about OSPF is the capability to quickly adapt to topology changes. There are two components of routing convergence:

- **Detection of topology changes**—OSPF uses two mechanisms to detect topology changes. The first mechanism is to monitor interface status change (such as carrier failure on a serial link). The second mechanism is to monitor failure of OSPF to receive a Hello packet from its neighbor within a timing window called a dead timer. After this timer expires, the router assumes that the neighbor is down. The dead timer is configured using the **ip ospf dead-interval** interface configuration command. The default value of the dead timer is four times the value of the Hello interval. That results in a dead timer default of 40 seconds for broadcast networks and two minutes for nonbroadcast networks.

- **Recalculation of routes**—After a failure has been detected, the router that detected the failure sends a link-state packet with the change information to all routers in the area. All the routers recalculate all their routes by using the Dykstra (or SPF) algorithm. The time required to run the algorithm depends on a combination of the size of the area and the number of routes in the database.

OSPF Network Scalability

Your ability to scale an OSPF network depends on your overall network structure and addressing scheme. As outlined in the preceding discussions concerning network topology and route summarization, adopting a hierarchical addressing environment and a structured address assignment will be the most important factors in determining the scalability of your network. Network scalability is affected by operational and technical considerations:

- Operationally, OSPF networks should be designed so that areas do not need to be split to accommodate growth. Address space should be reserved to permit the addition of new areas.

- Technically, scaling is determined by the utilization of three resources: memory, CPU, and bandwidth; all discussed in the following sections.

Memory

An OSPF router stores all the link states for all the areas that it is in. In addition, it can store summaries and externals. Careful use of summarization and stub areas can reduce memory use substantially.

CPU

An OSPF router uses CPU cycles whenever a link-state change occurs. Keeping areas small and using summarization dramatically reduces CPU use and creates a more stable environment for OSPF.

Bandwidth

OSPF sends partial updates when a link-state change occurs. The updates are flooded to all routers in the area. In a quiet network, OSPF is a quiet protocol. In a network with substantial topology changes, OSPF minimizes the amount of bandwidth used.

OSPF Security

Two kinds of security are applicable to routing protocols:

- **Controlling the routers that participate in an OSPF network**—OSPF contains an optional authentication field. All routers within an area must agree on the value of the authentication field. Because OSPF is a standard protocol available on many platforms, including some hosts, using the authentication field prevents the inadvertent startup of OSPF in an uncontrolled platform on your network, and reduces the potential for instability.

- **Controlling the routing information that routers exchange**—All routers must have the same data within an OSPF area. As a result, it is not possible to use route filters in an OSPF network to provide security.

OSPF NSSA (Not-So-Stubby Area) Overview

Prior to NSSA, to disable an area from receiving external (Type 5) link-state advertisements (LSAs), the area needed to be defined as a stub area. Area Border Routers (ABRs) that connect stub areas do not flood any external routes they receive into the stub areas. To return packets to destinations outside of the stub area, a default route through the ABR is used.

RFC 1587 defines a hybrid area called the not-so-stubby area (NSSA). An OSPF NSSA is similar to an OSPF stub area, but allows for the following capabilities:

- Importing (redistribution) of external routes as Type 7 LSAs into NSSAs by NSSA Autonomous System Boundary Routers (ASBRs).

- Translation of specific Type 7 LSAs routes into Type 5 LSAs by NSSA ABRs.

Using OSPF NSSA

Use OSPF NSSA when you want to summarize or filter Type 5 LSAs before they are forwarded into an OSPF area. The OSPF specification (RFC 1583) prohibits the summarizing or filtering of Type 5 LSAs. It is an OSPF requirement that Type 5 LSAs always be flooding throughout a routing domain. When you define an NSSA, you can import specific external routes as Type 7 LSAs into the NSSA. In addition, when translating Type 7 LSAs to be imported into nonstub areas, you can summarize or filter the LSAs before exporting them as Type 5 LSAs.

In Figure 3-14, the central site and branch office are interconnected through a slow WAN link. The branch office is not using OSPF, but the central site is. Rather than define a RIP domain to connect the sites, you can define an NSSA.

Figure 3-14 *OSPF NSSA Operation*

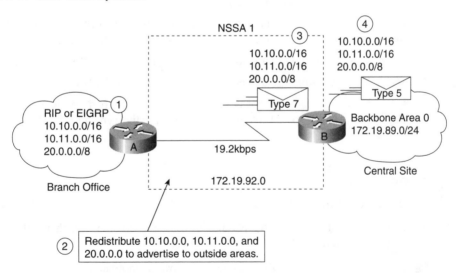

In this scenario, Router A is defined as an ASBR. It is configured to redistribute any routes within the RIP/EIGRP domain to the NSSA. When the area between the connecting routers is defined as an NSSA, the following happens:

1 Router A receives RIP or EIGRP routes for networks 10.10.0.0/16, 10.11.0.0/16, and 20.0.0.0/8.

2 Because Router A is also connected to an NSSA, it redistributes the RIP or EIGRP routers as Type 7 LSAs into the NSSA.

3 Router B, an ABR between the NSSA and the Backbone Area 0, receives the Type 7 LSAs.

4 After the SPF calculation on the forwarding database, Router B translates the Type 7 LSAs into Type 5 LSAs and then floods them throughout backbone Area 0. At this point, Router B could have summarized routes 10.10.0.0/16 and 10.11.0.0/16 as 10.0.0.0/8, or could have filtered one or more of the routes.

Type 7 LSA Characteristics

Type 7 LSAs have the following characteristics:

- They are originated only by ASBRs connected between the NSSA and autonomous system domain.

- They include a forwarding address field. This field is retained when a Type 7 LSA is translated as a Type 5 LSA.

- They are advertised only within an NSSA.

- They are not flooded beyond an NSSA. The ABR that connects to another nonstub area reconverts the Type 7 LSA into a Type 5 LSA before flooding it.

- NSSA ABRs can be configured to summarize or filter Type 7 LSAs into Type 5 LSAs.

- NSSA ABRs can advertise a Type 7 default route into the NSSA.

- Type 7 LSAs have a lower priority than Type 5 LSAs; so when a route is learned with a Type 5 LSA and Type 7 LSA, the route defined in the Type 5 LSA will be selected first.

Configuring OSPF NSSA

The steps used to configure OSPF NSSA are as follows:

Step 1 Configure standard OSPF operation on one or more interfaces that will be attached to NSSAs.

Step 2 Configure an area as NSSA using the following command:

```
router(config)#area area-id nssa
```

Step 3 (Optional) Control the summarization or filtering during the translation. Figure 3-15 shows how Router B will summarize routes using the following command:

```
router(config)#summary-address prefix mask [not-advertise]
[tag tag]
```

Figure 3-15 *Configuring OSPF NSSA*

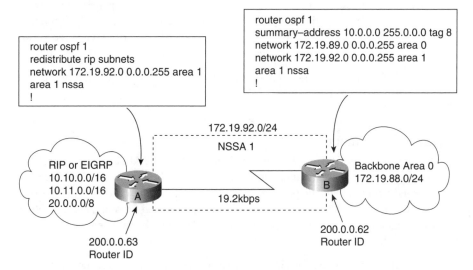

NSSA Implementation Considerations

Be sure to evaluate these considerations before implementing NSSA. As shown in Figure 3-15, you can set a Type 7 default route that can be used to reach external destinations. The command to issue a Type 7 default route is as follows:

```
router(config)#area area-id nssa [default-information-originate]
```

When configured, the router generates a Type 7 default into the NSSA by the NSSA ABR. Every router within the same area must agree that the area is NSSA; otherwise, the routers will not be able to communicate with one another.

If possible, avoid doing explicit redistribution on NSSA ABR because you could get confused about which packets are being translated by which router.

OSPF On-Demand Circuit

OSPF on-demand circuit is an enhancement to the OSPF protocol that allows efficient operation over on-demand circuits such as ISDN, X.25 SVCs, and dialup lines. This feature supports RFC 1793, "Extending OSPF to Support Demand Circuits." This RFC explains the operation of OSPF on-demand circuits. It has good examples and explains the operation of OSPF in this type of environment.

Prior to this feature, OSPF periodic Hello and LSA updates would be exchanged between routers that connected the on-demand link, even when there were no changes in the Hello or LSA information.

With OSPF on-demand circuit, periodic Hellos are suppressed and periodic refreshes of LSAs are not flooded over demand circuits. These packets bring up the links when they are exchanged for the first time only, or when there is a change in the information they contain. This operation allows the underlying data link layer to be closed when the network topology is stable, thus keeping the cost of the demand circuit to a minimum.

This feature is a standards-based mechanism similar to the Cisco Snapshot feature used for distance-vector protocols such as RIP.

Why Use OSPF On-Demand Circuit?

This feature is useful when you want to have an OSPF backbone at the central site, and you want to connect telecommuters or branch offices to the central site. In this case, OSPF on-demand circuit allows the benefits of OSPF over the entire domain without excessive connection costs. Periodic refreshes of Hello updates and LSA updates, and other protocol overhead are prevented from enabling the on-demand circuit when there is no "real" data to transmit.

Overhead protocols such as Hellos and LSAs are transferred over the on-demand circuit upon initial setup only and when they reflect a change in the topology. This means that topology-critical changes that require new SPF calculations are transmitted to maintain network topology integrity, but that periodic refreshes that do not include changes are not transmitted across the link.

OSPF On-Demand Circuit Operation

Figure 3-16 shows the network that will form the basis for the following overview of OSPF on-demand circuit operation:

Figure 3-16 *OSPF Area*

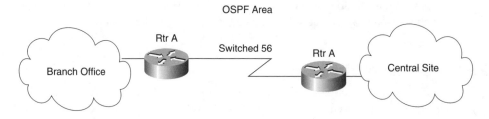

1 Upon initialization, Router A brings up the on-demand circuit to exchange Hellos and synchronize LSA databases with Router B. Because both routers are configured for OSPF on-demand circuit, each router's Hello packets and database description packets have the demand circuit (DC) bit set. As a result, both routers know to suppress periodic Hello packet updates. When each router floods LSAs over the

network, the LSAs will have the DoNotAge (DNA) bit set. This means that the LSAs will not age. They can be updated if a new LSA is received with changed information, but no periodic LSA refreshes will be issued over the demand circuit.

2 When Router A receives refreshed LSAs for existing entries in its database, it will determine whether the LSAs include changed information. If not, Router A will update the existing LSA entries, but it will not flood the information to Router B. Therefore, both routers will have the same entries, but the entry sequence numbers may not be identical.

3 When Router A does receive an LSA for a new route or an LSA that includes changed information, it will update its LSA database, bring up the on-demand circuit, and flood the information to Router B. At this point, both routers will have identical sequence numbers for this LSA entry.

4 If there is no data to transfer while the link is up for the updates, the link is terminated.

5 When a host on either side needs to transfer data to another host at the remote site, the link will be brought up.

Configuring OSPF On-Demand Circuit

The steps used to configure OSPF on-demand circuit are summarized as follows:

Step 1 Configure your on-demand circuit. For example:

```
interface bri 0
ip address 10.1.1.1 255.255.255.0
encapsulation ppp
dialer idle-timeout 3600
dialer map ip name rtra 10.1.1.2 broadcast 1234
dialer group 1
ppp authentication chap
dialer list 1 protocol ip permit
```

Step 2 Enable OSPF operation, as follows:

```
router(config)#router ospf process-id
```

Step 3 Configure OSPF on an on-demand circuit using the following interface command:

```
interface bri 0
ip ospf demand-circuit
```

If the router is part of a point-to-point topology, only one end of the demand circuit needs to be configured with this command, but both routers need to have this feature loaded. All routers that are part of a point-to-multipoint topology need to be configured with this command.

Implementation Considerations for OSPF On-Demand Circuit

Consider the following before implementing OSPF on-demand circuit:

1 Because LSAs indicating topology changes are flooded over an on-demand circuit, you are advised to put demand circuits within OSPF stub areas or within NSSAs to isolate the demand circuits from as many topology changes as possible.

2 To take advantage of the on-demand circuit functionality within a stub area or NSSA, every router in the area must have this feature loaded. If this feature is deployed within a regular area, all other regular areas must also support this feature before the demand-circuit functionality can take effect. This is because external LSAs are flooded throughout all areas.

3 Do not enable this feature on a broadcast-based network topology because Hellos cannot be successfully suppressed, which means the link will remain up.

OSPF Over Nonbroadcast Networks

NBMA networks are those networks that support many (more than two) routers, but have no broadcast capability. Neighboring routers are maintained on these nets using OSPF's Hello protocol. Due to the lack of broadcast capability, however, some configuration information may be necessary to aid in the discovery of neighbors. On nonbroadcast networks, OSPF protocol packets that are normally multicast need to be sent to each neighboring router, in turn. An X.25 Public Data Network (PDN) is an example of a nonbroadcast network. Note the following:

- OSPF runs in one of two modes over nonbroadcast networks. The first mode, called nonbroadcast multiaccess (NBMA), simulates the operation of OSPF on a broadcast network. The second mode, called point-to-multipoint, treats the nonbroadcast network as a collection of point-to-point links. Nonbroadcast networks are referred to as NBMA networks or point-to-multipoint networks, depending on OSPF's mode of operation over the network.

- In NBMA mode, OSPF emulates operation over a broadcast network. A designated router is elected for the NBMA network, and the designated router originates an LSA for the network. The graph representation for broadcast networks and NBMA networks is identical.

NBMA Mode

NBMA mode is the most efficient way to run OSPF over nonbroadcast networks, both in terms of link-state database size and in terms of the amount of routing-protocol traffic. However, it has one significant restriction: It requires all routers attached to the NBMA network to be able to communicate directly. Although this restriction may be met on some nonbroadcast networks, such as an ATM subnet utilizing SVCs, it is often not met on other nonbroadcast networks, such as PVC-only Frame Relay networks.

On nonbroadcast networks in which not all routers can communicate directly, you can break the nonbroadcast network into logical subnets, with the routers on each subnet being able to communicate directly. Then, each separate subnet can be run as an NBMA network or a point-to-point network if each virtual circuit is defined as a separate logical subnet. This setup requires quite a bit of administrative overhead, however, and is prone to misconfiguration. It is probably better to run such a nonbroadcast network in point-to-multipoint mode.

Point-to-Multipoint Mode

Point-to-multipoint networks have been designed to work simply and naturally when faced with partial mesh connectivity. In point-to-multipoint mode, OSPF treats all router-to-router connections over the nonbroadcast network as if they were point-to-point links. No designated router is elected for the network, nor is there an LSA generated for the network. It may be necessary to configure the set of neighbors that are directly reachable over the point-to-multipoint network. Each neighbor is identified by its IP address on the point-to-multipoint network. Because no designated routers are elected on point-to-multipoint networks, the designated-router eligibility of configured neighbors is undefined.

Alternatively, neighbors on point-to-multipoint networks may be dynamically discovered by lower-level protocols such as Inverse ARP. In contrast to NBMA networks, point-to-multipoint networks have the following properties:

1 Adjacencies are established between all neighboring routers. There is no designated router or backup designated router for a point-to-multipoint network. No network LSA is originated for point-to-multipoint networks. Router priority is *not* configured for either point-to-multipoint interfaces or for neighbors on point-to-multipoint networks.

2 When originating a router LSA, point-to-multipoint interface is reported as a collection of "point-to-point links" to all the interface's adjacent neighbors, together with a single stub link advertising the interface's IP address with a cost of 0.

3 When flooding out a nonbroadcast interface (when in either NBMA or point-to-multipoint mode) the link-state update or link-state acknowledgment packet must be replicated in order to be sent to each of the interface's neighbors.

The following is an example of point-to-multipoint configuration on an NBMA (Frame Relay, in this case) network. Attached is the resulting routing table and router link state, along with other pertinent information:

```
interface Ethernet0
 ip address 130.10.6.1 255.255.255.0
 !
interface Serial0
```

```
 no ip address
 encapsulation frame-relay
 frame-relay lmi-type ansi
!
interface Serial0.1 multipoint
 ip address 130.10.10.3 255.255.255.0
 ip ospf network point-to-multipoint
 ip ospf priority 10
 frame-relay map ip 130.10.10.1 140 broadcast
 frame-relay map ip 130.10.10.2 150 broadcast
!
router ospf 2
 network 130.10.10.0 0.0.0.255 area 0
 network 130.10.6.0 0.0.0.255 area 1

R6#sh ip ospf int s 0.1
Serial0.1 is up, line protocol is up
Internet Address 130.10.10.3/24, Area 0
Process ID 2, Router ID 140.10.1.1, Network Type POINT_TO_MULTIPOINT, Cost: 6,
Timer intervals configured, Hello 30, Dead 120, Wait 120, Retransmit 5
Hello due in 00:00:18
Neighbor Count is 2, Adjacent neighbor count is 2
Adjacent with neighbor 130.10.10.2
Adjacent with neighbor 130.10.5.129

R6#sh ip ospf ne

Neighbor ID       Pri     State     Dead Time     Address         Interface
130.10.10.2        0      FULL/     00:01:37      130.10.10.2     Serial0.1
130.10.5.129       0      FULL/     00:01:53      130.10.10.1     Serial0.1
R6#

R6#sh ip ro
Codes: C - connected, S - static, I - IGRP, R - RIP, M - mobile, B - BGP
       D - EIGRP, EX - EIGRP external, O - OSPF, IA - OSPF inter area
       E1 - OSPF external type 1, E2 - OSPF external type 2, E - EGP
       i - IS-IS, L1 - IS-IS level-1, L2 - IS-IS level-2, * - candidate default
       U - per-user static route

Gateway of last resort is not set

130.10.0.0/16 is variably subnetted, 9 subnets, 3 masks
O       130.10.10.2/32 [110/64] via 130.10.10.2, 00:03:28, Serial0.1
C       130.10.10.0/24 is directly connected, Serial0.1
O       130.10.10.1/32 [110/64] via 130.10.10.1, 00:03:28, Serial0.1
O IA    130.10.0.0/22 [110/74] via 130.10.10.1, 00:03:28, Serial0.1
O       130.10.4.0/24 [110/74] via 130.10.10.2, 00:03:28, Serial0.1
C       130.10.6.0/24 is directly connected, Ethernet0

R6#sh ip ospf data router 140.10.1.1

        OSPF Router with ID (140.10.1.1) (Process ID 2)
Router Link States (Area 0)

 LS age: 806
 Options: (No TOS-capability)
 LS Type: Router Links
 Link State ID: 140.10.1.1
 Advertising Router: 140.10.1.1
 LS Seq Number: 80000009
 Checksum: 0x42C1
 Length: 60
 Area Border Router
  Number of Links: 3
```

```
Link connected to: another Router (point-to-point)
 (Link ID) Neighboring Router ID: 130.10.10.2
 (Link Data) Router Interface address: 130.10.10.3
 Number of TOS metrics: 0
  TOS 0 Metrics: 64

Link connected to: another Router (point-to-point)
 (Link ID) Neighboring Router ID: 130.10.5.129
 (Link Data) Router Interface address: 130.10.10.3
 Number of TOS metrics: 0
  TOS 0 Metrics: 64

Link connected to: a Stub Network
 (Link ID) Network/subnet number: 130.10.10.3
 (Link Data) Network Mask: 255.255.255.255
 Number of TOS metrics: 0
  TOS 0 Metrics: 0
```

On-Demand Routing

On-Demand Routing (ODR) is a mechanism that provides minimum-overhead IP routing for stub sites. The overhead of a general dynamic routing protocol is avoided, without incurring the configuration and management overhead of using static routing.

A stub router is the peripheral router in a hub-and-spoke network topology. Stub routers commonly have a WAN connection to the hub router and a small number of LAN network segments (stub networks) connected directly to the stub router. To provide full connectivity, the hub routers can be statically configured to know that a particular stub network is reachable via a specified access router. If there are multiple hub routers, many stub networks, or asynchronous connections between hubs and spokes, however, the overhead required to statically configure knowledge of the stub networks on the hub routers becomes too great.

On-Demand Routing allows stub routers to advertise their connected stub networks using CDP (Cisco Discovery Protocol).

ODR requires stub routers to be configured statically with default routes pointing to hub routers. The hub router is configured to accept remote stub networks via CDP. Once ODR is enabled on a hub router, the router begins installing stub network routes in the IP forwarding table. The hub router can also be configured to redistribute these routes into any configured dynamic IP routing protocols. No IP routing protocol is configured on the stub routers. With ODR, a router is automatically considered to be a stub when no IP routing protocols have been configured on it. The following is an ODR configuration command required on a hub router:

```
router odr
```

No configuration is required on the remote router because CDP is enabled by default.

The suggested Frame Relay configuration is point-to-point subinterface. Point-to-point subinterface configuration is used on the Frame Relay cloud because remote routers are configured with static defaults that point to the other end of the Frame Relay cloud—that is, the IP address of the hub router. When the PVC between the remote and the hub routers goes down, the point-to-point subinterface goes down and the static default route is no longer valid. If it is a multipoint configuration on the Frame Relay, the interface on the cloud does not go down when a PVC is inactive, and hence static default black holes the traffic.

Benefits of On-Demand Routing

The benefits of ODR are as follows:

- ODR is a mechanism that provides minimum-overhead IP routing for stub sites. The overhead of a general dynamic routing protocol is avoided, without incurring the configuration and management overhead of using static routing.

- ODR simplifies installation of IP stub networks in which the hub routers dynamically maintain routes to the stub networks. This is accomplished without requiring the configuration of an IP routing protocol at the stub routers. With ODR, the stub advertises IP prefixes corresponding to the IP networks configured on its directly connected interfaces. Because ODR advertises IP prefixes rather than IP network numbers, ODR can carry variable-length subnet mask (VLSM) information.

- ODR minimizes the configuration and bandwidth overhead required to provide full routing connectivity. Moreover, it eliminates the need to configure an IP routing protocol at the stub routers.

Considerations When Using ODR

You should consider the following when using ODR:

- ODR propagates routes between routers using CDP. Therefore, ODR is partially controlled by the configuration of CDP. If CDP is disabled, the propagation of ODR routing information will cease.

- By default, CDP sends updates every 60 seconds. This update interval may not be frequent enough to provide fast reconvergence. If faster convergence is required, the CDP update interval may need to be changed.

- Limit of number of interfaces on the hub.

- CDP is not yet supported on ATM.

Summary

Recall the following design implications of EIGRP and OSPF:

- Network topology
- Addressing and route summarization
- Route selection
- Convergence
- Network scalability
- Security

This chapter also covered On-Demand Routing (ODR), a mechanism that provides minimum-overhead IP routing for stub sites. The overhead of a general dynamic routing protocol is avoided, without incurring the configuration and management overhead of using static routing. ODR minimizes the configuration and bandwidth overhead required to provide full routing connectivity. Moreover, it eliminates the need to configure an IP routing protocol at the stub routers.

CHAPTER 4

Designing Large-Scale IP Networks with BGP

Edited by Atif Khan

The Border Gateway Protocol (BGP) is an interautonomous system routing protocol. The primary function of a BGP-speaking system is to exchange network reachability information with other BGP systems. This network reachability information includes the list of autonomous systems (ASs) that reachability information traverses. BGP4 provides a set of mechanisms for supporting classless interdomain routing. These mechanisms include support for advertising an IP prefix and eliminate the concept of network *class* within BGP. BGP4 also introduces mechanisms that allow aggregation of routes, including aggregation of AS paths. These changes provide support for the proposed supernetting scheme. This chapter describes how BGP works and how it can be used to participate in routing with other networks that run BGP. The following topics are covered:

- BGP Operation
- BGP Attributes
- BGP Path Selection Criteria
- Understanding and Defining BGP Routing Policies

BGP Operation

This section presents fundamental information about BGP, including the following topics:

- Internal BGP (IBGP)
- External BGP (EBGP)
- BGP and Route Maps
- Advertising Networks

Routers that belong to the same AS and exchange BGP updates are said to be running internal BGP (IBGP). Routers that belong to different ASs and exchange BGP updates are said to be running external BGP (EBGP).

With the exception of the neighbor **ebgp-multihop** command, the commands for configuring EBGP and IBGP are the same. This chapter uses the terms EBGP and IBGP as a reminder that, for any particular context, routing updates are being exchanged between ASs (EBGP) or within an AS (IBGP). Figure 4-1 shows a network that demonstrates the difference between EBGP and IBGP.

Figure 4-1 *EBGP, IBGP, and Multiple ASs*

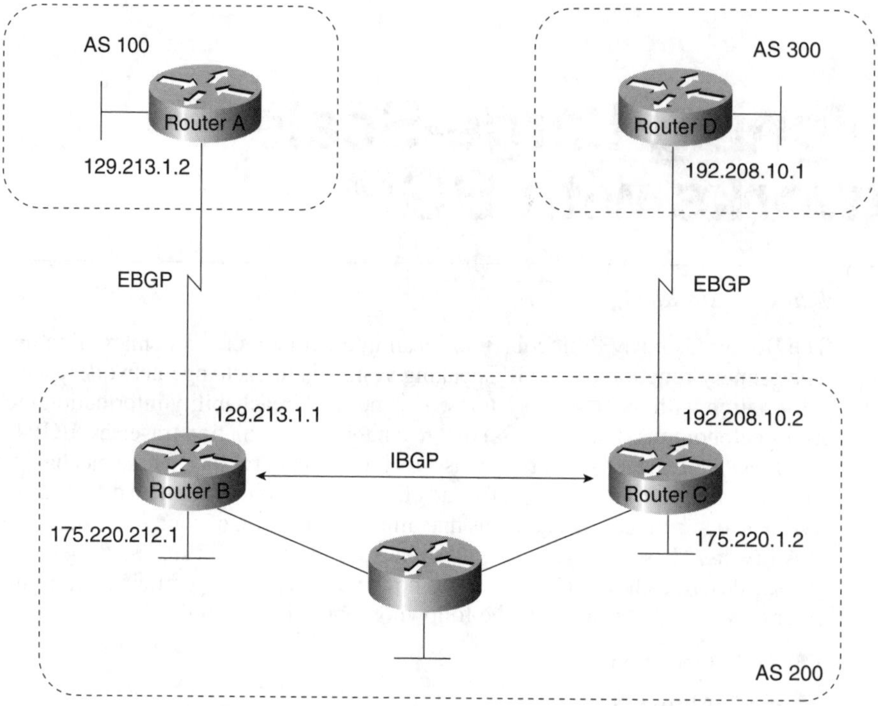

Before it exchanges information with an external AS, BGP ensures that networks within the AS are reachable. This is done by a combination of internal BGP peering among routers within the AS and by redistributing BGP routing information to Interior Gateway Protocols (IGPs) that run within the AS, such as Enhanced Interior Gateway Routing Protocol (EIGRP), Interior Gateway Routing Protocol (IGRP), Intermediate System–to–Intermediate System (IS-IS), Routing Information Protocol (RIP), and Open Shortest Path First (OSPF).

BGP uses the Transmission Control Protocol (TCP) as its transport protocol (specifically, port 179). Any two routers that have opened a TCP connection to each other for the purpose of exchanging routing information are known as peers or neighbors. In Figure 4-1, Routers A and B are BGP peers, as are Routers B and C, and Routers C and D. The routing information consists of a series of AS numbers that describe the full path to the destination network. BGP uses this information to construct a loop-free map of ASs. Note that within an AS, BGP peers do not have to be directly connected.

BGP peers initially exchange their full BGP routing tables. Thereafter, BGP peers send incremental updates only. BGP peers also exchange keepalive messages (to ensure that the connection is up) and notification messages (in response to errors or special conditions).

NOTE   Routers A and B are running EBGP, and Routers B and C are running IBGP, as shown in Figure 4-1. Note that the EBGP peers are directly connected and that the IBGP peers are not. So long as there is an IGP running that allows the two neighbors to reach each other, IBGP peers do not have to be directly connected.

All BGP speakers within an AS must establish a peer relationship with one another. That is, the BGP speakers within an AS must be fully meshed logically. BGP4 provides two techniques that alleviate the requirement for a logical full mesh: confederations and route reflectors. For information about these techniques, see the sections titled "Confederations" and "Route Reflectors" later in this chapter.

AS 200 is a transit AS for AS 100 and AS 300. That is, AS 200 is used to transfer packets between AS 100 and AS 300.

Internal BGP

Internal BGP is the form of BGP that exchanges BGP updates within an AS. Instead of IBGP, the routes learned via EBGP could be redistributed into IGP within the AS and then redistributed again into another AS. However, IBGP is more flexible, more scalable, and provides more efficient ways of controlling the exchange of information within the AS. It also presents a consistent view of the AS to external neighbors. For example, IBGP provides ways to control the exit point from an AS. Figure 4-2 shows a topology that demonstrates IBGP.

When a BGP speaker receives an update from other BGP speakers in its own AS (that is, via IBGP), the receiving BGP speaker uses EBGP to forward the update to external BGP speakers only. This behavior of IBGP is why it is necessary for BGP speakers within an AS to be fully meshed.

In Figure 4-2, for example, if no IBGP session existed between Routers B and D, Router A would send updates from Router B to Router E, but not to Router D. If you want Router D to receive updates from Router B, Router B must be configured so that Router D is a BGP peer.

Figure 4-2 *Internal BGP Example*

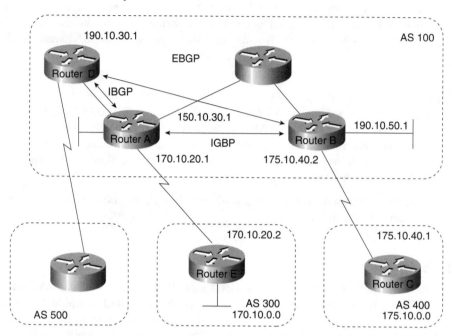

Loopback interfaces are often used by IBGP peers. The advantage of using loopback interfaces is that they eliminate a dependency that would otherwise occur when you use the IP address of a physical interface to configure BGP. Figure 4-3 shows a network in which using the loopback interface is advantageous.

Figure 4-3 *Use of Loopback Interfaces*

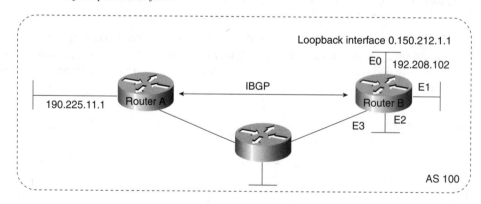

In Figure 4-3, Routers A and B are running IBGP within AS 100. If Router A were to specify the IP address of Ethernet interface 0, 1, 2, or 3 in the **neighbor remote-as**

command, and if the specified interface were to become unavailable, Router A would not be able to establish a TCP connection with Router B. Instead, Router A specifies the IP address of the loopback interface that Router B defines. When the loopback interface is used, BGP does not have to rely on the availability of a particular interface for making TCP connections.

NOTE   Loopback interfaces are rarely used between EBGP peers because EBGP peers are usually directly connected and, therefore, depend on a particular physical interface for connectivity.

External BGP

When two BGP speakers that are not in the same AS run BGP to exchange routing information, they are said to be running EBGP.

Synchronization

When an AS provides transit service to other ASs when there are non-BGP routers in the AS, transit traffic might be dropped if the intermediate non-BGP routers have not learned routes for that traffic via an IGP. The BGP synchronization rule states that if an AS provides transit service to another AS, BGP should not advertise a route until all the routers within the AS have learned about the route via an IGP. The topology shown in Figure 4-4 demonstrates this synchronization rule.

In Figure 4-4, Router C sends updates about network 170.10.0.0 to Router A. Routers A and B are running IBGP, so Router B receives updates about network 170.10.0.0 via IBGP. If Router B wants to reach network 170.10.0.0, it sends traffic to Router E. If Router A does not redistribute network 170.10.0.0 into an IGP, Router E has no way of knowing that network 170.10.0.0 exists and will drop the packets.

If Router B advertises to AS 400 that it can reach 170.10.0.0 before Router E learns about the network via IGP, traffic coming from Router D to Router B with a destination of 170.10.0.0 will flow to Router E and be dropped.

This situation is handled by the synchronization rule of BGP. It states that if an AS (such as AS 100 in Figure 4-4) passes traffic from one AS to another AS, BGP does not advertise a route before all routers within the AS (in this case, AS 100) have learned about the route via an IGP. In this case, Router B waits to hear about network 170.10.0.0 via an IGP before it sends an update to Router D.

Figure 4-4 *EBGP Synchronization Rule*

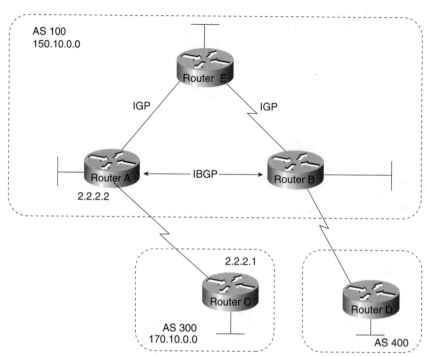

Disabling Synchronization

In some cases, you might want to disable synchronization. Disabling synchronization allows BGP to converge more quickly, but it might result in dropped transit packets. You can disable synchronization if one of the following conditions is true:

- Your AS does not pass traffic from one AS to another AS.
- All the transit routers in your AS run BGP.

BGP and Route Maps

Route maps are used with BGP to control and modify routing information and to define the conditions by which routes are redistributed between routing domains. The format of a route map is as follows:

```
route-map map-tag [[permit | deny] | [sequence-number]]
```

The *map-tag* is a name that identifies the route map, and the *sequence-number* indicates the position that an instance of the route map is to have in relation to other instances of the same route map. (Instances are ordered sequentially.) For example, you might use the following commands to define a route map named MYMAP:

```
route-map MYMAP permit 10
! First set of conditions goes here.
route-map MYMAP permit 20
! Second set of conditions goes here.
```

When BGP applies MYMAP to routing updates, it applies the lowest instance first (in this case, instance 10). If the first set of conditions is not met, the second instance is applied, and so on, until either a set of conditions has been met, or there are no more sets of conditions to apply.

The **match** and **set route map** configuration commands are used to define the condition portion of a route map. The **match** command specifies a criteria that must be matched, and the **set** command specifies an action that is to be taken if the routing update meets the condition defined by the **match** command. The following is an example of a simple route map:

```
route-map MYMAP permit 10
match ip address 1.1.1.1
set metric 5
```

When an update matches the IP address 1.1.1.1, BGP sets the metric for the update to 5, sends the update (because of the **permit** keyword), and breaks out of the list of route-map instances. When an update does not meet the criteria of an instance, BGP applies the next instance of the route map to the update, and so on, until an action is taken, or until there are no more route-map instances to apply. If the update does not meet any criteria, the update is not redistributed or controlled.

When an update meets the match criteria, and the route map specifies the **deny** keyword, BGP breaks out of the list of instances, and the update is not redistributed or controlled. Figure 4-5 shows a topology that demonstrates the use of route maps.

Figure 4-5   *Route Map Example*

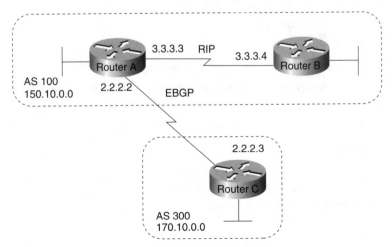

In Figure 4-5, Routers A and B run RIP with each other, and Routers A and C run BGP with each other. If you want Router A to redistribute routes from 170.10.0.0 with a metric of 2 and to redistribute all other routes with a metric of 5, use the following commands for Router A:

```
!Router A
router rip
network 3.0.0.0
network 2.0.0.0
network 150.10.0.0
passive-interface serial 0
redistribute bgp 100 route-map SETMETRIC
!
router bgp 100
neighbor 2.2.2.3 remote-as 300
network 150.10.0.0
!
route-map SETMETRIC permit 10
match ip-address 1
set metric 2
!
route-map SETMETRIC permit 20
set metric 5
!
access-list 1 permit 170.10.0.0 0.0.255.255
```

When a route matches the IP address 170.10.0.0, it is redistributed with a metric of 2. When a route does not match the IP address 170.10.0.0, its metric is set to 5, and the route is redistributed.

Assume that on Router C you want to set to 300 the community attribute of outgoing updates for network 170.10.0.0. The following commands apply a route map to outgoing updates on Router C:

```
!Router C
router bgp 300
network 170.10.0.0
neighbor 2.2.2.2 remote-as 100
neighbor 2.2.2.2 route-map SETCOMMUNITY out
!
route-map SETCOMMUNITY permit 10
match ip address 1
set community 300
!
access-list 1 permit 0.0.0.0 255.255.255.255
```

Access list 1 denies any update for network 170.10.0.0 and permits updates for any other network.

Advertising Networks

A network that resides within an AS is said to originate from that network. To inform other ASs about its networks, the AS advertises them. BGP provides three ways for an AS to advertise the networks that it originates:

- Redistributing static routes
- Redistributing dynamic routes
- Using the **network** command

This section uses the topology shown in Figure 4-6 to demonstrate how networks that originate from an AS can be advertised.

Figure 4-6   *Network Advertisement Example 1*

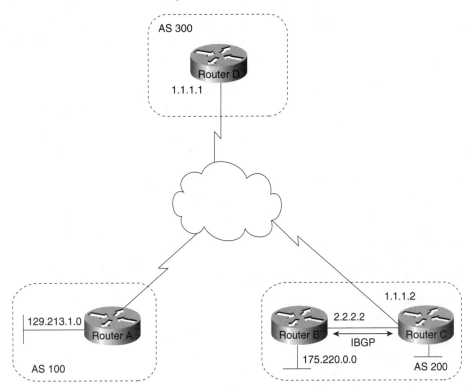

Redistributing Static Routes

One way to advertise that a network or a subnet originates from an AS is to redistribute static routes into BGP. The only difference between advertising a static route and advertising a dynamic route is that when you redistribute a static route, BGP sets the origin attribute of updates for the route to Incomplete. (For a discussion of other values that can be assigned to the origin attribute, see the section titled "Origin Attribute" later in this chapter.) To configure Router C in Figure 4-6 to originate network 175.220.0.0 into BGP, use these commands:

```
!Router C
router bgp 200
neighbor 1.1.1.1 remote-as 300
redistribute static
!
ip route 175.220.0.0 0.0.255.255 null 0
```

The **redistribute** command and the **static** keyword cause all static routes to be redistributed into BGP. The **ip route** command establishes a static route for network 175.220.0.0. In theory, the specification of the null 0 interface would cause a packet destined for network 175.220.0.0 to be discarded. In practice, there will be a more specific match for the packet than 175.220.0.0, and the router will send it out the appropriate interface. Redistributing a static route is the best way to advertise a supernet because it prevents the route from flapping.

NOTE   Regardless of route type (static or dynamic), the **redistribute** command is the only way to inject BGP routes into an IGP.

Redistributing Dynamic Routes

Another way to advertise networks is to redistribute dynamic routes. Typically, you redistribute IGP routes (such as Enhanced IGRP, IGRP, IS-IS, OSPF, and RIP routes) into BGP. Some of your IGP routes might have been learned from BGP, so you need to use access lists to prevent the redistribution of routes back into BGP. Assume that in Figure 4-6, Routers B and C are running IBGP, that Router C is learning 129.213.1.0 via BGP, and that Router B is redistributing 129.213.1.0 back into EIGRP. The following commands configure Router C:

```
!Router C
router eigrp 10
network 175.220.0.0
redistribute bgp 200
redistributed connected
default-metric 1000 100 250 100 1500
!
router bgp 200
neighbor 1.1.1.1 remote-as 300
neighbor 2.2.2.2 remote-as 200
neighbor 1.1.1.1 distribute-list 1 out
redistribute eigrp 10
!
access-list 1 permit 175.220.0.0 0.0.255.255
```

The **redistribute** command with the **eigrp** keyword redistributes Enhanced IGRP routes for process ID 10 into BGP. (Normally, distributing BGP into IGP should be avoided because too many routes would be injected into the AS.) The **neighbor distribute-list** command applies access list 1 to outgoing advertisements to the neighbor whose IP address is 1.1.1.1 (that is, Router D). Access list 1 specifies that network 175.220.0.0 is to be advertised. All other networks, such as network 129.213.1.0, are implicitly prevented from

being advertised. The access list prevents network 129.213.1.0 from being injected back
into BGP as if it originated from AS 200 and allows BGP to advertise network 175.220.0.0
as originating from AS 200.

Using the **network** Command

Another way to advertise networks is to use the **network** command. When used with BGP,
the **network** command specifies the networks that the AS originates. (By way of contrast,
when used with an IGP such as RIP, the **network** command identifies the interfaces on
which the IGP is to run.) The **network** command works for networks that the router learns
dynamically or that are configured as static routes. The origin attribute of routes that are
injected into BGP by means of the **network** command is set to IGP. The following
commands configure Router C to advertise network 175.220.0.0:

```
!Router C
router bgp 200
neighbor 1.1.1.1 remote-as 300
network 175.220.0.0
```

The **network** command causes Router C to generate an entry in the BGP routing table for
network 175.220.0.0. Figure 4-7 shows another topology that demonstrates the effects of
the **network** command.

Figure 4-7   *Network Advertisement Example 2*

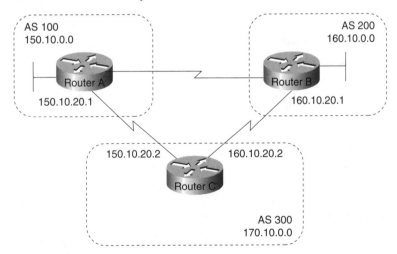

The following configurations use the **network** command to configure the routers shown in
Figure 4-7:

```
!Router A
router bgp 100
neighbor 150.10.20.2 remote-as 300
network 150.10.0.0
```

```
!Router B
router bgp 200
neighbor 160.10.20.2 remote-as 300
network 160.10.0.0
!Router C
router bgp 300
neighbor 150.10.20.1 remote-as 100
neighbor 160.10.20.1 remote-as 200
network 170.10.0.0
```

To ensure a loop-free interdomain topology, BGP does not accept updates that originated from its own AS. In Figure 4-7, for example, if Router A generates an update for network 150.10.0.0 with the origin set to AS 100 and sends it to Router C, Router C will pass the update to Router B with the origin still set to AS 100. Router B will send the update (with the origin still set to AS 100) to Router A, which will recognize that the update originated from its own AS and will ignore it.

BGP Attributes

When a BGP speaker receives updates from multiple ASs that describe different paths to the same destination, it must choose the single best path for reaching that destination. Once chosen, BGP propagates the best path to its neighbors. The decision is based on the value of attributes (such as next hop, administrative weights, local preference, the origin of the route, and path length) that the update contains and other BGP-configurable factors. This section describes the following attributes and factors that BGP uses in the decision-making process:

- AS_path Attribute
- Origin Attribute
- Next Hop Attribute
- Weight Attribute
- Local Preference Attribute
- Multi-Exit Discriminator Attribute
- Community Attribute

AS_path Attribute

Whenever an update passes through an AS, BGP prepends its AS number to the update. The AS_path attribute is the list of AS numbers that an update has traversed to reach a destination. An AS-SET is a mathematical set of all the ASs that have been traversed. Consider the network shown in Figure 4-8.

Figure 4-8   *AS_path Attribute*

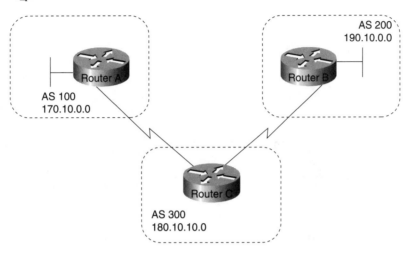

Origin Attribute

The origin attribute provides information about the origin of the route. The origin of a route can be one of three values:

- **IGP**—The route is interior to the originating AS. This value is set when the **network** command is used to inject the route into BGP. The IGP origin type is represented by the letter *i* in the output of the **show ip bgp** EXEC command.

- **EGP**—The route is learned via the Exterior Gateway Protocol (EGP). The EGP origin type is represented by the letter *e* in the output of the **show ip bgp** EXEC command.

- **Incomplete**—The origin of the route is unknown or learned in some other way. An origin of Incomplete occurs when a route is redistributed into BGP. The Incomplete origin type is represented by the question mark symbol (?) in the output of the **show ip bgp** EXEC command.

Figure 4-9 shows a network that demonstrates the value of the origin attribute.

Figure 4-9 *Origin Attribute*

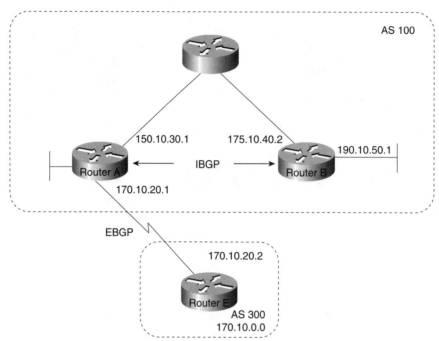

Next Hop Attribute

The BGP next hop attribute is the IP address of the next hop that is going to be used to reach a certain destination. For EBGP, the next hop is usually the IP address of the neighbor specified by the **neighbor remote-as** command. (The exception is when the next hop is on a multiaccess medium, in which case the next hop could be the IP address of the router in the same subnet.) Consider the network shown in Figure 4-10.

In Figure 4-10, Router C advertises network 170.10.0.0 to Router A with a next hop attribute of 170.10.20.2, and Router A advertises network 150.10.0.0 to Router C with a next hop attribute of 170.10.20.1.

BGP specifies that the next hop of EBGP-learned routes should be carried without modification into IBGP. Because of that rule, Router A advertises 170.10.0.0 to its IBGP peer (Router B) with a next hop attribute of 170.10.20.2. As a result, according to Router B, the next hop to reach 170.10.0.0 is 170.10.20.2, rather than 150.10.30.1. For that reason, the configuration must ensure that Router B can reach 170.10.20.2 via an IGP. Otherwise, Router B will drop packets destined for 170.10.0.0 because the next hop address is inaccessible.

Figure 4-10 *Next Hop Attribute*

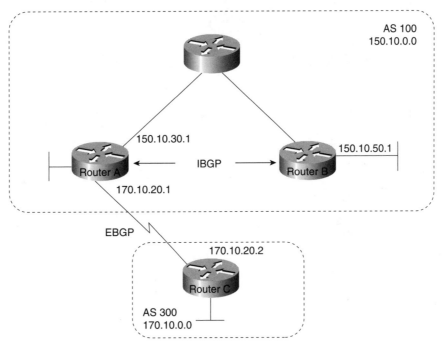

If Router B runs IGRP, for example, Router A should run IGRP on network 170.10.0.0. You might want to make IGRP passive on the link to Router C so that only BGP updates are exchanged.

Next Hop Attribute and Multiaccess Media

BGP might set the value of the next hop attribute differently on multiaccess media, such as Ethernet. Consider the network shown in Figure 4-11.

In Figure 4-11, Routers C and D in AS 300 are running OSPF. Router C is running BGP with Router A. Router C can reach network 180.20.0.0 via 170.10.20.3. When Router C sends a BGP update to Router A regarding 180.20.0.0, it sets the next hop attribute to 170.10.20.3, rather than its own IP address (170.10.20.2). This is because Routers A, B, and C are in the same subnet, and it makes more sense for Router A to use Router D as the next hop instead of taking an extra hop via Router C.

Figure 4-11 *Multiaccess Media Network*

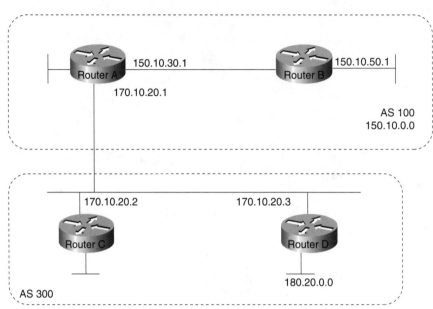

Next Hop Attribute and Nonbroadcast Media Access

In Figure 4-12, three networks are connected by a nonbroadcast media access (NBMA) cloud, such as Frame Relay.

If Routers A, C, and D use a common medium such as Frame Relay (or any NBMA cloud), Router C advertises 180.20.0.0 to Router A with a next hop of 170.10.20.3, just as it would do if the common medium were Ethernet. The problem is that Router A does not have a direct permanent virtual connection (PVC) to Router D and cannot reach the next hop, so routing will fail. To remedy this situation, use the **neighbor next-hop-self** command, as shown in the following configuration for Router C:

```
!Router C
router bgp 300
neighbor 170.10.20.1 remote-as 100
neighbor 170.10.20.1 next-hop-self
```

The **neighbor next-hop-self** command causes Router C to advertise 180.20.0.0 with the next hop attribute set to 170.10.20.2.

Figure 4-12 *Next Hop Attribute and Nonbroadcast Media Access*

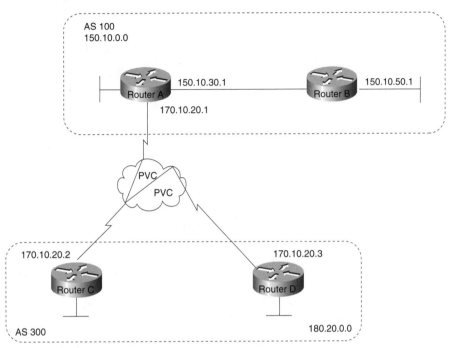

Weight Attribute

The weight attribute is a special Cisco attribute used in the path selection process when there is more than one route to the same destination. The weight attribute is local to the router on which it is assigned, and it is not propagated in routing updates. By default, the weight attribute is 32768 for paths that the router originates and zero for other paths. Routes with a higher weight are preferred when there are multiple routes to the same destination. Consider the network shown in Figure 4-13.

In Figure 4-13, Routers A and B learn about network 175.10.0.0 from AS 400, and each propagates the update to Router C. Router C has two routes for reaching 175.10.0.0 and has to decide which route to use. If, on Router C, you set the weight of the updates coming in from Router A to be higher than the updates coming in from Router B, Router C will use Router A as the next hop to reach network 175.10.0.0. There are three ways to set the weight for updates coming in from Router A:

- Using an access list to set the weight attribute
- Using a route map to set the weight attribute
- Using the **neighbor weight** command to set the weight attribute

Figure 4-13 *Weight Attribute Example*

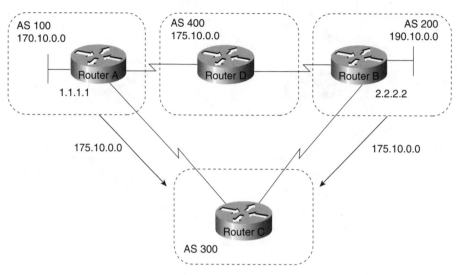

Using an Access List to Set the Weight Attribute

The following commands on Router C use access lists and the value of the AS_path attribute to assign a weight to route updates:

```
!Router C
router bgp 300
neighbor 1.1.1.1 remote-as 100
neighbor 1.1.1.1 filter-list 5 weight 2000
neighbor 2.2.2.2 remote-as 200
neighbor 2.2.2.2 filter-list 6 weight 1000
!
ip as-path access-list 5 permit ^100$
ip as-path access-list 6 permit ^200$
```

In this example, 2000 is assigned to the weight attribute of updates from the neighbor at IP address 1.1.1.1 that are permitted by access list 5. Access list 5 permits updates whose AS_path attribute starts with 100 (as specified by ^) and ends with 100 (as specified by $). (The ^ and $ symbols are used to form regular expressions.) This example also assigns 1000 to the weight attribute of updates from the neighbor at IP address 2.2.2.2 that are permitted by access list 6. Access list 6 permits updates whose AS_path attribute starts with 200 and ends with 200.

In effect, this configuration assigns 2000 to the weight attribute of all route updates received from AS 100 and assigns 1000 to the weight attribute of all route updates from AS 200.

Using a Route Map to Set the Weight Attribute

The following commands on Router C use a route map to assign a weight to route updates:

```
!Router C
router bgp 300
neighbor 1.1.1.1 remote-as 100
neighbor 1.1.1.1 route-map SETWEIGHTIN in
neighbor 2.2.2.2 remote-as 200
neighbor 2.2.2.2 route-map SETWEIGHTIN in
!
ip as-path access-list 5 permit ^100$
!
route-map SETWEIGHTIN permit 10
match as-path 5
set weight 2000
route-map SETWEIGHTIN permit 20
set weight 1000
```

This first instance of the SETWEIGHTIN route map assigns 2000 to any route update from AS 100, and the second instance of the SETWEIGHTIN route map assigns 1000 to route updates from any other AS.

Using the **neighbor weight** Command to Set the Weight Attribute

The following configuration for Router C uses the **neighbor weight** command:

```
!Router C
router bgp 300
neighbor 1.1.1.1 remote-as 100
neighbor 1.1.1.1 weight 2000
neighbor 2.2.2.2 remote-as 200
neighbor 2.2.2.2 weight 1000
```

This configuration sets the weight of all route updates from AS 100 to 2000, and the weight of all route updates coming from AS 200 to 1000. The higher weight assigned to route updates from AS 100 causes Router C to send traffic through Router A.

Local Preference Attribute

When there are multiple paths to the same destination, the local preference attribute indicates the preferred path. The path with the higher preference is preferred. (The default value of the local preference attribute is 100.) Unlike the weight attribute, which is relevant only to the local router, the local preference attribute is part of the routing update and is exchanged among routers in the same AS. The network shown in Figure 4-14 demonstrates the local preference attribute.

In Figure 4-14, AS 256 receives route updates for network 170.10.0.0 from AS 100 and AS 300. There are two ways to set local preference:

- Using the **bgp default local-preference** command
- Using a route map to set local preference

Figure 4-14 *Local Preference*

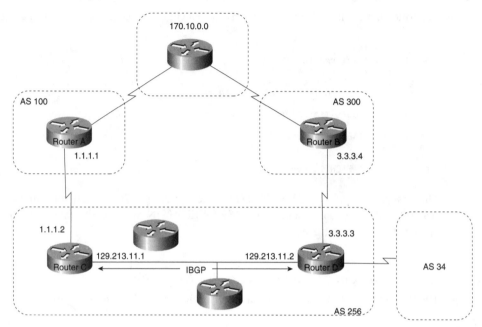

Using the **bgp default local-preference** Command

The following configurations use the **bgp default local-preference** command to set the local preference attribute on Routers C and D:

```
!Router C
router bgp 256
neighbor 1.1.1.1 remote-as 100
neighbor 128.213.11.2 remote-as 256
bgp default local-preference 150
!Router D
router bgp 256
neighbor 3.3.3.4 remote-as 300
neighbor 128.213.11.1 remote-as 256
bgp default local-preference 200
```

The configuration for Router C causes it to set the local preference of all updates from AS 300 to 150, and the configuration for Router D causes it to set the local preference for all updates from AS 100 to 200. Because local preference is exchanged within the AS, both Routers C and D determine that updates regarding network 170.10.0.0 have a higher local preference when they come from AS 300 than when they come from AS 100. As a result, all traffic in AS 256 destined for network 170.10.0.0 is sent to Router D as the exit point.

Using a Route Map to Set Local Preference

Route maps provide more flexibility than the **bgp default local-preference** command. When the **bgp default local-preference** command is used on Router D in Figure 4-14, the local preference attribute of all updates received by Router D will be set to 200, including updates from AS 34.

The following configuration uses a route map to set the local preference attribute on Router D specifically for updates regarding AS 300:

```
!Router D
router bgp 256
neighbor 3.3.3.4 remote-as 300
route-map SETLOCALIN in
neighbor 128.213.11.1 remote-as 256
!
ip as-path 7 permit ^300$
route-map SETLOCALIN permit 10
match as-path 7
set local-preference 200
!
route-map SETLOCALIN permit 20
```

With this configuration, the local preference attribute of any update coming from AS 300 is set to 200. Instance 20 of the SETLOCALIN route map accepts all other routes.

Multi-Exit Discriminator Attribute

The multi-exit discriminator (MED) attribute is a hint to external neighbors about the preferred path into an AS when there are multiple entry points into the AS. A lower MED value is preferred over a higher MED value. The default value of the MED attribute is 0.

NOTE   In BGP4, MED is known as Inter-AS_Metric.

Unlike local preference, the MED attribute is exchanged between ASs, but a MED attribute that comes into an AS does not leave the AS. When an update enters the AS with a certain MED value, that value is used for decision making within the AS. When BGP sends that update to another AS, the MED is reset to 0.

Unless otherwise specified, the router compares MED attributes for paths from external neighbors that are in the same AS. If you want MED attributes from neighbors in other ASs to be compared, you must configure the **bgp always-compare-med** command. The network shown in Figure 4-15 demonstrates the use of the MED attribute.

Figure 4-15 *MED Example*

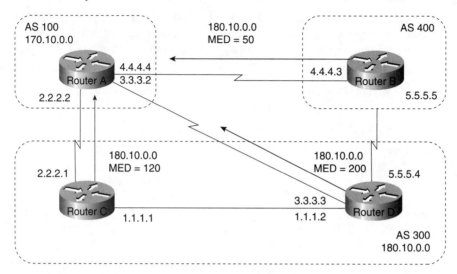

In Figure 4-15, AS 100 receives updates regarding network 180.10.0.0 from Routers B, C, and D. Routers C and D are in AS 300, and Router B is in AS 400. The following commands configure Routers A, B, C, and D:

```
!Router A
router bgp 100
neighbor 2.2.2.1 remote-as 300
neighbor 3.3.3.3 remote-as 300
neighbor 4.4.4.3 remote-as 400

!Router B
router bgp 400
neighbor 4.4.4.4 remote-as 100
neighbor 4.4.4.4 route-map SETMEDOUT out
neighbor 5.5.5.4 remote-as 300
!
route-map SETMEDOUT permit 10
set metric 50

!Router C
router bgp 300
neighbor 2.2.2.2 remote-as 100
neighbor 2.2.2.2 route-map SETMEDOUT out
neighbor 1.1.1.2 remote-as 300
!
route-map SETMEDOUT permit 10
set metric 120

!Router D
router bgp 300
neighbor 3.3.3.2 remote-as 100
neighbor 3.3.3.2 route map SETMEDOUT out
neighbor 5.5.5.5 remote-as 400
neighbor 1.1.1.1 remote-as 300
route-map SETMEDOUT permit 10
set metric 200
```

By default, BGP compares the MED attributes of routes coming from neighbors in the same external AS (such as AS 300 in Figure 4-15). Router A can only compare the MED attribute coming from Router C (120) to the MED attribute coming from Router D (200), even though the update coming from Router B has the lowest MED value.

Router A will choose Router C as the best path for reaching network 180.10.0.0. To force Router A to include updates for network 180.10.0.0 from Router B in the comparison, use the **bgp always-compare-med** command, as in the following modified configuration for Router A:

```
!Router A
router bgp 100
neighbor 2.2.2.1 remote-as 300
neighbor 3.3.3.3 remote-as 300
neighbor 4.4.4.3 remote-as 400
bgp always-compare-med
```

Router A will choose Router B as the best next hop for reaching network 180.10.0.0 (assuming that all other attributes are the same).

You can also set the MED attribute when you configure the redistribution of routes into BGP. On Router B you can inject the static route into BGP with a MED of 50, for example, as in the following configuration:

```
!Router B
router bgp 400
redistribute static
default-metric 50
!
ip route 160.10.0.0 255.255.0.0 null 0
```

The preceding configuration causes Router B to send out updates for 160.10.0.0 with a MED attribute of 50.

Community Attribute

The community attribute provides a way of grouping destinations (called communities) to which routing decisions (such as acceptance, preference, and redistribution) can be applied. Route maps are used to set the community attribute. Table 4-1 lists a few predefined communities.

Table 4-1   *Predefined Communities*

Community	Meaning
no-export	Do not advertise this route to EBGP peers.
no-advertised	Do not advertise this route to any peer.
internet	Advertise this route to the Internet community; all routers in the network belong to it.

The following route maps set the value of the community attribute:

```
route-map COMMUNITYMAP
match ip address 1
set community no-advertise
!
route-map SETCOMMUNITY
match as-path 1
set community 200 additive
```

If you specify the **additive** keyword, the specified community value is added to the existing value of the community attribute. Otherwise, the specified community value replaces any community value that was set previously. To send the community attribute to a neighbor, you must use the **neighbor send-community** command, as in the following example:

```
router bgp 100
neighbor 3.3.3.3 remote-as 300
neighbor 3.3.3.3 send-community
neighbor 3.3.3.3 route-map setcommunity out
```

For examples of how the community attribute is used to filter updates, see the section titled "Community Filtering" later in this chapter.

BGP Path Selection Criteria

BGP selects only one path as the best path. When the path is selected, BGP puts the selected path in its routing table and propagates the path to its neighbors. BGP uses the following criteria, in the order presented, to select a path for a destination:

1 If the path specifies a next hop that is inaccessible, drop the update.

2 Prefer the path with the largest weight.

3 If the weights are the same, prefer the path with the largest local preference.

4 If the local preferences are the same, prefer the path that was originated by BGP running on this router.

5 If no route was originated, prefer the route that has the shortest AS_path.

6 If all paths have the same AS_path length, prefer the path with the lowest origin type (where IGP is lower than EGP, and EGP is lower than Incomplete).

7 If the origin codes are the same, prefer the path with the lowest MED attribute.

8 If the paths have the same MED, prefer the external path over the internal path.

9 If the paths are still the same, prefer the path through the closest IGP neighbor.

10 Prefer the path with the lowest IP address, as specified by the BGP router ID.

Understanding and Defining BGP Routing Policies

This section describes how to understand and define BGP policies to control the flow of BGP updates. The techniques include the following:

- Administrative distance
- BGP filtering
- BGP peer groups
- CIDR and Aggregate addresses
- Confederations
- Route reflectors
- Route flap dampening

Administrative Distance

Normally, a route could be learned via more than one protocol. Administrative distance is used to discriminate between routes learned from more than one protocol. The route with the lowest administrative distance is installed in the IP routing table. By default, BGP uses the administrative distances shown in Table 4-2.

Table 4-2   *BGP Administrative Distances*

Distance	Default Value	Function
External	20	Applied to routes learned from EBGP
Internal	200	Applied to routes learned from IBGP
Local	200	Applied to routes originated by the router

NOTE   Distance does not influence the BGP path selection algorithm, but it does influence whether BGP-learned routes are installed in the IP routing table.

BGP Filtering

You can control the sending and receiving of updates by using the following filtering methods:

- Prefix filtering
- AS_path filtering
- Route map filtering
- Community filtering

Each method can be used to achieve the same result—the choice of method depends on the specific network configuration.

Prefix Filtering

The prefix list is implemented for the purpose of efficient route filtering (currently with only BGP). Compared to using the (extended) access list in route filtering, there are several advantages to using the prefix list:

- Significant performance improvement in loading and route lookup of large lists
- Support for incremental updates
- More user-friendly command line interface

Several key features with the access list are preserved in the prefix list:

- Configuration of either permit or deny
- Order dependency—first match wins
- Filtering on prefix length—both exact match and range match

However, noncontiguous masks are not supported in the prefix list.

The full syntax of a prefix list is as follows:

```
ip prefix-list [seq] deny¦permit prefix le¦ge
```

The following command can be used to delete a prefix list:

```
no ip prefix-list
```

seq is optional. It can be used to specify the sequence number of an entry of a prefix list.

By default, the entries of a prefix list have sequence values of 5, 10, 15, and so on. In the absence of a specified sequence value, the entry would be assigned with a sequence number of (Current_Max + 5).

If a given prefix matches multiple entries of a prefix list, the one with the smallest sequence number is considered the match.

deny or **permit** specifies an action taken once a match is found.

Multiple policies (exact match or range match) with different sequence numbers can be configured for the same prefix.

ge indicates greater than or equal to. **le** indicates less than or equal to. Both **ge** and **le** are optional. They can be used to specify the range of the prefix length to be matched for prefixes.

Exact match is assumed when neither **ge** nor **le** is specified.

The range is assumed to be from *ge value* to 32 if only the **ge** attribute is specified. The range is assumed to be from *len* to *le value* if only the **le** attribute is specified.

As usual, an implicit deny is assumed at the end of a prefix list.

The following are configuration examples for an exact match:

```
ip prefix-list aaa deny 0.0.0.0/0
ip prefix-list aaa permit 35.0.0.0/8
```

The following list shows configuration commands for a prefix length match:

- In 192/8, accept up to /24:

  ```
  ip prefix-list aaa permit 192.0.0.0/8 le 24
  ```

- In 192/8, deny /25+:

  ```
  ip prefix-list aaa deny 192.0.0.0/8 ge 25
  ```

- In all address space, deny /0 through /7:

  ```
  ip prefix-list aaa deny 0.0.0.0/0 le 7
  ```

- In all address space, deny /25+:

  ```
  ip prefix-list aaa deny 0.0.0.0/0 ge 25
  ```

- In 10/8, deny all:

  ```
  ip prefix-list aaa deny 10.0.0.0/8 le 32
  ```

- In 204.70.1/24, deny /25+:

  ```
  ip prefix-list aaa deny 204.70.1.0/24 ge 25
  ```

- Permit all:

  ```
  ip prefix-list aaa permit 0.0.0.0/0 le 32
  ```

Incremental updates are possible with prefix lists. As opposed to the normal access list where one **no** command will erase the whole access list, a prefix list can be modified incrementally. To change a prefix list from A to B, for example, only the difference between B and A needs to be deployed to the router.

From A:

- `ip prefix-list aaa deny 0.0.0.0/0 le 7`
- `ip prefix-list aaa deny 0.0.0.0/0 ge 25`
- `ip prefix-list aaa permit 35.0.0.0/8`
- `ip prefix-list aaa permit 204.70.0.0/15`

To B:

- `ip prefix-list aaa deny 0.0.0.0/0 le 7`
- `ip prefix-list aaa deny 0.0.0.0/0 ge 25`
- `ip prefix-list aaa permit 35.0.0.0/8`
- `ip prefix-list aaa permit 198.0.0.0/8`

by deploying the difference:

- `no ip prefix-list aaa permit 204.70.0.0/15`
- `ip prefix-list aaa permit 198.0.0.0/8`

AS_path Filtering

You can specify an access list on both incoming and outgoing updates based on the value of the AS_path attribute. The network shown in Figure 4-16 demonstrates the usefulness of AS_path filters:

```
!Router C
neighbor 3.3.3.3 remote-as 200
neighbor 2.2.2.2 remote-as 100
neighbor 2.2.2.2 filter-list 1 out
!
ip as-path access-list 1 deny ^200$
ip as-path access-list 1 permit .*
```

Figure 4-16 *AS_path Filtering*

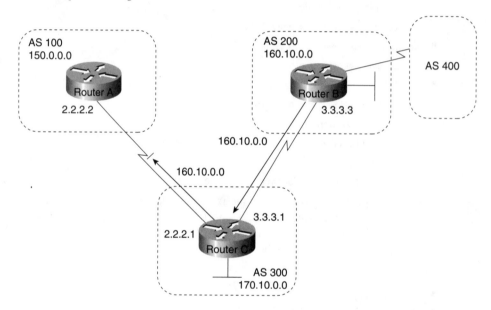

In this example, access list 1 denies any update whose AS_path attribute starts with 200 (as specified by ^) and ends with 200 (as specified by $). Because Router B sends updates about 160.10.0.0 whose AS_path attributes start with 200 and end with 200, such updates will match the access list and will be denied. By specifying that the update must also end with 200, the access list permits updates from AS 400 (whose AS_path attribute is 200, 400). If the access list specified ^200 as the regular expression, updates from AS 400 would be denied.

In the second access list statement, the period symbol (.) means any character, and the asterisk symbol (*) means a repetition of that character. Together, .* matches any value of the AS_path attribute, which in effect permits any update that has not been denied by the previous access list statement. If you want to verify that your regular expressions work as intended, use the following EXEC command:

```
show ip bgp regexp regular-expression
```

The router displays all the paths that match the specified regular expression.

Route Map Filtering

The **neighbor route-map** command can be used to apply a route map to incoming and outgoing routes. The network shown in Figure 4-17 demonstrates using route maps to filter BGP updates.

Figure 4-17 *BGP Route Map Filtering*

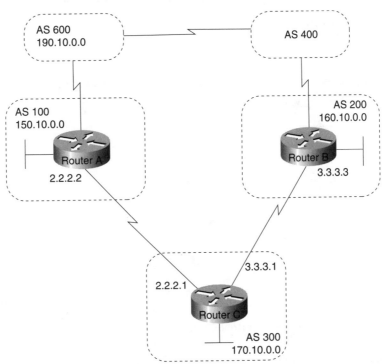

Assume that in Figure 4-17 you want Router C to learn about networks that are local to AS 200 only. (That is, you do not want Router C to learn about AS 100, AS 400, or AS 600 from AS 200.) Also, on those routes that Router C accepts from AS 200, you want the weight attribute to be set to 20. The following configuration for Router C accomplishes this goal:

```
!Router C
router bgp 300
network 170.10.0.0
neighbor 3.3.3.3 remote-as 200
neighbor 3.3.3.3 route-map STAMP in
!
route-map STAMP permit 10
match as-path 1
set weight 20
!
ip as-path access-list 1 permit ^200$
```

In the preceding configuration, access list 1 permits any update whose AS_path attribute begins with 200 and ends with 200 (that is, access list 1 permits updates that originate in AS 200). The weight attribute of the permitted updates is set to 20. All other updates are denied and dropped.

Community Filtering

The network shown in Figure 4-18 demonstrates the usefulness of community filters.

Figure 4-18 *Community Filtering*

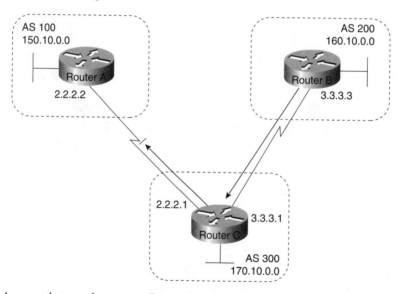

Assume that you do not want Router C to propagate routes learned from Router B to Router A. You can do this by setting the community attribute on updates that Router B sends to Router C, as in the following configuration for Router B:

```
!Router B
router bgp 200
network 160.10.0.0
neighbor 3.3.3.1 remote-as 300
neighbor 3.3.3.1 send-community
neighbor 3.3.3.1 route-map SETCOMMUNITY out
```

```
!
route-map SETCOMMUNITY permit 10
match ip address 1
set community no-export
!
route-map SETCOMMUNITY permit 20
!
access list 1 permit 0.0.0.0 255.255.255.255
```

For routes sent to the neighbor at IP address 3.3.3.1 (Router C), Router B applies the route map named SETCOMMUNITY. The SETCOMMUNITY route map sets the community attribute of any update (by means of access list 1) destined for 3.3.3.1 to no-export. The **neighbor send-community** command is required to include the community attribute in updates sent to the neighbor at IP address 3.3.3.1. When Router C receives the updates from Router B, it does not propagate them to Router A because the value of the community attribute is no-export.

Another way to filter updates based on the value of the community attribute is to use the **ip community-list** global configuration command. Assume that Router B has been configured as follows:

```
!Router B
router bgp 200
network 160.10.0.0
neighbor 3.3.3.1 remote-as 300
neighbor 3.3.3.1 send-community
neighbor 3.3.3.1 route-map SETCOMMUNITY out
!
route-map SETCOMMUNITY permit 10
match ip address 2
set community 100 200 additive
route-map SETCOMMUNITY permit 20
!
access list 2 permit 0.0.0.0 255.255.255.255
```

In the preceding configuration, Router B adds 100 and 200 to the community value of any update destined for the neighbor at IP address 3.3.3.1. To configure Router C to use the **ip community-list** command, set the value of the weight attribute. Based on whether the community attribute contains 100 or 200, use the following configuration:

```
!Router C
router bgp 300
neighbor 3.3.3.3 remote-as 200
neighbor 3.3.3.3 route-map check-community in
!
route-map check-community permit 10
match community 1
set weight 20
!
route-map check-community permit 20
match community 2 exact
set weight 10
!
route-map check-community permit 30
match community 3
!
ip community-list 1 permit 100
ip community-list 2 permit 200
ip community-list 3 permit internet
```

In the preceding configuration, any route that has 100 in its community attribute matches community list 1 and has its weight set to 20. Any route whose community attribute is only 200 (by virtue of the **exact** keyword) matches community list 2 and has its weight set to 10. In the last community list (list 3), the use of the **internet** keyword permits all other updates without changing the value of an attribute. (The **internet** keyword specifies all routes because all routes are members of the Internet community.)

BGP Peer Groups

A BGP *peer group* is a group of BGP neighbors that share the same update policies. Update policies are usually set by route maps, distribution lists, and filter lists. Instead of defining the same policies for each individual neighbor, you define a peer group name and assign policies to the peer group.

Members of a peer group inherit all the configuration options of the peer group. Peer group members can also be configured to override configuration options if the options do not affect outgoing updates. That is, you can override options set only for incoming updates. The network shown in Figure 4-19 demonstrates the use of BGP peer groups.

Figure 4-19 *BGP Peer Groups*

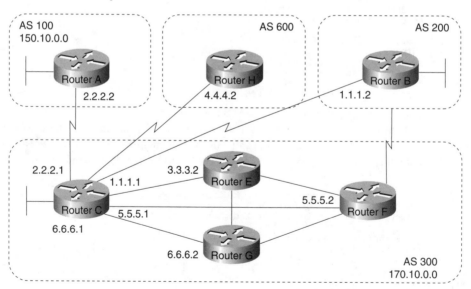

The following commands configure a BGP peer group named INTERNALMAP on Router C and apply it to the other routers in AS 300:

```
!Router C
router bgp 300
neighbor INTERNALMAP peer-group
neighbor INTERNALMAP remote-as 300
```

```
neighbor INTERNALMAP route-map INTERNAL out
neighbor INTERNALMAP filter-list 1 out
neighbor INTERNALMAP filter-list 2 in
neighbor 5.5.5.2 peer-group INTERNALMAP
neighbor 6.6.6.2 peer-group INTERNALMAP
neighbor 3.3.3.2 peer-group INTERNALMAP
neighbor 3.3.3.2 filter-list 3 in
```

The preceding configuration defines the following policies for the INTERNALMAP peer group:

```
A route map named INTERNAL
A filter list for outgoing updates (filter list 1)
A filter list for incoming updates (filter list 2)
```

The configuration applies the peer group to all internal neighbors—Routers E, F, and G. The configuration also defines a filter list for incoming updates from the neighbor at IP address 3.3.3.2 (Router E). This filter list can be used only to override options that affect incoming updates.

The following commands configure a BGP peer group named EXTERNALMAP on Router C and apply it to routers in AS 100, 200, and 600:

```
!Router C
router bgp 300
neighbor EXTERNALMAP peer-group
neighbor EXTERNALMAP route-map SETMED
neighbor EXTERNALMAP filter-list 1 out
neighbor EXTERNALMAP filter-list 2 in
neighbor 2.2.2.2 remote-as 100
neighbor 2.2.2.2 peer-group EXTERNALMAP
neighbor 4.4.4.2 remote-as 600
neighbor 4.4.4.2 peer-group EXTERNALMAP
neighbor 1.1.1.2 remote-as 200
neighbor 1.1.1.2 peer-group EXTERNALMAP
neighbor 1.1.1.2 filter-list 3 in
```

In the preceding configuration, the **neighbor remote-as** commands are placed outside of the **neighbor peer-group** commands because different external ASs have to be defined. Also note that this configuration defines filter list 3, which can be used to override configuration options for incoming updates from the neighbor at IP address 1.1.1.2 (Router B).

CIDR and Aggregate Addresses

BGP4 supports classless interdomain routing (CIDR). CIDR is a new way of looking at IP addresses that eliminates the concept of classes (Class A, Class B, and so on). Network 192.213.0.0, which is an illegal Class C network number, for example, is a legal supernet when it is represented in CIDR notation as 192.213.0.0/16. The /16 indicates that the subnet mask consists of 16 bits (counting from the left). Therefore, 192.213.0.0/16 is similar to 192.213.0.0 255.255.0.0.

CIDR makes it easy to aggregate routes. Aggregation is the process of combining several different routes in such a way that a single route can be advertised, which minimizes the size of routing tables. Consider the network shown in Figure 4-20.

Figure 4-20 *Aggregation Example*

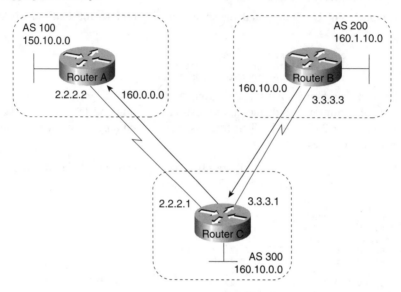

In Figure 4-20, Router B in AS 200 is originating network 160.11.0.0 and advertising it to Router C in AS 300. To configure Router C to propagate the aggregate address 160.0.0.0 to Router A, use the following commands:

```
!Router C
router bgp 300
neighbor 3.3.3.3 remote-as 200
neighbor 2.2.2.2 remote-as 100
network 160.10.0.0
aggregate-address 160.0.0.0 255.0.0.0
```

The **aggregate-address** command advertises the prefix route (in this case, 160.0.0.0/8) and all the more-specific routes. If you want Router C to propagate the prefix route only, and you do not want it to propagate a more specific route, use the following command:

```
aggregate-address 160.0.0.0 255.0.0.0 summary-only
```

This command propagates the prefix (160.0.0.0/8) and suppresses any more-specific routes that the router may have in its BGP routing table. If you want to suppress specific routes when aggregating routes, you can define a route map and apply it to the aggregate. If, for example, you want Router C in Figure 4-20 to aggregate 160.0.0.0 and suppress the specific route 160.20.0.0, but propagate route 160.10.0.0, use the following commands:

```
!Router C
router bgp 300
neighbor 3.3.3.3 remote-as 200
```

```
neighbor 2.2.2.2 remote-as 100
network 160.10.0.0
aggregate-address 160.0.0.0 255.0.0.0 suppress-map CHECK
!
route-map CHECK permit 10
match ip address 1
!
access-list 1 deny 160.20.0.0 0.0.255.255
access-list 1 permit 0.0.0.0 255.255.255.255
```

If you want the router to set the value of an attribute when it propagates the aggregate route, use an attribute map, as demonstrated by the following commands:

```
route-map SETORIGIN permit 10
set origin igp
!
aggregate-address 160.0.0.0 255.0.0.0 attribute-map SETORIGIN
```

Aggregation and AS-SET

When aggregates are generated from more-specific routes, the AS_path attributes of the more-specific routes are combined to form a set called the AS-SET. This set is useful for preventing routing information loops.

Confederations

A confederation is a technique for reducing the IBGP mesh inside the AS. Consider the network shown in Figure 4-21.

In Figure 4-21, AS 500 consists of nine BGP speakers (although there might be other routers not configured for BGP). Without confederations, BGP would require that the routers in AS 500 be fully meshed. That is, each router would need to run IBGP with each of the other eight routers, and each router would need to connect to an external AS and run EBGP, for a total of nine peers for each router.

Confederations reduce the number of peers within the AS, as shown in Figure 4-21. You use confederations to divide the AS into multiple mini-ASs and assign the mini-ASs to a confederation. Each mini-AS is fully meshed, and IBGP is run among its members. Each mini-AS has a connection to the other mini-ASs within the confederation. Even though the mini-ASs have EBGP peers to ASs within the confederation, they exchange routing updates as if they were using IBGP. That is, the next hop, MED, and local preference information is preserved. To the outside world, the confederation looks like a single AS. The following commands configure Router C:

```
!Router C
router bgp 65050
bgp confederation identifier 500
bgp confederation peers 65060 65070
neighbor 128.213.10.1 remote-as 65050
neighbor 128.213.20.1 remote-as 65050
neighbor 128.210.11.1 remote-as 65060
neighbor 135.212.14.1 remote-as 65070
neighbor 5.5.5.5 remote-as 100
```

Figure 4-21 *Example of Confederations*

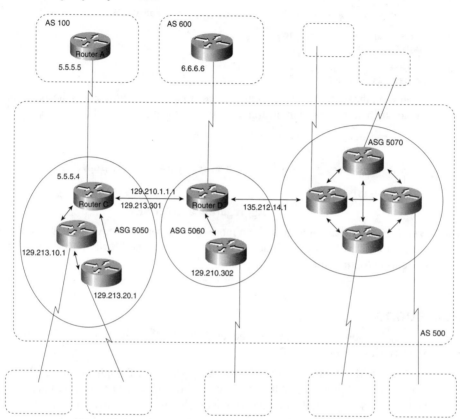

The **router bgp** command specifies that Router C belongs to AS 50.

The **bgp confederation identifier** command specifies that Router C belongs to confederation 500. The first two **neighbor remote-as** commands establish IBGP connections to the other two routers within AS 65050. The second two **neighbor remote-as** commands establish BGP connections with confederation peers 65060 and 65070. The last **neighbor remote-as** command establishes an EBGP connection with external AS 100. The following commands configure Router D:

```
!Router D
router bgp 65060
bgp confederation identifier 500
bgp confederation peers 65050 65070
neighbor 129.210.30.2 remote-as 65060
neighbor 128.213.30.1 remote-as 65050
neighbor 135.212.14.1 remote-as 65070
neighbor 6.6.6.6 remote-as 600
```

The **router bgp** command specifies that Router D belongs to AS 65060. The **bgp confederation identifier** command specifies that Router D belongs to confederation 500.

The first **neighbor remote-as** command establishes an IBGP connection to the other router within AS 65060. The second two **neighbor remote-as** commands establish BGP connections with confederation peers 65050 and 65070. The last **neighbor remote-as** command establishes an EBGP connection with AS 600. The following commands configure Router A:

```
!Router A
router bgp 100
neighbor 5.5.5.4 remote-as 500
```

The **neighbor remote-as** command establishes an EBGP connection with Router C. Router A is unaware of AS 65050, AS 65060, or AS 65070. Router A only has knowledge of AS 500.

Route Reflectors

Route reflectors are another solution for the explosion of IBGP peering within an AS. As described earlier in the section titled "Synchronization," a BGP speaker does not advertise a route learned from another IBGP speaker to a third IBGP speaker. Route reflectors ease this limitation and allow a router to advertise (reflect) IBGP-learned routes to other IBGP speakers, thereby reducing the number of IBGP peers within an AS. The network shown in Figure 4-22 demonstrates how route reflectors work.

Without a route reflector, the network shown in Figure 4-22 would require a full IBGP mesh (that is, Router A would have to be a peer of Router B). If Router C is configured as a route reflector, IBGP peering between Routers A and B is not required, because Router C will reflect updates from Router A to Router B and from Router B to Router A. To configure Router C as a route reflector, use the following commands:

```
!Router C
router bgp 100
neighbor 1.1.1.1 remote-as 100
neighbor 1.1.1.1 route-reflector-client
neighbor 2.2.2.2 remote-as 100
neighbor 2.2.2.2 route-reflector-client
```

The router whose configuration includes **neighbor route-reflector-client** commands is the route reflector. The routers identified by the **neighbor route-reflector-client** commands are clients of the route reflector. When considered as a whole, the route reflector and its clients are called a cluster. Other IBGP peers of the route reflector that are not clients are called nonclients.

Figure 4-22 *Simple Route Reflector Example*

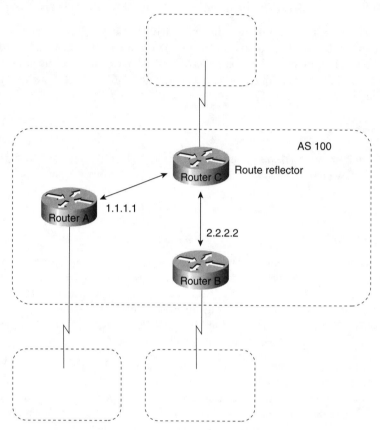

An AS can have more than one route reflector. When an AS has more than one route reflector, each route reflector treats other route reflectors as normal IBGP speakers. There can be more than one route reflector in a cluster, and there can be more than one cluster in an AS.

Route Flap Dampening

Route flap dampening (introduced in Cisco IOS Release 11.0) is a mechanism for minimizing the instability caused by route flapping. The following terms are used to describe route flap dampening:

- **Penalty**—A numeric value assigned to a route when it flaps.

- **Half-life time**—A configurable numeric value that describes the time required to reduce the penalty by one-half.

- **Suppress limit**—A numeric value that is compared with the penalty. If the penalty is greater than the suppress limit, the route is suppressed.

- **Suppressed**—A route that is not advertised even though it is up. A route is suppressed if the penalty is more than the suppressed limit.

- **Reuse limit**—A configurable numeric value that is compared with the penalty. If the penalty is less than the reuse limit, a suppressed route that is up will no longer be suppressed.

- **History entry**—An entry that is used to store flap information about a route that is down.

A route that is flapping receives a penalty of 1000 for each flap. When the accumulated penalty reaches a configurable limit, BGP suppresses advertisement of the route even if the route is up. The accumulated penalty is decremented by the half-life time. When the accumulated penalty is less than the reuse limit, the route is advertised again (if it is still up).

Summary

The primary function of a BGP system is to exchange network reachability information with other BGP systems. This information is used to construct a graph of AS connectivity from which routing loops are pruned and with which AS-level policy decisions are enforced. BGP provides a number of techniques for controlling the flow of BGP updates, such as route, path, and community filtering. It also provides techniques for consolidating routing information, such as CIDR aggregation, confederations, and route reflectors. BGP is a powerful tool for providing loop-free interdomain routing within and between ASs.

CHAPTER 5

Designing ATM Networks

Edited by Ron McCarty

This chapter describes current Asynchronous Transfer Mode (ATM) technology that network designers can use in their networks today, as well as future ATM technology to watch. This chapter also covers implementation considerations for leveraging Cisco products while deploying ATM solutions in existing LAN and WAN environments.

ATM Overview

ATM is a mature but evolving technology designed for the high-speed transfer of voice, video, and data through public and private networks in a cost-effective manner.

ATM is based on the efforts of Study Group XVIII of the International Telecommunication Union Telecommunication Standardization Sector (ITU-T, formerly the Consultative Committee for International Telegraph and Telephone [CCITT]) and the American National Standards Institute (ANSI). Their goals have been to apply very large-scale integration (VLSI) technology to the transfer of data within public networks.

Current efforts to bring ATM technology to private networks and to encourage interoperability between private and public networks is being done by the ATM Forum, which was jointly founded by Cisco Systems, NET/ADAPTIVE, Northern Telecom, and Sprint in 1991. The ATM Forum's current membership includes more than 600 organizations wishing to promote ATM technology and solutions. Members include network operating systems vendors, telecommunication vendors and value-added resellers, and LAN/WAN hardware vendors.

Role of ATM in Networks

The network is the critical tool for information flow in today's computing environment. Applications require larger data pipes than earlier generations, networks must scale to meet immediate business needs, and networks must provide redundancy and quick recovery from failures.

The Internet has been the major force in bringing multimedia to the desktop. Besides the Internet's limitless supply of multimedia, WAN connections are now expected to carry voice and data streams. LAN applications are also being deployed across WAN and VPN links. In addition, multimedia applications based on core business needs, including voice and video applications, are wanted at the desktop. This growth in bandwidth needs and blurring of traditional LAN/WAN applications' borders encourages exploiting technologies that are not limited by traditional LAN/WAN design limitations. The integration of voice, video, and data over single circuits also pressures networks to cost less than comparable nonintegrated solutions, yet still support the larger applications and provide the necessary bandwidth to support voice and video.

Integration of voice, video, and data creates quality of service (QoS) issues that network designers have not had to consider as a major design issue with TCP/IP-based networks— bandwidth was either adequate or upgraded on LANs to provide a "good enough" environment for interactive programs. WAN connectivity, for example, despite limited bandwidth, worked using TCP's connection-oriented, sliding-window mechanism that provided a robust-enough connection for noninteractive WAN applications. In those cases where the connection was so poor that TCP could not maintain a connection, most applications recovered gracefully and attempted the connection later.

Multimedia applications must receive a guaranteed minimum bandwidth or QoS to be effective. Users will accept a certain amount of loss and noise; however, a timeout during delivery and later retry is usually not acceptable. QoS issues and integration of services (voice, video, and data) are the deciding factors to consider when designing or expanding networks to include ATM networking.

This section discusses the following ATM concepts:

- ATM Functional Layers
- ATM Addressing
- ATM Media
- Multiservice Networks

ATM Functional Layers

Just as the *Open System Interconnection* (OSI) reference model describes how two computers communicate over a network, the ATM protocol model describes how two end systems communicate through ATM switches. The ATM protocol model consists of the following three functional layers:

- ATM physical layer
- ATM layer
- ATM adaptation layer (AAL)

As Figure 5-1 shows, these three layers correspond roughly to Layer 1 and parts of Layer 2 (such as error control and data framing) of the OSI reference model.

Figure 5-1   *Relationship of ATM Functional Layers to the OSI Reference Model*

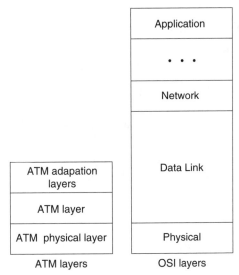

Physical Layer

The ATM physical layer controls transmission and receipt of bits on the physical medium. It also keeps track of ATM cell boundaries and packages cells into the appropriate type of frame for the physical medium being used. The ATM physical layer is divided into two parts:

- Physical medium sublayer
- Transmission convergence sublayer

Physical Medium Sublayer

The physical medium sublayer is responsible for sending and receiving a continuous flow of bits with associated timing information to synchronize transmission and reception. Because it includes only physical medium–dependent functions, its specification depends on the physical medium used. Some existing standards that can carry ATM cells are Category 5 copper wiring, SONET (Synchronous Optical Network)/SDH, DS-3/E3, 100-Mbps local fiber (Fiber Distributed Data Interface [FDDI] physical layer), and 155-Mbps local fiber (Fiber Channel physical layer).

Transmission Convergence Sublayer

The transmission convergence sublayer is responsible for the following:

- **Cell delineation**—Maintains ATM cell boundaries.

- **Header error-control sequence generation and verification**—Generates and checks the header error-control code to ensure valid data.

- **Cell-rate decoupling**—Inserts or suppresses idle (unassigned) ATM cells to adapt the rate of valid ATM cells to the payload capacity of the transmission system.

- **Transmission-frame adaptation**—Packages ATM cells into frames acceptable to the particular physical layer implementation.

- **Transmission-frame generation and recovery**—Generates and maintains the appropriate physical layer frame structure.

ATM Layer

The ATM layer establishes virtual connections and passes ATM cells through the ATM network. To do this, it uses the information contained in the header of each ATM cell. The ATM layer is responsible for performing the following functions:

- Delivers the 48-byte payload on an established ATM connection.

- Multiplexes and demultiplexes the cells of different virtual connections. These connections are identified by their virtual channel identifier (VCI) and virtual path identifier (VPI) values.

- Performs cell identification to determine cell type and priority.

The ATM layer is a complex layer for network designers more accustomed to other networking fundamentals. This complexity arises from the QoS issues traditionally only seen within telecommunication switches. The complexity is further compounded because of the granularity needed to support traffic with various QoS needs (from stringent to no QoS needed).

QoS is based on performance parameters formerly defined by the ATM Forum. The following parameters may be negotiated during session setup:

- **Peak-to-peak cell delay variation (peak-to-peak CDV)**—The difference between the best cell transfer delay and the worst cell transfer delay. The worst case is based on a predefined probability-based value.

- **Maximum cell transmission delay (maxCTD)**—The predefined low probable maximum cell transmission delay.

- **Cell loss ration (CLR)**—The ration of lost cells to total cells. A CLR can be negotiated for each class of cells (high or low priority) or all cells.

In addition to the negotiable parameters just listed, there are also parameters based on statistical data; these are, therefore, not negotiated:

- **Cell error ration (CER)**—Ratio of errors to total cells.

- **Cell misinsertion rate (CMR)**—Rate of misinserted cells. This is the number of cells that were received, but that should have been sent to another ATM device.

- **Severely errored cell block ratio (SECBR)**—Ratio of severely errored cell blocks to total cell blocks.

ATM Adaptation Layer (AAL)

The AAL is responsible for segmentation and reassembly of upper-layer data. The AAL must provide a payload of 48 bytes to the ATM layer. In addition to the segmentation and reassembly, the AAL also provides specific services to the upper layers. The ITU-T recommends four service classes: Class A, Class B, Class C, and Class D; these classes are based on characteristics of the requested session:

- **Class A**—Connection-oriented, constant bit rate, delay-/time-sensitive session

- **Class B**—Connection-oriented, variable bit rate, delay-/time-sensitive session

- **Class C**—Connection-oriented, variable bit rate, no delay-/time-sensitive relation required

- **Class D**—Connectionless-oriented, variable bit rate, no delay-/time-sensitive relation required

To implement the four service types, four AAL layers (protocols) have been specified.

Table 5-1 summarizes the characteristics of each AAL.

Table 5-1   *ATM Adapter Layers*

Characteristics	AAL1	AAL2	AAL3/4	AAL5
Requires timing between source and destination	Yes	Yes	No	No
Data rate	Constant	Variable	Variable	Variable
Connection mode	Connection oriented	Connection oriented	Connection oriented	Connection oriented
Traffic types	Voice and circuit emulation	Voice (telephone quality)	Data	Data

AAL1

AAL1 is appropriate for transporting telephone traffic and uncompressed video traffic. It requires timing synchronization between the source and destination and, for that reason, depends on a medium that supports clocking, such as SONET. Clock recovery is performed by the receiver using the clock recovery bit in the header.

AAL1 uses bits of the payload to define additional fields. The payload data consists of a synchronous sample (for example, one byte of data generated at a sampling rate of 125 microseconds); the sequence number (SN) field; and sequence number protection (SNP) fields, which provide the receiving AAL1 ordering information to ensure proper reassembly. A three-bit cyclic redundancy check also provides error detection and recovery.

AAL2

AAL2 is designed to provide services to low–bit-rate, delay-sensitive applications such as telephone-quality voice services. Because the traffic in these types of applications is of variable length, Logical Link Controls (LLCs) were designed to provide virtual point-to-point connections that use the LLC field and length field to assemble the smaller variable-length packets into ATM cells.

AAL3/4

AAL3/4 was designed for network service providers and is closely aligned with Switched Multimegabit Data Service (SMDS). AAL3/4 is used to transmit SMDS packets over an ATM network.

AAL3/4 uses field identifiers for the following:

- **Type**—Identifies whether the cell is the beginning of a message, continuation of a message, or end of a message.

- **Sequence number**—Identifies the order in which cells should be reassembled.

- **Multiplexing identifier**—Identifies cells from different traffic sources interleaved on the same virtual circuit connection (VCC), so that the correct cells are reassembled at the destination.

- **CRC trailer**—Provides error detection and correction.

Figure 5-2 shows how the cells are prepared for AAL3/4.

Figure 5-2   *AAL3/4 Cell Preparation*

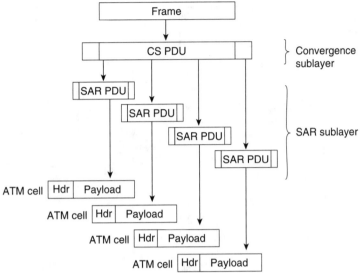

AAL5

AAL5 prepares a cell for transmission, as shown in Figure 5-3.

First, the convergence sublayer of AAL5 appends a variable-length pad and an eight-byte trailer to a frame. The pad is long enough to ensure that the resulting PDU falls on the 48-byte boundary of the ATM cell. The trailer includes the length of the frame and a 32-bit CRC computed across the entire PDU, which allows AAL5 at the destination to detect bit errors and lost cells, or cells that are out of sequence.

Next, the segmentation and reassembly sections the CS PDU into 48-byte blocks. Then, the ATM layer places each block into the payload field of an ATM cell. For all cells except the last cell, a bit in the PT field is set to zero to indicate that the cell is not the last cell in a series that represents a single frame. For the last cell, the bit in the PT field is set to one. When the cell arrives at its destination, the ATM layer extracts the payload field from the cell; the SAR sublayer reassembles the CS PDU; and the CS uses the CRC and the length field to verify that the frame has been transmitted and reassembled correctly.

AAL5 is the adaptation layer used to transfer most non-SMDS data, such as classical IP over ATM and local-area network (LAN) emulation.

Figure 5-3   *AAL5 Cell Preparation*

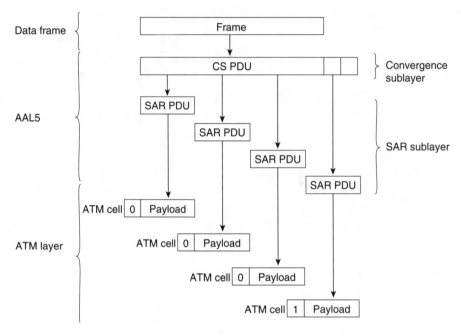

ATM Addressing

ATM addressing uses the ATM layer for addressing. Unlike an IP node, this addressing requires that the end ATM node know the complete path to the destination. ATM addressing bypasses the overhead associated with in-transit routing decisions; however, ATM devices must, at least within ATM edge switches, provide Layer 3 logical addressing.

Several ATM address formats have been developed. Public ATM networks typically use E.164 numbers, which are also used by narrowband ISDN (N-ISDN) networks.

Figure 5-4 shows the format of private-network ATM addresses. The three formats are Data Country Code (DCC), International Code Designator (ICD), and Network Service Access Point (NSAP)–encapsulated E.164 addresses.

Figure 5-4   *ATM Address Formats*

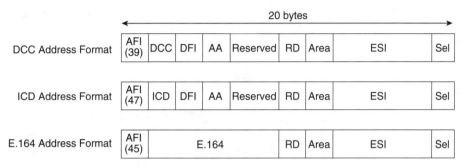

Fields of an ATM Address

The fields of an ATM address are as follows:

- **AFI**—One byte of authority and format identifier. The AFI field identifies the type of address. The defined values are 45, 47, and 39 for E.164, ICD, and DCC addresses, respectively.

- **DCC**—Two bytes of DCC.

- **DFI**—One byte of domain specific part (DSP) format identifier.

- **AA**—Three bytes of administrative authority.

- **RD**—Two bytes of routing domain.

- **Area**—Two bytes of area identifier.

- **ESI**—Six bytes of end-system identifier, which is an IEEE 802 Media Access Control (MAC) address.

- **Sel**—One byte of NSAP selector.

- **ICD**—Two bytes of ICD.

- **E.164**—Eight bytes of ISDN telephone number.

The ATM address formats are modeled on ISO NSAP addresses, but they identify Subnetwork Point of Attachment (SNPA) addresses. Incorporating the MAC address into the ATM address makes it easy to map ATM addresses into existing LANs.

ATM Media

The ATM Forum has defined multiple standards for encoding ATM over various types of media. Table 5-2 lists the framing types and data rates for the various media, including unshielded twisted-pair (UTP) supported by Cisco products.

Table 5-2 *ATM Physical Rates*

Framing	Data Rate (Mbps)	Multimode Fiber	Single Mode Fiber	Coaxial Cable	UTP-3	UTP-5	STP
DS-1	1.544			X			
E1	2.048			X			
DS-3	45			X			
E3	34			X			
STS-1	51				X		
SONET STS3c SDH STM1	155	X	X	X		X	
SONET STS12c SDH STM4	622	X	X				
TAXI 4B/5B	100	X					
8B/10B (Fiber Channel)	155	X					X

There are two standards for running ATM over copper cable: Category 3 and Category 5. Category 5 supports 155 Mbps with NRZI encoding; Category 3 supports 51 Mbps with CAP-16 encoding. CAP-16 is more difficult to implement; so, although it may be cheaper to wire with UTP-3 cable, workstation cards designed for CAP-16–based UTP-3 may be more expensive and will offer less bandwidth.

ATM's support of fiber and copper cable will ease future migrations by organizations with large investments in fiber and copper.

Multiservice Networks

ATM has emerged as one of the technologies for integrating services as well as for providing WAN services to connect LANs. ATM is also a LAN; however, its LAN usage has not been as popular because of Ethernet's continued growth in the 100-Megabit and Gigabit arena. ATM supports various traffic types in separate or mixed streams, delay-sensitive traffic, and nondelay-sensitive traffic, as shown in Figure 5-5.

Figure 5-5   *ATM Support of Various Traffic Types*

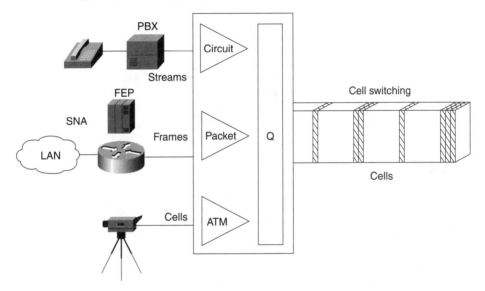

ATM supports various speeds from 1.54 Mbps to 622 Mbps. ATM has been adopted by the industry's equipment vendors, from LAN to private branch exchange (PBX) to international carriers. With ATM, Cisco's ATM switches, and ATM edge routers, network designers can integrate services, provide LAN-to-WAN connectivity, and cost-effectively support emerging applications for their enterprises.

Integrated Solutions

The trend in networking is to give network designers greater flexibility to solve multiple networking problems without creating multiple networks or writing off existing data-communications investments. Routers can provide a reliable, secure network and act as a barrier against inadvertent broadcast storms in the local networks. Switches, which can be divided into two main categories—LAN switches and WAN switches—can be deployed at the workgroup, campus backbone, or WAN level, as shown in Figure 5-6.

Figure 5-6 *The Role of ATM Switches in a Network*

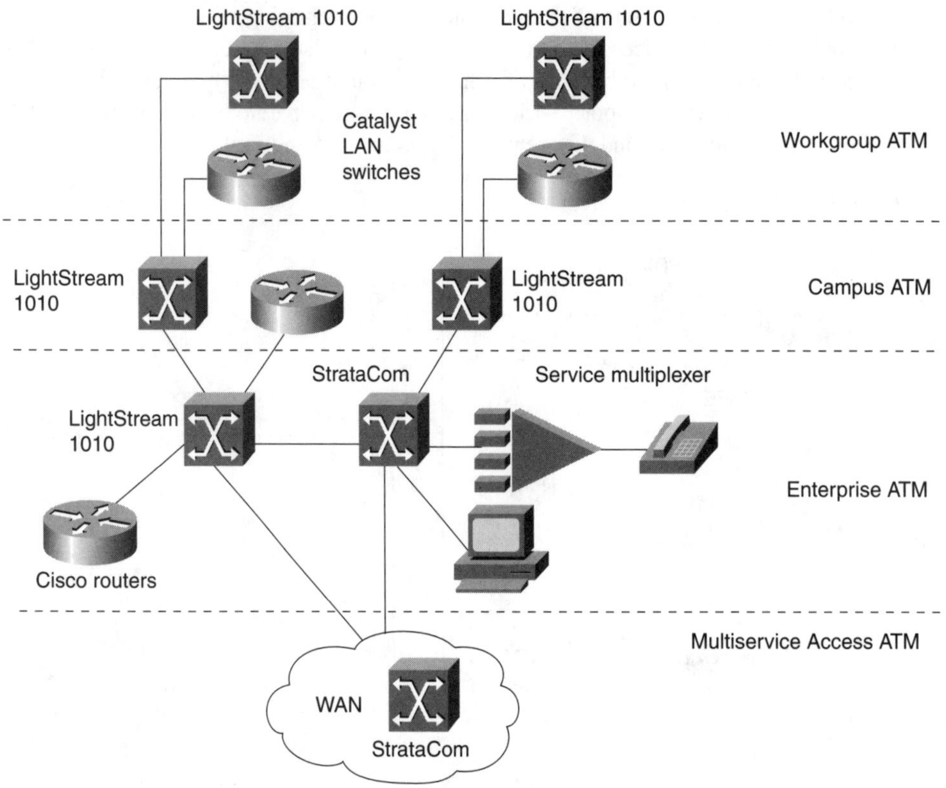

Underlying and integrating all Cisco products is the Cisco IOS software. The Cisco IOS software enables disparate groups, diverse devices, and multiple protocols all to be integrated into a highly reliable and scalable network.

Different Types of ATM Switches

Even though all ATM switches perform cell relay, ATM switches differ markedly in the following ways:

- Variety of interfaces and services that are supported
- Redundancy
- Depth of ATM networking software
- Sophistication of traffic-management mechanism

Just as there are routers and LAN switches available at various price/performance points with different levels of functionality, ATM switches also come in various configurations to support various ATM integration into workgroups, campuses, and the enterprise.

Workgroup and Campus ATM Switches

Workgroup ATM switches are often characterized as having Ethernet switch ports and an ATM uplink to connect to a campus ATM switch; however, due to the popularity of switched 100-Mb Ethernet, campus and enterprise ATM switches are also supporting Ethernet ports. An example of a workgroup ATM switch is the Cisco Catalyst 5000 family of switches.

The Catalyst 5500 switch provides high-performance switching in workgroup and campus environments. The Catalyst 5500 LAN has a 13-slot chassis. Slot 1 is reserved for the supervisor engine module, which provides switching, local and remote management, and dual Fast Ethernet uplinks. Slot 2 is available for a second redundant supervisor engine or any of the other supported modules. Slots 3–12 support Ethernet, Fast Ethernet, Gigabit Ethernet, Fiber Distributed Data Interface (FDDI), Copper Distributed Data Interface (CDDI), and ATM modules. Slot 13 can be populated only with a LightStream 1010 ATM Switch Processor (ASP). If an ASP is present in slot 13, slots 9–12 support any of the standard LightStream 1010 ATM switch port adapter modules (PAMs).

The Catalyst 5500 has a 10-Gbps media-independent switch fabric and a 40-Gbps cell-switch fabric. The backplane provides the connection between power supplies, supervisor engine, interface modules, and backbone module. The 3.6-Gbps media-independent fabric supports Ethernet, Fast Ethernet, FDDI/CDDI, ATM LAN Emulation, and RSM modules. The 5-Gbps cell-based fabric supports a LightStream 1010 ASP module and ATM PAMs.

Campus ATM switches are generally used for small-scale ATM backbones (for instance, to link ATM routers or LAN switches). This use of ATM switches can alleviate current backbone congestion while supporting the deployment of virtual LANs (VLANs). Campus switches need to support a wide variety of both local backbone and WAN types, but also need to be price/performance optimized for the local backbone function. In this class of switches, ATM routing capabilities that allow multiple switches to be tied together are very important. Congestion-control mechanisms for optimizing backbone performance are also important.

Cisco's expansion of campus ATM switches includes the Catalyst 8500 family of products.

The Catalyst 8540 supports 40 Gbps of nonblocking switch-fabric performance. The first three slots are reserved for the processor modules. Two modules are required, and the third redundant module can be used in the third slot. The remaining 10 ports support Ethernet, Fast Ethernet, Gigabit Ethernet, and OC3c (155 Mbps) and OC12c (622 Mbps) ATM.

Enterprise ATM Switches and Routers

Enterprise ATM switches are sophisticated multiservice, multimedium, and multiprotocol devices designed to form the core backbones of large enterprise networks. They are intended to complement, and in some cases replace, the role of today's high-end multiprotocol routers. Enterprise ATM switches are used to interconnect campus ATM switches. Enterprise class switches, however, can act not only as ATM backbones, but can also serve as the single point of integration for all the disparate services and technology found in enterprise backbones today. By integrating all these services onto a common platform and a common ATM transport infrastructure, network designers can gain greater manageability and eliminate the need for multiple overlay networks.

Cisco's LightStream 1010 is an enterprise switch that can support the enterprise backbone or provide edge ATM services to the enterprise. The LightStream 1010 ATM switch comes with a five-slot modular chassis that supports dual fault-tolerant load-sharing power supplies. The ATM switch processor is located in the central slot, and the switch fabric supports speed up to 5 Gbps. The LightStream 1010 family of ATM switches is an example of a campus ATM switch with support for multiple ATM segments. The LightStream 1010 will support up to 32 switched OC-3 ATM ports in a standard 19-inch (48-centimeter) rack. For more information on deploying workgroup and campus ATM switches in your network, see Chapter 12, "Designing Switched LAN Networks."

Cisco's BPX 8600 is a powerful broadband ATM edge switch designed to meet the demanding, high-traffic needs of a large private enterprise or public service provider. The switch has 15 slots, two of which support the redundant broadband control cards made up of the switching fabric and control system. An additional slot is used by the status monitor. The remaining 12 cards can be used to support BPX, IGX, MGX, or ATM UNI and NNI interfaces. The switch's performance is optimized through the use of both input and output switch buffers.

IP networking requires high-performance routers, as well as ATM switching services.

The Cisco 7500 router incorporates distributed switching functions that enable network designers to provide the high-performance routing necessary to support networks using ATM, multilayer LAN switching, emulated LAN (ELAN), and virtual LAN (VLAN) technologies.

The Cisco 7500 family of routers offers broad support for high-speed ATM and WAN interfaces. The high port densities supported by the Cisco 7500 series easily handle the large number of interfaces required for remote-site connectivity. Network designers can deploy the Cisco 7500 series in the WAN environment to access multiple types of carrier-service offerings, including ATM backbones. The router provides 2.1 Gbps of throughput.

The Cisco 7500 also provides the redundant power supplies expected of high-end routers and a redundant Route Switch Processor (RSP), as well as load sharing for IP (other protocols are planned) if the redundant RSP is present. The Cisco 7500 has proved to be the enterprise router of choice; and with its ATM support, it can act as a campus or enterprise edge ATM router.

Carrier Class Switches

Beyond private networks, ATM platforms are also widely deployed by service providers, both as customer premises' equipment and within public networks. Such equipment supports multiple WAN services, including Frame Relay switching, IP-based services, ATM NNI interconnect, and public ATM services exploiting a common ATM infrastructure. These high-end enterprise ATM switches, often referred to as carrier class, will often be used in these public-network applications because of their emphasis on high availability and redundancy, their support of multiple interfaces, and their capability to integrate voice and data. The Cisco BPX 8600, discussed earlier, is an example of a carrier class ATM switch. As the telecommunications industry further expands, especially in Europe, the demand for carrier class switches will also expand.

Structure of an ATM Network

ATM is based on the concept of two endpoint devices communicating by means of intermediate switches. As Figure 5-7 shows, an ATM network is made up of a series of switches and endpoint devices. The endpoint devices can be ATM-attached end stations, ATM-attached servers, or ATM-attached routers.

Figure 5-7   *Components of an ATM Network*

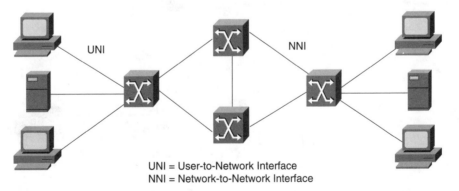

UNI = User-to-Network Interface
NNI = Network-to-Network Interface

As Figure 5-7 shows, an ATM network has two types of interfaces:

- User-to-Network Interface (UNI)
- Network-to-Network Interface (NNI)

The UNI connection is made up of an endpoint device, and a private or public ATM switch. Early ATM developers were mostly concerned with the UNI interface to bring products to market.

The NNI is the connection between two ATM switches. The UNI and NNI connections can be carried by different physical connections.

In addition to the UNI and NNI protocols, the ATM Forum has defined protocols to support LAN Emulation (LANE). LANE is a technology network that designers use to network LANs, such as Ethernet and Token Ring, with ATM-attached devices. The need to connect Ethernet and Token Ring networks to ATM networks has created the largest market for ATM edge switches. (Early ATM designers assumed that Ethernet and Token Ring would be phased out as soon as ATM gained popularity, but switched 100-Mb and Gigabit Ethernet have ensured Ethernet's continued growth.)

Operation on an ATM Network

In an ATM network, a connection must be established between two endpoints before any data transfer can occur. This connection is accomplished through a signaling protocol, as shown in Figure 5-8.

Figure 5-8   *Establishing a Connection in an ATM Network*

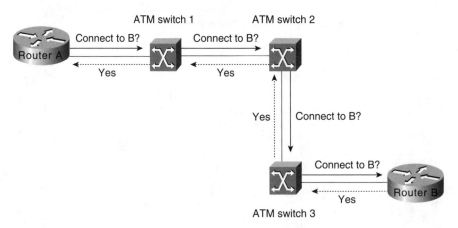

As Figure 5-8 shows, for Router A to connect to Router B, the following must occur:

1 Router A sends a signaling request packet to its directly connected ATM switch (ATM switch 1).

   This request contains the ATM address of Router B, as well as any QoS parameters described later required for the connection.

2 ATM switch 1 reassembles the signaling packet from Router A, and then examines it.

3 If ATM switch 1 has an entry for Router B's ATM address in its switch table, and it can accommodate the QoS requested for the connection, it sets up the virtual connection and forwards the request to the next switch (ATM switch 2) along the path.

4 Every switch along the path to Router B reassembles and examines the signaling packet, and then forwards it to the next switch if the QoS parameters can be supported. Each switch also sets up the virtual connection as the signaling packet is forwarded.

If any switch along the path cannot accommodate the requested QoS parameters, the request is rejected and a rejection message is sent back to Router A with a possible lower QoS available.

5 When the signaling packet arrives at Router B, Router B reassembles it and evaluates the packet. If Router B can support the requested QoS, it responds with an accept message. As the accept message is propagated back to Router A, the switches set up a virtual circuit.

NOTE   A virtual channel is equivalent to a virtual circuit—that is, both terms describe a logical connection between the two ends of a communications connection. A virtual path is a logical grouping of virtual circuits that allows an ATM switch to perform operations on groups of virtual circuits.

---

6 Router A receives the accept message from its directly connected ATM switch (ATM switch 1), as well as the virtual path identifier (VPI) and virtual channel identifier (VCI) values that it should use for cells sent to Router B.

NOTE   ATM cells consist of five bytes of header information and 48 bytes of payload data. The VPI and VCI fields in the ATM header are used to route cells through ATM networks. The VPI and VCI fields of the cell header identify the next network segment that a cell needs to transmit on its way to its final destination.

Role of LANE

The ATM Forum has defined a standard for LANE. LANE is a technology that network designers can deploy to network existing Ethernet and Token Ring LANs with ATM networks. LANE provides MAC encapsulation (OSI Layer 2) to support the highest number of existing OSI Layer 3 protocols. The end result is that all devices attached to an emulated LAN (ELAN) appear to be on one bridged segment. In this way, AppleTalk, IPX,

IP, and other protocols will have similar performance characteristics as in a traditional bridged environment using the same media; however, network communications between ELANs still have to communicate through a Layer 3 router. Because communicating through the Layer 3 router adds unnecessary latency in an ATM network that would not normally require Layer 3 services except to support the existing Ethernet and Token Ring LANs, the ATM Forum defined Multiprotocol over ATM.

Figure 5-9 shows an example of an ATM LANE network that uses routers for inter-ELAN communications.

Figure 5-9   *Components of an ATM LANE Network*

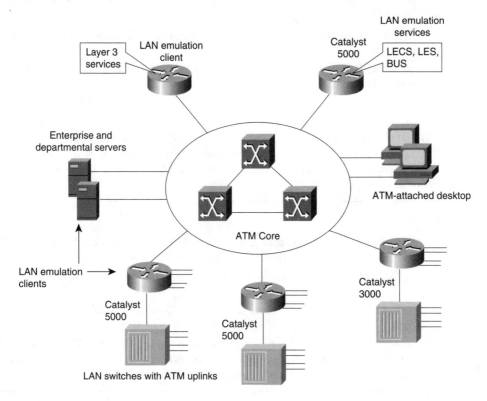

Using Multiprotocol over ATM, the ATM stations realize that inter-ELAN communication is taking place and build a direct "shortcut" to the receiving station, effectively bypassing the latency that occurs in the topology shown in Figure 5-9.

LANE Components

LANE components include the following:

- **LAN Emulation Client (LEC)**—ATM systems that support both the LAN, such as Ethernet or Token Ring, and ATM LANE—for example, the Catalyst family of switches and Cisco 7500, 7000, 4500, and 4000 series routers that support ATM attachments. The LEC emulates an interface to a legacy LAN to the higher-level protocols, as well as performs data forwarding, address resolution, and registration of MAC addresses with the LAN Emulation server (LES). The LEC communicates with other LECs via ATM virtual channel connections (VCCs).

- **LAN Emulation Configuration Server (LECS)**—The LECS maintains a database of ELANs and the ATM addresses of the LESs that control the ELANs. An LECS accepts queries from LECs and responds with the ATM address of the LES that serves the appropriate ELAN.

- **LAN Emulation Server (LES)**—The LES provides a central control point for all LECs. LECs maintain a Control Direct VCC to the LES to forward registration and control information. The LES maintains a point-to-multipoint VCC, known as the Control Distribute VCC, to all LECs. The Control Distribute VCC is used only to forward control information. As new LECs join the ATM ELAN, each LEC is added as a leaf to the Control Distribute tree.

- **Broadcast and Unknown Server (BUS)**—The BUS acts as a central point for distributing broadcasts and multicasts. ATM is a point-to-point technology without broadcast support. LANE solves this problem by centralizing the broadcast support in the BUS. Each LEC must set up a Multicast Send VCC to the BUS. The BUS then adds the LEC as a leaf to its point-to-multipoint VCC (known as the Multicast Forward VCC).

  The BUS also acts as a multicast server. LANE is defined on ATM adaptation layer 5 (AAL5), which specifies a simple trailer to be appended to a frame before it is broken into ATM cells. The problem is that there is no way to differentiate between ATM cells from different senders when multiplexed on a virtual channel. It is assumed that cells received will be in sequence, and when the End of Message (EOM) cell arrives, you should just have to reassemble all the cells that have already arrived.

  The BUS takes the sequence of cells on each Multicast Send VCC and reassembles them into frames. When a full frame is received, it is queued for sending to all the LECs on the Multicast Forward VCC. This guarantees that all the cells from a particular data frame will be sent in order and not interleaved with cells from any other data frames on the point-to-multipoint VCC.

Note that because LANE is defined at OSI Layer 2, the LECS is the only security checkpoint available. After it has been told where to find the LES and it has successfully joined the ELAN, the LEC is free to send any traffic (whether malicious or not) into the bridged ELAN. The only place for any OSI Layer 3 security filters is in the router that routes this ELAN to other ELANs, and this security is bypassed once Multiprotocol over ATM has completed a "shortcut" to bypass the router. Therefore, the larger the ELAN, the greater the exposure to security violations.

How LANE Works

An ELAN provides Layer 2 communication between all users on an ELAN. One or more ELANs can run on the same ATM network. However, each ELAN is independent of the others and users on separate ELANs cannot communicate directly. As mentioned, routers or MPOA is required for inter-ELAN communication.

Because an ELAN provides Layer 2 communication, it can be equated to a broadcast domain. In addition, IP subnets and IPX networks that are defined on Layer 3–capable devices such as routers frequently map into broadcast domains (barring secondary addressing). This makes it possible to assign an IP subnetwork or an IP network to an ELAN.

An ELAN is controlled by a single LES/BUS pair, and the mapping of an ELAN to its LES ATM address is defined in the LEC's database. ELANs consist of multiple LECs and can be Ethernet or Token Ring, but not both at the same time.

For ELAN to operate properly, the LECs on that ELAN need to be operational. Each LEC goes through a boot-up sequence, as described in the following sections.

LANE Operation

In a typical LANE operation, the LEC must first find the LECS to discover which ELAN it should join. Specifically, the LEC is looking for the ATM address of the LECS that serves the desired ELAN.

Finding the LECS

To resolve the ATM address of the LECS, the LEC does the following:

1 Queries the ATM switch via Interim Local Management Interface (ILMI). The switch has a MIB variable set up with the ATM address of the LECS. The LEC can then use UNI signaling to contact the LECS.

2 Looks for a fixed ATM address specified by the ATM Forum as the LECS ATM address.

3 Accesses permanent virtual circuit (PVC) 0/17, a well-known PVC.

Contacting the LECS

The LEC creates a signaling packet with the ATM address of the LECS. It signals a Configure Direct VCC and then issues an LE_CONFIGURE_REQUEST on that VCC. The information in this request is compared with the data in the LECS database. The source ATM address is most commonly used to place an LEC into a specific ELAN. If a matching entry is found, a successful LE_CONFIGURE_RESPONSE is returned with the ATM address of the LES that serves the desired ELAN.

Configuring the LECS Database

You can configure the LECS database in any of the following three ways:

- **Configure ELAN names at the LEC**—In this configuration, all the LECs are configured with an ELAN name that they can embed in their Configure_Requests. This is the most basic form of the LECS database, and it needs only to contain the list of ELANs and their corresponding LES ATM addresses. In this configuration, all LECs that specifically request to join a given ELAN are returned the ATM address of the corresponding LES. An LEC that does not know which ELAN to join can be assigned to a default ELAN if one is configured in the LECS database.

  The following is an example of LEC-to-ELAN mapping at the LEC:

  ```
  lane database test-1
  name finance server-atm-address 47.0091.8100.0000.0800.200c.1001.
     0800.200c.1001.01
  name marketing server-atm-address 47.0091.8100.0000.0800.200c.1001.
     0800.200c.1001.02
  default-name finance
  ```

- **Configure LEC to ELAN assignment in the LECS database**—In this configuration, all the information is centralized in the LECS database. The LECs do not need intelligence, and they can just query the LECS to determine which ELAN they should join. Although this is a more time-intensive configuration, it provides tighter control over all the ELANs. Consequently, it can be used to tighten security.

  With this method, the LECs are identified by their ATM addresses or MAC addresses. Because wildcarding of ATM address prefixes is also supported, it is useful to make such relationships as, "Assign any LEC joining with a prefix of A to ELAN X." The following is an example of LEC-to-ELAN mapping in the LECS database:

  ```
  lane database test-2
  name finance server-atm-address 47.0091.8100.0000.0800.200c.1001.
     0800.200c.1001.01
  name marketing server-atm-address 47.0091.8100.0000.0800.200c.1001.
     0800.200c.1001.02
  default-name finance
  client-atm-address  47.0091.8100.0000.08  name finance
  client-atm-address  47.0091.8100.0000.09  name marketing
  mac-address 00c0.0000.0100 name finance
  mac-address 00c0.1111.2222 name marketing
  ```

- **Hybrid combination**—You can configure a combination of the preceding two methods.

Joining the LES

After the LEC has discovered the ATM address of the desired LES, it drops the connection to the LECS, creates a signaling packet with the ATM address of the LES, and signals a Control Direct VCC. Upon successful VCC setup, the LES sends an LE_JOIN_REQUEST. This request contains the LEC ATM address, as well as a MAC address that the LEC wants to register with the ELAN. This information is maintained so that no two LECs can register the same MAC or ATM addresses.

Upon receipt of the LE_JOIN_REQUEST, the LES checks with the LECS via its own open connection with the LECS, and verifies the request, thus confirming the client's membership. Upon successful verification, the LES adds the LEC as a leaf of its point-to-multipoint Control Distribute VCC. Finally, the LES issues the LEC a successful LE_JOIN_RESPONSE that contains a LANE client ID (LECID), which is an identifier unique to the new client. This ID is used by the LEC to filter its own broadcasts from the BUS. Figure 5-10 shows examples of LES connections.

Figure 5-10 *LAN Emulation Server (LES) Connections*

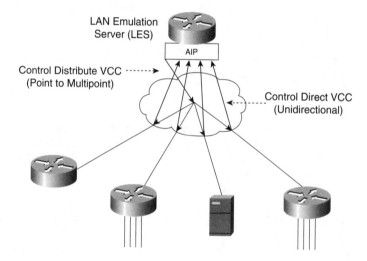

Finding the BUS

After the LEC has successfully joined the LES, its first task is to resolve the ATM address of the BUS and join the broadcast group. The LEC creates an LE_ARP_REQUEST packet with the MAC address 0xFFFFFFFF. This special LE_ARP packet is sent on the Control Direct VCC to the LES. The LES recognizes that the LEC is looking for the BUS, responds with the ATM address of the BUS, and forwards that response on the Control Distribute VCC.

Joining the BUS

When the LEC has the ATM address of the BUS, its next action is to create a signaling packet with that address and signal a Multicast Send VCC. Upon receipt of the signaling request, the BUS adds the LEC as a leaf on its point-to-multipoint Multicast Forward VCC. At this time, the LEC has become a member of the ELAN. Figure 5-11 shows examples of BUS connections.

Figure 5-11 *BUS Connections*

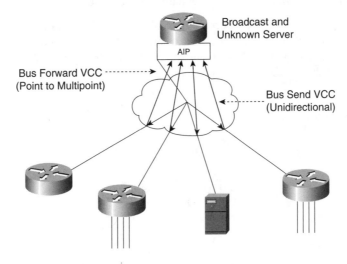

Address Resolution

The real value of LANE is the ATM forwarding path that it provides for unicast traffic between LECs. When an LEC has a data packet to send to an unknown destination, it issues an LE_ARP_REQUEST to the LES on the Control Direct VCC. The LES forwards the request on the Control Distribute VCC, so all LEC stations hear it. In parallel, the unicast data packets are sent to the BUS, to be forwarded to all endpoints. This flooding is not the optimal path for unicast traffic, and this transmission path is limited to 10 packets per second (per the LANE standard). Unicast packets continue using the BUS until the LE_ARP_REQUEST has been resolved.

If bridging or switching devices with LEC software participate in the ELAN, they translate and forward the ARP on their LAN interfaces. One of the LECs should issue an LE_ARP_RESPONSE and send it to the LES, which forwards it to the Control Distribute VCC so that all LECs can learn the new MAC-to-ATM address binding. The 10 packet per second flooding is then no longer needed.

When the requesting LEC receives the LE_ARP_RESPONSE, it has the ATM address of the LEC that represents the MAC address being sought. The LEC should now signal the other LEC directly and set up a Data Direct VCC that will be used for unicast data between the LECs.

While waiting for LE_ARP resolution, the LEC forwards unicasts to the BUS. With LE_ARP resolution, a new optimal path becomes available. If the LEC switches immediately to the new path, it runs the risk of packets arriving out of order. To guard against this situation, the LANE standard provides a flush packet.

When the Data Direct VCC becomes available, the LEC generates a flush packet and sends it to the BUS. When the LEC receives its own flush packet on the Multicast Forward VCC, it knows that all previously sent unicasts must have already been forwarded. It is now safe to begin using the Data Direct VCC. Figure 5-12 shows an example of a fully connected ELAN.

Figure 5-12 *Fully Connected ELAN*

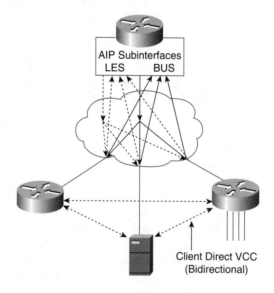

LANE Implementation

As Table 5-3 indicates, the LANE functionality (the LECS, LEC, LES, and BUS) can be implemented in different Cisco devices.

Table 5-3   *Cisco LANE Implementation*

Cisco Product	Available LANE Components	Required Software Release
Family of Catalyst 5000 switches	LECS, LES, BUS, LEC	ATM Module Software Version 2.0 or later
Family of Catalyst 3000 switches	LECS, LES, BUS, LEC	ATM Module Software Version 2.1 or later
Family of Cisco 7000 routers	LECS, LES, BUS, LEC	Cisco IOS Software Release 11.0 or later
Family of Cisco 7500 routers	LECS, LES, BUS, LEC	Cisco IOS Software Release 11.1 or later
Family of Cisco 4500 and 4000 routers	LECS, LES, BUS, LEC	Cisco IOS Software Release 11.1 or later

These functions will be defined on ATM physical interfaces and subinterfaces. A *subinterface* can be defined as a logical interface, and is a part of a physical interface such as an Optical Carrier 3 (OC-3) fiber. ATM interfaces on the Cisco routers and the ATM module on the Catalyst 5000 switch can be logically divided into up to 255 logical subinterfaces.

This section examines the implementation of ATM LANE networks and covers the following topics:

- LANE Design Considerations
- LANE Redundancy

LANE Design Considerations

The following are some general LANE design considerations:

- The ATM Interface Processor (AIP) provides an interface to ATM switching fabrics for transmitting and receiving data. The data rate is determined by the physical layer interface module (PLIM).
- One active LECS supports all ELANs.
- In each ELAN, there is one LES/BUS pair and some number of LECs.

- The LES and BUS functionality must be defined on the same subinterface and cannot be separated.

- There can be only one active LES/BUS pair per subinterface.

- There can be only one LES/BUS pair per ELAN.

- The current LANE Phase 1 standard does not provide for any LES/BUS redundancy.

- The LECS and LES/BUS can be different routers, bridges, or workstations.

- VCCs can be either switched virtual circuits (SVCs) or permanent virtual circuits (PVCs), although PVC design configuration and complexity might make anything more than a very small network prohibitively unmanageable and complex.

- If an LEC on a router subinterface is assigned an IP, IPX, or AppleTalk address, that protocol is routable over that LEC. If there are multiple LECs on a router and they are assigned protocol addresses, routing will occur between the ELANs. For routing between ELANs to function correctly, an ELAN should be in only one subnet for a particular protocol.

PNNI in LANE Networks

Network designers can deploy PNNI as a Layer 2 routing protocol for bandwidth management, traffic distribution, and path redundancy for LANE networks. PNNI is an ATM routing protocol used for routing call setups, and is implemented in the ATM switches. Most LANE networks consist of multiple ATM switches and typically employ the PNNI protocol.

NOTE   Although PNNI is an advanced routing protocol and supports QoS-based routing, this particular aspect of PNNI is not discussed in this chapter because most LANE networks are based on the best-effort traffic category.

Some PNNI-related features that can be useful in scaling LANE networks are the following:

- Support of load-balance call setup requests across multiple paths between two end stations

- Support of load-balance call setups across multiple parallel links

- Support for link and path redundancy with fast convergence

- Excellent call setup performance across multiple hops using the background routing feature

Figure 5-13 shows how the LightStream 1010 switch supports load balancing.

Figure 5-13 *Load-Balancing Calls across Multiple Paths and Multiple Links*

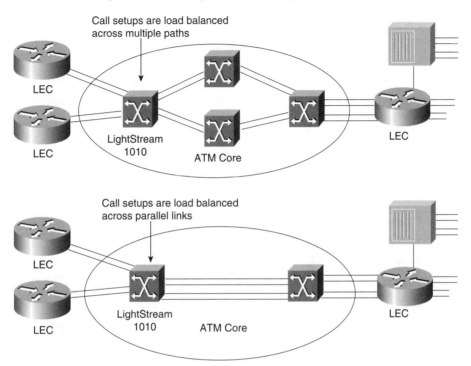

As Figure 5-13 shows, load balancing of calls is enabled by default on the LightStream 1010 switch. Background routing, however, is not enabled by default. Background routing can be thought of as routing of call setups using a path from a precomputed route database. The background routing process computes a list of all possible paths, to all destinations, and across all the service categories (for example, constant bit rate [CBR], virtual bit rate-real time [VBR-RT], virtual bit rate and non-real time [VBR-NRT], and available bit rate-unspecified bit rate [ABR-UBR]).

When a call is placed from Point A to Point B, PNNI picks a cached routed from the background route table instead of computing a route on demand. This eases the CPU load and provides a faster rate of processing the call setups.

Background routing can be useful in networks that have a stable topology with respect to QoS. It is, however, not very effective in networks that have rapidly changing topologies (for example, Internet service provider [ISP] networks or carrier networks). Campus LANE networks can use this feature effectively because all the SVCs in the network belong to the UBR or ABR category. To enable this feature, use the following command:

```
atm router pnni
  node 1 level 56
  bg-routes
```

The current implementation of PNNI on the LightStream 1010 switch is fully ATM Forum-PNNI Version 1-compliant. The LightStream default PNNI image license supports a single level of hierarchy, in which multiple peer groups can be interconnected by IISP or by other switches that support full PNNI hierarchy; extra PNNI image licenses will support multiple levels of routing hierarchy.

The PNNI protocols have been designed to scale across all sizes of ATM networks, from small campus networks of a handful of switches, to the possible global ATM Internet of millions of switches. This level of scalability is greater than that of any existing routing protocol, and requires very significant complexity in the PNNI protocol.

Specifically, such scalability mandates the support of multiple levels of routing hierarchy, based on the use of prefixes of the 20-byte ATM address space. The lowest level of the PNNI routing hierarchy consists of a single peer group within which all switches flood all reachability and QoS metrics to one another. This is analogous, for instance, to a single area in the OSPF protocol.

Subsequently, multiple peer groups at one level of the hierarchy are aggregated into higher-level peer groups, within which each lower-level peer group is represented by a single *peer group leader*, and so on iteratively up the PNNI hierarchy. Each level of the hierarchy is identified by a prefix of the ATM address space, implying that PNNI could theoretically contain more than 100 levels of routing hierarchy. However, a handful of levels would be adequate for most networks. The price to be paid for such scalability is the need for highly complex mechanisms for supporting and bringing up the multiple levels of hierarchy, and for electing the peer-group leaders within each peer group at each level.

Scaling an ELAN—Spanning-Tree Protocol Issues

Spanning-Tree Protocol is a Layer 2 protocol supported by switches and bridges to prevent temporary loops in networks with redundant links. Because an LEC bridges Ethernet/Token Ring traffic over an ATM backbone, the spanning-tree bridge protocol data units (BPDUs) are transmitted over the entire ELAN. The ATM network appears as a shared Ethernet/Token Ring network to the spanning-tree process at the edge of the Layer 2 switches.

The spanning-tree topology of a LANE-based network is substantially simpler than a pure frame-switched network that employs the Spanning-Tree Protocol. It follows that spanning-tree convergence times, which can be a major issue in large frame-switched networks, can be less of an issue in LANE networks. Note that spanning tree must reconverge if there are failures at the edge devices or inside the ATM network. If there is a need to tune the convergence time to a lower or higher value, the forward delay parameter can be used.

LANE Redundancy

Although LANE enables network designers to connect their legacy LANs to an ATM network, LANE Version 1.0 does not define mechanisms for building redundancy and fault tolerance into the LANE services. Consequently, this makes the LANE services a single point of failure. Moreover, router redundancy and path/link redundancy are also issues that the network designer needs to consider.

Network designers can use the following techniques to build fault-tolerant and resilient LANE networks:

- Simple Server Replication Protocol (SSRP) for LANE provides redundancy that works with Cisco and any third-party LECs.
- Hot Standby Router Protocol (HSRP) over LANE provides redundancy for the default router configured at IP end stations.
- Redundant modules supported by Cisco ATM switches.
- Spanning-Tree Protocol on the Ethernet-ATM switches.

The following subsections examine these various mechanisms and highlight design rules and issues to consider while implementing redundant LANE networks. The discussion begins by examining SSRP, which was developed to provide redundant LANE services.

Although many vendors implemented redundant LANE services early on, the services violated the LANE 1.0 specification and therefore were not interoperable with other third-party implementations. SSRP supports the LANE 1.0 specification, however, and is interoperable with third-party LEC implementations, which is important when implementing an interoperable ATM network.

The SSRP discussion is followed by a description of HSRP over LANE, which provides a mechanism for building router redundancy. Following this is an examination of the Spanning-Tree Protocol and other product-specific features that can be used to build link and path redundancy into edge devices.

Issues in a LANE Network

A major concern with LANE 1.0 networks is that only one set of LANE service components can be accessed by an LEC at any given time. This results in the following limitations:

- Only a single LECS supports all ELANs.
- There can be only one LES/BUS pair per ELAN.

A failure in any of these service components has the following impact on network operation:

- **LECS failure**—A failed LECS impacts all the ELANs under its control because it provides access control for all its ELANs. Although the existing ELANs would continue to work normally (assuming only Cisco LECs), no new LEC can join any ELAN under the control of that LECS. Also, any LEC that needs to rejoin its ELAN or change its membership to another ELAN cannot because the LES cannot verify any LEC trying to join an ELAN.

- **LES/BUS failure**—The LES/BUS pair is needed to maintain an operational ELAN. The LES provides the LE_ARP service for ATM-MAC address mappings, and the BUS provides broadcast and unknown services for a given ELAN. Therefore, a failure of either the LES or the BUS immediately affects normal communication on the ELAN. However, a LES/BUS failure impacts only the ELAN served by that pair.

It is clear that these issues can be limiting to networks in which resiliency and robustness are required; therefore, these issues might even be deciding factors as to whether to implement LANE-based ATM networks. In addition, other design considerations can have implications on the overall robustness of the LANE environment (the placement of the LANE service components within an ATM network, for example).

Resiliency in LANE Networks

Increasing the resiliency of a LANE-based network essentially includes delivering increased robustness in the LANE service components such as the LECS, LES, and BUS. Such robustness is provided by SSRP through a primary-secondary combination of the LANE services. For LECS redundancy, one primary LECS is backed up by multiple secondary LECSs. LES/BUS redundancy is also handled in a similar fashion, where one primary LES/BUS pair is backed up by multiple secondaries. Note that the LES/BUS functions are always co-located in a Cisco implementation and the pair is handled as one unit with respect to redundancy.

LECS Redundancy

In the LANE 1.0 specification, the first step for an LEC during initialization is to connect with the LECS to obtain the LES ATM address for the ELAN it wants to join. For the LEC to connect to the LECS, multiple mechanisms are defined. First, the LEC should query the ATM switch it is attached to for the LECS address. This address discovery process is done using the ILMI protocol on VPI, VCI - 0, 16.

The following is an example of the configuration command to add an LECS address to a LightStream 1010 switch:

```
atm lecs-address <LECS NSAP address> <index>
```

With SSRP, multiple LECS addresses are configured into the ATM switches. An LEC, which requests the LECS address from the ATM switch, gets the entire table of LECS addresses in response. The LEC first attempts to connect to the highest-ranking LECS address. If this fails, it tries the next one in the list and so on until it connects to the LECS.

Whereas the LEC always tries to connect to the highest-ranking LECS available, SSRP ensures that there is only a single primary that responds to the Configure Request queries coming from the LEC. The establishment of a primary LECS and the placement of the others in backup go to the heart of SSRP. The following describes the way SSRP establishes a primary LECS. Upon initialization, an LECS obtains the LECS address table from the switch and then tries to connect to all the LECSs below itself in rank. The rank is derived from the index entry in the LECS address table.

If an LECS has a connection (VCC) from an LECS whose rank is higher than its own, it is in backup mode. The highest-ranking LECS does not have any other LECS that connects to it from above and assumes the role of the primary LECS.

Figure 5-14 shows the procedure of a backup taking over in the case of a failed primary LECS. The LANE network shown in Figure 5-14 has four LECS entities (LECS A, B, C, and D). All the ATM switches in the network are configured with the same LECS address table. After startup, LECS A obtains the LECS address table from the ATM switch it is attached to and finds that it has three LECSs below itself, and therefore tries to connect to LECS B, C, and D. LECS B connects to LECS C and LECS D, and LECS C connects to LECS D. There is a downward establishment of VCCs. Because LECS A does not have any VCCs from above, it becomes the primary LECS.

Figure 5-14 *LECS Redundancy*

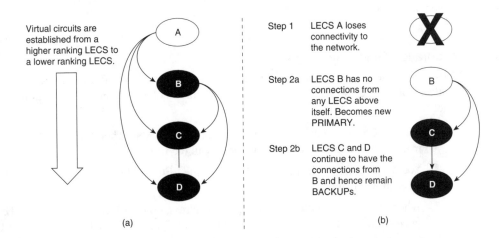

(a)   (b)

During normal network operation, LECS A responds to all configure requests, and the backup LECSs (LECS B, C, and D) do not respond to any queries. If for some reason the primary LECS (LECS A) fails because of such conditions as a box failure, LECS B loses its VCC from LECS A, as do the other LECS.

At this point, LECS B does not have any VCCs from above and therefore is now the highest-ranking available LECS in the network. LECS B now becomes the primary LECS. LECS C and LECS D still have connections from higher-ranking LECSs, and therefore continue to operate in backup mode, as shown in Step 2b of Figure 5-14.

LES/BUS Redundancy

The LES/BUS redundancy portion of SSRP supports the configuration of multiple LES/BUS pairs that work in a primary-secondary fashion. However, the mechanisms used here are different from those used for the LECS redundancy described in the preceding section.

Multiple LES/BUS pairs for a given ELAN are first configured into the LECS database. Within this database, each LES/BUS pair is assigned a priority. After initialization, each LES/BUS opens a VCC with the primary LECS using the LECS address discovery mechanism. The LES/BUS pair with the highest priority that has an open VCC to the LECS is assigned as the primary LES/BUS by the primary LECS.

SSRP Usage Guidelines

There are no theoretical limits on the number of LECSs that can be configured using SSRP; however, a recommended number is two (one primary and one backup) or three LECSs (one primary and two backups). Any more redundancy should be implemented only after very careful consideration because it will add significant complexity to the network. This added complexity might result in a substantial increase in management time to troubleshoot such networks.

SSRP Configuration Guidelines

To support the LECS redundancy scheme, you must adhere to the following configuration rules. Failure to do so will result in improper operation of SSRP and a malfunctioning network.

* Each LECS must maintain the same database of ELANs. Therefore, you must maintain the same ELAN database across all the LECSs.

* You must configure the LECS addresses in the LECS address table in the same order on each ATM switch in the network.

* When using SSRP with the Well Known Address, do not place two LECSs on the same ATM switch. If you place two LECs on the same ATM switch, only one LECS can register the Well Known Address with the ATM switch (through ILMI) and this can cause problems during initialization.

SSRP Interoperability Notes

SSRP can be used with independent third-party LECs if the third-party LECs use ILMI for LECS address discovery and can appropriately handle multiple LECS addresses returned by the ATM switch. The LEC should step through connecting to the list of LECS addresses returned by the ATM switch, for example. The first LECS that responds to the configuration request is the master LECS.

Behavior of SSRP with the Well Known LECS Address

SSRP also works with LECS Well Known Address (47.0079....) defined in the LANE 1.0 specification. The Cisco LECS can listen on multiple ATM addresses at the same time. Therefore, it can listen on the Well Known Address and the autoconfigured ATM address, which can be displayed using the **show lane default** command.

When the LECS is enabled to listen on the Well Known Address, it registers the Well Known Address with the ATM switch so that the ATM switches can advertise routes to the Well Known Address and route any call setup requests to the correct place.

Under SSRP, there are multiple LECSs in the network. If each LECS registers the Well Known Address to the ATM switches that it is connected to, call setups are routed to different places in the network. Consequently, under SSRP you must configure an autoconfigured address so that the negotiation of the master first takes place, and then the master registers the Well Known Address with the ATM switch. If the master fails, the Well Known Address moves with the master LECS. The PNNI code on the LightStream 1010 switch takes care of advertising the new route to the Well Known Address when there is a change of LECS mastership. Therefore, third-party LECs that use only the Well Known Address can also interpolate with SSRP. SSRP is the only redundancy scheme that can be used with almost any LEC in the industry.

To implement SSRP with the Well Known Address, follow these steps:

Step 1   Configure the LECS to listen on the autoconfigured address (or on a separate ATM address that you have predetermined). This autoconfigured (or other) address should be programmed into the ATM switches for the LECS address discovery mechanism.

Step 2   Configure each LECS to listen on the Well Known Address using the **lane config fixed-config-atm-address** command. After the master LECS is determined using the LECS redundancy procedure, the master registers the Well Known Address to the ATM switch.

NOTE	SSRP with the Well Known Address does not work properly under certain circumstances (during failure) if two LECS are attached to the same ATM switch, because of the possibility of duplicate address registration on the same switch (which ILMI does not allow). Make sure each LECS is on a separate ATM switch.

Behavior of SSRP in Network Partitions

In the event of network partitions in which two separate ATM clouds are formed due to an interconnecting link or switch failure, each cloud has its own set of LANE services if SSRP is configured to handle network partitions.

When configuring SSRP, use the following guidelines to accommodate the possibility of network partition:

- Configure each partition with its own LANE services that can become active during a network partition. If you are connecting two sites or campuses across a MAN and you want the same ELANs at both locations, for example, configure each campus/site with its own LANE services.

- Routing behavior should be carefully examined during a network partition in the case where an ELAN maps to a Layer 3 network (for example, an IP subnet or IPX network) because there are now two routes to the same subnet (assuming there are redundant routers in the network). If there are no redundant routers, one of the partitions will be effectively isolated from the rest of the network. Intra-ELAN traffic will continue to behave properly.

HSRP over LANE

HSRP is a protocol that network designers can use to guard against router failures in the network. The HSRP protocol is exchanged between two routers and one of them is elected as the primary router interface (or subinterface) for a given subnet. The other router acts as the *hot standby* router.

In HSRP, a default IP address and a default virtual MAC address are shared between the two routers exchanging the HSRP protocol. All IP end stations use this default IP address as the default gateway to communicate with end stations outside their immediate subnet. Therefore, when there is a primary router failure, the hot standby router takes over the default gateway address and the MAC address so that the end station can continue communicating with end stations that are not in its immediate subnet.

Because HSRP is a Layer 2 mechanism and needs a MAC address–based Layer 2 network, it is possible to implement HSRP-style recovery over LANE. The mechanisms used are the same as for any Ethernet interface and can be configured at a subinterface level.

Redundant Modules for Cisco ATM Switches

Another aspect of addressing the redundancy needs from a physical network perspective is the addition of redundant modules in ATM switches. Cisco ATM switches support redundant power supplies, as well as redundant switch and interface modules.

Summary

ATM technology, ATM networks, and ATM integration into current networks have been covered in this chapter.

ATM has three functional layers: the ATM physical layer, the ATM layer, and the ATM adaptation layer. ATM supports multiple media at the physical layer. The ATM layer is responsible for payload delivery, virtual connections, and cell identification.

ATM manages QoS issues at the ATM adaptation layer. The adaptation layer's four traffic classifications—AAL1, AAL2, AAL3/4, and AAL5—impact QoS decisions.

In addition to ATM technology, other design considerations were covered (LANE and ATM switch sizing, for example). This chapter also discussed Cisco ATM offerings.

CHAPTER 6

Designing Packet Service Networks and Voice over Frame Relay Networks

Edited by Christopher Beveridge

This chapter focuses on the implementation of packet-switching services, and addresses network design in terms of the following packet-switching service topics:

- Hierarchical network design
- Topology design
- Broadcast issues
- Performance issues

Information provided in this chapter is organized around these central topics. An introductory discussion outlines the general issues; subsequent discussions focus on considerations for the specific packet-switching technologies.

This chapter focuses on general packet-switching considerations and Frame Relay networks. Frame Relay was selected as the focus for this chapter because it presents a comprehensive illustration of design considerations for interconnection to packet-switching services. Also included in this chapter is an introductory discussion of design and performance issues when integrating data and voice on a Frame Relay network.

Understanding Packet-Switched Network Design

The chief trade-off in linking local-area networks (LANs) and private wide-area networks (WANs) into packet-switching data network (PSDN) services is between cost and performance. An ideal design optimizes packet services. Service optimization does not necessarily translate into picking the service mix that represents the lowest possible tariffs. Successful packet-service implementations result from adhering to two basic rules:

- When implementing a packet-switching solution, be sure to balance the cost savings derived by instituting PSDN interconnections against your computing community's performance requirements.
- Build an environment that is manageable and that can scale up as more WAN links are required.

These rules recur as underlying themes in the discussions that follow. The introductory sections outline the overall issues that influence the ways in which packet-switched networks are designed.

Hierarchical Design

The objective of a hierarchical network design is to modularize the elements of a large network into layers of networking. The general model of this hierarchy is described in Chapter 2, "Network Design Basics." The key functional layers in this model are the access, distribution, and backbone (or core) routing layers. In essence, a hierarchical approach strives to split networks into subnetworks so that traffic and nodes can be more easily managed. Hierarchical designs also facilitate scaling of networks because new subnetwork modules and networking technologies can be integrated into the overall scheme without disrupting the existing backbone. Figure 6-1 illustrates the basic approach to hierarchical design.

Figure 6-1 *Hierarchical Packet-Switched Interconnection*

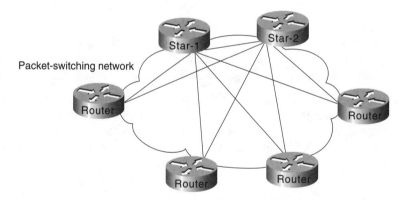

Three basic advantages tilt the design decision in favor of a hierarchical approach:

* Scalability of Hierarchical Networks
* Manageability of Hierarchical Networks
* Optimization of Broadcast and Multicast Control Traffic

Scalability of Hierarchical Networks

Scalability is a primary advantage that supports using a hierarchical approach to packet-service connections. Hierarchical networks are more scalable because they enable you to grow your network in incremental modules without running into the limitations that are quickly encountered with a flat, nonhierarchical structure.

Hierarchical networks raise certain issues that require careful planning, however. These issues include the costs of virtual circuits, the complexity inherent in a hierarchical design (particularly when integrated with a meshed topology), and the need for additional router interfaces to separate layers in your hierarchy.

To take advantage of a hierarchical design, you must match your hierarchy of networks with a complementary approach in your regional topologies. Design specifics depend on the packet services you implement, as well as on your requirements for fault tolerance, cost, and overall performance.

Manageability of Hierarchical Networks

Hierarchical designs offer several management advantages:

- **Network simplicity**—Adopting a hierarchical design reduces the overall complexity of a network by partitioning elements into smaller units. This partitioning of elements makes troubleshooting easier, while providing inherent protection against the propagation of broadcast storms, routing loops, or other potential problems.

- **Design flexibility**—Hierarchical network designs provide greater flexibility in the use of WAN packet services. Most networks benefit from using a hybrid approach to the overall network structure. In many cases, leased lines can be implemented in the backbone, with packet-switching services used in the distribution and access networks.

- **Router management**—With the use of a layered, hierarchical approach to router implementation, the complexity of individual router configurations is substantially reduced because each router has fewer neighbors or peers with which to communicate.

Optimization of Broadcast and Multicast Control Traffic

The effect of broadcasting in packet-service networks (discussed in "Broadcast Issues," later in this chapter) requires you to implement smaller groups of routers. Typical examples of broadcast traffic are the routing updates and Novell Service Advertisement Protocol (SAP) updates broadcast between routers on a PSDN. An excessively high population of routers in any area or layer of the overall network might result in traffic bottlenecks brought on by broadcast replication. A hierarchical scheme enables you to limit the level of broadcasting between regions and into your backbone.

Topology Design

After you have established your overall network scheme, you must settle on an approach for handling interconnections among sites within the same administrative region or area. In designing any regional WAN, whether it is based on packet-switching services or point-to-point interconnections, you can adopt three basic design approaches:

- Star Topologies
- Fully Meshed Topologies
- Partially Meshed Topologies

The following discussions introduce these topologies. Technology-specific discussions presented in this chapter address the applicability of these topologies for the specific packet-switching services.

Illustrations in this chapter use lines to show the interconnections of specific routers on the PSDN network. These interconnections are virtual connections, facilitated by mapping features within the routers. Actual physical connections generally are made to switches within the PSDN. Unless otherwise specified, the connecting lines represent these virtual connections in the PSDN.

Star Topologies

A star topology features a single networking hub, providing access from leaf networks into the backbone and access to each other only through the core router. Figure 6-2 illustrates a packet-switched star topology for a regional network.

The advantages of a star approach are simplified management and minimized tariff costs. However, the disadvantages are significant. First, the core router represents a single point of failure. Second, the core router limits overall performance for access to backbone resources because it is a single pipe through which all traffic intended for the backbone (or for the other regional routers) must pass. Third, this topology is not scalable.

Figure 6-2   *Star Topology for a Regional Network*

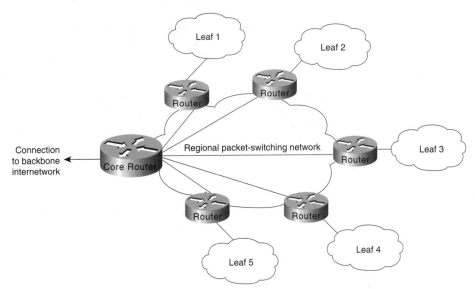

Fully Meshed Topologies

A fully meshed topology means that each routing node on the periphery of a given packet-switching network has a direct path to every other node on the cloud. Figure 6-3 illustrates this kind of arrangement.

Figure 6-3   *Fully Meshed Topology*

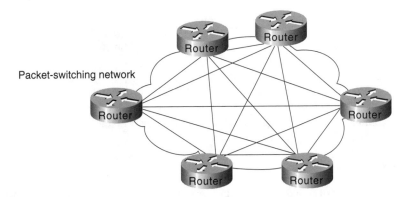

The key rationale for creating a fully meshed environment is to provide a high level of redundancy. Although a fully meshed topology facilitates support of all network protocols, it is not tenable in large packet-switched networks. Key issues are the large number of virtual circuits required (one for every connection between routers), problems associated with the large number of packet/broadcast replications required, and the configuration complexity for routers in the absence of multicast support in nonbroadcast environments.

By combining fully meshed and star approaches into a partially meshed environment, you can improve fault tolerance without encountering the performance and management problems associated with a fully meshed approach. The next section discusses the partially meshed approach.

Partially Meshed Topologies

A partially meshed topology reduces the number of routers within a region that have direct connections to all other nodes in the region. All nodes are not connected to all other nodes. For a nonmeshed node to communicate with another nonmeshed node, it must send traffic through one of the collection point routers. Figure 6-4 illustrates such a situation.

Figure 6-4   *Partially Meshed Topology*

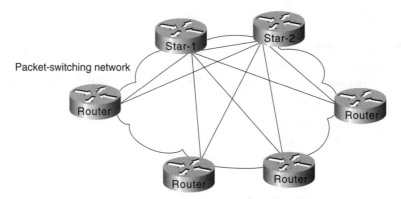

There are many forms of partially meshed topologies. In general, partially meshed approaches are considered to provide the best balance for regional topologies in terms of the number of virtual circuits, redundancy, and performance.

Broadcast Issues

The existence of broadcast traffic can present problems when introduced into packet-service networks. Broadcasts are necessary for a station to reach multiple stations with a single packet when the sending node does not know the specific address of each intended recipient. Table 6-1 lists common networking protocols and the general level of broadcast traffic associated with each, assuming a large-scale network with many routing nodes.

Table 6-1 *Broadcast Traffic Levels of Protocols in Large-Scale Networks*

Network Protocol	Routing Protocol	Relative Broadcast Traffic Level
AppleTalk	Routing Table Maintenance Protocol (RTMP)	High
	Enhanced Interior Gateway Routing Protocol (Enhanced IGRP)	Low
Novell Internetwork Packet Exchange (IPX)	Routing Information Protocol (RIP)	High
	Service Advertisement Protocol (SAP)	High
	Enhanced IGRP	Low
Internet Protocol (IP)	RIP	High
	Interior Gateway Routing Protocol (IGRP)	High
	Open Shortest Path First (OSPF)	Low
	Intermediate System-to-Intermediate System (IS-IS)	Low
	Enhanced IGRP	Low
	Border Gateway Protocol (BGP)	None
	Exterior Gateway Protocol (EGP)	None
DECnet Phase IV	DECnet Routing	High
DECnet Phase V	IS-IS	Low
International Organization for Standardization (ISO) Connectionless Network Service (CLNS)	IS-IS	Low
	ISO-IGRP	High
Xerox Network Systems (XNS)	RIP	High
Banyan Virtual Integrated Network Service (VINES)	Routing Table Protocol (RTP)	High
	Sequenced RTP	Low

The relative values *high* and *low* in Table 6-1 provide a general range for these protocols. Your situation and implementation will determine the magnitude of broadcast traffic. For example, the level of broadcast traffic generated in an AppleTalk Enhanced IGRP environment depends on the setting of the Enhanced IGRP hello-timer interval. Another issue relates to the size of the network. In a small-scale network, the amount of broadcast traffic generated by Enhanced IGRP nodes might be higher than with a comparable RTMP-based network. For large-scale networks, however, Enhanced IGRP nodes generate substantially less broadcast traffic than RTMP-based nodes.

Managing packet replication is an important design consideration when integrating broadcast-type LANs (such as Ethernet) with nonbroadcast packet services (such as X.25). With the multiple virtual circuits, characteristic of connections to packet-switched environments, routers must replicate broadcasts for each virtual circuit on a given physical line.

With highly meshed environments, replicating broadcasts can be expensive in terms of increased required bandwidth and the number of CPU cycles. Despite the advantages that meshed topologies offer, they are generally impractical for large packet-switching networks. Nonetheless, some level of circuit meshing is essential to ensure fault tolerance. The key is to balance the trade-off in performance against requirements for circuit redundancy.

Performance Issues

When designing a WAN around a specific packet-service type, you must consider the individual characteristics of the virtual circuit. Performance under certain conditions will depend on a given virtual circuit's capability to accommodate mixed protocol traffic, for example. Depending on how the multiprotocol traffic is queued and streamed from one node to the next, certain protocols may require special handling. One solution might be to assign specific virtual circuits to specific protocol types. Performance concerns for specific packet-switching services include committed information rates (CIR) in Frame Relay networks and window size limitations in X.25 networks. (The CIR corresponds to the maximum average rate per connection [PVC] for a period of time.)

Frame Relay Network Design

One of the chief concerns when designing a Frame Relay implementation is scalability. As your requirements for remote interconnections grow, your network must be able to grow to accommodate changes. The network must also provide an acceptable level of performance, while minimizing maintenance and management requirements. Meeting all these objectives simultaneously can be quite a balancing act. The discussions that follow focus on several important factors for Frame Relay networks:

- Hierarchical design
- Regional topologies
- Broadcast issues
- Performance issues

The guidelines and suggestions that follow are intended to provide a foundation for constructing scalable Frame Relay networks that balance performance, fault tolerance, and cost.

Hierarchical Design for Frame Relay Networks

In general, the arguments supporting hierarchical design for packet-switching networks, discussed in the section titled "Hierarchical Design" earlier in this chapter, apply to hierarchical design for Frame Relay networks. To review, the three factors driving the recommendation for implementing a hierarchical design are the following:

- Scalability of hierarchical networks

- Manageability of hierarchical networks

- Optimization of broadcast and multicast control traffic

The method by which many Frame Relay vendors tariff services is by Data Link Connection Identifier (DLCI), which identifies a Frame Relay permanent virtual connection. A Frame Relay permanent virtual connection is equivalent to an X.25 permanent virtual circuit, which, in X.25 terminology, is identified by a logical channel number (LCN). The DLCI defines the interconnection between Frame Relay elements. For any given network implementation, the number of Frame Relay permanent virtual connections is highly dependent on the protocols in use and actual traffic patterns.

How many DLCIs can be configured per serial port? It varies, depending on the traffic level. You can use all of them (about 1,000), but in common use, 200–300 is a typical maximum. If you broadcast on the DLCIs, 30–50 is more realistic due to CPU overhead in generating broadcasts. Specific guidelines are difficult because overhead varies by configuration. On low-end boxes (4,500 and below), however, the architecture is bound by the available I/O memory. The specific number depends on several factors that should be considered together:

- **Protocols being routed**—Any broadcast-intensive protocol constrains the number of assignable DLCIs. For example, AppleTalk is a protocol characterized by high levels of broadcast overhead. Another example is Novell IPX, which sends both routing and service updates resulting in higher broadcast bandwidth overhead. In contrast, IGRP is less broadcast-intensive because it sends routing updates less often (by default, every 90 seconds). However, IGRP can become broadcast-intensive if its IGRP timers are modified so that updates are sent more frequently.

- **Broadcast traffic**—Broadcasts, such as routing updates, are the single most important consideration in determining the number of DLCIs that can be defined. The amount and type of broadcast traffic will guide your ability to assign DLCIs within this general recommended range. Refer to Table 6-1, earlier in this chapter, for a list of the relative level of broadcast traffic associated with common protocols.

- **Speed of lines**—If broadcast traffic levels are expected to be high, you should consider faster lines and DLCIs with higher CIR and excess burst (Be) limits. You should also implement fewer DLCIs.

- **Static routes**—If static routing is implemented, you can use a larger number of DLCIs per line because a larger number of DLCIs reduces the level of broadcasting.

- **Size of routing protocol and SAP updates**—The larger the network, the larger the size of these updates. The larger the updates, the fewer the number of DLCIs that you can assign.

Two forms of hierarchical design can be implemented:

- Hierarchical Meshed Frame Relay Networks
- Hybrid-Meshed Frame Relay Networks

Both designs have advantages and disadvantages. The brief discussions that follow contrast these two approaches.

Hierarchical Meshed Frame Relay Networks

The objectives of implementing a hierarchical mesh for Frame Relay environments are to avoid implementing excessively large numbers of DLCIs and to provide a manageable, segmented environment. The hierarchical meshed environment features full meshing within the core PSDN and full meshing throughout the peripheral networks. The hierarchy is created by strategically locating routers between network elements in the hierarchy.

Figure 6-5 illustrates a simple hierarchical mesh. The network illustrated in Figure 6-5 illustrates a fully meshed backbone, with meshed regional networks and broadcast networks at the outer periphery.

The key advantages of the hierarchical mesh are that it scales well and localizes traffic. By placing routers between fully meshed portions of the network, you limit the number of DLCIs per physical interface, segment your network, and make the network more manageable. However, consider the following two issues when implementing a hierarchical mesh:

- **Broadcast and packet replication**—In an environment that has a large number of multiple DLCIs per router interface, excessive broadcast and packet replication can impair overall performance. With a high level of meshing throughout a hierarchical mesh, excessive broadcast and packet replication is a significant concern. In the backbone, where traffic throughput requirements are typically high, preventing bandwidth loss due to broadcast traffic and packet replication is particularly important.

- **Increased costs associated with additional router interfaces**—Compared with a fully meshed topology, additional routers are needed to separate the meshed backbone from the meshed peripheral networks. By using these routers, however, you can create much larger networks that scale almost indefinitely in comparison to a fully meshed network.

Figure 6-5 *Fully Meshed Hierarchical Frame Relay Environment*

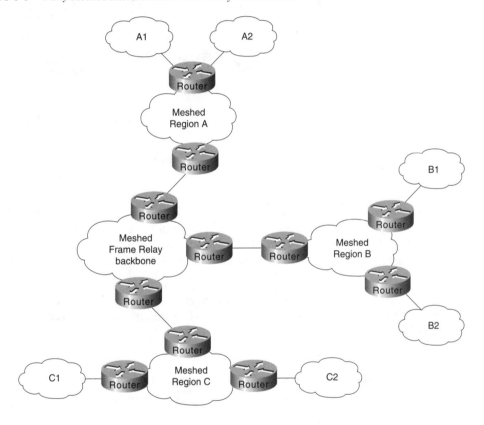

Hybrid-Meshed Frame Relay Networks

The economic and strategic importance of backbone environments often force network designers to implement a hybrid-meshed approach to WAN networks. Hybrid-meshed networks feature redundant, meshed leased lines in the WAN backbone and partially (or fully) meshed Frame Relay PSDNs in the periphery. Routers separate the two elements. Figure 6-6 illustrates such a hybrid arrangement.

Figure 6-6 *Hybrid Hierarchical Frame Relay Network*

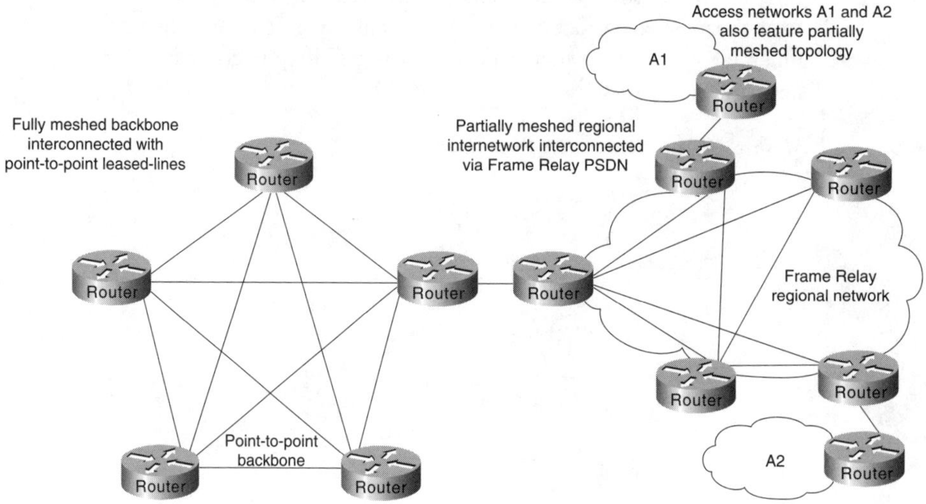

Hybrid hierarchical meshes have the advantages of providing higher performance on the backbone, localizing traffic, and simplifying scaling of the network. In addition, hybrid-meshed networks for Frame Relay are attractive because they can provide better traffic control in the backbone and they allow the backbone to be made of dedicated links, resulting in greater stability.

The disadvantages of hybrid hierarchical meshes include the high costs associated with the leased lines, as well as broadcast and packet replication that can be significant in access networks.

Regional Topologies for Frame Relay Networks

You can adopt one of three basic design approaches for a Frame Relay–based packet service regional network:

- Star Topologies
- Fully Meshed Topologies
- Partially Meshed Topologies

Each of these is discussed in the following sections. In general, emphasis is placed on partially meshed topologies integrated into a hierarchical environment. Star and fully meshed topologies are discussed for structural context.

Star Topologies

The general form of the star topology is addressed in the section titled "Topology Design," earlier in this chapter. Stars are attractive because they minimize the number of DLCIs required and result in a low-cost solution. A star topology presents some inherent bandwidth limitations, however. Consider an environment in which a backbone router is attached to a Frame Relay cloud at 256 kbps, whereas the remote sites are attached at 56 kbps. Such a topology will throttle traffic coming off the backbone intended for the remote sites.

As suggested in the general discussion, a strict star topology does not offer the fault tolerance needed for many networking situations. If the link from the hub router to a specific leaf router is lost, all connectivity to the leaf router is lost.

Fully Meshed Topologies

A fully meshed topology mandates that every routing node connected to a Frame Relay network be logically linked via an assigned DLCI to every other node on the cloud. This topology is not tenable for larger Frame Relay networks for several reasons:

- Large, fully meshed Frame Relay networks require many DLCIs. One is required for each logical link between nodes. As shown in Figure 6-7, a fully connected topology requires the assignment of $[n(n-1)]/2$ DLCIs, where n is the number of routers to be directly connected.

Figure 6-7   *Fully Meshed Frame Relay*

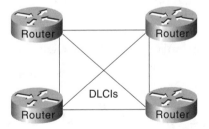

- Broadcast replication will choke networks in large, meshed Frame Relay topologies. Routers inherently treat Frame Relay as a broadcast medium. Each time a router sends a multicast frame (such as a routing update, spanning-tree update, or SAP update), the router must copy the frame to each DLCI for that Frame Relay interface.

These problems combine to make fully meshed topologies unworkable and unscalable for all but relatively small Frame Relay implementations.

Partially Meshed Topologies

Combining the concepts of the star topology and the fully meshed topology results in the partially meshed topology. Partially meshed topologies are generally recommended for Frame Relay regional environments because they offer superior fault tolerance (through redundant stars) and are less expensive than a fully meshed environment. In general, you should implement the minimum meshing to eliminate single point-of-failure risk.

Figure 6-8 illustrates a twin-star, partially meshed approach. This arrangement is supported in Frame Relay networks running IP, ISO CLNS, DECnet, Novell IPX, AppleTalk, and bridging.

Figure 6-8   *Twin-Star, Partially Meshed Frame Relay Network*

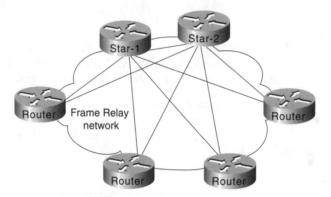

A feature called virtual interfaces (introduced with Software Release 9.21) enables you to create networks using partially meshed Frame Relay designs, as shown in Figure 6-8.

To create this type of network, individual physical interfaces are split into multiple virtual (logical) interfaces. The implication for Frame Relay is that DLCIs can be grouped or separated to maximize utility. Small fully meshed clouds of Frame Relay–connected routers can travel over a group of four DLCIs clustered on a single virtual interface, for example, whereas a fifth DLCI on a separate virtual interface provides connectivity to a completely separate network. All this connectivity occurs over a single physical interface connected to the Frame Relay service.

Prior to Software Release 9.21, virtual interfaces were not available and partially meshed topologies posed potential problems, depending on the network protocols used. Consider the topology illustrated in Figure 6-9.

Figure 6-9   *Partially Meshed Frame Relay Network*

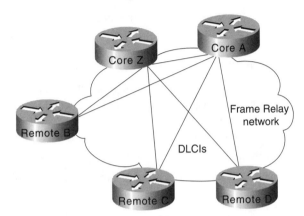

Given a standard router configuration and router software predating Software Release 9.21, the connectivity available in the network shown in Figure 6-9 can be characterized as follows:

- Core A and Core Z can reach all the remote routers.

- Remote B, Remote C, and Remote D cannot reach each other.

For Frame Relay implementations running software prior to Software Release 9.21, the only way to permit connectivity among all these routers is by using a distance vector routing protocol that can disable split horizon, such as RIP or IGRP for IP. Any other network protocol, such as AppleTalk or ISO CLNS, does not work. The following configuration listing illustrates an IGRP configuration to support a partially meshed arrangement:

```
router igrp 20
network 45.0.0.0
!
interface serial 3
encapsulation frame-relay
ip address 45.1.2.3 255.255.255.0
no ip split-horizon
```

This topology works with distance vector routing protocols, assuming that you want to establish connectivity from Remote B, C, or D to Core A or Core Z only, but not across paths. This topology does not work with link-state routing protocols because the router cannot verify complete adjacencies. Note that you will see routes and services of the leaf nodes that cannot be reached.

Broadcast Issues for Frame Relay Networks

Routers treat Frame Relay as a broadcast medium, which means that each time the router sends a multicast frame (such as a routing update, spanning-tree update, or SAP update), the router must replicate the frame to each DLCI for the Frame Relay interface. Frame replication results in substantial overhead for the router and for the physical interface.

Consider a Novell IPX environment with multiple DLCIs configured for a single physical serial interface. Every time a SAP update is detected, which occurs every 60 seconds, the router must replicate it and send it down the virtual interface associated with each DLCI. Each SAP frame contains up to seven service entries, and each update is 64 bytes. Figure 6-10 illustrates this situation.

One way to reduce broadcasts is to implement more efficient routing protocols, such as Enhanced IGRP, and to adjust timers on lower-speed Frame Relay services.

Figure 6-10   *SAP Replication in Frame Relay Virtual Interface Environment*

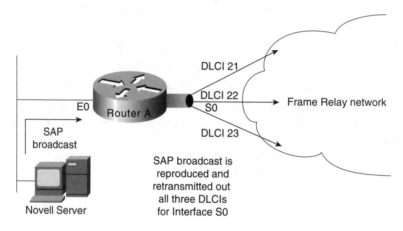

Creating a Broadcast Queue for an Interface

Very large Frame Relay networks might have performance problems when many DLCIs terminate in a single router or access server that must replicate routing updates and service advertising updates on each DLCI. The updates can consume access-link bandwidth and cause significant latency variations in user traffic; the updates can also consume interface buffers and lead to higher packet-rate loss for both user data and routing updates.

To avoid such problems, you can create a special broadcast queue for an interface. The broadcast queue is managed independently of the normal interface queue, has its own buffers, and has a configurable size and service rate.

A broadcast queue is given a maximum transmission rate (throughput) limit, measured in both bytes per second and packets per second. The queue is serviced to ensure that no more than this maximum is provided. The broadcast queue has priority when transmitting at a rate below the configured maximum, and hence has a guaranteed minimum bandwidth allocation. The two transmission rate limits are intended to avoid flooding the interface with broadcasts. The actual transmission-rate limit in any second is the first of the two rate limits that is reached.

Performance Issues for Frame Relay Networks

Two important performance concerns must be addressed when you are implementing a Frame Relay network:

- Packet-Switched Service Provider Tariff Metrics
- Multiprotocol Traffic Management Requirements

Each of these must be considered during the network planning process. The following sections briefly discuss the impact that tariff metrics and multiprotocol traffic management can have on overall Frame Relay performance.

Packet-Switched Service Provider Tariff Metrics

When you contract with Frame Relay packet-switched service providers for specific capabilities, CIR (measured in bits per second) is one of the key negotiated tariff metrics. CIR is the maximum permitted traffic level that the carrier will allow on a specific DLCI into the packet-switching environment. CIR can be anything up to the capacity of the physical limitation of the connecting line.

Other key metrics are committed burst (B_c) and excess burst (B_e). B_c is the number of bits that the Frame Relay network is committed to accept and transmit at the CIR. B_e sets the absolute limit for a DLCI in bits. This is the number of bits that the Frame Relay network will attempt to transmit after B_c is accommodated. B_e determines a peak or maximum Frame Relay data rate (Max_R), where $Max_R = (B_c + B_e)/B_c \times CIR$, measured in bits per second.

Consider the situation illustrated in Figure 6-11. In this environment, DLCIs 21, 22, and 23 are assigned CIRs of 56 kbps. Assume that the Max_R for each line is 112 kbps (double the CIR). The serial line to which Router A is connected is a T1 line capable of 1.544 Mbps total throughput. Given that the type of traffic being sent into the Frame Relay network consists of FTP file transfers, the potential is high that the router will attempt to transmit at a rate in excess of Max_R. If this occurs, traffic might be dropped without notification if the B_e buffers (allocated at the Frame Relay switch) overflow.

Figure 6-11   *Example of a CIR and CBR Traffic-Limiting Situation*

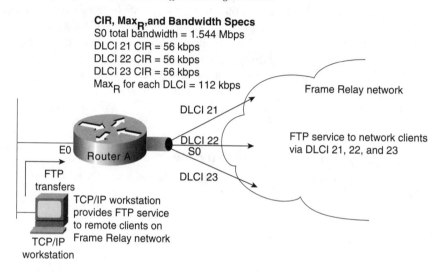

Unfortunately, there are relatively few ways to automatically prevent traffic on a line from exceeding the Max_R. Although Frame Relay itself uses the Forward Explicit Congestion Notification (FECN) and Backward Explicit Congestion Notification (BECN) protocols to control traffic in the Frame Relay network, there is no formally standardized mapping between the Frame Relay (link) level and most upper-layer protocols. At this time, an FECN bit detected by a router is mapped to the congestion notification byte for DECnet Phase IV or ISO CLNS. No other protocols are supported.

The actual effect of exceeding specified CIR and derived Max_R settings depends on the types of application running on the network. TCP/IP's backoff algorithm will see dropped packets as a congestion indication, for instance, and sending hosts might reduce output. NFS has no backoff algorithm, however, and dropped packets will result in lost connections. When determining the CIR, B_c, and B_e for Frame Relay connection, you should consider the actual line speed and applications to be supported.

Most Frame Relay carriers provide an appropriate level of buffering to handle instances when traffic exceeds the CIR for a given DLCI. These buffers allow excess packets to be spooled at the CIR and reduce packet loss, given a robust transport protocol such as TCP. Nonetheless, overflows can happen. Remember that although routers can prioritize traffic, Frame Relay switches cannot. You can specify which Frame Relay packets have low priority or low time sensitivity and will be the first to be dropped when a Frame Relay switch is congested. The mechanism that allows a Frame Relay switch to identify such packets is the discard eligibility (DE) bit.

This feature requires that the Frame Relay network be able to interpret the DE bit. Some networks take no action when the DE bit is set. Other networks use the DE bit to determine which packets to discard. The most desirable interpretation is to use the DE bit to determine which packets should be dropped first and also which packets have lower time sensitivity. You can define DE lists that identify the characteristics of packets to be eligible for discarding, and you can also specify DE groups to identify the DLCI that is affected.

You can specify DE lists based on the protocol or the interface, and on characteristics such as fragmentation of the packet, a specific TCP or User Datagram Protocol (UDP) port, an access list number, or a packet size.

NOTE   To avoid packet loss, implement unacknowledged application protocols (such as packetized video) carefully. With these protocols, there is a greater potential for buffer overflow.

Multiprotocol Traffic-Management Requirements

With multiple protocols being transmitted into a Frame Relay network through a single physical interface, you might find it useful to separate traffic among different DLCIs, based on protocol type. To split traffic in this way, you must assign specific protocols to specific DLCIs. This can be done by specifying static mapping on a per–virtual interface basis or by defining only specific types of encapsulations for specific virtual interfaces.

Figure 6-12 illustrates the use of virtual interfaces (assigned using subinterface configuration commands) to allocate traffic to specific DLCIs. In this case, traffic of each configured protocol is sent down a specific DLCI and segregated on a per-circuit basis. In addition, each protocol can be assigned a separate CIR and a separate level of buffering by the Frame Relay service provider.

Figure 6-12 *Virtual Interfaces Assigned Specific Protocols*

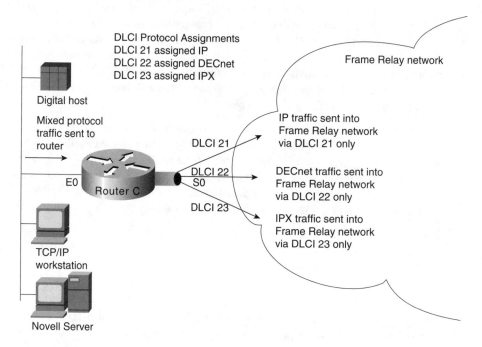

Figure 6-13 provides a listing of the subinterface configuration commands needed to support the configuration illustrated in Figure 6-12. The command listing in Figure 6-13 illustrates the enabling of the relevant protocols and the assignment of the protocols to the specific subinterfaces and associated Frame Relay DLCIs. Software Release 9.1 and later uses Frame Relay Inverse Address Resolution Protocol (IARP) to map protocol addresses to Frame Relay DLCIs dynamically. For that reason, Figure 6-13 does not show Frame Relay mappings.

Figure 6-13 *Virtual Interface Configuration Example*

```
interface Ethernet 0
ip address 192.198.78-9 255.255.255.0
ipx network AC
decnet cost 4
no mcp enabled
!
interface Serial0
no ip address
encapsulation frame–relay
!
interface Serial0.1 point–to–point
ip address 131.108.3.12.255.255.255.0
frame–relay interface–dlci 21 broadcast
frame-relay inverse-asp IP 21
no frame–relay inverse–arp NOVELL 21
no frame–relay inverse–arp APPLETALK 21
no frame–relay inverse–arp INS 21
!
interface Serial0.2 point–to–point
no ip address
decnet cost 10
frame–relay interface–dlci 22 broadcast
no frame–relay inverse–arp IP 22
no frame–relay inverse–arp NOVELL 22
no frame–relay inverse–arp APPLETALK 22
no frame–relay inverse–arp INS 22
!
interface Serial0.3 point–to–point
no ip address
ipx network A3
frame–relay interface–dlci 23 broadcast
no frame–relay inverse–arp IP 23
frame–relay inverse–arp NOVELL 23
no frame-relay inverse-asp APPLETALK 23
no frame–relay inverse–arp INS 23
!
router igrp 109
network 192.198.78.0
!
ip name–server 255.255.255.255
!
snmp–server community
!
line con 0
line aux 0
line vty 0 4
end
```

Subinterface command configuration defining Frame Relay DLCIs and assigning protocols to specific DLCIs

You can use the following commands in Software Release 9.1 and later to achieve a configuration similar to the configuration shown in Figure 6-13:

```
Version 9.1
interface serial 0
ip address 131.108.3.12 255.255.255.0
decnet cost 10
novell network A3
frame-relay map IP 131.108.3.62 21 broadcast
frame-relay map DECNET 10.3 22 broadcast
frame-relay map NOVELL C09845 23 broadcast
```

Configuring Frame Relay Traffic Shaping

Beginning with Release 11.2, Cisco IOS supports Frame Relay traffic shaping, which provides the following features:

- **Rate enforcement on a per-virtual circuit basis**—The peak rate for outbound traffic can be set to the CIR or some other user-configurable rate.

- **Dynamic traffic throttling on a per-virtual circuit basis**—When BECN packets indicate congestion on the network, the outbound traffic rate is automatically stepped down; when congestion eases, the outbound traffic rate is stepped up again. This feature is enabled by default.

- **Enhanced queuing support on a per-virtual circuit basis**—Either custom queuing or priority queuing can be configured for individual virtual circuits.

By defining separate virtual circuits for different types of traffic, and specifying queuing and an outbound traffic rate for each virtual circuit, you can provide guaranteed bandwidth for each type of traffic. By specifying different traffic rates for different virtual circuits over the same time, you can perform virtual time division multiplexing. By throttling outbound traffic from high-speed lines in central offices to low-speed lines in remote locations, you can ease congestion and data loss in the network; enhanced queuing also prevents congestion-caused data loss. Traffic shaping applies to both PVCs and SVCs.

Voice over Frame Relay Design

Unlike most data applications, which can tolerate delay, voice communications must be performed in near real time. This means that transmission and network delays must be kept low enough and constant enough to remain imperceptible to the user. Historically, packetized voice transmission was impossible, due to the voice bandwidth requirements and transmission delays associated with packet-based networks. Also, integrating voice over data networks has only recently been well understood because of the challenges of designing and building a network that can accommodate the two very different types of traffic: data and voice. The remainder of this chapter is an introduction to the design and implementation characteristics of voice traffic and its behavior on a Frame Relay network.

Human Speech Characteristics

Human speech contains a significant amount of redundant information that is necessary for communications to occur in a conversation between persons in the same room, but which is not needed for a conversation to occur over a communications network. Typically, only 20% of a conversation consists of essential speech components that need to be transmitted for a successful voice conversation. The balance is made up of pauses, background noise, and repetitive patterns.

Packetized voice is possible and higher bandwidth efficiencies are attained by analyzing and processing only the essential components of the voice sample, instead of attempting to digitize the entire voice sample (with all the associated pauses and repetitive patterns). Current speech-processing technology takes the voice-digitizing process several steps further than conventional encoding methods.

Removing Repetition in Voice Conversations

Repetitive sounds are part of human speech, and are easily compressed. In a normal conversation, only about half of what is spoken will reach the listener's ear. In a typical communications network, however, all speech content is encoded and transmitted. Transmission of these identical sounds is not necessary and their removal can increase bandwidth efficiency.

Silence Suppression in Voice Conversations

A person speaking does not provide a continuous stream of information. Pauses between words and sentences, and those gaps that come at the end of one person talking but before the other begins, also can be removed to increase bandwidth efficiency. The pauses may be represented in compressed form, and then can be regenerated at the destination to maintain the natural quality of the spoken communication.

Voice Frame Formation and Fragmentation

After the removal of repetitive patterns and silent periods, the remaining speech information may then be digitized and placed into voice packets suitable for transmission over Frame Relay networks. These packets or frames also tend to be smaller than average data frames. These frame sizes and the compression algorithms are specified in the Frame Relay Forum specifications FRF.11 and FRF.12 (see Figure 6-14).

Figure 6-14 *FRF.11 and FRF.12 Specifications*

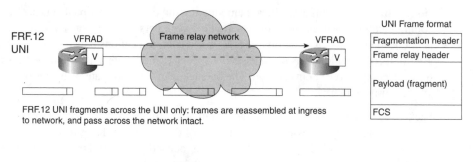

FRF.12 UNI fragments across the UNI only: frames are reassembled at ingress to network, and pass across the network intact.

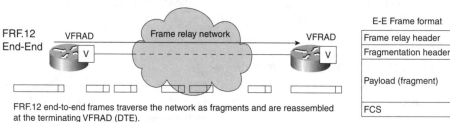

FRF.12 end-to-end frames traverse the network as fragments and are reassembled at the terminating VFRAD (DTE).

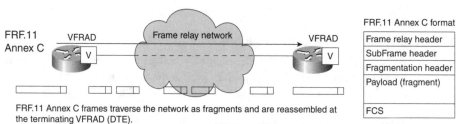

FRF.11 Annex C frames traverse the network as fragments and are reassembled at the terminating VFRAD (DTE).
However, FRF.11 Annex C allows for a subframe header which allows many different channels of different types to be multiplexed onto a single network PVC.

The frame size is encoded using the encoding and compression algorithm used in ITU (International Telecommunications Union) standard number G.729, Conjugate-Structure-Algebraic Code-Excited-Linear-Predictive (CSA-CELP). Then, the frame is typically fragmented to remove large variable delay components. The use of smaller packets helps to reduce overall transmission delay and variability of delay across a Frame Relay network, and the compression algorithm reduces the overall bandwidth requirement.

Voice Compression Algorithms

Compression of voice involves the removal of silent periods, removing redundant information found in human speech, and applying specific algorithms to the coded bitstream of sampled voice traffic. Uncompressed digitized voice and fax require a large amount of bandwidth, typically 64 kbps. The 64-kbps rate is arrived at by multiplying the sampling rate (8000 samples per second) by the number of bits per sample (8). One of the methods to achieve lower bit rates is requiring fewer bits per sample, such as 5, 4, 3, or even 2 bits per sample (as specified in ITU G.726, Adaptive Differential Pulse Code Modulation, or ADPCM). The use of low bit-rate voice compression algorithms can make it possible to provide high-quality speech while using bandwidth efficiently.

Various algorithms are used to sample the speech pattern and reduce the information sent— all while retaining the highest voice-quality level possible. There are three basic types of voice coders: waveform coders, vocoders, and hybrid coders. Pulse Code Modulation (PCM) is an ITU standard (G.711) waveform coder, consumes 64 kbps, and is optimized for speech quality. PCM is the voice-encoding algorithm commonly used in telephone networks today. The Adaptive Differential Pulse Code Modulation (ADPCM) algorithm is an ITU standard (G.726) waveform coder. ADPCM can reduce the speech data rate to at least half that of PCM, and may be used in place of PCM while maintaining about the same voice quality. See Table 6-2 for various compression algorithms and their associated bandwidth requirements. (The bandwidth requirements in Table 6-2 are from the ITU G series specifications.)

Table 6-2   *Compression Algorithms*

ITU Encoding/Compression	Result Bit Rate
G.711 PCM	64 kbps (DS0)
A-Law/μ-Law	
G.726 ADPCM	16, 24, 32, 40 kbps
G.729 CS-ACELP	8 kbps
G.728 LD-CELP	16 kbps
G.723.1 CELP	6.3/5.3 kbps variable

Reducing the speech bandwidth requirements further and maintaining good voice quality through the use of vocoders and hybrid coders require the use of advanced compression algorithms made possible by the use of digital signal processors (DSPs). A DSP is a microprocessor designed specifically to process digitized signals such as those found in voice applications. Significant advances in the design of DSPs have occurred, and there are a number of standard low bit-rate voice-compression algorithms (such as the ITU G.729 hybrid coder) that provide significant reductions in the amount of information required to compress and reproduce speech. A G.729 coder generates only an 8 kbps bitstream from the 64 kbps origin PCM bitstream, for example, yielding 8:1 compression. Other algorithms such as ITU G.723.1 compress further, to as low as 5.3 kbps.

As the available bit rate is reduced from 64 kbps to 32, 16, or 8 kbps or below, DSP processors and other advanced compression algorithms allow the possibility of accomplishing voice compression within Voice over Frame Relay–capable devices at lower and lower bit rates.

Echo Phenomenon and Echo Cancelers

Echo is a phenomenon found in voice networks. Echo occurs when the transmitted voice is reflected back to the point from which it was transmitted. Echo is typically caused by a reflection of voice energy within a device called a hybrid, which converts a two-wire local loop copper pair to a four-wire interface for long-distance transmission. When there is an impedance mismatch between the two–wire and the four-wire interfaces, the voice energy that cannot be passed along the path of transmission is reflected back to the source (see Figure 6-15).

Figure 6-15 *Echo Phenomenon*

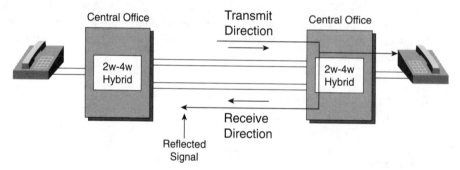

In voice networks, echo cancellation devices are used within a carrier's network when the propagation delay increases to the point where echo is made worse as a result of the combination of the reflected energy and a significant delay component of the end-to-end transmission of a voice conversation. Figure 6-16 shows echo as a function of delay and power levels.

Figure 6-16 *Echo and Delay/Power Levels*

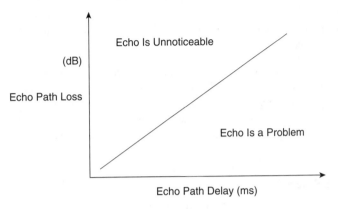

The longer the distance of the voice transmission, the more delay is expected and the more likely that echo will result. Voice transmitted over a Frame Relay network will also face propagation delays. As the end-to-end delay increases, the echo becomes noticeable to the end user if it is not canceled (see Figure 6-17).

Figure 6-17 *Echo Canceler Function*

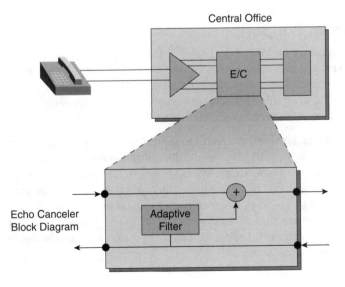

Delay and Delay Variation Transport Issues

The bursty nature and variable frame sizes of Frame Relay may result in variable delays between consecutive packets. The variation in the time difference between each arriving packet is called *jitter*.

Jitter can cause the equipment at the receiving end customer's premises to have difficulty regenerating voice in a smooth and even fashion. Because voice is inherently a continuous wave form, a large gap between the regenerated voice packets will result in a distorted sound. To avoid dropping frames, data can be buffered at the speech decoder sufficiently to account for the worst-case delay variation through the network.

Frame Loss Issues

The application of Voice over Frame Relay networks can usually withstand infrequent packet loss better than data. If a Voice over Frame Relay packet is lost, the user will most likely not notice. If excessive frame loss occurs, it is equally unacceptable for Voice over Frame Relay and data traffic. Packet loss can occur as a result of queue overflow or when bit errors are introduced into the frame along the transmission path and the CRC (cyclic redundancy check) error-checking mechanism detects errors and drops the frame. In either case, the voice transmission can be sufficiently degraded as to be unusable.

Fax and Modem Support

It is necessary for Voice over Frame Relay to support fax and data modem services. Voice band fax and data modem signals can be demodulated and transmitted as digital data in packet format. This is typically referred to as *fax relay*, and can add efficiency to the overall support of fax traffic on a data network, without the requirement to modulate and demodulate fax over a voice channel at 64 kbps.

It is difficult, however, to reliably compress fax and data modem signals over voice channels to achieve the low-bandwidth utilization often necessary for the most efficient integration over Frame Relay. Typical Frame Relay switch interfaces use a scheme in which voice is compressed to a low bit rate, but upon detection of a fax tone, the bandwidth is reallocated to a 64 kbps rate to allow for support of higher-speed fax transmission. The typical requirement is a 64 kbps channel, supporting Group 3 fax at 14.4 kbps. If the equipment supports fax relay, the bit rate of the fax transmission remains 14.4 kbps across the entire transmission path.

Traffic Prioritization across Frame Relay Transport

Voice, fax, and some data types are delay-sensitive. This means that if the end-to-end delay or delay variation exceeds a specified limit, the service level will degrade. To minimize the potential for service degradation, one can employ a variety of mechanisms and techniques.

To minimize voice traffic delay, a prioritization mechanism that provides service to the delay-sensitive traffic first can be employed. Equipment capable of integrating Voice over Frame Relay may provide a variety of proprietary mechanisms to ensure a balance between voice and data transmission needs. These may include custom, priority, or weighted queuing. Although they may differ, the concept remains the same. For example, each input traffic type may be configured into one of several priority queues. Voice and fax traffic can be placed in the highest-priority queue, and lower-priority data traffic can be queued until the higher-priority voice and fax packets are sent.

Prioritization places delay-sensitive traffic, such as voice, ahead of lower-priority data transmissions.

Delay Control Using Frame Fragmentation

Fragmentation is used to break up larger blocks of data into smaller, more predictable and manageable frames. Fragmentation attempts to ensure an even flow of voice frames into the network, minimizing delay (see Figure 6-14).

Fragmentation ensures that high-priority traffic such as voice does not have to wait to be sent. Long data packets can be interrupted to send a voice packet.

The fragmentation often affects all the data in the network to retain consistent voice quality. This is because even if the voice information is fragmented, delay will still occur if a voice frame is held up in the middle of the network behind a large data frame. This fragmentation of data packets ensures that voice and fax packets are not unacceptably delayed behind large data packets. Additionally, fragmentation reduces jitter because voice packets can be sent and received more regularly. Fragmentation, especially when used with prioritization techniques, is used to ensure a consistent flow of voice information. The objective of this technique is to enable Voice over Frame Relay technology to provide service approaching toll voice quality, while allowing the data transmission on the same network to use the remaining bandwidth efficiently.

Silence Removal Using Digital Speech Interpolation

Digital speech interpolation (DSI) is also known as voice activity detection (VAD). The nature of speech communication includes pauses between words and sentences. VAD-compression algorithms, which identify and remove these periods of silence, effectively reduce the overall amount of speech information to be transmitted. DSI uses advanced voice-processing techniques to detect silent periods and suppress transmission of this information. By taking advantage of this technique, bandwidth consumption may be reduced (see Figure 6-18).

Figure 6-18 *VAD Silence Removal*

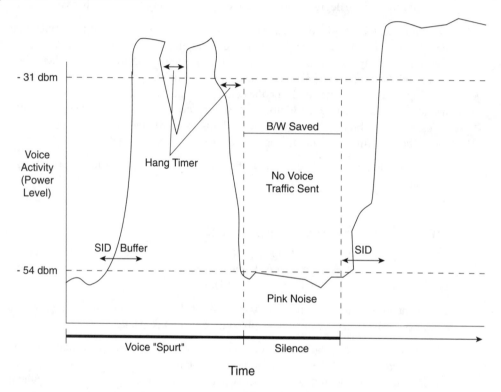

Bandwidth Optimization Using Multiplexing Techniques

Some equipment vendors offer voice Frame Relay Access Devices (FRADs) that use different bandwidth-optimization multiplexing techniques, such as logical link multiplexing and subchannel multiplexing. Logical link multiplexing allows voice and data frames to share the same PVC, and thus enables the user to save on carrier PVC charges and to increase the utilization of the PVC.

Subchannel multiplexing is a technique used to combine multiple voice conversations within the same frame. By allowing multiple voice payloads to be sent in a single frame, packet overhead is reduced. This may offer increased performance on low-speed links. This technique can allow slow-speed connections to transport small voice packets efficiently across the Frame Relay network.

Summary

This chapter focused on the implementation of packet-switching services and addressed network design in terms of the packet-switching service topics, including hierarchical network design, topology design, broadcast issues, and performance issues. Also covered were Voice over Frame Relay networking design considerations.

CHAPTER 7

Designing APPN Networks

Edited by Nicole Park

Advanced Peer-to-Peer Networking (APPN) is a second generation of the Systems Network Architecture (SNA) from IBM. It moves SNA from a hierarchical, mainframe-centric environment to a peer-to-peer environment. It provides capabilities similar to other LAN protocols, such as dynamic resource definition and route discovery.

This chapter focuses on developing the network design and planning a successful migration to APPN. It covers the following topics:

- Evolution of SNA
- When to Use APPN as Part of a Network Design
- When to Use APPN Versus Alternative Methods of SNA Transport
- Overview of APPN
- Scalability Issues
- Backup Techniques in an APPN Network
- APPN in a Multiprotocol Environment
- Network Management
- Configuration Examples

Although this chapter does discuss using APPN with DLSw+, for detailed information on using DLSw+, refer to Chapter 8, "Designing DLSw+ Networks."

Evolution of SNA

Introduced in 1974, subarea SNA made the mainframe computer running Advanced Communications Function/Virtual Telecommunication Access Method (ACF/VTAM) the hub of the network. The mainframe was responsible for establishing all sessions (a connection between two resources over which data can be sent), activating resources, and deactivating resources. The design point of subarea SNA was reliable delivery of information across low-speed analog lines. Resources were explicitly predefined. This eliminated the need for broadcast traffic and minimized header overhead.

Many enterprises today maintain two networks: a traditional, hierarchical SNA subarea network and an interconnected LAN network based on connectionless, dynamic protocols. The advantage of the subarea SNA network is that it is manageable and provides predictable response time. The disadvantages are that it requires extensive system definition and does not take advantage of the capabilities of intelligent devices (for example, the PCs and workstations).

Role of APPN

With APPN, you can consolidate the two networks (an SNA subarea network and an interconnected LAN network) because APPN has many of the characteristics of the LAN networks and still offers the advantages of an SNA network. The major benefits of using APPN include the following:

- Connections are peer-to-peer, allowing any end user to initiate a connection with any other end user without the mainframe (VTAM) involvement.

- APPN supports subarea applications as well as newer peer-to-peer applications over a single network.

- APPN provides an effective routing protocol to allow SNA traffic to flow natively and concurrently with other protocols in a single network.

- Traditional SNA class of service (CoS)/transmission priority can be maintained.

As SNA has evolved, one feature has remained critical to many users: CoS. This feature provides traffic prioritization on an SNA session basis on the backbone. This, in turn, allows a single user to have sessions with multiple applications, each with a different CoS. In APPN, this feature offers more granularity and extends this capability all the way to the end node rather than just between communication controllers.

Types of APPN Nodes

An APPN network has three types of nodes: LEN nodes, end nodes (ENs), and network nodes (NNs), as shown in Figure 7-1.

Throughout the rest of this chapter, the abbreviations EN and NN are used occasionally and stand for end node and network node, respectfully.

Table 7-1 describes these different types of APPN nodes. The control point (CP), which is responsible for managing a node's resources and adjacent node communication in APPN, is key to an APPN node. The APPN control point is the APPN equivalent of the SSCP.

Figure 7-1   *Different Types of APPN Nodes*

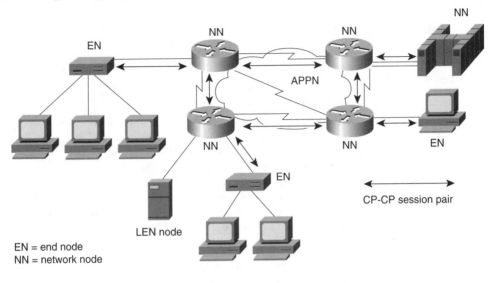

EN = end node
NN = network node

SSCP: System Service Control Point

In traditional SNA networking (also known as subarea routing), VTAM is the main component that controls all SNA resources such as application subsystems (CICS, TSO, and IMS), control units (3174, 3274), FEP, terminals, and printers. SSCP function of VTAM defines and activates/deactivates those resources.

Table 7-1   *Different Types of APPN Nodes*

Type of APPN Node	Description
Local Entry Networking (LEN) nodes	LEN nodes are pre-APPN, peer-to-peer nodes. They can participate in an APPN network by using the services provided by an adjacent network node. The CP of the LEN node manages the local resources but does not establish a CP-CP session with the adjacent network node. Session partners must be predefined to the LEN node, and the LEN node must be predefined to the adjacent network node. LEN nodes are also referred to as SNA node type 2.1, physical unit (PU) type 2.1, or PU2.1.
End nodes	End nodes contain a subset of full APPN functionality. They access the network through an adjacent network node and use the adjacent network node's routing services. An end node establishes a CP-CP session with an adjacent network node, and then uses that session to register resources, request directory services, and request routing information.

continues

Table 7-1   *Different Types of APPN Nodes (Continued)*

Type of APPN Node	Description
	An end node selects network-node server (NNS) when multiple candidate NNSs are available. The architecture doesn't define how to select NNS.
	It can be done by preferred NNS list or first-available NNS. It's up to the vendor implementation.
Network nodes	Network nodes contain full APPN functionality. The CP in a network node is responsible for managing the resources of the network node along with the attached end nodes and LEN nodes. The CP establishes CP-CP sessions with adjacent end nodes and network nodes. It also maintains network topology and directory databases, which are created and updated by dynamically gathering information from adjacent network nodes and end nodes over CP-CP sessions. In an APPN environment, network nodes are connected by transmission groups (TGs), which, in the current APPN architecture, refers to a single link. Consequently, the network topology is a combination of network nodes and transmission groups.

For more background information on APPN, refer to the section "Overview of APPN," later in this chapter.

When to Use APPN as Part of a Network Design

APPN has two key advantages over other protocols:

- Native SNA routing
- CoS for guaranteed service delivery

APPN, like Transmission Control Protocol/Internet Protocol (TCP/IP), is a routable protocol in which routing decisions are made at the network nodes. Although only the network node adjacent to the originator of the session selects the session path, every network node contributes to the process by keeping every other network node informed about the network topology. The network node adjacent to the destination also participates by providing detailed information about the destination. Only routers running as APPN network nodes can make routing decisions.

LEN and EN are always the end points of sessions. They rely on NN for routing decisions. NN computes the best route for sessions.

You need APPN in your network when a routing decision (for example, which data center or path) must be made. Figure 7-2 helps to illustrate the criteria you use to determine where APPN should be used in a network.

Figure 7-2   *Determining Where to Use APPN in a Network*

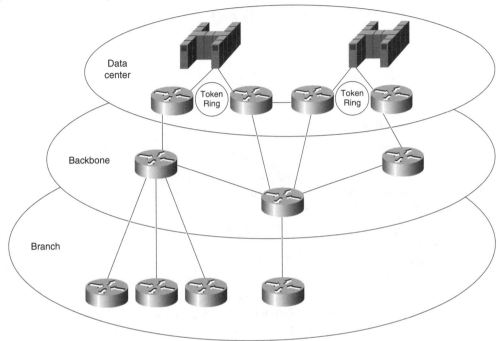

In Figure 7-2, a single link connects the branch office to the backbone. Therefore, a routing decision does not need to be made at the branch office. Consequently, an APPN network node might not be necessary at those sites.

Because there are two data centers, however, the routing decision about which data center to send the message to must be made. This routing decision can be made either at the data center or at the backbone routers. If you want this routing decision made at the data center, all messages are sent to a single data center using DLSw+, for example, and then routed to the correct data center, using APPN only in the routers in the data center. If you want the routing decision to be made at the backbone routers, place the APPN network node in the backbone routers, where alternative paths are available for routing decisions outside of the data center. In this example, this latter approach is preferred because it isolates the function at the data centers' routers to channel attachment, reduces the number of hops to the second data center, and provides a path to a backup data center if something catastrophic occurs.

Because APPN requires more memory and additional software, it is generally a more expensive solution. The advantages of direct APPN routing and CoS, however, often offset the added expense. In this case, the added expense to add APPN to the backbone and data-center routers might be justifiable, whereas added expense at the branch might not be justifiable.

APPN Network Node at Every Branch

Adding an APPN network node at every branch can be cost justified under the following circumstances:

- When CoS is required
- When branch-to-branch routing is required

When CoS Is Required

CoS implies that the user accesses multiple applications and must be able to prioritize traffic at an application level. Although other priority schemes, such as custom queuing, might be able to prioritize by end user, they cannot prioritize among applications for an individual user. If this capability is critical, APPN network nodes must be placed in the individual branches to consolidate the traffic among multiple users using CoS. CoS can ensure, for example, that credit-card verification always gets priority over batch receipts to a retail company's central site.

It is important to understand where CoS is used in the network today. If the network is a subarea SNA network, CoS is used only between front-end processors (FEPs) and ACF/VTAMs between two ACF/VTAMs, and between FEPs. Unless there is already an FEP at the branch office, they do not have traffic prioritization from the branch, although traffic can be prioritized from the FEP out. In this case, adding an APPN network node at the branch office would prioritize the traffic destined for the data center sooner rather than waiting until it reaches the FEP-adding function over what is available today.

When Branch-to-Branch Routing Is Required

If branch-to-branch traffic is required, you can send all traffic to the central site and let those APPN network nodes route to the appropriate branch office. This is the obvious solution when both data-center and branch-to-branch traffic are required and the branch is connected to the backbone over a single link. If a separate direct link to another branch is cost-justifiable, however, routing all traffic to the data center is unacceptable. In this case, making the routing decision at the branch is necessary. Using an APPN network node at the branch, data-center traffic is sent over the data-center link and branch-to-branch traffic is sent over the direct link.

In the example in Figure 7-3, each branch has two links to alternative routers at the data center. This is a case where APPN network nodes might be required at the branches so that the appropriate link can be selected. This can also be the design for branch-to-branch routing, adding a single hop rather than creating a full mesh of lines. This provides more direct routing than sending everything through the data center.

Figure 7-3   *Sample Network for Which Branch-to-Branch Routing Is Required*

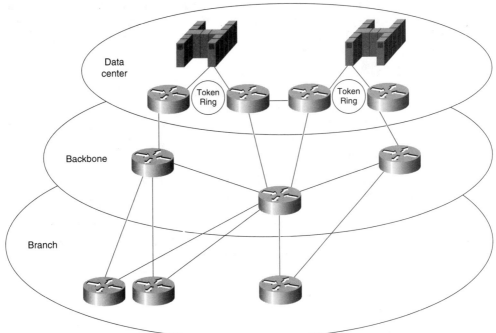

As you also learn in this chapter, scalability issues make it advantageous to keep the number of network nodes as small as possible. Understanding where native routing and CoS is needed is key to minimizing the number of network nodes.

In summary, choosing where to implement APPN must be decided based on cost, scalability, and where native routing and CoS are needed. Implementing APPN everywhere in your network might seem to be an obvious solution, even when not necessary. It must be understood, however, that if you were to deploy APPN everywhere in your network, it probably would be a more costly solution than necessary and may potentially lead to scalability problems. Consequently, the best solution is to deploy APPN only where it is truly needed in your network.

When to Use APPN Versus Alternative Methods of SNA Transport

APPN and boundary network node (BNN)/boundary access node (BAN) over Frame Relay using RFC 1490 are the two methods of native SNA transport, where SNA is not encapsulated in another protocol. BAN and BNN allow direct connection to an FEP, using the Frame Relay network to switch messages, rather than providing direct SNA routing.

Although *native* might seem to be the appropriate strategy, APPN comes at the price of cost and network scalability, as indicated in the preceding section. With BNN/BAN, additional cost is required to provide multiprotocol networking because the FEP does not handle multiple protocols. This implies that additional routers are required in the data center for other protocols, and separate virtual circuits are required to guarantee service delivery for the SNA or APPN traffic.

DLSw+ provides encapsulation of SNA, where the entire APPN message is carried as data inside a TCP/IP message. There is often concern about the extra 40 bytes of header associated with TCP/IP. Because Cisco offers alternatives such as data-link switching lite, Fast-Sequenced Transport (FST), and Direct Transport, which have shorter headers, header length is deemed noncritical to this discussion.

DLSw+ is attractive for those networks in which the end stations and data center will remain SNA-centric, but the backbone will be TCP/IP. This allows a single protocol across the backbone, while maintaining access to all SNA applications.

With the 11.3 CoS Priority Mapping feature, APPN CoS priority can be tied to IP precedence priority when you run APPN and DLSw+ on the same router to enable this feature.

Consequently, DLSw+ is preferable for networks, in which cost is a key criterion, that have the following characteristics:

- A single data center or mainframe
- Single links from the branches

In general, DLSw+ is a lower-cost solution that requires less memory and software. In the vast majority of networks, DLSw+ will be combined with APPN, using APPN only where routing decisions are critical. With TCP/IP encapsulation, the TCP layer provides the same reliable delivery as SNA/APPN, but does not provide the native routing and CoS.

TN3270 transports 3270 data stream inside a TCP/IP packet without SNA headers. Therefore, this solution assumes that the end station has only a TCP/IP protocol stack and no SNA. Therefore, TN3270 is not an alternative to APPN because APPN assumes that the end station has an SNA protocol stack. APPN, like DLSw+, may still be required in the network to route between TN3270 servers and multiple mainframes or data centers.

In summary, APPN will frequently be used with DLSw+ in networks when a single backbone protocol is desired. BAN/BNN provides direct connectivity to the FEP but lacks the multiprotocol capabilities of other solutions. TN3270 is used only for TCP/IP end stations.

Overview of APPN

This section provides an overview of APPN and covers the following topics:

- Defining Nodes
- Establishing APPN Sessions
- Understanding Intermediate Session Routing
- Using Dependent Logical Unit Requester/Server

Defining Nodes

Nodes, such as ACF/VTAM, OS/400, and Communications Server/2 (CS/2), can be defined as either network nodes or end nodes. When you have a choice, consider the following issues:

- **Network size**—How large is the network? Building large APPN networks can introduce scalability issues. Reducing the number of network nodes is one solution for avoiding scalability problems. For more information on reducing the number of network nodes, see the section titled "Reducing the Number of Network nodes," later in this chapter.
- **Role of the node**—Is it preferable to have this node performing routing functions as well as application processing? A separate network node can reduce processing cycles and memory requirements in an application processor.

Generally, you should define a network node whenever a routing decision needs to be made.

APPN Node Identifiers

An APPN node is identified by its network-qualified CP name, which has the format netid.name. The network identifier (netid) is an eight-character name that identifies the network or subnetwork in which the resource is located. The network identifier and name must be a combination of uppercase letters (A through Z), digits (0 through 9), and special characters ($, #, or @); but cannot have a digit as the first character.

Establishing APPN Sessions

For an APPN session to be established, the following must occur:

1. The end user requests a session with an application, which causes the end node to begin the process of session establishment by sending a LOCATE message to its network-node server. For session initiation, the network-node server provides the path to the destination end node, which allows the originating end node to send messages directly to the destination. This is true for EN but not for LEN. LEN sends BIND to NNS. NNS does directory service (sending LOCATE to other NNs and ENs).

2 The network node uses directory services to locate the destination by first checking its internal directories. If the destination is not included in the internal directory, the network node sends a LOCATE request to the central directory server (CDS) if one is available. If a central directory server is not available, the network node sends a LOCATE broadcast to the adjacent network nodes that in turn propagate the LOCATE throughout the network. The network-node server of the destination returns a reply that indicates the location of the destination. NN finds CDS the location stored in the topology database.

3 Based on the location of the destination, the CoS requested by the originator of the session, the topology database, and the CoS tables, the network-node server of the originator selects the least-expensive path that provides the appropriate level of service.

4 The originating network-node server sends a LOCATE reply to the originating end node. The LOCATE reply provides the path to the destination.

5 The originating end node is then responsible for initiating the session. A BIND is sent from the originating end node to the destination end node, requesting a session. After the destination replies to the BIND, session traffic can flow.

Understanding Intermediate Session Routing

Session connectors are used in place of routing tables in APPN. The unique session identifier and port from one side of the node are mapped to the unique session identifier and port on the other side. As data traffic passes through the node, the unique session identifier in the header is swapped for the outgoing identifier and sent out on the appropriate port, as shown in Figure 7-4.

Figure 7-4 *Intermediate Session Routing Label Swap*

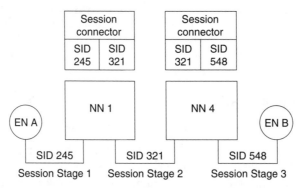

This routing algorithm is called *intermediate session routing* (ISR). It supports dynamic route definition and incorporates the following legacy features:

- **Node-to-node error and flow-control processing**—This reflects the 1970s method of packet-switching, in which many line errors dictated error and flow control at each node. Given the current high-quality digital facilities in many locations, this redundant processing is unnecessary and significantly reduces end-to-end throughput. End-to-end processing provides better performance and still delivers the necessary reliability.

- **Disruptive session switching around network failures**—Whenever a network outage occurs, all sessions using the path fail and have to be restarted to use an alternative path.

Because these features are undesirable in most high-speed networks today, a newer routing algorithm—High-Performance Routing (HPR)—has been added to APPN that supports nondisruptive rerouting around failures and end-to-end error control, flow control, and segmentation. Cisco routers support both ISR and HPR.

Using Dependent Logical Unit Requester/Server

Dependent Logical Unit Requester/Server (DLUR/DLUS) is an APPN feature that allows legacy traffic to flow on an APPN network. Prior to the introduction of this feature, the APPN architecture assumed that all nodes in a network could initiate peer-to-peer traffic (for example, sending the BIND to start the session). Many legacy terminals that are referred to as dependent logical units (DLUs) cannot do this and require VTAM to notify the application, which then sends the BIND.

Getting the legacy sessions initiated requires a client/server relationship between ACF/VTAM (Dependent LU Server—DLUS) and the Cisco router (Dependent LU Requester—DLUR). A pair of logical unit (LU) type 6.2 sessions are established between the DLUR and DLUS—one session is established by each end point. These sessions are used to transport the legacy control messages that must flow to activate the legacy resources and initiate their logical unit to logical unit (LU-LU) sessions. An LU-LU session is the connection formed when the five steps, described earlier in the section "Establishing APPN Sessions," are completed.

An activate logical unit (ACTLU) message must be sent to the LU to activate a legacy LU, for example. Because this message is not recognized in an APPN environment, it is carried as encapsulated data on the LU 6.2 session. DLUR then de-encapsulates it, and passes it to the legacy LU. Likewise, the DLU session request is passed to the ACF/VTAM DLUS, where it is processed as legacy traffic. DLUS then sends a message to the application host, which is responsible for sending the BIND. After the legacy LU-LU session is established, the legacy data flows natively with the APPN traffic, as shown in Figure 7-5.

Figure 7-5 *DLU Session Processing*

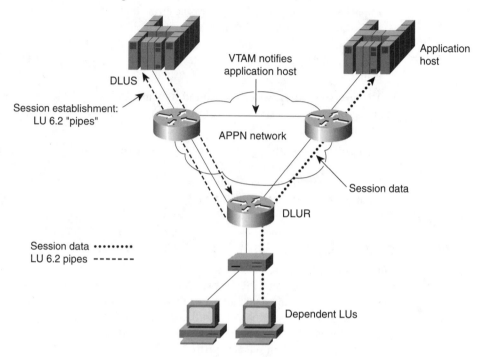

Cisco Implementation of APPN

This section provides an overview of Cisco's implementation of APPN and discusses where APPN resides in the Cisco IOS software. Cisco licensed the APPN source code from IBM and then ported it to the Cisco IOS software using network services from the data-link controls (DLCs).

Applications use APPN to provide network transport. APPN runs on top of the Cisco IOS software. APPN is a higher-layer protocol stack that requires network services from DLC. Cisco's APPN implementation is compliant with the APPN architecture of record. When used with other features in the Cisco IOS software, APPN provides the following unique features:

- APPN can use DLSw+ or RSRB as a network transport, thereby supporting APPN over a native TCP/IP network.

- APPN can be used with downstream physical unit concentration (DSPU) to reduce the number of downstream PUs visible to VTAM. This reduces VTAM definition and network restart times.

- In addition to CoS, priority queuing, custom queuing, and weighted fair queuing can be used with CoS to ensure traffic prioritization and bandwidth reservation between protocols.

- Network management options are supported that include native SNA management services, using Native Service Point (NSP) in the Cisco router, and the Simple Network Management Protocol (SNMP) management, using CiscoWorks Blue applications.

- Using Channel Interface Processor (CIP) or Channel Port Adapter (CPA), the Cisco APPN network node can interface directly with ACF/VTAM across the channel. VTAM can be defined either as an end node or network node.

Scalability Issues

As a single-network link-state architecture, the network topology is updated as changes occur. This results in significant network traffic if instability occurs, and significant memory and processing to maintain the large topology databases and CoS tables. Similarly, in large networks, dynamic discovery of resources can consume significant bandwidth and processing. For these reasons, scalability becomes a concern as network size increases. The number of nodes that are too large depends on the following:

- Amount of traffic

- Network stability

- The number of the techniques, which are described in this section, being used to control traffic and processing

Essentially, to allow growth of APPN networks, the network design must focus on reducing the number of topology database updates (TDUs) and LOCATE search requests.

Topology Database Update Reduction

APPN is a link-state protocol. Like other link-state–based algorithms, it maintains a database of the entire topology information of the network. Every APPN network node in the network sends out TDU packets that describe the current state of all its links to its adjacent network nodes. The TDU contains information that identifies the following:

- The characteristics of the sending node

- The node and link characteristics of the various resources in the network

- The sequence number of the most recent update for each described resource

Network nodes originate TDUs when TG is activated, when TG or network node change occurs, and periodically (every five days) even if there is no change.

A network node that receives a TDU packet propagates this information to its adjacent network nodes using a flow-reduction technique. Each APPN network node maintains full knowledge of the network and how the network is interconnected. When a network node detects a change to the network (either a change to the link, or the node), it floods TDUs throughout the network to ensure rapid convergence. If there is an unstable link in the network, it can potentially cause many TDU flows in a network.

As the number of network nodes and links increases, so does the number of TDU flows in your network. This type of distributing topology can consume significant CPU cycles, memory, and bandwidth. Maintaining routes and a large, complete topology subnet can require a significant amount of dynamic memory.

You can use the following techniques to reduce the amount of TDU flows in the network:

- Reduce the number of links
- Reduce the number of CP-CP sessions
- Reduce the number of network nodes in the network

Reducing the Number of Links

The first technique for reducing the amount of TDU flows in the network is to reduce the number of links in your network. In some configurations, it might be possible to use the concept of *connection network* to reduce the number of predefined links in your network. Because network nodes exchange information about their links, the fewer links you define, the fewer TDU flows can occur.

Figure 7-6 shows the physical view of an APPN network. In this network, NN1, NN2, and NN3 are routers attached to an FDDI LAN.

The network-node server (NNS), EN1, and EN2 hosts are attached to the same FDDI LAN via a CIP router or a cluster controller. These nodes on the FDDI LAN have any-to-any connectivity. To reflect any-to-any connectivity in APPN, NN1 needs to define a link to NN2, NN3, NNS (VTAM host), EN1 (VTAM data host), and EN2 (EN data host). The transmission groups connecting network nodes are contained in the network topology database. For every link defined to the network node, TDUs are broadcast.

Throughout the rest of this chapter, the abbreviation NNS is used in the illustrations. When the text refers to an NNS icon in an illustration, the abbreviation is also used; otherwise, the full term (network-node server) is used within the text for clarity.

Figure 7-6   *Physical View of an APPN Network*

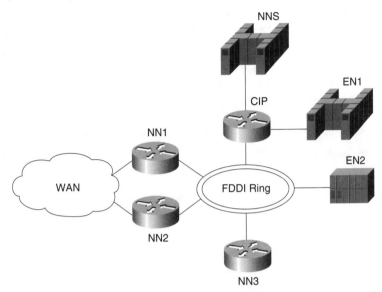

Figure 7-7 shows the logical view of the APPN network, shown earlier in Figure 7-6. When NN1 first joins the network, NN1 activates the links to NN2, NN3, NNS, EN1, and EN2. CP-CP sessions are established with the adjacent network nodes. Each adjacent network node sends a copy of the current topology database to NN1. Similarly, NN1 creates a TDU about itself and its links to other network nodes and sends this information over the CP-CP sessions to NN2, NN3, and NNS. When NN2 receives the TDU from NN1, it forwards the TDU to its adjacent network nodes, which are NN3 and NNS. Similarly, NN3 and NNS receive the TDU from NN1 and broadcast this TDU to their adjacent network nodes. The result is that every network node receives multiple copies of the TDU.

Figure 7-7   *Logical View of an APPN Network without Connection Network Deployed*

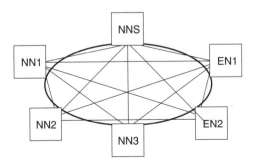

The transmission groups that connect the end nodes are not contained in the network topology database. Consequently, no TDUs are broadcast for the two links to EN1 and EN2. If the number of transmission groups connecting network nodes can be reduced, the number of TDU flows can also be reduced.

By using the concept of connection networks, you can eliminate the transmission group definitions, and therefore reduce TDU flows. A connection network is a single virtual routing node (VRN), which provides any-to-any connectivity for any of its attached nodes. The VRN is not a physical node, it is a logical entity that indicates that nodes are using a connection network and a direct routing path can be selected.

Figure 7-8 shows the APPN network shown in Figure 7-6 with connection network deployed.

Figure 7-8 *Logical View of an APPN Network with Connection Network Deployed*

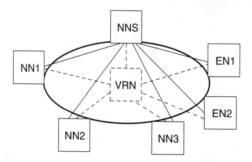

NN1, NN2, and NN3 define a link to the network-node server (NNS) and a link to the VRN. When the link between NN1 and NNS is activated, NNS sends a copy of the current network topology database to NN1. NN1 creates a TDU about itself, its link to NNS, and its link to the VRN. It then sends this information to NNS. NN1 does not have a link defined to NN2 and NN3; therefore, there are no TDUs sent to NN2 and NN3 from NN1. When NNS receives the TDU information from NN1, NNS forwards it to NN2 and NN3. Neither NN2 nor NN3 forwards the TDU information because they only have a connection to NNS. This significantly reduces the number of TDU flows in the network.

When a session is activated between resources on the connection network, the network-node server recognizes that this is a connection network and selects a direct route rather than routing through its own network nodes. Cisco recommends that you apply the concept of connection networks whenever possible. Not only does it reduce the number of TDU flows in the network, it also greatly reduces system definitions.

As shown in the example, a LAN (Ethernet, Token Ring, or FDDI) can be defined as a connection network. With ATM LAN Emulation (LANE) services, you can interconnect ATM networks with traditional LANs. From APPN's perspective, because an ATM-emulated LAN is just another LAN, a connection network can be applied. In addition to LANs, the concept of connection networks can apply to X.25, Frame Relay, and ATM networks. It should also be noted that technologies such as RSRB and DLSw appear as LANs to APPN. You can also use connection networks in these environments. APPN, in conjunction with DLSw+ or RSRB, provides a synergy between routing and bridging for SNA traffic.

Reducing the Number of CP-CP Sessions

The second technique for reducing the amount of TDU flows in the network is to reduce the number of CP-CP sessions in your network. Network nodes exchange topology updates over CP-CP sessions. The number of CP-CP sessions has a direct impact on the number of TDU flows in the network.

In Figure 7-9, for example, NN2, NN3, NN4, and NN5 are in a fully meshed network. Every network node establishes CP-CP sessions with its adjacent network nodes. This means that NN2 establishes CP-CP sessions with NN3, NN4, and NN5. NN3 establishes CP-CP sessions with NN2, NN4, NN5, and so forth.

Figure 7-9   *Fully Meshed CP-CP Sessions*

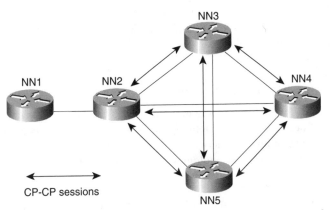

If the link fails between NN1 and NN2, TDU updates are broadcast from NN2 to NN3, NN4, and NN5. When NN3 receives the TDU update, it resends this information to NN4 and NN5. Similarly, when NN5 receives the TDU update, it resends this information to NN3 and NN4. This means that NN4 receives the same information three times. You should keep the number of CP-CP sessions to a minimum so that duplicate TDU information will not be received.

In Figure 7-10, CP-CP sessions exist only between NN2 and NN3, NN2 and NN4, and NN2 and NN5; no other CP-CP sessions exist. When the link fails between NN1 and NN2, NN2 broadcasts transmission group updates to NN3, NN4, and NN5. None of the three NNs forwards this information to the rest of the network because CP-CP sessions do not exist. Although this minimizes the TDU flows, if the link between NN2 and NN3 fails, this becomes a disjointed APPN network and NN3 is isolated.

Figure 7-10 *Single Pair of CP-CP Sessions*

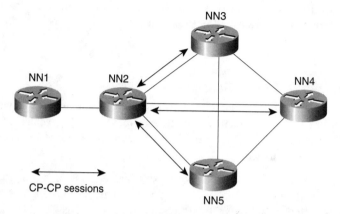

Figure 7-11 shows a more efficient design that also provides redundancy. Every network node has CP-CP sessions with two adjacent network nodes. NN2 has CP-CP sessions with NN3 and NN5. If the link between NN2 and NN3 fails, TDU updates will be sent via NN5 and NN4.

For redundancy purposes, each network node should have CP-CP sessions to two other network nodes if possible.

Reducing the Number of Network Nodes

The third technique for reducing the amount of TDU flows in the network is to reduce the number of network nodes by defining APPN nodes only at the edges of the network. Minimizing the number of network nodes also reduces the size of the network topology. The following are some technologies for reducing the number of network nodes:

- APPN over DLSw+
- APPN over Frame Relay Access Server (FRAS)/BNN or BAN
- APPN over RSRB

Figure 7-11 *Dual Pair of CP-CP Sessions*

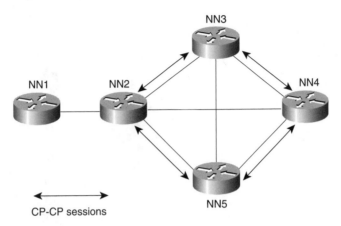

CP-CP sessions

APPN over DLSw+

Data-link switching is one way to reduce the number of network nodes in the network. DLSw+ is a means of transporting APPN traffic across a WAN, in which APPN network nodes or end nodes are defined only at the edges of the network. Intermediate routing is through DLSw+ and not via native SNA.

DLSw+ defines a standard to integrate SNA/APPN and LAN networks by encapsulating these protocols within IP. Cisco's implementation of DLSw, known as DLSw+, is a superset of the current DLSw architecture. DLSw+ has many value-added features not available in other vendors' DLSw implementations. APPN, when used with DLSw, can benefit from the many scalability enhancements implemented in DLSw+, such as border peer, on-demand peers, caching algorithms, and explorer firewalls.

In Figure 7-12, sessions between end-node workstations and the host are transported over the DLSw+ network.

Figure 7-12 *APPN with DLSw+*

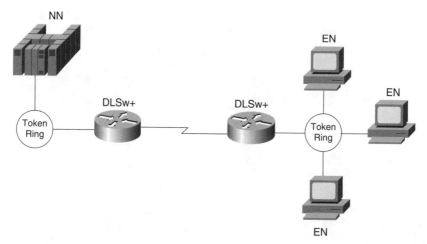

VTAM acts as the network-node server for remote end-node workstations. Optionally, if multiple VTAMs or data centers exist, APPN on the channel-attached router(s) or on other routers in the data center can offload VTAM by providing the SNA routing capability, as shown in Figure 7-13.

Figure 7-13 *APPN with DLSw+ Using a Channel-Attached Router*

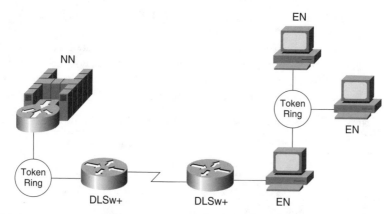

DLSw+ also brings nondisruptive rerouting in the event of a WAN failure. Using DLSw+ as a transport reduces the number of network nodes in the network. A disadvantage is that remote end-node workstations require WAN connections for NNS services. Another disadvantage is that without APPN in the routers, APPN transmission priority is lost when traffic enters the DLSw+ network.

For detailed information on DLSw and DLSw+, refer to Chapter 8, "Designing DLSw+ Networks."

APPN over FRAS BNN/BAN

If the APPN network is based on a Frame Relay network, one option is to use the FRAS/BNN or the Frame Relay BAN function for host access. Both BNN and BAN allow a Cisco router to attach directly to a FEP. When you use FRAS/BNN, you are assuming that the Frame Relay network is performing the switching and that native routing is not used within the Frame Relay network. For an example of how APPN with FRAS BNN/BAN can be used in your network design, see the section "Example of APPN with FRAS BNN," later in this chapter.

APPN over RSRB

Using RSRB, the SNA traffic can be bridged from a remote site to a data center. The use of RSRB significantly reduces the total number of network nodes in the network, thus reducing the number of TDU flows in the network. Another advantage of using RSRB is that it provides nondisruptive routing in the event of a link failure.

LOCATE Search Reduction

This section describes the broadcast traffic in an APPN network and how LOCATE searches can become a scalability issue in an APPN network. The impact of LOCATE searches in an APPN network varies from one network to the other. This section first identifies some of the causes of an excessive number of LOCATE searches, and then discusses the following four techniques you can use to minimize them:

- Safe-Store of Directory Cache
- Partial Directory Entries
- Central Directory Server (CDS)/Client
- Central Resource Registration

An APPN network node provides dynamic location of network resources. Every network node maintains dynamic knowledge of the resources in its own directory database. The distributed directory database contains a list of all the resources in the network. The LOCATE search request allows one network node to search the directory database of all other network nodes in the network.

When an end-node resource requests a session with a target resource that it has no knowledge of, it uses the distributed search capabilities of its network-node server to locate the target resource. If the network node does not have any knowledge of the target resource, the network node forwards the LOCATE search request to all its adjacent network nodes, requesting these nodes to assist the network-node server to locate the resource. These adjacent network nodes propagate these LOCATE search requests to their adjacent network nodes. This search process is known as *broadcast search*.

Although several mechanisms are put into place to reduce the LOCATE broadcast searches (for example, resource registration and resource caching), there might still be an excessive amount of LOCATE flows in a network for such reasons as the network resources no longer exist, there is a mixture of subarea networks and APPN networks, or the resources are temporarily unavailable.

Safe-Store of Directory Cache

The first technique that you can use to minimize the LOCATE flows in your APPN network is the safe-store of directory cache, which is supported by the Cisco network-node implementation. Cache entries in a network node's directory database can be periodically written to a permanent storage medium: a tftp host. This speeds recovery after a network-node outage or initial power loss. Resources do not have to be relearned through a LOCATE broadcast search after a router failure. This reduces spikes of broadcasts that might otherwise occur when the APPN network is restarted.

Partial Directory Entries

The second technique that you can use to minimize the LOCATE flows in your APPN network is to define the resources in the local directory database by identifying the end node or network node where the particular resource is located.

The following is a sample configuration:

```
appn partner-lu-location CISCO.LU21
owning-cp CISCO.CP2
complete
```

The preceding example defines the location of a LU named CISCO.LU21 that is located with end node or network node CISCO.CP2. This command improves network performance by allowing directed LOCATE rather than a broadcast. The disadvantage is that definitions must be created. To alleviate this definition problem, it may be possible to use partially specified names to define multiple resources.

The following is a sample configuration:

```
Sample configuration:
appn partner-lu-location CISCO.LU
owning-cp CISCO.CP2
wildcard
complete
```

The preceding example defines the location of all the LUs prefixed with the characters LU. Obviously, a naming convention is essential to the success of this type of node definition.

Central Directory Server (CDS)/Client

The third technique that you can use to minimize the LOCATE flows in your APPN network is to use the CDS/client function. The APPN architecture specifies a CDS that allows a designated network node to act as a focal point for locating network resources. In current APPN networks, every network node can potentially perform a broadcast search for a resource. This is because the directory services database is not replicated on every network node.

The CDS function allows a network node, with central directory client support, to send a directed LOCATE search to a CDS. If the CDS has no knowledge of the resource, it performs one broadcast search to find the resource. After the resource is found, the CDS caches the results in its directory. Subsequently, the CDS can provide the location of the resource to other network nodes without performing another broadcast search. The Cisco network-node implementation supports the central directory client function. VTAM is the only product that currently implements the CDS function.

Using the CDS means that there is a maximum of one broadcast search per resource in the network. This significantly reduces the amount of network traffic used for resource broadcast searching. You can define multiple CDSs in an APPN network. A network node learns the existence of a CDS via TDU exchange. If more than one CDS exists, the nearest one is used based on the number of hop counts. If a CDS fails, the route to the nearest alternative CDS is calculated automatically.

Central Resource Registration

The fourth technique that you can use to minimize the LOCATE flows in your APPN network is to use the central resource registration function. An end node registers its local resources at its network-node server. If every resource is registered, all network nodes can query the CDS, which eliminates the need for broadcast searches.

Activation of the CP-CP session and subsequent activation of a major node causes registration to take place.

Major nodes that include resources have a register parameter that determines whether the resources are to be registered with the network-node server or central directory server, or not registered at all.

Backup Techniques in an APPN Network

This section provides an overview of the various backup techniques in an APPN network. The backup and recovery scenarios are representative of common environments and requirements. The following three backup scenarios are discussed:

- A secondary WAN link as a backup to a primary WAN link
- Dual WAN links and dual routers providing full redundancy
- APPN DLUR backup support using a Cisco CIP router

Link Backup

The first backup technique that you can use in your APPN network is to use a secondary WAN link as a backup to your primary WAN link. By using the concept of auto-activation on demand, you can back up a primary WAN link with a secondary WAN link by using any supported protocols (for example, Point-to-Point [PPP], Switched Multimegabit Data Service [SMDS], and X.25), as shown in Figure 7-14.

Figure 7-14 *Link Backup*

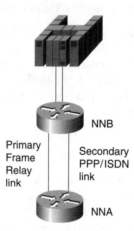

In Figure 7-14, the Frame Relay link is the primary link and the ISDN dial link is the backup link. The requirement is that the ISDN link provides instantaneous backup for the primary link and it remains inactive until the primary link goes down. No manual intervention is needed. To support this, NNA needs to define two parallel transmission groups to NNB.

The primary link is defined by using the following configuration command:

```
appn link-station PRIMARY
port FRAME_RELAY
fr-dest-address 35
retry-limit infinite
complete
```

The secondary link is defined as supporting auto-activation by using the following configuration command:

```
appn link-station SECONDARY
port PPP
no connect-at-startup
adjacent-cp-name NETA.NNB
activate-on-demand
complete
```

By specifying **no connect-at-startup**, the secondary link is not activated upon APPN node startup. To indicate auto-activation support, specify **adjacent-cp-name** and **activate-on-demand**.

When the primary link fails, APPN detects the link failure and CP-CP session's failure, which is disruptive to any existing LU-LU sessions. Because there are multiple links from NNA to NNB, NNA attempts to re-establish the CP-CP sessions over the secondary link. The CP-CP session's request will activate the secondary dial link automatically.

To ensure that the Frame Relay link is used as primary and the dial PPP link is used as the backup, define the transmission group characteristics to reflect that. Use the **cost-per-connect-time** parameter, for example, to define the relative cost of using the dial PPP/ISDN link.

```
cost-per-connect-time 5
```

This will make the primary Frame Relay link a lower-cost route. Therefore, it is a more desirable route than the secondary dial link because the default cost-per-connect-time is zero. When the primary link becomes active, there is no mechanism in place to automatically switch the sessions back to the primary link. Manual intervention is required.

Full Redundancy

The second backup technique that you can use in your APPN network is dual WAN links and dual routers for full redundancy. In some cases, for example, complete fault tolerance is required for mission-critical applications across the network. You can have dual routers and dual links installed to provide protection against any kind of communications failure.

Figure 7-15 shows how you can use duplicate virtual MAC addresses via RSRB to provide full redundancy and load sharing.

Figure 7-15 *Full Redundancy*

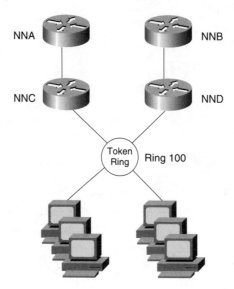

The router configuration for NNC is as follows:

```
source-bridge ring-group 200
!
interface TokenRing0
 ring-speed 16
 source 100 1 200
!
appn control-point NETA.NNC
  complete
!
appn port RSRB rsrb
  rsrb-virtual-station 4000.1000.2000 50 2 200
  complete
```

The router configuration for NND is as follows:

```
source-bridge ring-group 300
!
interface TokenRing0
 ring-speed 16
 source 100 5 300
!
appn control-point NETA.NND
  complete
!
appn port RSRB rsrb
  rsrb-virtual-station 4000.1000.2000 60 3 300
  complete
```

Both NNC and NND define an RSRB port with the same virtual MAC address. Every workstation will define the RSRB virtual MAC address as its destination MAC address of its network-node server. Essentially, a workstation can use either NNC or NND as its network-node server, depending on which node answers the test explorer frame first. The route to NNC consists of the following routing information:

```
Ring 100 -> Bridge 1 -> Ring 200 -> Bridge 2 -> Ring 50
```

The route to NND will consist of the following routing information:

```
Ring 100 > Bridge 5 -> Ring 300 -> Bridge 3 -> Ring 60
```

When NND fails, sessions on NND can be re-established over NNC instantaneously. This is analogous to the duplicate Token Ring Interface Coupler (TIC) support on the FEP, except that no hardware is required. In Cisco's RSRB implementation, as shown in Figure 7-15, Segment 20 and Bridge 1, and Segment 30 and Bridge 2 are virtual. Duplicate MAC addresses can be supported without the hardware in place.

SSCP Takeover

The third backup technique is to use APPN DLUR with a Cisco CIP router to support transfer of resource ownership from one system services control point (SSCP) (VTAM) to another when a failure occurs. This includes maintaining existing sessions over the failure. DLUS/DLUR can provide the capability to transfer SSCP ownership from the primary SSCP to the backup SSCP. It then examines how DLUR can provide the capability to obtain SSCP services from the backup SSCP without terminating LU-LU sessions that are in progress.

Figure 7-16 illustrates how the FEP can be replaced with a CIP router running CIP SNA (CSNA).

Figure 7-16 *SSCP Takeover with APPN and CIP*

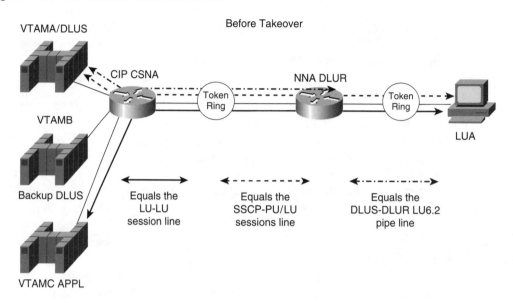

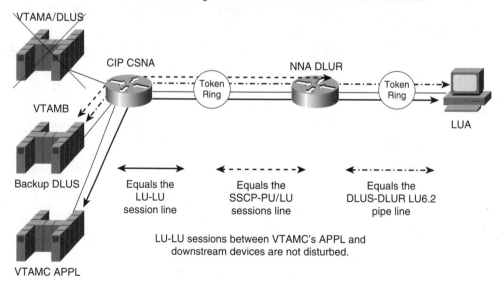

In this example, VTAMA is the primary DLUS, VTAMB is the backup DLUS, and NNA is configured as the DLUR. Assume that LUA requests to log on to an application residing on VTAMB. When VTAMA and the DLUS to DLUR connections fail, the DLUR node attempts to establish a session with VTAMC, which is configured as backup DLUS. When the control sessions to the DLUS are active, the DLUR node notifies VTAMB to activate downstream physical and logical units by sending REQACTPU and REQACTLU. VTAMB sends **activate physical unit (ACTPU)** and **activate logical unit (ACTLU)** commands to these downstream devices. This transfers the resource ownership from VTAMA to VTAMB.

After the SSCP-PU and SSCP-LU sessions are re-established with VTAMB, new LU-LU sessions are possible. In addition, the DLUR node notifies VTAMB about all the dependent logical units that have active sessions.

The LU-LU path between VTAMC and LUA would be VTAMB → NNB → NNA → LUA. When VTAMA fails, LU-LU sessions are not disrupted because VTAMA is not part of the LU-LU session path. In fact, LUA has no knowledge that the owning SSCP (VTAMA) failed and a new SSCP became the new owner. This process is transparent to LUA.

APPN in a Multiprotocol Environment

The trend in networking is to provide network designers with greater flexibility in building multiprotocol networks. Cisco provides the following two mechanisms to transport SNA traffic over a network:

- Encapsulation
- Natively via APPN

The key to building multiprotocol networks is to implement some kind of traffic priority or bandwidth reservation to ensure acceptable response time for mission-critical traffic while maintaining some networking resource for less delay-sensitive traffic.

Bandwidth Management and Queuing

The following are some Cisco bandwidth-management and queuing features that can enhance the overall performance of your network:

- Priority queuing
- Custom queuing
- Weighted fair queuing
- APPN buffer and memory management

For many years, the mainframe has been the dominant environment for processing business-critical applications. Increasingly powerful intelligent workstations, the creation of client/server computing environments, and higher-bandwidth applications are changing network topologies. With the proliferation of LAN-based client/server applications, many corporate networks are migrating from purely hierarchical SNA-based networks to all-purpose multiprotocol networks that can accommodate the rapidly changing network requirements. This is not an easy transition. Network designers must understand how well the different protocols use shared network resources without causing excessive contentions among them.

Cisco has for many years provided technologies that encapsulate SNA traffic and allow consolidation of SNA with multiprotocol networks. APPN on the Cisco router provides an additional option in multiprotocol networks, in which SNA traffic can now flow natively and concurrently with other protocols. Regardless of the technology used in a multiprotocol environment, network performance is the key consideration.

Some of the major factors affecting network performance in a multiprotocol environment are as follows:

- **Media access speed**—The time it takes for a frame to be sent over a link. The capacity requirement of the network must be understood. Insufficient network capacity is the primary contributor to poor performance. Whether you have a single protocol network or a multiprotocol network, sufficient bandwidth is required.

- **Congestion control**—The router must have sufficient buffering capacity to handle instantaneous bursts of data. To support a multiprotocol environment, buffer management plays an important role to ensure that one protocol does not monopolize the buffer memory.

- **Latency in the intermediate routers**—This includes packet processing time while traversing a router and queuing delay. The former constitutes a minor part of the total delay. The latter is the major factor because client/server traffic is bursty.

Typically, subarea SNA traffic is highly predictable and has low bandwidth requirements. Compared to SNA traffic, client/server traffic tends to be bursty in nature and has high bandwidth requirements. Unless there is a mechanism in place to protect mission-critical SNA traffic, network performance could be impacted.

Cisco provides many networking solutions to enterprise networks by allowing the two types of traffic with different characteristics to coexist and share bandwidth and at the same time provide protection for mission-critical SNA data against less delay-sensitive client/server data. This is achieved through the use of several priority queuing or bandwidth-reservation mechanisms.

Interface priority output queuing provides a way to prioritize packets transmitted on a per-interface basis. The four possible queues associated with priority queuing—high, medium, normal, and low—are shown in Figure 7-17. Priorities can be established based on the protocol type, particular interface, SDLC address, and so forth.

Figure 7-17 *Four Queues of Priority Queuing*

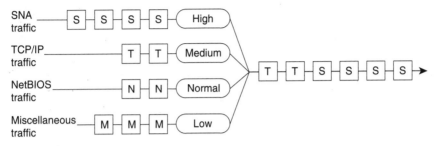

In Figure 7-18, SNA, TCP/IP, NetBIOS, and other miscellaneous traffic are sharing the media. The SNA traffic is prioritized ahead of all other traffic, followed by TCP/IP, NetBIOS, and finally other miscellaneous traffic. There is no aging algorithm associated with this type of queuing. Packets queued to the high priority queue are always serviced prior to the medium queue, the medium queue is always serviced before the normal queue, and so forth.

Priority queuing, however, introduces a fairness problem in that packets classified to lower-priority queues might not get serviced in a timely manner, or at all. Custom queuing is designed to address this problem. Custom queuing allows more granularity than priority queuing. In fact, this feature is commonly used in the networking environment in which multiple higher-layer protocols are supported. Custom queuing reserves bandwidth for a specific protocol, thus allowing mission-critical traffic to receive a guaranteed minimum amount of bandwidth at any time.

The intent is to reserve bandwidth for a particular type of traffic. In Figure 7-18, for example, SNA has 40% of the bandwidth reserved using custom queuing, TCP/IP has 20%, NetBIOS has 20%, and the remaining protocols have 20%. The APPN protocol itself has the concept of CoS that determines the transmission priority for every message. APPN prioritizes the traffic before sending it to the DLC transmission queue.

Custom queuing prioritizes multiprotocol traffic. A maximum of 16 queues can be built with custom queuing. Each queue is serviced sequentially until the number of bytes sent exceeds the configurable byte count or the queue is empty. One important function of custom queuing is that if SNA traffic uses only 20% of the link, the remaining 20% allocated to SNA can be shared by the other traffic.

Custom queuing is designed for environments that want to ensure a minimum level of service for all protocols. In today's multiprotocol network environment, this important feature allows protocols of different characteristics to share the media. For an overview of how to use the other types of queuing to allow multiple protocols to coexist within a router, review Chapter 2, "Network Design Basics."

Figure 7-18 *Example of Custom Queuing*

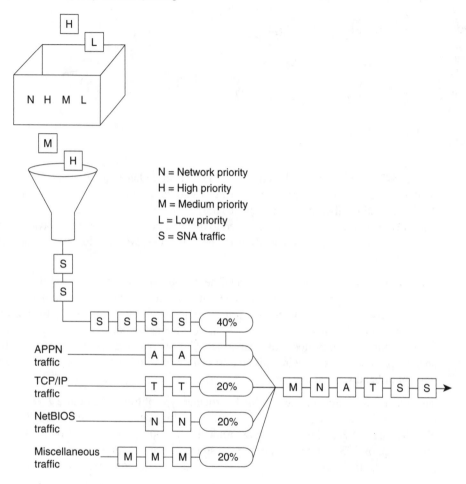

N = Network priority
H = High priority
M = Medium priority
L = Low priority
S = SNA traffic

Other Considerations with a Multiprotocol Environment

The memory requirement to support APPN is considerably higher than other protocols because of its large CoS tables, network topology databases, and directory databases. To ensure that APPN will coexist with other network protocols when operating in a multiprotocol environment, users can define the maximum amount of memory available to APPN. The following is the sample configuration command:

```
appn control-point CISCONET.EARTH
   maximum-memory 16
   complete
```

The preceding command specifies that APPN will not use more than 16 megabytes (MB) of memory. The memory is then managed locally by APPN. You can also specify the amount of memory reserved for APPN by using the following command:

```
appn control-point CISCONET.EARTH
  minimum-memory 32
  complete
```

Memory dedicated to APPN is not available for other processing. Use this command with caution.

Although memory determines factors such as the number of sessions that APPN can support, buffer memory is required to regulate traffic sent to and from the router. To ensure that APPN has adequate buffers to support the traffic flows, you can define the percentage of buffer memory reserved for use by APPN. This prevents APPN from monopolizing the buffer memory available in the router.

The following is the sample configuration command:

```
appn control-point CISCONET.EARTH
  buffer-percent 60
  complete
```

APPN uses a statistical buffering algorithm to manage the buffer usage. When buffer memory is constrained, APPN uses various flow-control mechanisms to protect itself from severe congestion or deadlock conditions as a result of buffer shortage.

Network Management

As networks grow in size and complexity, there are many ways to provide network management for an enterprise. Table 7-2 summarizes Cisco's management products.

Table 7-2 *Network Management Tools Available for APPN Networks*

Application	Description
Show commands	A common challenge in APPN networks is to understand the topology and status of the resources in the network. Show commands take advantage of the fact that all network nodes in a network (or subnetwork) have a fully replicated network topology database. Only a single network node is required to get a view of the APPN subnet, and it should not matter which network node is chosen. To obtain more detailed information, such as attached end nodes and LEN nodes, and local ports and link stations, additional network nodes should be checked. The Cisco router supports the RFC1593, APPN MIB, which is used by the IBM 6611 router, so it can be an agent for SNMP APPN applications. Most APPN nodes can show much of this information in tabular form. In the Cisco router, the **show appn topo** command displays the topology database in tabular form. The **show appn?** command lists all the options available.

continues

Table 7-2   *Network Management Tools Available for APPN Networks (Continued)*

Application	Description
CiscoWorks Blue Maps	A CiscoWorks application that shows logical maps of APPN, RSRB, and DLSw+ networks. It runs on the HP/UX, SunOS, and AIX operating systems. The APPN map is a manager for APPN SNMP agents, and displays the APPN network. The application can handle only a single network topology agent. If there are multiple subnets, the application can be started multiple times.
Native Service Point (NSP)	In SNA, a session between an SSCP and a PU is referred to as an SSCP-PU session. SSCPs use SSCP-PU sessions to send requests and receive status information from individual nodes. This information is then used to control the network configuration. NSP in the router can be used to send alerts and respond to requests from NetView on the mainframe computer. A service point allows NetView to establish a session to the router with the help of Cisco's applications that run on NetView. These applications cause commands to be sent to the router, and the router returns the reply. Currently, this is supported only over the SSCP-PU session, but DLUR can be used to accomplish this over an APPN network.
Alerts and traps	NetView is the primary destination of alerts. It supports receiving alerts from both APPN and on the SSCP-PU session used by NSP. The Cisco router can send alerts on each session. At this time, two sessions are required: one for APPN-unique alerts and one for all other alerts. The new APPN MIB allows for APPN alerts to be sent as traps as well, with the Alert ID and affected resource included in the trap. To send alerts to NetView, the following command must be entered at NetView: **FOCALPT CHANGE, FPCAT=ALERT, TARGET=NETA.ROUTER**.

Configuration Examples

This section provides the following APPN network configuration examples:

- Simple APPN network
- APPN network with end stations
- APPN over DLSw+

It also provides the following examples of using APPN when designing your network:

- Subarea to APPN migration
- APPN/CIP in a Sysplex environment
- APPN with FRAS BNN

As the following examples show, the minimal configuration for an APPN node includes an APPN control-point statement for the node and a port statement for each interface.

Simple APPN Network Configuration

Figure 7-19 shows an example of a simple APPN network that consists of four network nodes: Routers A, B, C, and D. Router A is responsible for initiating the connections to Routers B, C, and D. Consequently, it needs to define APPN logical links specifying the FDDI address of Router C, the ATM address of Router D, and so forth. For Routers B, C, and D, they can dynamically create the link-station definitions when Router A connects.

Figure 7-19 *Example of a Simple APPN Network Configuration*

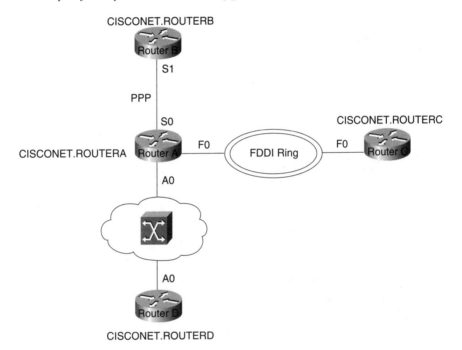

Sample Configurations

This section provides sample configurations for each of these four network nodes (Routers A, B, C, and D) shown in Figure 7-19.

Router A Configuration

The following is a sample configuration for Router A, shown in Figure 7-19. Note that all link stations are defined in Router A and are dynamically discovered by the other routers. A link station connects two resources and must be defined with the destination address in one of the resources:

```
!
hostname routera
!
interface Serial0
 ip address 10.11.1.1 255.255.255.0
 encapsulation ppp
 no keepalive
 no fair-queue
 clockrate 4000000
!
interface Fddi0
 no ip address
 no keepalive
!
interface ATM0
 no ip address
 atm clock INTERNAL
 atm pvc 1 1 32 aal5nlpid
!
appn control-point CISCONET.ROUTERA
   complete
!
appn port PPP Serial0
   complete
!
appn port FDDI Fddi0
   desired-max-send-btu-size 3849
   max-rcv-btu-size 3849
   complete
!
appn port ATM ATM0
   complete
!
appn link-station LINKTOB
   port PPP
   complete
!
appn link-station LINKTOC
   port FDDI
   lan-dest-address 0000.6f85.a8a5
   no connect-at-startup
   retry-limit infinite 5
   complete
!
appn link-station LINKTOD
   port ATM
   atm-dest-address 1
   no connect-at-startup
   retry-limit infinite 5
   complete
!
```

Router B Configuration

The following is a sample configuration for Router B, shown in Figure 7-19:

```
!
hostname routerb
!
interface Serial1
 ip address 10.11.1.2 255.255.255.0
 encapsulation ppp
 no keepalive
```

```
 no fair-queue
!
appn control-point CISCONET.ROUTERB
  complete
!
appn port PPP Serial1
  complete
!
appn routing
!
end
```

Router C Configuration

The following is a sample configuration for Router C, shown in Figure 7-19:

```
!
hostname routerc
!
interface Fddi0
 no ip address
 no keepalive
!
appn control-point CISCONET.ROUTERC
  complete
!
appn port FDDI Fddi0
  desired-max-send-btu-size 3849
  max-rcv-btu-size 3849
  complete
!
appn routing
!
end
```

Router D Configuration

The following is a sample configuration for Router D, shown in Figure 7-19:

```
!
hostname routerd
!
interface ATM0
 ip address 100.39.15.3 255.255.255.0
 atm pvc 1 1 32 aal5nlpid
!
appn control-point CISCONET.ROUTERD
  complete
!
appn port ATM ATM0
  complete
!
appn routing
!
end
```

APPN Network Configuration with End Stations

Figure 7-20 shows an example of an APPN network with end stations. At the remote location, Router B initiates the APPN connection to Router A at the data center.

Figure 7-20 *Example of an APPN Network with End Stations*

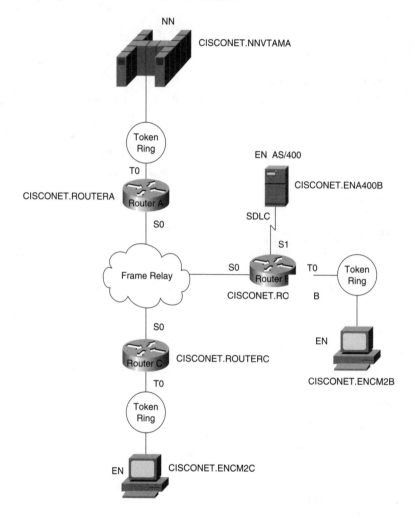

Sample Configurations

This section provides sample configurations for Routers A, B, and C, shown in Figure 7-20.

Sample Configuration for Router A

The following is a sample configuration for Router A, shown in Figure 7-20, which is responsible for initiating the APPN connection to the VTAM host:

```
hostname routera
!
interface TokenRing0
 no ip address
 mac-address 4000.1000.1000
 ring-speed 16
!
interface Serial0
 mtu 4096
 encapsulation frame-relay IETF
 keepalive 12
 frame-relay lmi-type ansi
 frame-relay map llc2  35
!
appn control-point CISCONET.ROUTERA
  complete
!
appn port FR0 Serial0
  complete
!
appn port TR0 TokenRing0
  complete
!
appn link-station TOVTAM
  port TR0
  lan-dest-address 4000.3745.0000
  complete
!
end
```

Sample Configuration for Router B

The following is a sample configuration for Router B, shown in Figure 7-20. At the remote location, Router B initiates the APPN connection to Router A at the data center and EN AS/400. Because a link station is not defined in Router B for CISCONET.ENCM2B, a link station must be defined in ENCM2B for Router B:

```
!hostname routerb
!
interface TokenRing0
 mac-address 4000.1000.2000
 no ip address
 ring-speed 16
!
interface Serial0
 mtu 4096
 encapsulation frame-relay IETF
 keepalive 12
 frame-relay lmi-type ansi
 frame-relay map llc2  35
!
interface Serial1
no ip address
 encapsulation sdlc
 no keepalive
```

```
   clockrate 19200
   sdlc role prim-xid-poll
   sdlc address 01
!
appn control-point CISCONET.ROUTERB
  complete
!
appn port FR0 Serial0
  complete
!
appn port SDLC Serial1
  sdlc-sec-addr 1
  complete
!
appn port TR0 TokenRing0
  complete
!
appn link-station AS400
  port SDLC
  role primary
  sdlc-dest-address 1
  complete
!
appn link-station ROUTERA
  port FR0
  fr-dest-address 35
  complete
!
end
```

Sample Configuration for Router C

The following is a sample configuration for Router C, shown in Figure 7-20. Router C
initiates an APPN connection to Router A. Because there is not a link station for
CISCONET.ENCMC2C, one must be defined in the configuration for ENCM2C:

```
hostname routerc
!
interface TokenRing0
 mac-address 4000.1000.3000
 no ip address
 ring-speed 16
!
interface Serial0
 mtu 4096
 encapsulation frame-relay IETF
 keepalive 12
 frame-relay lmi-type ansi
 frame-relay map llc2 36
!
appn control-point CISCONET.ROUTERC
  complete
!
appn port FR0 Serial0
  complete
!
appn port TR0 TokenRing0
  complete
!
appn link-station TORTRA
  port FR0
```

```
      fr-dest-address 36
      complete
   !
   end
```

APPN over DLSw+ Configuration Example

Figure 7-21 shows an example of APPN with DLSw+. ROUTERA is a DLSw+ router with no APPN functions and ROUTERB is running DLSw+ and APPN.

Figure 7-21 *Example of APPN with DLSw+*

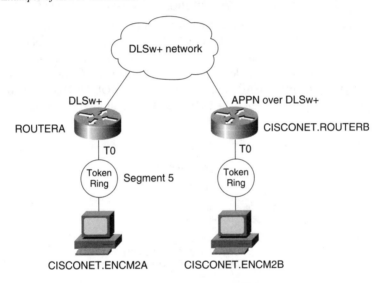

Sample Configurations of DLSw+ Router A

The following section provides sample configurations for ROUTERA and ROUTERB and the two workstations, shown in Figure 7-21.

Sample Configuration of DLSw+ ROUTERA

The following is a sample configuration for the DLSw+ ROUTERA, shown in Figure 7-21:

```
hostname routera
!
source-bridge ring-group 100
dlsw local-peer peer-id 10.4.21.3
dlsw remote-peer 0 tcp 10.4.21.1
!
interface Serial0
 mtu 4096
 ip address 10.4.21.3 255.255.255.0
```

```
encapsulation frame-relay IETF
keepalive 12
no fair-queue
frame-relay lmi-type ansi
frame-relay map llc2  56
!
interface TokenRing0
 ip address 10.4.22.2 255.255.255.0
 ring-speed 16
 multiring all
 source-bridge 5 1 100
!
```

Sample Configuration for Workstation Attached to ROUTERA

The following is a sample CS/2 configuration for the OS/2 workstation named
CISCONET.ENCM2A, shown in Figure 7-21. This workstation is attached to the DLSw+
router named ROUTERA. The workstation is configured as an end node, and it uses
ROUTERB as the network-node server. The destination MAC address configured on this
workstation is the virtual MAC address configured in ROUTERB on the **appn port**
statement. A sample of the DLSw+ ROUTERB configuration is provided in the next
section.

```
DEFINE_LOCAL_CP   FQ_CP_NAME(CISCONET.ENCM2A)
                  CP_ALIAS(ENCM2C)
                  NAU_ADDRESS(INDEPENDENT_LU)
                  NODE_TYPE(EN)
                  NODE_ID(X'05D00000')
                  NW_FP_SUPPORT(NONE)
                  HOST_FP_SUPPORT(YES)
                  MAX_COMP_LEVEL(NONE)
                  MAX_COMP_TOKENS(0);
    DEFINE_LOGICAL_LINK  LINK_NAME(TORTRB)
                  ADJACENT_NODE_TYPE(LEARN)
                  PREFERRED_NN_SERVER(YES)
                  DLC_NAME(IBMTRNET)
                  ADAPTER_NUMBER(0)
                  DESTINATION_ADDRESS(X'400010001112')
                  ETHERNET_FORMAT(NO)
                  CP_CP_SESSION_SUPPORT(YES)
                  SOLICIT_SSCP_SESSION(YES)
                  NODE_ID(X'05D00000')
                  ACTIVATE_AT_STARTUP(YES)
                  USE_PUNAME_AS_CPNAME(NO)
                  LIMITED_RESOURCE(NO)
                  LINK_STATION_ROLE(USE_ADAPTER_DEFINITION)
                  MAX_ACTIVATION_ATTEMPTS(USE_ADAPTER_DEFINITION)
                  EFFECTIVE_CAPACITY(USE_ADAPTER_DEFINITION)
                  COST_PER_CONNECT_TIME(USE_ADAPTER_DEFINITION)
                  COST_PER_BYTE(USE_ADAPTER_DEFINITION)
                  SECURITY(USE_ADAPTER_DEFINITION)
                  PROPAGATION_DELAY(USE_ADAPTER_DEFINITION)
                  USER_DEFINED_1(USE_ADAPTER_DEFINITION)
                  USER_DEFINED_2(USE_ADAPTER_DEFINITION)
                  USER_DEFINED_3(USE_ADAPTER_DEFINITION);
    DEFINE_DEFAULTS   IMPLICIT_INBOUND_PLU_SUPPORT(YES)
                  DEFAULT_MODE_NAME(BLANK)
                  MAX_MC_LL_SEND_SIZE(32767)
                  DIRECTORY_FOR_INBOUND_ATTACHES(*)
                  DEFAULT_TP_OPERATION(NONQUEUED_AM_STARTED)
```

```
                              DEFAULT_TP_PROGRAM_TYPE(BACKGROUND)
                              DEFAULT_TP_CONV_SECURITY_RQD(NO)
                              MAX_HELD_ALERTS(10);
                 START_ATTACH_MANAGER;
```

Sample Configuration for DLSw+ ROUTERB

ROUTERB, shown in Figure 7-21, is an APPN router that uses the APPN over DLSw+
feature. The VDLC operand on the port statement indicates that APPN is carried over
DLSw+. The following is a sample configuration for this router:

```
hostname routerb
!
source-bridge ring-group 100
dlsw local-peer peer-id 10.4.21.1
dlsw remote-peer 0 tcp 10.4.21.3
!
interface Serial2/0
 mtu 4096
 ip address 10.4.21.1 255.255.255.0
 encapsulation frame-relay IETF
 keepalive 12
 no fair-queue
 frame-relay map llc2  35
!
interface TokenRing0
 no ip address
 ring-speed 16
 mac-address 4000.5000.6000
source-bridge 10 1 100
!
appn control-point CISCONET.ROUTERB
  complete
!
appn port VDLC vdlc
  vdlc 100 vmac 4000.1000.1112
  complete
!
appn port tr0  TokenRing 0
complete
```

Sample Configuration for Workstation Attached to ROUTERB

The following is a sample CS/2 configuration for the OS/2 workstation named
CISCONET.ENCM2B, shown in Figure 7-21. This workstation is attached to the DLSw+
router named ROUTERB:

```
DEFINE_LOCAL_CP   FQ_CP_NAME(CISCONET.ENCM2B)
                  CP_ALIAS(ENCM2C)
                  NAU_ADDRESS(INDEPENDENT_LU)
                  NODE_TYPE(EN)
                  NODE_ID(X'05D00000')
                  NW_FP_SUPPORT(NONE)
                  HOST_FP_SUPPORT(YES)
                  MAX_COMP_LEVEL(NONE)
                  MAX_COMP_TOKENS(0);
   DEFINE_LOGICAL_LINK  LINK_NAME(TORTRB)
                  ADJACENT_NODE_TYPE(LEARN)
```

```
                             PREFERRED_NN_SERVER(YES)
                             DLC_NAME(IBMTRNET)
                             ADAPTER_NUMBER(0)
                             DESTINATION_ADDRESS(X'400050006000')
                             ETHERNET_FORMAT(NO)
                             CP_CP_SESSION_SUPPORT(YES)
                             SOLICIT_SSCP_SESSION(YES)
                             NODE_ID(X'05D00000')
                             ACTIVATE_AT_STARTUP(YES)
                             USE_PUNAME_AS_CPNAME(NO)
                             LIMITED_RESOURCE(NO)
                             LINK_STATION_ROLE(USE_ADAPTER_DEFINITION)
                             MAX_ACTIVATION_ATTEMPTS(USE_ADAPTER_DEFINITION)
                             EFFECTIVE_CAPACITY(USE_ADAPTER_DEFINITION)
                             COST_PER_CONNECT_TIME(USE_ADAPTER_DEFINITION)
                             COST_PER_BYTE(USE_ADAPTER_DEFINITION)
                             SECURITY(USE_ADAPTER_DEFINITION)
                             PROPAGATION_DELAY(USE_ADAPTER_DEFINITION)
                             USER_DEFINED_1(USE_ADAPTER_DEFINITION)
                             USER_DEFINED_2(USE_ADAPTER_DEFINITION)
                             USER_DEFINED_3(USE_ADAPTER_DEFINITION);
       DEFINE_DEFAULTS  IMPLICIT_INBOUND_PLU_SUPPORT(YES)
                             DEFAULT_MODE_NAME(BLANK)
                             MAX_MC_LL_SEND_SIZE(32767)
                             DIRECTORY_FOR_INBOUND_ATTACHES(*)
                             DEFAULT_TP_OPERATION(NONQUEUED_AM_STARTED)
                             DEFAULT_TP_PROGRAM_TYPE(BACKGROUND)
                             DEFAULT_TP_CONV_SECURITY_RQD(NO)
                             MAX_HELD_ALERTS(10);
       START_ATTACH_MANAGER;
```

For more information on DLSw+, see Chapter 8, "Designing DLSw+ Networks."

Example of Subarea to APPN Migration

This section provides an overview of the implementation and conversion of the SNA
network from subarea FEP-based to APPN router-based. It explores the use of DLSw+ as
a migration technology from traditional SNA to APPN, and covers the migration steps. The
example involves a large insurance company in Europe. The company plans to replace the
FEPs with Cisco routers, migrating from subarea to APPN routing.

Figure 7-22 shows the company's current SNA network. The network consists of two
mainframe sites running four VTAM images with a Communications Management
Complex (CMC) host in each data center, as shown in Figure 7-22. In every data center,
four NCR Comten FEPs (IBM 3745–compatible) support traffic from multiple regional
offices. There are also two NCR Comten FEPs that provide SNA Network Interconnect
(SNI) support.

Figure 7-22 *SNA FEP-Based Network*

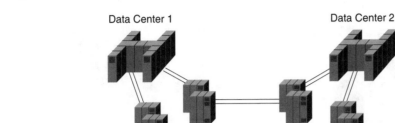

There are 22 regional offices across the country. Every regional office has two NCR Comten FEPs installed, one connecting to Data Center 1 and the other connecting to Data Center 2. The remote FEPs have dual Token Rings connected via a bridge; duplicate TIC address support is implemented for backup and redundancy. This means that a PU2.0 station can connect to the host through any one of the two FEPs. If one FEP fails, PU2.0 stations can access the host via the other FEP.

In addition to the Token Ring–attached devices (approximately 15 per regional office), the two FEPs also run NCP Packet-Switching Interface (NPSI), supporting over 200 remotely attached devices via the public X.25 network. The total number of LUs supported per regional office is approximately 1,800, with 1,500 active LU-LU sessions at any one time. The estimated traffic rate is 15 transactions per second.

The first migration step is to implement Cisco CIP routers at one of the data centers, replacing the channel-attached FEPs. A remote router is then installed in one of the regional offices. The two routers are connected using DLSw+, as shown in Figure 7-23.

Figure 7-23 *Subarea to APPN Migration—Phase One*

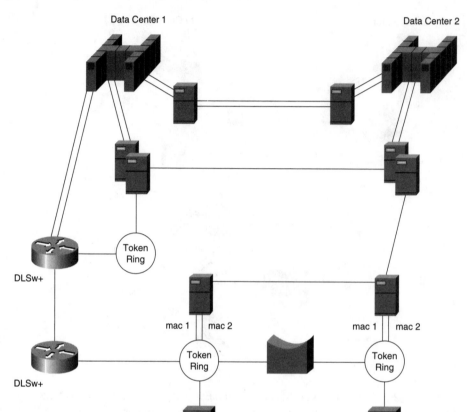

As Figure 7-23 shows, the FEPs at the regional office continue to provide boundary functions to the Token Ring– and X.25-attached devices. The two DLSw+ routers handle the traffic between the FEP at Data Center 1 and the FEP at the regional office. SNA CoS is preserved in this environment.

After the stability of the routers is ensured, the network designer proceeds to the next phase. As Figure 7-24 shows, this phase involves installation of a second router in Data Center 2 and the regional office. At this point, FEP-to-FEP communications between regional offices and data centers are handled by the routers via DLSw+.

Figure 7-24 *Subarea to APPN Migration—Phase Two*

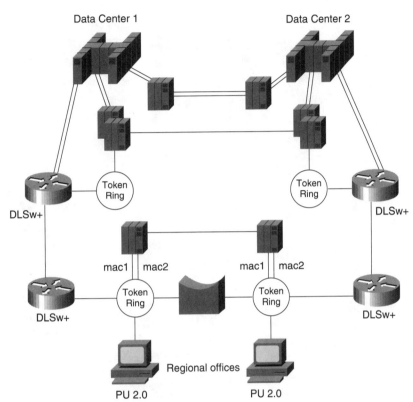

Continuing with the migration plan, the network designer's next step is to install an additional CIP router in each data center to support traffic between the two data centers. As shown in Figure 7-25, the links connecting the FEPs in Data Center 1 and Data Center 2 are moved one by one to the routers.

Figure 7-25 *Subarea to APPN Migration—Phase Three*

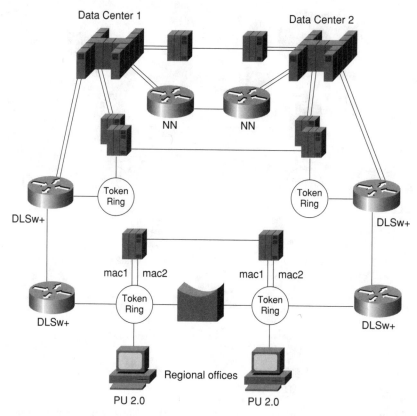

APPN will be enabled to support the traffic between Data Center 1 and Data Center 2. Eventually, the FEP-based network will become a router-based network. The NCR Comten processors will become obsolete. Two of the NCR Comten processors will be kept to provide SNI support to external organizations. Figure 7-26 illustrates the new router-based network.

Figure 7-26 *Subarea to APPN Migration—Phase Four*

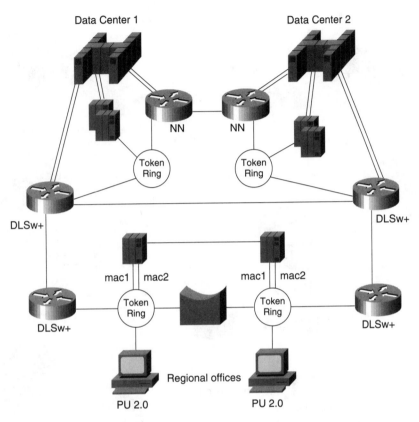

The communication links that formerly connected the FEPs in the two data centers are now moved to the routers. The FEPs at the data centers can be eliminated. The FEPs at the regional offices are merely providing the boundary functions for dependent LU devices, thus allowing SNA CoS to be maintained. The next phase is to migrate the SNA boundary functions support from the FEP to the remote router at the regional office by enabling APPN and DLUR. After this is complete, all the FEPs can be eliminated.

The next step is to migrate from DLSw+ to APPN between the data-center routers and the regional-office routers. This is done region by region, until stability of the network is ensured. As shown in Figure 7-27, DLUR is enabled to support the dependent PU devices in the regional offices. X.25-attached dependent PU2.0 devices that were formerly connected to the FEPs using NPSI are supported via Qualified Logical Link Control (QLLC) in the router. QLLC is the standard for SNA encapsulation for X.25.

Figure 7-27 *Subarea to APPN Migration—Phase Five*

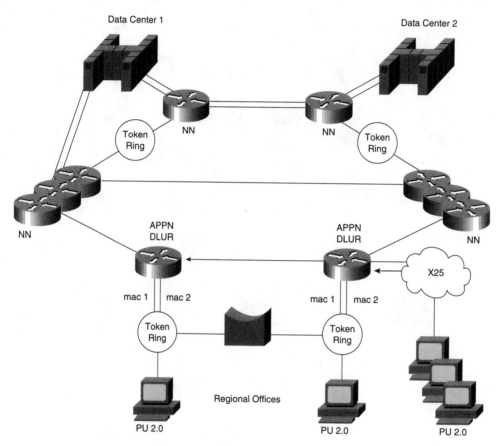

Example of APPN/CIP in a Sysplex Environment

This section examines APPN and the CIP routers in a Sysplex (system complex) environment. It provides an overview of the Sysplex environment and its relationship with APPN, along with a description of how to use the following three approaches to support the Sysplex environment:

- Sysplex with APPN Using Subarea Routing–Option One
- Sysplex Using Subarea/APPN Routing–Option Two
- Sysplex Using APPN Routing–Option Three

It also describes how APPN provides fault tolerance and load-sharing capabilities in the data center.

Sysplex Overview

Sysplex provides a means to centrally operate and manage a group of multiple virtual storage (MVS) systems by coupling hardware elements and software services. Many data-processing centers have multiple MVS systems to support their business, and these systems often share data and applications. Sysplex is designed to provide a cost-effective solution to meet a company's expanding requirements by allowing MVS systems to be added and managed efficiently.

A Sysplex environment consists of multiple 9672 CMOS processors, and each CMOS processor presents a VTAM domain. The concept of multiprocessors introduces a problem. Today, users are accustomed to single images. IMS (Information Management System) running on the mainframe can serve the entire organization on a single host image, for example. With the multiprocessor concept, you would not want to instruct User A to establish the session with IMS on System A and User B to establish the session with IMS on System B because IMS might run on either system.

To resolve this, a function called *generic resource* was created. The generic resource function enables multiple application programs, which provide the same function, to be known and accessed by a single generic name. This means that User A might sometimes get IMS on System A, and sometimes get IMS on System B. Because both systems have access to the same shared data in the Sysplex, this switching of systems is transparent to the users. VTAM is responsible for resolving the generic name and determining which application program is used to establish the session. This function enables VTAM to provide workload balancing by distributing incoming session initiations among a number of identical application programs running on different processors.

Generic resource runs only on VTAM with APPN support. To achieve session load balancing across the different processors, users must migrate VTAM from subarea SNA to APPN. The rest of this section examines three options for supporting the Sysplex environment.

Sysplex with APPN Using Subarea Routing—Option One

The first option to support the Sysplex environment is to convert the CMC host to a composite network node. Traditionally, the CMC host was the VTAM that owned all the network's SNA resources. With this approach, the composite network node is used to describe the combination of VTAM and Network Control Program (NCP). This means that VTAM and NCP function together as a single network node. In Figure 7-28, the CMC host and the FEPs are configured as the composite network node.

Figure 7-28 *CMC Composite Network Node with Subarea Routing—Option One*

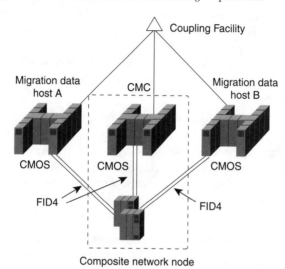

Composite network node

The VTAM CMC host owns the FEPs. Each FEP is connected to the 9672 CMOS processors through a parallel channel. Each 9672 CMOS processor is configured as a migration data host, and maintains both an APPN and subarea appearance.

Each migration data host establishes subarea connections to the FEPs using Virtual Route Transmission Group (VRTG), which allows APPN to be transported over traditional subarea routing. CP-CP sessions between the CMC host and the 9672 migration data hosts are established using VRTG. Generic resource function is performed in APPN, but all routing is subarea routing. This is the most conservative way to migrate to a Sysplex.

The disadvantage of this approach is that using subarea routing does not provide dynamic implementation of topology changes in APPN, which is available with APPN connection. If you need to add a CMOS processor, subarea PATH changes to every subarea node are required. Another drawback of this approach is that running APPN over subarea routing introduces complexity to your network.

Sysplex Using Subarea/APPN Routing—Option Two

The second option to support the Sysplex environment is to use subarea/APPN routing. This approach is similar to Option One, which was described in the preceding section. With this second approach, the CMC host and the FEPs are converted to a composite network node, as shown in Figure 7-29.

Figure 7-29 *CMC Composite Network Node with APPN Routing—Option Two*

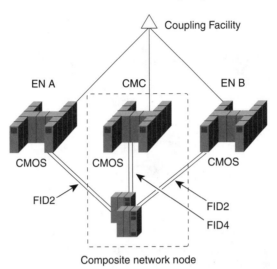

As shown in Figure 7-29, the two 9672 CMOS processors are converted to pure end nodes (EN A and EN B). APPN connections are established between the 9672s and the FEPs. Sessions come into the CMC in the usual way and the CMC does a subarea/APPN interchange function. This means that sessions are converted from subarea routing to APPN routing on the links between the FEPs and the 9672s.

A disadvantage of this second approach is that it performs poorly because the FEPs must perform an extra conversion. This approach also requires more NCP cycles and memory. Although this is very easy to configure and it does not require any changes to the basic subarea routing, the cost of the NCP upgrades can be expensive.

Sysplex Using APPN Routing—Option Three

The third option to support the Sysplex environment is to use APPN routing. With this approach, you use DLUR as a front end to the CMC-owned logical units. Figure 7-30 illustrates this configuration.

Figure 7-30 *Sysplex with DLUR Using CIP—Option Three*

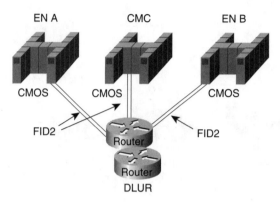

As shown in Figure 7-30, this is a pure APPN network with APPN routing only. Each CMOS end-node processor is attached to the DLUR routers through APPN. Note that the DLUR routers could be remote and not directly next to the mainframe computers (for example, there could be intervening routers).

This is the preferred approach for implementing the Sysplex environment for the company used in this sample scenario. The following section provides more details on this sample implementation.

The Company's Network

The company used in this example has a very large IP backbone and a very large SNA network. Today, its multiprotocol and SNA network are separate. The company's goal is to consolidate the traffic across the multiprotocol Internet. The company has chosen IP as its strategic backbone protocol of choice. To transport the SNA traffic, DLSw+ is used.

In the data center, the company plans to support five different IBM Sysplex environments. Its objective is to have the highest degree of redundancy and fault tolerance. The administrators decided not to run APPN throughout their existing multiprotocol network, but chose APPN in the data center to provide the required level of redundancy.

Figure 7-31 shows the configuration of the company's data center. The diagram on the top right in this figure is a logical view of one Sysplex environment and how it is connected to the multiprotocol network through the CIP/CSNA routers and the APPN routers. Each CIP/CSNA router has two parallel channel adapters to each Sysplex host (Sysplex 1 and Sysplex 2) through separate ESCON Directors. To meet the company's high-availability requirement, this configuration has no single points of failure.

Figure 7-31 *Example of APPN in the Data Center*

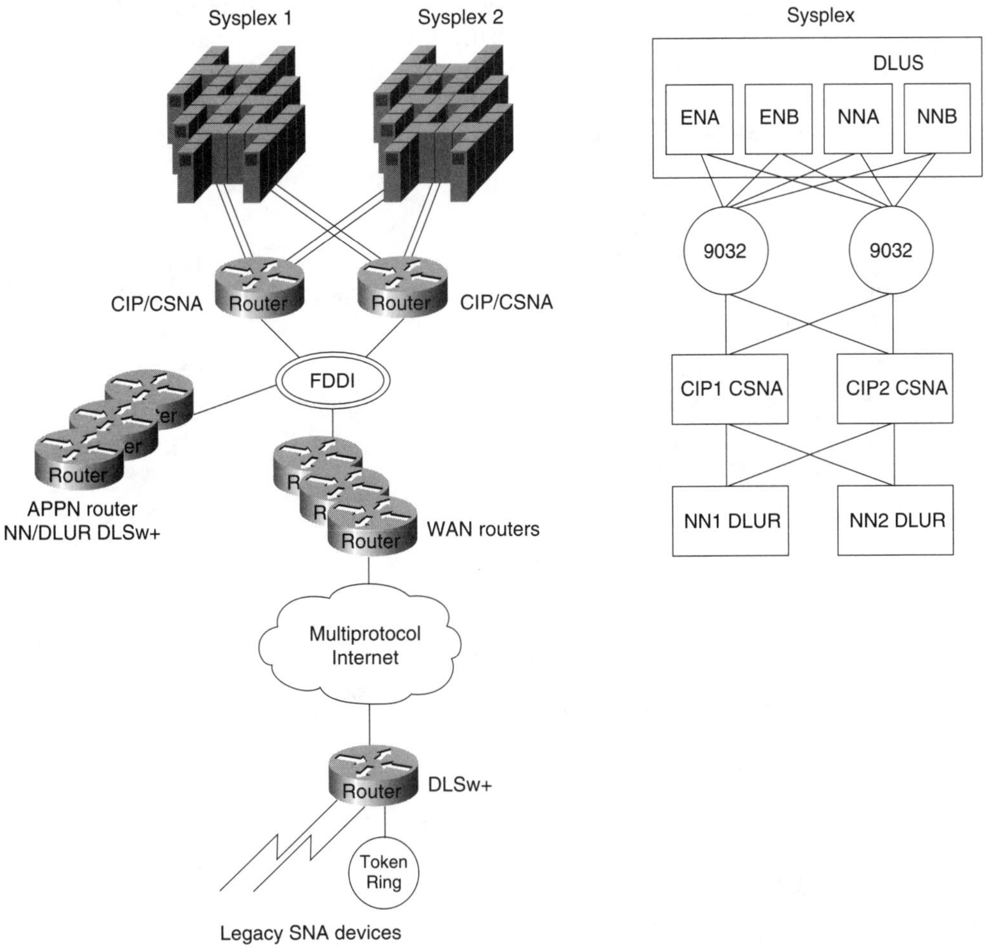

In each Sysplex environment, at least two network nodes per Sysplex act as a DLUS. VTAM NNA is designated as the primary DLUS node. NNB is designated the backup DLUS. The remaining hosts are data hosts configured as end nodes. These end node data hosts use NNA as the network-node server.

There are two CIP routers to support every Sysplex environment and at least two APPN routers running DLUR to provide boundary-functions support for remote devices. The traffic is expected to load share across the two CIP routers. Consequently, APPN provides load balancing and redundancy in this environment.

Sample Configuration

From an APPN standpoint, NNA in Figure 7-31 can be configured as the primary DLUS. NNB can be configured as the backup DLUS. The following is a configuration example for NN1. NN2 would be configured similarly.

```
!
appn control-point CISCONET.NN1
  dlus CISCONET.NNA
  backup-dlus CISCONET.NNB
  dlur
  complete
```

When the primary DLUS host goes out of service for any reason, the DLUR node is disconnected from its serving DLUS. The DLUR node retries the DLUS/DLUR pipe with NNA. If unsuccessful, it tries its backup DLUS.

To achieve load balancing, every DLUR router defines two parallel APPN transmission groups with equal weights to every VTAM host by using the following configuration:

```
!
! Link to VTAM ENA via CIP router 1
!
appn link-station LINK1ENA
  port FDDI0
  lan-dest-address 4000.3000.1001
  complete
!
! Link to VTAM ENA via CIP router 2
!
appn link-station LINK2ENA
  port FDDI0
  lan-dest-address 4000.3000.2001
  complete
!
! Link to VTAM ENB via CIP router 1
!
appn link-station LINK1ENB
  port FDDI0
  lan-dest-address 4000.3000.1002
  complete
!
! Link to VTAM ENB via CIP router 2
!
appn link-station LINK2ENB
  port FDDI0
  lan-dest-address 4000.3000.2002
  complete
!
! Link to Primary DLUS NNA via CIP router 1
!
appn link-station LINK1NNA
  port FDDI0
  lan-dest-address 4000.3000.1003
  complete
!
! Link to Primary DLUS NNA via CIP router 2
!
appn link-station LINK2NNA
  port FDDI0
  lan-dest-address 4000.3000.2003
```

```
  complete
!
! Link to Backup DLUS NNB via CIP router 1
!
appn link-station LINK1NNB
  port FDDI0
  lan-dest-address 4000.3000.1004
  complete
!
! Link to Backup DLUS NNB via CIP router 2
!
appn link-station LINK2NNB
  port FDDI0
  lan-dest-address 4000.3000.2004
  complete
```

As shown in the preceding configuration, NN1 defines two APPN transmission groups to ENA, ENB, NNA, and NNB. There are two channel attachments to each host, and each attachment is connected to separate hardware (for example, a CIP card, CIP router, and ESCON Director). Reasons to have duplicate hardware include provision for the loss of any physical component; if this happens, the host is still accessible using the alternative path.

From an APPN perspective, two transmission groups connect a DLUR router and every host. One transmission group traverses CIP Router 1 and the other traverses CIP Router 2. When one path fails, the APPN transmission group becomes inoperative. The second transmission group provides an alternative route for host connection through the other path.

All the subarea SSCP/PU and SSCP/LU sessions flow on one of the transmission groups between the DLUR router and the primary DLUS host. As for the LU-LU sessions, the two possible routes between the DLUR router and a VTAM host are available. The DLUR router and a VTAM host select one of these two routes at random for the LU-LU sessions. This randomization provides a certain amount of load distribution across the two CIP routers, although it might not necessarily be statistically load-balanced.

Multiple DLUR routers support downstream SNA devices. The following is a sample configuration for DLUR router NN1:

```
source-bridge ring-group 100
dlsw local-peer peer-id 172.18.3.111 promiscuous
!
interface FDDI0
 ip address 172.18.3.111 255.255.255.0
!
appn control-point CISCONET..NN1
dlus CISCONET.NNA
backup-dlus CISCONET.NNB
dlur
complete
!
appn port VDLC1 vdlc
  vdlc 100 4000.1000.2000
  complete
```

The following is a sample configuration for DLUR router NN2:

```
source-bridge ring-group 200
dlsw local-peer peer-id 172.18.3.112 promiscuous
```

```
!
interface FDDI0
 ip address 172.18.3.112 255.255.255.0
!
appn control-point CISCONET.NN2
  complete
!
appn port VDLC2 vdlc
  vdlc 200 4000.1000.2000
  complete
```

A workstation gains access to the host through the DLUR router. A workstation defines 4000.1000.2000 as the destination MAC address in the emulation software. This virtual MAC address is defined to every DLUR router. When initiating a connection, a workstation sends an all-routes broadcast Test command frame to the MAC address to which it wants to connect. The remote DLSw+ router sends an explorer frame to its peers. Both NN1 and NN2 respond with **ICANREACH**. The DLSw+ router is configured to use the load-balancing mode. This means that the DLSw+ router caches both NN1 and NN2 as peers that can reach the host. Host sessions are established through NN1 and NN2 in a round-robin fashion. This allows the company to spread its SNA traffic over two or more DLUR routers. If NN1 becomes unavailable, sessions that traverse NN1 are disruptive but they can be reestablished through NN2 with negligible impact.

This design increases overall availability by using duplicate virtual MAC address on the DLUR router. The dual paths provide the option for a secondary path to be available for use when the primary path is unavailable. Another advantage is that this design allows for easy scaling. When the number of SNA devices increases, for example, buffer memory might become a constraint on the DLUR routers. The company can add a DLUR router to support the increased session load. This topology change does not require any network administration from any remote routers or the data-center routers.

Example of APPN with FRAS BNN

This section describes the design considerations when building a large enterprise APPN network. It lists the current technologies that allow the company in this example to build a large APPN network. Each option is discussed in detail. FRAS BNN is chosen as an interim scalability solution to reduce the number of network nodes in the network. This allows the network to scale to meet the company's expanding requirements.

In this example, a government agency has a network that consists of one data center and approximately 100 remote sites. Within the next few years, its network is expected to increase to 500 remote sites.

Figure 7-32 shows a simplified version of the agency's current APPN network.

Figure 7-32 *Sample APPN Network for a Government Agency*

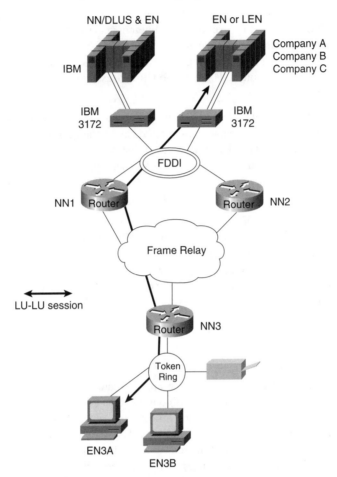

The data center consists of 20 mainframe processors from IBM and a variety of other vendors. The IBM mainframes are MVS-based and are running VTAM. They are also configured as NN/DLUS and EN data hosts. No subarea protocol exists in this network. Other non-IBM mainframes are configured as either an EN or LEN node.

The user platform is OS/2 running Communications Server at all the remote sites with connectivity needs to the data-center mainframe computers. Initially, there are no any-to-any communication requirements in this network. The applications supported are LU type 2 and LU6.2.

APPN in the Data Center

The host mainframes in Figure 7-32 are connected using the external communication adapter (XCA) connection over the 3172 Interconnect Controllers. The non-IBM data hosts (Companies A, B, and C) use the VTAM IBM mainframe as the network-node server. To keep the amount of TDU flows to a minimum, CP-CP sessions exist only between VTAM and the data-center routers. There are no CP-CP sessions among the routers located at the data center.

To achieve the optimal route calculation without explicitly defining meshed-connection definitions, every end node and network node at the data center is connected to the same connection network. This allows a session to be directly established between two data-center resources without traversing the VTAM network node. As Figure 7-32 shows, when an LU-LU session between resources at EN3A and Company A's mainframe is set up, the optimal route is directly through the FDDI ring to NN1 and NN3.

To reduce the number of broadcast searches to a maximum of one per resource, VTAM is configured as the CDS in this network. The CDS function is very effective in this network because the resources in the network require access only to resources at the host mainframes in the data center. These host mainframes register their resources with VTAM, which is their network-node server. Consequently, VTAM always has location information for every resource at the data center. This means that VTAM never has to perform LOCATE broadcast searches.

APPN in the Remote Site

The network depicted in Figure 7-32 has approximately 30 to 40 CS/2 workstations in every remote site. Every user workstation is configured as an end node. Each end node supports eight independent LU6.2 sessions and four dependent LU sessions. A Cisco router at every location forwards the traffic to the data center. The router's network node function provides the intermediate routing node function for the independent LUs. The DLUR function provides the dependent LU routing function for the dependent LUs.

Future Configuration

This network will eventually consist of 500 remote network-node routers, 100 data-center routers, and eight mainframe computers. Typically, a 600-node APPN network will have scalability issues. The rest of this section examines the following two options that you can use to address scalability issues in an APPN network:

- Implementing Border Node on VTAM to Partition the Network into Smaller Subnets
- Using FRAS BNN to Reduce the Number of Network Nodes in the Network

Using Border Node on VTAM to Partition the Network into Smaller Subnets

By implementing the concept of border node on VTAM, a peripheral subnetwork boundary is introduced between NN1 and VTAM, and between NN2 and VTAM, as shown in Figure 7-33.

Figure 7-33 *APPN Network with VTAM Extended Border Node*

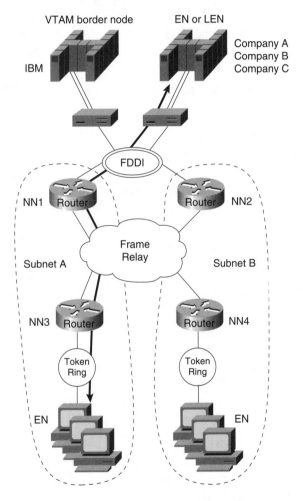

There would be no topology information exchange between VTAM and the data-center NN routers. The eight mainframe computers would be in the same subnet. Every data-center router would support multiple-access routers and they would form their own subnet. Each subnet is limited to a maximum of 100 network nodes. This configuration would prevent topology information from being sent from one subnet to another, thus allowing the network to scale to over 600 network nodes.

Although this approach addresses the TDU flow issue, there is a considerable loss of functions, however, by configuring VTAM as a border node in this environment. First, two APPN subnetworks cannot be connected through a connection network. LU-LU sessions between resources at Company A's host and remote resources would be set up through an indirect route through the VTAM border node. This is clearly not an optimal route. Second, the central directory server function is lost because the VTAM border node portrays an end node image to NN1. This prevents NN1 from discovering the central directory server in the network.

The next section examines an alternative approach of using FRAS BNN to reduce the number of network nodes in the network.

Using FRAS BNN to Reduce the Number of Network Nodes

Figure 7-34 shows how FRAS BNN can be used to reduce the number of network nodes in the company's network. All the server applications are on the mainframe computers and devices require only host access. APPN routing is not essential for this company.

Implementing FRAS BNN rather than a full APPN network node on the access routers directly reduces the number of network nodes. This allows the network to scale without the concern of TDU flows. This is proven to be a viable solution for this company for the time being because LAN-to-LAN connectivity is not an immediate requirement. The remote routers can be migrated to support APPN border node when it becomes available.

In this environment, CP-CP sessions are supported over the Frame Relay network. The central directory server and the concept of connection network are fully supported. LU-LU sessions can be set up using the direct route without traversing VTAM, as shown in Figure 7-34. The only function lost with FRAS BNN is CoS for traffic traveling from the remote FRAS BNN router to the data center.

Figure 7-34 *APPN Network with FRAS BNN*

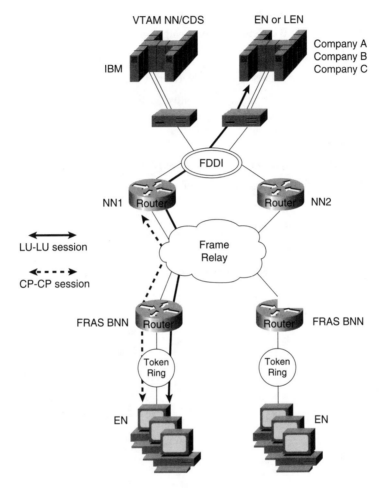

Summary

Recall that this chapter discussed developing the network design and planning a successful migration to APPN. It covered the following topics:

- Evolution of SNA
- When to Use APPN as Part of a Network Design
- When to Use APPN versus Alternative Methods of SNA Transport
- Overview of APPN
- Scalability Issues
- Backup Techniques in an APPN Network
- APPN in a Multiprotocol Environment
- Network Management
- Configuration Examples

CHAPTER 8

Designing DLSw+ Networks

Edited by Nicole Park

This chapter contains the following information:

- Introduction to DLSw+
- Getting Started with DLSw+
- DLSw+ Advanced Features

Introduction to DLSw+

This section describes *data-link switching plus* (DLSw+), and provides configuration examples to enable you to quickly design and configure simple DLSw+ networks. It reviews the key components of the data-link switching (DLSw) features and describes the extensions to the standard that are included in DLSw+. This section also describes advanced features, tells when to use them, and includes examples of how to use these features. It provides tuning, hierarchical design, meshed design, debug, and migration guidance. Finally, it recommends how to proceed with designing your network. This section can be used as a reference only (for configuration examples), as a tuning guide, or as a guide to design a complete DLSw+ network.

DLSw+ Defined

DLSw+ is a means of transporting Systems Network Architecture (SNA) and NetBIOS traffic over a campus or wide-area network (WAN). The end systems can attach to the network over Token Ring, Ethernet, Synchronous Data Link Control (SDLC) protocol, Qualified Logical Link Control (QLLC), or Fiber Distributed Data Interface (FDDI). (FDDI is supported on the Cisco 7000 series only, and requires Cisco IOS Release 11.2 or later.) DLSw+ switches between diverse media and locally terminates the data links, keeping acknowledgments, keepalives, and polling off the WAN. Local termination of data links also eliminates data-link control timeouts that can occur during transient network congestion or when rerouting around failed links. Finally, DLSw+ provides a mechanism for dynamically searching a network for SNA or NetBIOS resources, and includes caching algorithms that minimize broadcast traffic.

In this document, DLSw+ routers are referred to as peer routers, peers, or partners. The connection between two DLSw+ routers is referred to as a peer connection. A DLSw+ circuit compromises the data-link control connection between the originating end system and the originating router, the connection between the two routers (typically a Transport Control Protocol [TCP] connection), and the data-link control connection between the target router and the target end system. A single peer connection can carry multiple circuits.

DLSw+ supports circuits between SNA physical units (PUs), or between NetBIOS clients and servers. The SNA PU connectivity supported is PU 2.0/2.1–to–PU 4 (attached via any supported data-link controls), PU 1–to–PU 4 (SDLC only), PU 4–to–PU 4 (Token Ring only), and PU 2.1–to–PU 2.1 (any supported data-link control).

PU 4–to–PU 4 connectivity supports only a single path between front-end processors (FEPs) because of an idiosyncrasy in the way FEPs treat duplicate source-route bridged paths. In addition, remote load is not supported.

DLSw Standard

The DLSw standard was defined at the Advanced Peer-to-Peer Networking (APPN) Implementers Workshop (AIW) in the DLSw-related interest group. The current standard is Version 1, which is documented in RFC 1795. RFC 1795 makes RFC 1434 obsolete, which described IBM's original 6611 implementation of DLSw.

The DLSw standard describes the Switch-to-Switch Protocol (SSP) used between routers (called data-link switches) to establish DLSw peer connections, locate resources, forward data, handle flow control, and perform error recovery. RFC 1795 requires that data-link connections be terminated at the peer routers—that is, the data-link connections are locally acknowledged and, in the case of Token Ring, the routing information field (RIF) ends at a virtual ring in the peering router.

By locally terminating data-link control connections, the DLSw standard eliminates the requirement for link-layer acknowledgments and keepalive messages to flow across the WAN. In addition, because link-layer frames are acknowledged locally, link-layer timeouts should not occur. It is the responsibility of the DLSw routers to multiplex the traffic of multiple data-link controls to the appropriate TCP pipe and to transport the data reliably across an IP backbone. Before any end-system communication can occur over DLSw, the following must take place:

- Establish Peer Connections
- Exchange Capabilities
- Establish Circuit

Establish Peer Connections

Before two routers can switch SNA or NetBIOS traffic, they must establish two TCP connections between them. The standard allows one of these TCP connections to be dropped if it is not required. (Cisco routers will drop the extra TCP connection unless they are communicating with another vendor's router that requires two TCP connections.) The standard also allows additional TCP connections to be made to allow for different levels of priority.

Exchange Capabilities

After the TCP connections are established, the routers exchange their capabilities. Capabilities include the DLSw version number, initial pacing windows (receive window size), NetBIOS support, list of supported link service access points (SAPs), and the number of TCP sessions supported. Media Access Control (MAC) address lists and NetBIOS name lists can also be exchanged at this time, and, if desired, a DLSw partner can specify that it does not want to receive certain types of search frames. It is possible to configure the MAC addresses and NetBIOS names of all resources that will use DLSw and thereby avoid any broadcasts. After the capabilities exchange, the DLSw partners are ready to establish circuits between SNA or NetBIOS end systems.

Establish Circuit

Circuit establishment between a pair of end systems includes locating the target resource (based on its destination MAC address or NetBIOS name) and setting up data-link control connections between each end system and its data-link switch (local router). SNA and NetBIOS are handled differently. SNA devices on a LAN find other SNA devices by sending an explorer frame (a TEST or an exchange identification [XID] frame) with the MAC address of the target SNA device. When a DLSw router receives an explorer frame, the router sends a *canureach frame* to each of the DLSw partners. If one of its DLSw partners can reach the specified MAC address, the partner replies with an *icanreach frame*. The specific sequence includes a *canureach ex* (explorer) to find the resource and a *canureach cs* (circuit setup) that triggers the peering routers to establish a circuit.

At this point, the DLSw partners establish a *circuit* that consists of three connections: the two data-link control connections between each router and the locally attached SNA end system, and the TCP connection between the DLSw partners. This circuit is uniquely identified by the source and destination circuit IDs, which are carried in all steady state data frames in lieu of data-link control addresses such as MAC addresses. Each circuit ID is defined by the destination and source MAC addresses, destination and source-link service access points (LSAPs), and a data-link control port ID. The circuit concept simplifies management, and is important in error processing and cleanup. After the circuit is established, information frames can flow over the circuit.

NetBIOS circuit establishment is similar, but instead of forwarding a canureach frame that specifies a MAC address, DLSw routers send a name query (NetBIOS NAME-QUERY) frame that specifies a NetBIOS name. Instead of an icanreach frame, there is a *name recognized* (NetBIOS NAME-RECOGNIZED) frame.

Most DLSw implementations cache information learned as part of the explorer processing so that subsequent searches for the same resource do not result in the sending of additional explorer frames.

Flow Control

The DLSw standard describes adaptive pacing between DLSw routers, but does not indicate how to map this to the native data-link flow control on the edges. The DLSw standard specifies flow control on a per-circuit basis and calls for two independent, unidirectional circuit flow-control mechanisms. Flow control is handled by a windowing mechanism that can dynamically adapt to buffer availability, TCP transmit queue depth, and end-station flow-control mechanisms. Windows can be incremented, decremented, halved, or reset to zero.

The granted units (the number of units that the sender has permission to send) are incremented with a flow-control indication from the receiver (similar to classic SNA session-level pacing). Flow-control indicators can be one of the following types:

- *Repeat*—Increment granted units by the current window size
- *Increment*—Increment the window size by one, and increment granted units by the new window size
- *Decrement*—Decrement window size by one, and increment granted units by the new window size
- *Reset*—Decrease window to zero, and set granted units to zero to stop all transmission in one direction until an increment flow-control indicator is sent
- *Half*—Cut the current window size in half, and increment granted units by the new window size

Flow-control indicators and flow-control acknowledgments can be piggybacked on information frames or can be sent as independent flow-control messages, but reset indicators are always sent as independent messages.

DLSw+ Features

DLSw+ is Cisco's implementation of DLSw. It goes beyond the standard to include the advanced features of Cisco's current remote source-route bridging (RSRB) and provides additional functionality to increase the overall scalability of DLSw. DLSw+ includes enhancements in the following areas:

- *Scalability*—Constructs IBM networks in a way that reduces the amount of broadcast traffic and therefore enhances their scalability

- *Availability*—Dynamically finds alternative paths quickly; and optionally load balances across multiple active peers, ports, and channel gateways

- *Transport flexibility*—Higher-performance transport options when there is enough bandwidth to handle the traffic load without risk of timeouts, and the option to use lower-overhead solutions when bandwidth is at a premium and nondisruptive rerouting is not required

- *Modes of operation*—Dynamically detects the capabilities of the peer router, and operates according to those capabilities

DLSw+ Improved Scalability

One of the most significant factors that limits the size of LAN networks is the amount of explorer traffic that traverses the WAN. Several optimizations in DLSw+ reduce the number of explorers.

Peer-Group Concept

Perhaps the most significant optimization in DLSw+ is a feature known as the *peer group*. Peer groups are designed to address the broadcast replication that occurs in a fully meshed network. When any-to-any communication is required (for example, for NetBIOS or APPN environments), RSRB or standard DLSw implementations require peer connections between every pair of routers.

This setup is not only difficult to configure, it also results in branch access routers having to replicate search requests for each peer connection. This wastes bandwidth and router cycles. A better concept is to group routers into clusters and designate a focal router to be responsible for broadcast replication. This capability is included in DLSw+.

With DLSw+, a cluster of routers in a region or a division of a company can be combined into a peer group. Within a peer group, one or more of the routers are designated to be the *border peers*. Instead of all routers peering to one another, each router within a group peers to the border peer; border peers establish peer connections with each other (see Figure 8-1). When a DLSw+ router receives a TEST frame or NetBIOS NAME-QUERY, it sends a single explorer frame to its border peer. The border peer forwards the explorer on behalf of the peer-group member. This setup eliminates duplicate explorers on the access links and minimizes the processing required in access routers.

Figure 8-1   *The Peer-Group Concept Can Be Used to Simplify and Scale Any-to-Any Networks*

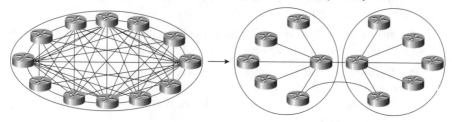

When the correct destination router is found, an end-to-end peer connection (TCP or IP) is established to carry end-system traffic. This connection remains active as long as there is end-system traffic on it; and it is dynamically torn down when not in use, permitting casual, any-to-any communication without the burden of specifying peer connections in advance. It also allows any-to-any routing in large networks in which persistent TCP connections between every pair of routers would not be possible.

Explorer Firewalls

To further reduce the amount of explorer traffic that enters the WAN, there are a number of filter and firewall techniques to terminate the explorer traffic at the DLSw+ router. A key feature is the explorer firewall.

An explorer firewall permits only a single explorer for a particular destination MAC address to be sent across the WAN. While an explorer is outstanding and awaiting a response from the destination, subsequent explorers for that MAC address are not propagated. After the explorer response is received at the originating DLSw+, all subsequent explorers receive an immediate local response. This eliminates the start-of-day explorer storm that many networks experience.

DLSw+ Enhanced Availability

One way DLSw+ offers enhanced availability is by maintaining a reachability cache of multiple paths for local and remote destination MAC addresses or NetBIOS names. For remote resources, the path specifies the peer to use to reach this resource. For local resources, the path specifies a port number. If there are multiple paths to reach a resource, the router will mark one path preferred and all other paths capable. If the preferred path is not available, the next available path is promoted to the new preferred path, and recovery over an alternative path is initiated immediately. The way that multiple capable paths are handled with DLSw+ can be biased to meet the needs of the network:

- *Fault tolerance*—Biases circuit establishment over a preferred path, but also rapidly reconnect on an active alternative path if the preferred path is lost

- *Load balancing*—Distributes circuit establishment over multiple DLSw+ peers in the network or ports on the router

The default for DLSw+ is to use fault-tolerant mode. In this mode, when a DLSw+ peer receives a TEST frame for a remote resource, it checks its cache. If it finds an entry and the entry is fresh (that is, if it is not verified within the last verify interval), the DLSw+ peer responds immediately to the TEST frame and does not send a canureach frame across the network. If the cache entry is stale, the originating DLSw+ peer sends a canureach directly to each peer in the cache to validate the cache entries (this is known as a directed verify). If any peer does not respond within SNA-EXPLORER-TIMEOUT, it is deleted from the list. There is no retry on the WAN. This may result in reordering the cache. The SNA-VERIFY-INTERVAL is configurable and is the length of time a router waits before marking the cache entry stale. The SNA-CACHE-TIMEOUT is the interval that cache entries are maintained before they are deleted. It defaults to 16 minutes and is configurable.

At the destination DLSw+ router, a slightly different procedure is followed using the local-cache entries. If the cache entry is fresh, the response is sent immediately. If the cache entry is stale, a single-route broadcast TEST frame is sent over all the ports in the cache. If a positive response is received, an icanreach frame is sent to the originating router. TEST frames are sent every 30 seconds (SNA-RETRY-INTERVAL) for a three-minute period (SNA-EXPLORER-TIMEOUT). These timers are configurable.

Alternatively, when there are duplicate paths to the destination end system, you can configure load balancing, which causes DLSw+ to alternate new circuit requests in a round-robin fashion through the list of capable peers or ports.

This feature is especially attractive in SNA networks. A very common practice used in the hierarchical SNA environment is assigning the same MAC address to different mainframe channel gateways—for example, FEPs or Cisco routers with Channel Interface Processors (CIPs). If one channel gateway is unavailable, alternative channel gateways are dynamically located without any operator intervention. Duplicate MAC addressing also allows load balancing across multiple active channel gateways or Token Ring adapters.

DLSw+ ensures that duplicate MAC addresses are found, and it caches up to four DLSw peers or interface ports that can be used to find the MAC address. This technique can be used for fault tolerance and load balancing. When using this technique for fault tolerance, it facilitates a timely reconnection after circuit outages. When using this technique for load balancing, it improves overall SNA performance by spreading traffic across multiple active routers, Token Ring or FDDI adapters, or channel gateways, as shown in Figure 8-2. Load balancing not only enhances performance, it also speeds up recovery from the loss of any component in a path through the network because a smaller portion of the network is affected by the loss of any single component.

Figure 8-2 *DLSw+ Caching Techniques Provide Load Balancing across Multiple Central-Site Routers, Token Rings, and Channel Gateways*

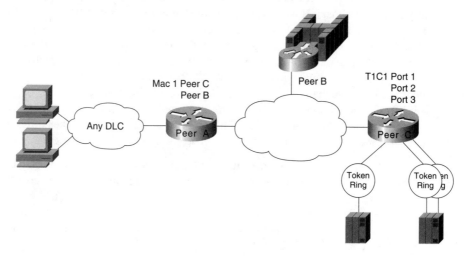

In addition to supporting multiple active peers, DLSw+ supports *backup peers*, which are connected only when the primary peer is unreachable.

DLSw+ Transport Flexibility

The transport connection between DLSw+ routers can vary according to the needs of the network, and is not tied to TCP/IP as the DLSw standard is. Cisco supports four transport protocols between DLSw+ routers:

- *TCP/IP*—Transports SNA and NetBIOS traffic across WANs when local acknowledgment is required to minimize unnecessary traffic and prevent data-link control timeouts, and when nondisruptive rerouting around link failures is critical; this transport option is required when DLSw+ is operating in DLSw standard mode.

- *FST/IP*—Transports SNA and NetBIOS traffic across WANs with an arbitrary topology; this solution allows rerouting around link failures, but recovery may be disruptive, depending on the time required to find an alternative path; this option does not support local acknowledgment of frames.

- *Direct*—Transports SNA and NetBIOS traffic across a point-to-point or Frame Relay connection when the benefits of an arbitrary topology are not important and when nondisruptive rerouting around link failures is not required; this option does not support local acknowledgment of frames.

- *DLSw Lite*—Transports SNA and NetBIOS traffic across a point-to-point connection (currently only Frame Relay is supported) when local acknowledgment and reliable transport are important, but when nondisruptive rerouting around link failures is not required; DLSw Lite uses RFC 1490 encapsulation of Logical Link Control type 2 (LLC2).

DLSw+ Modes of Operation

Cisco has been shipping IBM networking products for many years. There is a substantial installed base of Cisco routers running RSRB today. Therefore, it is essential for DLSw+ and RSRB to coexist in the same network and in the same router. In addition, because DLSw+ is based on the new DLSw standard, it must also interoperate with other vendors' implementations that are based on that DLSw standard.

There are three modes of operation for DLSw+:

- *Dual mode*—A Cisco router can communicate with some remote peers using RSRB and with others using DLSw+, providing a smooth migration path from RSRB to DLSw+. In dual mode, RSRB and DLSw+ coexist on the same box; the local peer must be configured for both RSRB and DLSw+; and the remote peers must be configured for either RSRB or DLSw, but not both.

- *Standards-compliance mode*—DLSw+ can detect automatically (via the DLSw capabilities exchange) if the participating router is manufactured by another vendor, therefore operating in DLSw standard mode.

- *Enhanced mode*—DLSw+ can detect automatically that the participating router is another DLSw+ router, therefore operating in enhanced mode, making all the features of DLSw+ available to the SNA and NetBIOS end systems.

Some of the enhanced DLSw+ features are also available when a Cisco router is operating in standards-compliance mode with another vendor's router. In particular, enhancements that are locally controlled options on a router can be accessed, even though the remote router does not have DLSw+. These enhancements include load balancing, local learning (the capability to determine whether a destination is on a LAN before sending canureach frames across a WAN), explorer firewalls, and media conversion.

How to Proceed

If you have a simple hierarchical network with a small volume of SNA traffic, read the "Getting Started with DLSw+" section, which describes the configuration commands required in all DLSw+ implementations and provides configuration examples for SDLC, Token Ring, Ethernet, and QLLC. After reading the "Getting Started" section, you can read about advanced features, customization, and bandwidth management.

This chapter describes how to use DLSw+ in conjunction with downstream physical unit (DSPU) concentration, LAN Network Manager, APPN, and native client interface architecture (NCIA).

Getting Started with DLSw+

This section describes the basic configuration commands required for a DLSw+ network. It begins with a description of the minimum required configuration, and then provides examples for Token Ring, Ethernet, SDLC, and QLLC environments. If you are unfamiliar with router configuration, you should also review the examples in Appendix A, "Subnetting an IP Address Space." These examples illustrate how to configure not only routers, but also the attaching end systems. They show how to configure canonical addresses, static routes, and loopback addresses.

Minimum Required Configuration

Configuring DLSw+ on most networks is not difficult. Every router that supports DLSw+ must have a **dlsw local-peer** command; **dlsw remote-peer** commands are optional, but usually at least one side of a peer connection must configure a remote peer. If a DLSw+ peer configuration omits **dlsw remote-peer** commands, the **dlsw local-peer** command must specify the **promiscuous** keyword. Promiscuous routers will accept peer-connection requests from routers that are not preconfigured. This feature enables you to minimize changes to central-site routers when branch offices are added or deleted. It also minimizes required coordination of configurations.

If you have used RSRB in the past, you need to know what *not* to configure. With DLSw+, you do not need proxy explorer, NetBIOS name caching, SDLC-to-LLC2 conversion (SDLLC), or source-route translational bridging (SR/TLB). All these features are built in to DLSw+.

In Figure 8-3, the branch router specifies both a **dlsw local-peer** and a **dlsw remote-peer** command. The headquarters router specifies only a **dlsw local-peer** command, but it specifies **promiscuous** on the **dlsw local-peer** command to allow it to dynamically accept connections from branch routers. The peer ID specified on the **dlsw local-peer** command is the router's IP address. It can be a loopback address configured via **interface loopback 0** or the IP address associated with a specific LAN or WAN interface. If you use a LAN or WAN IP address, however, the interface must be up for DLSw to work.

Figure 8-3   *Example of* **dlsw local-peer** *and* **dlsw remote-peer** *Commands*

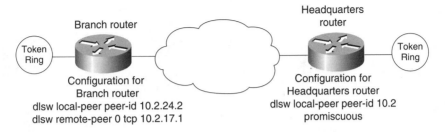

Configuration for
Branch router
dlsw local-peer peer-id 10.2.24.2
dlsw remote-peer 0 tcp 10.2.17.1

Configuration for
Headquarters router
dlsw local-peer peer-id 10.2
promiscuous

The number following **dlsw remote-peer** is the ring list number. Ring lists are an advanced topic, so for now, specify zero in this space, which indicates that ring lists are not in use. There are other options on the **dlsw local-peer** and **dlsw remote-peer** commands, but they are not required. These options are covered in the "DLSw+ Advanced Features" section, later in this chapter.

In addition to specifying local and remote peers, you must map the following local data-link controls to DLSw:

- *Token Ring*—Define a virtual ring using the **source-bridge ring-group** command and include a **source-bridge** command that tells the router to bridge from the external Token Ring to that virtual ring.

- *Ethernet*—Map a specific Ethernet bridge group to DLSw.

- *SDLC*—Define the SDLC devices and map the SDLC addresses to DLSw+ virtual MAC addresses.

- *QLLC*—Define the X.25 devices and map the X.25 addresses to DLSw+ virtual MAC addresses.

- *FDDI*—Define a virtual ring using the **source-bridge ring-group** command and include an SRB statement that tells the router to bridge from the external FDDI to that virtual ring; FDDI is supported in Cisco IOS Release 11.2 on the Cisco 7000 series.

The rest of this section provides sample configurations for Token Ring, Ethernet, SDLC, and QLLC.

Token Ring

Figure 8-4 shows a sample DLSw+ configuration for Token Ring. Traffic that originates on Token Ring is source-route bridged from the local ring onto a source-bridge ring group, and then picked up by DLSw+. You must include a **source-bridge ring-group** command that specifies a virtual ring number. In addition, you must include a **source-bridge** command that tells the router to bridge from the physical Token Ring to the virtual ring.

Figure 8-4 *Simple Token Ring DLSw+ Configuration*

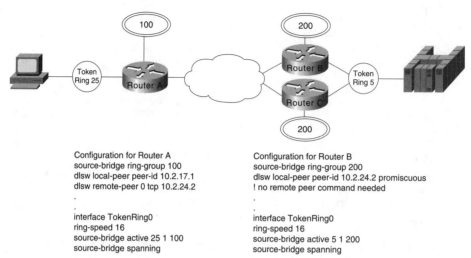

Configuration for Router A
source-bridge ring-group 100
dlsw local-peer peer-id 10.2.17.1
dlsw remote-peer 0 tcp 10.2.24.2
.
.
interface TokenRing0
ring-speed 16
source-bridge active 25 1 100
source-bridge spanning

Configuration for Router B
source-bridge ring-group 200
dlsw local-peer peer-id 10.2.24.2 promiscuous
! no remote peer command needed
.
.
interface TokenRing0
ring-speed 16
source-bridge active 5 1 200
source-bridge spanning

DLSw+ supports RIF termination, which means that all remote devices appear to be attached to the virtual ring specified in the **source-bridge** command. In Figure 8-4, from the host end, all the devices attached to Router A appear to reside on Virtual Ring 200. Conversely, from the remote site, the FEP appears to reside on Virtual Ring 100. As illustrated in this figure, the virtual rings specified in peer routers do not have to match. If multiple routers are attached to the same physical ring, as shown in Routers B and C, by specifying the same ring group number in each of them, you can prevent explorers from coming in from the WAN and being forwarded back onto the WAN.

Ethernet

Traffic that originates on Ethernet is picked up from the local Ethernet bridge group and transported across the DLSw network. DLSw always transfers data in noncanonical format. In Figure 8-5, you do not need to configure the left router for translational bridging or worry about what media reside on the other side of the WAN. DLSw will automatically make the correct MAC address conversion, depending on the destination media. When DLSw+ receives a MAC address from an Ethernet-attached device, it assumes that it is canonical, and converts it to noncanonical for transport to the remote peer. At the remote peer, the address is either passed unchanged to Token Ring–attached end systems or converted back to canonical if the destination media is Ethernet. Note that when an SNA resource resides on Ethernet, if you configure a destination SNA address in that device, you must use canonical format. For example, Ethernet-attached 3174s must specify the MAC address of the FEP in canonical format. If the Token Ring or noncanonical format of the MAC address of the FEP is 4000.3745.0001, the canonical format is 0200.ECA2.0080

In Figure 8-5, the data is transferred directly to a Cisco router with a Channel Interface Processor (CIP), but it can be any DLSw-compliant router, and the upstream SNA end system can reside on any supported media.

Figure 8-5 *Simple Ethernet DLSw+ Configuration*

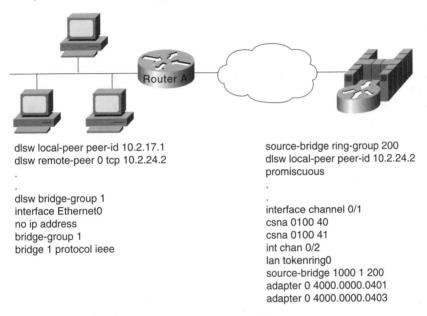

dlsw local-peer peer-id 10.2.17.1
dlsw remote-peer 0 tcp 10.2.24.2
.
.
.
dlsw bridge-group 1
interface Ethernet0
no ip address
bridge-group 1
bridge 1 protocol ieee

source-bridge ring-group 200
dlsw local-peer peer-id 10.2.24.2
promiscuous
.
.
.
interface channel 0/1
csna 0100 40
csna 0100 41
int chan 0/2
lan tokenring0
source-bridge 1000 1 200
adapter 0 4000.0000.0401
adapter 0 4000.0000.0403

SDLC

Configuring SDLC devices is a bit more complicated. For SDLC devices, you must know whether the device is a PU 1, PU 2.0, or PU 2.1. For PU 2.0 devices, you must know the IDBLK and IDNUM that was specified in the virtual telecommunications access method (VTAM) for that device because the router plays a greater role in XID processing when SDLC PU 2.0 is involved. You must know whether the router is the primary or secondary end of the SDLC line. In addition, if the attachment to the upstream SNA device is over a LAN, you must configure the MAC address of the destination upstream SNA device. In all cases, you must configure a virtual MAC address that will be mapped to an SDLC polling address.

In Figure 8-6, the SDLC-attached devices are each given a common base virtual MAC address of 4000.3174.0000. The router will replace the last two digits of the virtual MAC address with the SDLC address of the device. The device at SDLC address C1 appears to have MAC address 4000.3174.00C1, and the device at SDLC address C2 appears to have MAC address 4000.3174.00C2. In this example, both devices are PU 2.0 devices, so their XID must be configured, and it must match what is specified as the IDBLK and IDNUM in

VTAM. In addition, the router always assumes the primary role when attaching upstream from PU 2.0 devices.

Figure 8-6 *Simple SDLC DLSw+ Configuration*

```
Configuration for Router A
dlsw local-peer peer-id 10.2.17.1
dlsw remote-peer 0 tcp 10.2.24.2
Interface serial 0
encapsulation sdlc
sdlc role primary
sdlc vmac 4000.3174.0000
sdlc address c1
sdlc xid c1 01712345
sdlc partner 4000.3745.0001 c1
sdlc dlsw c1
```

```
interface serial1
encapsulation sdlc
sdlc role primary
sdlc vmac 4000.3174.1000
sdlc address c2
sdlc xid c1 01767890
sdlc partner 4000.3745.0001 c2
sdlc dlsw c2
```

The router can be the secondary end of an SDLC line (for example, when connecting to a FEP over SDLC). In this case, specify **secondary** in the **sdlc role** command; and for PU 2.1 devices, specify **xid-passthru** in the **sdlc address** command. In Cisco IOS Release 11.0 and later, DLSw+ supports multidrop PU 2.0/2.1. In Figure 8-7, the multidrop PU 2.0 configuration includes an **sdlc xid** command for each PU 2.0 device.

For multidrop lines with a mix of PU 2.1 and 2.0 devices, specify **primary** in the **sdlc role** command. For PU 2.0 devices, you must code the IDBLK and IDNUM in the **sdlc xid** command. For PU 2.1 devices, you can omit the **sdlc xid** command. In the **sdlc address** command, however, you need to specify **xid-poll**. Alternatively, when all devices on a line are PU 2.1, you can specify **sdlc role prim-xid-poll**, in which case you do not need to specify **xid-poll** in each **sdlc address** command.

Figure 8-7   *Multidrop SDLC DLSw+ Configuration*

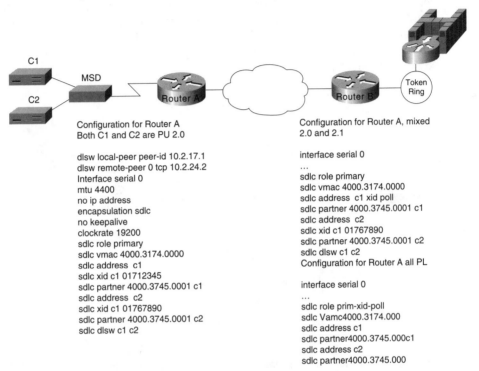

Configuration for Router A
Both C1 and C2 are PU 2.0

dlsw local-peer peer-id 10.2.17.1
dlsw remote-peer 0 tcp 10.2.24.2
Interface serial 0
mtu 4400
no ip address
encapsulation sdlc
no keepalive
clockrate 19200
sdlc role primary
sdlc vmac 4000.3174.0000
sdlc address c1
sdlc xid c1 01712345
sdlc partner 4000.3745.0001 c1
sdlc address c2
sdlc xid c1 01767890
sdlc partner 4000.3745.0001 c2
sdlc dlsw c1 c2

Configuration for Router A, mixed
2.0 and 2.1

interface serial 0
...
sdlc role primary
sdlc vmac 4000.3174.0000
sdlc address c1 xid poll
sdlc partner 4000.3745.0001 c1
sdlc address c2
sdlc xid c1 01767890
sdlc partner 4000.3745.0001 c2
sdlc dlsw c1 c2
Configuration for Router A all PL

interface serial 0
...
sdlc role prim-xid-poll
sdlc Vamc4000.3174.000
sdlc address c1
sdlc partner4000.3745.000c1
sdlc address c2
sdlc partner4000.3745.000

QLLC

QLLC is the data link used by SNA devices when connecting to X.25 networks. QLLC is a legacy protocol developed by IBM to allow the Network Control Program (NCP) to support remote connections over X.25. The software feature on NCP that supports QLLC is called Network Packet-Switching Interface. The QLLC protocol derives its name from using the Q-bit in the X.25 header to identify QLLC protocol primitives. QLLC essentially emulates SDLC over X.25. Thus, DLSw+ performs QLLC conversion in a manner similar to SDLC conversion. Cisco's DLSw+ implementation added support for QLLC in Cisco IOS Release 11.0. Because QLLC is more complicated than Token Ring, Ethernet, or SDLC, three examples are included here.

Figure 8-8 shows DLSw+ being used to allow remote devices to connect to a DLSw+ network over an X.25 public packet-switched network. In this example, all QLLC traffic is addressed to destination address 4000.1161.1234, which is the MAC address of the FEP. The remote X.25-attached 3174 is given a virtual MAC address of 1000.0000.0001. This virtual MAC address is mapped to the X.121 address of the 3174 (31104150101) in the X.25-attached router.

Figure 8-8   *QLLC DSLw+ Configuration to a Single LAN-Attached Upstream Device*

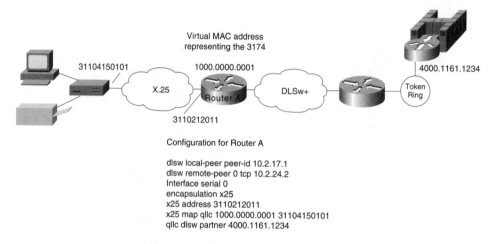

In Figure 8-9, a single 3174 needs to communicate with both an AS/400 and a FEP. The FEP is associated with subaddress 150101, and the AS/400 is associated with subaddress 150102. If an X.25 call comes in for 33204150101, the call is mapped to the FEP and forwarded to MAC address 4000.1161.1234. The 3174 appears to the FEP as a Token Ring–attached resource with MAC address 1000.0000.0001. The 3174 uses a source SAP of 04 when communicating with the FEP.

If an X.25 call comes in for 33204150102, the call is mapped to the AS/400 and forwarded to MAC address 4000.2034.5678. The 3174 appears to the AS/400 as a Token Ring–attached resource with MAC address 1000.0000.0001. The 3174 uses a source SAP of 08 when communicating with the AS/400.

In Figure 8-10, two X.25 resources want to communicate over X.25 to the same FEP. In the router attached to the X.25 network, every X.25 connection request for X.121 address 31102150101 is directed to DLSw+. The **qllc dlsw** command creates a pool of two virtual MAC addresses, starting with 1000.0000.0001. The first switched virtual circuit (SVC) established will be mapped to virtual MAC address 1000.0000.0001. The second SVC will be mapped to virtual MAC address 1000.0000.0002.

Figure 8-9 *QLLC DLSw+ Configuration for Support of Multiple Upstream LAN-Attached Devices*

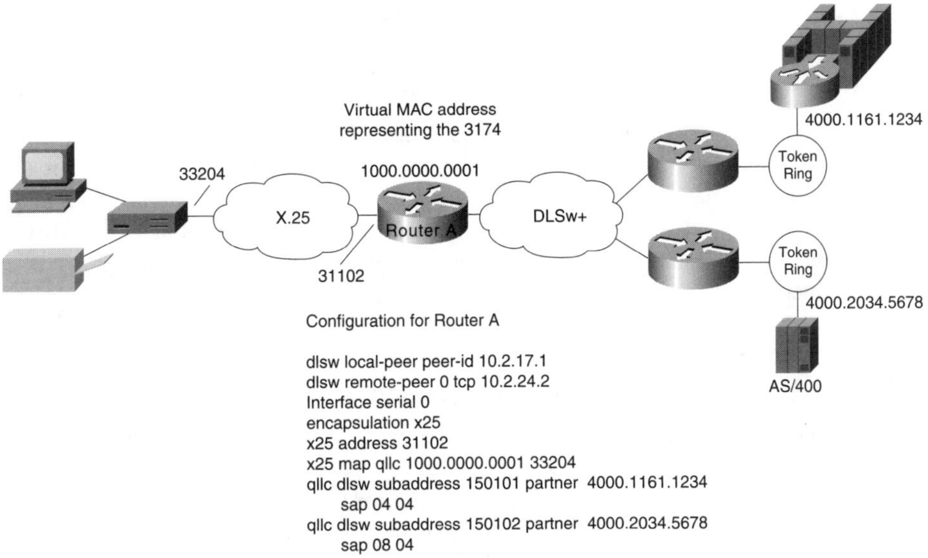

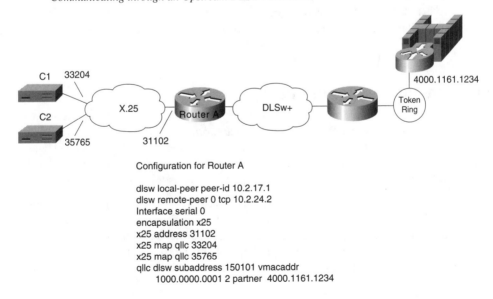

Virtual MAC address
representing the 3174

4000.1161.1234

33204

1000.0000.0001

X.25

Router A

DLSw+

Token
Ring

Token
Ring

31102

4000.2034.5678

AS/400

Configuration for Router A

dlsw local-peer peer-id 10.2.17.1
dlsw remote-peer 0 tcp 10.2.24.2
Interface serial 0
encapsulation x25
x25 address 31102
x25 map qllc 1000.0000.0001 33204
qllc dlsw subaddress 150101 partner 4000.1161.1234
       sap 04 04
qllc dlsw subaddress 150102 partner 4000.2034.5678
       sap 08 04

Figure 8-10 *QLLC DLSw+ Configuration for Support of Multiple Downstream X.25-Attached Devices Communicating through an Upstream DLSw+ Network*

4000.1161.1234

C1 33204

X.25

Router A

DLSw+

Token
Ring

C2

35765

31102

Configuration for Router A

dlsw local-peer peer-id 10.2.17.1
dlsw remote-peer 0 tcp 10.2.24.2
Interface serial 0
encapsulation x25
x25 address 31102
x25 map qllc 33204
x25 map qllc 35765
qllc dlsw subaddress 150101 vmacaddr
       1000.0000.0001 2 partner 4000.1161.1234

DLSw+ Advanced Features

This section describes advanced features of DLSw+, the benefits they provide, and a brief description of when and how to use them. Use this section to determine which options you want to use and to learn how to configure those options to address your requirements.

DLSw+ includes features to enhance availability (load balancing, redundancy, and backup peers), improve performance (encapsulation options), minimize broadcasts (ring lists), and build meshed networks (border peers and peer groups). DLSw+ also provides a feature to maximize central-site resources and minimize carrier costs (dynamic peers). Advanced features are optional and do not apply in all networks. Each feature includes a description of where it should be used.

How DLSw+ Peers Establish Connections

To understand load balancing, it is useful to understand how DLSw+ peers establish peer connections and find resources. When DLSw+ routers are activated, the first thing they do is establish peer connections with each configured remote peer (unless **passive** is specified, in which case a peer will wait for the remote peer to initiate a peer connection). The routers then exchange their capabilities. Included in the capabilities exchange are any resources configured in **dlsw icanreach** or **dlsw icannotreach** commands. After the capabilities exchange, the DLSw+ peers are idle until an end system sends an explorer frame (explorer frames are SNA TEST or XID frames, or NetBIOS NAME-QUERY or ADD NAME-QUERY frames). Explorer frames are forwarded to every active peer and any local ports (other than the port it was received on). It is possible that an end system can be found through multiple remote peers or local ports. The path selected for a given circuit depends on certain advanced configuration options described in this section.

Load Balancing and Redundancy

If you have multiple central-site routers supporting DLSw+ for either load balancing or redundancy, this section contains important information. It describes how to balance traffic across multiple central-site routers or multiple ports on a single router. Load balancing in this case does not refer to balancing traffic across multiple WAN links or IP paths. That load balancing is done by the underlying IP protocol and is transparent to DLSw+.

If DLSw+ gets multiple positive replies to an explorer, it will cache up to four peers that can be used to reach a remote end system, and up to four ports that can be used to reach a local end system. How these cache entries are used depends on whether load balancing is specified on the **dlsw duplicate-path-bias** command. If load balancing is specified, each new circuit request is established over the next path (remote peer or local port) in the cache in a round-robin fashion.

If load balancing is not specified, the peer selects the first path in the cache and sets up all circuits via that path unless the path is unavailable. The first path in the cache list can be one of the following:

- Peer from which the first positive response was received
- Peer with the least cost
- Port over which the first positive response was received

Cost can be specified on either a **dlsw local-peer** or a **dlsw remote-peer** command. When specified on a **dlsw local-peer** command, it is exchanged with remote DLSw+ peers as part of the capabilities exchange. The following example shows how cost can be used to control the path that sessions use.

In Figure 8-11, two channel gateways and three Token Ring adapters can be used to access mainframe applications. All three adapters have been assigned the same MAC address. Assigning duplicate addresses is a common technique for providing load balancing and redundancy in SRB environments. It works because SRB assumes that there are three paths to find the same device and not duplicate LAN addresses. (This technique does not work with transparent bridging.)

In this example, Peer A has **dlsw remote-peer** commands for both Peer B and Peer C. Peer B specifies a cost of four in its **dlsw local-peer** command, and Peer C specifies a cost of two. This cost information is exchanged with Peer A during the capabilities exchange.

When the SNA end system (that is, the PU) on the left sends an explorer packet, Peer A forwards the explorer to both Peer B and Peer C. Peer B and Peer C forward the explorer on their LAN. Peer B will receive a positive reply to the explorer and send a positive response back to Peer A. Peer C will receive two positive replies (one from each port) and will send a positive reply back to Peer A. Peer C records that it has two ports it can use to reach the MAC address of the channel gateway, and Peer A records that it has two peers it can use to reach the MAC address of the channel gateway.

Peer A will forward a positive response to the SNA PU and then establish an end-to-end circuit using Peer C. Peer C is selected because it has a lower cost specified. When the next PU attempts to set up a connection to the same MAC address, it will be set up using Peer C, if available. This is the default method to handle duplicate paths in DLSw+.

At Peer C, the first circuit will be established using Port 1, but the next circuit will use Port 2. This is because Peer C has specified load balancing in the **dlsw duplicate-path-bias** command. Each new SNA PU will use the next path in the list in a round-robin fashion.

Figure 8-11 *Possible Configuration and the Resulting Cache Entries Created when All Channel Gateways Have the Same MAC Address*

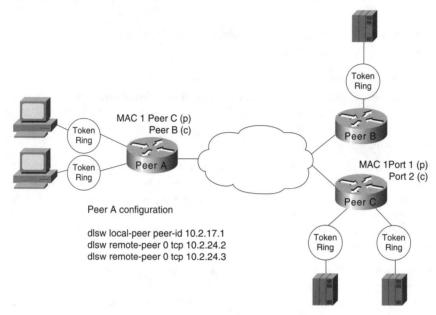

Peer A configuration

dlsw local-peer peer-id 10.2.17.1
dlsw remote-peer 0 tcp 10.2.24.2
dlsw remote-peer 0 tcp 10.2.24.3

Peer B configuration
dlsw local-peer peer-id 10.2.24.3 cost 4 promiscuous

Peer C configuration
dlsw local-peer peer-id 10.2.24.2 cost 2 promiscuous
dlsw duplicate-path-bias load-balance

Figure 8-11 shows how to cause all remote connections to prefer one peer over another, but the central site load balances traffic across all the LAN adapters on a given channel gateway. Alternatively, load balancing can be specified everywhere to load balance traffic across all central-site routers, channel gateways, and LANs. Note that this feature does not require the end systems to be Token Ring–attached. The remote end systems can connect over SDLC, Ethernet, or QLLC; and this feature will still work. The central-site channel gateway must be LAN-attached (preferably Token Ring–attached). Duplicate MAC addresses for channel gateways on Ethernet will work only when 1) you have a unique bridged Ethernet segment and a unique DLSw+ router for each duplicate MAC address, and 2) you load balance from the remote sites. (Ethernet has no provision to prevent loops, so care must be taken when building redundant networks with Ethernet LANs. Token Ring networks can rely on SRB for loop prevention.)

An alternative way to specify cost is to use the **dlsw remote-peer** command, as shown in Figure 8-12. Specifying **cost** in the **dlsw remote-peer** commands allows different divisions or parts of the country to favor different central-site gateways. In addition, you must specify **cost** if you want to split SNA traffic across multiple central-site routers, but each remote site has only a single SNA PU (all logical unit sessions flow over the same circuit that the PU session flows over). In Figure 8-12, Peer A always favors Peer B, and Peer D always favors Peer C.

Figure 8-12 *Configuration Where Cost Is Specified in the* **disw remote-peer** *Command Rather than the* **disw local-peer** *Command*

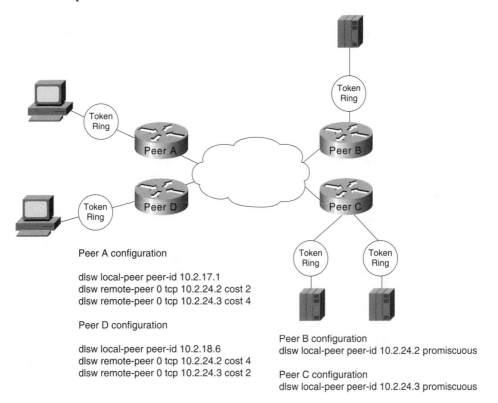

Peer A configuration

dlsw local-peer peer-id 10.2.17.1
dlsw remote-peer 0 tcp 10.2.24.2 cost 2
dlsw remote-peer 0 tcp 10.2.24.3 cost 4

Peer D configuration

dlsw local-peer peer-id 10.2.18.6
dlsw remote-peer 0 tcp 10.2.24.2 cost 4
dlsw remote-peer 0 tcp 10.2.24.3 cost 2

Peer B configuration
dlsw local-peer peer-id 10.2.24.2 promiscuous

Peer C configuration
dlsw local-peer peer-id 10.2.24.3 promiscuous

Controlling Peer Selection

A higher-cost peer can be used for a connection, even when the lower-cost peer is active, if the higher-cost peer responds to the explorer before the lower-cost peer. If your network configuration allows this possibility, you can prevent it by adjusting a timer.

Setting the **dlsw explorer-wait-time** command causes DLSw+ to wait the specified amount of time (for example, one second) before selecting a peer to use for connections. This timer can be set in Cisco IOS Release 11.0 and later. Prior to Cisco IOS Release 11.0, this timer did not exist.

Backup Peers

Having multiple active peers is one way to provide dynamic and immediate recovery from the loss of a central-site router. In some configurations, however, you may prefer the alternative peer to be active only when required. This may be the case when the backup router resides at a disaster-recovery site, or when there are more than 300 to 400 remote sites and a single central-site router is providing backup for multiple central-site routers.

In this case, use the backup peer capability (first available in Cisco IOS Release 10.3, but enhanced in Release 11.1). Figure 8-13 illustrates how to configure a backup peer. To use backup peers, the encapsulation method used to access the primary peer must be either TCP or Fast-Sequenced Transport (FST).

Figure 8-13   *How to Use Backup Peers to Enhance Availability In a Large DLSw+ Network*

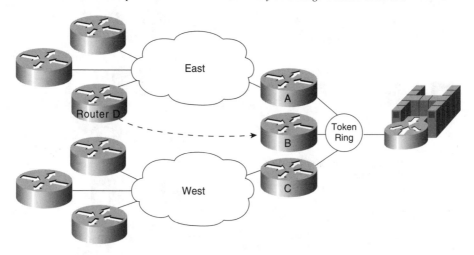

Router D configuration

```
dlsw local-peer peer-id 10.2.17.1
dlsw remote-peer 0 tcp 10.2.24.2
dlsw remote-peer 0 tcp 10.2.24.3 backup-peer 10.2.24.2 linger 20
```

In this example, there are 400 remote sites. All the routers on the East Coast use Router A as the primary router, and all the routers on the West Coast use Router C as the primary router. In either case, the backup router is Router B. The configuration shown is the configuration in Router D, an East Coast router. (All the East Coast routers will have the same two **dlsw remote-peer** commands.) Both the primary router (Router A) and the backup router (Router B) are configured in **dlsw remote-peer** commands. Router B is configured as a backup only, and the IP address of the router it is backing up is specified.

In the event of a failure in Router A, all SNA sessions are terminated and will re-establish through Router B. When Router A becomes available again, all new sessions are established through Router A, but sessions active on Router B will remain on Router B until the linger timer expires. Omitting the **linger** keyword will cause sessions on Router B to remain active until they terminate on their own. The **linger** keyword can be used to minimize line costs if the backup peer is accessed over dial lines, but will provide enough time for an operator warning to be sent to all the SNA end users.

Prior to Cisco IOS Release 11.1, when the primary peer was activated again, all sessions using the backup peer were terminated immediately and re-established over the primary router. If that is not the action you want to take, and you are running a level of Cisco IOS software earlier than Release 11.1, consider using duplicate active peers instead (described in the preceding section).

Backup Peers Compared to Multiple Active Peers

Backup peers and multiple active peers (with one preferred and others capable) are two ways to ensure that a capable peer can back up the failure of a primary peer. One of the key differences in backup peers is that the peer connections are not active until they are needed. Suppose you have 1,000 branch offices, and you want to design a network at minimal cost that will recover dynamically from the failure of any single central-site router. Assume that four routers at the central site can handle your traffic load. You can install four primary routers at the central site and define 250 branches to peer to each central-site router.

To address your availability requirement, one option is multiple concurrently active peer connections. In this case, you configure each remote router to have two peer connections: one to a preferred router and one to a capable router. The preferred router is the router configured with lower cost. The capable router can be the same router for all remote sites, but in that case, it has 1,000 peer connections. The largest number of peering routers we have seen is 400, and that was in an environment with extremely low traffic. Although 1,000 idle peer connections are conceivable, as soon as the capable router takes over for another router, those peer connections could put a strain on the router. The other alternative is to have multiple central-site routers as capable routers, but this is not the most cost-effective design.

By using a **backup peer** statement in each remote branch instead of concurrently peering to two routers, a single backup router at a central site can easily back up any other central-site router. There is no work on a backup router until a primary router fails.

Encapsulation Options

DLSw+ offers four encapsulation options. These options vary in terms of the processing path they use, their WAN overhead, and the media they support. The encapsulation options are TCP, Fast-Sequenced Transport (FST), direct, and LLC2.

TCP Encapsulation

TCP is the standard DLSw encapsulation method and is the only encapsulation method supported by RFC 1795. TCP offers the most functionality of the encapsulation options. It provides reliable delivery of frames and local acknowledgment. It is the only option that offers nondisruptive rerouting around link failures. With TCP encapsulation, you can take advantage of dial-on-demand to dynamically dial additional bandwidth if primary links reach a preconfigured amount of congestion. In most environments, it is the recommended encapsulation because its performance is generally more than adequate, it offers the highest availability, and the overhead generally has no negative impact on response time or throughput.

TCP is process-switched, so it uses more cycles than FST or direct encapsulation. A Cisco 4700 router running DLSw+ with TCP encapsulation can switch up to 8 Mbps of data, so TCP encapsulation addresses the processing requirements of most SNA environments. When higher throughput is required, additional routers or alternative encapsulation options can be used.

TCP encapsulation adds the most overhead to each frame (20 bytes for TCP and 20 bytes for IP, in addition to the 16-byte DLSw header). TCP header compression or payload compression can be used to reduce the amount of bandwidth required, if necessary. At 56 kbps or higher line speeds, the 40 bytes of overhead add fewer than 5.7 ms to the round-trip delay, so its impact is negligible.

DLSw+ with TCP encapsulation provides local acknowledgment and local polling, and minimizes keepalive traffic across the WAN. It supports any local media and any WAN media. Load balancing across multiple WAN links or IP paths is possible because TCP resequences traffic before forwarding the traffic.

When using TCP encapsulation, you can assign different types of traffic to different TCP ports so that queuing can be granular. LLC2 traffic can be distinguished by SAP (to distinguish NetBIOS and SNA traffic), and SNA devices can be prioritized by LOCADDR or a MAC/SAP pair. The following is a sample **dlsw remote-peer** command specifying TCP encapsulation:

```
dlsw remote-peer 0 tcp 10.2.24.3
```

FST Encapsulation

FST is a high-performance option used over higher-speed links (256 kbps or higher) when high throughput is required. FST uses an IP header with sequencing numbers to ensure that all frames are delivered in sequence. (Out-of-order frames are discarded and the end system must retransmit them.)

FST is fast-switched, not process-switched, so using this encapsulation allows DLSw+ to process more packets per second than TCP encapsulation. FST does not use TCP, so the header is 20 bytes smaller.

FST, however, provides neither reliable delivery of frames nor local acknowledgment. All keepalive frames flow end to end. FST is supported only when the end systems reside on Token Ring. Two FST peers can connect over High-Level Data Link Control (HDLC), Ethernet, Token Ring, FDDI, Asynchronous Transfer Mode (ATM), or Frame Relay. (Some transport media are not available with early maintenance releases. See Appendix B, "IBM Serial Link Implementation," for details.) FST will reroute around link failures, but rerouting may be disruptive. In addition, load balancing across multiple WAN links or IP paths is not recommended with FST because frames may arrive out of order and FST will discard them, causing end systems to retransmit and reducing overall network performance.

Finally, queuing is not as granular with FST because you cannot assign different types of traffic to different TCP ports. This means that when using FST encapsulation, queuing algorithms cannot be distinguished by SAP (so NetBIOS and SNA are treated as LLC2 traffic), and they cannot be distinguished by LOCADDR or MAC address. The following is a sample **dlsw remote-peer fst** command specifying FST encapsulation:

```
dlsw remote-peer 0 fst 10.2.24.3
```

Direct Encapsulation

Direct encapsulation is a minimal-overhead option for transport across point-to-point lines when rerouting is not required. Direct encapsulation is supported over HDLC lines and Frame Relay. It includes a DLSw 16-byte header and the data-link control header. Direct encapsulation is fast-switched, not process-switched, so using this encapsulation allows DLSw+ to process more packets per second than TCP encapsulation.

Direct encapsulation provides neither reliable delivery of frames nor local acknowledgment. All keepalive frames flow end to end. Direct encapsulation is supported only when the end systems reside on Token Ring. Direct encapsulation does not provide any rerouting.

Finally, queuing is not as granular with direct encapsulation because you cannot assign different types of traffic to different TCP ports. This means that when using direct encapsulation, queuing algorithms cannot be distinguished by SAP (so NetBIOS and SNA are treated as LLC2 traffic), and they cannot be distinguished by SDLC or MAC address.

Direct encapsulation is sometimes considered for very-low-speed lines to minimize overhead, but TCP encapsulation with payload compression may offer lower WAN overhead without the limitations of direct encapsulation. The following is a sample **dlsw remote-peer interface** command specifying direct encapsulation on an HDLC line:

```
dlsw remote-peer 0 interface serial 01
```

The following is a sample **dlsw remote-peer frame relay** command specifying direct encapsulation on a Frame Relay line:

```
dlsw remote-peer 0 frame-relay interface serial 01 33 pass-thru
frame-relay map dlsw 33
```

In this example, data-link connection identifier (DLCI) 33 on serial interface 1 is used to transport DLSw traffic. Specifying **pass-thru** implies that the traffic is not locally acknowledged. Leaving **pass-thru** off causes the traffic to be locally acknowledged, which means it is transported in LLC2 to ensure reliable delivery. The next section describes LLC2 encapsulation.

LLC2 Encapsulation (DLSw Lite)

DLSw+ with LLC2 encapsulation is also known as DLSw Lite. It supports many DLSw+ features, including local acknowledgment, media conversion, minimizing keepalive traffic, and reliable delivery of frames; but it uses less overhead (16 bytes of DLSw header and four bytes of LLC2). It is currently supported over Frame Relay and assumes a point-to-point configuration over Frame Relay (that is, the peering router at the central site is also the WAN router). DLSw Lite supports Token Ring–, SDLC-, QLLC-, or Ethernet-attached end systems. DLSw Lite is process-switched and processes approximately the same traffic volume as TCP encapsulation.

With DLSw Lite, link failures are disruptive. Availability can be achieved by having multiple active central-site peers, which allows for dynamic, but disruptive, recovery from the loss of either a link or a central-site peer. Backup peers are not yet supported for DLSw Lite.

Queuing with DLSw Lite is not as granular as with TCP encapsulation because you cannot assign different types of traffic to different TCP ports. This means that when using DLSw Lite, queuing algorithms cannot distinguish traffic by SAP (so NetBIOS and SNA are treated as LLC2 traffic), and they cannot distinguish traffic by SDLC or MAC address. The following is a sample **dlsw remote-peer frame-relay** command specifying LLC2 encapsulation on a Frame Relay line:

```
dlsw remote-peer 0 frame-relay interface serial 01 33
frame-relay map llc2 33
```

NOTE   The **frame-relay map llc2** command will not work on point-to-point subinterfaces. Instead, you must provide the DLCI number in the **frame-relay interface-dlci** command and specify the same DLCI number in the **dlsw remote-peer frame relay** command.

The following is a sample **dlsw remote-peer** command for point-to-point subinterfaces:

```
dlsw remote-peer 0 frame-relay interface serial 0.1 60
interface s0.1 point-to-point
frame-relay interface-dlci 60
```

Encapsulation Overhead

Different types of encapsulation incur different amounts of overhead on a per-frame basis. But with TCP and LLC2, local acknowledgment and keepalive traffic are removed from the WAN, reducing the number of packets. Also, such techniques as payload or header compression, and packing multiple SNA frames in a single TCP packet can further reduce the overhead. The percentage of overhead created by DLSw depends on the encapsulation method used.

Figure 8-14 illustrates the frame format for TCP, FST, DLSw Lite, and direct encapsulation. The percentage shown is the amount of overhead, assuming SNA transactions of 40 in, 1,920 out (a screen refresh) and 40 in, 1,200 out. With smaller transactions, the overhead is larger. The TCP encapsulation numbers are worst-case numbers because they assume that each SNA path information unit (PIU) is encapsulated in a separate TCP packet. In fact, if there is more than one SNA PIU in the output queue, multiple frames will be encapsulated in a single TCP packet, reducing the overhead. The percentages in Figure 8-14 do not take into consideration the fact that DLSw+ eliminates keepalive packets and acknowledgments.

Figure 8-14 *Frame Format and Per-Packet Overhead of Various Encapsulation Types and Transaction Sizes*

Encapsulation		40/1920 SDLC	40/1920 LAN	40/1200 SDLC	40/1200 LAN
TCP	DLC | IP | TCP | DLSw | Data	5.7%	4.5%	9%	7%
FST	DLC | IP | DLSw | Data	3.7%	2.4%	5.8%	3.9%
Lite	FR | LLC2 | DLSw | Data	2%	1%	3.2%	1.3%
Direct	FR | DLSw | Data	1.8%	.6%	2.9%	1%

The effective per-packet overhead of DLSw for LAN traffic is lower than SDLC because DLSw+ eliminates the need to carry MAC addresses and RIFs in every frame. DLSw does not carry this data because the DLSw circuit ID (part of the 16-byte DLSw header) is used for circuit correlation. The overhead of MAC addresses and RIFs can range from 12 to 28 bytes of data. The percentages in Figure 8-14 assume the minimum overhead (no RIF).

Port Lists

Port lists enable you to create virtual LANs (VLANs) or broadcast domains in a DLSw+ network. Using port lists, you can control where broadcasts are forwarded. In Figure 8-15, for example, there are three rings at the distribution site (where Peer A resides).

All the rings have SNA end systems, but Ring 15 is the only ring with NetBIOS servers. The branch with Peer B needs access port lists:DLSw+;DLSw+:port lists to the NetBIOS servers on Ring 15, but does not need access to other rings. Port lists enable you keep all broadcasts from Peer B off Rings 12 and 22 (and prevent Peer B from communicating with devices on Rings 12 or 22).

You can distinguish between different Token Ring ports and serial ports using port lists, but all Ethernet ports are treated as a single entity (Ethernet bridge group).

Figure 8-15   *Ring Lists Used to Limit Broadcast Domains in a DLSw+ Network*

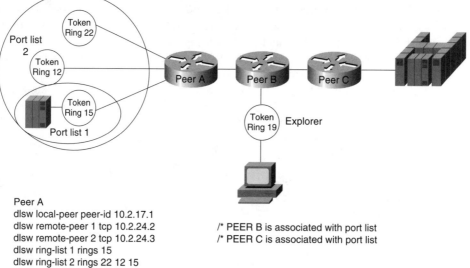

Peer A
dlsw local-peer peer-id 10.2.17.1
dlsw remote-peer 1 tcp 10.2.24.2
dlsw remote-peer 2 tcp 10.2.24.3
dlsw ring-list 1 rings 15
dlsw ring-list 2 rings 22 12 15

/* PEER B is associated with port list
/* PEER C is associated with port list

Peer Groups, Border Peers, and On-Demand Peers

Peer groups and border peers can be used to minimize the number of peer connections required for any-to-any communication. Prior to the introduction of border peers, any two DLSw routers that required connectivity needed a peer connection active at all times. This peer connection is used to find resources and to carry circuit traffic. In a fully meshed network of n routers, this requires $nx(n-1)/2$ TCP connections. This is complex to configure and can result in unnecessary explorer traffic. To address this issue, DLSw+ supports the concept of peer groups and border peers. Peer groups are arbitrary groups of routers with one or more designated border peers. Border peers form peer connections with every router in their group and with border peers in other groups. The role of a border peer is to forward explorers on behalf of other routers.

Use peer groups and border peers only when you need branch-to-branch communication between NetBIOS or APPN end systems. In Figure 8-16, the "before" network shows the required TCP connections for fully meshed connectivity without using border peers.

Without border peers, any time a router wants to find a resource that is not in its cache, it must create an explorer frame and replicate it for each TCP connection. This creates excessive explorer traffic on the WAN links and processing load on the router.

Figure 8-16 *Using Border Peers and Peer Groups to Minimize the Number of Required Tcp Connections While Maintaining Full Any-to-Any Connectivity*

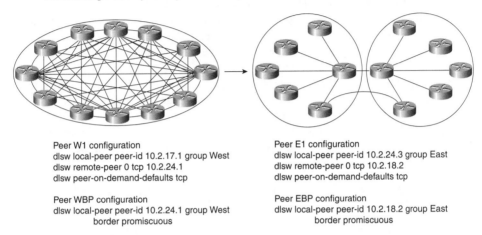

Peer W1 configuration
dlsw local-peer peer-id 10.2.17.1 group West
dlsw remote-peer 0 tcp 10.2.24.1
dlsw peer-on-demand-defaults tcp

Peer WBP configuration
dlsw local-peer peer-id 10.2.24.1 group West
       border promiscuous

Peer E1 configuration
dlsw local-peer peer-id 10.2.24.3 group East
dlsw remote-peer 0 tcp 10.2.18.2
dlsw peer-on-demand-defaults tcp

Peer EBP configuration
dlsw local-peer peer-id 10.2.18.2 group East
       border promiscuous

After configuring border peers and peer groups, the same fully meshed connectivity is possible without the overhead. In the "after" network, two peer groups are defined (West Group and East Group). Within each group, one or more peers are configured as border peers. Every peer within the West Group establishes a peer connection with the west border peer (WBP). Every peer within the East Group establishes a peer connection with the east border peer (EBP). The border peers establish a peer connection with each other. When a peer in the West Group wants to find a resource, it sends a single explorer to its border peer. The border peer forwards this explorer to every peer in its group and to every other border peer. The EBP, after receiving this explorer, forwards it to every peer in its group. When the resource is found (in this case at E1), a positive reply flows back to the origin (W1) via the two border peers. At this point, W1 establishes a direct peer connection to E1. Peer connections established via border peers without the benefit of preconfiguration are called peer-on-demand connections. The rules for establishing on-demand peers are defined in the **dlsw peer-on-demand-defaults tcp** commands in each router.

Dynamic Peers

Dynamic peers (available in Cisco IOS Release 11.1 and later) are configured remote peers that are connected only when circuits use them. When a **dlsw remote-peer** command specifies **dynamic**, the remote peer is activated only when an end system sends an explorer frame that passes all the filter conditions specified in the **dlsw remote-peer** command. After the dynamic peer connection is established, the explorer is forwarded to the remote peer. If the resource is found, a circuit is established, and the remote peer will remain active until all circuits using that remote peer terminate and 5 minutes elapse. You can specify the **no-llc** keyword to modify the elapsed time to something other than five minutes. Optionally, the remote peer can be configured to disconnect when there is no activity on any of the circuits for a prespecified amount of time (inactivity timer).

Filters that minimize how many explorers are sent to a remote peer can be included in **dlsw remote-peer** commands. In the case of dynamic peers, these filters are also used to prevent the dynamic peer from being activated. The **remote peer** statement enables you to point to lists of SAPs, MAC addresses, NetBIOS names, or byte offset filters. You can also specify a MAC address on the **dlsw remote-peer** command for a dynamic peer, in which case that remote peer is activated only when there is an explorer for the specified MAC address. Figure 8-17 shows an example of how to use this feature. In Figure 8-17, the dynamic peer is established only if an explorer frame is received that is destined for the MAC address of the FEP. After the peer connection is established, if there is no activity on this peer connection for 20 minutes, the peer connection and any circuits using the connection are terminated because **inactivity 20** was specified.

Figure 8-17 *DLSw+ Routers Configure to Take Advantage of the Dynamic Peer Feature*

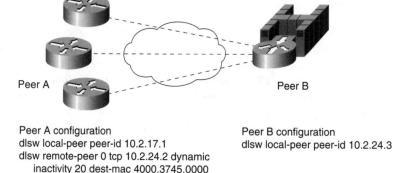

Peer A

Peer B

Peer A configuration
dlsw local-peer peer-id 10.2.17.1
dlsw remote-peer 0 tcp 10.2.24.2 dynamic
inactivity 20 dest-mac 4000.3745.0000

Peer B configuration
dlsw local-peer peer-id 10.2.24.3

When to Use Dynamic Peers

Use dynamic peers if you have a large network, but do not require all remote sites to be connected at the same time. By using dynamic peers, you can minimize the number of central-site routers needed to support the network. You can also use dynamic peers for occasional communication between a pair of remote sites. Dynamic peers differ from on-demand peers because they must be preconfigured. Finally, for small networks, dynamic peers can be used to dial out during error recovery.

SNA Dial-on-Demand Routing

SNA dial-on-demand routing (DDR) refers to the capability for DLSw+ to transfer SNA data over a dialup connection and automatically drop the dial connection when there is no data to send. The SNA session remains active. To use SNA DDR, configure the following on the **dlsw remote-peer** command:

```
dlsw remote-peer list-number tcp ip-address dynamic keepalive 0 timeout seconds
```

The **dynamic** keyword is optional but recommended because it will prevent the remote peer connection from being established unnecessarily. The **dynamic** option is described in the previous section and can be used in conjunction with the **dmac-out** or **dmac-output-list** options on the **dlsw remote-peer** command to ensure that peer connections are brought up only when desired (for example, when a device is trying to locate the FEP).

The **keepalive** keyword is required. DLSw+ locally acknowledges SNA (or more precisely, SDLC or LLC2) traffic, so no data-link control acknowledgments or receiver ready frames will bring up the dial connection. However, DLSw+ peers send peer keepalives to each other periodically, and these keepalives will bring up the dial connection.

The **keepalive** parameter refers to how often DLSw+ peers send peer keepalives to each other. If you set this to zero, no keepalives are sent, and the peer keepalive will not keep the dial line up. This parameter must be specified in *both* peers, which means that you must either specify the remote peers at both the local and remote DLSw+ routers, or you must use the **dlsw prom-peer-default** command to set keepalive to zero for all promiscuous peer connections. The **dlsw prom-peer-default** command is similar to the **dlsw peer-on-demand-defaults** command and is available in the later maintenance releases of all DLSw+ releases.

The **timeout** keyword is recommended. Without peer keepalives, DLSw+ is dependent on TCP timers to determine when the SNA session has come down. TCP will only determine that it has lost a partner if it does not get an acknowledgment after it sends data. By default, TCP may wait up to 15 minutes for an acknowledgment before tearing down the TCP connection. Therefore, when **keepalive 0** is specified, you should also set the **timeout** keyword, which is the number of seconds that TCP will wait for an acknowledgment before tearing down the connection. Timeout should be long enough to allow acknowledgments to get through in periods of moderate-to-heavy congestion, but short enough to minimize the time it takes to recover from a network outage. SNA data-link control connections typically wait 150 to 250 seconds before timing out.

Other Considerations

In addition to preventing keepalive traffic from bringing up the Integrated Services Digital Network (ISDN) lines, you need to worry about routing updates. In hub and spoke environments, to prevent route table updates from bringing up the dial connections, use static routes. Alternatively, you can use Routing Interface Protocol (RIP) Version 2 or on-demand routing for IP routing from the dialup branches to the central site. On-demand routing (ODR) is a mechanism that provides minimum-overhead IP routing for subsites. Define RIP Version 2 or on-demand routing on the ISDN interface of the central router as passive mode. Then, redistribute RIP Version 2 or ODR routes into the main routing protocol (Enhanced Interior Gateway Routing Protocol [IGRP] or Open Shortest Path First [OSPF]). This enables you to have multiple routers at the central site for load balancing or redundancy. Whichever router receives the call from the remote site will have the route installed dynamically. At the remote site, the routing protocol (RIP or ODR) must be denied from the dialer list.

For meshed topologies, you can minimize routing-table updates by using a distance-vector protocol, such as RIP or IGRP, in combination with Cisco's snapshot routing feature. Snapshot routing prevents regular routing updates from bringing up the ISDN connection. The changes in routing tables are sent either when the link is opened by end-user traffic or at a regular configurable interval. Snapshot routing supports not only IP routing updates, but also Novell's IPX routing and SAP updates.

Many NetBIOS implementations use a session keepalive (in addition to a data-link control keepalive) to maintain sessions, so DDR may not work with NetBIOS. (The session-level keepalive will keep the dial line up.)

Local Switching

Local switching (available in Cisco IOS Release 11.1 and later) allows a single router to provide media conversion between SDLC and Token Ring, and between QLLC and LAN. This is useful in environments that need simplified SNA network design and improved availability. By converting SDLC to Token Ring, for example, fewer FEP expansion frames are required; moves, adds, and changes are easier; and recovery from a FEP or Token Ring interface coupler (TIC) failure can be automatic (by using duplicate TIC addresses). Local switching can be used to connect SDLC devices directly to a Cisco router with a CIP card. Local switching can also be used over a WAN, in which the remote branch has SNA devices on LANs, but the central-site FEP still requires serial connectivity (for example, when the FEP is a Cisco 3725 router). To use local switching, omit **dlsw remote-peer** commands. In the **dlsw local-peer** command, the peer ID is unnecessary. Figure 8-18 shows a sample network and its configuration.

Figure 8-18 *Local-Switching Configuration in a Mixed PU 2.0 and PU 2.1 Environment*

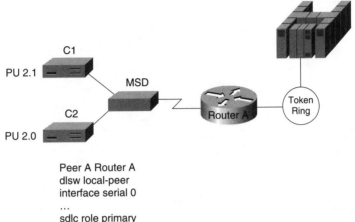

```
Peer A Router A
dlsw local-peer
interface serial 0
…
sdlc role primary
sdlc vmac 4000.3174.0000
sdlc address c1 xid-poll
sdlc partner 4000.3745.0001 c1
sdlc address c2
sdlc xid c2 01767890
sdlc partner 4000.3745.0001 c2
sdlc dlsw c1 c2
```

Summary

This chapter provided an introduction to DLSw+, including a description of DLSw+ and configuration examples to enable you to quickly design and configure simple DLSw+ networks. It reviewed the key components of the data-link switching (DLSw+) features and described the extensions to the standard that are included in DLSw+. Finally, advanced features of DLSw+, the benefits they provide, and a brief description of when and how to use them were discussed.

CHAPTER 9

CIP Design and Configuration

By George Sackett and Nancy Sackett

This chapter appears in the book Internetworking SNA with Cisco Solutions *published by Cisco Press* (ISBN: 1-57870-083-3).

The Cisco *Channel Interface Processor (CIP)* and the *Channel Port Adapter (CPA)* enable direct channel connection to the IBM mainframe. The CIP is available on Cisco 7000 and 7500 router platforms. The CPA is available only on the Cisco 7200 router platform. For purposes of this text, we will refer only to the CIP for connecting to the mainframe. However, all features, functions, and commands used for connecting resources to the mainframe through a Cisco router using the CPA are supported and specified as discussed for the CIP.

Direct connection of a channel-attached Cisco router to the mainframe enables a Cisco router to perform functions previously only available to IBM 3745 FEPs and IBM 3172 Interconnect Controllers. These features are as follows:

- Connection of LAN-attached devices to TCP/IP or SNA applications residing on the mainframe
- Support for the TCP/IP Offload facility of IBM TCP/IP for MVS or Cisco IOS for S/390
- Support for the Multipath Channel (MPC) feature
- Common Link Access for Workstations (CLAW) for TCP/IP access to mainframes
- Cisco SNA (CSNA) which allows the transport of SNA, APPN ISR to VTAM
- Cisco Multipath Channel (CMPC) for the support of APPN ISR and APPN HPR data to VTAM
- Attachment via a parallel channel adapter (PCA)
- Attachment via an Enterprise System Connection (ESCON) channel adapter (ECA)

In addition to these features, the Cisco IOS software support advances connectivity options through the following supported features not found on the IBM 3745 FEP or IBM 3172 Interconnect Controller. These enhancements are as follows:

- TCP Assist for offloading mainframe TCP/IP checksum processing cycles
- Support for a TN3270 server residing on the router
- IP precedence and IP TOS mapping for TN3270 connections
- Support for APPN/HPR on the Cisco router

- Support for NCIA server on the Cisco router
- Support for DLSw+ on the Cisco router
- Support for APPN DLUR/DLUS

Full support of all these features along with all the features previously discussed for transporting SNA data over multimedia WANs enables the Cisco channel-attached router as a full-function replacement of an IBM 3745 or IBM 3172 and most other gateway channel devices.

NOTE   Although the CIP supports SNA, APPN, and TCP/IP connectivity concurrently to the mainframe, this chapter discusses SNA and APPN connectivity options only.

Design Criteria

The Cisco CIP supports many features for connecting to the IBM mainframe for SNA. The capability to use ESCON allows for multiple IBM mainframe connectivity from one Cisco CIP, and thereby increases availability for downstream SNA sessions. The mainframe must be using EMIF to allow the CIP to connect multiple logical partitions (LPARs) using a single channel connection. The following concerns are some of the criteria that must be addressed when implementing Cisco CIP:

- Which of the many SNA transport features supported by Cisco IOS software are currently implemented and which features are planned?
- Which layer of the Cisco router internetworking architecture is most appropriate for supporting the SNA transport to the Cisco CIP router: core, access, or distribution?
- How many CIP routers and CIP interfaces are required to support the SNA traffic to the mainframe?
- What is the impact on the router processing memory and CIP memory requirements to support the SNA traffic over the CIP connection? This is important when LLC2 frames are to be transported to the CIP connection via a bridging methodology.
- Is the SNA network a mix of SNA sub-area routing and APPN ISR/HPR or a variant of this configuration?
- What is the need of uninterrupted or automated recovery to the mainframe through high-availability configurations?

There are three typical functional configurations for implementing Cisco CIP routers, as discussed in the following sections.

All in One

The Cisco CIP router provides all the functions necessary for connecting to the mainframe. This may include all the varied SNA transport features: DLSw+, RSRB, SDLLC, STUN, Frame Relay, and APPN, along with TCP/IP support. Figure 9-1 depicts this type of configuration. If this solution is entertained, it is best for use in small networks with a maximum of 50 remote locations. In addition, to ensure availability, more than one CIP router must be employed to provide primary support for some of the remote locations.

Figure 9-1   *All-in-One CIP Connectivity to the IBM Mainframe*

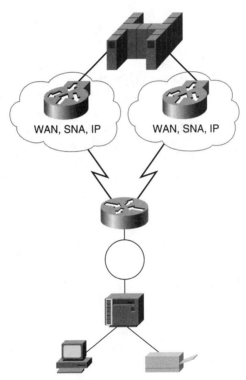

CIP and SNA Combined

In networks where minimal non-SNA connections are used through the CIP (that is, FTP, TCP) to the mainframe, offloading the WAN processing to LAN-attached routers ensures performance and throughput of the CIP router. Using the configuration illustrated in Figure 9-2, the CIP router can support hundreds of remote locations. This functional design segregates multiprotocol broadcast replication from the SNA processing. In addition, it increases the options for availability design by having a data-center backbone LAN with multiple CIP routers attached to multiple WAN routers for connecting to the WAN locations. In this configuration, the CIP routers are processing LLC2 frames along with IP packets.

CIP Solo

Using the CIP for processing SRB LLC2 traffic and IP only is possible through further segregation of services. SRB traffic in a router is switched instead of DLSw+ or APPN/ DLUR, which are processed by the router's main processor. In such a configuration, as shown in Figure 9-3, SNA-only routers on the data-center backbone LAN are the DLSw+ peers for the remote locations. These routers then transport the SNA frames to the CIP routers using SRB. Meanwhile, WAN routers deliver IP-based traffic directly to the CIP router. The CIP can handle upwards of 6,000 SNA PU sessions when using this type of connection.

Figure 9-2   *CIP and SNA Connectivity to the IBM Mainframe*

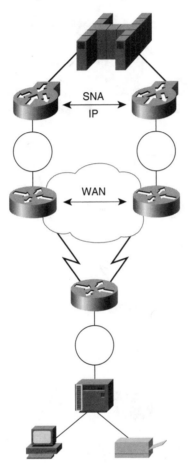

Figure 9-3   *SRB and IP-only Connectivity to the IBM Mainframe*

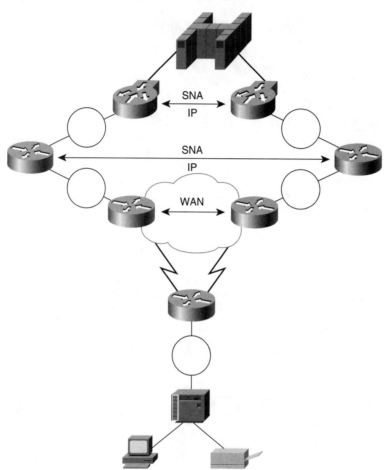

Design Configurations

The design configuration shown here represents the use of a Cisco CIP router for mainframe connectivity in place of the IBM 3745 FEP. The configurations cover many of the previous SNA transport mechanisms discussed by using the CIP rather than the IBM 3745 as the destination MAC address for the SNA connection establishment.

ESCON, PCA and MPC Configurations

Figure 9-4 illustrates using the mainframe via the various connectivity options from a Cisco CIP router to the IBM mainframe. Router R1 connects directly to the IBM mainframe using a bus-and-tag Parallel Channel Adapter (PCA) connection. Throughput on a PCA connection is approximately 4.5MBps.

Router 2 in Figure 9-4 diagrams the CIP connection using ESCON Channel Adapters (ECAs). The one CIP connection from R2 connects directly to the mainframe using ECA. The second CIP connection on the R2 router connects to a mainframe using the ESCON Director. *ESCON Directors* allow access to multiple logical partitions (LPARs) or multiple mainframes using a single ESCON connection from the router. In essence, the ESCON Director is a switch. Both PCA and ECA adapters use a single channel for reading and writing to the mainframe.

NOTE	The CIP also works with EMIF to allow access to multiple LPARs without using an ESCON Director.

The router R3 in the diagram depicts the use of Cisco MPC (CMPC) support for connecting to the mainframe over ESCON. CMPC enables the use of a pair of channels. One channel of the pair is used for reading; the second channel in the pair is used for writing. The pair of channels is referred to as a *transmission group (TG)*. If you have a CIP with two channel adapters installed, one adapter can be dedicated to reading and the other can be dedicated to writing. CMPC can also use a subchannel pair within a single physical channel.

High Availability Using RSRB to Mainframe Using Dual CIP Routers

RSRB caches the RIF field for all destination MAC address connections successfully made through the router. Figure 9-5 shows the use of RSRB between a remote location serviced by router R3 and two data-center routers R1 and R2 channel attached to the mainframe using a Cisco CIP. The internal LAN definitions on the CIP routers address connectivity to the mainframe using the same internal MAC address of `4000.7513.0001` on different internal CIP ring numbers.

The cache in R3 will maintain two RIF entries to the destination MAC address: one through R1 and one through R2. The first entry in the cache is the entry used by the remote location. If the router R1 or its channel connection were to fail the cache entry, the R1 router will expire and all new sessions will establish their SNA connectivity through the R2 router.

Figure 9-4   *PCA, ESCON, and MPC Connectivity Configurations for CIP to Mainframe*

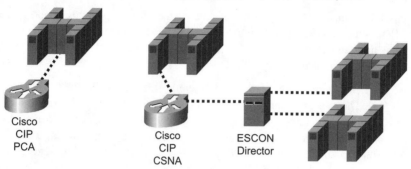

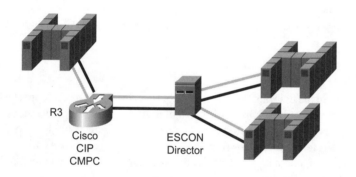

Figure 9-5   *High Availability Using RSRB and Duplicate MAC Addresses on Two Cisco CIP Routers through ESCON Directors*

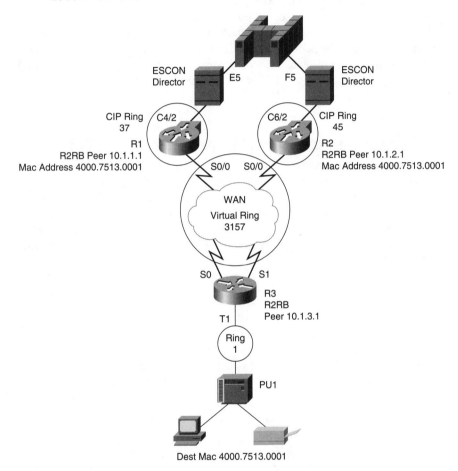

High Availability and Load Balancing Using DLSw+ to Dual CIP Routers

In Figure 9-6, we can answer the RIF cache problem by implementing DLSw+-to-WAN routers and using SRB to connect to the CIP routers. In this scenario, the remote location PU1 connects to MAC address 4000.7513.0001 using DLSw+. The DLSw+ learns of two unique paths through the network. The data-center routers R4 and R5 will provide round-robin connectivity over the dual Token Rings that attach the WAN routers R4 and R5 to the channel-attached routers R1 and R2. Recall that the round-robin is pertinent to SNA session establishment only.

VTAM-to-VTAM Communications Through a Single CIP Router with Two CIPs

VTAM-VTAM communications is often used in networks with more than one VTAM running. Figure 9-7 illustrates the use of VTAM-VTAM connectivity over two CIPs in the same router. The performance is enhanced through the use of the CMPC protocol. This configuration can also be accomplished by using two different CIP routers with a single connection to one of the VTAMs. These routers would then communicate over a high-speed backbone such as Fast Ethernet, ATM, or FDDI using the same mechanism as shown with the single CIP router configuration.

Figure 9-6   *High Availability Using Duplicate MAC Addresses with Load Balancing via DLSw+ on Two Cisco CIP Routers through ESCON Directors*

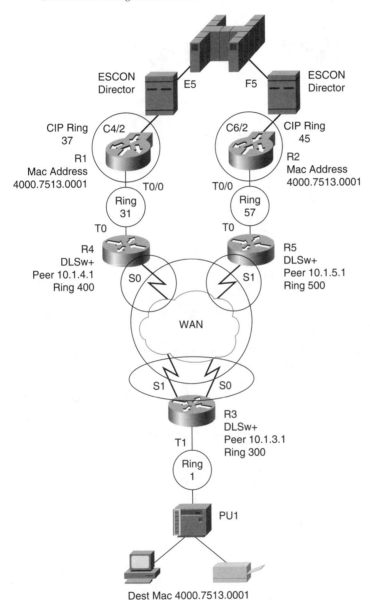

Dest Mac 4000.7513.0001

Figure 9-7 *VTAM-VTAM Communications over a Single CIP Router with Two CIPs*

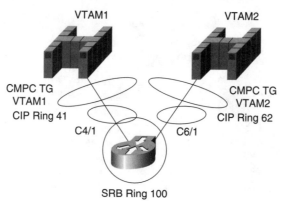

TN3270 Session Switching Using DLUR/DLUS with VTAM Host Redundancy

The Cisco CIP support for TN3270 enables IBM 3270 data stream traffic to pass through an IP backbone. The TN3270 server support on the Cisco CIP offloads TCP/IP processing from TN3270 termination on the mainframe and presents the TN3270 connections to VTAM as LUs of a LAN-attached PU.

Figure 9-8 illustrates the use of TN3270 server functionality with the added functionality of switching TN3270 connections from one VTAM to another should the primary VTAM become inoperative. The switched major nodes on VTAM must represent the direct PU connections for the TN3270 server along with a definition used for session switching. The configuration uses the APPN Virtual Routing Node for connecting the three mainframe APPN nodes. The transport between the two CIP routers is DLSw+.

Figure 9-8 *TN3270 Session Switching Using DLUR/DLUS and Host Redundancy*

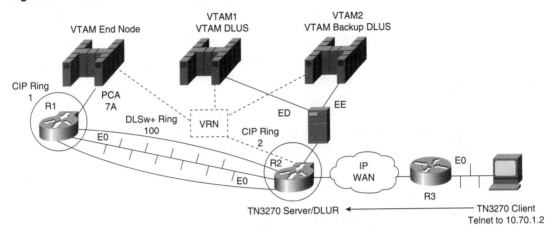

CMPC ESCON Connection for APPN HPR to VTAM

In this configuration, Figure 9-9, the CIP router communicates with VTAM and the APPN WAN using HPR. The CIP router defines the channel and Token-Ring ports as APPN links to establish the end-to-end connection. This same connection can also support APPN ISR. The CIP router does not have to be an APPN NN in this configuration; it is labeled as such to show function.

Figure 9-9 *ESCON CMPC Channel Configuration Using APPN HPR*

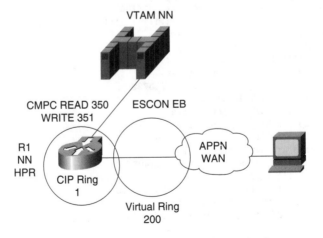

Loading the CIP Microcode

As of Cisco IOS Software Release 11.1, microcode for the CIP (or *CIP image*) is unbundled from the Cisco IOS software release. The route processor (RP) of the Cisco 7000 or the router switch processor (RSP) of the Cisco 7200/7500 router must have flash memory installed. A minimum of 8MB of RAM is required on the CIP itself to use the IBM channel attach features of Cisco IOS Software Release 11.1 and later.

NOTE The CIP image is preloaded on flash cards for all Cisco 7000 with RSP7000, Cisco 7500, and Cisco 7200 series routers ordered with the CIP/CPA option for Cisco IOS Software Release 11.1 and later.

The Cisco CIP microcode is found on the Cisco Web site under "Support." After finding the appropriate microcode for your CIP or CPA, it is TFTP'd to a viable TFTP server within your network. Execute the following commands in Example 9-1 to transfer the CIP microcode from a TFTP server to a flash card on the router.

Example 9-1 *Example of transferring the CIP microcode to the CIP router*

```
Router-r1#copy tftp slot0:
Enter source file name: cip25-8.bin
6843800 bytes available on device slot0, proceed? [confirm]
Address or name of remote host [tftpserver.domain.com]? 10.1.254.2
Accessing file "cip25-8.bin" on 10.1.254.2 ...FOUND
Loading cip25-8.bin from 10.1.254.2 (via Ethernet2/3): !
--- expanding multi-segment file ---
slot0:cip25-8.bin_kernel_hw4 size = 257888
!!!!!!!!!!!!!!!!!!!!!!!!!!!!!!!!!!!!!!!!!!!!!!!!!!!!CCCCCCC
--- expanding multi-segment file ---
slot0:cip25-8.bin_kernel_hw5 size = 256914
!!!!!!!!!!!!!!!!!!!!!!!!!!!!!!!!!!!!!!!!!!!!!!!!!!!CCCCCCC
--- expanding multi-segment file ---
slot0:cip25-8.bin_seg_802 size = 233792
!!!!!!!!!!!!!!!!!!!!!!!!!!!!!!!!!!!!!!!!!!!!!!!!!!CCCCCCC
--- expanding multi-segment file ---
slot0:cip25-8.bin_seg_csna size = 85896
!!!!!!!!!!!!!!!!!!!!CC
--- expanding multi-segment file ---
slot0:cip25-8.bin_seg_eca size = 461408
!!!!!!!!!!!!!!!!!!!!!!!!!!!!!!!!!!!!!!!!!!!!!!!!!!!!!!!!!
!!!!!!!!!!!!!!!!!!!!!!!!!!!!!!!!!!!CCCCCCCCCCCCCCCC
--- expanding multi-segment file ---
slot0:cip25-8.bin_seg_offload size = 64656
!!!!!!!!!!!!!!C
--- expanding multi-segment file ---
slot0:cip25-8.bin_seg_pca size = 69360
```

continues

Example 9-1   *Example of transferring the CIP microcode to the CIP router (Continued)*

```
!!!!!!!!!!!!!!CC
--- expanding multi-segment file ---
slot0:cip25-8.bin_seg_push size = 13752
!!!
--- expanding multi-segment file ---
slot0:cip25-8.bin_seg_tcpip size = 182032
!!!!!!!!!!!!!!!!!!!!!!!!!!!!!!!!!!!!!!!!!CCCCC
--- expanding multi-segment file --
slot0:cip25-8.bin_seg_tn3270 size = 542392
!!!!!!!!!!!!!!!!!!!!!!!!!!!!!!!!!!!!!!!!!!!!!!!!!!!!!!!!!!!!!!
!!!!!!!!!!!!!!!!!!!!!!!!!!!!!!!!!!!!!!!!!!!!!!!!!!CCCCCCCCCCCCCCCCC
```

The router configuration file must have a pointer to the CIP microcode name and location. This is accomplished by entering configuration mode on the router and entering the `microcode` configuration command as shown in Example 9-2.

Example 9-2   *Configuration command to point to CIP microcode*

```
microcode CIP flash slot0:cip25-8.bin
microcode reload
```

The `microcode` global command defines the interface processor being loaded, where the microcode resides, and the name of the microcode to load. The `microcode reload` global command will load the CIP immediately.

Defining CSNA Support

The Cisco SNA (CSNA) feature communicates with VTAM on the mainframe using the External Channel Adapter (XCA) driver of VTAM. In support of SNA, the CSNA uses a single channel address for reading and writing to the mainframe. The CSNA function utilizes the CIP virtual interface x/2 for defining internal virtual LANs used for connectivity through LLC2.

Assigning CSNA to an I/O Device Address

The `cnsa` command uses the channel path and the device address. The format of the `csna` interface command is as follows:

```
csna path device [maxpiu value] [time-delay value] [length-delay value]
```

The `csna` *path* parameter is subdivided into three arguments: logical path, channel logical address, and control unit address.

- The logical path (2 hexadecimal digits) constitutes the address of the physical connection from the mainframe point of view, one hexadecimal digit for the control unit address, and one hexadecimal digit for the device address. The PCA channel connections require the first two digits of the path value to be 01. The second two digits are configured in the IOCP generation file and should correspond to the appropriate device.

- The ESCON *logical-channel* argument of the csna *path* parameter must match the ESCON PATH input port value as defined in the IOCP generation. When using ESCON Directors, this is the port connecting to the mainframe. Without ESCON Directors (direct ESCON attachment to the mainframe), the *logical-channel* argument is 01. The IOCP/HCD macro definition CHPID points to the logical partition by a named value on the PART parameter. The IOCP/HCD RESOURCE macro defining the named partition specifies the LPAR number of the partition. Coding a value of shared for the channel path identifier (CHPID) macro requires the specification of the LPAR number attaching to the csna definition through a ESCON Director. If an ESCON Director is not used, the path value is 01.

- The *control-unit-address* argument of the csna *path* parameter is a single hexadecimal digit that must match the IOCP/HCD CUADD parameter of the CNTLUNIT macro. If the CUADD parameter was not coded in the IOCP/HCD CNTLUNIT macro for this channel, the default value of 0 is used for the *control-unit-address* argument of the csna *path* parameter.

- The csna *device* parameter represents the position of the CIP interface as a device attached to the channel. The value here is from the UNITADD parameter of the CTLUNIT macro in the IOCP/HCD definitions.

If given, the IOCP IODEVICE address of EB2 and the UNITADD parameter of the corresponding CTLUNIT macro specified EB0 and the UNITADD IOCP parameter begins at 00. The csna interface command would be defined as follows:

```
csna E220 02
```

where the ESCON port address connecting to the mainframe is E2. The LPAR using this connection is LPAR number 2 and the CUADD value defaults to 0. The CIP is connected as the third device on the channel (counting from 0) because the device parameter is 02.

Suppose the IODEVICE address is 97A. The IODEVICE ADDRESS parameter specifies a beginning IO address of 920 for 64 addresses (IODEVICE ADDRESS=(0920,64)). The corresponding UNITADD parameter begins at 20 for 64 devices (UNITADD=((20,64))). The csna device parameter is the difference between 7A and 20, which equals 5A. The corresponding csna command would be coded as follows:

```
csna E220 5A
```

The optional maxpiu keyword value denotes the largest packet size in bytes that can be placed on the channel being defined. This can be thought of as equivalent to SNA

MAXDATA and IP MTU size. The value defaults to `20470` if not coded and ranges from 4096 to 65535 bytes. The format is as follows:

```
maxpiu value
```

The optional `time-delay` keyword value is in milliseconds and specifies the delay used prior to transmitting a received packet on the interface. The default is 10 milliseconds, with a range of 0 to 100 milliseconds. The format is as follows:

```
time-delay value
```

The optional `length-delay` keyword value is the number of bytes to buffer before placing the data on the interface for transmission. The default is `20470` and the valid range is 0 to 65535. The format is as follows:

```
length-delay value
```

Defining the Internal Virtual LAN

SNA communications over the CIP with CSNA requires an internal virtual LAN definition. Define the internal virtual LAN under the ENABLE mode using the `CONFIG TERM` terminal operator command. Example 9-3 illustrates a sample configuration using internal virtual LAN.

Example 9-3 *Internal virtual LAN definition for CSNA services*

```
source-bridge ring-group 4
!
interface Channel 4/0
no ip address
csna E220 02
!
interface Channel4/2
 no ip address
 no keepalive
   LAN Tokenring 0
   source-bridge 6 1 4
   adapter 0 4000.C15C.0001
```

Using the listing, the CIP virtual interface Channel 4/2 is used for defining the internal virtual LAN. CSNA does not require an IP address for connectivity to the mainframe and therefore it is not defined. This is denoted by the command `no ip address`. Because this is a virtual interface and is considered up and active only when the physical interface Channel 4/0 is up, there is no need for keepalive messages. We denote this by using the `no keepalive` command.

NOTE   The CPA of a Cisco 7200 router does not use a virtual interface. Therefore, the commands discussed under the CIP virtual interface will hold true for a physical interface on the CPA.

The internal virtual LAN interface is defined using the `LAN` command. The `LAN` command can specify `FDDI`, `Ethernet`, and `Tokenring`. `Tokenring` is currently the only supported internal LAN at this time. The value `0` following the `LAN Tokenring` parameter indicates to the CIP that this is virtual LAN interface 0. The number of LAN interfaces can range from 0–31. The virtual Channel 4/2 interface can have multiple virtual LAN interfaces assigned to it.

The `source-bridge` statement following the `LAN Tokenring` statement defines the connection between this LAN virtual ring and the WAN virtual ring. The WAN virtual ring is the value defined on the `source-bridge ring-group` global command. The statement in Example 9-3 identifies ring number 6 as the ring number for the LAN virtual ring segment. The `source-bridge` statement therefore in Example 9-3 defines connectivity between the internal LAN virtual ring segment (ring number 6) and the WAN virtual ring segment (4) through bridge 1.

The last statement required for CSNA connectivity is the `adapter` statement. The `adapter` statement identifies the relative adapter number (RAN) and the MAC address assigned to the RAN for use on the internal virtual LAN segment. The `RAN` value ranges from 0–17 and must match the VTAM XCA major node parameter `ADAPNO`. The CIP allows multiple virtual adapters defined to the internal LAN virtual Token-Ring segment.

The internal LAN virtual MAC address as defined in Example 9-3 is `4000.C15C.0001` on adapter 0. This MAC address will be the destination MAC address for devices connecting to the mainframe using SNA.

Defining the VTAM XCA Major Node

The CIP2 communicates with VTAM using an *External Communications Adapter (XCA)*. Four parameters in the XCA definition are pertinent to establishing communications with the CIP2. These are the `ADAPNO`, `CUADDR`, `SAPADDR`, and `MEDIUM`.

Example 9-4 details an XCA definition for the CIP2 CSNA defined in Example 9-3. The `PORT` statement identifies the RAN using the `ADAPNO` parameter. The value coded for the XCA `ADAPNO` parameter must match the value defined for the first variable on the CIP `adapter` command. For the examples shown, this value is `0`.

The XCA `CUADDR` parameter on the `PORT` statement specifies the I/O device address VTAM will use to communicate with the CIP. The value specified in Example 9-4 is `EB2`. This value must be the I/O device address referenced by the `device-address` variable of the CSNA statement defined for the CIP Channel 4/0 interface.

The `SAPADDR` parameter on the `PORT` statement specifies the Service Access Point (SAP) address this VTAM XCA major node will use for communicating with devices over the channel connection. The `SAPADDR` value of 4 specified on the XCA must be matched in the SNA PU controller definitions of the devices that will communicate with VTAM through the CIP2.

The final parameter of the XCA PORT statement, MEDIUM, specifies the type of LAN in use. This value must reflect the type of virtual LAN defined on the CIP for communicating to VTAM. In the examples given, the value RING on the XCA identifies the use of a Token-Ring LAN defined by the LAN statement on the CIP2 virtual interface Channel 4/2.

Example 9-4 *Example of the VTAM XCA Major Node definition for CIP connection*

```
XCAR1     VBUILD TYPE=XCA
CIPEB21  PORT    ADAPNO=0,CUADDR=EB2,SAPADDR=4,MEDIUM=RING,TIMER=60
*  PU2/PU2.1 SWITCHED RESOURCES *
GEB2101  GROUP DIAL=YES,ISTATUS=ACTIVE,AUTOGEN=(50,L,P)
```

Defining TN3270 Server Support

The modifications to the CSNA configuration in supporting TN3270 server functions involve the following additions:

- An IP address for the Channel 4/2 interface
- A second virtual adapter for use on the virtual Token-Ring interface
- TN3270 PU definitions to represent the PU functions for the LUs assigned by VTAM using Dynamic Definition Dependent LUs (DDDLUs)

The assignment of an IP address to the virtual Channel 4/2 interface enables IP services as seen in Example 9-5. The statement max-llc2-sessions specifies the maximum number of active SNA LLC2 sessions at any given time through this virtual Channel 4/2 interface. The TN3270 server uses a second virtual adapter on the virtual LAN. RAN 1 and MAC address 4000.3270.7006 define the addresses for the TN3270 server adapter.

Example 9-5 *Additional statements required on the CIP Channel 4/2 interface for TN3270 server function*

```
source-bridge ring-group 4
interface channel 4/0
csna 0110 00
!
interface Channel 4/2
 ip address 192.168.6.1 255.255.255.0
 no keepalive
 max-llc2-sessions 2000
  LAN Tokenring 0
  source-bridge 6 1 4
  adapter 0 4000.0000.7006
  adapter 1 4000.3270.7006
 tn3270-server
  maximum-lus 4000
  pu PUEB2001 017FABC0 192.168.6.2 token-adapter 1 04 luseed LUTNS###
```

Entering the tn3270-server command enables the TN3270 server functions. The TN3270 server may handle a maximum of 30,000 LU sessions. The maximum-lus statement limits the number of LUs supported by the TN3270 server. In the example, the maximum number of LUs is 4000. The previous `max-llc2-sessions` value thereby limits the number of active LUs to only 2000 at any given time.

The core of the TN3270 server functions is the definition of the SNA PU. The `PU` statement defines the variables required to establish PU and LU sessions with the VTAM on the mainframe. The format of the statement is as follows:

`PU` *puname idblkidnum ip-address adapter-type ran lsap* `luseed` *lunamestem*

The *puname* on the TN3270 PU statement for the router matches the name of the VTAM switched PU name. The *idblkidnum* value must match the `IDBLK` and `IDNUM` values specified on the VTAM PU definition statement defined for the TN3270 PU representation. The *ip-address* is the IP address used by the TN3270 client for connecting to the TN3270 server PU. This IP address is known as the *IP Listening Address*. The `adapter-type` value must match the virtual LAN type defined for the Channel 4/2 interface. The *ran* value identifies the adapter used for connectivity to the mainframe.

The *lsap* variable of the TN3270 PU statement identifies the SAP used for communication over this virtual interface for this specific PU. If a second PU were defined under the TN3270 server using the same virtual adapter, a different SAP value would be assigned to the second PU definition. Usually, the SAP value for SNA begins with `04` and increments by four. Therefore, a second PU using the same `rmac` address would use a `lsap` value of `08`. Because it is customary to use SAP 04 for the CSNA connections, a value of SAP `08` is more appropriate for the TN3270 connection.

The `luseed` keyword indicates that the VTAM DDDLU feature will be used to define LU names and their associated characteristics dynamically. The names are based on the value given to the *lunamestem* variable. In Example 9-6, the suggested variable for dynamic LU names is `LUTNS###`. The `###` positions are replaced by VTAM during definition time with the decimal value of the LU's local address (`LOCADDR`) value as assigned by VTAM in the switched major node. The `###` `LUSEED` will output the seed in decimal. Using only two hashes —`##`—can generate a hex output for the LU name. If `LUSEED` is used, it is recommended that the seeds specified in VTAM and on the server match.

Example 9-6 *Switched PU definition to support DDDLU for TN3270 server*

```
* CIP switch DEFINTIION
SWEB200   VBUILD TYPE=SWNET,MAXGRP=4,MAXNO=80
PUEB2001 PU  ADDR=01,PUTYPE=2,MAXPATH=4,ANS=CONT,LOGAPPL=NMT,
                ISTATUS=ACTIVE,MAXDATA=521,IRETRY=YES,MAXOUT=7,
                PASSLIM=5,IDBLK=017,IDNUM=FABC0,MODETAB=SDLCTAB,
                LUSEED=LUTNS###,LUGROUP=EB2LUGRP,USSTAB=TESTUSS
  PATHEB2  PATH   DIALNO=01400032707006,GRPNM=GEB2001
 *LUTNS001  LU     LOCADDR=1
 *LUTNS002  LU     LOCADDR=2
 *LUTNS003  LU     LOCADDR=3
 *LUTNS004  LU     LOCADDR=4
```

Example 9-6 illustrates the resulting LU name for the first four LUs on the switched major node representing the TN3270 server PU defined in the router. The * denotes a comment line to VTAM. Note that the router *luseed* value must match the LUSEED value specified in the VTAM switched major node. The LUGROUP value in the switched major node points to a list that identifies the LU model type.

Example 9-7 lists a sample LUGROUP major node for VTAM.

Example 9-7   *VTAM LUGROUP major node definition to support DDDLU model types for TN3270 server*

```
TN3270G  VBUILD TYPE=LUGROUP
*
*   PU2/PU2.1 SWITCHED RESOURCES *
*                                               *
*   THIS IS A TEST XCA LUGROUP MAJOR NODE FOR CISCO CIP  *
*   TN3270 SESSIONS                             *
*
EB2LUGRP LUGROUP
327802   LU    DLOGMOD=D4C32782,
               MODETAB=ISTINCLM,SSCPFM=USS3270,LOGAPPL=NMT
327803   LU    DLOGMOD=D4C32783,
               MODETAB=ISTINCLM,SSCPFM=USS3270,LOGAPPL=NMT
327804   LU    DLOGMOD=D4C32784,
               MODETAB=ISTINCLM,SSCPFM=USS3270,LOGAPPL=NMT
327805   LU    DLOGMOD=D4C32785,
               MODETAB=ISTINCLM,SSCPFM=USS3270,LOGAPPL=NMT
327902   LU    DLOGMOD=D4C32782,
               MODETAB=ISTINCLM,SSCPFM=USS3270,LOGAPPL=NMT
327903   LU    DLOGMOD=D4C32783,
               MODETAB=ISTINCLM,SSCPFM=USS3270,LOGAPPL=NMT
327904   LU    DLOGMOD=D4C32784,
               MODETAB=ISTINCLM,SSCPFM=USS3270,LOGAPPL=NMT
327905   LU    DLOGMOD=D4C32785,
               MODETAB=ISTINCLM,SSCPFM=USS3270,LOGAPPL=NMT
327802E  LU    DLOGMOD=SNX32702,
               MODETAB=ISTINCLM,SSCPFM=USS3270,LOGAPPL=NMT
327803E  LU    DLOGMOD=SNX32703,
               MODETAB=ISTINCLM,SSCPFM=USS3270,LOGAPPL=NMT
327804E  LU    DLOGMOD=SNX32704,
               MODETAB=ISTINCLM,SSCPFM=USS3270,LOGAPPL=NMT
327805E  LU    DLOGMOD=SNX32705,
               MODETAB=ISTINCLM,SSCPFM=USS3270,LOGAPPL=NMT
327902E  LU    DLOGMOD=SNX32702,
               MODETAB=ISTINCLM,SSCPFM=USS3270,LOGAPPL=NMT
327903E  LU    DLOGMOD=SNX32703,
               MODETAB=ISTINCLM,SSCPFM=USS3270,LOGAPPL=NMT
327904E  LU    DLOGMOD=SNX32704,
               MODETAB=ISTINCLM,SSCPFM=USS3270,LOGAPPL=NMT
327905E  LU    DLOGMOD=SNX32705,
               MODETAB=ISTINCLM,SSCPFM=USS3270,LOGAPPL=NMT
3278S2   LU    DLOGMOD=D4C32782,
```

continues

Example 9-7 *VTAM LUGROUP major node definition to support DDDLU model types for TN3270 server (Continued)*

```
                           MODETAB=ISTINCLM,SSCPFM=USSSCS,LOGAPPL=NMT
        3278S3   LU        DLOGMOD=D4C32783,
                           MODETAB=ISTINCLM,SSCPFM=USSSCS,LOGAPPL=NMT
        3278S4   LU        DLOGMOD=D4C32784,
                           MODETAB=ISTINCLM,SSCPFM=USSSCS,LOGAPPL=NMT
        3278S5   LU        DLOGMOD=D4C32785,
                           MODETAB=ISTINCLM,SSCPFM=USSSCS,LOGAPPL=NMT
        3279S2   LU        DLOGMOD=D4C32782,
                           MODETAB=ISTINCLM,SSCPFM=USSSCS,LOGAPPL=NMT
        3279S3   LU        DLOGMOD=D4C32783,
                           MODETAB=ISTINCLM,SSCPFM=USSSCS,LOGAPPL=NMT
        3279S4   LU        DLOGMOD=D4C32784,
                           MODETAB=ISTINCLM,SSCPFM=USSSCS,LOGAPPL=NMT
        3279S5   LU        DLOGMOD=D4C32785,
                           MODETAB=ISTINCLM,SSCPFM=USSSCS,LOGAPPL=NMT
        3278S2E  LU        DLOGMOD=SNX32702,
                           MODETAB=ISTINCLM,SSCPFM=USSSCS,LOGAPPL=NMT
        3278S3E  LU        DLOGMOD=SNX32703,
                           MODETAB=ISTINCLM,SSCPFM=USSSCS,LOGAPPL=NMT
        3278S4E  LU        DLOGMOD=SNX32704,
                           MODETAB=ISTINCLM,SSCPFM=USSSCS,LOGAPPL=NMT
        3278S5E  LU        DLOGMOD=SNX32705,
                           MODETAB=ISTINCLM,SSCPFM=USSSCS,LOGAPPL=NMT
        3279S2E  LU        DLOGMOD=SNX32702,
                         MODETAB=ISTINCLM,SSCPFM=USSSCS,LOGAPPL=NMT
        3279S3E  LU        DLOGMOD=SNX32703,
                           MODETAB=ISTINCLM,SSCPFM=USSSCS,LOGAPPL=NMT
        3279S4E  LU        DLOGMOD=SNX32704,
                           MODETAB=ISTINCLM,SSCPFM=USSSCS,LOGAPPL=NMT
        3279S5E  LU        DLOGMOD=SNX32705,
                           MODETAB=ISTINCLM,SSCPFM=USSSCS,LOGAPPL=NMT
        @        LU        DLOGMOD=D4C32782,
                           MODETAB=ISTINCLM,SSCPFM=USSSCS,LOGAPPL=NMT
```

TN3270 with DLUR/DLUS Support

The TN3270 server function can also be employed by using the DLUR/DLUS features of
Cisco IOS and VTAM. The DLUR function of the TN3270 feature allows the TN3270 PU
to appear as an APPN end node. The commands applicable to DLUR are as follows:

```
dlur fq-cpname fq-dlusname
dlus-backup dlusname2
preferred-nnserver name
lsap type adapter-number [lsap]
link name [rmac rmac] [rsap rsap]
vrn vrn-name
pu pu-name idblk-idnum ip-address
```

The dlur command follows the usage as discussed for APPN connections. The *fq-cpname*
is a fully qualified control-point name (netid) and the LU name used for the session
switching. The *fq-dlusname* is the name of the control point providing the DLUS services.

The `dlus-backup` command identifies the fully qualified CP name of the VTAM DLUS providing backup. There can be only one `dlus-backup` per CIP.

The `preferred-nnserver` *name* specifies the name of the APPN network node server to which this DLUR definition belongs. The name is the CP name of an adjoining NN. This is an optional parameter and is not required for SNA switching to take place.

The `lsap` *type adapter-number* [*lsap*] is the local SAP address definition for the DLUR end node. The *type* parameter identifies the type of internal LAN adapter in use for the DLUR. The only valid value at this time is `token-adapter`. The *adapter-number* parameter identifies which adapter on the internal LAN is being used for the DLUR connection. The optional *lsap* variable is the local SAP address used by the DLUR ranging from 04 to FC in multiples of four. The value selected must be unique for all LLC2 connections traversing the adapter. The default value is C0.

The link name [`rmac` *rmac*] [`rsap` *rsap*] command defines an APPN link to the host for the end node DLUR. The *name* parameter is the eight-character alphanumeric string identifying the link. This name must be unique for the DLUR being defined. The *rmac* value is optional and defines the remote MAC address used for connecting the end node. The *rsap* value is the SAP address used for communicating to the DLUS over the link. The default here is 04 and ranges from 04 to FC in multiples of four.

The `vrn` *vrn-name* identifies the name of the virtual routing node for connecting the DLUR to the DLUS and possible backup DLUS. The `DLUS` and `backup-DLUS` must have the same VRN name specified in the VTAM switched major node representing the DLUR; otherwise, the switch will fail.

The `pu` *pu-name idblk-idnum ip-address* command defines the TN3270 DLUR PU used for connecting TN3270 clients. The *pu-name* parameter is a unique PU name assigned to the `PU` command. For operational and documentation purposes, the name should match the VTAM PU switch major node name defined for supporting the TN3270 PU definition. The *idblk-idnum* parameter must match the unique `IDBLK` and `IDNUM` parameters of the PU definition statement in VTAM that represents this TN3270 connection. The *ip-address* is the IP address used by the TN3270 client for connecting to the TN3270 server.

CIP CMPC Definition

In taking advantage of IBM's Multipath Channel architecture, the following tasks must be completed on both VTAM and on the CIP router:

1 Define the VTAM Transport Resource List (TRL) major node.

2 Define a local SNA major node.

3 Specify the CMPC subchannels.

4 Specify the CMPC TGs.

5 Define the internal CIP virtual LAN for CMPC. The LAN interface definition parameters are the same as those used by CSNA.

Transport Resource List Major Node

The *VTAM TRL major node* identifies to VTAM that the MPC line control is to be employed on IO device address 2F0 and 2F1. The TRLE statement defines which IO device address is for reading (READ) and which is for writing (WRITE). These IO device address values and properties must be matched on the CMPC definition within the CIP router. Example 9-8 is a sample TRL major node.

Example 9-8 *VTAM TRL major node for CMPC support.*

```
CIPTRL   VBUILD TYPE=TRL
TRL2F0     TRLE  LNCTL=MPC,MAXBFRU=8,REPLYTO=3.0,              X
                 READ=(97A),                                   X
                 WRITE=(97B)
```

NOTE   Although an even/odd address pair is not required, it is prudent for understanding the relationships and to maintain IO address continuity.

Define the Local SNA Major Node

Because CMPC support is only for APPN, a MPC channel link is defined on the VTAM host for connecting to the CMPC router through the definition of a local SNA major node. The PU statement shown in Example 9-9 points to the previously defined TRL major node. The TRLE parameter of the PU statement specifies the corresponding TRLE definition statement found on a previously defined TRL major node. In this example, the TRLE parameter points to the TRLE statement named TRL2F0. Also note that this local SNA major node defines the PU for XID required with CP-CP sessions using HPR routing.

Example 9-9 *Local SNA major node for MPC channel link configuration to CMPC router from VTAM*

```
LAGLNA   VBUILD TYPE=LOCAL
  LAGPUA     PU  TRLE=LAGTRLEA,                                X
                 ISTATUS=ACTIVE,                               X
                 XID=YES,CONNTYPE=APPN,CPCP=YES,HPR=YES
```

Defining the CMPC Subchannels

The cmpc command is specified on the physical interfaces of the CIP and not the logical interface x/2. This is because CMPC pairs subchannel addresses, so each subchannel may be defined on separate physical CIP interface ports of the same CIP. The format of the cmpc command is as follows:

```
cmpc path device tg-name {read ¦ write}
```

The cmpc *path* and *device* parameters are defined exactly like that described for csna. The cmpc *tg-name* variable is a name associated with the subchannel being defined. A read and write subchannel must be defined to use CMPC. The *tg-name* value ties the two cmcp definitions together to form the CMPC TG. An example of coding the cmpc command is as follows:

```
interface channel 4/0
!
cmpc 97A 5A R1CIP read
cmpc 97B 5B R1CIP write
```

Defining the CMPC Transmission Group

The CMPC transmission group is defined by using the tg command under the virtual channel interface x/2 definition. The format of the tg command is as follows:

```
tg name llc type adapter-number lsap [rmac rmac] [rsap rsap]
```

The *name* parameter is the TG name used for a previously defined cmpc statement. This name ties the subchannel pair to the LLC2 driver for the internal LAN.

The llc keyword denotes connectivity to the LLC stack on the CIP.

The *type* parameter specifies the type of internal LAN defined for use by the TG. The only value allowed at this time is token-adapter.

The *adapter-number* parameter identifies which internal virtual LAN adapter definition is used by the TG.

The *lsap* parameter defines the local SAP address used for communicating to the host. The SAP address value used here must be unique within the router and host, along with any IEEE 802.2 clients using the specified adapter. The default is 04. However, it may be wise to specify the high end of the allowable range, FC, and move down for additional CMPC connections to avoid any unknown conflicts. The value is a multiple of four ranging from 04 to FC.

The optional keyword rmac and its associated variable *rmac* is a MAC address assigned for use by the CMPC driver for LLC2 connectivity.

The optional rsap keyword and variable *rsap* defaults to 04 and is the remote SAP address used by the driver for communications.

NOTE	To change any parameter on the tg command, the no tg command must first be entered. The new tg command with the altered parameters must then be entered for the definition to take effect.

CIP Configuration Examples

In this section, we address various network configurations using the Cisco CIP as the gateway to the mainframe. The configurations explore the use of the CIP with examples of the previously discussed SNA encapsulation techniques for connecting legacy SNA resources to the IBM mainframe.

High Availability Using RSRB to Mainframe Using Dual CIP Routers

In Figure 9-10 the CIP router acts as the gateway to the mainframe and also connects the WAN. RSRB is used for transporting the data from the remote locations to the mainframe through the CIP. Although RSRB and duplicate MAC addresses provide high availability, they do not enable load balancing. DLSw+ will support the load-balancing function.

Figure 9-10 *Using RSRB to CIP WAN Routers for High Availability*

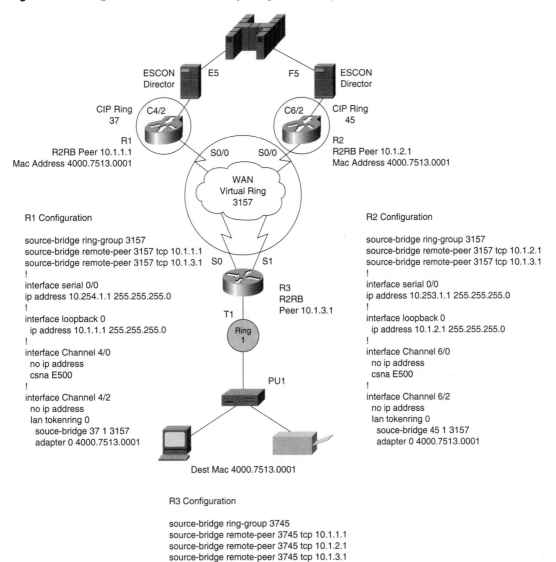

ESCON Director   E5   F5   ESCON Director

CIP Ring 37   C4/2   C6/2   CIP Ring 45

R1
R2RB Peer 10.1.1.1
Mac Address 4000.7513.0001

S0/0   S0/0

R2
R2RB Peer 10.1.2.1
Mac Address 4000.7513.0001

WAN
Virtual Ring
3157

R1 Configuration

source-bridge ring-group 3157
source-bridge remote-peer 3157 tcp 10.1.1.1
source-bridge remote-peer 3157 tcp 10.1.3.1
!
interface serial 0/0
ip address 10.254.1.1 255.255.255.0
!
interface loopback 0
  ip address 10.1.1.1 255.255.255.0
!
interface Channel 4/0
  no ip address
  csna E500
!
interface Channel 4/2
  no ip address
  lan tokenring 0
    souce-bridge 37 1 3157
    adapter 0 4000.7513.0001

S0   S1

R3
R2RB
Peer 10.1.3.1

T1

Ring 1

PU1

Dest Mac 4000.7513.0001

R2 Configuration

source-bridge ring-group 3157
source-bridge remote-peer 3157 tcp 10.1.2.1
source-bridge remote-peer 3157 tcp 10.1.3.1
!
interface serial 0/0
ip address 10.253.1.1 255.255.255.0
!
interface loopback 0
  ip address 10.1.2.1 255.255.255.0
!
interface Channel 6/0
  no ip address
  csna E500
!
interface Channel 6/2
  no ip address
  lan tokenring 0
    souce-bridge 45 1 3157
    adapter 0 4000.7513.0001

R3 Configuration

source-bridge ring-group 3745
source-bridge remote-peer 3745 tcp 10.1.1.1
source-bridge remote-peer 3745 tcp 10.1.2.1
source-bridge remote-peer 3745 tcp 10.1.3.1
!
interface tokenring 1
ip address 10.1.3.1
source-bridge 1 1 3157
!
interface serial 0
  ip address 10.254.1.2 255.255.255.0
!
interface serial 1
ip address 10.253.1.1 255.255.255.0

High Availability and Load Balancing Using DLSw+ to Dual CIP Routers

Figure 9-11 shows the router configurations necessary for supporting high availability and load balancing using DLSw+ and dual CIP routers. The WAN routers at the data center offload all processing from the CIP routers except for SRB. This type of configuration enables duplicate MAC addressing for load balancing and redundancy should either CIP router fail.

Figure 9-11 *High Availability Using Duplicate MAC Addresses with Load Balancing via DLSw+ on Two Cisco CIP Routers Through ESCON Directors*

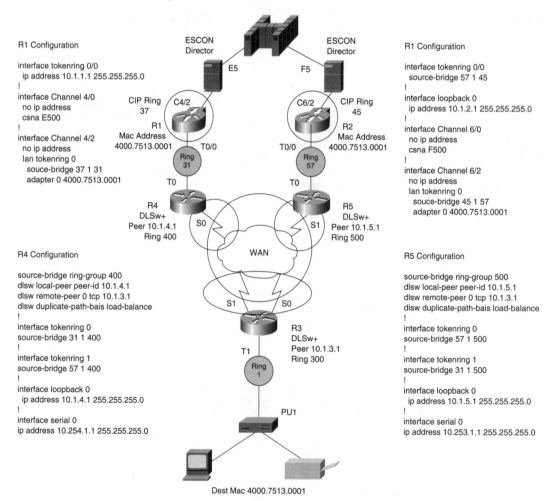

Dest Mac 4000.7513.0001

CMPC Connectivity Between TwoVTAMs over a Single CIP Router

Figure 9-12 shows an example of using a single CIP router for communications between two VTAMs. Each VTAM is connected to a different CIP on the same router. CMPC is used here to support APPN node-to-node communications between the VTAMs. The configuration shown demonstrates the use of the *rmac* and *rsap* values on the tg command. The tg named VTAM1 has the rmac point to the MAC address of the adapter used for connecting VTAM2. Likewise, the tg named VTAM2 has its rmac point to the MAC address of the adapter used for connecting VTAM1. Likewise, the *rsap* values reflect the SAP addresses used for the other VTAM connection to the CIP.

TN3270 Session Switching UsingDLUR/DLUS with VTAM Host Redundancy

The Cisco CIP support for TN3270 enables IBM 3270 data stream traffic to pass through an IP backbone. The TN3270 server support on the Cisco CIP offloads TCP/IP processing from TN3270 termination on the mainframe and presents the TN3270 connections to VTAM as LUs of a LAN-attached PU.

Figure 9-13 illustrates the use of TN3270 server functionality with the added functionality of switching TN3270 connections from one VTAM to another should the primary VTAM become inoperative. The switched major nodes on VTAM must represent the direct PU connections for the TN3270 server along with a definition used for session switching. The configuration uses the APPN virtual routing node for connecting the three mainframe APPN nodes. The transport between the two CIP routers is DLSw+.

VTAM-to-APPN NN Using HPR over CMPC

In this configuration, Figure 9-14, the CIP router uses an ESCON CMPC connection to VTAM. The CIP router uses HPR for communications to VTAM and the APPN network.

Figure 9-12 *CMPC Configuration for VTAM-VTAM Communications over a Single Router with Two CIPs*

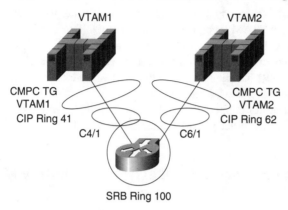

```
source-bridge ring-group 100

interface Channel4/1
 no ip address
 no keepalive
 cmpc C010 40 VTAM1 READ
 cmpc C010 41 VTAM1 WRITE
!
interface Channel4/2
 no ip address
 no keepalive
 lan TokenRing 0
 source-bridge 41  5  100
 adapter 4 4000.0000.CC42
 tg VTAM1 llc token-adapter 4 34 rmac 4000.000.CC62 rsap 30
!
interface Channel6/1
 no ip address
 no keepalive
 cmpc C020 F4  VTAM2 READ
 cmpc C010 F5 VTAM2 WRITE
!
interface Channel6/2
 lan TokenRing 0
 source-bridge 62 3 100
   adapter 6 4000.0000.CC62
 tg VTAM2 llc token-adapter 6  30 rmac 4000.000.CC42 rsap 34
```

Figure 9-13 *Configuration for TN3270 Session Switching using DLUR/DLUS and Host Redundancy*

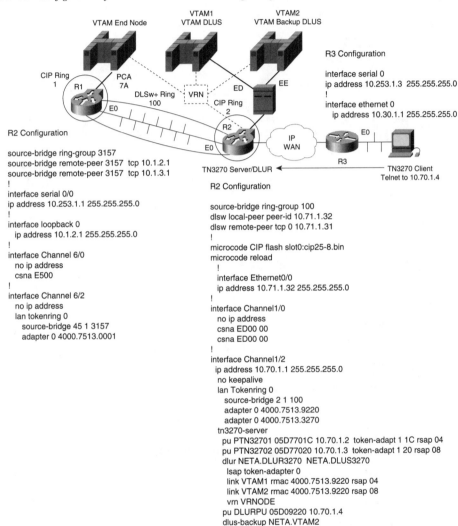

R3 Configuration

interface serial 0
ip address 10.253.1.3 255.255.255.0
!
interface ethernet 0
  ip address 10.30.1.1 255.255.255.0

R2 Configuration

source-bridge ring-group 3157
source-bridge remote-peer 3157 tcp 10.1.2.1
source-bridge remote-peer 3157 tcp 10.1.3.1
!
interface serial 0/0
ip address 10.253.1.1 255.255.255.0
!
interface loopback 0
  ip address 10.1.2.1 255.255.255.0
!
interface Channel 6/0
  no ip address
  csna E500
!
interface Channel 6/2
  no ip address
  lan tokenring 0
    source-bridge 45 1 3157
    adapter 0 4000.7513.0001

R2 Configuration

source-bridge ring-group 100
dlsw local-peer peer-id 10.71.1.32
dlsw remote-peer tcp 0 10.71.1.31
!
microcode CIP flash slot0:cip25-8.bin
microcode reload
  !
  interface Ethernet0/0
  ip address 10.71.1.32 255.255.255.0
!
interface Channel1/0
  no ip address
  csna ED00 00
  csna ED00 00
!
interface Channel1/2
  ip address 10.70.1.1 255.255.255.0
  no keepalive
  lan Tokenring 0
    source-bridge 2 1 100
    adapter 0 4000.7513.9220
    adapter 0 4000.7513.3270
  tn3270-server
    pu PTN32701 05D7701C 10.70.1.2 token-adapt 1 1C rsap 04
    pu PTN32702 05D77020 10.70.1.3 token-adapt 1 20 rsap 08
    dlur NETA.DLUR3270 NETA.DLUS3270
      lsap token-adapter 0
      link VTAM1 rmac 4000.7513.9220 rsap 04
      link VTAM2 rmac 4000.7513.9220 rsap 08
      vrn VRNODE
    pu DLURPU 05D09220 10.70.1.4
    dlus-backup NETA.VTAM2

Figure 9-14   *ESCON CMPC Configuration for Connecting the APPN WAN to VTAM Using HPR*

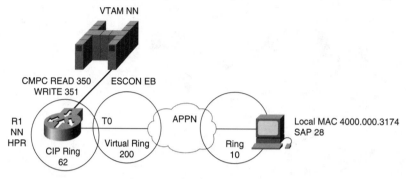

R1 Configuration

```
source-bridge ring-group 200
!
interface tokenring 0
 source-bridge 10  1  200
!
 interface Channel6/1
no ip address
no keepalive
cmpc EB10 50 VTAM1 READ
cmpc EB10 51 VTAM1 WRITE
!
interface Channel6/2
no ip address
no keepalive
lan Tokenring 0
  source-bridge 62   2   200
  adapter 0 4000.7513.0061
lan Tokenring 1
tg VTAM1 llc token-adapter 0  20 rmac 4000.7513.eb10 rsap  24
!
 appn control-point neta.R1
   hpr
   complete
!
appn port CMPC rsrb
   local-sap 24
   rsrb-virtual-station 4000.7513eb10  50  3  200
 complete
!
appn link-station PC
   port CMPC
   lan-dest-address 4000.0000.3174  28
complete
!
appn routing
```

CHAPTER 10

Designing DDR Networks

Edited by Salman Asad

Dial-on-demand routing (DDR) provides network connections across Public Switched Telephone Networks (PSTNs). Dedicated wide-area networks are typically implemented on leased lines or more modern service provider options such as Frame Relay, SMDS, or ATM. Dial-on-demand routing provides session control for wide-area connectivity over circuit-switched networks, which in turn provides on-demand services and decreased network costs.

DDR can be used over synchronous serial interfaces, Integrated Services Digital Network (ISDN) interfaces, or asynchronous serial interfaces. V.25bis and DTR dialing are used for Switched 56 CSU/DSUs, ISDN terminal adapters (TAs), or synchronous modems. Asynchronous serial lines are available on the auxiliary port on Cisco routers and on Cisco communication servers for connections to asynchronous modems. DDR is supported over ISDN using BRI and PRI interfaces.

Introduction to DDR

Cisco IOS dial-on-demand routing (DDR) provides several functions. First, DDR spoofs routing tables to provide the image of full-time connectivity using dialer interfaces. When the routing table forwards a packet to a dialer interface, DDR then filters out the interesting packets for establishing, maintaining, and releasing switched connections. Internetworking is achieved over the DDR-maintained connection using PPP or other WAN-encapsulation techniques (such as HDLC, X.25, and SLIP). Internetwork engineers can use the model presented in this chapter to construct scalable DDR internetworks that balance performance, fault tolerance, and cost.

DDR Design Stack

Similar to the model provided by the OSI for understanding and designing internetworking, a stacked approach, shown in Figure 10-1, can be used to design DDR networks.

Figure 10-1 *DDR Design Stack*

Dialer Clouds

The network formed by the interconnected DDR devices can generically be labeled the dialer media or dialer cloud. The scope of the dialer cloud includes only the intended interconnected devices, and does not include the entire switched media (the entire ISDN spans the globe and is beyond the scope of the dialer cloud). The exposure to the ISDN must be considered when designing security.

The fundamental characteristics of dialer clouds are as follows:

- Dialer clouds are collective bundles of potential and active point-to-point connections.

- On active connections, dialer clouds form an NBMA (nonbroadcast multiaccess) media similar to Frame Relay.

- For outbound dialing on switched circuits (such as ISDN), network-protocol address–to–directory-number mapping must be configured.

- Inactive DDR connections are spoofed to appear as active to routing tables.

- Unwanted broadcast or other traffic causing unneeded connections can be prohibitively expensive. Potential costs on tariffed media (such as ISDN) should be closely analyzed and monitored to prevent such loss.

The characteristics of dialer clouds affect every stage of DDR internetworking design. A solid understanding of network protocol addressing, routing, and filtering strategies can result in very robust and cost-effective internetworks.

Traffic and Topology of DDR

To determine the optimum topology, the DDR designer should perform a traffic analysis of internetworking applications that must be supported. This includes answering the following questions:

- How often does data traffic need to move between the DDR sites?
- What side of the DDR connection can establish the connection? How many remote sites?
- Is this a point-to-point solution or a multipoint solution?

Topologies

The most important factor in selecting the topology is the number of sites that will be supported. If only two sites will be involved, the point-to-point topology is used. If more than two sites are to be supported, the hub-and-spoke topology is typically used. For small numbers of sites with very low traffic volumes, the fully meshed topology may be the most appropriate solution.

Topologies for DDR covered in this section include the following:

- Point-to-point
- Fully meshed
- Hub-and-spoke

Point-to-Point Topology

In a simple point-to-point topology, two sites are connected to each other (see Figure 10-2). Each site has a dialer interface and maps the other site's address to a telephone number. If additional bandwidth is required, multiple links can be aggregated using MultiLink PPP.

Figure 10-2 *Point-to-Point Topology*

Fully Meshed Topology

The fully meshed configuration is recommended only for very small DDR networks (see Figure 10-3). Fully meshed topologies can streamline the dialing process for any-to-any connectivity because each site can call any other site directly, instead of having to call through a central site, which then places another call to the target site. The configuration for each site is more complex, however, because each site must have mapping information for every other site.

If load sharing is desired, interfaces can be configured for MultiLink PPP capability. In addition to the complexity of the configuration, either sufficient interfaces must be available on each device to deal with the possibility of all the other devices calling in, or the possibility of contention for interfaces needs to be understood and dealt with.

Figure 10-3 *Fully Meshed Topology*

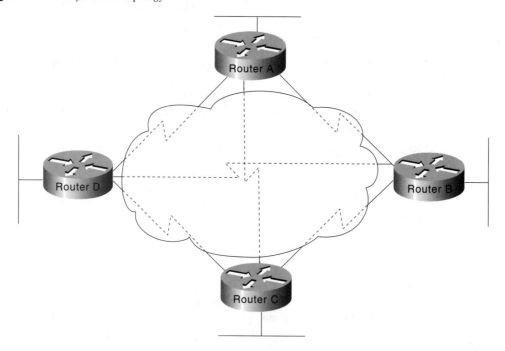

Hub-and-Spoke DDR Solutions

In a hub-and-spoke topology, a central site is connected to several remote sites (see Figure 10-4). The remote sites communicate with the central site directly; they do not call any of the other remote sites. This topology works very well for scaling large solutions.

Figure 10-4 *Hub-and-Spoke Topology*

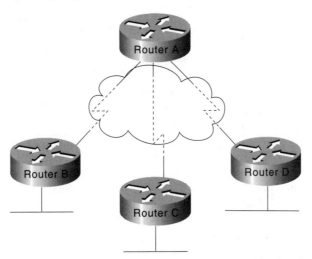

Hub-and-spoke topologies are easier to configure than fully meshed topologies when multipoint topologies are required because remote-site dialer interfaces are mapped only to the central site. This allows most of the design complexity (such as addressing, routing, and authentication) to be managed on the DDR hub. Configuration support of the remote sites can be greatly simplified (similar to one end of a point-to-point topology).

If any-to-any connectivity initiation is required between remote sites, routing behavior may need to be modified, depending on dialer-interface behavior. (That is, it may be necessary to disable split-horizon on distance-vector routing protocols.)

Multiple hubs can be used to provide further scaling of hub-and-spoke technologies. When using MultiLink PPP, as is very common in ISDN solutions, designers can implement Cisco IOS MultiChassis MultiLink PPP to scale the dial-in rotary group between multiple network access servers. MultiChassis MultiLink PPP (MMP) is discussed further in Chapter 11, "Designing ISDN Networks," in the section titled "ISDN Scaling Techniques."

Traffic Analysis

For traffic analysis, develop a chart that shows which protocols need to be able to support DDR-based dialing from which devices. This will form the basis of the rest of the DDR design.

Company KDT has selected a hub-and-spoke topology (to provide for scaling), for example, and has developed the needs shown in for its DDR cloud requirements.

Table 10-1   *DDR Protocol Connectivity Requirements for KDT*

Remote Site	Dial-In Protocols	Dial-Out Protocols	Notes
c700A	IP, IPX	None	
c700B	IP	None	
c1600A	IP, AppleTalk	IP	
c2500A	IP, IPX, AppleTalk	IP, IPX, AppleTalk	
c2500B	IP, IPX	IP	
NAS3600A	IP, IPX, AppleTalk	IP, IPX, AppleTalk	

The purpose of   is to identify which sites and protocols require the capability to initiate the DDR connections. After connectivity is established, each protocol requires two-way connectivity via routing tables and dialer cloud address mapping. Dial-in versus dial-out is from the perspective of the hub.

Often, a primary goal of a DDR network is to offer a cost improvement over WAN charges associated with dedicated connections. Additional traffic analysis must be performed for each protocol at this or the dialer-filtering design stage. Network applications use the infrastructure provided by the internetwork in many different and often unexpected ways. It is critical to perform a thorough analysis of real-world network traffic that will transit the dialer media to determine whether a DDR network can operate in a feasible manner. Packet capture and analysis tools provide the most valuable tool for this analysis.

Dialer Interfaces

Access to the dialer media is via Cisco ISO dialer interfaces. ISDN B channels, synchronous serial interfaces, and asynchronous interfaces can all be converted to dialer interfaces using dialer-interface configuration commands. To understand dialer interfaces, the following concepts are covered:

- Supported Physical Interfaces
- Dialer Rotary Groups
- Dialer Profiles
- Dialer Addressing
- Dialer Mapping

Dialer interfaces also provide the basis for support of routing-table spoofing and dialer filtering. This section focuses on lower-layer characteristics of dialer interfaces.

Supported Physical Interfaces

Several types of physical interfaces can be enabled as dialer interfaces.

Synchronous Serial Interfaces

Dialing on synchronous serial lines can be initiated using V.25bis dialing or DTR dialing. V.25bis is the ITU standard for in-band dialing. With in-band dialing, dialing information is sent over the same connection that carries the data. V.25bis is used with a variety of devices, including synchronous modems, ISDN terminal adapters (TAs), and Switched 56 DSU/CSUs.

With DTR dialing, the DTR signal on the physical interface is activated, which causes some devices to dial a number configured into that device. When using DTR dialing, the interface cannot receive calls. But using DTR dialing allows lower-cost devices to be used in cases where only a single number needs to be dialed. Synchronous serial lines support PPP, HDLC, and X.25 datagram encapsulation.

To convert a synchronous serial interface into a dialer interface, use the Cisco IOS command **dialer in-band** or **dialer dtr**.

ISDN Interfaces

All ISDN devices subscribe to services provided by an ISDN service provider, usually a telephone company. ISDN DDR connections are made on B channels at 56 or 64 kbps, depending on the bearer capabilities of the end-to-end ISDN switching fabric. MultiLink PPP is often used to allow BRI devices to aggregate both B channels for great bandwidth and throughput. See Chapter 11 for guidance when designing ISDN internetworks.

ISDN BRI and PRI interfaces are automatically configured as dialer in-band interfaces. ISDN can support PPP, HDLC, X.25, and V.120 encapsulation. Typically, PPP will be used for DDR solutions. ISDN interfaces are automatically configured as dialer in-band interfaces.

When examining a BRI interface on a Cisco IOS router, for example, you can see that it is in the spoofing (pretending to be up/up so that the routing table can point to this interface):

```
c1600A#sh int bri 0
BRI0 is up, line protocol is up (spoofing)
```

However, the physical interfaces are the individual B (BRI0:1 and BRI0:2) channels being managed by the dialer interface (BRI0):

```
c1600A#sh int bri 0 1
BRI0:1 is down, line protocol is down
  Hardware is BRI
  MTU 1500 bytes, BW 64 Kbit, DLY 20000 usec, rely 255/255, load 1/255
  Encapsulation PPP, loopback not set, keepalive set (10 sec)
  LCP Closed, multilink Closed
  Closed: IPCP, CDPCP
```

Asynchronous Modem Connections

Asynchronous connections are used by communication servers or through the auxiliary port on a router. Asynchronous DDR connections can be used to support multiple network layer protocols. When considering asynchronous DDR solutions, designers should consider whether the internetworking applications can tolerate the longer call setup time and lower throughput of analog modems (in comparison with ISDN). For some design applications, DDR over asynchronous modem connections may provide a very cost-effective option.

To dial out using asynchronous connections, chat scripts must be configured so that modem dialing and login commands are sent to remote systems. For design flexibility, multiple chat scripts can be configured on dialer maps. Modem scripts can be used to configure modems for outbound calls. Login scripts are intended to deal with logging in to remote systems and preparing the link for establishment of PPP. Chat scripts are configured with expect-send pairs and keywords to modify settings, as follows:

```
chat-script dialnum "" "atdt\T" TIMEOUT 60 CONNECT \c
```

If you are using asynchronous DDR and calling a system that requires a character-mode login, use the **system-script** keyword with the **dialer map** command.

Chat scripts often encounter problems with timing because they are run with much greater precision than when a human is controlling the connection. Sometimes, when a modem sends the CONNECT message, for example, it is not actually ready to send data, and may even disconnect if any data is received on the TX circuitry. To avoid such failure modes, pauses are added at the head of some send strings.

Each send string is terminated with a carriage return, even when it is a null string (""). Often, the chat script will be set up without the final "send" string. This may produce unexpected results. Ensure that all chat scripts have complete expect-send pairs. If the final element in the chat script logic turns out to be an expect (as in the preceding example), use the **\c** as the final send to suppress unwanted output.

Use the **debug chat** commands to troubleshoot chat script problems. Line-specific debugging can provide additional details when expect-send logic is failing. For an example of a large-scale async DDR solution, see Chapter 20, "Scaling Dial-on-Demand Routing."

Dialer Rotary Groups

For hub-and-spoke or fully meshed topologies that support multiple connections between sites, physical interfaces can be grouped into rotary groups with the **dialer rotary-group** command. Physical interfaces assigned to the dialer rotary group inherit their configuration from the corresponding interface dialer.

If one of the physical interfaces in a rotary group is busy, the next available interface can be used to place or receive a call. It is not necessary to configure rotary groups for BRI or PRI interfaces because ISDN B channels are automatically placed into a rotary group; however, multiple BRI or PRI interfaces can be grouped using **dialer rotary-group**.

Dialer Profiles

Dialer profiles introduced in Cisco IOS 11.2 offer additional design flexibility, such as multisite bridging over ISDN. Dialer profiles provide an alternative methodology for designing DDR networks by removing the logical definition of dialer sites from the physical dialer interfaces.

Encapsulation Methods

When a clear data link is established between two DDR peers, internetworking datagrams must be encapsulated and framed for transport across the dialer media. The encapsulation methods available depend on the physical interface being used. Cisco supports Point-to-Point Protocol (PPP), High-Level Data Link Control (HDLC), Serial Line Interface Protocol (SLIP), and X.25 data-link encapsulations for DDR:

- PPP is the recommended encapsulation method because it supports multiple protocols and is used for synchronous, asynchronous, or ISDN connections. In addition, PPP performs address negotiation and authentication and is interoperable with different vendors.

- HDLC is supported on synchronous serial lines and ISDN connections only. HDLC supports multiple protocols. HDLC does not provide authentication, however, which may be required if using dialer rotary groups.

- SLIP works on asynchronous interfaces only and is supported by IP only. Addresses must be configured manually. SLIP does not provide authentication and is interoperable only with other vendors that use SLIP.

- X.25 is supported on synchronous serial lines and a single ISDN B channel.

Addressing Dialer Clouds

There are two ways of setting up addressing on dialer clouds, as follows:

- Applying a subnet to the dialer cloud

  Each site connected to the dialer cloud is given a unique node address on a shared subnet for use on its dialer interface. This method is similar to numbering a LAN or multipoint WAN, and simplifies the addressing scheme and creation of static routes.

- Using unnumbered interfaces

  Similar to using unnumbered addressing on leased line point-to-point interfaces, the address of another interface on the router is borrowed for use on the dialer interface. Unnumbered addressing takes advantage of the fact that there are only two devices on the point-to-point link. The routing table points to an interface (the dialer interface) and a next-hop address (which must match a dialer map: static or dynamic).

  Building static routes for unnumbered interfaces can be a little more complex because the router must be configured with the interface that finds the next-hop out.

Dialer Maps

Similar to the function provided by an ARP table, **dialer map** statements translate next-hop protocol addresses to telephone numbers. Without statically configured dialer maps, DDR call initiation cannot occur. When the routing table points at a dialer interface, and the next-hop address is not found in a dialer map, the packet is dropped.

In the following example, packets received for a host on network 172.20.0.0 are routed to a next-hop address of 172.20.1.2, which is statically mapped to telephone number 555-1212:

```
interface dialer 1
ip address 172.20.1.1 255.255.255.0
dialer map ip 172.20.1.2 name c700A 5551212
!
ip route 172.20.0.0 255.255.255.0 172.20.1.2
```

Checks against **dialer map** statements for broadcasts will fail because a broadcast packet is transmitted with a next-hop address of the broadcast address. If you want broadcast packets transmitted to remote sites defined by **dialer map** statements, use the **broadcast** keyword with the **dialer map** command.

To configure whether calls are placed at 56 or 64 kbps for ISDN calls, you can use the speed option with the **dialer map** command when configuring interfaces. See Chapter 11 for details on ISDN media.

When setting up DDR between more than two sites, it is necessary to use PPP authentication and to use the **name** keyword with the **dialer map** command because dialer maps for inbound calls are maps between protocol addresses and authenticated usernames.

To facilitate the building of dialer maps, the internetwork designer should build an address-mapping table as an aid for configuration. In Table 10-1, the dialer cloud has been assigned IP subnet 172.20.1.0/24, IPX network 100, and an AppleTalk cable range 20-20. Table 10-1 forms the basis for building proper dialer maps for each site.

Table 10-2   *DDR Address Mapping Table for KDT*

Remote Site	Dial-In Protocols	Directory	Notes
c700A	IP: 172.20.1.2 IPX: 100.0000.0c00.0002	4085551212	
c700B	IP: 172.20.1.3	4155558888	56K
c1600A	IP: 172.20.1.4 AT: 20.4	5305551000	
c2500A	IP: 172.20.1.5 IPX: 100.0000.0c00.0005 AT: 20.5	5125558085	
c2500B	IP: 172.20.1.6 IPX: 100.0000.0c00.0006	2105552020	
NAS3600A	IP: 172.20.1.1 IPX: 100.0000.0c00.0001	8355558661	Hub

Because NAS3600A forms the hub in the hub-and-spoke topology, each remote site is configured with the dialer maps to get to the central site. For example, the dialer map configuration for c1600A would be as follows:

```
interface dialer1
encapsulation ppp
ip address 172.20.1.4 255.255.255.0
appletalk cable-range 20-20 20.4
appletalk zone ZZ DDR
dialer in-band
dialer map ip 172.20.1.1 name nas3600A speed 56 18355558661
dialer map appletalk 20.1 name nas3600A speed 56 18355558661
dialer-group 5
ppp authentication chap callin
```

The dialer map configuration for NAS3600A would be as follows:

```
interface dialer1
encapsulation ppp
ip address 172.20.1.1 255.255.255.0
appletalk cable-range 20-20 20.1
appletalk zone ZZ DDR
ipx network 100
dialer in-band
dialer map ip 172.20.1.2 name c700A
dialer map ipx 100.0000.0c00.0002 c700A
dialer map ip 172.20.1.3 name c700B
dialer map ip 172.20.1.4 name speed 56 c1600A 15305551000
dialer map appletalk 20.4 name c1600A
dialer map ip 172.20.1.5 name c2500A 15125558085
dialer map ipx 100.0000.0c00.0005 name c2500A 15125558085
dialer map appletalk 20.5 name c2500A 15125558085
dialer map ip 172.20.1.6 name c2500B 12105552020
dialer map ipx 100.0000.0c00.0006 name c2500B
```

```
dialer-group 5
ppp authentication chap callin
```

Note that dialer maps provide mapping between remote-site protocol addresses, remote-site names, and remote-site directory numbers. For dial-in only sites, directory numbers are not required, and can be left off to avoid inadvertent dialing. is used to determine which types of sites do not require dial-out support. For dial-in sites, the PPP authentication name is mapped to the protocol address to ensure that outbound packets are placed on the correct PPP connection.

Recent Cisco IOS releases can build dynamic dialer maps used for IP (using IPCP address negotiation) and IPX (using IPXCP address negotiation), eliminating the need for dialer maps for dial-in only sites.

The DDR designer should familiarize himself with the use of the Cisco IOS exec commands **show dialer** and **show dialer map** to examine the state of the DDR sites, the physical interfaces, and the dialer-map table. Use **debug dialer** to troubleshoot DDR connection problems.

```
c1600A#sh dialer
BRI0 - dialer type = ISDN
Dial String      Successes    Failures     Last called   Last status
1835558661 0           0       never            -
0 incoming call(s) have been screened.
BRI0:1 - dialer type = ISDN
Idle timer (60 secs), Fast idle timer (20 secs)
Wait for carrier (30 secs), Re-enable (5 secs)
Dialer state is idle
BRI0:2 - dialer type = ISDN
Idle timer (60 secs), Fast idle timer (20 secs)
Wait for carrier (30 secs), Re-enable (5 secs)
Dialer state is idle

c1600A#sh dialer map
Static dialer map ip 172.20.1.4 name nas (8355558661) on BRI0
```

Routing Strategies

The nature of DDR networks is that routing and some directory services tables must be maintained over idle connections. DDR designers may use a combination of static, dynamic, and snapshot routing techniques to meet design needs. Default routing and remote-node spoofing techniques (such as Cisco 700 Series PAT and Cisco IOS EZIP) can be used to greatly simplify routing design.

Often, the backbone at the NAS site will use a fast-converging routing protocol such as OSPF or EIGRP; however, these protocols do not operate easily on the dialer media due to their broadcast and link-state nature. Typically, static routing or distance-vector routing protocols are selected for the DDR connections. Routing redistribution may be required to support the propagation of routing information between the different routing protocols.

A complete discussion of routing redistribution techniques is beyond the scope of this chapter; however, DDR designers do need to develop and verify their routing strategy for each network protocol.

Static Routing

With static routes, network protocol routes are entered manually, eliminating the need for a routing protocol to broadcast routing updates across the DDR connection. Static routes can be effective in small networks that do not change often. Routing protocols can generate traffic that causes connections to be made unnecessarily.

When designing with IP unnumbered environments, older versions of Cisco IOS required multiple static routes for each site: one route to define the next-hop IP address and a second to define the interface on which to find the next hop (and dialer map). The following code

```
interface Dialer1
     ip unnumbered Ethernet0/0
     dialer in-band
     dialer map ip 172.17.1.100 name kdt-NAS speed 56 5558660
     dialer-group 5
     !
     ip classless
     ip route 0.0.0.0 0.0.0.0 172.17.1.100 200
     ip route 172.17.1.100 255.255.255.255 Dialer1 200
     dialer-list 5 protocol ip permit
```

creates the following routing table:

```
kdt-3640#sh ip route
     ...<snip>...
     Gateway of last resort is 172.17.1.100 to network 0.0.0.0
172.17.0.0/32 is subnetted, 1 subnets
     S        172.17.1.100 is directly connected, Dialer1
          172.20.0.0/24 is subnetted, 1 subnets
     S*   0.0.0.0/0 [200/0] via 172.17.1.100
```

Recent Cisco IOS versions allow configuration of this as one route. For example, the example configuration here

```
ip route 0.0.0.0 0.0.0.0 Dialer1 172.17.1.100 200 permanent
```

results in a simplified routing table, as follows:

```
kdt-3640#sh ip route
     ...<snip>...
     Gateway of last resort is 172.17.1.100 to network 0.0.0.0

172.20.0.0/24 is subnetted, 1 subnets
     C        172.20.1.0 is directly connected, Ethernet0/0
     S*   0.0.0.0/0 [200/0] via 172.17.1.100, Dialer1
```

It is typically necessary to configure the redistribution of static routes into the backbone dynamic routing protocol to ensure end-to-end connectivity. To redistribute the static route to other networks in IGRP autonomous system 20, for example, use the following configuration commands:

```
router igrp 20
 network 172.20.0.0
 redistribute static
```

Dynamic Routing

Dynamic routing can be used in DDR network design in a number of ways. Dynamic routing can be used with snapshot routing (as described in the "Snapshot Routing" section, later in this chapter) to cache routes learned by dynamic routing protocols, thus allowing the automation of static-routing maintenance. Dynamic routing can be used as a trigger for routing convergence in large and complex DDR designs.

When the DDR link is connected, routing updates will flow to the peer, allowing redundant designs to converge on the physical connection by redistribution of trigger-routing updates.

Selecting a Dynamic Routing Protocol

The routing protocol selected for DDR link is typical of a distance-vector protocol such as RIP, RIP II, EIGRP, IGRP, or RTMP. Selecting the simplest protocol that meets the needs of the internetwork design and that is supported by the DDR routers is recommended.

Passive Interfaces

Interfaces tagged as passive will not send routing updates. To prevent routing updates from establishing DDR connections on dialer interfaces that do not rely on dynamic routing information, configure DDR interfaces with the **passive-interface** command or use access lists, as described in the sections "IP Access Lists" and "IPX Access Lists," later in this chapter. Using either the **passive-interface** command or an access list prevents routing updates from triggering a call. If you want routing updates to be passed when the link is active, however, use an access list rather than the **passive-interface** command.

Split Horizons

Routers connected to broadcast-type IP networks and routers that use distance-vector routing protocols use split horizons to reduce the possibility of routing loops. When split horizons are enabled, information about routes that comes in on an interface is not advertised out on that same interface.

NOTE   If remote sites need to communicate with one another, split horizons should be disabled for hub-and-spoke topologies. In hub-and-spoke topologies, spokes learn about one another through the hub site to which they are connected by a single interface. For spokes to send and receive information to one another, split horizons may need to be disabled so that full routing tables are built at each site.

Dynamic Connected Routes

Dynamic connected routes include the following:

- *Per-user AAA installed routes*—AAA servers can install routes associated with users by using AAA authorization to download and install routes as remote sites connect.

- *PPP peer routes*—IPCP address negotiation installs host routes (/32 subnet mask) for the remote peer. This host route can be propagated to backbone routers to provide robust routing convergence. In most applications, the peer host route will be beneficial (or innocuous) to the internetwork design. If PPP peer host routes interact poorly with existing routing strategies, they can be turned off with the interface configuration command **no peer neighbor-route**.

Snapshot Routing

With snapshot routing, the router is configured for dynamic routing. Snapshot routing controls the update interval of the routing protocols. Snapshot routing works with the following distance-vector protocols:

- Routing Information Protocol (RIP) for IP

- Interior Gateway Routing Protocol (IGRP) for IP

- Routing Information Protocol (RIP) and Service Advertisement Protocol (SAP) for Novell Internet Packet Exchange (IPX)

- Routing Table Maintenance Protocol (RTMP) for AppleTalk

- Routing Table Protocol (RTP) for Banyan VINES

Under normal circumstances, these routing protocols broadcast updates every 10 to 60 seconds, so an ISDN link would be made every 10 to 60 seconds just to exchange routing information. From a cost perspective, this frequency is prohibitive. Snapshot routing solves this problem.

NOTE   Snapshot routing is available in Cisco IOS Software Release 10.2 or later.

Snapshot Model

Snapshot routing uses the client/server design model. When snapshot routing is configured, one router is designated as the snapshot server, and one or more routers are designated as snapshot clients. The server and clients exchange routing information during an active period. At the beginning of the active period, the client router dials the server router to exchange routing information. At the end of the active period, each router takes a snapshot of the entries in its routing table. These entries remain frozen during a quiet period. At the end of the quiet period, another active period begins, and the client router dials the server router to obtain the latest routing information. The client router determines the frequency at which it calls the server router. The quiet period can be as long as 100,000 minutes (approximately 69 days).

When the client router transitions from the quiet period to the active period, the line might be down or busy. If this happens, the router would have to wait through another entire quiet period before it could update its routing table, which might severely affect connectivity if the quiet period is very long. To avoid having to wait through the quiet period, snapshot routing supports a retry period. If the line is not available when the quiet period ends, the router waits for the amount of time specified by the retry period, and then transitions to an active period once again.

The retry period is also useful in dialup environments, in which there are more remote sites than interface lines. The central site might have one PRI (with 23 B channels available), for example, but might dial more than 23 remote sites. In this situation, there are more **dialer map** commands than available lines. The router tries the **dialer map** commands in order and uses the retry time for the lines that it cannot immediately access (see Figure 10-5).

Figure 10-5 *Snapshot Routers in Action*

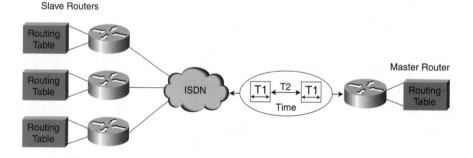

Enabling Snapshot Routing

Snapshot routing is enabled through interface configuration commands (see Figure 10-6). The central router is configured for snapshot routing by applying the **snapshot server** interface configuration command to its ISDN interfaces. The **snapshot server** command specifies the length of the active period and whether the router is allowed to dial remote sites to exchange routing updates in the absence of regular traffic.

The remote routers are configured for snapshot routing by applying the **snapshot client** command to each ISDN interface. The **snapshot client** interface configuration command specifies the following variables:

- The length of the active period (which must match the length specified on the central router)

- The length of the quiet period

- Whether the router can dial the central router to exchange routing updates in the absence of regular traffic

- Whether connections established to exchange user data can be used to exchange routing updates

When the backbone routing protocol is not supported by snapshot routing (for example, OSPF or EIGRP), standard routing redistribution techniques can be used to ensure that routing updates are propagated between routing protocols, as required. Care should be taken to ensure the redistribution of subnets if needed, and to avoid routing loops.

Figure 10-6 *AppleTalk Snapshot Routing*

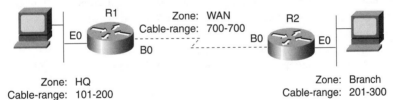

R1 configuration in Figure 10-6 is as follows:

```
username R2 password SECRET
appletalk routing
isdn switch-type basic-5ess
!
interface BRI0
 encapsulation ppp
 appletalk cable-range 700-700 700.1
 appletalk zone WAN
 dialer map appletalk 700.2 name R2 speed 56 broadcast 5552222
 dialer map snapshot 2 name R2 speed 56 broadcast 5552222
 dialer-group 1
 snapshot client 5 60 dialer
 isdn spid1 5550066
 ppp authentication chap
!
dialer-list 1 protocol appletalk permit
```

R2 configuration in Figure 10-6 is as follows:

```
username R1 password SECRET
appletalk routing
isdn switch-type basic-5ess
interface BRI0
 encapsulation ppp
 appletalk cable-range 700-700 700.2
 appletalk zone WAN
 dialer wait-for-carrier-time 60
 dialer map appletalk 700.1 name R1 speed 56 broadcast 5550066
 dialer-group 1
 snapshot server 5 dialer
 isdn spid1 5552222
 ppp authentication chap
 !
 dialer-list 1 protocol appletalk permit
```

For a further examination of snapshot routing, see Chapter 21, "Using ISDN Effectively in Multiprotocol Networks."

Dial Backup for Leased Lines

Dial backup protects against wide-area network (WAN) downtime by allowing a dedicated serial connection to be backed up by a circuit-switched connection. Dial backup can be performed in several ways: either with floating static routes or with backup interfaces.

Dial backup challenges the designer with traffic patterns different from DDR-supported SOHO and ROBO sites. When designing dial backup port densities, consider how many links might fail concurrently in a mass-failure scenario, as well as how many ports will be required on the central site in a worst-case scenario. Typical design involves selecting only dial-in or dial-out to avoid contention when both sides are trying to re-establish connectivity.

Backup Interfaces

A primary/dedicated serial line is configured to have a backup interface in the event of link failure or exceeded load thresholds. If the interface line or line protocol state goes down, the backup interface is used to establish a connection to the remote site.

When configured, the dial backup interface remains inactive until one of the following conditions is met:

1 *Line protocol on the primary link goes down*—The backup line is then activated, re-establishing the connection between the two sites.

2 *The traffic load on the primary line exceeds a defined limit*—The traffic load is monitored and a five-minute moving average is computed. If the average exceeds the user-defined value for the line, the backup line is activated. Depending on how the backup line is configured, some or all of the traffic flows onto it.

A Cisco IOS interface is placed into backup mode by applying the **backup interface** command:

- The **backup interface** interface configuration command specifies the interface that is to act as the backup.

- The **backup load** command specifies the traffic threshold at which the backup interface is to be activated and deactivated.

- The **backup delay** command specifies the amount of time that is to elapse before the backup interface is activated or deactivated after a transition on the primary interface.

Backup interfaces traditionally lock the backup interface into BACKUP state so that it is unavailable for other use. Dialer profiles eliminate this lock and allow the physical interface to be used for multiple purposes. Floating static-route DDR design also eliminates this lock on the dialer interface. In Figure 10-7, a leased line connects Router A to Router B, and BRI 0 on Router B is used as a backup line.

Figure 10-7 *Example of Dial Backup over ISDN*

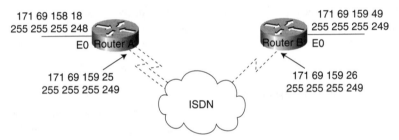

Using the configuration that follows, BRI 0 is activated only when serial interface 1/0 (the primary line) goes down. The **backup delay** command configures the backup connection to activate 30 seconds after serial interface 0 goes down and to remain activated for 60 seconds after the serial interface 1/0 comes up:

```
interface serial 1/0
    ip address 172.20.1.4 255.255.255.0
    backup interface bri 2/0
    backup delay 30 60
```

Using the configuration that follows, BRI 2/0 is activated only when the load on serial 0 (the primary line) exceeds 75% of its bandwidth. The backup line is deactivated when the aggregate load between the primary and backup lines is within 5% of the primary line's bandwidth:

```
interface serial 1/0
    ip address 172.20.1.4 255.255.255.0
    backup interface bri 2/0
    backup load 75 5
```

Using the following configuration, BRI 2/0 is activated only when serial interface 1/00 goes down or when traffic exceeds 25%. If serial interface 1/0 goes down, 10 seconds will elapse before BRI 0 becomes active. When serial interface 1/0 comes up, BRI 2/0 will remain active for 60 seconds. If BRI 2/ 0 is activated by the load threshold on serial interface 1/0, BRI 2/0 is deactivated when the aggregate load of serial interface 1/0 and BRI 2/0 returns to within 5% of the bandwidth of serial interface 1/0:

```
interface serial 1/0
ip address 172.20.1.4 255.255.255.0
backup interface bri 2/0
backup load 25 5
backup delay 10 60
```

Floating Static Routes

Backup interface operation is determined by the state of the line and line protocol on the primary link. It is possible that end-to-end connectivity is lost, but line protocol stays up. For example, line protocol on a Frame Relay link is determined by the status of ILMI messages between the Frame Relay DCE (switch). Connectivity to the Frame Relay DCE does not guarantee end-to-end connectivity.

Designing dial backup with floating static routes utilizes Cisco IOS routing-table maintenance and dynamic routing protocols. See Chapter 19, "Dial-on-Demand Routing," for examples of using floating static routes to provide backup to leased lines.

IPX Static Routes and SAP Updates

With DDR, you need to configure static routes because routing updates are not received across inactive DDR connections. To create static routes to specified destinations, use the **ipx route** command. You can also configure static Service Advertisement Protocol (SAP) updates with the **ipx sap** command so that clients can always find a particular server. In this way, you can determine the areas on your internetwork where SAP updates will establish DDR connections.

In the following example, traffic to network 50 will always be sent to address 45.0000.0c07.00d3. Traffic to network 75 will always be sent to address 45.0000.0c07.00de. The router will respond to GNS queries with the server WALT if there are no dynamic SAPs available:

```
ipx route 50 45.0000.0c07.00d3
ipx route 75 45.0000.0c07.00de
ipx sap 4 WALT 451 75.0000.0000.0001 15
```

Configuring AppleTalk Static Zones

Static AppleTalk routes and zones are created using the **appletalk static** command as in the following example:

```
appletalk static cable-range 110-110 to 45.2 zone Marketing
```

In many cases, manual configuration of static AppleTalk cable-ranges and zones will prove to be onerous. Snapshot routing should be investigated to provide automated route caching.

Dialer Filtering

Dialer filtering is used to classify all packets traversing the DDR connection as either *interesting* or *uninteresting* using access control lists (ACLs) (see Figure 10-8). Only interesting packets can bring up and keep up DDR connections. It is the task of the DDR designer to determine which kinds of packets are to be deemed uninteresting and develop ACLs to prevent these uninteresting packets from causing unnecessary DDR connections.

If a packet is uninteresting and there is no connection established, the packet is dropped. If the packet is uninteresting, but a connection is already established to the specified destination, the packet is sent across the connection, but the idle timer is not reset. If the packet is interesting, and there is no connection on the available interface, the router attempts to establish a connection.

Figure 10-8 *Dialer Filtering*

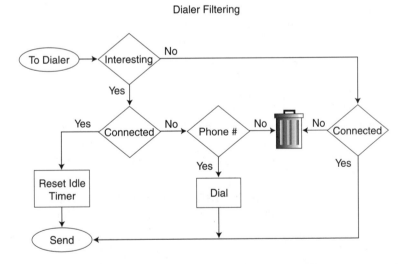

Each packet arriving at a dialer interface is filtered and determined to be interesting or uninteresting, based on **dialer-group** and **dialer-list** configuration. The following Cisco IOS configuration interface dialer 1 uses dialer group 5 to determine interesting packets, as defined by the **dialer-list 5** commands. Dialer group 5 is defined by **dialer-list 5** commands, which in this case deems all IP, IPX, and AppleTalk packets to be interesting.

```
interface Dialer1
dialer-group 5
!
dialer-list 5 protocol ip permit
```

```
dialer-list 5 protocol ipx permit
dialer-list 5 protocol appletalk permit
!
```

Cisco IOS now supports many dialer-filtering protocols, as seen by the dialer-list online help:

```
kdt-3640(config)#dialer-list 5 protocol ?
  appletalk         AppleTalk
  bridge            Bridging
  clns              OSI Connectionless Network Service
  clns_es           CLNS End System
  clns_is           CLNS Intermediate System
  decnet            DECnet
  decnet_node       DECnet node
  decnet_router-L1  DECnet router L1
  decnet_router-L2  DECnet router L2
  ip                IP
  ipx               Novell IPX
  llc2              LLC2
  vines             Banyan Vines
  xns               XNS
```

Defining Interesting Packets Using ACLs

Further dialer-filtering granularity is provided for each protocol by definition of Cisco IOS access control lists (ACLs). For example, the following configuration defines SNMP traffic as not interesting using dialer-list 3 and extended IP ACLs:

```
dialer-list protocol ip 3 list 101

!
access-list 101 deny udp any any eq snmp
access-list 101 permit ip any any
```

Routing updates and directory services effects on dialer interfaces can be managed by several techniques: static and default routing, passive interfaces, or nonbroadcast dialer maps. For solutions that require dynamic routing but cannot use snapshot, routing can still be supported on the ISDN link, and then deemed uninteresting by the dialer filtering.

If the internetwork design requires IGRP routing update packets, for example, the IGRP packets can be filtered with access lists to prevent unwanted DDR connections, as follows:

```
access-list 101 deny igrp 0.0.0.0 255.255.255.255 0.0.0.0 255.255.255.255
access-list 101 permit ip 0.0.0.0 255.255.255.255 0.0.0.0 255.255.255.255
```

You can use one of the following two access lists to classify Enhanced IGRP traffic as uninteresting:

```
access-list 101 deny eigrp any any
access-list 101 deny ip any 224.0.0.10 0.0.0.0
```

The first access list denies all Enhanced IGRP traffic, and the second access list denies the multicast address (224.0.0.10) that Enhanced IGRP uses for its updates. When you use access lists to control Enhanced IGRP traffic, you need to configure static routes to create routes across the ISDN link. When the DDR link is connected, routing updates will be able to flow across the line. In the design of DDR filtering, it is important to understand where updates and service requests are useful and where these packet types can be safely filtered.

It is important to consider closely the directory service protocols and the internetworking applications that need to be supported at each site. Numerous protocols and applications can cause DDR connections to be established and maintained, and may result in extraordinary WAN charges if not properly monitored and filtered. Don't wait until you get a phone bill surprise to perform careful traffic and costing analysis for your network. If you are concerned about WAN costs, implement network-monitoring tools to provide quick feedback on connection frequency and duration. Cost-containment issues are discussed in Chapter 11.

SNMP

Although SNMP can provide useful information about ISDN connections and how they are used, using SNMP can result in excessive uptime for ISDN links. For example, HP OpenView gathers information by regularly polling the network for SNMP events. These polls can cause the ISDN connections to be made frequently to check that the remote routers are there, which results in higher ISDN usage charges. To control ISDN charges, the central site should filter SNMP packets destined for remote sites over ISDN. Incoming SNMP packets from remote sites can still be permitted, which allows SNMP traps to flow to the SNMP management platform. That way, if an SNMP device fails at the remote site, the alarm will reach the SNMP management platform at the central site.

To control SNMP traffic, create an access list that denies SNMP packets. The following is an example of SNMP filtering:

```
access-list 101 deny tcp any any eq 161
access-list 101 deny udp any any eq snmp
access-list 101 permit ip any any
!
dialer-list 1 list 101
```

IPX Packets

On Novell IPX internetworks, it is important to consider filtering routing updates on DDR interfaces for the protocols listed in Table 10-2.

Table 10-3   *Novell IPX Update Packet Cycles*

Packet Type	Periodic Update Cycle
RIP	60 seconds
SAP	60 seconds
Serialization	66 seconds

You can use access lists to declare uninteresting packets intended for the Novell serialization socket (protocol number 0, socket number 457), RIP packets (protocol number 1, socket number 453), SAP packets (protocol number 4, socket number 452), and diagnostic packets generated by the autodiscovery feature (protocol number 4, socket number 456). Uninteresting packets are dropped and do not cause connections to be initiated. For a sample IPX access list, see Chapter 21.

IPX sends out several types of packets that, if not controlled, cause unnecessary connections: IPX watchdog packets and SPX keepalive packets. In addition, NetWare includes a time-synchronization protocol that, if not controlled, causes unnecessary connections.

Novell IPX internetworks use several types of update packets that may need to be filtered with access lists. Novell hosts broadcast serialization packets as a copy-protection precaution. Routing Information Protocol (RIP) routing-table updates and SAP advertisements are broadcast every 60 seconds. Serialization packets are sent approximately every 66 seconds.

In the following example, access list 901 classifies SAP (452), RIP (453), and serialization (457) packets as uninteresting; and classifies IPX packet types unknown/any (0), any or RIP (1), any or SAP (4), SPX (5), NCP (17), and NetBIOS (20) as interesting:

```
access-list 901 deny 0 FFFFFFFF 452
access-list 901 deny 4 FFFFFFFF 452
access-list 901 deny 0 FFFFFFFF 453
access-list 901 deny 1 FFFFFFFF 453
access-list 901 deny 0 FFFFFFFF 457
access-list 901 deny 0 FFFFFFFF 0 FFFFFFFF 452
access-list 901 deny 0 FFFFFFFF 0 FFFFFFFF 453
access-list 901 deny 0 FFFFFFFF 0 FFFFFFFF 457
access-list 901 permit 0
access-list 901 permit 1
access-list 901 permit 2
access-list 901 permit 4
access-list 901 permit 5
access-list 901 permit 17
```

You can permit any other type of IPX packet, as needed. With Cisco IOS 10.2, the configuration of Novell IPX access lists is improved with the support of wildcard (**-1**), so the previous example would be as follows:

```
access-list 901 deny -1 FFFFFFFF 452
access-list 901 deny -1 FFFFFFFF 453
access-list 901 deny -1 FFFFFFFF 457
access-list 901 deny -1 FFFFFFFF 0 FFFFFFFF 452
access-list 901 deny -1 FFFFFFFF 0 FFFFFFFF 453
access-list 901 deny -1 FFFFFFFF 0 FFFFFFFF 457
access-list 901 permit -1
```

Controlling IPX Watchdog Packets

NetWare servers send watchdog packets to clients and disconnect any clients that do not respond. When IPX watchdog spoofing is enabled, the router local to the NetWare server responds to watchdog packets on behalf of the server's clients. IPX watchdog spoofing allows clients to remain attached to servers without having to constantly send packets across the ISDN link to do so. This feature is particularly important when trying to control ISDN link uptime. The interface configuration command for enabling IPX watchdog spoofing is **ipx watchdog-spoof**.

Controlling SPX Keepalive Packets

Some Sequenced Packet Exchange (SPX)–based services in the Novell environment use SPX keepalive packets. These packets are used to verify the integrity of end-to-end communications when guaranteed and sequenced packet transmission is required. The keepalive packets are generated at a rate that can be adjusted by the user from a default of one every five seconds to a minimum of one every 15 minutes. SPX spoofing as implemented in the Cisco IOS software receives, recognizes, and successfully acknowledges keepalive packets, both at the server end and at the client end.

Time Server and NDS Replica Packets

NetWare 4.x includes a time-synchronization protocol that causes NetWare 4.x time servers to send an update every 10 minutes. To prevent the time server from generating update packets that would cause unwanted connections, you need to load a NetWare-loadable module (NLM) named TIMESYNC.NLM, which enables you to increase the update interval for these packets to several days.

A similar problem is caused by efforts to synchronize NDS replicas. NetWare 4.1 includes two NLMs: DSFILTER.NLM and PINGFILT.NLM. They work together to control NDS synchronization updates. Use these two modules to ensure that NDS synchronization traffic is sent to specified servers only at the specified times.

AppleTalk Filtering

AppleTalk's user-friendly directory services are based on zone names and the Name Binding Protocol (NBP). Applications (such as the MacOS Chooser) use NBP Lookups to look for services (such as AppleShare and Printing) by zone names. Some applications may abuse NBP services, assuming that DDR networks do not exist and send broadcasts to all zones. This in turn can cause excessive dial-on-demand triggers. Applications such as QuarkXpress and 4D use all zone NBP broadcasts to periodically probe the network, either for licensing purposes or to provide links to other networked resources. The **test appletalk:nbp lookup** command, combined with the **debug dialer** command, monitors NBP traffic and can help you determine the kinds of packets that cause connections to be made.

Beginning with Cisco IOS 11.0, you can filter NBP packets based on the name, type, and zone of the entity that originated the packet. AppleTalk NBP filtering allows Cisco routers to build firewalls, dial-on-demand triggers, and queuing options based on any NBP type or object. For a configuration example, see Chapter 21. Ultimately, if the applications that use NBP have been isolated, consult the individual vendors and ask for their advice on how to control or eliminate NBP traffic.

Some Macintosh applications periodically send out NBP Lookup to all zones for numerous reasons; checking same serial number for copy protection, automatic search of other servers, and so on. As a result, the ISDN link will get brought up frequently and waste usages. In 11.0(2.1) or later, Cisco routers enable the user to configure NBP Filtering for dialer lists to prevent this problem. To do this, you should replace this line on both routers

```
dialer-list 1 protocol appletalk permit
```

with these lines:

```
dialer-list 1 list 600
access-list 600 permit nbp 1 type AFPServer
access-list 600 permit nbp 2 type LaserWriter
access-list 600 deny other-nbps
access-list 600 permit other-access broadcast-deny
```

The preceding example indicates that you want to permit only two kinds of service for NBP Lookup to bring up the ISDN line. If you want to permit additional types, add to the example before the **denyother-nbps** statement. Make sure you have a different sequence number; otherwise, it will overwrite the previous one. If you want to also permit NBP Lookup for DeskWriter to bring up the line, for example, the list will look like this:

```
dialer-list 1 list 600
access-list 600 permit nbp 1 type AFPServer
access-list 600 permit nbp 2 type LaserWriter
access-list 600 permit nbp 3 type DeskWriter
access-list 600 deny other-nbps
access-list 600 permit other-access broadcast-deny
```

NOTE   AppleShare servers use the Apple Filing Protocol (AFP) to send out tickles approximately every 30 seconds to connected AppleShare clients. These tickles will cause DDR connections to stay up. To avoid unwanted DDR connections, you must manually unmount AppleTalk servers or install software on the servers that automatically disconnect idle users after a timeout period.

Banyan VINES, DECnet IV, and OSI Packets

Cisco IOS 10.3 introduced access lists for Banyan VINES, DECnet IV, and the Open Systems Integration (OSI) protocol. When a dialer map is configured for these protocols, access lists can be used to define interesting packets (that is, packets that will trigger the DDR link).

Dial-on-Demand and PPP

Several aspects of DDR are used to provide DDR capabilities between local and remote routers. The main features are dialer map, PPP encapsulation, CHAP, dialer rotary groups, and the **pulse-time** command. The comment lines in the following example explain the uses of these features:

```
interface dialer 1
ip address  130.100.120.10 255.255.255.0
!
!Encapsulation  type is PPP on interface dialer 1.
encapsulation ppp
!
!Authentication type for PPP is CHAP on interface dialer 1.
ppp authentication chap
!
!Following command makes the interface a DDR interface
dialer in-band
!
!Following command ties this interface to the dialer access group, which is
!defined with the dialer-list command
dialer group 1
!
! Following dialer map command allows remote site sanjose and the
! central site to call each other. The dialer string 5555555 is the remote
! site phone number which is used to dial the remote site.  The name
! sanjose is used when the remote site dials the central site.
dialer map ip  130.100.120.15 name sanjose 5555555
!
! Following dialer map command, has no dialer string defined, which allows
! the remote site sanjose to call the central site
! but the central site can not call
! remote site sanjose , since there is no dialer string defined.
dialer map ip 130.120.100.15  name sanjose
!
! Following command defines the DTR pulse signals for five seconds on the DDR
! interfaces in dialer group 1. This holds the DTR low so
! the modem can recognize that DTR has been dropped.
pulse-time 5
!
! Place asynchronous serial interfaces 1 and 2 in dialer rotary group 1. The
! interface subcommands applied to dialer rotary group 1 (for example,
! PPP encapsulation and CHAP) apply to these interfaces.
interface async 1
dialer rotary-group 1
interface async 2
dialer rotary-group 1
! CHAP passwords are specified for remote servers.
username sanjose password cisco
username rtp password cisco
```

Authentication

Authentication in DDR network design provides two functions: security and dialer state. Because most DDR networks connect to the Public Switched Telephone Network, it is imperative that a strong security model be implemented to prevent unauthorized access to sensitive resources. Authentication also allows the DDR code to keep track of what sites are currently connected, and provides for the building of MultiLink PPP bundles. The following issues are addressed:

- PPP Authentication
- CHAP
- PAP
- ISDN Security
- DDR Callback
- IPX Access Lists

PPP Authentication

PPP authentication via CHAP or PAP (as described in RFC 1334) should be used to provide security on DDR connections. PPP authentication occurs after LCP is negotiated on the DDR connection, but before any network protocols are allowed to flow. PPP authentication is negotiated as an LCP option, and is bidirectional, meaning each side can authenticate the other. In some environments, it may be necessary to enable PPP authentication on the call-in side only (meaning the calling side does not authenticate the called side).

CHAP

With CHAP, a remote device attempting to connect to the local router is presented with a CHAP challenge containing the host name and a challenge seed. When the remote router receives the challenge, it looks up the host name received in the challenge, and replies with the host name and a CHAP response derived from the challenge seed and the password for that host name. The passwords must be identical on the remote device and the local router. The names and passwords are configured using the **username** command. In the following example, Router nas3600A will allow Router c1600A to call in using the password *bubble*:

```
hostname nas3600A
username c1600A password bubble
!
interface dialer 1
ppp authentication chap callin
```

In the following example, Router Macduff will allow Router Macbeth to call in using the password *bubble*:

```
hostname c1600A
username nas3600A password bubble
!
interface dialer 1
encapsulation ppp
dialer in-band
dialer-group 5
dialer map ip 172.20.1.1 name nas3600A 18355558661
ppp authentication chap callin
```

The following steps illustrate the CHAP process:

Step 1 c1600A calls nas3600A, and LCP is negotiated.

Step 2 nas3600A challenges c1600A with <nas3600A/challenge_string>.

Step 3 c1600A looks up the password for username nas3600A and generates a response string.

Step 4 c1600A sends response to c3600A: <nas1600A/response_string>.

Step 5 c3600A looks up the password for username c1600A and generates the expected response string. If the response string received matches the response string expected, PPP authorization passes, and the PPP can negotiate the network-control protocols (such as IPCP). If it fails, the remote site is disconnected.

PAP

Like CHAP, PAP is an authentication protocol used with PPP. However, PAP is less secure than CHAP. CHAP passes an encrypted version of the password on the physical link, but PAP passes the password in clear text, which makes it susceptible to sniffer attack.

When being authenticated with PAP, the router looks up the username that matches the dialer map used to initiate the call. When being authenticated with PAP on a receiving call, PAP looks up the username associated with its host name (because no dialer map was used to initiate the connection).

In the following configuration, the NAS router will authenticate the peer with PAP when answering the DDR call, and compare the result to the local database:

```
hostname nas3600A
aaa new-model
aaa authentication ppp default local
username c2500A password freedom
username nas3600A password texas
!
interface Dialer1
encapsualtion ppp
ppp authentication pap
```

ISDN Security

ISDN DDR can use caller ID for enhanced security by configuring ISDN caller on the incoming ISDN interfaces. Incoming calls are screened to verify that the calling-line ID is from an expected origin. However, caller-ID screening requires an end-to-end ISDN connection that can deliver the caller ID to the router.

DDR Callback

DDR environments can be configured for callback operations. When a remote site dials in to a central site (or the opposite), the central site can be configured to disconnect and initiate an outbound DDR connection to the remote site.

DDR callback provides enhanced security by ensuring that the remote site can connect only from a single location, as defined by the callback number. DDR callback can also enhance administration by centralizing billing for remote DDR connections.

IPX Access Lists

Access lists determine whether packets are interesting or uninteresting. Interesting packets activate DDR connections automatically. Uninteresting packets do not trigger DDR connections; although if a DDR connection is already active, uninteresting packets will travel across the existing connection.

Summary

When designing DDR internetworks, consider the topology type: point-to-point, hub-and-spoke, and fully meshed. With the topology type, consider the type of addressing scheme used and security issues. Keep in mind that media choice affects how packets are sent. Define where packets are sent by configuring static routes, zones, and services. Determine how packets reach their destination by configuring dialer interfaces and mapping addresses to telephone numbers. Finally, determine when the router should connect by configuring interesting versus uninteresting packets, eliminating unwanted AppleTalk broadcasts, and spoofing IPX watchdog packets. Following these guidelines will help you construct scalable DDR internetworks that balance performance, fault tolerance, and cost.

For further guidance on building DDR networks, including protocol-specific examples, see Chapter 11, "Designing ISDN Networks," Chapter 20, "Scaling Dial-on-Demand Routing," and Chapter 21, "Using ISDN Effectively in Multiprotocol Networks."

Designing ISDN Networks

Edited by Salman Asad

The Public Switched Telephone Network (PSTN) has been transformed into an Integrated Systems Digital Network (ISDN). Implementation of Signaling System 7 (SS7) in the PSTN backbone has made possible such widespread services as caller ID and dialed-number delivery, 800-Directory number lookup, calling-card services, and digital data services. Using BRI and PRI services, ISDN call switching can be extended to customer premises equipment (CPE), and can provide end-to-end digital paths.

Prior to ISDN availability, data connectivity over the Public Switched Telephone Network (PSTN) was via Plain Old Telephone Service (POTS) using analog modems. Connectivity over ISDN offers the networking designer increased bandwidth, reduced call setup time, reduced latency, and lower signal/noise ratios.

ISDN is now being deployed rapidly in numerous applications, including dial-on-demand routing, dial backup, small office/home office (SOHO) and remote office/branch office (ROBO) connectivity, and modem-pool aggregation. This chapter covers the design of these applications. The purpose of this chapter is to discuss the design issues associated with building ISDN networks. For specific examples, see the relevant case-study chapters.

Figure 11-1 shows ISDN being used to concurrently serve ISDN- and POTS (analog modem)–connected remote sites in a hybrid dial solution.

Figure 11-1 *ISDN Can Support Hybrid (Analog and Digital) Dial Solutions*

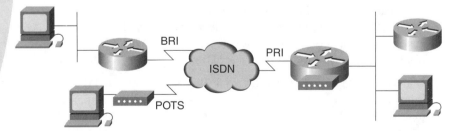

Applications of ISDN in Networking

ISDN has many applications in networking. The Cisco IOS has long been building dial-on-demand routing and dial backup solutions for remote office/branch office connectivity. Recently, ISDN has seen incredible growth in the support of mass small office/home office dialup connectivity. For the purposes of this book, the ISDN calling side will be referred to as SOHO, and the answering side will be referred to as the network access server (NAS) unless otherwise stated. This section addresses the following issues:

- Dial-On-Demand Routing
- Dial Backup
- SOHO Connectivity
- Modem Aggregation

Dial-On-Demand Routing

Full-time connectivity across the ISDN is spoofed by Cisco IOS routers using DDR. When qualified packets arrive at a dialer interface, connectivity is established over the ISDN. After a configured period of inactivity, the ISDN connection is disconnected. Additional ISDN B channels can be added and removed from the MultiLink PPP bundles using configurable thresholds. Figure 11-2 illustrates the use of DDR for networking between ISDN-connected sites.

Figure 11-2 *DDR Creates Connectivity between ISDN Sites*

Dial Backup

ISDN can be used as a backup service for a leased-line connection between the remote and central offices. If the primary connectivity goes down, an ISDN circuit-switched connection is established and traffic is rerouted over ISDN. When the primary link is restored, traffic is redirected to the leased line, and the ISDN call is released.

Dial backup can be accomplished with floating static routes and DDR, or by using the **interface backup** commands. ISDN dial backup can also be configured based on traffic thresholds as a dedicated primary link. If traffic load exceeds a user-defined value on the primary link, the ISDN link is activated to increase bandwidth between the two sites, as shown in Figure 11-3.

Figure 11-3 *ISDN Can Back Up Primary Connectivity between Sites*

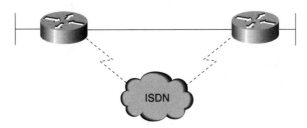

SOHO Connectivity

Small office and home office sites can now be economically supported with ISDN BRI services. This offers to the casual or full-time SOHO sites the capability to connect to their corporate site or the Internet at much higher speeds than those available over POTS and modems.

SOHO designs typically involve dialup only (SOHO-initiated connections), and can take advantage of emerging address-translation technology (such as Cisco 700 series PAT and Cisco IOS EZIP) to simplify design and support. Using these features, the SOHO site can support multiple devices, but appears to the Cisco IOS NAS as a single IP address, as shown in Figure 11-4.

Figure 11-4 *SOHO Sites Can Appear to the Cisco IOS NAS as a Single IP Node*

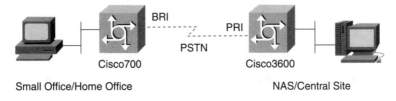

Modem Aggregation

Modem racking and cabling have been eliminated by the integration of digital modem cards on Cisco IOS network access servers (NAS). Digital integration of modems makes possible 56-kbps modem technologies. Hybrid dial solutions can be built using a single phone number to provide analog modem and ISDN conductivity, as shown in Figure 11-1.

Building Blocks of ISDN Solutions

ISDN itself does not solve networking problems. By using either DDR or user-initiated sessions, ISDN can provide the network designer a clear data path over which to negotiate

PPP links. A Public Switched Telephone Network to provide network connectivity requires careful consideration of network security and cost containment.

This section includes overviews of the following ISDN design issues, which are then covered more fully in the following main sections of this chapter:

- ISDN Connectivity
- Datagram Encapsulation
- DDR: Dial-On-Demand Routing
- Security Issues
- Cost-Containment Issues

ISDN Connectivity

Connectivity to ISDN is provided by physical PRI and BRI interfaces. A single PRI or BRI interface provides a multiplexed bundle of B and D channels. The B channel provides bearer services such as high-bandwidth data (up to 64 kbps per B channel) or voice services. The D channel provides the signaling and control channel, and can also be used for low-bandwidth data applications.

BRI service is provided over a groomed local loop, traditionally used for switching to analog phone service. BRI delivers to the subscriber two 64-kbps B channels and one 16-kbps D channel (2B+D).

PRI service is provided on traditional T1 and E1 leased lines between the customer premise equipment (CPE) and the ISDN switch:

- T1-based PRI provides 23 B channels and one D channel (23B+D).
- E1-based PRI provides 30 64-kbps B channels and one 64-kbps D channel (30B+D).

Provisioning of both PRI and BRI services entails very stringent requirements for the physical equipment and cabling in the path from ISDN switch to ISDN CPE. Typical installations can require additional lead times as well as require working with dedicated support groups within your ISDN service-provider organizations (see Figure 11-5).

Figure 11-5 *Connectivity to ISDN Using BRI and PRI*

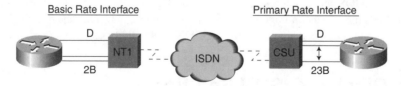

Datagram Encapsulation

When DDR (or a user) creates an end-to-end path over the ISDN, some method of datagram encapsulation is needed to provide data connectivity. Available encapsulations for ISDN designs are PPP, HDLC, X.25, and V.120. X.25 can also be used for datagram delivery over the D channel.

Most networking designs use PPP as the encapsulation. The Point-to-Point Protocol (PPP) is a powerful and modular peer-to-peer mechanism to establish data links, provide security, and encapsulate data traffic. PPP is negotiated between the networking peers each time a connection is established. PPP links can then be used by network protocols such as IP and IPX to establish network connectivity. PPP solutions can support bandwidth aggregation using MultiLink PPP to provide greater throughput for networking applications.

DDR: Dial-On-Demand Routing

When building networking applications, designers must determine how ISDN connections will be initiated, maintained, and released. DDR is a sophisticated set of Cisco IOS features that intelligently establishes and releases circuit-switched connections, as needed by networking traffic. DDR can spoof network routing and directory services in numerous ways to provide the illusion of full-time connectivity over circuit-switched connections. Refer to Chapter 10, "Designing DDR Networks," for a discussion of DDR design.

Security Issues

Because your network devices can now be connected to over the PSTN, it is imperative to design and confirm a robust security model for protecting your network. Cisco IOS uses the AAA model for implementing security. ISDN offers the use of caller ID and DNIS information to provide additional security-design flexibility.

Cost-Containment Issues

A primary goal of selecting ISDN for your network is to avoid the cost of full-time data services (such as leased lines or Frame Relay). As such, it is very important to evaluate your data traffic profiles and monitor your ISDN usage patterns to ensure your WAN costs are controlled. Dialer callback can also be implemented to centralize billing.

Each of these building blocks of ISDN (connectivity, data encapsulation, DDR, security, and cost containment) is discussed in further detail in the remaining sections of this chapter.

ISDN Connectivity Issues

Based on application need and traffic engineering, BRI or PRI services are selected for ISDN connectivity from each site. Traffic engineering may require multiple BRI services or multiple PRIs at some sites. Once connected to the ISDN fabric by BRI or PRI interfaces, design of ISDN end-to-end services must be implemented. This section covers the following issues related to ISDN connectivity:

- Establishing BRI Connectivity
- Establishing ISDN Primary Rate Interface (PRI)
- ISDN End-to-End Considerations
- Datagram-Encapsulation Issues

Establishing BRI Connectivity

The BRI local loop is terminated at the customer premise at an NT1. The interface of the local loop at the NT1 is called the U reference point. On the customer premise side of the NT1 is the S/T reference point. The S/T reference point can support a multipoint bus of ISDN devices (terminal adapters). Figure 11-6 shows a typical BRI installation.

Figure 11-6 *The BRI Local Loop Connected to ISDN*

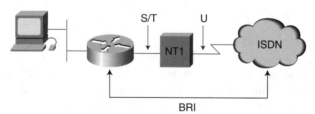

BRI Hardware

Two common types of ISDN CPE are available for BRI services: ISDN routers and PC terminal adapters. Some BRI devices offer integrated NT1s and integrated terminal adapters for analog telephones.

- *LAN routers*—ISDN routers provide routing between ISDN BRI and the LAN by using dial-on-demand routing (DDR).

  DDR automatically establishes and releases circuit-switched calls, providing transparent connectivity to remote sites, based on networking traffic. DDR also controls establishing and releasing secondary B channels, based on load thresholds. MultiLink PPP is used to provide bandwidth aggregation when using multiple B channels. For more information on DDR, see Chapter 10.

Some ISDN applications may require the SOHO user to take direct control over ISDN calls. Emerging Cisco IOS features can bring this control to the user desktop. New Cisco 700 models provide a call button on the front of the router for direct control.

Cisco 700 series and Cisco IOS–based 1000, 1600, 2500 routers provide single BRI interfaces. Multiple-BRI interfaces are available for the Cisco 3600 and Cisco 4x00 series.

- *PC terminal adapters (PC-TA)*—These devices connect to PC workstations either by the PC bus or externally through the communications ports (such as RS-232), and can be used similar to analog (such as V.34) internal and external modems.

PC terminal adapters can provide a single PC user with direct control over ISDN session initiation and release, similar to using an analog modem. Automated mechanisms must be provided to support the addition and removal of the secondary B channel. Cisco 200 Series PC Cards can provide ISDN services to a PC.

BRI Configuration

BRI configuration involves configuration of ISDN switch type and ISDN SPIDs, as follows:

- *ISDN switch types*—ISDN central-office switches (also known as local-exchange equipment) provide two functions at the local exchange: local termination and exchange termination. The local-termination function deals with the transmission facility and termination of the local loop. The exchange-termination function deals with the switching portion of the local exchange. First, the exchange-termination function demultiplexes the bits on the B and D channels. Next, B-channel information is routed to the first stage of the circuit switch, and D-channel packets are routed to D-channel packet-separation circuitry.

For proper ISDN operation, it is imperative that the correct switch type be configured on the ISDN device. For Cisco IOS releases up to 11.2, the configured ISDN switch type is a global command. (Note that this also means you cannot use BRI and PRI cards in the same Cisco IOS chassis.) In Cisco IOS 11.3T or later, multiple switch types in a single Cisco IOS chassis are now supported.

Cisco IOS switch types—The following Cisco IOS command helps illustrate the supported BRI switch types. In North America, the most common types are 5ESS, DMS100, and NI-1.

```
kdt-3640(config)#isdn switch-type ?
  basic-1tr6     1TR6 switch type for Germany
  basic-5ess     AT&T 5ESS switch type for the U.S.
  basic-dms100   Northern DMS-100 switch type
```

```
basic-net3    NET3 switch type for UK and Europe
basic-ni1     National ISDN-1 switch type
basic-nwnet3  NET3 switch type for Norway
basic-nznet3  NET3 switch type for New Zealand
basic-ts013   TS013 switch type for Australia
ntt           NTT switch type for Japan
vn2           VN2 switch type for France
vn3           VN3 and VN4 switch types for France
```

Cisco 700 switch types—On Cisco 700 series routers, use the **set switch** command, which has the following options when running the U.S. software image:

```
SEt SWitch 5ESS ¦ DMS ¦ NI-1 ¦ PERM64 ¦ PERM128
```

- *Service profile identifiers (SPIDs)*—A service profile identifier (SPID) is a number provided by the ISDN carrier to identify the line configuration of the BRI service. SPIDs allow multiple ISDN devices, such as voice and data, to share the local loop. SPIDs are required by DMS-100 and National ISDN-1 switches. Depending on the software version it runs, an AT&T 5ESS switch might require SPIDs as well.

Each SPID points to line setup and configuration information. When a device attempts to connect to the ISDN network, it performs a D-channel Layer 2 initialization process that causes a TEI to be assigned to the device. The device then attempts D-channel Layer 3 initialization. If SPIDs are necessary, but not configured or configured incorrectly on the device, the Layer 3 initialization fails, and the ISDN services cannot be used.

The AT&T 5ESS switch supports up to eight SPIDs per BRI. Because multiple SPIDs can be applied to a single B channel, multiple services can be supported simultaneously. The first B channel can be configured for data, for example, and the second B channel can be configured for both voice (using an ISDN telephone) and data.

DMS-100 and National ISDN-1 switches support only two SPIDs per BRI: one SPID for each B channel. If both B channels will be used for data only, configure the router for both SPIDs (one for each B channel). You cannot run data and voice over the same B channel simultaneously. The absence or presence of a channel's SPID in the router's configuration dictates whether the second B channel can be used for data or voice.

NOTE   There is no standard format for SPID numbers. As a result, SPID numbers vary, depending on the switch vendor and the carrier.

- A typical Cisco IOS SPID configuration is as follows:

```
interface BRI0
isdn spid1 0835866201 8358662
isdn spid2 0835866401 8358664
```

These commands also specify the local directory number (LDN), which is the seven-digit number assigned by the service provider and used for call routing. The LDN is not necessary for establishing ISDN-based connections, but it must be specified if you want to receive incoming calls on B channel 2. The LDN is required only when two SPIDs are configured (for example, when connecting to a DMS or NI1 switch). Each SPID is associated with an LDN. Configuring the LDN causes incoming calls to B channel 2 to be answered properly. If the LDN is not configured, incoming calls to B channel 2 may fail.

- A typical Cisco 700 Series SPID configuration is as follows:

```
SET 1 SPID 51255500660101
SET 1 DIRECTORYNUMBER 5550066
SET PHONE1 = 5550066
SET 2 SPID 51255500670101
```

Confirming BRI Operations

To confirm BRI operations in Cisco IOS, use the **show isdn status** command to inspect the status of your BRI interfaces. In the following example, the TEIs have been successfully negotiated and ISDN Layer 3 (end to end) is ready to make or receive calls:

```
kdt-1600#sh isdn status
The current ISDN Switchtype = basic-ni1
ISDN BRI0 interface
    Layer 1 Status:
        ACTIVE
    Layer 2 Status:
        TEI = 109, State = MULTIPLE_FRAME_ESTABLISHED
        TEI = 110, State = MULTIPLE_FRAME_ESTABLISHED
    Spid Status:
        TEI 109, ces = 1, state = 8(established)
            spid1 configured, spid1 sent, spid1 valid
            Endpoint ID Info: epsf = 0, usid = 1, tid = 1
        TEI 110, ces = 2, state = 8(established)
            spid2 configured, spid2 sent, spid2 valid
            Endpoint ID Info: epsf = 0, usid = 3, tid = 1
    Layer 3 Status:
        0 Active Layer 3 Call(s)
    Activated dsl 0 CCBs = 0
    Total Allocated ISDN CCBs = 0
```

Troubleshooting SPID problems is done with the **debug isdn q921** command. In the example that follows, you can see that **isdn spid1** was rejected by the ISDN switch:

```
kdt-1600#debug isdn q921
ISDN Q921 packets debugging is on
kdt-1600#clear int bri 0
kdt-1600#
*Mar  1 00:09:03.728: ISDN BR0: TX -> SABMEp sapi = 0  tei = 113
```

```
*Mar  1 00:09:04.014: ISDN BR0: RX <-  IDREM  ri = 0  ai = 127
*Mar  1 00:09:04.018: %ISDN-6-LAYER2DOWN:
              Layer 2 for Interface BRI0, TEI 113 changed to down
*Mar  1 00:09:04.022: %ISDN-6-LAYER2DOWN:
              Layer 2 for Interface BR0, TEI 113 changed to down
*Mar  1 00:09:04.046: ISDN BR0: TX ->  IDREQ  ri = 44602  ai = 127
*Mar  1 00:09:04.049: ISDN BR0: RX <-  IDCKRQ  ri = 0  ai = 113
*Mar  1 00:09:05.038: ISDN BR0: RX <-  IDCKRQ  ri = 0  ai = 113
*Mar  1 00:09:06.030: ISDN BR0: TX ->  IDREQ  ri = 37339  ai = 127
*Mar  1 00:09:06.149: ISDN BR0: RX <-  IDREM  ri = 0  ai = 113
*Mar  1 00:09:06.156: ISDN BR0: RX <-  IDASSN  ri = 37339  ai = 114
*Mar  1 00:09:06.164: ISDN BR0: TX ->  SABMEp sapi = 0  tei = 114
*Mar  1 00:09:06.188: ISDN BR0: RX <-  UAf sapi = 0  tei = 114
*Mar  1 00:09:06.188: %ISDN-6-LAYER2UP:
              Layer 2 for Interface BR0, TEI 114 changed to up
*Mar  1 00:09:06.200: ISDN BR0: TX ->
              INFOc sapi = 0  tei = 114  ns = 0  nr = 0  i = 0x08007B3A06383932393833
*Mar  1 00:09:06.276: ISDN BR0: RX <-
              INFOc sapi = 0  tei = 114  ns = 0  nr = 1  i = 0x08007B080382E43A
*Mar  1 00:09:06.283: ISDN BR0: TX ->  RRr sapi = 0  tei = 114  nr = 1
*Mar  1 00:09:06.287: %ISDN-4-INVALID_SPID: Interface BR0, Spid1 was rejected
```

Check the status of the Cisco 700 ISDN line with the **show status** command, as follows:

```
kdt-776> sh status
Status     01/04/1995 18:15:15
Line Status
  Line Activated
  Terminal Identifier Assigned    SPID Accepted
  Terminal Identifier Assigned    SPID Accepted
Port Status                               Interface Connection Link
  Ch:  1      Waiting for Call
  Ch:  2      Waiting for Call
```

BRI Notes

Note the following issues regarding BRI configuration that must be addressed:

- *TEI negotiation*—Some switches deactivate Layer 2 of the D channel when no calls are active, so the router must be configured to perform TEI negotiation at the first call rather than at router power up (the default). To enable TEI negotiation at the first call, use the following global configuration command:

  ```
  isdn tei-negotiation first-call
  ```

- *ISDN subaddressing*—The S/T bus is a point-to-multipoint bus. Multiple ISDN CPE devices can share the same S/T bus. Call routing to individual devices on an S/T bus is achieved by using ISDN subaddressing.

- *Voice routing*—Cisco 700 Series routers can provide POTS jacks for connecting traditional analog telephone sets. SOHO sites can benefit from the capability to concurrently route data and voice calls over the same ISDN BRI interface. Voice-port phone numbers and voice priority must be configured for the needs of the SOHO site. The example that follows shows the voice-routing setup for a typical Cisco 700:

```
SET SWITCH NI-1
SET 1 SPID 51255500660101
SET 1 DIRECTORYNUMBER 5550066
SET PHONE1 = 5550066
SET 2 SPID 51255500670101
SET 2 DIRECTORYNUMBER 5550067
SET PHONE2 = 5550067
SET VOICEPRIORITY INCOMING INTERFACE PHONE1 NEVER
SET VOICEPRIORITY OUTGOING INTERFACE PHONE1 NEVER
SET CALLWAITING INTERFACE PHONE1 OFF
SET VOICEPRIORITY INCOMING INTERFACE PHONE2 ALWAYS
SET VOICEPRIORITY OUTGOING INTERFACE PHONE2 ALWAYS
SET CALLWAITING INTERFACE PHONE2 ON
kdt-776> sh voicerouting
Interface     VoicePriority  VoicePriority  Call     Directory  Ring
              In             Out            Waiting  Number     Cadence
    PHONE1    NEVER          NEVER          OFF      6720066
    PHONE2    ALWAYS         ALWAYS         ON       6720067
    DOV       N/A            N/A            N/A
    UNSPECIFIED  N/A         N/A            N/A
```

Establishing ISDN Primary Rate Interface (PRI)

Cisco IOS routers support PRI interfaces using MultiChannel Interface Processor (MIP) cards. MIP cards can support Channelized T1/E1 or PRI timeslots. MIP cards are available for Cisco 4x000, Cisco 36x0, Cisco 5x00, and Cisco 7x00 Series routers.

To specify that the MIP card is to be used as an ISDN PRI, use the **pri-group timeslots** controller configuration command.

Cisco IOS routers supporting PRI interfaces become network access servers. Cisco 5x00 and 36x0 Series routers support hybrid dial solutions (POTS and ISDN) by providing access to analog modems over the NAS backplane.

PRI Configuration

Configure the ISDN switch type for the PRI interface using the **isdn switch-type** command:

```
AS5200-2(config)#isdn switch-type ?
  primary-4ess     AT&T 4ESS switch type for the U.S.
  primary-5ess     AT&T 5ESS switch type for the U.S.
  primary-dms100   Northern Telecom switch type for the U.S.
  primary-net5     European switch type for NET5
  primary-ntt      Japan switch type
  primary-ts014    Australia switch type
```

Normally, this is a global configuration command. Cisco IOS 11.3T or later will provide support for multiple switch types in a single Cisco IOS chassis. Enable PRI services on the Cisco IOS NAS by configuring the T1 (or E1) controllers. The configuration that follows shows a typical T1 controller configuration on a Cisco 5200:

```
controller T1 0
 framing esf
 clock source line primary
 linecode b8zs
 pri-group timeslots 1-24
 !
controller T1 1
 framing esf
 clock source line secondary
 linecode b8zs
 pri-group timeslots 1-24
 !
```

Note that PRI channels 0–23 map to **pri-group timeslots 1-24**. The same +1 mapping is used on E1-based PRI.

To configure a T1-based PRI, apply the configuration commands to the PRI D channel—that is, interface Serial0:23. All B channels in an ISDN PRI (or BRI) interface are automatically bundled into a dialer interface. When calls are made or received on the B channels, the configuration is cloned from the dialer interface (Serial0:23). If a NAS contains multiple PRIs, these PRIs can be grouped into a single dialer interface by the **dialer rotary-group** interface command, as shown in this example:

```
interface Serial0:23
 dialer rotary-group 1
 !
interface Serial1:23
 dialer rotary-group 1
 !
interface Dialer1
 ip unnumbered Ethernet0
 encapsulation ppp
 peer default ip address pool default
 dialer in-band
 dialer idle-timeout 120
 dialer-group 1
 no fair-queue
 no cdp enable
 ppp authentication pap chap
 ppp multilink
```

With this configuration, every B channel configuration or MultiLink PPP bundle is cloned from **interface Dialer1**.

Confirming PRI Operations

The state of the T1 controller is inspected with the Cisco IOS exec command **show controller t1**, as follows:

```
AS5200-1#sh contr t1
T1 0 is up.
  No alarms detected.
  Version info of slot 0:  HW: 2, Firmware: 14, NEAT PLD: 14, NR Bus PLD: 22
  Framing is ESF, Line Code is B8ZS, Clock Source is Line Primary.
```

```
Data in current interval (685 seconds elapsed):
    0 Line Code Violations, 0 Path Code Violations
    0 Slip Secs, 0 Fr Loss Secs, 0 Line Err Secs, 0 Degraded Mins
    0 Errored Secs, 0 Bursty Err Secs, 0 Severely Err Secs, 0 Unavail Secs
Total Data (last 24 hours)
    0 Line Code Violations, 0 Path Code Violations,
    0 Slip Secs, 0 Fr Loss Secs, 0 Line Err Secs, 8 Degraded Mins,
    0 Errored Secs, 0 Bursty Err Secs, 0 Severely Err Secs, 0 Unavail Secs
T1 1 is up.
No alarms detected.
Version info of slot 0:  HW: 2, Firmware: 14, NEAT PLD: 14, NR Bus PLD: 22
Framing is ESF, Line Code is B8ZS, Clock Source is Line Secondary.
Data in current interval (197 seconds elapsed):
    0 Line Code Violations, 0 Path Code Violations
    0 Slip Secs, 0 Fr Loss Secs, 0 Line Err Secs, 0 Degraded Mins
    0 Errored Secs, 0 Bursty Err Secs, 0 Severely Err Secs, 0 Unavail Secs
Total Data (last 24 hours)
    0 Line Code Violations, 0 Path Code Violations,
    0 Slip Secs, 0 Fr Loss Secs, 0 Line Err Secs, 4 Degraded Mins,
    0 Errored Secs, 0 Bursty Err Secs, 0 Severely Err Secs, 0 Unavail Secs
```

Excessive line-code violations and other errors will cause significant performance loss. Work with your ISDN PRI service provider to ensure that these counters show a relatively clean operation. Use the Cisco IOS exec command **show isdn status** to verify that ISDN is operational, as follows:

```
AS5200-1#sh isdn status
The current ISDN Switchtype = primary-dms100
ISDN Serial0:23 interface
    Layer 1 Status:
        ACTIVE
    Layer 2 Status:
        TEI = 0, State = MULTIPLE_FRAME_ESTABLISHED
    Layer 3 Status:
        0 Active Layer 3 Call(s)
    Activated dsl 0 CCBs = 0
ISDN Serial1:23 interface
    Layer 1 Status:
        ACTIVE
    Layer 2 Status:
        TEI = 0, State = MULTIPLE_FRAME_ESTABLISHED
    Layer 3 Status:
        0 Active Layer 3 Call(s)
    Activated dsl 1 CCBs = 0
    Total Allocated ISDN CCBs = 0
```

Inspect B-channel status with the **show isdn service** exec command, as follows:

```
AS5200-1#sh isdn service
PRI Channel Statistics:
ISDN Se0:23, Channel (1-31)
  Activated dsl 0
  State (0=Idle 1=Propose 2=Busy 3=Reserved 4=Restart 5=Maint)
  0 0 0 0 0 0 0 0 0 0 0 0 0 0 0 0 0 0 0 0 0 0 3 3 3 3 3 3 3
  Channel (1-31) Service (0=Inservice 1=Maint 2=Outofservice)
  0 0 0 0 0 0 0 0 0 0 0 0 0 0 0 0 0 0 0 0 0 0 0 0 0 0 0 0 0 0
ISDN Se1:23, Channel (1-31)
```

```
Activated dsl 1
State (0=Idle 1=Propose 2=Busy 3=Reserved 4=Restart 5=Maint)
0 0 0 0 0 0 0 0 0 0 0 0 0 0 0 0 0 0 0 0 0 0 0 3 3 3 3 3 3 3
Channel (1-31) Service (0=Inservice 1=Maint 2=Outofservice)
0 0 0 0 0 0 0 0 0 0 0 0 0 0 0 0 0 0 0 0 0 0 0 0 0 0 0 0 0 0
```

ISDN End-to-End Considerations

This section discusses the following ISDN end-to-end considerations:

- Signaling System 7 (SS7)
- Data-Path Speed

Signaling System 7

Signaling System 7 (SS7) provides telephone switches with out-of-band signaling capabilities for telephony trunks (switch-to-switch DS0 connections). End-to-end call management (such as setup and teardown) uses ITU specification Q.931 and is extended to PRI/BRI networking devices over the ISDN D channel.

Out-of-band signaling via SS7 provides numerous benefits to networking design, including reduced call setup time, bearer capability and other progress indicators, 64-kbps data paths, caller ID, and dialed number information (DNIS). The output that follows (of Cisco IOS **debug isdn q931**) shows typical ISDN Q.931 SETUP messages received by an NAS.

The Q.931 SETUP message includes a bearer-capability information element (IE), which indicates to the ISDN fabric and receiving side the type of application carried on the B channel. It is the responsibility of the ISDN to provide an end-to-end channel capable of carrying the bearer service, and to provide to the receiving side progress indication to help it better utilize the ISDN connection.

The Cisco IOS **debug isdn q931** output has different bearer capabilities for each incoming call type, as follows:

- Incoming 64-kbps data call

    ```
    ISDN Se0:23: RX <-  SETUP pd = 8  callref = 0x0470
            Bearer Capability i = 0x8890
            Channel ID i = 0xA98382
            Calling Party Number i = '!', 0x83, '5125558084'
            Called Party Number i = 0xC9, '52000'
    ```
- Incoming 56-kbps data call

    ```
    ISDN Se0:23: RX <- SETUP pd = 8  callref = 0x05DC
            Bearer Capability i = 0x8890218F
            Channel ID i = 0xA98382
            Calling Party Number i = '!', 0x83, '5125558084'
            Called Party Number i = 0xC9, '52000'
    ```

• Incoming voice call

```
ISDN Se0:23: RX <-  SETUP pd = 8  callref = 0x015C
        Bearer Capability i = 0x8090A2
        Channel ID i = 0xA98383
        Progress Ind i = 0x8283 - Origination address is non-ISDN
        Called Party Number i = 0xC1, '5552000'
```

To support the routing of voice calls to integrated modem cards, use the Cisco IOS interface configuration command **isdn incoming-voice modem**. In some network designs, data calls can be made with the Q.931 SETUP message, indicating that it is a voice call. In some regions, ISDN tariff structures may make this type of call more cost-effective. (This design is commonly referred to as ISDN data-over-voice.) However, indicating to the ISDN switching fabric that the bearer capability is voice allows the call to be placed through nondigital trunks. Designers, therefore, must carefully consider the potential risk in such a design. To support incoming ISDN data-over-voice calls on the Cisco IOS, use the configuration command **isdn incoming-voice data**, as follows:

```
NAS-522(config)#int serial 0:23
NAS-522(config-if)#isdn incoming ?
  data   Incoming voice calls will be handled as data.
  modem  Incoming voice calls will be handled as modems.
```

Data-Path Speed

Prior to SS7 implementation, end-to-end call-management signaling was provided in-band by robbing bits from the DS0 trunks. Utilizing the occasional eighth and least significant bit of each voice byte was not detrimental to voice quality, but provided switch-to-switch signaling. End-to-end, out-of-band signaling via SS7 and PRI/BRI D channels allows data calls to be placed through ISDN networks utilizing the full DS0 trunk (64 kbps). Some trunks of the PSTN still do not support out-of-band signaling, and can provide only robbed-bit trunking (Channelized T1/E1), limiting the available data channel to 56 kbps.

It is the responsibility of the ISDN switching fabric to provide an end-to-end path matching the requirement of the bearer capability. If a call is made at 64 kbps and there is not a 64-kbps clear, end-to-end path for the call, a busy signal should be received. Network designers must consider the possibility of occasional ISDN call blocking at 64 kbps. Robust design may require that some sites be supported with 56-kbps data calls. Table 11-11 shows outgoing speeds.

Table 11-1   *Outgoing Speeds and the Cisco IOS Dialer Maps and Profiles*

Outgoing Speed	Cisco IOS Dialer Maps	Cisco IOS Dialer Profile	Cisco 700
64 kbps	Dialer map ... speed 64 (default)	??	Set speed 64
56 kbps	Dialer map ... speed 56	??	Set speed 56
Auto	Multiple Dialer Maps	??	Set speed auto (default)

When originating calls are made at 64 kbps and improperly delivered to the destination by the ISDN network over a 56-kbps path, the transmitted data will be corrupted. The troubleshooting indication will be that **debug isdn q931** shows the call being delivered, but no output is ever seen as being received from **debug ppp negotiation** on one side. The packets have been corrupted and are being discarded. If calls are being delivered and PPP is not negotiating LCP, it is always a prudent idea to test outgoing calls at 56 kbps.

- Outgoing call speed

  Cisco IOS speed configuration—Use the **speed** parameter on the **dialer map** configuration command to make outgoing calls at 56 kbps, as in the following example:

  ```
  int dialer 1
  dialer map ip 172.20.1.1 name nas speed 56 5558084
  ```

  Cisco IOS dialer profiles speed configuration—The following example illustrates how to configure a Cisco IOS dialer profile to make outgoing calls at 56 kbps:

  ```
  interface dialer 1
  dialer remote-name nas
  dialer string 5558084 class unameit
  !
  map-class dialer unameit
  dialer isdn speed 56
  ```

  Cisco 700 speed configuration—Use the Cisco 700 series **set speed** configuration command to control the speed for outgoing calls.

- Incoming call speed

  The ISDN Q.931 bearer capability and other IEs are used to determine the speed of the incoming call, and will operate properly in most circumstances. In some country-to-country applications, however, the incoming call SETUP message will be delivered with a bearer capability that does not match the originating call. If an **isdn not end-to-end** IE is also received, it can be used to override the received bearer capability using the Cisco IOS configuration command **isdn not end-to-end**.

Datagram-Encapsulation Issues

ISDN can use PPP, HDLC, or X.25 for encapsulation. PPP is used most frequently because it provides an excellent mechanism for authentication and negotiation of compatible link and protocol configuration.

Point-to-Point Protocol (PPP)

PPP provides a standard method for transporting multiprotocol packets over point-to-point links. PPP is defined in RFC 1661. PPP consists of several components, each of which are of concern to the network designer:

- PPP framing

  RFC 1662 discusses the implementation of PPP in HDLC-like framing. There are differences in the way PPP is implemented on asynchronous and synchronous links.

  When one end of the link uses synchronous PPP (such as an ISDN router) and the other uses asynchronous PPP (such as an ISDN TA connected to a PC serial port), two techniques are available to provide framing compatibility. The preferable method is to enable synchronous-to-asynchronous PPP frame conversion in the ISDN TA. If this is not available, V.120 can be used to encapsulate the asynchronous PPP frames for transport across the ISDN.

- Link Control Protocol (LCP)

  The PPP LCP provides a method of establishing, configuring, maintaining, and terminating the point-to-point connection. Before any network layer datagrams (for example, IP) can be exchanged, LCP must first open the connection and negotiate configuration parameters. This phase is complete when a configuration acknowledgment frame has been both sent and received.

- PPP authentication

  The PPP authentication protocols (PAP and CHAP) are defined in RFC 1334. After LCP has established the PPP connection, an optional authentication protocol can be implemented before proceeding to the negotiation and establishment of the Network Control Protocols. If authentication is desired, it must be negotiated as an option at the LCP establishment phase. Authentication can be bidirectional (both sides authenticate the other) or unidirectional (one side, typically the called side, authenticates the other).

  Most ISDN designs require the called device to authenticate the calling device. Besides the obvious security benefits, authentication also provides a sense of state for DDR and MultiLink PPP bundling.

- Network Control Protocols (NCPs)

  This is a family of NCPs for establishing and configuring different network layer protocols. PPP is designed to allow the simultaneous use of multiple network layer protocols.

After LCP has been established and authentication has passed, the PPP nodes send NCP frames to negotiate and establish connectivity for one or more network layer protocols. To support IP over a PPP connection, for example, the IPCP is negotiated and established as per RFC 1332. After IPCP is successfully established, IP datagrams can be transmitted over the PPP connection.

- MultiLink PPP (MP)

  MultiLink PPP is a standard for aggregating multiple PPP links that allows for multivendor interoperability, and is defined in RFC 1717. MP defines a way of sequencing and transmitting packets over multiple physical interfaces. To reduce potential latency issues, MP also defines a method of fragmenting and reassembling large packets. Figure 11-7 provides a conceptual view of MP in action.

Figure 11-7 *MultiLink PPP in Action*

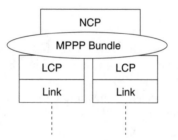

When an NCP packet arrives at an MLP master interface for transmitting and is larger than 30 bytes, it is fragmented and sent on each physical link in the MLP bundle. When MLP packet fragments arrive on PPP destination, MLP reassembles the original packets and sequences them correctly in the data stream.

Using MP, BRI devices can double their connection bandwidth across the link: from 56/64 kbps to 112/128 kbps. MPPP is supported as long as all devices are part of the same dialer rotary group or pool.

Cisco IOS and Cisco 700 DDR intelligence is used to determine when to add and remove links from the MP master interface. Cisco IOS DDR provides a load-threshold configuration to determine when to add and remove the additional link. The load factor can be calculated on incoming, outgoing, or two-way traffic.

The following partial configuration for NAS places two BRI interfaces into a dialer rotary group, enables MP support, and defines a load threshold for determining when to bring up additional B channels.

```
interface BRI2/0
 encapsulation ppp
 dialer rotary-group 1
 isdn spid1 0835866201
 isdn spid2 0835866401
!
interface BRI2/1
 encapsulation ppp
 dialer rotary-group 1
 isdn spid1 0835867201
 isdn spid2 0835967401
!
interface Dialer1
 ip unnumbered Ethernet0/0
 encapsulation ppp
 dialer in-band
 dialer map ip 172.20.2.1 name kdt-nas 8358661
 dialer load-threshold 100 either
 dialer-group 1
 ppp authentication chap callin
 ppp multilink
```

MP state and sessions can be investigated using the **show user** and the **show ppp multilink** commands:

```
KDT-5200#sh user
     Line    User      Host(s)                Idle Location
 * 51 vty 1  admin     idle                   00:00:00
     Vi1     jack-isdn Virtual PPP (Bundle)    00:00:46
     Vi9     cisco776  Virtual PPP (Bundle)    00:00:46
     Se0:18  jack-isd  Sync PPP               00:09:06
     Se0:21  cisco776  Sync PPP               00:18:59
     Se0:22  jack-isdn Sync PPP               00:08:49


KDT-AS5200#sh ppp multi

Bundle cisco776, 1 member, Master link is Virtual-Access9
Dialer Interface is Dialer1
  0 lost fragments, 3 reordered, 0 unassigned, sequence 0x2068/0x1A7C rcvd/
  sent
  0 discarded, 0 lost received, 1/255 load

Member Link: 1
Serial0:21

Bundle jack-isdn, 2 members, Master link is Virtual-Access1
Dialer Interface is Dialer1
  0 lost fragments, 8 reordered, 0 unassigned, sequence 0x5DEB/0x1D7E4 rcvd/
  sent
  0 discarded, 0 lost received, 1/255 load

Member Links: 2
Serial0:18
Serial0:22
```

As seen previously, MP uses the PPP authentication name to build and maintain MP bundles. To enable MP on a Cisco 700, apply the following configuration command:

```
set ppp multilink on
```

* Compression Control Protocol (CCP)

  The Point-to-Point (PPP) Compression Control Protocol (CCP) is an Internet Engineering Task Force (IETF) draft RFC that defines a method for negotiating data compression over PPP links. These links can be either leased lines or circuit-switched WAN links, including ISDN. Compression increases throughput and shortens file transfer times.

  Use the **compress** interface configuration command at both ends of the link to enable compression. Use the **stac** keyword to enable the Stacker (LZS) compression algorithm or the **predictor** keyword to enable the RAND algorithm (a predictor algorithm). The Stacker algorithm is appropriate for LAPB and PPP encapsulation, and the RAND algorithm is appropriate for HDLC and PPP encapsulation. The Stacker algorithm is preferred for PPP encapsulation.

On the Cisco IOS, to determine what components have been negotiated (such as LCP, IPCP, CCP, and so on), use the **show interface** command on the master interface. To troubleshoot PPP negotiation problems, use **debug ppp negotiation** and **debug ppp authentication**.

ISDN Security

Using SS7, the ISDN can deliver end-to-end information elements such as caller ID and dialed number information service (DNIS). This information can be used to provide additional security when designing ISDN solutions. It is recommended that PPP authentication always be implemented.

* PPP authentication

  PPP authentication is used to provide primary security on ISDN and other PPP-encapsulated links. The authenticated username is also used by MultiLink PPP to maintain bundles and by DDR to determine which dialer sites are currently connected.

  PPP authentication is enabled with the **ppp authentication** interface command. PAP and/or CHAP can be used to authenticate the remote connection. CHAP is considered a superior authentication protocol because it uses a three-way handshake to avoid sending the password in clear text on the PPP link.

  Often, it may be necessary to authenticate the remote side only when receiving calls (not when originating).

- Caller-ID screening

  The **isdn caller** interface configuration command configures caller-ID screening. For example, the following command configures an ISDN to accept a call with a delivered caller ID having 41555512 and any numbers in the last two positions.

  ```
  isdn caller 41555512xx
  ```

  Multiple **isdn caller** commands can be entered as needed. If a call is received that does not contain a caller ID or does not match a configured **isdn caller** statement, the call will be rejected.

- Dialer callback

  Callback allows a router (typically a remote router) to initiate a circuit-switched WAN link to another device and request that device to call back. The device, such as a central-site router, responds to the callback request by calling the device that made the initial call. Callback uses the Point-to-Point Protocol (PPP) and the facilities specified in RFC 1570. Figure 11-8 shows a typical negotiation.

Figure 11-8 *ISDN Callback*

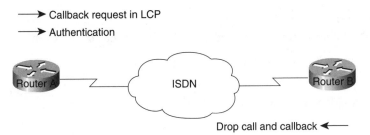

In Figure 11-8, callback is completed in the following sequence of steps:

Step 1 Router A brings up a circuit-switched connection to Router B.

Step 2 Routers A and B negotiate PPP Link Control Protocol (LCP). Router A can request a callback, or Router B can initiate a callback.

Step 3 Router A authenticates itself to Router B using PPP PAP or CHAP. Router B can optionally authenticate itself to Router A.

Step 4 Both routers drop the circuit-switched connection.

Step 5 Router B brings up a circuit-switched connection to Router A.

Callback provides centralized billing for synchronous dialup services. It also enables you to take advantage of tariff disparities on both a national and international basis. Because callback requires a circuit-switched connection to be established before the callback request can be passed, however, a small charge (dependent on local tariffing) is always incurred by the router initiating the call that requests a callback.

See Chapter 10 for a further discussion of DDR callback. See Chapter 21, "Using ISDN Effectively in Multiprotocol Networks," for a callback configuration example.

- Called-party number verification

  When multiple devices and a router share the same ISDN local loop, you can ensure that the correct device answers an incoming call. This is done by configuring the device to verify the called-party number and the subaddress delivered by the switch as part of the SETUP message against the device's configured number and subaddress.

  To configure called-party number verification on the router, apply the **isdn answer1** or **isdn answer2** interface configuration commands to the BRI. These commands enable you to specify the called-party number, the subaddress number, or both. If you do not use either the **isdn answer1** command or the **isdn answer2** command, the router processes and accepts all incoming calls.

ISDN Scaling Techniques

ISDN scaling techniques covered in this section include the following:

- Virtual Remote Nodes
- Virtual Profiles
- MultiChassis MultiLink PPP (MMP)

Virtual Remote Nodes

By using network address translations (NAT) features such as Cisco 700 PAT and Cisco IOS EZIP, remote sites can appear to the ISDN NAS as a single remote node IP address. This alleviates IP address–consumption problems and the routing-design complexity often associated with large-scale ISDN DDR deployment, while still supporting a LAN and DDR-based connectivity from the remote site.

These NAT features use the IP address received from the NAS during IPCP negotiation. All packets routed between the LAN and the PPP link have their individual IP addresses translated to a single IP address. Different UDP/TCP port numbers are used with the single IP address to determine which packets need to be returned to which IP addresses on the LAN. The port number translation is used to determine which packets need to be returned to which IP addresses on the LAN. The following Cisco 700 configuration commands set NAT up for PAT.

Cisco 700 PAT and DHCP

The following configuration sets up a Cisco 700 for PAT and DHCP service:

```
cd internal
set ip address 172.24.4.254
set ip netmask 255.255.255.0
set ip routing on
set ip rip update off
cd
set user access-gw1
set ip routing on
set ip framing none
set number 18005552626
set ip rip update off
set encap ppp
set ip route destination 0.0.0.0 gateway 0.0.0.0
set ip pat on
cd lan
set bridging on
set encaps ppp
set ip routing on
cd
set ip pat porthandler default 172.24.4.1
set ip pat porthandler http 172.24.4.1
set bridging on
set dhcp server
set dhcp domain cisco.com
set dhcp address 172.24.1.1 10
set dhcp netmask 255.255.255.0
set dhcp gateway primary 172.24.4.254
set dhcp dns primary 172.30.1.100
set dhcp dns secondary 172.30.2.100
set dhcp wins primary 172.30.1.101
set dhcp wins secondary 172.30.2.101
set ppp authentication incoming chap
set ppp authentication outgoing chap
set ppp secret client
 <insert_secret>
 <insert_secret>
set ppp secret host
 <insert_secret>
 <insert_secret>
```

If support is required for outbound-initiated network connections to the remote site, port-handler configuration can be added so that the SOHO router knows which IP address to forward packets on to for individual connection types.

```
kdt-776> sh ip pat
Dropped - icmp 0, udp 0, tcp 0, map 0, frag 0
Timeout - udp 5 minutes, tcp 30 minutes
Port handlers [default 172.24.4.1]:
Port    Handler         Service
------------------------------------
0       172.24.4.1      DEFAULT
23      Router          TELNET
67      Router          DHCP Server
```

```
68       Router        DHCP Client
69       Router        TFTP
80       172.24.4.1    HTTP
161      Router        SNMP
162      Router        SNMP-TRAP
520      Router        RIP

Translation Table - 11 Entries.
Inside          Outside         Orig. Port/ID    Trans. Port/ID  Timeout
- - - - - - - - - - - - - - - - - - - - - - - - - - - - - - - - - - - - - - - - -
172.24.4.1      172.17.190.5    0x414            0xff7d                1
172.24.4.1      172.17.190.5    0x415            0xff7c               30
172.24.4.1      172.17.190.26   0x40d            0xff88               27
172.24.4.1      172.17.114.11   0x416            0xff7b                4
172.24.4.1      172.17.114.11   0x417            0xff7a                4
172.24.4.1      172.17.114.11   0x40f            0xff82                4
172.24.4.1      172.17.190.19   0x418            0xff79                1
172.24.4.1      172.17.190.5    0x410            0xff81                1
172.24.4.1      172.17.114.11   0x411            0xff80                4
172.24.4.1      172.17.114.11   0x412            0xff7f                4
172.24.4.1      172.17.190.5    0x413            0xff7e                1
```

Virtual Profiles

Virtual profiles (introduced in Cisco IOS 11.3) are PPP applications that create virtual-access interfaces for each connected user. Virtual profiles allow additional design flexibility when building ISDN networks for SOHO support. Using virtual profiles for dial-in can provide simplified node addressing and address mapping that was previously provided by using DDR on ISDN interfaces. (As of Cisco IOS 11.3, virtual profile–based dial-out is not supported.)

The virtual-access interface configuration can be cloned from a dialer or virtual template. To learn more about virtual-access interfaces, see http://cio.cisco.com/warp/customer/131/4.html. Virtual profiles use virtual templates and can use AAA based on per-user configuration to create virtual-access interfaces. Per-user configuration can be added to meet the specific protocol needs of individual users or groups.

Cisco IOS virtual-access interfaces can simplify remote node support for IPX and AppleTalk by using the same configuration used on traditional group-async interfaces. The following configuration provides peer addressing for IP, IPX, and AppleTalk using a virtual-template interface:

```
interface Virtual-Template1
 ip unnumbered Ethernet0/0
 appletalk client-mode
 ipx ppp-client Loopback0
 peer default ip address pool default
```

MultiChassis MultiLink PPP (MMP)

When designing MultiLink PPP without MultiChassis support, telco hunt groups cannot span more than a single Cisco IOS NAS; otherwise, there exists a risk that the multiple B channels will not be reassembled. An AS5300 can support up to four PRI interfaces, for example, providing a maximum of 120 B channels (E1 based) in a single dial-in hunt group. Additional NAS capacity would need to be provided by configuring a new hunt group (with a new pilot directory number) for each network access server, as shown in Figure 11-9. This has the negative effect of fragmenting the dialup pool.

Figure 11-9 *MMP Allows a Telco Hunt Group to Span More than a Single NAS*

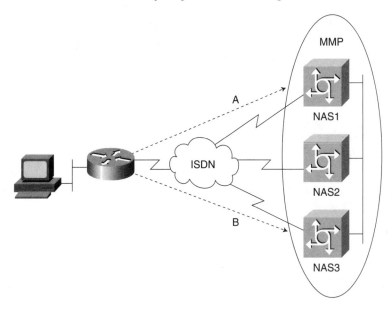

Cisco recognized that no matter what size NAS they can develop, there will always be customers needing larger pools of access ports. As such, Cisco IOS 11.2 released MultiChassis MultiLink Point-to-Point Protocol (MMP), which extends MultiLink PPP (MLP) by providing a mechanism to aggregate B channels transparently across multiple NASs.

MMP consists of two primary components to complement MLP, as follows:

- *The dial StackGroup*—NASs that operate as a group when receiving MLP calls. Every MLP session receiving any NAS is sent out to bid using the Stack Group Bidding Protocol (SGBP). Primarily, this allows secondary MLP links to be bundled to the MLP master interface. Different bidding strategies (such as off load and load sharing) can be used to determine who should win master-interface bidding.

- *Level 2 Forwarding (L2F) protocol*—A draft IETF standard, L2F provides for tunneling of the MLP fragments between the MLP physical interface and the MLP master interface.

By using MMP, MLP capacity can be easily added and removed from large dial pools as needed. CPU processing capacity can be added to dialup pools through the use of off-load servers. Tasks such as MLP fragmentation and reassembly, PPP compression, and encryption can be intensive and may benefit from execution in off-load servers (see Figure 11-10).

To configure MMP on a Cisco IOS NAS, use the **sgbp** commands, as follows:

```
kdt-3640(config)#sgbp ?
  group        SGBP group name
  member       SGBP group member configuration
  ppp-forward  SGBP participation for non-Multilink PPP also
  seed-bid     mastership query seed bid
  source-ip    SGBP source ip address
```

To monitor and troubleshoot MMP, use both SGBP and VPDN (for L2F):

```
sh sgbp
sh vpdn
debug sgbp
debug vpdn
```

MMP provides an interoperable multivendor solution because it does not require any special software capabilities at the remote sites. The only remote requirement is support for the industry standard MLP (RFC 1717).

Figure 11-10 *Active MMP Sessions*

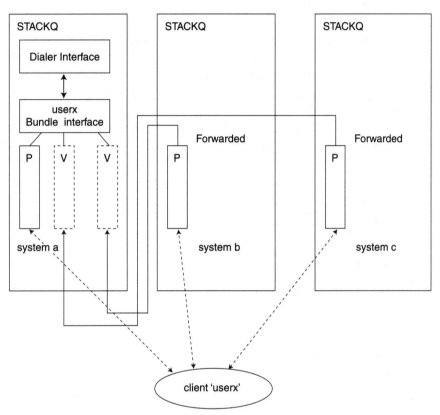

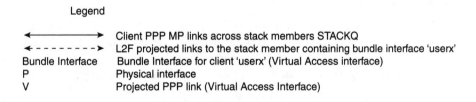

Legend

←――――――――→	Client PPP MP links across stack members STACKQ
←‑ ‑ ‑ ‑ ‑ ‑ ‑ ‑→	L2F projected links to the stack member containing bundle interface 'userx'
Bundle Interface	Bundle Interface for client 'userx' (Virtual Access interface)
P	Physical interface
V	Projected PPP link (Virtual Access Interface)

ISDN Cost-Containment Issues

As a circuit-switched connection, ISDN is billed, or tariffed, based on usage. Given this model, the configuration goal is to minimize uptime by controlling the kinds of packets that bring the link up. Minimizing uptime becomes a challenge when routing protocols are used because of their need to send regular broadcasts that contain routing information.

ISDN charges in some installations have easily exceeded $4,000/month for a single site as a result of being poorly designed and managed. When the outrageous phone bill is received, it is too late; the cost has been incurred. Cisco highly recommends the use of proper network management to back up careful design, to ensure that excessive charges are not experienced. Depending on the protocols your network runs, you might want to use a combination of the techniques described in this section, which are as follows:

- Traffic Analysis
- Tariff Structure
- User Education
- Using SNMP
- Cisco Enterprise Accounting (CEA) for ISDN
- AAA Accounting

Traffic Analysis

Most ISDN solutions can remain cost-effective only as long as the ISDN B channels are kept idle most of the day. The general rule-of-thumb is that Frame Relay will make a more cost-effective solution at some application-dependent number of hours per day. (The point at which it is more cost-effective to use a leased-line solution depends on the cost structures for each point-to-point application.)

Each networking application and protocol has its own set of challenges. E-mail clients may be set to periodically poll POP servers. Network Time Protocol might be desired to support clock synchronization. To provide total control over when the DDR connections are made, the network designer must carefully consider the following issues:

- Which sites can initiate connections based on traffic?
- Is dial-out required to SOHO sites? For network or workstation management?
- Which sites can terminate connections based on idle links?
- How are directory services and routing tables supported across an idle connection?
- What applications need to be supported over DDR connections? For how many users?
- What unexpected protocols might cause DDR connections? Can they be filtered?
- Are dialer filters performing as expected?

Guidelines should be provided to users about how to avoid and/or eliminate excessive ISDN charges. These guidelines will be the result of first determining what applications are required over these connections. Packet-tracing tools can be used very effectively to determine how to minimize or eliminate unnecessary DDR connections. For example:

- Sending and receiving e-mail should be manual, if possible.
- Windows Networking may require periodic directory services traffic.
- AppleShare servers will need to be disconnected to avoid tickle packets.
- DB-accessing applications, such as scheduling software, may require logging out when not in use.

Tariff Structure

Some ISDN service providers charge a per-connection and per-minute charge, even for local calls. It is important to consider local and long-distance tariff charges when selecting DDR design and parameters. ISDN callback can be used to centralize long-distance charges, which can significantly reduce administrative overhead and provide opportunities for reduced rate structures. ISDN callback can also enhance the security environment.

User Education

End users should be trained to keep their ISDN routers visible and monitor the status of their B-channel LEDs on their BRI devices. If B channels are up when they are not using networking applications, they should alert network managers. User education can be very effective in helping to avoid excessive ISDN charges.

Using SNMP

The Simple Network Management Protocol (SNMP) uses Management Information Bases (MIBs) to store information about network events. Currently, no industry-standard ISDN MIB is available, but as of Cisco IOS Software Release 10.3(3), two Cisco ISDN MIBs are available. With these MIBs, SNMP-compliant management platforms (for example, HP OpenView or SunNet Manager) can query Cisco routers for ISDN-related statistics.

The Cisco ISDN MIB focuses primarily on ISDN interface and neighbor information. It defines two MIB groups: demandNbrTable and demandNbrEntry. Table 11-2 lists some of the MIB variables available in the ISDN MIB. Cisco Enterprise Accounting for ISDN can provide management access to Call History Data using this MIB.

Table 11-2   *Cisco ISDN MIB Variables*

MIB Object	Description
demandNbrPhysIf	Index value of the physical interface that the neighbor will be called on; on an ISDN interface, this is the ifIndex value of the D channel.
demandNbrMaxduration	Maximum call duration in seconds.
demandNbrLastduration	Duration of last call in seconds.
demandNbrAcceptCalls	Number of calls accepted from the neighbor.
demandNbrRefuseCalls	Number of calls from neighbor that the router has refused.

The Cisco Call History MIB stores call information for accounting purposes. The goal is to provide an historical view of an ISDN interface, including the number of calls that have been placed and call length. Most Call History MIB variables are in the ciscoCallHistory MIB group. Table 11-3 lists some of the MIB variables.

Table 11-3   *Cisco Call History Variables*

MIB Object	Description
ciscoCallHistoryStartTime	The value of sysUpTime when this call history entry was created; this variable can be used to retrieve all calls after a specific time.
ciscoCallHistoryCalledNumber	The number that was used to place this call.
ciscoCallHistoryCallConnection Time	The value of sysUpTime when the call was connected.
ciscoCallHistoryCallDisconnect Time	The value of sysUpTime when the call was disconnected.

The Cisco ISDN MIBs assume SNMP support on the network. If an SNMP-compliant management platform is present, the Cisco ISDN MIBs deliver valuable information about ISDN links. In particular, the Call History MIB provides critical information about ISDN uptime, which is useful for tracking ISDN charges.

Cisco offers a wide range of ISDN-based products in response to a variety of networking needs. The Cisco IOS software provides a number of features that maximize ISDN performance and minimize ISDN usage charges, such as snapshot routing, access lists, NBP filtering (for AppleTalk), and watchdog and keepalive packet control (for IPX).

Cisco Enterprise Accounting (CEA) for ISDN

CEA for ISDN is a software application that runs on Windows NT. CEA for ISDN can be used to monitor the ISDN Call History-MIB and provide network managers with Call Detail Records, including cost estimates.

AAA Accounting

AAA Accounting can be implemented to provide feedback of PPP session connect times. AAA Accounting is transported to TACACS+ or RADIUS servers, where the data can often be accessed with standard SQL tools for scheduled and immediate reporting. The following command enables AAA Accounting records for PPP sessions:

```
aaa accounting network stop-only
```

Troubleshooting ISDN

When troubleshooting ISDN, it is important to keep in mind the ISDN protocol architecture and how it relates to the OSI reference model. ISDN works on the lower three layers of the OSI reference model: the physical, data link, and network layers. On the physical layer, there are protocols, such as I.430 for BRI and I.431 for PRI, which are shared between both the B and D channels. On the data link layer, PPP is used as the B-channel protocol. HDLC could be used too, but there are more advantages to using PPP. LAPD, which is also known as Q.921, is used as the D-channel protocol on the data link layer. On the network layer, there are protocols such as IP, IPX, and so on, which are used on B channels; and Q.931, which is used on the D channel.

When troubleshooting ISDN, this structure is important. It is important to be systematic and go step-by-step. Troubleshoot physical layer issues first, before troubleshooting the data link layer or network layer problems. Always troubleshoot both ends of the ISDN connection; you'll actually clear up a lot of issues (discussed in more detail later) when troubleshooting these links.

Before troubleshooting the ISDN link, you must first ping the remote ISDN interface. If you can ping the remote ISDN interface, your ISDN connection is working fine. If you cannot ping the remote ISDN interface, then at this point do not bother to look at the routing or cost issues. Keep in mind that an ISDN interface is a DDR interface, and in Cisco IOS the DDR interface does not come up unless there are some interesting packets to trigger the ISDN link. To check on the router configuration and see whether there is any interesting traffic, you can use the following debug commands on the router:

- **debug dialer events**
- **debug dialer packets**

Use the preceding debug commands to monitor and see whether there are any packets triggering the ISDN link. In the following **debug dialer events** command, you can see that there are interesting packets to bring up the ISDN link, and you can also see the source and destination IP address:

```
Router # debug dialer events
Dialing cause: BRI0: ip (s=20.20.20.20 d20.20.22.22)
Router # debug dialer packets
BRI0: ip (s=20.20.20.20, d=20.20.22.22), 100 bytes, interesting (ip PERMIT)
```

Troubleshooting the Physical Layer

Always begin your troubleshooting at the physical layer first, before troubleshooting the data link layer or network layer problems. A very handy command in IOS gives a snapshot of the status of all three layers. By looking at the **show isdn status** command, you can jump to the appropriate layer and troubleshoot that particular layer. The following is the output of the **show isdn status** command, and it shows the status of all three layers in case of PRI or BRI. Notice that in the following output the Layer 1 status is deactivated and that there is something wrong on the physical layer. Remember that if a layer is not active, none of the upper layers are going to be active.

```
Router # show isdn status
ISDN BRI0 interface
    Layer 1 Status:
  DEACTIVATED
    Layer 2 Status:
     Layer 2 NOT Activated
    Layer 3 Status:
     No Active Layer 3 Call(s)
    Activated dsl 0 CCBs are 0, Allocated = 0
```

Two things could be wrong in this case: an external problem or an internal problem to the router. If the problem is external, it could be a cable problem, telco problem, NT1 problem; or perhaps, the network has never acknowledged the router's request to activate the ISDN interface. An internal problem to the router means that the router never requested the network to activate the ISDN interface.

The **debug bri** Command

A very handy debug command in IOS shows whether the problem is internal to the router or external to the router. The command is called **debug bri**. The **debug bri** command is a communication between the IOS and ISDN chipset on the ISDN interface. The **write_sid** commands are sent to the ISDN chipset. Different types of Cisco routers show different wrote values, such as **wrote = E**, **wrote = 1B**, and so on. In other words, when you see **write_sid**, it means that the router is trying to activate the line and is instructing the ISDN chipset to generate the HDLC flags. **wrote = 1B** means that the ISDN chipset is sending these HDLC flags. If everything is working okay, these **write_sid** are followed by SID interrupts with a status **reg = C**. These SID interrupts are sent from the chipset to the IOS indicating status **reg = C**—where C means that the activation bit (A bit) just turned from 0 to 1, which is received from the network. In the newer IOS versions, you will also see a message-received activation indication, which also means that the activation bit (A bit) just turned from 0 to 1, which is received from the network. In the following debug outputs, the router is doing its job and the network is also doing its job by replying to the router request:

```
BRI: write_sid: scp = 0, wrote = 1B
BRI: write_sid: scp = 0, wrote = 20
BRI: write_sid: scp = 0, wrote = 3
SID interrupt. status reg = C
BRI: Received activation indication…
BRI: write_sid: scp = 0, wrote = E
BRI: write_sid: scp = 0, wrote = E
```

When things are not working okay, you see something like the following on the same **debug bri** output. T3 is the descriptor block in the IOS, and you can notice in the following debug output, the router is sending the **write_sid**, which means that the router is trying to activate the line and instructing the ISDN chipset to generate the HDLC flags. **wrote = 3** means that the ISDN chipset is sending these HDLC flags. When the router is tired of sending the HDLC flags, it starts the T3 timer and tries to send some more HDLC flags. Then the T3 timers expire, and the router puts the BRI interface to deactivation state. In the following debug output, the router is doing its job, but the network is not doing its job because the network is not replying by turning the activation bit (A bit) from 0 to 1. Now the problem has been identified as external to the router. In most cases, this problem is related to the cable, NT1, or the telco.

```
BRI: Starting Power Up timer for unit = 2
BRI: write_sid: wrote 3 for subunit 2, slot 1
BRI: Starting T3 timer after expiry of Power
Up timeout for unit = 2, current state is F4 (…)
BRI: write_sid: wrote 92 for subunit 2, slot 1
BRI: write_sid: wrote 93 for subunit 2, slot 1
BRI: T3 timer expired for unit = 2, current state is F2
BRI: write_sid: wrote 1 for subunit 2, slot 1
BRI: write_sid: wrote 0 for subunit 2, slot 1
BRI: Forced interrupt for subunit 2, slot 1 is F
BRI: write_sid: wrote FF for subunit 2, slot 1
BRI: write_sid: wrote 1 for subunit 2, slot 1
BRI: write_sid: wrote 0 for subunit 2, slot 1
BRI: Deactivation for unit = 2, current state is F2
```

When the physical layer has no problems and Layer 1 is activated, you would see the following from **show isdn status** or **show controller bri**:

```
Layer 1 Status: ACTIVATED
```

or

```
Layer 1 is ACTIVATED
```

Troubleshooting PRI Layer 1 Problems

Troubleshooting PRI Layer 1 problems is not specific to ISDN. You would troubleshoot the PRI interface in exactly the same way as you would troubleshoot a T1 connection. When things are okay, it means that no alarms are detected on the T1. Make sure that you see the following under the **show controller t1** output:

```
Router # show controller t1
T1 2/0 is up
     Description: Primary Rate Interface to DMS-100
     No alarms detected
     Framing is ESF, Line Code is B8ZS, Clock Source is Line
     Data in current interval (165 seconds elapsed):
     0 Line Code Violations, 0 Path Code Violations
     0 Slip Secs, 1 Fr Loss Secs, 0 Line Err Secs, 0 Degraded Mins
     0 Errored Secs, 0 Bursty Err Secs, 0 Severely Err Secs, 12 Unavail Secs
```

When things are not okay, you would see that the transmitter is sending remote alarms, which is not a good sign. The main items to look at in the preceding output are the status of the line, alarms, line-code and path-code violations, and slip secs. The line status will tell whether the T1 is up, down, or administratively down. The alarms section is very important; it tells what type of problem may be present on the line. The presence of any alarm indicates a major problem on the line. Therefore, whenever you encounter a T1 in an alarm state, you should verify the configuration accuracy of the framing and line-coding parameters. You would see the following when there is something wrong on the physical layer in a PRI environment:

```
Router # show controller t1
T1 2/1 is down
     Transmitter is sending remote alarm
     Receiver has loss of signal
     Framing is ESF, Line Code is B8ZS, Clock Source is Line
     Data in current interval (160 seconds elapsed):
     0 Line Code Violations, 0 Path Code Violations
     0 Slip Secs, 0 Fr Loss Secs, 0 Line Err Secs,
     0 Errored Secs, 0 Bursty Err Secs, 0 Severely Err Secs, 160 Unavail Secs
```

Troubleshooting the Data Link Layer

Now that you have seen what kind of problems can occur on the physical layer and how to solve them, it is time to consider data link layer (Layer 2) issues. If the **show isdn status** on the router produces the following output, the Layer 1 status is active (which is good), but now the Layer 2 status is not active:

```
Router # show isdn status
The current ISDN Switchtype = basic-net3
ISDN BRI0 interface
Layer 1 Status:
Activated
Layer 2 Status:
Layer 2 NOT Activated
Layer 3 Status:
```

```
No Active Layer 3 Call(s)
Activated dsl 0 CCBs are 0, Allocated = 0
```

If you recall from the previous discussion, two types of protocols run on this layer: PPP (B channel) and LAPD (D channel) protocols. Troubleshoot the Layer 2 problems separately for B and D channels. The ISDN standard does not define a particular Layer 2 protocol for the B channel. In most of the cases, PPP is used because of its versatile nature. On the D channel, LAPD (Link Access Procedure on D channel) should be used according to the ISDN standard. LAPD is also known as Q.921. The Q.921 signaling is used between the local router and the local ISDN switch. Q.921 signaling is not end-to-end.

Troubleshooting the TEI Process

In the BRI environment, the terminal endpoint identifier (TEI) process takes place on Layer 2. The reason for the TEI assignment in a BRI environment is that on an S/T connection on a single BRI interface you can connect up to eight devices, and each device can have a unique TEI number, which is assigned from the local ISDN switch. By TEI assignment, the switch can differentiate between the multiple devices connected to the S/T bus on the BRI interface. The router sends an identification request (IDREQ) to the switch; and if everything is working okay, the switch acknowledges the IDREQ with an identification assigned (IDASSN).

The IDREQ and IDASSN packets contain two important values: the action indicator (AI) and the reference indicator (RI). Whenever the router sends an IDREQ to the switch, the AI is always set to 127, which is a wildcard and means that router is asking the switch to assign any TEI value. Valid TEI values range from 64 to 126 and are assigned from the switch. TEI values from 0 to 63 are reserved for fixed TEI. In the early days of ISDN, people used to configure TEI values manually; now, however, all the TEI negotiation and assignment are dynamic. Always keep in mind that in a PRI environment, only one device is connected to the ISDN interface, so there is no need for TEI; therefore, you would always notice that the TEI value is 0.

RI in the IDREQ packet always has a random number attached to it. This number should always match in the IDREQ and IDASSN messages. The IDASSN message from the switch must be the response to the same IDREQ message sent to the switch. Enabling **debug isdn q921** on the router reveals the assignment process. The following debug output shows that the router is sending the IDREQ with RI = 15454 (which is a random value) and AI = 127 (which is a wildcard). The IDASSN from the switch has RI = 15454 (which is the same random value sent by the router) and AI = 64. TEI 64 is assigned by the switch and is a valid TEI value.

```
Router # debug isdn q921
TX ->  IDREQ  ri = 15454  ai = 127
RX <-  IDASSN  ri = 15454  ai = 64
```

When something is wrong on Layer 2, the IDREQ is retransmitted with different random RI values and with an AI value of 127 (which is a wildcard); but still there is no IDASSN message from the switch. In such a case, the router is doing its job, but the local switch is not replying with an IDASSN message. Also keep in mind that sometimes the switch does reply with the IDASSN message, but assigns an invalid TEI value to the router, which is also a malfunctioning of the switch.

```
Router # debug isdn q921
TX ->  IDREQ  ri = 89898  ai = 127
TX ->  IDREQ  ri = 90976  ai = 127
TX ->  IDREQ  ri = 23434  ai = 127
```

After the local switch assigns the router a valid TEI, the router attempts to set up an HDLC connection with the switch. This is traditional HDLC. The router sends a set asynchronous balance mode extended (SABME) message on the TEI value 64 (which was just assigned by the local switch). SAPI (service access point identifier) behaves like a type field in Ethernet. It identifies the upper-layer protocol. If you see the **debug q921** output, you would see that the value of SAPI is 0, which means the Layer 3 D-channel protocol is Q.931. The SABME message is answered by a UA message, which is sent by the local switch. UA means that the SABME ID was accepted by the switch.

```
Router # debug isdn q921
TX ->  SABMEp  sapi = 0  tei = 64
RX <-  UAf  sapi = 0  tei = 64
```

After the data-link connection is established, information (INFO) frames are exchanged between the router and the local switch. INFO frames get acknowledged by other INFO frames or receive ready (RR) frames. Keep in mind that these INFO frames, which are sent on the D channel, have the Q.931 signaling messages. INFO frames have NS (send sequence number) and NR (next expected sequence number) fields.

```
Router # debug isdn q921
RX <-  INFOc  sapi = 0  tei = 64  ns = 0  nr = 0
TX ->  RRr  sapi = 0  tei = 64  nr = 1
TX ->  INFOc  sapi = 0  tei = 64  ns = 0  nr = 1
```

If no INFO frames are exchanged between the router and local switch, you would see the periodic exchange of RR frames. Exchange of RR frames is like a keepalive mechanism between the router and the local switch—that is, the Layer 2 connection is established, but there are no INFO frames to send. You would see something like the following in the debug output:

```
Router # debug isdn q921
RX <-  RRp  sapi = 0  tei = 80  nr = 5
TX ->  RRf  sapi = 0  tei = 80  nr = 4
RX <-  RRp  sapi = 0  tei = 80  nr = 5
TX ->  RRf  sapi = 0  tei = 80  nr = 4
RX <-  RRp  sapi = 0  tei = 80  nr = 5
TX ->  RRf  sapi = 0  tei = 80  nr = 4
RX <-  RRp  sapi = 0  tei = 80  nr = 5
TX ->  RRf  sapi = 0  tei = 80  nr = 4
```

When everything is working well on Layer 2, you should see something like the following on the **debug isdn q921** output. All these fields are explained in the previous discussion.

```
Router # debug isdn q921
TX ->  IDREQ  ri = 15454  ai = 127
RX <-  IDASSN  ri = 15454  ai = 64
TX ->  SABMEp  sapi = 0  tei = 64
RX <-  UAf  sapi = 0  tei = 64
RX <-  INFOc  sapi = 0  tei = 64  ns = 0  nr = 0
TX ->  RRr  sapi = 0  tei = 64  nr = 1
TX ->  INFOc  sapi = 0  tei = 64  ns = 0  nr = 1
```

Now, the **show isdn status** command will reveal the TEI value and the Layer 2 status shows that **state = MULTIPLE_FRAME_ESTABLISHED**:

```
Router # show isdn status
Layer 1 Status:
    ACTIVE
Layer 2 Status:
    TEI = 0, State =
MULTIPLE_FRAME_ESTABLISHED
Layer 3 Status:
    0 Active Layer 3 Call(s)
    Activated dsl 0 CCBs = 0
```

Notice in the preceding output that the TEI = 0, which means it is a PRI link; notice also, however, that state = MULTIPLE_FRAME_ESTABLISHED on Layer 2. If it were a BRI environment, you would see a valid TEI value (as stated earlier, a value between 64 and 126). This output also shows that Layer 3 is not active.

Troubleshooting the Network Layer

Now it is important to consider Layer 3 D-channel issues. If you recall from the previous discussion, two types of protocols run on this layer: IP, IPX, and such (B-channel) protocols; and Q.931 (D-channel) protocols. Troubleshoot the Layer 2 problems separately for B and D channels. The ISDN standard does not define a particular Layer 2 protocol for the B channel; IP, IPX, and other Layer 3 protocols could be used, depending on the Layer 2 B-channel protocol. On the D channel, Q.931 should be used according to the ISDN standard. The Q.931 signaling is used between the local router and the local ISDN switch. Q.931 enables you to tell the switch that you want to dial a number; the switch then tries to make that call. Q.931 signals get translated to corresponding SS7 signals at the local switch (because inside the ISDN network, SS7 signaling is used). These SS7 signals again get translated to the corresponding Q.931 signals at the remote ISDN switch. Q.931 signaling is not end-to-end.

Q.931

Q.931 is a Layer 3 signaling protocol for D channels in an ISDN environment. Q.931 comes in different "flavors"; because in the beginning of the ISDN era, Q.931 was not standardized and several major telcos wrote their own versions of it. Although these different versions of Q.931 are similar, you need to make sure that you are configuring exactly the same switch type on the router as is configured on the local ISDN switch (this does, after all, concern data communication). If the switch is configured for ISDN switch type basic-ni1, the router should be configured for the same switch type, of which several are currently available. There are efforts to standardize basic-net3 as the Pan-European standard and basic-ni1 as the North American standard.

Q.931 has 37 different ways for call setup. It is a very flexible and wide protocol. Frame Relay SVC signaling and ATM UNI signaling are based on Q.931 signaling. **debug isdn q931** can be activated on the router to see the Q.931 signals and see where there is a failure. To see the whole picture, you need to turn on this debug command on both sides of the connection. All the Layer 3 Q.931 signals get transmitted into Layer 2 INFO frames.

```
Router # debug isdn q931
TX ->  INFOc  sapi = 0  tei = 80  ns = 6  nr = 6
    SETUP pd = 8  callref = 0x02
        Bearer Capability i = 0x8890
        Channel ID i = 0x83
        Called Party Number i = 0x80, '555555'
RX <-  INFOc  sapi = 0  tei = 80  ns = 6  nr = 7
    CALL_PROC pd = 8  callref = 0x82
        Channel ID i = 0x89
RX <-  INFOc  sapi = 0  tei = 80  ns = 7  nr = 7
    CONNECT pd = 8  callref = 0x82
```

Every time the router places a call, it must send a setup packet out. The setup packet always has a protocol descriptor of pd = 8, and it generates a random hex value for the callref. The callref is used to track the call. If two calls are placed, for example, it can tell which call the RX (received) message is for. 0x8890 means a 64-kbps data call. 0x8890218F means it is a 56-kbps data call, and 0x8090A2 means it is a voice call. Channel ID 0x83 means that the router is asking the switch to assign it a B channel. Called-party number is 5555555.

CALL_PROC means that the call is proceeding. The callref uses a different value for the first digit (to differentiate between TX and RX); the second digit is the same (SETUP had a 2 for the last digit and CALL_PROC also has a 2). Channel ID i = 0x89 means B channel one; 0x8A is B channel two. This sequence of events is the same every time a call is placed. The router is completely dependent on the phone company to assign a B channel. If the switch doesn't assign the router a channel, the call won't work. In this case, a CONNECT message with the same reference number as received for CALL_PROC (0x82) is received from the switch.

SPIDs

After Layer 1 and Layer 2 are up, the first thing that happens before any of the Layer 3 SETUP messages are sent is that the router sends the service profile identifier (SPID) to the switch. SPIDs are assigned by the service provider and they should be configured on the router in exactly the same way as they are provided by the service provider. SPIDs are usually 12 to 14 digits long and are comprised of the 10-digit telephone number plus some extra digits. SPIDs are used only in North America, and only a few switch types require

SPIDs (for example, dms-100 and ni-1). Not all the switch types require the SPID number. SPIDs are used only in the BRI environment.

SPIDs are used to bind a specific terminal to a specific service profile. SPIDs are validated by the switch with a handshake between the router and the local ISDN switch. A valid SPID is acknowledged by an endpoint ID; if the SPID is rejected by the switch, you get an "Invalid IE contents" message from the switch. This negotiation can be seen by using **debug isdn q931**. In the following debug output, you can see that the router is sending SPIDs to the switch one by one. Both the SPIDs are acknowledged by the switch because there is an endpoint ID for each SPID sent. These SPID numbers are ASCII-coded, where 36 means 3, 31 means 1, and so on. In the following output, **pd** means protocol descriptor. Sometimes, you must configure the LDN after the SPIDs. LDN is configured to receive incoming calls on the second B channel.

```
Router # debug isdn q931
TX ->  INFORMATION pd = 8  callref = (null)
SPID Information i = 0x36313337383535323631323030
RX <-  INFORMATION pd = 8  callref = (null)
ENDPOINT IDent i = 0xF180
TX ->  INFORMATION pd = 8  callref = (null)
SPID Information i = 0x36313337383535323631333030
RX <-  INFORMATION pd = 8  callref = (null)
ENDPOINT IDent i = 0xF080
```

In the following debug output, you can see that the SPID sent to the switch is rejected and there is an "Invalid IE contents" message from the switch. This indicates that the SPIDs are incorrect; in such a case, you must determine that the router and the switch are configured for the correct SPIDs.

```
TX ->  INFORMATION pd = 8  callref = (null)
SPID Information i = 0x31323334353536373736
RX <-  INFORMATION pd = 8  callref = (null)
Cause i = 0x82E43A-Invalid IE contents
```

The command **sh isdn status** at this point will show the status of the SPIDs. In the following output, both SPIDs are rejected because they are invalid:

```
Router # show isdn status
Layer 1 Status:
ACTIVE
Layer 2 Status:
TEI = 88, State = MULTIPLE_FRAME_ESTABLISHED
Spid Status:
TEI 88, ces = 1, state = 6(not initialized)
spid1 configured, no LDN, spid1 sent, spid1 NOT valid
TEI Not Assigned, ces = 2, state = 1(terminal down)
spid2 configured, no LDN, spid2 NOT sent, spid2 NOT valid
Layer 3 Status:
0 Active Layer 3 Call(s)
Activated dsl 1 CCBs = 0
```

RELEASE_COMP Messages

After the switch validates the SPIDs, you can place a call. Call can be refused for several reasons. If the other end is set up for call screening and only allows certain numbers, and you are not one of those, your call might fail. There could also be something wrong inside the network. In the following **debug isdn q931** output, the ISDN connection was never made, not even for the one second. If you send the SETUP message, you can get a RELEASE_COMP message right away with a cause ID for the call rejection. As the following debug output shows, this is a Q.931 layer issue. It is important to distinguish between the connection that never came up (which points to the Q.931 issue) and the connection that came up for a couple of seconds but then got disconnected (which means that the Q.931 is okay, but that there are PPP issues).

```
Router # debug isdn q931
TX -> SETUP pd = 8  callref = 0x01
Bearer Capability i = 0x8890
Channel ID i = 0x83
Called Party Number i = 0x80, '4839625'
RX <- RELEASE_COMP pd = 8  callref = 0x81
Cause i = 0x8295 - Call rejected
```

RELEASE_COMP messages are followed by a cause ID for the call rejection. The cause ID is a hex value, and this value has a meaning. You can find the real cause by decoding the hex value and following up with your provider. If the call is connecting and then disconnecting after a couple of seconds, the Q.931 is okay, but you are running into PPP issues. PPP runs on the B channel of ISDN, and it is transparent to the carrier. PPP is based on RFC 1548 and others. Three main components comprise PPP: multiprotocol encapsulation, Link Control Protocol (LCP), and Network Control Protocols (NCPs). LCP is used to establish and maintain the data link and option negotiation (such as, use CHAP). NCPs are used to establish and configure network layer protocols, including protocol-specific option negotiation (addresses) and different Layer 3 protocols (IPCP, IPXCP, ATCP, and so on). In PPP negotiation, the LCP options are negotiated, and then the NCP options are negotiated.

Link Control Protocol

In LCP negotiation, the Configure-Req proposes certain options; if all options are acceptable, the remote station returns a Configure-ACK. All PPP negotiations are double negotiation, or two-way negotiation. You can see this PPP negotiation by turning on certain debugs on the Cisco routers. The following debug output shows an incoming CONFREQ and an outgoing CONFACK message. *I* means incoming, and *O* means outgoing.

```
Router # debug ppp packet
PPP BRI: B-Channel 1: I LCP CONFREQ(1) id 2 (4)
PPP BRI: B-Channel 1: O LCP CONFACK(2) id 2 (4)
```

The following debug output shows the negotiation for the PAP authentication type (value = C023) and the magic number for the loop avoidance in the connection. If it were a CHAP authentication, you would see a hex value = C223.

```
Router # debug ppp negotiation
ppp: sending CONFREQ, type = 3 (CI_AUTHTYPE), value = C023/0
ppp: sending CONFREQ, type = 5 (CI_MAGICNUMBER), value = 8C01B4
ppp: config ACK received, type = 3 (CI_AUTHTYPE), value = C023
ppp: config ACK received, type = 5 (CI_MAGICNUMBER), value = 8C01B4
```

show interface bri 0 1 tells whether the state of LCP is open or closed. If the options are negotiated, the state should be open. The following output indicates that the LCP state is open, but that the NCP options have not yet been negotiated:

```
Router # show interface bri 0 1

BRI0: B-Channel 1 is up, line protocol is up
   Hardware is BRI
   MTU 1500 bytes, BW 64 Kbit, DLY 20000 usec, rely 255/255, load 1/255
   Encapsulation PPP, loopback not set, keepalive set (10 sec)
   lcp state = OPEN
   ncp ipcp state = REQSENT    ncp osicp state = NOT NEGOTIATED
   ncp ipxcp state = NOT NEGOTIATED    ncp xnscp state = NOT NEGOTIATED
   ncp vinescp state = NOT NEGOTIATED   ncp deccp state = NOT NEGOTIATED
   ncp bridgecp state = NOT NEGOTIATED   ncp atalkcp state = NOT NEGOTIATED
   Last input 0:00:00, output 0:00:00, output hang never
   Last clearing of "show interface" counters never
   Output queue 0/40, 0 drops; input queue 0/75, 0 drops
   Five minute input rate 0 bits/sec, 0 packets/sec
   Five minute output rate 0 bits/sec, 1 packets/sec
   9099 packets input, 855915 bytes, 0 no buffer
```

If the LCP state is closed, the PPP options are mismatched on both of the devices (unless it is a 56-kbps link). Most of the long-distance connections in North America and international connections to and from North America force you down to 56 kbps. Sometimes over these connections, the high-order bit of the data you send is overwritten by the signaling information, possibly changing the data and making CRC errors "visible" to the device on the other end. In this case, you would use the V.110 spec for 56 kbps. In V.110, of the eight bit positions for every B channel, only seven bits are used for data transfer; the eighth bit is filled with junk, thus saving data from corruption.

In several cases, the interswitch connections may limit the speed to 56 kbps. There are different types of bearer capabilities, and they specify whether the call is a 56-kbps call and whether it is using V.110 rate adaptation. If the international signaling protocol in the ISDN network is adapted to ISDN, this 56-kbps indication will be carried all the way to the remote subscriber and the remote subscriber will treat the call as 56 kbps. Sometimes, on international links the carrier eats up this 56-kbps indication because the carrier might be using an old version of SS7. The receiving side thinks that the call is 64 kbps. The **dialer map** statement on the Cisco router enables you to specify the speed of the outgoing call. The default is 64 kbps. On the **debug isdn q931**, you might see a message that says "Call not end-to-end ISDN." If you see this message, you can configure **isdn not-end-to-end 56** on the router; then the router treats the call as a 56-kbps call.

```
Router # debug isdn q931
TX -> SETUP pd = 8  callref = 0x02
         Bearer Capability i = 0x8890
         Channel ID i = 0x83
         Called Party Number i = 0x80, '5555555'
RX <- CALL_PROC pd = 8
         callref = 0x82
         Channel ID i = 0x89
         Locking Shift to Codeset 5
         Codeset 5 IE 0x2A  i = 0x808E0C, 'OUTSIDE CALL'
RX <- PROGRESS pd = 8  callref = 0x82
         Progress Ind i = 0x8A81 -
      Call not end-to-end ISDN
RX <- CONNECT pd = 8  callref = 0x82
         Progress Ind i = 0x8482 - Destination address is non-ISDN
```

PPP Authentication Type

After LCP and 56 K issues have been dealt with, the next thing to consider is the PPP authentication type. HDLC could be used for Layer 2 B-channel protocol, but it does not support any authentication type. Some do this to get the ISDN up and running first, and then worry about the authentication later, which is the wrong approach because PAP or CHAP resolve the prefix issues. CHAP is always preferred over PAP authentication because CHAP performs MD5 hash function. If you turn on **debug ppp chap** on the router, you can see the handshaking process:

```
Router # debug ppp chap
ISDN Event: Connected to 5555555 on B1 at 64 kbps
BRI0: B-Channel 1: PPP AUTH CHAP input code = 1 id = 10 len = 14
BRI0: B-Channel 1: PPP AUTH CHAP input code = 2 id = 16 len = 26
BRI0: B-Channel 1: remote passed CHAP authentication
BRI0: B-Channel 1: PPP AUTH CHAP input code = 3 id = 10 len = 4
BRI0: B-Channel 1: Passed CHAP authentication with remote…
```

Also, you can use a **show dialer** command on both sides and see whether the remote router's name is in the output. If you see this name on both sides, CHAP or PAP is passed because it learns this name via PAP or CHAP. If you are failing authentication, make sure that your password for authentication is exactly the same on both sides, and keep in mind that the passwords are case-sensitive. In the following example, you know that the CHAP or PAP is passed because the name is displayed (SANJOSE) via PAP or CHAP:

```
Router #  show dialer
BRI0 - dialer type = ISDN
Dial String      Successes    Failures    Last called   Last status
4085555555          0            0                       never
0 incoming call(s) have been screened
BRI0: B-Channel 1 - dialer type = ISDN
Rotary group 0, priority = 0
Idle timer (120 secs), Fast idle timer (20 secs)
Wait for carrier (30 secs), Re-enable (15 secs)
```

```
Time until disconnect 85 secs
Connected to 4085555555 (SANJOSE)
```

PAP or CHAP enables you to know which site is connected. Without PAP or CHAP, this would be based on the ISDN calling number, which is often problematic because the calling number may not have been presented, or the calling number may be presented with or without prefixes. The carriers can change the numbers; sometimes they remove a prefix and sometimes they add a prefix. Sometimes they remove a number and sometimes they add a number, and you do not want to rely on the prefix for an ISDN connection. When you introduce CHAP or PAP, you resolve this prefix issue because you are not relying on a prefix anymore. With PAP or CHAP, you are relying on the host name of the remote router, which is learned by CHAP or PAP.

Network Control Protocols

After the LCP and authentication issues are considered, you run into NCP issues. NCPs negotiate and verify network-level parameters. There is a different NCP for each different network protocol (such as IPCP for IP, IPXCP for IPX, and so on). An NCP configure-request is sent for an NCP to the other side, which is acknowledged by an NCP configure-acknowledge message if that NCP is supported by the other side. If the other side does not support that NCP, the sending side gets a "NCP configure-not-acknowledge" message. Both sides exchange these messages and agree on NCPs that are supported by both ends. The negotiation is shown in the following debug output, in which IPCP is negotiated between both ends, where O means outgoing, and I means incoming:

```
Router # debug ppp negotiation
BRI0: B-Channel 1: O IPCP CONFREQ id D (10) Type3 (6) 147 211 117 40
BRI0: B-Channel 1: I IPCP CONFREQ id C (10) Type3 (6) 147 211 117 1
BRI0: B-Channel 1: O IPCP CONFACK id C (10) Type3 (6) 147 211 117 1
BRI0: B-Channel 1: I IPCP CONFACK id D (10) Type3 (6) 147 211 117 40
```

The NCP state is also in the following output command. In the following output, the IPCP is negotiated between both ends, and the IPCP state is open. OSICP and XNSCP are not negotiated because they have not been tried. IPXCP is in request state, which means that a negotiation was tried but did not work, maybe because the IPX network number on the remote ISDN interface was not configured.

```
Router #  show interface bri 0 1
BRI0: B-Channel 1 is up, line protocol is up
Hardware is BRI
MTU 1500 bytes, BW 64 Kbit, DLY 20000 usec, rely 255/255, load 1/255
Encapsulation PPP, loopback not set, keepalive set (10 sec)
lcp state = OPEN
ncp ipcp state = OPEN
ncp osicp state = NOT NEGOTIATED
ncp ipxcp state = REQSENT
ncp xnscp state = NOT NEGOTIATED
```

Because all three layers are up and running, you should now be able to ping the remote IP address of the ISDN interface. Now that you can ping the remote ISDN interface, you can look at the routing issues. At this point, if you cannot ping an IP address somewhere behind the remote side ISDN interface, the problem is not related to ISDN connectivity. Also, make sure that you have the interesting traffic and dialer filters defined correctly and do not wait for the first ISDN bill. Use **show dialer**, **debug dialer**, and **show isdn history** IOS commands to monitor the interesting traffic.

Summary

Increasing availability and decreasing costs are making ISDN an excellent choice for many networking applications. Cisco IOS features allow the building of large and flexible ISDN solutions. DDR is used for call initiation and termination. Virtual profiles can be used to easily scale mass ISDN dial-in solutions. Extra care must be taken, however, to ensure that ISDN costs are controlled. Troubleshooting ISDN is also discussed in detail in this chapter.

CHAPTER 12

Designing Switched LAN Networks

Edited by Christophe Paggen

This chapter describes the following three technologies that network designers can use to design switched LAN networks:

- LAN switching (Ethernet, Fast Ethernet, and Gigabit Ethernet)
- Virtual LANs (VLANs)
- ATM switching (LAN Emulation, Multiprotocol over ATM)

Current scalable campus network-design practices will also be discussed.

Evolution from Shared to Switched Networks

The LAN business is in constant evolution, driven by the desktop's need for more and more bandwidth. It is remarkable that even those working in the LAN domain for just more than a couple of years can actually refer to how things used to be "in the old days." A few years ago, the goal of a high-capacity LAN was to provide high aggregate capacity that could be shared among several devices. It was assumed that not all stations needed this capacity in a sustainable fashion; however, the total bandwidth was available on a time-share basis to whoever had to communicate. Shared LANs were very effective in providing a logical fully connected mesh topology without supporting the cost of several hundred point-to-point connections. A properly designed shared LAN maximized the probability of channel availability (that is, the sum of the stations' communication needs should be smaller than the channel's capacity). Huge increases in desktop computing power during the late 1980s meant that 10 Mbps could easily become the bottleneck in transmissions. Also, the constantly increasing number of devices per segment continued to contribute to the overall channel utilization. To improve user performance, network administrators began to segment shared LANs using bridges. LAN bridges have been available since 1984, but their internal bridging capacity remained the limiting factor, and wire-speed bridging was a luxury. With the progress made in the field of semiconductors in the 1990s, application-specific integrated circuits (ASICs) started to emerge, making it possible to build multiport LAN bridges capable of forwarding frames at wire rate. The bridges were launched on the market as *switches*. Network designers were prompted to replace their legacy hubs in the wiring closets with switches, as shown in Figure 12-1.

Figure 12-1   *Evolution from Shared to Switched Networks*

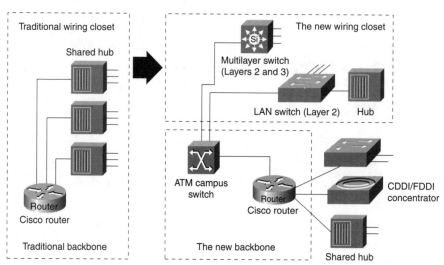

This strategy enabled network managers to protect their existing wiring investments and boost network performance with dedicated bandwidth to the desktop for each user. Coinciding with the wiring-closet evolution is a similar trend in the network backbone. Today, the role of Fast Ethernet, ATM (Asynchronous Transfer Mode), and lately Gigabit Ethernet is constantly increasing. Several protocols have now been standardized, such as LAN Emulation (LANE), 802.1q/p, and 802.3z and 802.3ab (1000BaseTX). Network designers are collapsing their router backbones with high-performance multilayer switches, switching routers, or ATM switches, to offer the greater backbone bandwidth required by high-throughput data services.

Technologies for Building Switched LAN Networks

With the advent of such technologies as Layer 2 switching, Layer 3 and 4 switching, and VLANs, building campus LANs is becoming more complex than in the past. Today, the following four technologies are required to build successful campus networks:

- LAN switching technologies

  Ethernet, Fast Ethernet, and Gigabit Ethernet switching provide Layer 2 switching and offer broadcast domain segmentation using VLANs. This is the base fabric of the network. Token Ring switching offers the same functionality as Ethernet switching but uses 16 Mbps Token Ring technology. You can use a Token Ring switch as either a transparent bridge or source-route bridge. Ethernet has become a more popular medium than Token Ring today, however, and is preferred over the legacy bus technology.

- Link aggregation for higher bandwidth

  The aggregation of individual Fast Ethernet links makes it possible to create 800-Mbps channels. Gigabit Ethernet interfaces can also be bundled to provide multigigabit pipes that rival and even surpass the highest speeds offered by today's ATM solutions. These channels are treated as a single logical link from a switch's perspective, thus providing seamless integration with the Spanning-Tree Protocol.

- ATM switching technologies

  ATM switching offers high-speed switching technology for voice, video, and data. Aggregated bandwidths of up to OC-48 speeds (roughly 2.480 Mbps) are emerging today, while OC-12 (roughly 620 Mbps) interfaces are a reality in many networks. ATM operation is almost similar to LAN switching technologies for data operations.

- Routing technologies

  Routing is a key technology for connecting LANs in a campus network. Many of today's routers can achieve wire-speed routing; therefore, they are frequently referred to as Layer 3 or 4 switching routers. Layer 3 (or 4) switching is nothing more than regular routing highly optimized for speed.

NOTE	Switched LAN networks are also referred to as campus LANs.

Role of LAN Switching Technology in Campus Networks

Most network designers have integrated switching devices into their existing shared-media networks to achieve the following goals:

- Increase the bandwidth available to each user, thereby alleviating congestion in their shared-media networks. 10/100-Mbps links to the desktop are common today. Some vendors have already started to manufacture Gigabit Ethernet NICs.

- Employ the manageability of VLANs along with the flexibility and scalability of routing. This, combined with the use of Dynamic Host Resolution Protocol (DHRP) servers, can reduce the cost of moves, adds, and changes.

- Deploy emerging multimedia applications across different switching platforms and technologies, making them available to a variety of users. This type of software makes extensive use of IP multicast. An example of such an application is the IP/TV software.

- Provide a smooth evolution path to high-performance switching solutions, such as Gigabit Ethernet and high-speed ATM.

Segmenting shared-media LANs divides the users into two or more separate LAN segments, reducing the number of users contending for bandwidth. LAN switching technology, which builds on this trend, employs *microsegmentation*, which further segments the LAN to fewer users and ultimately to a single user with a dedicated LAN segment. Each switch port provides a dedicated 10/100/1000-Mbps Ethernet segment or a dedicated 4/16-Mbps Token Ring segment for legacy environments.

Segments (also referred to as VLANs) are interconnected by networking devices that enable communication between LANs while blocking other types of traffic, typically routers. Switches have the intelligence to monitor traffic and build address tables based on source MAC addresses, which then allows them to forward packets directly to specific ports. Switches also usually provide nonblocking service, which allows multiple conversations (traffic between two ports) to occur simultaneously. A switch architecture is said to be nonblocking when its switching fabric's bandwidth exceeds the aggregate bandwidth of all its ports (that is, a 12-Gbps backplane for 96 10/100-Mbps ports).

Switching technology has become the preferred solution for improving LAN traffic for the following reasons:

- Unlike hubs and repeaters, switches allow multiple data streams to pass simultaneously (a switch is equal to multiple independent two-port bridges) and independently.

- Switches have the capability through microsegmentation to support the increased speed and bandwidth requirements of emerging technologies (that is, a VLAN is a broadcast domain).

- Switches deliver dedicated bandwidth to users through high-density group-switched and switched 10/100 fiber- or copper-based Ethernet, Fast EtherChannel, Gigabit Ethernet, Gigabit EtherChannel and ATM LAN Emulation (LANE), or Multiprotocol over ATM (MPOA).

Switched Network Solutions

To be successful, a switched network solution should accomplish the following:

- Leverage strategic investments in the existing communications infrastructure while increasing available bandwidth (for example, reutilization of the existing wiring scheme).

- Reduce the costs of managing network operations.

- Offer options to support multimedia applications and other high-demand traffic across a variety of platforms (for example, IGMP snooping). This implies the support of quality of service (QoS) features to provide preferential treatment to certain patterns of traffic (for example, differentiation based on IP precedence or 802.1q priority).

- Provide scalability, traffic control, and security at least as well as or better than today's router-based networks (for example, protocol filtering and port security).
- Provide support for the embedded remote monitoring (RMON) agent.

The key to achieving these benefits is to understand the role of the networking software infrastructure within the switched network. Within today's networks, routers allow for the interconnection of disparate LAN and WAN technologies, while also implementing security filters and logical firewalls. It is these capabilities that have allowed current networks to scale globally while remaining stable and robust. Routers also limit the radiation scope of broadcasts—that is, an all-ones broadcast does not cross a router unless specifically instructed to do so.

As networks evolve toward switched networks, similar logical networking capabilities are required for stability and scalability. Although LAN and ATM switches provide great performance improvements, they also raise new networking challenges. Switched networks must integrate with existing LAN and WAN networks, as well as with future multiservice networks capable of simultaneously carrying voice and data traffic.

A true switched network, therefore, is more than a collection of boxes. Rather, it consists of a system of devices integrated and supported by an intelligent networking software infrastructure. What used to be centralized within routers is now becoming available on high-end multilayer LAN switches. With the advent of switched networks, the intelligence is often dispersed throughout the network, reflecting the decentralized nature of switching systems. The need for a networking infrastructure, however, remains.

Components of the Switched Networking Model

The following three basic components make up a switched network:

- Physical switching platforms
- A common software infrastructure
- Network-management tools and applications

Cisco provides network designers with a complete, end-to-end solution for implementing and managing scalable, robust, switched networks.

Scalable Switching Platforms

The first component of the switched networking model is the physical switching platform. This can be an ATM switch, a multilayer LAN switch, or a switching router.

ATM Switches

Cisco Systems' Enterprise Multiservice Asynchronous Transfer Mode (ATM) Switch family offers mid-range ATM switches for ATM workgroups and campus backbones, metropolitan-area networks (MANs), and alternative service provider backbones. This series of switches spans from 5 to 40 Gbps in performance. The Enterprise Multiservice ATM Switches provide services optimized for both cell- and packet-based applications, including support for all ATM traffic classes and up to OC-48 switching capabilities. As the family expands, new members of the product family can take advantage of the existing set of carrier adapter modules (CAMs), port adapter modules (PAMs), and switch software, or use upgraded CAMs and PAMs specifically designed for those products. This forward compatibility protects existing equipment and software investments while facilitating network evolution.

For campus networks, the product family currently includes the following:

- **LightStream 1010 (LS1010)**—A 5-Gbps fully nonblocking modular ATM switch supporting a wide range of interfaces ranging from T1/E1 speeds up to 622-Mbps OC-12c

- **Catalyst 8510 (Cat8510)**—An L2/L3/ATM 10-Gbps wire-speed nonblocking modular switch with up to OC-12c interface switching speed currently, and support for both Fast and Gigabit Ethernet

- **Catalyst 8540 (Cat8540)**—An L2/L3/ATM 40-Gbps modular switch with up to OC-12 switching speed currently, support for both Fast and Gigabit Ethernet, and optional switching fabric and CPU redundancy

Just as there are routers and LAN switches available at various price/performance points with different levels of functionality, ATM switches can be segmented into the following four distinct types that reflect the needs of particular applications and markets:

- Workgroup ATM switches
- Campus ATM switches
- Enterprise ATM switches
- Multiservice ATM switches

Workgroup and Campus ATM Switches

Workgroup ATM switches are optimized for deploying ATM to the desktop over low-cost ATM desktop interfaces, with ATM signaling interoperability for ATM adapters and QoS support for multimedia applications.

Campus ATM switches are generally used for small-scale ATM backbones (for example, to link ATM routers or LAN switches). This use of ATM switches can alleviate current backbone congestion while enabling the deployment of such services as VLANs. Campus switches need to support a wide variety of both local backbone and WAN types but also need to be price/performance optimized for the local backbone function. In this class of switches, ATM routing capabilities that allow multiple switches to be tied together are very important. Congestion-control mechanisms for optimizing backbone performance are also important.

Enterprise and Multiservice ATM Switches

Enterprise and *Multiservice ATM switches* are sophisticated devices designed to form the core backbones of large enterprise networks. They are intended to complement the role played by today's high-end multiprotocol routers. Enterprise ATM switches, much like campus ATM switches, are used to interconnect workgroup ATM switches and other ATM-connected devices, such as LAN switches. They provide cell and frame services, along with advanced QoS and dynamic routing features. Enterprise-class switches, however, cannot only act as ATM backbones but can also serve as the single point of integration for all the disparate services and technology found in enterprise backbones today (such as voice, video, and data). By integrating all these services onto a common platform and a common ATM transport infrastructure, network designers can gain greater manageability while eliminating the need for multiple overlay networks.

LAN Switches

A LAN switch is a device that typically consists of many ports that connect LAN segments (typically 10/100-Mbps Ethernet) and several high-speed ports (such as 100-Mbps Fast Ethernet, OC-12/48 ATM, or Gigabit Ethernet). These high-speed ports, in turn, connect the LAN switch to other devices in the network. The three main categories of LAN switches are as follows:

- **Wiring-closet switch**—A device to provide host access at the edge of the network (for example, the Catalyst 2900XL, the Catalyst 400 series of switches, or even the Catalyst 5x00 series)

- **Multilayer switch**—A Layer 2, 3, or 4 device that provides various interfaces, high port densities, and a wide range of functions that make it suitable for the distribution of core layers of the network (for example, the Catalyst 5500 or 6000 family of switches)

- **Switching router**—A Layer 2, 3, or 4 device primarily focused at the core layer of the network, providing wire-speed multiservice switching on all its interfaces (for example, the Catalyst 8500)

A LAN switch has dedicated bandwidth per port, and each port represents a different segment. For best performance, network designers often assign just one host to a port, giving that host dedicated bandwidth of 10 Mbps, 100 Mbps, or even 1 Gbps, as shown in Figure 12-2, or 16 Mbps for legacy Token Ring networks.

Figure 12-2 *Sample LAN Switch Configuration*

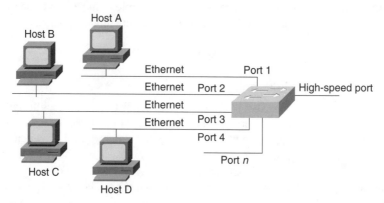

When a LAN switch first starts up, and as the devices connected to it request services from other devices, the switch builds a table that associates the *source* MAC address of each local device with the port number on which that device was heard. That way, when Host A on Port 1 needs to transmit to Host B on Port 2, the LAN switch forwards frames from Port 1 to Port 2, thus sparing other hosts on Port 3 from responding to frames destined for Host B. If Host C needs to send data to Host D at the same time that Host A sends data to Host B, it can do so because the LAN switch can forward frames from Port 3 to Port 4 at the same time it forwards frames from Port 1 to Port 2.

Whenever a device connected to the LAN switch sends a packet to an address that is not in the LAN switch's table (this table is sometimes referred to as the CAM table), or whenever the device sends a broadcast or multicast packet, the LAN switch sends the packet out all ports (except for the port from which the packet originated)—a technique known as *flooding*. Several techniques exist to constrain the flooding of multicast traffic to certain ports only, including the Cisco Group Management Protocol (CGMP) and the Internet Group Management Protocol (IGMP) snooping for Layer 3–capable switches. These protocols act on multicast packets only, not broadcast. Another feature called *broadcast suppression* can help alleviate the adverse effects of broadcast storms.

Because they work like traditional "transparent" bridges, LAN switches dissolve previously well-defined workgroup or department boundaries. A network built and designed only with LAN switches appears as a *flat* network topology consisting of a single broadcast domain. Consequently, these networks are liable to suffer the problems inherent in flat (or *bridged*) networks—that is, they do not scale well. Note, however, that LAN switches that support VLANs are more scalable than traditional bridges. The scalability problem is primarily associated with a very useful protocol found in almost every redundant Layer 2 network: the IEEE 802.1d Spanning-Tree Protocol.

Multiservice Access Switches

Beyond private networks, ATM platforms will also be widely deployed by service providers both as customer premises equipment (CPE) and within public networks. Such equipment will be used to support multiple MAN and WAN services—for example, Frame Relay switching, LAN interconnect, or public ATM services—on a common ATM infrastructure. Enterprise ATM switches will often be used in these public network applications because of their emphasis on high availability and redundancy, and their support of multiple interfaces.

Routing Platforms

In addition to LAN switches and ATM switches, network designers use routers as one of the key components in a switched network infrastructure. While LAN switches are being added to wiring closets to increase bandwidth and to reduce congestion in existing shared-media hubs, high-speed backbone technologies such as Gigabit Ethernet switching (or ATM switching) are being deployed in the backbone. Within a switched network, routing platforms allow for the interconnection of disparate LAN and WAN technologies while also implementing broadcast filters and logical firewalls. In general, if you need advanced networking services, such as broadcast firewalling and communication between dissimilar LANs, routers are necessary. Also, switching routers play a very significant role in today's campus networks: They limit the scope of VLANs and, more particularly, limit the scope of the spanning-tree domains. With the creation of centralized server farms, traffic patterns now demand wire-rate switching routers, and various techniques are available to achieve this (for example, Multilayer LAN Switching [MLS], Cisco Express Forwarding [CEF], and Multiprocol over ATM [MPOA]). Routers (or switching routers, or multilayer switches) play a very important role in the scalability of today's campus networks. This trend is making flat networks implemented by campus-wide VLANs disappear.

Common Software Infrastructure

The second level of a switched networking model is a common software infrastructure. The function of this software infrastructure is to unify the variety of physical switching platforms: multilayer LAN switches, ATM switches, and multiprotocol routers. Specifically, the software infrastructure should perform the following tasks:

- Monitor the logical topology of the network
- Logically route and reroute the traffic
- Manage and control sensitive traffic
- Provide firewalls, gateways, filtering, and protocol translation

Cisco offers network designers Cisco Internetwork Operating System (Cisco IOS) switching software. This subset of the Cisco IOS software is optimized for switching and provides the unifying element to Cisco's line of switching platforms in a switched network. The Cisco IOS software is found on stand-alone routers, router modules for shared-media hubs, multilayer switches, multiservice WAN access switches, LAN switches, ATM switches, and ATM-capable PBXs. It provides optional levels of routing and switching across a switched network in addition to new capabilities, such as VLANs trunking, ATM networking software services, wire-speed multilayer switching, extensions to support new networked multimedia applications (IP multicast and so on), traffic management and analysis tools, and many other features.

VLANs

A VLAN typically consists of several end systems, either hosts or network equipment (such as switches and routers), all of which are members of a single logical broadcast domain. A VLAN does not have physical proximity constraints for the broadcast domain. A VLAN is supported on various pieces of network equipment (for example, LAN switches) that support VLAN trunking protocols between them. Each VLAN supports a separate spanning tree (IEEE 802.1d), allowing various logical topologies with only a single physical network (that is, VLAN load balancing on equal-cost trunks and so forth). It is a common practice to implement VLANs so that they map to a Layer 3 protocol subnet.

First-generation VLANs are based on various OSI Layer 2 multiplexing mechanisms— such as IEEE 802.10 for FDDI interfaces, LAN Emulation (LANE) on ATM links, Inter-Switch Link (ISL), or IEEE 802.1q on Ethernet—that allow the formation of multiple, disjointed, overlaid broadcast groups on a single network infrastructure. (That is, it is possible to carry multiple VLANs across a single physical interface, also known as a *trunk*.) Figure 12-3 shows an example of a switched LAN network that uses campus-wide VLANs (a concept that started to emerge in 1996). Layer 2 of the OSI reference model provides reliable transit of data across a physical link. The data link layer is concerned with physical addressing, network topology, line discipline, error notification, ordered delivery frames, and flow control. The IEEE has divided this layer into two sublayers: the MAC sublayer and the LLC sublayer, sometimes simply called the link layer.

In Figure 12-3, 10/100-Mbps Ethernet connects the hosts on each floor to Switches A, B, C, and D. 100-Mbps Fast Ethernet or Gigabit Ethernet connects these to Switch E. VLAN 10 consists of those hosts on Ports 6 and 8 of Switch A and Port 2 on Switch B. VLAN 20 consists of those hosts that are on Port 1 of Switch A and Ports 1 and 3 of Switch B.

VLANs can be used to group a set of related users, regardless of their physical connectivity. They can be located across a campus environment or even across geographically dispersed locations.

Figure 12-3 *Typical VLAN Topology*

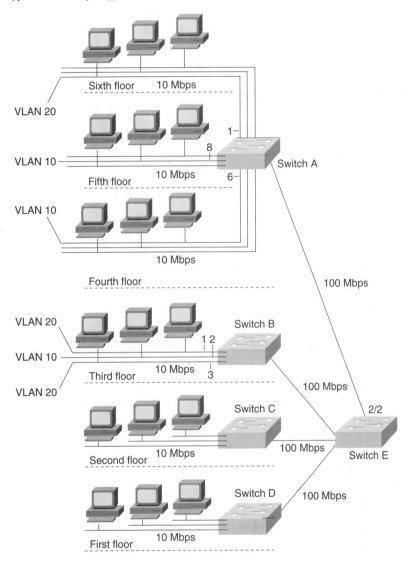

Problems Inherent to the Spanning-Tree Protocol

Although deploying campus-wide VLANs was a very common practice a year ago, it is a design technique that is quickly becoming obsolete, mostly because this model does not scale well. The scalability problem is partly inherent to the Spanning-Tree Protocol (STP), a protocol used to break logical loops at Layer 2 of the OSI model. Because there is no Time To Live (TTL) field in the Layer 2 header, it is possible to have packets looping in the network for an infinite amount of time! Contrary to popular belief, there is no need for a broadcast packet to create an infinite loop—it is absolutely possible to have a unicast storm in a Layer 2 network. Even though STP is supposed to break these logical loops, it puts a burden on the switches' CPU. When the STP operation becomes impaired for any reason (lack of CPU resources and so forth), it is possible to suffer from a network meltdown. The following are characteristics of the STP broadcast domain:

- Redundant links are blocked and carry no data traffic.

- Suboptimal paths exist between different points.

- The Spanning-Tree Protocol convergence typically takes 50 seconds (2 × Forward_Delay + Max Age = 2 × 15 + 20 = 50). Although the minimum IEEE values allow for a minimum convergence time of 14 seconds (2 × 4 + 6), it is certainly not recommended to apply these minimal values in most networks.

- Broadcast traffic within the Layer 2 domain interrupts every host.

- Broadcast or unicast storms with the Layer 2 domain affect the whole domain. A local problem quickly becomes a global issue.

- Isolating the problem is cumbersome and time-consuming.

- Network security offered at Layer 2 of the OSI model is limited.

Without a router, hosts in one VLAN cannot communicate with hosts in another VLAN. Compared with STP, routing protocols have the following characteristics:

- Load balancing across many equal-cost paths (up to six on certain Cisco platforms)

- Optimal or lower-cost paths between networks

- Faster convergence than STP with intelligent protocols such as EIGRP, IS-IS, and OSPF

- Summarized (and therefore scalable) reachability information

- Isolating a problem at Layer 3 is easier than at Layer 2.

Network Management Tools and Applications

The third and last component of a switched networking model consists of network-management tools and applications. As switching is integrated throughout the network, network management becomes crucial at both the workgroup and backbone levels.

Managing a switch-based network requires a radically different approach than managing traditional hub- and router-based LANs.

As part of designing a switched network, network designers must ensure that their design takes into account network-management applications needed to monitor, configure, plan, and analyze switched network devices and services. Cisco offers such tools for emerging switched networks.

Switched LAN Network Designs

Now that the various components of switched campus networks have been introduced, several campus network-design possibilities will be examined and discussed. Scalability factors, as well as migrations from legacy environments to highly efficient switched networks, will be thoroughly analyzed too.

The Hub-and-Router Model

Figure 12-4 shows a campus with the traditional hub-and-router design. The access layer devices are hubs that act as Layer 1 repeaters. The distribution layer consists of routers. The core layer contains FDDI concentrators or other hubs that act as Layer 1 repeaters. Routers in the distribution layer provide broadcast control and segmentation. Each wiring-closet hub corresponds to a logical network or subnet and homes to a router port. Alternatively, several hubs can be cascaded or bridged together to form one logical subnet or network.

The hub-and-router model is scalable because of the advantages of intelligent routing protocols such as OSPF and Enhanced IGRP. The distribution layer is the demarcation between networks in the access layer and networks in the core.

Distribution layer routers provide segmentation and terminate collision domains as well as broadcast domains. The model is consistent and deterministic, which simplifies troubleshooting and administration. This model also maps well to all the network protocols, such as Novell IPX, AppleTalk, DECnet, and TCP/IP.

The hub-and-router model is straightforward to configure and maintain because of its modularity. Each router within the distribution layer is programmed with the same features. Common configuration elements can be cut and pasted across the layer. Because each router is programmed the same way, its behavior is predictable, which makes troubleshooting easier.

Layer 3 packet-switching load and middleware services are shared among all the routers in the distribution layer.

The traditional hub-and-router campus model can be upgraded as performance demands increase. The shared media in the access layer and core can be upgraded to Layer 2 switching, and the distribution layer can be upgraded to Layer 3 switching with multilayer switching. Upgrading shared Layer 1 media to switched Layer 2 media does not change the network addressing, the logical design, or the programming of the routers.

Figure 12-4 *Traditional Hub and Router Campus*

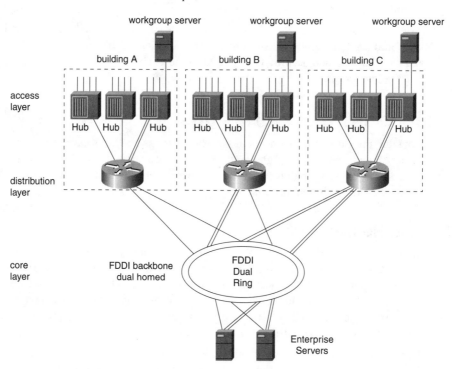

The Campus-Wide VLAN Model

Figure 12-5 shows a conventional legacy campus-wide VLAN design. Layer 2 switching is used in the access, distribution, and core layers. Four workgroups represented by the colors blue, red, purple, and green are distributed across several access layer switches. Connectivity between workgroups is by Router X, which connects to all four VLANs. Layer 3 switching and services are concentrated at Router X. Enterprise servers are shown behind the router on different logical networks indicated by the lines.

The various VLAN connections to Router X could be replaced with an ISL trunk. In either case, Router X is typically referred to as a "router on a stick" or a "one-armed router." More routers can be used to distribute the load, and each router attaches to several or all VLANs. Traffic between workgroups must traverse the campus in the source VLAN to a port on the gateway router, and then back out into the destination VLAN.

Figure 12-5 *Campus-Wide VLAN Design*

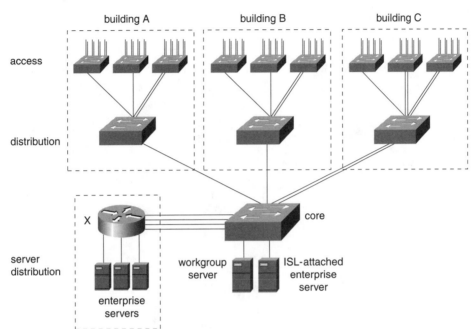

Figure 12-6 shows an updated version of the campus-wide VLAN model that takes advantage of multilayer switching. The switch marked X is a Catalyst 5000 family multilayer switch. The one-armed router is replaced by an RSM and the hardware-based Layer 3 switching of the NetFlow Feature Card. Enterprise servers in the server farm may be attached by Fast Ethernet at 100 Mbps, or by Fast EtherChannel to increase the bandwidth to 200-Mbps FDX or 400-Mbps FDX.

The campus-wide VLAN model is highly dependent on the 80/20 rule. If 80% of the traffic is within a workgroup, 80% of the packets are switched at Layer 2 from client to server. If 90% of the traffic goes to the enterprise servers in the server farm, however, 90% of the packets are switched by the one-armed router. The scalability and performance of the VLAN model are limited by the characteristics of STP. Each VLAN is equivalent to a flat bridged network.

Figure 12-6 *Campus-Wide VLANs with Multilayer Switching*

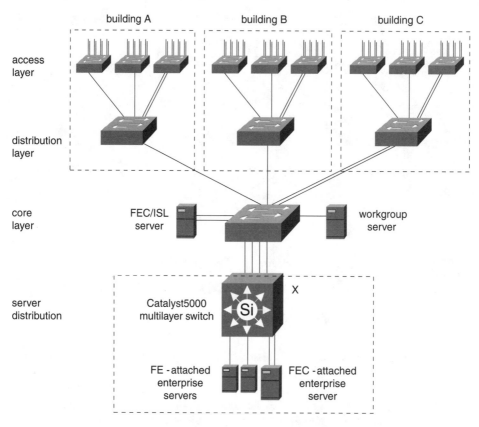

The campus-wide VLAN model provides the flexibility to have statically configured end stations move to a different floor or building within the campus. Cisco's VLAN Membership Policy Server (VMPS) and the VLAN Trunking Protocol (VTP) make this possible. A mobile user plugs a laptop PC into a LAN port in another building. The local Catalyst switch sends a query to the VMPS to determine the access policy and VLAN membership for the user. Then the Catalyst switch adds the user's port to the appropriate VLAN.

Multiprotocol over ATM

Multiprotocol over ATM (MPOA) adds Layer 3 cut-through switching to ATM LANE. The ATM infrastructure is the same as in ATM LANE. The LECS and the LES/BUS for each ELAN are configured the usual way. Figure 12-7 shows the elements of a small MPOA campus design.

Figure 12-7 *MPOA Campus Design*

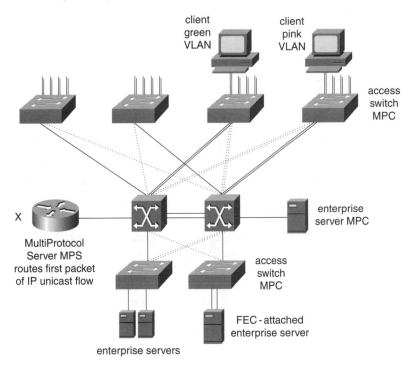

With MPOA, the new elements are the multiprotocol client (MPC) hardware and software on the access switches as well as the multiprotocol server (MPS), which is implemented in software on Router X. When the client in the pink VLAN talks to an enterprise server in the server farm, the first packet goes from the MPC in the access switch to the MPS using LANE. The MPS forwards the packet to the destination MPC using LANE. Then the MPS tells the two MPCs to establish a direct switched virtual circuit (SVC) path between the green subnet and the server farm subnet.

With MPOA, IP unicast packets take the cut-through SVC as indicated. Multicast packets, however, are sent to the BUS to be flooded in the originating ELAN. Then Router X copies the multicast to the BUS in every ELAN that needs to receive the packet as determined by multicast routing. In turn, each BUS floods the packet again within each destination ELAN.

Packets of protocols other than IP always proceed LANE to router to LANE without establishing a direct cut-through SVC. MPOA design must consider the amount of broadcast, multicast, and non-IP traffic in relation to the performance of the router. MPOA should be considered for networks with predominately IP unicast traffic and ATM trunks to the wiring-closet switch.

The Multilayer Model

One of the key concepts in building highly efficient and scalable campus networks is to think of the network as a big modular puzzle—a puzzle where it is possible to easily add new pieces—a piece being either a new building, a new group of users, or a server farm, for example. To achieve this, layers need to be introduced into the picture. This is what the multilayer model addresses.

The New 80/20 Rule

The conventional wisdom of the 80/20 rule underlies the traditional design models discussed in the preceding section. With the campus-wide VLAN model, the logical workgroup is dispersed across the campus but is still organized such that 80% of traffic is contained within the VLAN. The remaining 20% of traffic leaves the network or subnet through a router.

The traditional 80/20 traffic model arose because each department or workgroup had a local server on the LAN. The local server was used as a file server, logon server, and application server for the workgroup. The 80/20 traffic pattern has been changing rapidly with the rise of corporate intranets and applications that rely on distributed IP services. Many new and existing applications are moving to distributed World Wide Web (WWW)–based data storage and retrieval. The traffic pattern is moving toward what is now referred to as the 20/80 model. In the 20/80 model, only 20% of traffic is local to the workgroup LAN, and 80% of the traffic leaves.

Components of the Multilayer Model

The performance of multilayer switching matches the requirements of the new 20/80 traffic model. The two components of multilayer switching on the Catalyst 5000 family are the RSM and the NetFlow Feature Card. The RSM is a Cisco IOS-based multiprotocol router on a card. It has performance and features similar to a Cisco 7500 RSP/2 router. The NetFlow Feature Card (NFFC/NFFC-2) is a daughter-card upgrade to the Supervisor Engine of the Catalyst 5000 family of switches. It performs both Layer 3 for IP, IP Multicast, or IPX and Layer 2 switching in hardware with specialized ASICs. It is important to note that there is no performance penalty associated with Layer 3 switching versus Layer 2 switching with the NetFlow Feature Card. An alternative is the more powerful Catalyst 6000 family and its multilayer switching module (MSM), based on the Catalyst 8510 SRP, with performance figures in the neighborhood of 6 million packets per second for IP and IPX. For even more performance, the Catalyst 6000's future Multiprotocol Switching Feature Card (MSFC) can be used, boosting the performance to 15 million packets per second for IP and IPX.

Figure 12-8 illustrates a simple multilayer campus network design. The campus consists of three buildings, A, B, and C, connected by a backbone called the core. The distribution layer consists of Catalyst 5000 or 6000 family multilayer switches. The multilayer design takes advantage of the Layer 2 switching performance and features of the Catalyst family switches in the access layer and backbone and uses multilayer switching in the distribution layer. The multilayer model preserves the existing logical network design and addressing, as in the traditional hub-and-router model. Access layer subnets terminate at the distribution layer. From the other side, backbone subnets also terminate at the distribution layer. So the multilayer model does not consist of campus-wide VLANs but does take advantage of VLAN trunking, as discussed later.

Figure 12-8 *Multilayer Campus Design with Multilayer Switching*

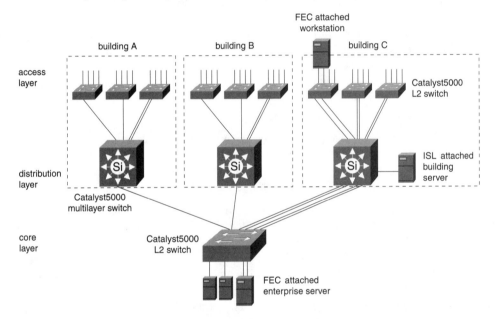

Because Layer 3 switching is used in the distribution layer of the multilayer model, this is where many of the characteristic advantages of routing apply. The distribution layer forms a broadcast boundary so that broadcasts don't pass from a building to the backbone or vice versa. Value-added features of the Cisco IOS software apply at the distribution layer. The distribution layer switches cache information about Novell servers, for example, and respond to Get Nearest Server queries from Novell clients in the building. Another example is forwarding Dynamic Host Configuration Protocol (DHCP) messages from mobile IP workstations to a DHCP server.

Another Cisco IOS feature implemented at the multilayer switches in the distribution layer is called Local-Area Mobility (LAM). LAM is valuable for campus intranets that have not deployed DHCP services and permits workstations with statically configured IP addresses and gateways to move throughout the campus. LAM works by propagating the address of the mobile hosts (via host or /32 routes) out into the Layer 3 routing table.

Actually, hundreds of valuable Cisco IOS features improve the stability, scalability, and manageability of enterprise networks. These features apply to all the protocols found in the campus, including DECnet, AppleTalk, IBM SNA, Novell IPX, TCP/IP, and many others. One characteristic shared by most of these features is that they are "out of the box." Out-of-the-box features apply to the functioning of the network as a whole. They are in contrast with "inside-the-box" features, such as port density or performance, that apply to a single box rather than to the network as a whole. Inside-the-box features have little to do with the stability, scalability, or manageability of enterprise networks.

The greatest strengths of the multilayer model arise from its hierarchical and modular nature. It is hierarchical because the layers are clearly defined and specialized. It is modular because every part within a layer performs the same logical function. One key advantage of modular design is that different technologies can be deployed with no impact on the logical structure of the model. Token Ring can be replaced by Ethernet, for example. FDDI can be replaced by Switched Fast Ethernet. Hubs can be replaced by Layer 2 switches. Fast Ethernet can be substituted for ATM LANE. ATM LANE can be substituted for Gigabit Ethernet, and so on. So modularity makes both migration and integration of legacy technologies much easier.

Another key advantage of modular design is that each device within a layer is programmed the same way and performs the same job, making configuration much easier. Troubleshooting is also easier, because the whole design is highly deterministic in terms of performance, path determination, and failure recovery.

In the access layer, a subnet corresponds to a VLAN. A VLAN may map to a single Layer 2 switch, or it may appear at several switches. Conversely, one or more VLANs may appear at a given Layer 2 switch. If Catalyst 4000, 5000, or 6000 family switches are used in the access layer, VLAN trunking (ISL or 802.1q) provides flexible allocation of networks and subnets across more than one switch. Examples later in this chapter show two VLANs per switch, to illustrate how to use VLAN trunking to achieve load balancing and fast failure recovery between the access layer and the distribution layer.

In its simplest form, the core layer is a single logical network or VLAN. The examples in this chapter show the core layer as a simple switched Layer 2 infrastructure with no loops. It is advantageous to avoid spanning-tree loops in the core. This discussion focuses on taking advantage of the load balancing and fast convergence of Layer 3 routing protocols such as OSPF and Enhanced IGRP to handle path determination and failure recovery across the backbone. Therefore, all the path determination and failure recovery is handled at the distribution layer in the multilayer model.

Redundancy and Load Balancing

A distribution layer switch in Figure 12-8 represents a point of failure at the building level. One thousand users in Building A could lose their connections to the backbone in the event of a power failure. If a link from a wiring-closet switch to the distribution layer switch is disconnected, 100 users on a floor could lose their connections to the backbone. Figure 12-9 shows a multilayer design that addresses these issues.

Multilayer Switches A and B provide redundant connectivity to domain North. Redundant links from each access layer switch connect to distribution layer switches A and B. Redundancy in the backbone is achieved by installing two or more Catalyst switches in the core. Redundant links from the distribution layer provide failover as well as load balancing over multiple paths across the backbone.

Redundant links connect access layer switches to a pair of Catalyst multilayer switches in the distribution layer. Fast failover at Layer 3 is achieved with Cisco's Hot Standby Router Protocol. The two distribution layer switches cooperate to provide HSRP gateway routers for all the IP hosts in the building. Fast failover at Layer 2 is achieved by Cisco's UplinkFast feature. UplinkFast is a convergence algorithm that achieves link failover from the forwarding link to the backup link in about three seconds.

Load balancing across the core is achieved by intelligent Layer 3 routing protocols implemented in the Cisco IOS software. In this picture, there are four equal-cost paths between any two buildings. In Figure 12-9, the four paths from domain North to domain West are AXC, AXYD, BYD, and BYXC. These four Layer 2 paths are considered equal by Layer 3 routing protocols. Note that all paths from domains North, West, and South to the backbone are single, logical hops. The Cisco IOS software supports load balancing over up to six equal-cost paths for IP (this is currently not possible on the Catalyst 8500 family of switching routers; two equal-cost paths are supported, however), and over many paths for other protocols.

Figure 12-10 shows the redundant multilayer model with an enterprise server farm. The server farm is implemented as a modular building block using multilayer switching. The Gigabit Ethernet trunk labeled A carries the server-to-server traffic. The Fast EtherChannel trunk labeled B carries the backbone traffic. All server-to-server traffic is kept off the backbone, which has both security and performance advantages. The enterprise servers have fast HSRP redundancy between the multilayer switches X and Y. Access policy to the server farm can be controlled by access lists on X and Y. In Figure 12-10, the Layer 2 core switches V and W are shown separate from server distribution switches X and Y for clarity. In a network of this size, V and W would collapse into X and Y.

Putting servers in a server farm also avoids problems associated with IP redirect and selecting the best gateway router when servers are directly attached to the backbone subnet, as shown in Figure 12-9. In particular, HSRP would not be used for the enterprise servers in Figure 12-9; they would use proxy Address Resolution Protocol (ARP), Internet Router Discovery Protocol (IRDP), Gateway Discovery Protocol (GDP), or Routing Information Protocol (RIP) snooping to populate their routing tables.

Figure 12-9 *Redundant Multilayer Campus Design*

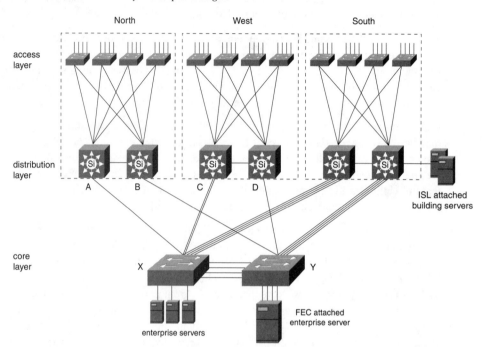

Figure 12-11 shows HSRP operating between two distribution layer switches. Host systems connect at a switch port in the access layer. The even-numbered subnets map to even-numbered VLANs, and the odd-numbered subnets map to odd-numbered VLANs. The HSRP primary for the even-numbered subnets is distribution layer Switch X, and the HSRP primary for the odd-numbered subnets is Switch Y. The HSRP backup for even-numbered subnets is Switch Y, and the HSRP backup for odd-numbered subnets is Switch X. The convention followed here is that every HSRP gateway router always has host address 100— so the HSRP gateway for subnet 15.0 is 15.100. If gateway 15.100 loses power or is disconnected, Switch X assumes the address 15.100 as well as the HSRP MAC address within about two seconds.

Figure 12-10   *Multilayer Model with Server Farm*

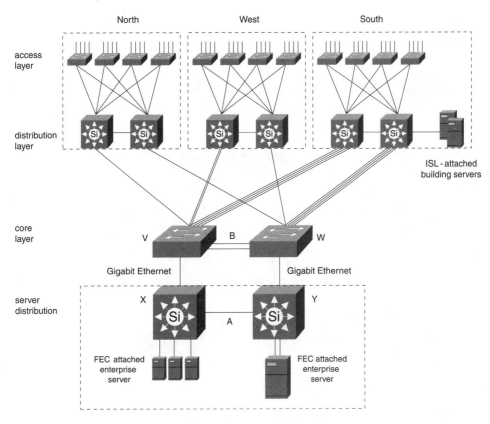

Figure 12-12 shows load balancing between the access layer and the distribution layer using Cisco's ISL (or IEEE 802.1q) VLAN trunking protocol. In this example, VLANs 10 and 11 are allocated to access layer Switch A, and VLANs 12 and 13 to Switch B. Each access layer switch has two trunks to the distribution layer. The STP puts redundant links in blocking mode as shown. Load distribution is achieved by making one trunk the active forwarding path for even-numbered VLANs and the other trunk the active forwarding path for odd-numbered VLANs.

Figure 12-11 *Redundancy with HSRP*

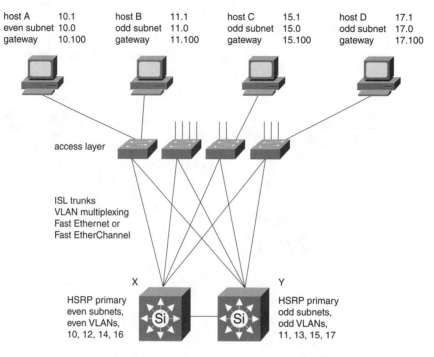

Figure 12-12 *VLAN Trunking for Load Balancing*

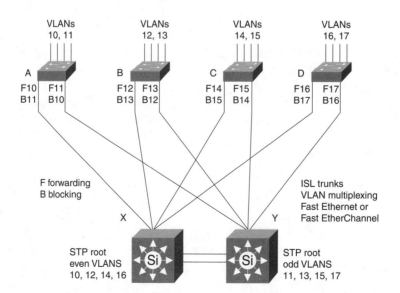

On Switch A, the left trunk is labeled F10, which means that it is the forwarding path for VLAN 10. The right trunk is labeled F11, which means that it is the forwarding path for VLAN 11. The left trunk is also labeled B11, which means that it is the blocking path for VLAN 11, and the right trunk is B10, which means that it is the blocking for VLAN 10. This is accomplished by making X the root for even VLANs and Y the root for odd VLANs.

Figure 12-13 shows Figure 12-12 after a link failure, which is indicated by the big *X*. UplinkFast changes the left trunk on Switch A to be the active forwarding path for VLAN 11. Traffic is switched across Fast EtherChannel Trunk Z if required. Trunk Z is the Layer 2 backup path for all VLANs in the domain and also carries some of the return traffic that is load-balanced between Switch X and Switch Y. With conventional STP, convergence would take 40 to 50 seconds. With UplinkFast, failover takes about three seconds.

Figure 12-13   *VLAN Trunking with Uplink Fast Failover*

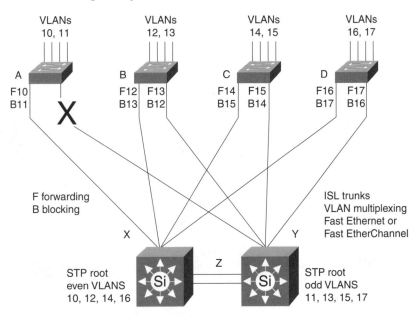

Scaling Bandwidth

Ethernet trunk capacity in the multilayer model can be scaled in several ways. Ethernet can be migrated to Fast Ethernet. Fast Ethernet can be migrated to Fast EtherChannel or Gigabit Ethernet or Gigabit EtherChannel. Access layer switches can be partitioned into multiple VLANs with multiple trunks. VLAN multiplexing with ISL or 802.1q can be used in combination with the different trunks.

Fast EtherChannel combines up to eight Fast Ethernet links into a single high-capacity trunk. Fast EtherChannel is supported by the Cisco 7500 and 8500 family of routers. It is supported on Catalyst 4000, 5000, and 6000 switches. Fast EtherChannel support has been announced by several partners, including Adaptec, Auspex, Compaq, Hewlett-Packard, Intel, Sun Microsystems, and Znyx. With Fast EtherChannel trunking, a high-capacity server can be connected to the core backbone at 400-Mbps FDX for 800-Mbps total throughput. High-end Cisco routers also support Gigabit EtherChannel, and several vendors have also announced Gigabit NICs.

Figure 12-14 shows three ways to scale bandwidth between an access layer switch and a distribution layer switch. On the configuration labeled "A Best," all VLANs are combined over Fast EtherChannel with ISL or 802.1q. In the middle configuration, labeled "B Good," a combination of segmentation and ISL trunking is used. On the configuration labeled "C OK," simple segmentation is used.

Figure 12-14 *Scaling Ethernet Trunk Bandwidth*

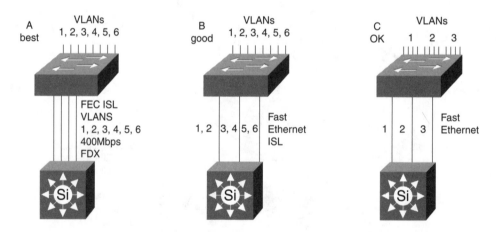

You should use model A if possible, because Fast EtherChannel provides more efficient bandwidth utilization by multiplexing traffic from multiple VLANs over one trunk. If a Fast EtherChannel line card is not available, use model B if possible. If neither Fast EtherChannel nor ISL/802.1q trunking are possible, use model C. With simple segmentation, each VLAN uses one trunk, so one can be congested while another is unused. More ports will be required to get the same performance. Scale bandwidth within ATM backbones by adding more OC-3, OC-12, or OC-48 trunks as required. The intelligent routing provided by Private Network-to-Network Interface (PNNI) handles load balancing and fast failover.

Policy in the Core

With Layer 3 switching in the distribution layer, it is possible to implement the backbone as a single logical network or multiple logical networks as required. VLAN technology can be used to create separate logical networks that can be used for different purposes. One IP core VLAN could be created for management traffic and another for enterprise servers. A different policy could be implemented for each core VLAN. Policy is applied with access lists at the distribution layer. In this way, access to management traffic and management ports on network devices is carefully controlled.

Another way to logically partition the core is by protocol. Create one VLAN for enterprise IP servers and another for enterprise IPX or DECnet servers. The logical partition can be extended to become complete physical separation on multiple core switches if dictated by security policies. Figure 12-15 shows the core separated physically into two switches. VLAN 100 on Switch V corresponds to IP subnet 131.108.1.0 where the World Wide Web (WWW) server farm attaches. VLAN 200 on Switch W corresponds to IPX network BEEF0001 where the Novell server farm attaches.

Figure 12-15 *Logical of Physical Partitioning of the Core*

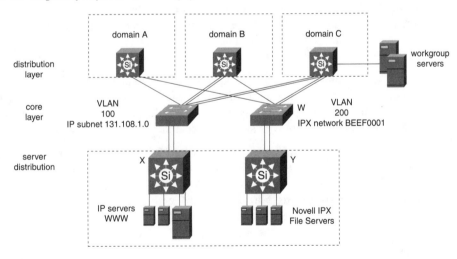

Of course, the simpler the backbone topology, the better. A small number of VLANs or ELANs is preferred. A discussion of the scaling issues related to large numbers of Layer 3 switches peered across many networks appears later in the section titled "Scaling Considerations."

Positioning Servers

It is very common for an enterprise to centralize servers. In some cases, services are consolidated into a single server. In other cases, servers are grouped at a data center for physical security or easier administration. At the same time, it is increasingly common for workgroups or individuals to publish a Web page locally and make it accessible to the enterprise.

With centralized servers directly attached to the backbone, all client/server traffic crosses one hop from a subnet in the access layer to a subnet in the core. Policy-based control of access to enterprise servers is implemented by access lists applied at the distribution layer. In Figure 12-16, Server W is Fast Ethernet attached to the core subnet. Server X is Fast EtherChannel attached to the core subnet. As mentioned, servers attached directly to the core must use proxy ARP, IRDP, GDP, or RIP snooping to populate their routing tables. HSRP would not be used within core subnets, because switches in the distribution layer all connect to different parts of the campus.

Enterprise servers Y and Z are placed in a server farm by implementing multilayer switching in a server distribution building block. Server Y is Fast Ethernet attached, and server Z is Fast EtherChannel attached. Policy controlling access to these servers is implemented with access lists on the core switches. Another big advantage of the server distribution model is that HSRP can be used to provide redundancy with fast failover. The server distribution model also keeps all server-to-server traffic off the backbone.

Server M is within workgroup D, which corresponds to one VLAN. Server M is Fast Ethernet attached at a port on an access layer switch, because most of the traffic to the server is local to the workgroup. This follows the conventional 80/20 rule. Server M could be hidden from the enterprise with an access list at the distribution layer switch H if required.

Server N attaches to a distribution layer at switch H. Server N is a building-level server that communicates with clients in VLANs A, B, C, and D. A direct Layer 2 switched path between server N and clients in VLANs A, B, C, and D can be achieved in two ways. With four network interface cards (NICs), it can be directly attached to each VLAN. With an ISL NIC, server N can talk directly to all four VLANs over a VLAN trunk. Server N can be selectively hidden from the rest of the enterprise with an access list on distribution layer switch H if required.

Figure 12-16 *Server Attachment in the Multilayer Model*

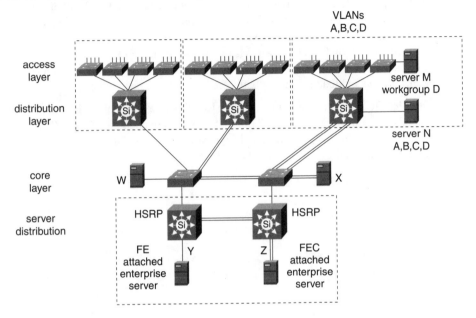

ATM/LANE Backbone

Figure 12-17 shows the multilayer campus model with ATM LANE in the backbone. For customers that require guaranteed quality of service (QoS), ATM is a good alternative. Real-time voice and video applications may mandate ATM features such as per-flow queuing, which provides granular control of delay and jitter.

Each Catalyst 5000 multilayer switch in the distribution layer is equipped with a LANE card. The LANE card acts as LEC so that the distribution layer switches can communicate across the backbone. The LANE card has a redundant ATM OC-3 or OC-12 physical interface called dual-PHY. In Figure 12-17, the solid lines represent the active link, and the dotted lines represent the hot-standby link. Two LightStream 1010 switches form the ATM core. Routers and servers with native ATM interfaces attach directly to ATM ports in the backbone. Enterprise servers in the server farm attach to multilayer Catalyst 5000 switches X and Y. Servers may be Fast Ethernet or Fast EtherChannel attached. These Catalyst 5000 switches are also equipped with LANE cards and act as LECS that connect Ethernet-based enterprise servers to the ATM ELAN in the core.

The trunks between the two LightStream 1010 core switches can be OC-3, OC-12, or OC-48, as required. The LightStream 1010 can be replaced by the Catalyst 8500 Multiservice router if higher capacity is needed. The PNNI protocol handles load balancing and intelligent routing between the ATM switches. Intelligent routing is increasingly important as the core scales up from two switches to many switches. STP is not used in the backbone. Intelligent Layer 3 routing protocols such as OSPF and Enhanced IGRP manage path determination and load balancing between distribution layer switches.

Cisco has implemented the Simple Server Redundancy Protocol (SSRP) to provide redundancy of the LECS and the LES/BUS. SSRP is available on Cisco 7500 routers, the Catalyst 5000 family of switches, and LightStream 1010 ATM switches. SSRP is compatible with all LANE 1.0 standard LECS.

Figure 12-17 *Multilayer Model with ATM LANE Core*

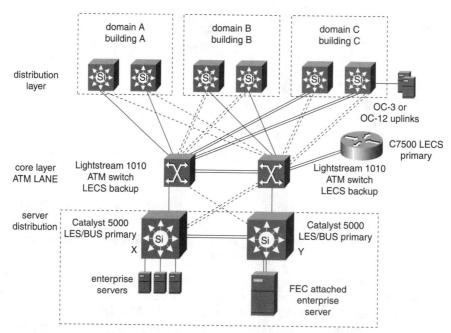

The LANE card for the Catalyst 5000 family is an efficient BUS with broadcast performance of 120 kbps. This is enough capacity for the largest campus networks. Figure 12-17 shows the primary LES/BUS on Switch X and the backup LES/BUS on Switch Y. For a small campus SSRP, LES/BUS failover takes only a few seconds. For a very large campus, LES/BUS failover can take several minutes. In large campus designs, dual ELAN backbones are frequently used to provide fast convergence in the event of a LES/BUS failure.

As an example, two ELANs, Red and Blue, are created in the backbone. If the LES/BUS for ELAN Red is disconnected, traffic is quickly rerouted over ELAN Blue until ELAN Red recovers. After ELAN Red recovers, the multilayer switches in the distribution layer reestablish contact across ELAN Red and start load balancing between Red and Blue again. This process applies to routed protocols, but not to bridged protocols.

The primary and backup LECS database is configured on the LightStream 1010 ATM switches because of their central position. When the ELAN is operating in steady state, there is no overhead CPU utilization on the LECS. The LECS is contacted only when a new LEC joins an ELAN. For this reason, there are few performance considerations associated with placing the primary and backup LECS. A good choice for a primary LECS would be a Cisco 7500 router with direct ATM attachment to the backbone, because it would not be affected by ATM signaling traffic in the event of a LES/BUS failover.

Figure 12-18 shows an alternative implementation of the LANE core using the Catalyst 5500 switch. Here the Catalyst 5500 operates as an ATM switch with the addition of the ATM Switch Processor (ASP) card. It is configured as a LEC with the addition of the OC-12 LANE/MPOA card. It is configured as an Ethernet frame switch with the addition of the appropriate Ethernet or Fast Ethernet line cards. The server farm is implemented with the addition of multilayer switching. The Catalyst 5500 combines the functionality of the LightStream 1010 and the Catalyst 5000 in a single chassis. It is also possible, thanks to the ATM fabric integration module (ATM FIM), to combine the functionality of the Catalyst 8510 SRP and the Catalyst 5500 in one chassis.

Figure 12-18 *ATM LANE Core with Catalyst 5500 Switches*

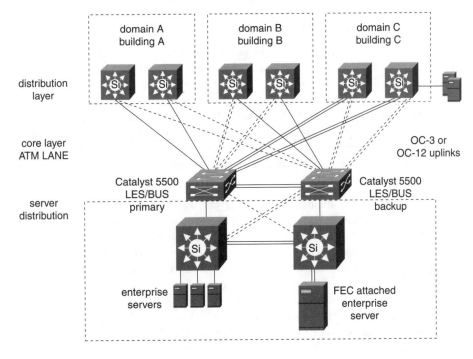

IP Multicast

Applications based on IP multicast represent a small but rapidly growing component of corporate intranets. Applications such as IPTV, Microsoft NetShow, and NetMeeting are being tried and deployed. There are several aspects to handling multicasts effectively:

- Multicast routing, protocol-independent multicast (PIM) dense mode, sparse mode, or sparse-dense mode

- Clients and servers join multicast groups with Internet Group Management Protocol (IGMP)

- Pruning multicast trees with Cisco Group Multicast Protocol (CGMP) or IGMP snooping

- Switch and router multicast performance

- Multicast policy

The preferred routing protocol for multicast is PIM. PIM sparse mode is described in RFC 2117, and PIM dense mode is on the standards track. PIM is being widely deployed in the Internet as well as in corporate intranets. As its name suggests, PIM works with various unicast routing protocols, such as OSPF and Enhanced IGRP. PIM routers may also be required to interact with the Distance Vector Multicast Routing Protocol (DVMRP). DVMRP is a legacy multicast routing protocol deployed in the Internet multicast backbone (MBONE). Currently 50% of the MBONE has converted to PIM, and it is expected that PIM will replace DVMRP over time.

PIM can operate in dense mode, sparse mode, or sparse-dense. Dense-mode operation is used for an application such as IPTV where there is a multicast server with many clients throughout the campus. Sparse-mode operation is used for workgroup applications such as NetMeeting. In either case, PIM builds efficient multicast trees that minimize the amount of traffic on the network. This is particularly important for high-bandwidth applications such as real-time video. In most environments, PIM is configured as sparse-dense and automatically uses either sparse mode or dense mode as required: The interface is treated as dense mode if the group is in dense mode; the interface is treated as sparse mode if the group is in sparse mode.

IGMP is used by multicast clients and servers to join or advertise multicast groups. The local gateway router makes a multicast available on subnets with active listeners, but blocks the traffic if no listeners are present. CGMP extends multicast pruning down to the Catalyst switch. A Cisco router sends out a CGMP message to advertise all the host MAC addresses that belong to a multicast group. Catalyst switches receive the CGMP message and forward multicast traffic only to ports with the specific MAC address in the forwarding table. This blocks multicast packets from all switch ports that don't have group members downstream. For Layer 3–capable switches, IGMP snooping is a more efficient alternative to CGMP, giving the switch enough intelligence to parse the IGMP packets originated from the clients and create the appropriate forwarding table entries.

Catalyst switches have an architecture that forwards multicast streams to one port, many ports, or all ports with no performance penalty. Catalyst switches will support one or many multicast groups operating at wire-speed concurrently.

One way to implement multicast policy is to place multicast servers in a server farm behind multilayer Catalyst Switch X, as shown in Figure 12-19. Switch X acts as a multicast firewall that enforces rate limiting and controls access to multicast sessions. To further isolate multicast traffic, create a separate multicast VLAN/subnet in the core. The multicast VLAN in the core could be a logical partition of existing core switches or a dedicated switch if traffic is very high. Switch X is a logical place to implement the PIM rendezvous point. The rendezvous point is like the root of the multicast tree.

Figure 12-19   *Multicast Firewall and Backbone*

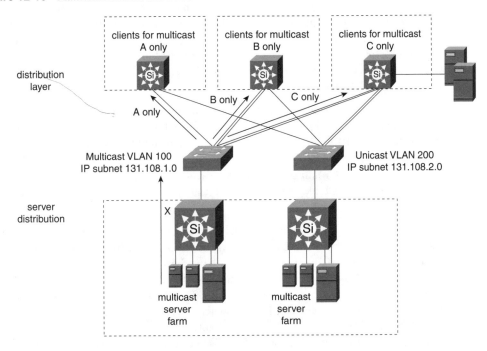

Scaling Considerations

The multilayer design model is inherently scalable. Layer 3 switching performance scales because it is distributed. Backbone performance scales as you add more links or more switches. The individual switch domains or buildings scale to more than 1,000 client devices with two distribution layer switches in a typical redundant configuration. More building blocks or server blocks can be added to the campus without changing the design model. Because the multilayer design model is highly structured and deterministic, it is also scalable from a management and administration perspective.

In all the multilayer designs discussed, STP loops in the backbone have been avoided. STP takes 40 to 50 seconds to converge and does not support load balancing across multiple paths. Within Ethernet backbones, no loops are configured. For ATM backbones, PNNI handles load balancing. In all cases, intelligent Layer 3 routing protocols such as OSPF and Enhanced IGRP handle path determination and load balancing over multiple paths in the backbone.

OSPF overhead in the backbone rises linearly as the number of distribution layer switches rises. This is because OSPF elects one designated router and one backup designated router to peer with all the other Layer 3 switches in the distribution layer. If two VLANs or ELANs are created in the backbone, a designated router and a backup are elected for each. Therefore, the OSPF routing traffic and CPU overhead increase as the number of backbone VLANs or ELANs increases. For this reason, it is recommended to keep the number of VLANs or ELANs in the backbone small. For large ATM/LANE backbones, it is recommended to create two ELANs in the backbone, as discussed earlier in the section titled "ATM/LANE Backbone."

Another important consideration for OSPF scalability is summarization. For a large campus, make each building an OSPF area and make the distribution layer switches Area Border Routers (ABRs). Pick all the subnets within the building from a contiguous block of addresses and summarize with a single summary advertisement at the ABRs. This reduces the amount of routing information throughout the campus and increases the stability of the routing table. Enhanced IGRP can be configured for summarization in the same way.

Not all routing protocols are created equal, however. AppleTalk Routing Table Maintenance Protocol (RTMP), Novell Server Advertisement Protocol (SAP), and Novell Routing Information Protocol (RIP) are protocols with overhead that increases as the square of the number of peers. Assume, for example, that 12 distribution layer switches are attached to the backbone and are running Novell SAP. If 100 SAP services are being advertised throughout the campus, each distribution switch injects $100/7 = 15$ SAP packets into the backbone every 60 seconds. All 12 distribution layer switches receive and process $12 \times 15 = 180$ SAP packets every 60 seconds. The Cisco IOS software provides features such as SAP filtering to contain SAP advertisements from local servers where appropriate. The 180 packets are a reasonable number, but consider what happens with 100 distribution layer switches advertising 1,000 SAP services.

Figure 12-20 shows a design for a large hierarchical, redundant ATM campus backbone. The ATM core designated B consists of eight LightStream 1010 switches with a partial mesh of OC-12 trunks. Domain C consists of three pairs of LightStream 1010 switches. Domain C can be configured with an ATM prefix address that is summarized where it connects to the core B. On this scale, manual ATM address summarization would have little benefit. The default summarization would have just 26 routing entries corresponding to the

26 switches in Figure 12-20. In domain A, pairs of distribution layer switches attach to the ATM fabric with OC-3 LANE. A server farm behind Catalyst switches X and Y attaches directly to the core with OC-12 LANE/MPOA cards.

Figure 12-20 *Hierarchical Redundant ATM Campus Backbone*

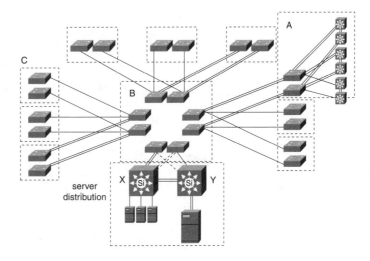

Migration Strategies

The multilayer design model describes the logical structure of the campus. The addressing and Layer 3 design are independent of choice of media. The logical design principles are the same whether implemented with Ethernet, Token Ring, FDDI, or ATM. This is not always true in the case of bridged protocols such as NetBIOS and Systems Network Architecture (SNA), which are media-dependent. In particular, Token Ring applications with frame sizes larger than the 1500 bytes allowed by Ethernet need to be considered.

Figure 12-21 shows a multilayer campus with a parallel FDDI backbone. The FDDI backbone could be bridged to the Switched Fast Ethernet backbone with translational bridging implemented at the distribution layer. Alternatively, the FDDI backbone could be configured as a separate logical network. There are several possible reasons for keeping an existing FDDI backbone in place. FDDI supports 4500-byte frames, while Ethernet frames can be no larger than 1500 bytes. This is important for bridged protocols that originate on Token Ring end systems that generate 4500-byte frames. Another reason to maintain an FDDI backbone is for enterprise servers that have FDDI network interface cards.

Figure 12-21 *FDDI and Token Ring Migration*

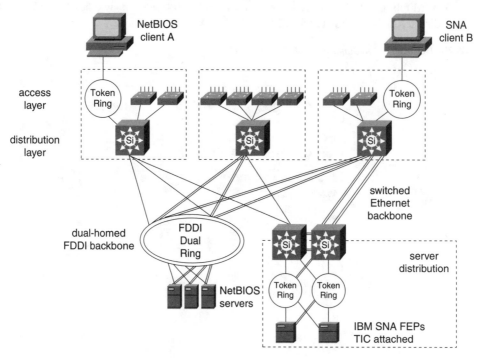

Data-link switching plus (DLSw+) is Cisco's implementation of standard DLSw. SNA frames from native SNA client B are encapsulated in TCP/IP by a router or a distribution layer switch in the multilayer model. A distribution switch deencapsulates the SNA traffic out to a Token Ring–attached front-end processor (FEP) at a data center. Multilayer switches can be attached to Token Ring with the Versatile Interface Processor (VIP) card and the Token Ring port adapter (PA).

Security in the Multilayer Model

Access control lists are supported by multilayer switching with no performance degradation. Because all traffic passes through the distribution layer, this is the best place to implement policy with access control lists. These lists can also be used in the control plane of the network to restrict access to the switches themselves. In addition, the TACACS+ and RADIUS protocols provide centralized access control to switches. The Cisco IOS software also provides multiple levels of authorization with password encryption. Network managers can be assigned to a particular level at which a specific set of commands are enabled.

Implementing Layer 2 switching at the access layer and in the server farm has immediate security benefits. With shared media, all packets are visible to all users on the logical network. It is possible for a user to capture clear-text passwords or files. On a switched network, conversations are visible only to the sender and receiver. And within a server farm, all server-to-server traffic is kept off the campus backbone.

WAN security is implemented in firewalls. A firewall consists of one or more routers and bastion host systems on a special network called a demilitarized zone (DMZ). Specialized Web-caching servers and other firewall devices may attach to the DMZ. The inner firewall routers connect to the campus backbone in what can be considered a WAN distribution layer.

Figure 12-22 shows a WAN distribution building block with firewall components.

Figure 12-22 *WAN Distribution to the Internet*

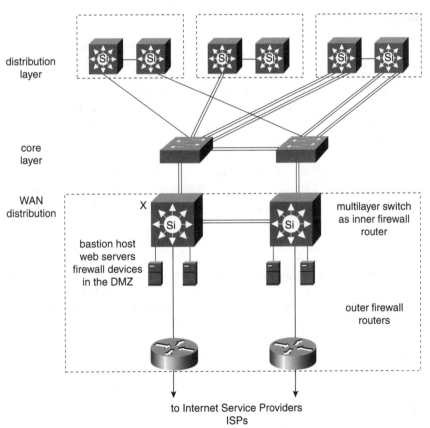

Bridging in the Multilayer Model

For nonrouted protocols, bridging is configured. Bridging between access layer VLANs and the backbone is handled by the RSM, the Catalyst 6000 MSM/MSFC, or the 8500 switching router. Because each access layer VLAN is running IEEE spanning tree, the RSM must not be configured with an IEEE bridge group. The effect of running IEEE bridging on the RSM is to collapse all the spanning trees of all the VLANs into a single spanning tree with a single root bridge. Configure the RSM with a DEC STP bridge group to keep all the IEEE spanning trees separate. Remember that LAN switches run the IEEE STP only. It is recommended to run a recent version of IOS on the RSM (or MSM, or SRP) to allow the DEC bridge protocol data units (BPDUs) to pass between RSMs through the Catalyst Layer 2 switches in a transparent fashion.

Advantages of the Multilayer Model

This chapter has discussed several variations of the multilayer campus design model. Whether implemented with frame-switched Ethernet backbones or cell-switched ATM backbones, all share the same basic advantages. The model is highly deterministic, which makes it easy to troubleshoot as it scales. The modular building-block approach scales easily as new buildings or server farms are added to the campus. Intelligent Layer 3 routing protocols such as OSPF and Enhanced IGRP handle load balancing and fast convergence across the backbone. The logical structure and addressing of the hub-and-router model are preserved, which makes migration much easier. Many value-added services of the Cisco IOS software, such as server proxy, tunneling, and summarization are implemented in the Catalyst multilayer switches at the distribution layer. Policy is also implemented with access lists at the distribution layer or at the server distribution switches.

Redundancy and fast convergence are provided by features such as UplinkFast and HSRP. Bandwidth scales from Fast Ethernet to Fast EtherChannel to Gigabit Ethernet without changing addressing or policy configuration. With the features of the Cisco IOS software, the multilayer model supports all common campus protocols, including TCP/IP, AppleTalk, Novell IPX, DECnet, IBM SNA, NetBIOS, and many more. Many of the largest and most successful campus intranets are built with the multilayer model. It avoids all the scaling problems associated with flat bridged or switched designs. And finally, the multilayer model with multilayer switching handles Layer 3 switching in hardware with no performance penalty compared with Layer 2 switching.

Summary

Campus LAN designs use switches to replace traditional hubs and use an appropriate mix of routers to minimize broadcast radiation. With the appropriate pieces of software and hardware in place, and adhering to good network design, it is possible to build topologies, such as the examples described in the "Switched LAN Network Designs" section earlier in this chapter.

CHAPTER 13

PIM Sparse Mode

By Beau Williamson

This chapter appears in the book Developing IP Multicast Networks, Volume I *by Cisco Press (ISBN 1-57870-077-9).*

For a review of multicast, see Appendix I, "Overview of IP Multicast."

Protocol Independent Multicast sparse mode (PIM-SM), like PIM dense mode (PIM-DM), uses the unicast routing table to perform the Reverse Path Forwarding (RPF) check function instead of maintaining a separate multicast route table. Therefore, regardless of which unicast routing protocol(s) is (are) used to populate the unicast routing table (including static routes), PIM-SM uses this information to perform multicast forwarding; hence, it too is protocol independent.

Some key characteristics of PIM-SM are

- Protocol independent (uses unicast route table for RPF check)
- No separate multicast routing protocol (à la Distance Vector Multicast Routing Protocol [DVMRP])
- Explicit Join behavior
- Classless (as long as classless unicast routing is in use)

This chapter provides an overview of the basic mechanisms used by PIM-SM, which include

- Explicit Join model
- Shared trees
- Shortest path trees (SPT)
- Source registration
- Designated Router (DR)
- SPT switchover
- State-Refresh
- Rendezvous point (RP) discovery

In addition, some of the mechanisms that are used in PIM-DM are also used by PIM-SM. These include

- PIM Neighbor Discovery
- PIM Asserts

This chapter does not repeat these topics. However, the reader is encouraged to review these topics before proceeding with this chapter. Finally, it's important to keep in mind that this chapter is strictly an overview of PIM-SM and covers only the basics.

Explicit Join Model

Just as its name implies, PIM-SM conforms to the sparse mode model where multicast traffic is only sent to locations of the network that specifically request it. In PIM-SM, this is accomplished via PIM Joins, which are sent hop by hop toward the root node of tree. (The root node of a tree in PIM-SM is the RP in the case of a shared tree or the first-hop router that is directly connected to the multicast source in the case of a SPT.) As this Join travels up the tree, routers along the path set up multicast forwarding state so that the requested multicast traffic will be forwarded back down the tree.

Likewise, when multicast traffic is no longer needed, a router sends a PIM Prune up the tree toward the root node to prune off the unnecessary traffic. As this PIM Prune travels hop by hop up the tree, each router updates its forwarding state appropriately. This update often results in the deletion of the forwarding state associated with a multicast group or source.

The key point here is that in the Explicit Join model, forwarding state in the routers is set up as a result of these Joins. This is a substantial departure from flood-and-prune protocols such as PIM-DM where router forwarding state is set up by the arrival of multicast data.

PIM-SM Shared Trees

PIM-SM operation centers around a single, unidirectional shared tree whose root node is called the rendezvous point (RP). These shared trees are sometimes called RP trees because they are rooted at the RP. (Shared trees or RP trees are frequently known as RPTs so as to avoid confusion with source trees, which are also known as shortest path trees; hence, the acronym SPTs.)

Last-hop routers (that is, routers that have a directly connected receiver for the multicast group) that need to receive the traffic from a specific multicast group, join this shared tree. When the last-hop router no longer needs the traffic of a specific multicast group (that is, when there are no longer any directly connected receivers for the multicast group), the router prunes itself from the shared tree.

Because PIM-SM uses a unidirectional shared tree where traffic can only flow down the tree, sources must register with the RP to get their multicast traffic to flow down the shared tree (via the RP). This registration process actually triggers an SPT Join by the RP toward the Source when there are active receivers for the group in the network. (SPT Joins are described in more detail in the section, "PIM-SM Shortest Path Trees," and registers are described in more detail in the "Source Registration" section.)

Shared Tree Joins

Figure 13-1 shows the first step of a Shared Tree Join in a sample PIM-SM. In this step, a single host (Receiver 1) has just joined multicast Group G via an Internet Group Membership Protocol (IGMP) Membership Report.

Figure 13-1 *PIM Shared Tree Joins—Step 1*

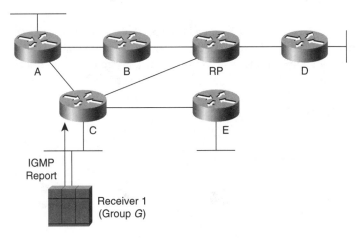

Because Receiver 1 is the first host to join the multicast group in the example, Router C had to create a (*, G) state entry in its multicast routing table for this multicast group. Router C then places the Ethernet interface in the outgoing interface list of the (*, G) entry as shown by the solid arrow in Figure 13-2. Because Router C had to create a new (*, G) state entry, it must also send a PIM (*, G) Join (indicated by the dashed arrow in Figure 13-2) toward the RP to join the shared tree. (Router C uses its unicast routing table to determine the interface toward the RP.)

Figure 13-2 *PIM Shared Tree Join—Step 2*

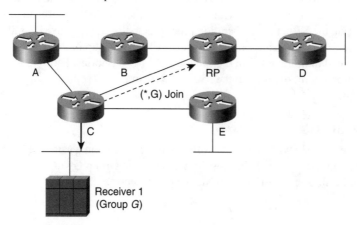

The RP receives the (*, G) Join, and because it too had no previous state for multicast group G, creates a (*, G) state entry in its multicast routing table and adds the link to Router C to the outgoing interface list. At this point, a shared tree for multicast Group G has been constructed from the RP to Router C and Receiver 1, as shown by the solid lines in Figure 13-3. Now, any traffic for multicast Group G that reaches the RP can flow down the shared tree to Receiver 1.

Figure 13-3 *Shared Tree Joins—Step 3*

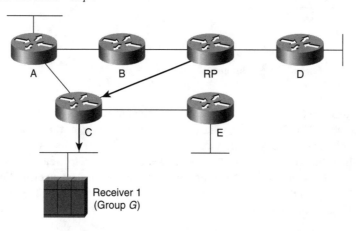

Let's continue the example and assume that another host (Receiver 2) joins the multicast group as shown in Figure 13-4. Again, the host has signaled its desire to join multicast Group G by using an IGMP Membership Report that was received by Router E.

Figure 13-4 *Shared Tree Joins—Step 4*

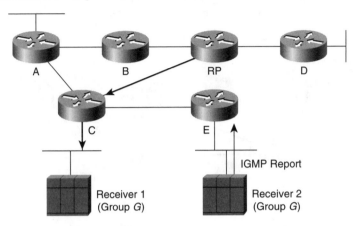

Because Router E didn't have any state for multicast Group G, it creates a (*, G) state entry in its multicast routing table and adds the Ethernet interface to its outgoing interface list (shown by the solid arrow in Figure 13-5). Because Router E had to create a new (*, G) entry, it sends a (*, G) Join (indicated by the dashed arrow in Figure 13-5) toward the RP to join the shared tree for Group G.

Figure 13-5 *Shared Tree Joins—Step 5*

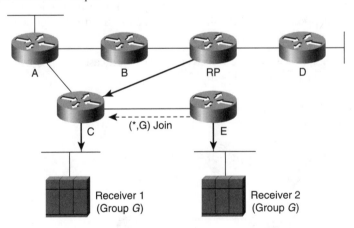

When Router C receives the (*, G) Join from Router E, it finds that it already has (*, G) state for Group G (that is, it's already on the shared tree for this group). As a result, Router C simply adds the link to Router E to the outgoing interface list in its (*, G) entry.

Figure 13-6 shows the resulting shared tree (indicated by the solid arrows) that includes Routers C and E along with their directly connected hosts (Receiver 1 and Receiver 2).

Figure 13-6 *Shared Tree Joins—Step 6*

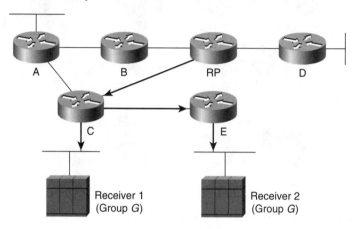

Shared Tree Prunes

Because PIM-SM uses the Explicit Join model to build distribution trees as needed, it also uses Prunes to tear down the trees when they are no longer needed. (We could just stop sending periodic Joins to refresh the tree and allow the tree branches to time out. However, that isn't a very efficient usage of network resources.)

As an example, assume that Receiver 2 leaves multicast Group G by sending an IGMP Leave message (shown in Figure 13-7).

Figure 13-7 *Shared Tree Prunes—Step 1*

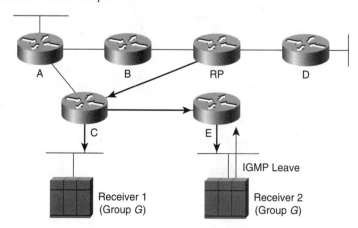

Because Receiver 2 was the only host joined to the group on Router E's Ethernet interface, this interface is removed from the outgoing interface list in its (*, G) entry. (This is represented by the removal of the arrow on Router E's Ethernet in Figure 7-8.) When the interface is removed, the outgoing interface list for this (*, G) entry is null (empty), which indicates that Router E no longer needs the traffic for this group. Router E responds to the fact that its outgoing interface list is now null by sending a (*, G) Prune (shown in Figure 13-8) toward the RP to prune itself off the shared tree.

Figure 13-8 *Shared Tree Prunes—Step 2*

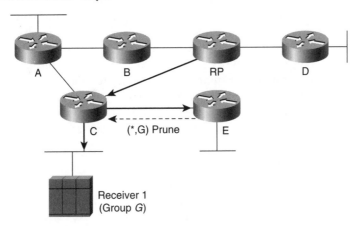

When Router C receives this Prune, it removes the link to Router E from the outgoing interface list of the (*, G) entry (as indicated by the removal of the arrow between Router C and Router E in Figure 13-9). However, because Router C still has a directly connected host for the group (Receiver 1), the outgoing interface list for the (*, G) entry is not null (empty). Therefore, Router C must remain on the shared tree, and a Prune is not sent up the shared tree toward the RP.

Figure 13-9 *Shared Tree Prunes—Step 3*

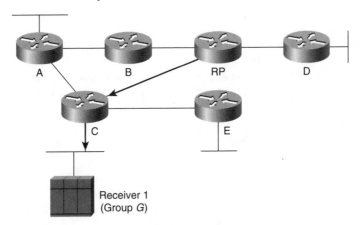

NOTE	The prune examples in this section did not cover the situation in which a (*, G) prune is being sent on a multi-access network (such as an Ethernet segment) with several other PIM-SM routers still joined to the same shared tree.

PIM-SM Shortest Path Trees

One of the primary advantages of PIM-SM is that, unlike other sparse mode protocols (such as core-based trees), it doesn't limit us to receiving multicast traffic only via the shared tree. Just as it is possible to use the Explicit Join mechanism to join the shared tree, whose root is the RP, this mechanism can be used to join the SPT whose root is a particular source. The advantage should be obvious. By joining the SPT, multicast traffic is routed directly to the receivers without having to go through the RP, thereby reducing network latency and possible congestion at the RP. On the other hand, the disadvantage is that routers must create and maintain (S, G) state entries in their multicast routing tables along the (S, G) SPT. This action, of course, consumes more router resources.

Still, the overall amount of (S, G) information maintained by the routers in a PIM-SM network that uses SPTs is generally much less than is necessary for dense mode protocols. The reason is that the Flood-and-Prune mechanism used by dense mode protocols results in all routers in the network maintaining (S, G) state entries in their multicast routing tables for all active sources. This is true even if there are no active receivers for the groups to which the sources are transmitting. By joining SPTs in PIM-SM, we gain the advantage of an optimal distribution tree without suffering from the overhead and inefficiencies associated with other dense mode protocols such as PIM-DM, DVMRP, and Multicast Open Shortest Path First (MOSPF). (By now, you are probably beginning to understand why PIM-SM is generally recommended over other dense mode protocols.)

This leads to an obvious question: If using SPTs in PIM-SM is so desirable, why join the shared tree in the first place? The problem is that without the shared tree to deliver the first few multicast packets from a source, routers have no way of knowing that a source is active.

NOTE	Several methods (including the use of dynamic Domain Name System [DNS] entries) have been proposed to tell routers which sources are currently active for which groups. Using this information, a router could immediately and directly join the SPT of all active sources in the group. This would eliminate the need for a shared tree and its associated Core or RP. Unfortunately, none of the methods proposed to date have met with much acceptance in the Internet community.

The sections that follow present the basic concepts of building SPTs using (S, G) Joins and Prunes. Keep in mind that the goal here is to understand the basic concepts of joining the SPT. The details as to why and when PIM-SM routers actually join the SPT are discussed later.

Shortest Path Tree Joins

As you recall from the section "Shared Tree Joins," routers send a (*, G) Join toward the RP to join the shared tree and receive multicast traffic for Group G. However, by sending an (S, G) Join toward Source S, a router can just as easily join the SPT for Source S and receive multicast traffic being sent by S to Group G.

Figure 13-10 shows an example of an (S, G) Join being sent toward an active source to join the SPT. (The solid arrows in the drawing indicate the path of the SPT down which traffic from Source S_1 flows.) In this example, Receiver 1 has already joined Group G (indicated by the solid arrow from Router E).

Figure 13-10   *SPT Join—Step 1*

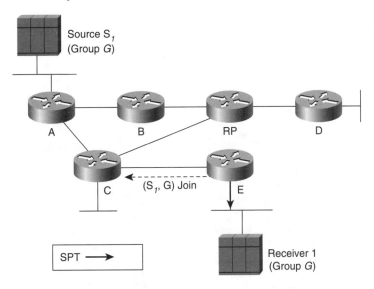

For the sake of this example, assume that Router E somehow magically knows that Source S_1 is active for Group G.

NOTE   In reality, Router E would have learned that Source S_1 is active because it would have received a packet from the source via the shared tree. However, to make the point that PIM SPTs are independent from shared trees (and to simplify this example), we are going to ignore this minor detail and concentrate on the fact that a router can explicitly join a SPT just as a router can join the shared tree.

Because Router E wants to join the SPT for Source S_1, it sends an (S_1, G) Join toward the source. Router E determines the correct interface to send this Join out by calculating the RPF interface toward Source S_1. (The RPF interface calculation uses the unicast routing table, which in turn indicates that Router C is the next-hop router to Source S_1.)

When Router C receives the (S_1, G) Join, it creates an (S_1, G) entry in its multicast forwarding table and adds the interface on which the Join was received to the entry's outgoing interface list (indicated by the solid arrow from Router C to Router E in Figure 13-11). Because Router C had to create state for (S_1, G), it also sends an (S_1, G) Join (as shown by the dashed arrow in Figure 13-11) toward the source.

Figure 13-11   *SPT Join—Step 2*

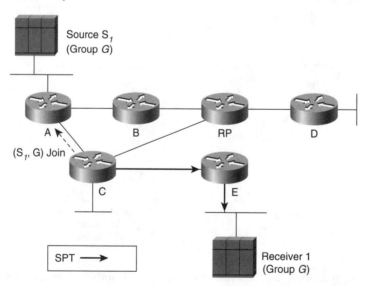

Finally, when Router A receives the (S_1, G) Join, it adds the link to Router C to the outgoing interface list of its existing (S_1, G) entry as shown by the solid arrow in Figure 13-12. (Router A is referred to as the first hop router for Source S_1 and would have already created an (S_1, G) entry as soon as it received the first packet from the source.)

Figure 13-12 *SPT Join—Step 3*

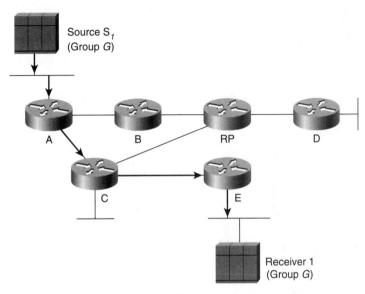

Shortest Path Tree Prunes

SPTs can be pruned by using (S_1, G) Prunes in the same manner that shared trees were pruned by using $(*, G)$ Prunes.

NOTE	Again, the prune examples in this section do not cover the situation where an (S, G) prune is being sent on a multi-access network (such as an Ethernet segment) with several other PIM-SM routers still joined to the same SPT.

Continuing with the SPT example, assume that Router E no longer has a directly connected receiver for Group G and therefore has no further need for (S_1, G) traffic. Therefore, Router E sends an (S_1, G) Prune toward Source S_1 (as shown by the dashed arrow in Figure 13-13).

Figure 13-13 *SPT Prunes—Step 1*

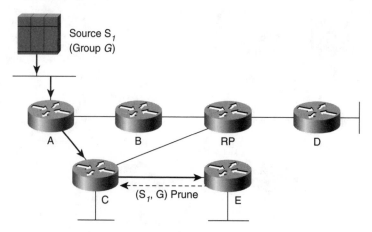

When Router C receives the (S_1, G) Prune from Router E, it removes the interface on which the message was received from the outgoing interface list of its (S_1, G) entry (indicated by the absence of the solid arrow between Routers C and E in Figure 7-14). This results in Router C's (S_1, G) entry having an empty outgoing interface list. Because the outgoing interface list is now empty, Router C has to send an (S_1, G) Prune toward the source S_1 (as shown by the dashed arrow in Figure 13-14).

Figure 13-14 *SPT Prunes—Step 2*

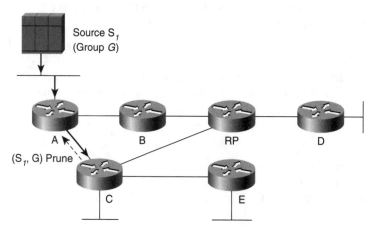

When Router A receives the (S_1, G) Prune from Router C, it removes the interface on which it received the Prune from the outgoing interface list of its (S_1, G) entry (indicated by the absence of the solid arrow between Routers A and C in Figure 13-15). However, because Router A is the first-hop router for Source S_1 (in other words, it is directly connected to the source), no further action is taken. (Router A simply continues to drop any packets from Source S$_1$ because the outgoing interface list in Router A's (S$_1$, G) entry is empty.)

Figure 13-15 *SPT Prunes—Step 3*

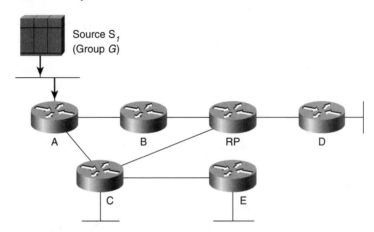

NOTE   To avoid being flamed by readers who are experienced PIM-SM users, I should point out that the previous SPT examples have been radically simplified to make the concepts of SPTs in PIM-SM easier to understand. Again, the key point here is that the PIM-SM explicit Join/Prune mechanism can be used to Join/Prune SPTs as well as shared trees. This capability becomes important in later sections on source registering and SPT switchover.

PIM Join/Prune Messages

Although we have been referring to PIM Prunes and Joins as if they were two individual message types, the reality is that there is only a single PIM Join/Prune message type. Each PIM Join/Prune message contains both a Join list and a Prune list, either one of which may be empty, depending on the information being conveyed up the distribution tree. By including multiple entries in the Join and/or Prune lists, a router may Join/Prune multiple sources and/or groups with a single PIM Join/Prune message. This greatly improves the efficiency of the periodic refresh mechanism because typically only a single message is necessary to refresh an upstream router's state.

The entries in the Join and Prune lists of PIM Join/Prune messages share a common format, containing (among other things) the following information:

- **Multicast source address**—IP address of the multicast source to Join/Prune. (If the Wildcard flag is set, this is the address of the RP.)
- **Multicast group address**—Class D multicast group address to Join/Prune.
- **WC bit (Wildcard flag)**—This entry is a shared tree (*, G) Join/Prune message.
- **RP bit (RP Tree flag)**—This Join/Prune information is applicable to and should be forwarded up the shared tree.

By manipulating the preceding information in each Join/Prune list entry, various requests may be signaled to an upstream router.

For example, a PIM Join/Prune message with an entry in the Join list of

Source address = 192.16.10.1
Group address = 224.1.1.1
Flags = WC, RP

indicates that this item is a (*, G) (denoted by the WC and RP flags being set) Join for Group 224.1.1.1 whose RP is 192.16.10.1.

A PIM Join/Prune message with an entry in the Prune list of

Source address = 191.1.2.1
Group address = 239.255.1.1
Flags = none

indicates that this is an (S, G) (denoted by the WC and RP flags being clear) Prune for source 191.1.2.1, Group 239.255.1.1.

NOTE   The reason that this information on the Join/Prune message contents is presented here is that it (particularly the part about the RP flag) will be important when we discuss pruning specific source traffic flows from the shared tree in the "Shortest Path Tree Switchover" section.

PIM-SM State-Refresh

To prevent a stale PIM-SM forwarding state from getting stuck in the routers, it is given a finite lifetime (3 minutes), after which it is deleted. (For example, if an upstream router loses a Prune because of congestion, the associated forwarding state could remain in the router for a long time.) The lifetime is established by associating a 3-minute expiration timer with each (*, G) and (S, G) state entry in the multicast routing table. When these timers expire, the state entry is deleted. As a result, downstream routers must periodically refresh this forwarding state to prevent it from timing out and being deleted. To do so, routers send PIM Join/Prune messages to the appropriate upstream neighbor once a minute. When the upstream neighbor receives the PIM Join/Prune message, it refreshes its existing multicast forwarding state and resets the 3-minute expiration timers.

Routers refresh shared trees by periodically (once a minute) sending (*, G) Joins to the upstream neighbor in the direction of the RP. Additionally, routers refresh SPTs by periodically (once a minute) sending (S, G) Joins to the upstream neighbor in the direction of the source.

These periodic (*, G) and (S, G) Joins are sent by routers as long as they have a nonempty outgoing interface list in their associated (*, G) and (S, G) entries (or a directly connected host for multicast Group G). If these periodic Joins were not sent, multicast state for G would eventually time out (after 3 minutes) and the distribution tree associated with the (*, G) and/or (S, G) multicast routing entry would be torn down.

NOTE   I find that this periodic refresh mechanism is one of the most frequently overlooked aspects of PIM-SM when students are initially learning PIM-SM fundamentals. This results in confusion regarding the maintenance of certain timers in the multicast forwarding table as well as confusion when this periodic Join message traffic is observed during debugging sessions.

Source Registration

In the section "PIM-SM Shared Trees," you learned how routers use (*, G) Joins to join the shared tree for multicast Group G. However, because PIM-SM uses a unidirectional shared tree, multicast traffic can only flow down this tree. Therefore, multicast sources must somehow get their traffic to the RP so that the traffic can flow down the shared tree. PIM-SM accomplishes this by having the RP join the SPT back to the source so it can receive the source's traffic. First, however, the RP must somehow be notified that the source exists. PIM-SM makes use of PIM Register and Register-Stop messages to implement a source registration process to accomplish this task.

NOTE   A common misconception is that a source must register before any receivers can join the shared tree. However, receivers can join the shared tree, even though there are currently no active sources. But when a source does become active, the RP then joins the SPT to the source and begins forwarding this traffic down the shared tree. By the same token, sources can register first even if there are no active receivers in the network. Later, when a receiver does join the group, the RP Joins the SPT toward all sources in the group and begins forwarding the group traffic down the shared tree.

The following sections discuss the mechanics of the source registration process that makes use of *PIM Register* and *PIM Register-Stop* messages. This process notifies an RP of an active source in the network and delivers the initial multicast packets to the RP to be forwarded down the shared tree. At the end of this section, a detailed, step-by-step example shows this process in action.

PIM Register Messages

PIM Register messages are sent by first-hop DRs (that is, a DR that is directly connected to a multicast source) to the RP. The purpose of the PIM Register message is twofold:

1 Notify the RP that Source S_1 is actively sending to Group G.

2 Deliver the initial multicast packet(s) sent by Source S_1 (each encapsulated inside of a single PIM Register message) to the RP for delivery down the shared tree.

Therefore, when a multicast source begins to transmit, the DR (to which the source is directly connected) receives the multicast packets sent by the source and creates an (S, G) state entry in its multicast routing table. In addition, because the source is directly connected (to the DR), the DR encapsulates each multicast packet in a separate PIM Register message and unicasts it to the RP. (How the DR learns the IP address of the RP is discussed in the "RP Discovery" section.)

NOTE Unlike the other PIM messages that are multicast on a local segment and travel hop by hop through the network, PIM Register messages and their close cousins, PIM Register-Stop messages (discussed in the next subsection) are unicast between the first-hop router and the RP.

When an RP receives a PIM Register message, it first de-encapsulates the message so it can examine the multicast packet inside. If the packet is for an active multicast group (that is, shared tree Joins for the group have been received), the RP forwards the packet down the shared tree. The RP then joins the SPT for Source S_1 so that it can receive (S_1, G) traffic natively instead of it being sent encapsulated inside of PIM Register messages. If, on the other hand, there is no active shared tree for the group, the RP simply discards the multicast packets and does not send a Join toward the source.

Does Anyone Know a Multicast Source?

Every time I describe the PIM Register process to students learning PIM-SM, I can't help but use an analogy of an elementary school class. Remember back when you were in elementary school, and a few kids in class always seemed to have the answer to the teacher's question and were dying to be called on? Their response to these questions would be to throw their hand high into the air while blurting out, "Oh, oh, me, me, ME!" (This was generally accompanied by painful facial expressions that were a result of attempts to raise their hand higher than anyone else in class, sometimes nearly to the point of dislocating a shoulder.) Now imagine that the teacher has just asked, "Who has multicast traffic for me?" I like to think of PIM Register messages as the "Oh, oh, me, me, ME!" message sent by first-hop DRs that are trying to notify the teacher (the RP) that they have multicast traffic. Of course, in PIM-SM first-hop DRs (just like many elementary students) don't wait to be called on before blurting out their "Oh, oh, me, me, ME!" Register messages.

PIM Register-Stop Messages

The RP unicasts PIM Register-Stop messages to the first-hop DR, instructing it to stop sending (S_1, G) Register messages under any of the following conditions:

- When the RP begins receiving multicast traffic from Source S_1 via the (S_1, G) SPT between the source and the RP.

- If the RP has no need for the traffic because there is no active shared tree for the group.

When a first-hop DR receives a Register-Stop message, the router knows that the RP has received the Register message and one of the two conditions above has been met. In either case, the first-hop DR terminates the Register process and stops encapsulating (S_1, G) packets in PIM Register messages.

Source Registration Example

Refer back to the point in the network example (see Figure 13-6) where two receivers have joined multicast Group G (as a result of receiving IGMP Membership Reports from directly connected hosts). At this point, Routers C and E have successfully joined the shared tree back to the RP. Let's now assume that multicast Source S_1 begins sending multicast traffic to Group G, as shown in Figure 13-16.

Figure 13-16   *Source Registration—Step 1*

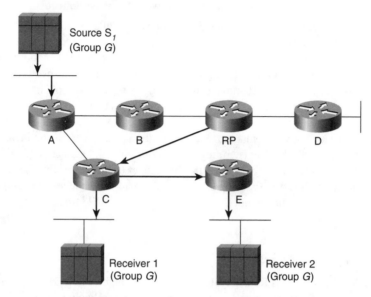

Because Router A is the first-hop DR, it responds to the incoming multicast traffic from Source S_1 by encapsulating the multicast packets in a PIM Register message and unicasting them (as shown by the dashed arrow in Figure 13-17) to the RP. (Note that Register messages are not sent hop by hop like other PIM messages, but are sent directly to the RP as a normal unicast packet.)

Figure 13-17   *Source Registration—Step 2*

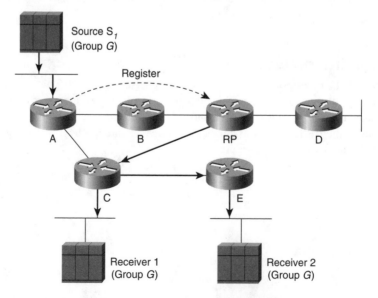

When the RP receives the Register message, the RP de-encapsulates the message and sees that the packet is addressed to multicast Group G. The RP also sees that an active shared tree with a nonempty outgoing interface list exists and therefore sends the de-encapsulated packet down the shared tree (depicted by the solid arrows in Figure 13-17). Furthermore, because an active shared tree exists for this group (with a nonempty outgoing interface list), the RP sends an (S_1, G) Join back toward Source S_1 to join the SPT and to pull the (S_1, G) traffic down to the RP. The (S_1, G) Join travels hop by hop back to the first-hop DR, Router A (see Figure 13-18).

Figure 13-18   *Source Registration—Step 3*

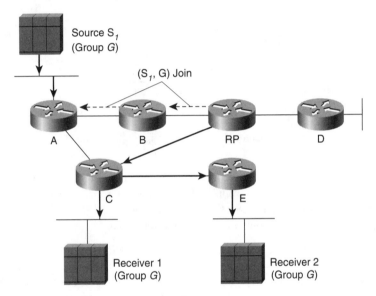

When the (S_1, G) Join reaches Router A, an (S_1, G) SPT has been built from Router A to the RP (indicated by the solid arrows from Router A to the RP in Figure 13-18). Now the (S_1, G) traffic begins to flow to the RP via this newly created (S_1, G) SPT.

At this point, the RP no longer needs to continue to receive the (S_1, G) traffic encapsulated in Register messages, so the RP unicasts a Register-Stop message back to the first-hop DR (Router A), as shown in Figure 13-19.

Figure 13-19 *Source Registration—Step 4*

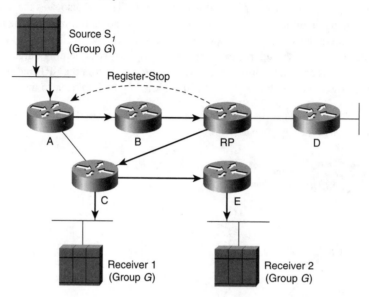

Let's continue with the example and assume another multicast source, S_2, connected to Router D begins sending to Group G. The same registration process would occur and would result in the RP joining the (S_2, G) SPT to pull the (S_1, G) traffic down to the RP so that it could be forwarded on down the shared tree for Group G.

At this point, the RP has joined both the (S_1, G) and (S_2, G) SPTs, (as seen in Figure 13-20) for the two active sources for Group G. This traffic is being forwarded down the $(*, G)$ shared tree to Receivers 1 and 2. Now, the paths are complete between the sources and the receivers, and multicast traffic is flowing properly.

Figure 13-20   *Source Registration—Step 5*

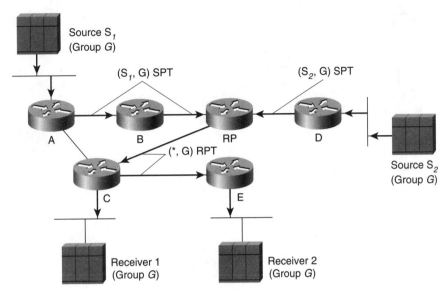

Shortest Path Tree Switchover

PIM-SM enables a last hop DR (that is, a DR with directly connected hosts that have joined a multicast group) to switch from the shared tree to the SPT for a specific source. This step is usually accomplished by specifying an SPT-Threshold in terms of bandwidth. If this threshold is exceeded, the last-hop DR joins the SPT. (Cisco routers have this threshold set to zero by default, which means that the SPT is joined as soon the first multicast packet from a source has been received via the shared tree.)

SPT Switchover Example

Let's return to the network example at the point where there are two receivers and two active sources (refer to Figure 13-20). Because Router C is a last-hop DR, it has the option of switching to the SPT's for Source S_1 and Source S_2. (For now, we are concentrating on Source S_1 because it is the more interesting case.) To accomplish this, Router C would send an (S_1, G) Join toward Source S_1, as shown by the dashed arrow in Figure 13-21.

Figure 13-21 *SPT Switchover—Step 1*

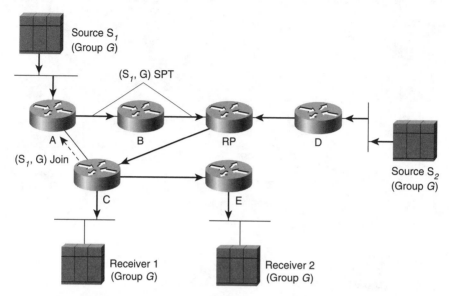

When Router A receives this Join, it adds the interface over which the Join was received to the outgoing interface list of the (S_1, G) entry in its multicast forwarding table. This effectively adds the link from Router A to Router C to the (S_1, G) SPT, as indicated in Figure 13-22. At this point, (S_1, G) multicast traffic can flow directly to Router C via the (S_1, G) SPT.

NOTE   Normally, Group SPT-Thresholds are configured consistently on all routers in the network. If this situation occurred in our example, Router E would also initiate a switch to the SPT by sending an (S, G) Join to the upstream router toward the source that, in this case, would be Router C. However, to keep the example simple, we only examined the case where Router C initiated the switch. Finally, remember that the routers, not the receivers, initiate the switchover to the SPT.

Figure 13-22 *SPT Switchover—Step 2*

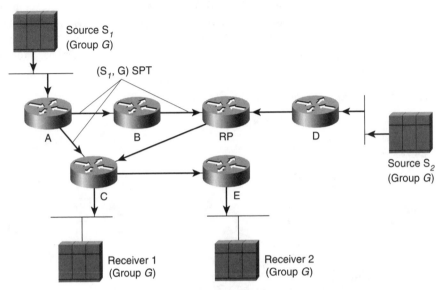

You have probably noticed that there are now two paths over which (S_1, G) multicast traffic can flow to reach Router C: the shared tree and the SPT. This would result in duplicate packets being delivered to Router C and is a waste of network bandwidth. So, we need to tell the RP to prune the (S_1, G) multicast traffic from the shared tree, which is precisely the topic of our next section.

Pruning Sources from the Shared Tree

When encountering the situation shown in Figure 13-22, in which source traffic is flowing down the shared tree that is also receiving via the SPT, a special type of Prune is used to tell the RP to prune this source's traffic from the shared tree. This special prune is referred to as an *(S, G) RP-bit Prune* because it has the RP flag set in the Prune list entry. As you recall from the section "PIM Join/Prune Messages," the RP flag (also referred to as the RP-bit) indicates that this message is applicable to the shared tree and should be forwarded up the shared tree toward the RP. Setting this flag/bit in an (S_1, G) Prune and sending it up the shared tree tells the routers along the shared tree to prune Source S_1 multicast traffic from the shared tree.

Referring to Figure 13-23, Router C sends an (S_1, G) RP-bit Prune up the shared tree toward the RP to prune S_1 multicast traffic from the shared tree. After receiving this special prune, the RP updates its multicast forwarding state so that (S_1, G) traffic is not forwarded down the link to Router C. However, because this link was the only interface on the shared tree that had (S_1, G) traffic flowing down it, the RP no longer has any need for the (S_1, G) traffic either.

Figure 13-23   *Pruning Sources from the Shared Tree—Step 1*

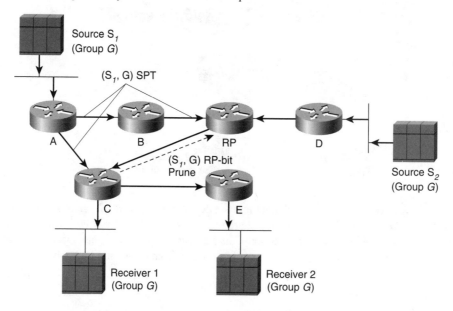

To shut off the now unneeded flow of (S_1, G) traffic, the RP sends an (S_1, G) Prune back toward Source S_1. This Prune (shown by the dashed arrows in Figure 13-24) travels hop by hop through Router B until it reaches the first-hop router, Router A.

Figure 13-24 *Pruning Sources from the Shared Tree—Step 2*

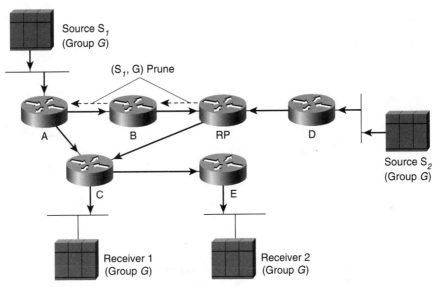

Figure 13-25 shows the result. Now, the (S_1, G) SPT has been pruned, leaving only the link between Router A and Router C. Note that Router E is still receiving (S_1, G) traffic from Router C (indicated by the solid arrow from C to E), although Router E is not aware that its upstream neighbor (Router C) has switched over to the SPT for Source S_1.

Figure 13-25 *Pruning Sources from the Shared Tree—Step 3*

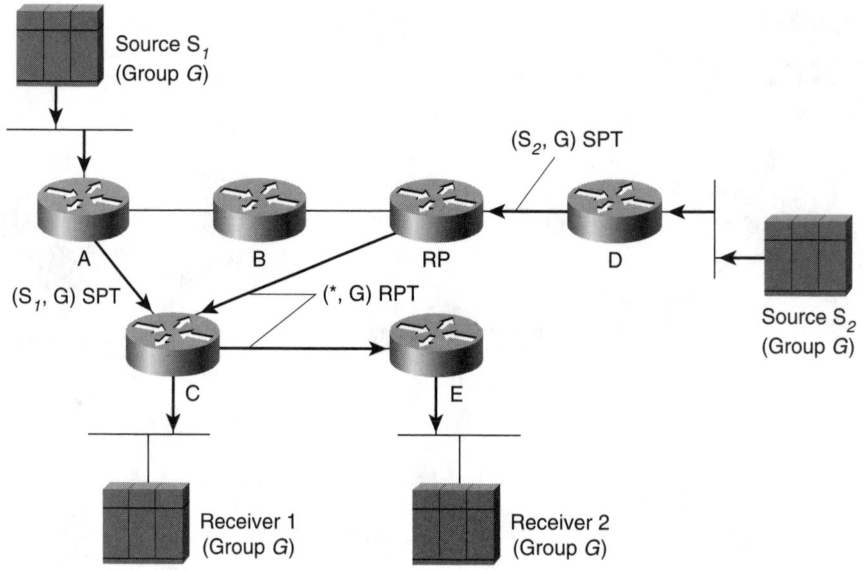

Also note in Figure 13-25 that (S_2, G) traffic is still flowing to the RP and down the shared tree to reach Receiver 1 and Receiver 2.

PIM-SM Designated Router

PIM elects a DR on each multi-access network (for example an Ethernet segment) using PIM Hello messages. In PIM-DM, the DR had meaning only if IGMPv1 was in use on the multi-access network because IGMPv1 does not have an IGMP Querier Election mechanism. In that case, the elected DR also functions as the IGMP Querier. However, in PIM-SM, the role of the DR is much more important, as you will see shortly.

The Role of the Designated Router

Consider the network example shown in Figure 13-26, in which two PIM-SM routers are connected to a common multi-access network with an active receiver for Group G. Because the Explicit Join model is used, only the DR (in this case, Router A) should send Joins to the RP to construct the shared tree for Group G. If both routers are permitted to send (*, G) Joins to the RP, parallel paths would be created and Host A would receive duplicate multicast traffic.

Figure 13-26   *PIM-SM Designated Router*

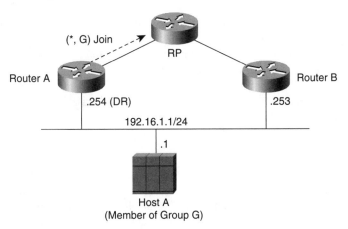

By the same token, if Host A begins to source multicast traffic to the group, the DR (Router A) is the router responsible for sending Register messages to the RP. Again, if both routers were permitted to send Register messages, the RP would receive duplicate multicast packets.

Designated Router Failover

When more than one router is connected to a LAN segment, PIM-SM provides not only a method to elect the DR but also a way to detect the failure of the current DR. If the current DR (Router A) shown in Figure 13-26 were to fail, Router B would detect this situation when its neighbor adjacency with Router A timed out. Now, a new DR election takes place, and Router B becomes the active DR for the network.

In this case, Router B is already aware that an active receiver (Host A) exists on the network because it has been hearing IGMP Membership Reports from the host. As a result, Router B already has IGMP state for Group G on this interface, which would cause B to send a Join to the RP as soon as it was elected the new DR. This step re-establishes traffic flow down a new branch of the shared tree via Router B. Additionally, if Host A were sourcing traffic, Router B would initiate a new Register process immediately after receiving the next multicast packet from Host A. This action would trigger the RP to join the SPT to Host A via a new branch through Router B.

RP Discovery

For PIM-SM to work properly, all routers within the PIM-SM domain must know the address of the RP. In small networks that use a single RP for all multicast groups, manually specifying the IP address of the RP in the configuration of each router might be possible. However, if the size of the network grows or if the RP changes frequently, manual configuration of every router becomes an administration nightmare. This problem is further compounded by the fact that different multicast groups use different RPs in other locations in the domain to either optimize the shared tree or spread the RP workload across multiple routers.

PIMv2 defines a *Bootstrap* mechanism that permits all PIM-SM routers within a domain to dynamically learn all *Group-to-RP* mappings and avoid the manual RP configuration problem. In addition, Cisco's PIM implementation has another mechanism, *Auto-RP*, which can accomplish the same thing. (Cisco's Auto-RP was developed before the PIMv2 specification was written so that existing Cisco PIM-SM networks could dynamically learn *Group-to-RP* mappings.)

PIM-SM Suitability/Scalability

Because PIM-SM uses the Explicit Join model, multicast traffic is better constrained to only those portions of the network where it is actually desired. Therefore, PIM-SM does not suffer from the inefficiencies found in flood-and-prune protocols such as DVMRP and PIM-DM. As a result, PIM-SM is better suited to multicast networks that have potential members at the end of WAN links.

In addition to the obvious advantages of the Explicit Join model, PIM-SM enables network engineers to use SPTs to reduce the network latency commonly associated with the use of shared trees. The decision to use or not use SPTs can be made on a group-by-group basis. For example, a low-rate, many-to-many multicast application (such as SDR) running over a star-topology network may not warrant the use of SPTs. In this case, the use of Infinity as the group's SPT-Threshold could force all group traffic to remain on the shared tree. This ability to control the use of SPTs gives network engineers greater control over the amount of state created in the routers in the network. Ultimately, the amount of state in the routers in the network is one of the primary factors that affects the scalability of any multicast routing protocol.

PIM-SM is arguably the best choice for an intra-domain multicast routing protocol for most general-purpose multicast networks. The possible exceptions are dedicated, special purpose networks that are designed to run very specific network applications under the complete control of the network administrators. (In these cases, PIM-SM may still be the best choice, although other protocols could possibly be made to work adequately given the tight controls that the network administrators have over the network and its applications.)

Summary

This chapter has presented an overview of the fundamentals of PIM-SM. The key points of PIM-SM are the use of an Explicit Join model to build shared trees and SPTs. In addition, because traffic only flows down the shared tree in traditional PIM-SM, there must be some way to get traffic from a source to the RP. This task is accomplished by the RP joining the SPT toward the source. However, first the RP must be made aware that the source exists, which requires the PIM Register mechanism. The final point, and possibly the most overlooked aspect of PIM-SM, is that routers with directly connected receivers usually immediately join the SPT to a newly detected source and bypass the RP.

Network Case Studies

CHAPTER 14

Switched Network Management

By Paul Della Maggiora, et. al.

This chapter is part of the basis for the forthcoming book Performance and Fault Management *from Cisco Press.*

This chapter provides a set of fault-monitoring and event-correlation guidelines, as applied to Cisco switches and routers, to help network administrators better manage their network of Cisco equipment. Switch- and router-management capabilities are first introduced, followed by more specific definitions of MIB objects, SNMP traps, and syslog messages associated with typical fault and performance conditions. These scenarios can be used to specify elements to monitor and to implement correlation rules. This chapter contains a Cisco knowledge base for Cisco switches and routers.

Also addressed is fault and event correlation for Cisco switches and routers, based on MIB objects and syslog messages. Because Cisco private MIBs are constantly evolving, some scenarios described in this chapter may not apply to your installation if these MIB objects and/or syslog messages are not supported or not applicable in your environment. The CCO Web site (www.cisco.com) contains a cross listing of all MIBs and syslog messages. The cross listing is organized to show the MIBs and syslog messages supported by particular platforms and by various IOS release versions.

This chapter was originally a white paper written by a group of Cisco's senior network engineers to address the concerns of customers as they migrated from router/shared hub networks to router/switched networks. They found that the network-management strategy that worked for shared networks did not scale to efficiently support and monitor switched networks.

The chapter concludes with a set of case study scenarios to assist you in switched-network management.

Overview

Within this chapter, you will find a consolidation of much information about the management of Cisco equipment for the purposes of helping end users better manage their networks, and helping network-management application vendors enhance their product offerings. It presents a set of network-monitoring and event-correlation guidelines for what the authors consider the most important conditions to monitor.

In addition to the description of the most important switch and router events to monitor within a single device, this chapter also describes a series of event-correlation scenarios to monitor across one or more devices, a VLAN or subnet, or the entire network. Cisco's event model is introduced along with a description of all possible means to gather information from a switch or router.

Audience for This Chapter

This chapter is written for network-management engineers who must implement network management for Cisco switches and routers. This chapter assumes the reader has a basic understanding of switching and routing theory, Simple Network Management (SNMP), and Cisco switches and routers. This chapter is also written for network-management platform and application vendors to enhance their product with specific monitoring and correlation rules for Cisco equipment.

Terms and Acronyms Used in This Chapter

Table 14-1 lists and explains the important terms you will find in this chapter.

Table 14-1   *Network Management Terms*

Term	Explanation
802.10	The 802.10 protocol incorporates a mechanism whereby LAN traffic can carry a VLAN identifier, thus allowing selective switching of packets with this identifier. This protocol is the IEEE 802.10 Interoperable LAN/MAN Security (SILS) standard, ratified in late 1992. It was originally conceived to address security within shared LAN/metropolitan-area network (MAN) environments.
ARP	Address Resolution Protocol.
ASIC	Application-Specific Integrated Circuit.
ATM	Asynchronous Transfer Mode.
BPDU	bridge protocol data unit.
BRI	Basic Rate Interface.
CAM	content-addressable memory.
CDP	Cisco Discovery Protocol.
CLI	command-line interface.
CPU	Central Processing Unit.

Table 14-1   *Network Management Terms (Continued)*

Term	Explanation
CRC	cyclic redundancy check.
CRM	Cisco Resource Manager.
CWSI	CiscoWorks for Switched Internetworks.
DBMS	Database Management System.
EARL	Enhanced Address Recognition Logic.
ECS	event-correlation system.
E-SPAN	Enhanced Switched Port Analyzer.
event	Typically, a message generated by a Cisco device for informational or error purposes.
FDDI	Fiber Distributed Data Interface.
GUI	graphical user interface.
ISDN	Integrated Services Digital Network.
ISL	Inter-Switch Link.
LANE	LAN Emulation.
LLC	Logical Link Control.
MAC	Media Access Control.
MAU	media attachment unit.
MIB	Management Information Base.
NIC	network interface card.
NMP	Network Management Processor.
NMS	network management system.
OID	Object Identifier.
OSI	Open System Interconnection.
PDU	protocol data unit.
PVID	Port VLAN ID.
RADIUS	Remote Access Dial-In User Service.
RMON	remote monitoring.
severity	The level of criticality of an event.
SLA	Service-Level Agreement.
SNAP	Subnetwork Access Protocol.
SNMP	Simple Network Management Protocol.

continues

Table 14-1   *Network Management Terms (Continued)*

Term	Explanation
SPAN	Switched Port Analyzer.
SRAM	static random-access memory. Type of RAM that retains its contents for as long as power is supplied. SRAM does not require constant refreshing.
STP	Spanning-Tree Protocol.
syslog	An error logging facility supported by IOS-based switches and routers.
syslogd	The *syslog* daemon logs system messages into a set of files described by the */etc/syslog.conf* configuration file.
TACACS	Terminal Access Controller Access Control System.
trap	An SNMP event.
VLAN	virtual LAN.
VMPS	VLAN Membership Policy Server.
VTP	VLAN Trunk Protocol—A Layer 2 messaging protocol that maintains VLAN configuration consistency throughout the network.

Other Catalyst 5000 Series acronyms can be found at the CCO Web site.

Network Management Overview

Network management is the art and science of managing network equipment such as switches, routers, hubs, and other communications equipment composing the network infrastructure.

ISO helped simplifying the partitioning of network-management activities by identifying five major areas (also known as FCAPS, for the initials of each functional area):

- Fault management
- Configuration management
- Accounting management
- Performance management
- Security management

An overview of these functional areas and an introduction to networking can be found at the CCO Web site.

Although several books have been written about network management, this chapter addresses only fault- and performance-management functional areas as applied to Cisco switches and routers.

Cisco Device Technical Overview

This section covers some background on how Cisco has implemented certain functions and protocols. This will be useful as background information for the material in this chapter.

Introduction to Switches

A Cisco Catalyst switch is a multiport bridging device. Cisco's switching architecture depends on the concept of multilayer switching, which combines the ease of use of Layer 2 switching (bridging) within a workgroup with the stability and security of Layer 3 switching (routing) among different workgroups.

Multilayer switching is important for sustainable growth in large switched environments for several reasons:

- It offers excellent throughput because it helps provide dedicated bandwidth to individual users.

- It obviates the bottlenecks that simple Layer 2 switching causes when multiple 10-Mbps segments all converge at single 10-Mbps connections to servers and routers.

Because switches are multiport bridges, each port is its own separate segment or ring with 10 MB of theoretical bandwidth available, as opposed to a hub that shares a single 10 MB of capacity among its various ports.

Because each port is bridged, each port sees only broadcast, some multicast, and unicast traffic destined to or sourced from the particular port. This means that if a device connected to switch port 2 talks with a device on switch port 3, no other switch ports will see that traffic. Therefore, a network analyzer connected to switch port 4 would not see the conversation going between switch ports 2 and 3.

This section explains the various components and protocols that make up a switch.

A thorough introduction to switching basics can be found at the CCO Web site.

Central Processing Unit (CPU) and Application-Specific Integrated Circuits (ASICs)

Switches, like routers, contain a CPU. Unlike routers, however, a switch performs most of the packet forwarding without impacting the CPU. Switching decisions are performed on the switch ASICs and, depending on the switch type, the bridging table may be stored on an ASIC as well.

Some of the operations performed by the switch's CPU include spanning tree, Telnet services, Cisco Discovery Protocol (CDP), security (such as Terminal Access Controller Access Control System [TACACS]), remote monitoring (RMON), VLAN Trunk Protocol (VTP), port aggregation, dynamic VLANs, and SNMP processing.

As such, measuring the CPU of a switch is of little importance when determining the switch's packet-forwarding performance of the switch.

Content-Addressable Memory (CAM) Table

Bridges/switches keep track of the ports from which they have received certain Media Access Control (MAC) addresses to isolate unicast conversations to the ports involved. The alternative is to forward all traffic, unicast and broadcast, to all switched ports, which would be excessive. This feature is traditionally done using a forwarding database (sometimes called a bridging table) and content-addressable memory (CAM) tables.

The forwarding database is usually a single centralized table or database on a bridge that contains all the MAC addresses (and their ports) the bridge has learned. It is used to forward packets to the correct ports.

The content of the CAM can be accessed using the contents rather than an address. A CAM typically exists at each physical port. In non-promiscuous mode (meaning not bridging), the CAM contains the burned-in MAC address of the network interface card (NIC), and is programmed with other addresses (like multicasts/broadcast) to which it needs to listen. Any packet that fails the CAM lookup is dropped by the NIC.

Bridges operate in promiscuous mode, which means the CAM on each port is cleared, so all MAC addresses are accepted. As the bridging table is built, the CAM is populated with destination MAC addresses of stations generating traffic on that port. In promiscuous mode, packets received on a port that have a destination MAC address that matches an entry in the CAM for that port are ignored. If MAC addresses are stored in the CAM, the MAC address is used to look up the entry, rather than a sequential search, because sequential searches are much slower. This makes the CAM quicker than the forwarding database. Many NICs have a CAM, but the Catalyst 5000 does not have CAM on Ethernet ports.

On the Catalyst 5000, the term "CAM" is used for historical reasons; no actual CAM is present. The Catalyst 5000 uses a central Enhanced Address Recognition Logic (EARL) for speed and additional functionality by combining the VLAN ID with the MAC address in the learning and lookup functions performed by the Catalyst 5000 hardware. The EARL combines the functions of the forwarding database (central complete list of MACs, VLANs, and ports) and the CAM (fast lookup using the contents of memory rather than a search). The MAC addresses are stored on an SRAM chip on the supervisor engine and do not impact memory or processor usage on the network-management processor (NMP). There is enough SRAM on the chip to store 16,000 MAC addresses.

The Path of a Packet

Generally, the path of a packet through a switch is as follows:

1 The switch receives a packet on a particular port.

2 The switch looks at the destination MAC address and compares it to the entries in its forwarding database. It also records the source MAC address and the port in which it was received in the CAM/bridging table.

3 If the destination address was a unicast address that was recorded in the CAM/ bridging table, the switch forwards the packet out the associated destination port if it is a different port.

4 If the destination address was not in the bridging table or if the destination was a broadcast or multicast address, the switch forwards the packet out all ports of the switch except the one on which it was received.

All of these operations are performed without impacting the switch's CPU at all.

Transparent Versus Translational Bridging

When bridging, Catalyst switches perform both transparent and translational bridging. Transparent bridging is the process of forwarding traffic from one port (such as Ethernet) to another common media port (such as another Ethernet port). The packet will not be modified in any form as it is taken from the receiving port and passed on to the destination port.

Translational bridging goes one step further by bridging traffic between two different media, such as from Ethernet to Fiber Distributed Data Interface (FDDI). Translational bridging requires a switch to take a received packet and "translate" it to a different media. This entails, at a minimum, the replacement of one topology's part of a packet with another. Translational switching requires extra processing time because a packet must be received, analyzed, and translated before sending the packet on to its final destination.

VLANs and VLAN Services

A VLAN is an administratively defined broadcast domain that can span multiple switches. Only end stations within the VLAN receive packets that are unicast, broadcast, or multicast (flooded). A VLAN enhances performance by limiting traffic; it allows the transmission of traffic among stations that belong to it and blocks traffic from other stations in other VLANs. VLANs can provide security barriers (firewalls) between end stations on different VLANs within the same switch.

In addition, some of the VLAN components supported on the Catalyst series include the following:

- **VLAN trunks**—Allow extending VLANs from one Catalyst series switch to one or more routers or other Catalyst series switches using high-speed interfaces, such as Fast Ethernet, FDDI, and Asynchronous Transfer Mode (ATM). Two trunking protocols are supported at this time: Inter-Switch Link (ISL) for Ethernet and Fast Ethernet, and 802.10 for FDDI.

- **Fast EtherChannel**—Allows parallel Fast Ethernet ISL trunks to split traffic among multiple trunks. By setting spanning-tree parameters on a VLAN basis, you can define which VLANs are active on a trunk and which should use the trunk as a backup if the active trunk fails.

- **VLAN Trunk Protocol (VTP)**—Allows VLAN naming consistency and connectivity between all devices in a management domain. When new VLANs are added to a Catalyst 5000 series switch in a management domain, the VTP automatically distributes this information to all the devices in the management domain. The VTP is transmitted on all trunk connections, including ISL, 802.10, and ATM LAN Emulation (LANE). By using multiple VTP servers through which global VLAN information is modified and maintained, you can configure redundancy in a network domain. Only a few VTP servers are required in a large network. In a small network, all devices are usually VTP servers. Catalyst 5000 Series Software Release 3.1 supports VTP version 2, an extension to VTP version 1.

Spanning-Tree Protocol (STP)

When creating fault-tolerant networks, a loop-free path must exist between all nodes in the network. A spanning-tree algorithm is used to calculate the best loop-free path through a Catalyst-switched network. Spanning-tree packets are sent and received by switches in the network at regular intervals. The packets are not forwarded by the switches participating in the spanning tree, but are instead processed to determine the spanning-tree itself. The IEEE 802.1D bridge protocol, called STP, performs this function for Catalyst switches.

The Catalyst series switches can use STP on all VLANs. The STP detects and breaks loops by placing some connections in a stand-by mode, which are activated in the event of a failure. A separate STP runs within each configured VLAN, ensuring valid Layer 2 topologies throughout the network.

The supported STP states are as follows:

- Disabled
- Forwarding
- Learning
- Listening
- Blocking

The state for each port is initially set by the configuration and later modified by the STP process. After the port state is set, the 802.1D bridge specification (RFC 1493) determines whether the port forwards or blocks packets.

Switched Port Analyzer (SPAN) Functionality and Purpose

The SPAN feature enables you to monitor traffic on any port for analysis by a network-analyzer device or RMON probe. Enhanced SPAN (E-SPAN) enables you to monitor traffic from multiple ports with the same VLAN.

SPAN redirects traffic from an Ethernet, Fast Ethernet, FDDI port, or VLAN to an Ethernet or Fast Ethernet monitor port for analysis and troubleshooting. You can monitor a single port or VLAN using a dedicated analyzer such as a Network General Sniffer, or an RMON probe such as a Cisco SwitchProbe.

Introduction to Routers

Routers are Layer 3 switching devices. Routing involves two basic activities: determination of optimal routing paths and the transport (or switching) of information groups (typically called packets) through a network. Switching is relatively straightforward. Path determination, on the other hand, can be very complex. Routing algorithms can be differentiated based on several key characteristics. First, the particular goals of the algorithm designer affect the operation of the resulting routing protocol. Second, there are various types of routing algorithms. Each algorithm has a different impact on network and router resources. Finally, routing algorithms use a variety of metrics that affect calculation of optimal routes.

A thorough overview of routing basics can be found at the CCO Web site.

Introduction to Layer 3 Switches

Layer 3 switches combine switch and routing technology to allow traffic switching at both Layer 2 and Layer 3.

Technology Common to Switches and Routers

This section covers two protocols that are common to switches and routers and that help build a complete view of Layer 2 and Layer 3 devices in the network.

Cisco Discovery Protocol (CDP)

CDP is media and protocol independent and runs on all Cisco-manufactured equipment, including routers, bridges, access and communication servers, and switches. With CDP, network-management applications can retrieve the device type and SNMP agent address of neighboring devices. This allows applications to send SNMP queries to neighboring devices.

CDP meets a need created by the existence of lower-level, virtually transparent protocols. CDP allows network-management applications to discover Cisco devices that are neighbors of already known devices, in particular neighbors running lower-layer, transparent protocols. CDP runs on all media that support the Subnetwork Access Protocol (SNAP), including LAN and Frame Relay. CDP runs over the data link layer only, not the network layer. With CDP, two systems that support different network layer protocols can learn about each other.

Cached CDP information is available to network-management applications. Cisco devices never forward a CDP packet. When new information is received, old information is discarded. CiscoWorks for Switched Internetworks (CWSI) uses this information during network discovery.

CDP is also very useful in troubleshooting. In a network of routers only, the Address Resolution Protocol (ARP) tables, routing tables, and other information are used to discover the topology, or to confirm the connectivity of the topology that is already known. In a network of bridges, these tables aren't used; instead, a forwarding database (which is not useful to discover bridges; it's for end stations) and spanning-tree information (which may be disabled, and gives information upstream toward the root only) are used. CDP will discover all Cisco devices that are neighbors and provide information such as host name, Cisco IOS version, and management IP address.

See the CCO Web site for information on how to configure CDP in a Catalyst 5000.

Embedded Remote Monitoring (RMON)

RFC 1757 defines a portion of the Management Information Base (MIB) for monitoring data link layer information of remote segments, in particular, traffic characteristics and error rates.

Remote network-monitoring devices, often called monitors or probes, are instruments that exist for the purpose of managing a network. Often these remote probes are standalone devices and devote significant internal resources for the sole purpose of managing a network. An organization may employ many of these devices, one per network segment, to manage its Internet. In addition, these devices may be used for a network-management service provider to access a client network, often geographically remote.

The objects defined in the RFC are intended as an interface between an RMON agent and an RMON management application and are not intended for direct manipulation by users.

Although some users may tolerate the direct display of some of these objects, few will tolerate the complexity of manually manipulating objects to accomplish row creation. These functions should be handled by the management application. Cisco provides applications to perform these functions.

RMON, as described in RFC 1757, is implemented on Cisco Catalyst products and routers as follows:

- Statistics, history, alarms, and events (of the nine RMON groups) on Ethernet segments in the 5000 or 5500 Workgroup Catalyst Switches with Software Release 2.1 and above and all 2900 Workgroup Catalyst Switches.

- Statistics, history, alarms, and events (of the nine RMON groups) on Ethernet segments in the Catalyst 1900 and Catalyst 2820 Switches with Software Release 5.33 and higher.

- Statistics, history, alarms, and events (of the nine RMON groups) on Ethernet segments in the 3000 Series (3000, 3100, and 3200) Workgroup Catalyst Switches.

- All nine RMON groups on Ethernet segments in the 1200 Workgroup Catalyst Switch with DMP and NMP Software Version 3.1 or higher.

- IOS Release 11.1 and higher supports the EtherStats, EtherHistory, Alarms, and Events MIB groups.

Network Management Protocols

This section covers how industry-standard network-management protocols can be used to manage Cisco networks.

Basic Protocols

Four types of network-management protocols are available to manage Cisco equipment:

- Telnet
- SNMP
- RMON
- Syslog

Telnet

Telnet (also known as CLI) allows direct login into a switch or router to have access to configuration and monitoring commands.

SNMP

As defined in RFC 1157, the Simple Network Management Protocol (SNMP) is based on the concept of a SNMP Manager communicating with one or more SNMP agents, using the SNMP. SNMP Get, Get-Next, and Set operations are performed by the SNMP Manager to the agent to either retrieve or set management variables supported by the SNMP agent. Management information is usually equally available from SNMP and through Telnet. SNMP agents can notify SNMP managers by issuing SNMP traps. Traps can contain any number of management information to better qualify the trap.

RMON

Based on the SNMP technology, the remote network monitoring capabilities are supported by a dedicated RMON (remote monitoring) data-collection and monitoring engine residing in a device. Communicating—for example, setting collection rules and receiving notifications from the engine—is performed through SNMP. RMON addresses ISO Layers 1 through 3, while RMON2 addresses ISO Layers 4 and above.

Syslog

The syslog protocol is used by Cisco devices to issue unsolicited notifications to a management station. Although similar in nature to SNMP traps, the syslog protocol is only used for event notification. The CISCO-SYSLOG-MIB is being implemented on Cisco devices as an alternative to issuing syslog messages, to allow any SNMP manager to receive all events through SNMP.

Event Model Overview

This section presents Cisco's conceptual event model as applied to Cisco equipment. But, first introduced are the event types available from Cisco switches and routers.

Event Types

All Cisco devices generate *SNMP traps* to notify NMS applications of activity and error conditions. In addition, IOS-based devices generate *syslog* messages.

Syslog Messages

Cisco's IOS syslog logging utility is identical to the UNIX syslog utility, namely a UDP-based logging mechanism for applications and operating systems to report activity or error conditions. All routers and most switches generate syslog messages. This means that any UNIX management workstation (preferably your UNIX network-management station) can serve as the syslog server for all your Cisco equipment. Every syslog message is associated, at the time of logging, with a time stamp, a facility, a severity, and a textual description.

SNMP Traps

See the CCO Web site for a listing of all SNMP traps supported by Cisco. Cisco-supported SNMP traps can also be found in Cisco-supported MIB files.

Public and Private SNMP Traps   All Cisco devices generate SNMP traps. In addition, because most Cisco devices support the standard RMON alarm and event MIB groups, additional localized polling of any MIB variables can be configured within a device to monitor for thresholds and generate SNMP traps as needed.

Syslog SNMP Traps   More and more Cisco routers implement the Cisco Syslog MIB as a means to generate SNMP traps in place of, or in addition to, syslog messages. This MIB enhances Cisco device management through SNMP by adding a greater number of unsolicited messages that an NMP may receive, and therefore enhance router manageability.

To enable syslog traps on a router, use the following command:

```
snmp-server enable traps syslog
```

In addition, the following command specifies the level of messages to be sent:

```
logging history level
```

Platform Events

SNMP platforms may generate their own events, or their own SNMP traps, as a result of performing remote polling of specific MIB objects and applying thresholds to these MIB objects. In addition, event-correlation engines and network-performance reporting applications may generate their own events to the NMP.

Event Processing

Event processing is characterized by the following four activities.

Event Collection

The basis for a comprehensive event-correlation engine is to feed it as many events as possible to get the maximum amount of filtering and correlation desired.

A high-performance event-collection engine is required to accept all events received. An event-collection engine needs to process SNMP traps and syslog messages.

Event Knowledge

Processing and reporting events must be accompanied by a comprehensive explanation of the event and how it relates to the operation of the device, and possibly of the network.

Event Filtering

Excessive and repetitive events are known to occur and clutter a network-management system to the point where network operators shut off the feature and rely on their intuition and user complaints. Therefore, it is important to provide an effective means to *reduce* the number of events reported to network operators by removing repetitive messages (for example, identical messages repeated within a given time period) and to *eliminate* low-priority events (for example, events not deemed to require operator notification).

Event Correlation

After events are filtered, it is still important to assess the critical nature of an event as it relates to a device or to other events. A router down event may be ignored temporarily, for example, if you know the router is restarting as a result of a software error. If the router does not come back online after 5 minutes, however, the operator should be notified immediately.

Cisco Event Model

This section introduces a model to manage a high volume of traps and syslog messages and correlate them to your network; so now the information becomes practical rather than overwhelming.

Theoretical Event Model

The following proposed event model is a conceptual model for correlating Cisco events. It assumes syslog messages as well as SNMP traps generated either directly by the device or as a result of SNMP thresholding through the RMON alarm and event groups. All these event types serve as input into the event model.

Events are first filtered to eliminate as many events deemed of no interest as possible, as driven from a knowledge database. This operation minimizes the processing required in the subsequent phases of the event model.

Events of interest are then normalized to a common form to ease the processing in the event-correlation engine. Normalization may also involve modifying the severity of an event to more accurately reflect the priority of an event at a specific site.

The event-correlation engine is composed of several correlation conditions that may eliminate events, pass them straight through at all times, only pass them straight through if one or more other conditions occur within a specific time window, modify events, or create new events. Each condition is specific to a device, a type of device, or to all devices depending on the scope of the correlation rules. Correlation rules can make use of external information such as physical or logical topology to better isolate a faulty device. Correlation rules can also issue additional requests to one or more devices if they need to obtain additional information at any point in a correlation rule.

Figure 14-1 illustrates the conceptual model.

Although Figure 14-1 shows CLI commands to communicate with a device, this option is usually not needed because syslog messages and SNMP MIBs provide all information needed to manage these devices.

Figure 14-1   *Conceptual Cisco Event Model*

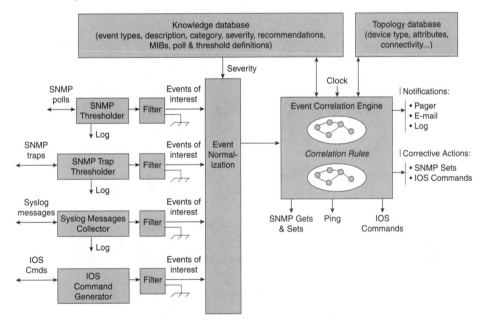

Commercial Event-Correlation Systems

Every event-correlation system (ECS) has its own way of mapping Cisco's event model to its own implementation. Implementing the event model in a third-party correlation engine may require custom programming or scripting depending on the engine capabilities.

Table 14-2 identifies where Cisco's event model components described earlier may exist in a third-party event-correlation engine.

Table 14-2 *Cisco Event Model Components*

Event Model Component	Event-Correlation Engine Mapping
Knowledge database	A relational database about all Cisco IOS syslog messages and recommendations, and Cisco SNMP traps. Would need to be populated from Cisco's existing syslog message knowledge base with additional severity mapping software/tables.
Topology database	This topology is usually available from the NMS platform through published APIs or an export facility.
SNMP thresholder	This is supported either through the platform or polling engine or through Cisco's built-in RMON alarm and event MIB groups.
SNMP trap collector	This is supported through the existing platform or correlation engine trap collector.
Syslog message collector	A custom module built to receive syslog messages and parse them appropriately.
IOS Command Generator	Typically a Telnet client. Can either be scripted or built in to the correlation engine.
Event Normalization	Every platform or engine has its own proprietary methods for normalizing an event.
SNMP Gets & Sets	Can either be scripted or built in to the NMS platform or correlation engine.
Ping (ICMP) queries	Can either be scripted or built in to the NMS platform or correlation engine.
IOS Commands	Typically a Telnet client. Can either be scripted or built in to the correlation engine.
MIBs	Cisco MIBs are available for uploading into the NMS or correlation engine and serve as the basis for the knowledge base.
Paging notifications	E-mail is usually supported either in the NMS platform or the correlation engine. Paging systems are usually available from third-party vendors.
Corrective actions	Can be invoked from within the NMS or correlation engine as a correlation rule becomes true, in an attempt to correct the faulty condition.

Because most fault management is about detecting faults and performing root-cause analysis, less emphasis is placed on automating corrective actions in this chapter.

Network Management Guidelines

This section is a series of steps to follow to implement effective management of your network.

Start with a Good Design and Secure Closets

Good network-management starts with good network design. This includes the following steps:

- Secure the wiring closets, and grant access in a controlled manner only. An unlocked closet is begging to be disturbed.

- Document the physical network, including the network equipment and the wiring. You need to know which devices are connected to which ports of each switch and router. You then must be able to identify which cables actually connect those devices.

- Define and adhere to move/add/change policies in which all network modifications are documented and planned in advance whenever possible. Physical maps and inventories should always reflect any changes.

Identify Critical Ports; Leave the Rest Alone

As switches become more affordable, they are replacing hubs and media attachment units (MAUs) in the wiring closet. Typically, customers migrate from hubbed to switched networks by replacing hub ports with switch ports. Users and servers are migrated incrementally by moving a connection from the hub to a switch port.

The traditional broadcast domain or segment of Ethernet that was commonly used to monitor no longer exists. It was a shared media that any one port would give users (through an analyzer) a complete picture of what was happening for *all* traffic. In a switched environment the broadcast domain (VLAN) may span multiple switches, closets, and buildings. Unicast traffic and sometimes multicast traffic is segregated to only the ports that need to see it.

Traditionally, a traffic analyzer could be used to look at all traffic on a segment and determine which devices were the busiest, overloaded, underutilized, and so forth. In a switched environment, that overall picture does not exist anywhere in the network. The traffic on each port of a VLAN is different (except for ports with only one active device— the switch). Even if a SPAN port is used, it gives only a picture of what exists on a single switch, which is only part of that same VLAN, which may coexist on multiple switches.

Although the broadcast rate still imposes a limit on the growth of a VLAN (just like it did on shared media), it is only part of the picture. Because it is not practical for most of us to monitor every single switched port (to get a complete picture), we need to identify, document, and maintain only the "critical" switched ports.

A "critical" switched port is one that is vital to the success of the network's operation. Examples of critical switched-port connections include the following:

- File/application servers ports
- Router ports
- Trunk ports
- Mahogany Row ports (those executives whose ports should never go down)

Client ports (with the exception of Mahogany Row) should never be considered critical. Trying to maintain management data for that many ports can be overwhelming and overload switch resources. In addition, getting an alert whenever a user turns off her PC does not provide useful data in comparison with a warning of a trunk or router port going down in an unplanned fashion.

After the critical ports have been identified, they should be documented, physically marked, and maintained through move/add/changes. If not, network operators run the risk of reacting to ports conditions that were once critical, but are now noncritical based on an undocumented change.

The remaining keys discuss management strategies for critical ports. Setting up network availability reports by device or by critical port of a switch can provide management with an important metric for decision making.

Set Up Fault Monitoring

Fault monitoring consists of availability monitoring, SNMP trap logging and processing, and syslog message logging and processing. If not already done, your network devices should be configured for SNMP access, SNMP trap generation, and syslog message generation with time stamps. Synchronize the clocks on your network devices and your network-management station (NMS) with NTP to greatly improve event-correlation capabilities.

Monitoring Availability

The simplest way to monitor device availability is to check responses to a **ping** (ICMP) or SNMP **get** request. Standard NMS products monitor all the objects they manage through these simple mechanisms. Although a **ping** response is not a guarantee that the switch is functioning properly, the lack of such a response is a definite sign of a problem. Using an NMS with availability monitoring linked to the color of a device on a topology map is the most common example of fault monitoring.

Setting Up Syslog

Configure routers and switches to send their console messages to a syslog server, typically being the NMS. A Catalyst 5000 series switch can buffer the last n syslog console messages it generates by saving them in a 1-KB buffer. Although these are useful for quick reference from the command-line interface (CLI), it is recommended to log these messages to a syslog server for persistence, later reference, and correlation.

Log messages are system messages that would normally be sent out on the console port; for example: "11/4/1996,13:52:54:SYS-5: Module 3 failed configuration". Cisco routers and switches generate many different kinds of system messages.

Switch syslog messages are formatted with two parameters: the facility and severity. You must choose one of eight facilities (local0–local7), and then choose the facility based on the facilities your syslog server is already logging. It is best to choose a facility that will be dedicated to your network devices. Cisco routers choose local7 by default, which is a good choice unless there is a conflict.

You can configure the severity level of each type of message you want the switch to send. You should log a severity level of "warning" and below of each type of system message so that you do not clog up the logs with superfluous messages that do not add useful information.

Although syslog information can be used for fault management, it is not a real-time fault alert mechanism like an SNMP trap (unless you do additional work to make it behave so). Syslog information is useful for event correlation, however. Parsing the syslog files for messages correlating to a certain event can provide useful insight to the cause of the problem. You can configure the syslog server to log messages of different severities to different log files or messages of all severities to one large file. You can then use tools such as Perl to search the syslog log files for the desired information. Tools such as Cisco Resource Manager (CRM) can gather syslog information and create reports based on severity and dates. Such tools can also summarize the syslog messages to make interpreting the messages easier.

Setting Up SNMP Traps

SNMP traps provide a mechanism for a device to unilaterally notify a network operator of a certain condition in real time. SNMP traps are unsolicited notifications, independent of any SNMP polling activities. The SNMP traps generated by Cisco switches and routers provide useful information on potentially harmful environmental conditions, processor status, and port status. Every device will also generate SNMP traps based on the features it supports. For example, a Cisco switch will generate SNMP spanning-tree topology changes SNMP traps when a spanning-tree configuration changes because of a trunk or switch being added or removed from the network.

Initially, it is recommended to enable the module, chassis, bridge, authentication, and port linkup/down traps. The port-level traps require enabling the port trap on the "critical" ports with this command:

```
set port trap module|port enable|disable
```

Many NMS products have trap receivers that log traps and can be configured to react to traps in fairly sophisticated ways. You can be informed of the trap through a pop-up window, an audible alarm, or an electronic page.

Collect Baseline Data

After documenting the network, identifying business critical switched ports, and enabling monitoring the status of your switches and routers, it is time to learn the true nature of your network by monitoring data over time and studying the traffic flows.

By collecting information for a baseline of the network, you gain an accurate picture of traffic flows through the network and have data for evaluating growth over time and estimating bottlenecks. Over time, this collection of data can serve as baseline data when determining threshold values for the next step (discussed under the heading, "Define and Set Thresholds"). Baselines are also valuable troubleshooting tools when you are trying to determine the cause of performance problems.

Baselining of the network is also essential because of the increasing importance of capacity planning. According to Optimal (www.optimal.com), 85% of new application deployments fail to meet service-level agreements. Of the several reasons for this, here are a few:

* Increased network complexity
* High-bandwidth multimedia applications and increased burstiness of applications
* Increased use of the network for nonbusiness applications (Internet and World Wide Web traffic)
* More organizations upgrading existing networks and applications rather than building new networks

Baselining is the key to capacity planning. It enables network administrators to understand their current level of capacity and performance, which is required to understand new network or application additions. Baselining should be done on at least a quarterly basis to identify capacity and trends.

First, determine what information you want to watch over time. Some examples are as follows:

* CPU utilization
* Memory consumption
* Interface utilization

- Error rate, particularly cyclic redundancy check (CRC) errors
- Multicast traffic
- Broadcast traffic

This information should be collected over a period of time. A 2-week period is the recommended minimum, but measurements for up to 2 months may show normal fluctuations that must be taken into account. This minimum allows the normal "rhythm" of the network traffic to be recorded. The longer the study, the higher the probability that the network's true traffic patterns will become apparent. The samples should be collected frequently enough to accurately capture traffic fluctuations, but not so frequently that the fluctuations skew the data.

After the data is collected, you can either write scripts or purchase software that will collate the data and provide "top-10" type reports to identify problem areas or areas of high activity.

Collect performance and error information from critical switch and router ports, for example, every 15 minutes over 2 weeks. After 2 weeks, analysis should reveal the baseline traffic and error rates for each critical port. These averages will be necessary for the following steps.

This baseline data can be gathered in several different ways:

- Use SNMP polling to gather the necessary data. Use NMS tools to establish baseline percentages of local and cross-campus traffic, and then allocate bandwidth appropriately. There are three types of traffic patterns that should be analyzed:
  - **Local traffic**—Traffic that remains within a small part of the network
  - **Cross-campus traffic**—Traffic that crosses the backbone of the network, travels through a router, or both.
  - **Campus-to-Internet traffic**—Traffic going out to the Internet from the campus and coming in to the campus from the Internet
- Use tools such as TrafficDirector with built-in RMON device capabilities or RMON external probes such as SwitchProbes to gather Ethernet, Token Ring, FDDI, and ATM statistics and histories from switches and routers. Although RMON 1 monitors traffic up to Layer 3, RMON 2 probes can be used to determine baselines at the higher layers of the Open System Interconnection (OSI) model. The baselining performed in a switch environment typically takes place only at the physical and data link layers of the OSI stack.
- Use the CLI via Telnet to gather the statistics. This would have to be done with scripts, such as Expect or Perl. NMS or other commercial collection applications can also be used to collect this data through SNMP.

Define and Set Thresholds

After your network is baselined, you should have an idea of what is "normal behavior" for different segments, particularly the critical ports. The next step is to set RMON thresholds. The RMON alarm and event groups enable you to set thresholds that cause the switch to send an SNMP trap when one of those thresholds is crossed.

To control the generation of alarms, two different threshold values must be defined:

- **Rising-threshold values**—These cause an alarm to be generated when the value of the sampled MIB object increases until it is greater than the rising threshold.

- **Falling-threshold values**—These cause an alarm to be generated when the value of the sample MIB object decreases until it is less than the falling threshold.

These alarms are not generated each time a threshold is crossed. There is a built-in hysteresis mechanism to limit the number of alarms generated. Each threshold acts as a re-arming mechanism to allow the opposite threshold to alarm again. A rising threshold on port utilization is set at 40%, for example, and the falling threshold is set at 25%. If port utilization is normally around 20% and suddenly rises to 50%, and then starts fluctuating between 35% and 50%, an alarm is generated only the first time the utilization crossed the rising threshold. Any subsequent time the utilization crosses from 35% to 50%, no alarm is generated. When utilization returns to around 20%, the falling threshold is crossed once again, causing a falling threshold alarm to be generated, and the rising threshold to be re-armed. This lets you know that the situation that caused the first alarm is over. This mechanism keeps you from receiving redundant traps informing you of a condition of which you are already aware. It also informs you when the incident is over.

Defining Threshold Values

To generate useful alarms you have to define sensible thresholds. Unfortunately, this is not always easy to do. In general, you should set thresholds on the data you have baselined. Set one threshold that will alert you when conditions are problematic and the opposite threshold to alert you when conditions have returned to normal.

Here is a list of guidelines for identifying appropriate thresholds:

- For port utilization, multicast and broadcast traffic levels use the baselines you have collected.

- Error thresholds for CRC errors should be very low—as low as one per hour. You should not have to baseline CRC errors, because the error rate for Ethernet is by specifications very low. Collisions are normal, so they should be baselined and the thresholds set accordingly.

- If you set the thresholds too low, many alarms will be generated. Although you want the operators to be notified of events on the network, you do not want them overwhelmed by the number of messages they receive. In addition, too many alarms can cause operators to just ignore them.

- If you set the thresholds too high, the operator will not notice important events early enough or the operator will have learned about a critical situation long after the trap is generated. It makes little sense, for example, to generate a trap when link utilization reaches 98% because end users will already have experienced a serious degradation in performance before the threshold has been reached.

Adjust Thresholds

Over the next few weeks, continue to observe collected data. By analyzing this data and monitoring the alarm rate, you can determine the effectiveness of your configured thresholds, and adjust them accordingly.

Adjusting the threshold rates is a process that continues as the network continues to grow and network traffic increases and changes.

Reduce Baseline Data Collection

With the introduction of alarms and events, it is no longer necessary to actively poll for traffic statistics because the device can monitor itself through the use of RMON events and alarms. Basic fault polling, such as ICMP or SNMP polling, is still necessary because if a device fails, it is not able to advertise its own failure.

Overall, you can disable RMON history collection as you move into the baseline phase of data collection. This reduces CPU and memory consumption on the switch. However, you will probably want to continue monitoring critical switch trunk ports.

Revisit and Gather Baseline Data on a Regular Basis

You may choose to collect further baseline data after defining your critical ports and alarm thresholds. Baseline data comes in handy if you want to study the network's growth over time and measure the performance of the switched network. Trend analysis and capacity planning come into play when actively baselining or polling your switched network.

Think carefully about the frequency with which you poll. Polling every 5 minutes for many switch ports is excessive, for example. See the sections "Network-Management Protocols" and "Cisco Catalyst Switch Recommendations" for specifics on what to actively monitor and poll on switches and routers, respectively, and how to gather this on-going information. SNMP polling, RMON alarms and events, and/or CLI commands can be used to gather this information.

Cisco Catalyst Switch Recommendations

So far, this chapter has outlined the data you need and the processes you should use to manage the switches in your network. This section provides the details of how to implement that strategy on Catalyst Series switches. Switch network management involves much more than just monitoring, SNMP polling, and MIB gathering. It needs to start from the very first switch design layout through the late deployment stages of the switched network. Several areas need to be addressed relating to managing a switched network: design and configuration recommendations, SNMP polling, SNMP traps, syslog, and RMON. See the CCO Web site for information on configuring network management in a Catalyst 5000.

Design and Configuration Recommendations

Prior to the rollout of switches into the network, the following network design and configuration recommendations need to be considered.

Network Design

Root bridges should be statically defined in the core distribution switches when using spanning tree. Spanning tree should be activated on all trunk ports. Optionally, you may want to activate spanning tree on end-user switch ports as well, in case a loop is mistakenly created in the network. Such a small precaution can prevent your network from grinding to a halt when a loop is created.

Data Acquisition

You can obtain the same data from a switch in a variety of ways. The method you use depends on many factors:

- The size of your network
- Your network-management needs
- The tools you have available to collect and process this data

For very small networks, the simple CLI may suffice. For larger, more complex networks, an NMS with SNMP pollers, SNMP trap processors, and a relational database may be necessary. For most situations, it will end up being a combination of both along with some Perl and Expect scripts to fill in the gaps. The following subsections cover what data to collect, how to get that data, and then how to turn that data into useful information. The following sections describe the data you can obtain from CLI commands and specific SNMP MIB objects.

This section also covers basic fault management through SNMP traps and syslog messages.

Telnet and the CLI

You can collect all the performance data you need for polling and monitoring by initiating a Telnet session to the switch and issuing various CLI commands. Traffic and error statistics for each port as well as critical data on the general health of the switch are available through the CLI. Obviously, this method does not scale for large numbers of switches or for continuous monitoring of any number of switches. It is an effective tool, however, for obtaining real-time data when troubleshooting a problem. It is also a necessary tool to obtain the data that is not available via SNMP. You can use scripting languages such as Expect and Perl to obtain this data on a periodic basis or in response to the detection of some fault condition. The CLI commands to obtain specific data are covered later in this section.

SNMP Polling

The most common method for collecting performance data is to use SNMP. Through SNMP polling, you can collect RMON MIB, MIB-2, and other enterprise-specific data. This data includes traffic statistics for your critical ports. It may also include enterprise-specific data for overall switch performance, such as backplane utilization.

Commercial NMS platforms are common methods of managing a network through SNMP. Typically, you can use the polling services in such a package to periodically poll your switches for specific information and store the data in some type of database. The database may be simple flat files or a relational database management system (DBMS). Generating reports from this data may consist of importing the flat files into a spreadsheet or using the reporting utilities of the DBMS. You may also opt for creating your own SNMP tools using a scripting language such as Perl. Perl is also useful for creating reports from flat files.

Cisco TrafficDirector is an example of additional specialized management packages. They are similar to the more general NMS products mentioned previously, but they specialize in a certain type of data, such as RMON or MIB-2 traffic statistics. These packages generally produce a number of basic reports with options for customizing them for your needs.

After you have the means to gather the data, you must decide what data to poll. More than one MIB object may contain the same data. For example, the RMON *etherStatsTable*, the MIB-2 *ifTable*, and the dot3 MIB all contain objects that provide similar traffic and error statistics on Ethernet ports. Which one is better to poll? We recommend using the *etherStatsTable* for most polling purposes. Many commercial applications already poll the *etherStatsTable* for this data and have ready-made tools for processing the data and generating reports. It is also easy to take advantage of the RMON history collection features to reduce polling overhead. Note that some Catalyst Cisco IOS versions allow the setting of RMON thresholds on objects in the *etherStatsTable* only. Because we want to baseline objects on which we can set RMON thresholds, the *etherStatsTable* is a good first choice. Some traffic statistics that are useful to baseline are total traffic (*etherStatsOctets*), multicast traffic (*etherStatsMulticastPkts*), and broadcast traffic (*etherStatsBroadcastPkts*).

Some error statistics to monitor are error frames (*etherStatsCRCAlignErrors*) and perhaps Ethernet fragments and jabbers (*etherStatsFragments* and *etherStatsJabbers*). Monitoring Ethernet collisions in a switched network is usually only useful on shared segments.

For detailed definitions of the MIB objects you are polling, there is no better source than the MIB document itself. All the MIB documents Cisco devices support are available in the public MIBs area on Cisco's Web site. The "v1" and "v2" directories contain ASN.1 MIBs complete with object definitions in SNMP v1 or SNMP v2 syntax, respectively. Most NMS stations can compile these files directly into a MIB database with no modification. The "oid" and "schema" directories are provided for other NMS stations that require the MIB data in this format. The "oid" directory is also handy for finding the full object identifier (OID) of a particular object if you are writing your own scripts to collect this data. The "support_list" directory is a loose guideline for determining which objects certain devices and Cisco IOS levels support.

After your switched network is installed and configured accordingly, you need to have an NMS station set up to do SNMP polling. SNMP polling for switches is similar to SNMP polling for routers; however, the amount of and type of MIB variables polled for are different. A great number of interface or port MIB variables will not be polled using SNMP, due to the density of the ports on switches and the unknown state of switch ports directly connected to PCs or workstations that may be turned off at any time. SNMP is very useful for monitoring switch and trunk port health. User ports can be managed by relying only on SNMP link up/down traps or by using the built-in RMON capabilities. The switch MIB variables addressed in this discussion come directly from the following MIBs: RFC1213, CISCO-STACK-MIB, ETHERLIKE-MIB, and BRIDGE-MIB.

The following three polling sections are taken directly from the "Guidelines for Polling MIB Variables" as it applies to routers. The same principles can be applied to a switched environment as well, but with different MIB variables.

Before discussing what to poll for, we must first determine what the purpose of polling is. Let's say that there are three major purposes for polling devices: to determine the availability of a device (monitor polling), to determine if an error condition has occurred or is approaching (threshold polling), and to analyze data for trends or performance measurements (performance polling).

Monitor Polling

The aim of monitor polling is to detect when network changes have occurred and to generate an immediate alarm. Monitor polling is to detect "hard errors" such as a device not responding or an interface status change. Any alarm generated by monitor polling should be acted on immediately. If your network management system is monitored on a 24×7 basis, a monitor polling alarm should create a visible and audible alarm on the system, so that the operator can take immediate action. If you do not have your network management system monitored on a 24×7 basis, it is recommended that any monitor polling alarm generate an alarm to the appropriate person, possibly via pager or e-mail.

Monitor polling applications are included with most commercial SNMP platforms and SNMP-based management applications. The purpose of monitor polling applications is to analyze the data points and generate an alarm when necessary.

Threshold Polling

The aim of threshold polling is to determine when escalating error conditions are occurring and take actions before performance is severely impacted. A wide variety of problems surface originally as increased error conditions. These conditions may eventually become a "hard error," or may present themselves as phantom problems that come and go. Threshold polling is a tool to detect these problems.

To implement threshold polling, the first decision is to determine which MIB variables to poll for (MIB variables for switches follow in this section). Users who are starting out with threshold polling may start with the suggested variables that follow, and then add any other applicable MIB variables that are appropriate for their network.

After the threshold MIB variables are decided upon, you must establish baseline values for these variables. This can be done by starting a poll process on the MIB variables for a period of time (1 week, for example). You must then review the data collected. Baselining should be performed during peak traffic patterns to be most representative of unusual conditions. The more static your network is (yearly adds, moves, and changes), the less baselining you need to perform, while the more dynamic your network is (monthly adds, moves, and changes), the more baselining you need to perform. With this data in hand, determine what values would be out of specification. A rule of thumb is to set thresholds 10%–20% higher than the maximum value seen.

The threshold values for any particular MIB variable may be applied uniformly across all switches, or they could be customized for groups of switches that have similar characteristics (for example, core, distribution).

Another decision to be made is what kind of notification is appropriate for threshold violations. Threshold violations are not indications of hard errors, so immediate notification is usually not in order. Logging all threshold values and reviewing on a daily basis is usually the most appropriate means of notification. It is very important that repeated threshold violations be investigated. It can then be determined if a problem has occurred that can be corrected, or if the violations are a result of the threshold values being too low for the circumstances.

Performance Polling

The aim of performance polling is to gather data that can be analyzed over time to determine trends and to aid in capacity planning. As with threshold polling, the determination of what MIB variables to poll for is the first consideration. Later in this section, some suggestions are made on which MIB variables would be most useful for performance polling of switches.

For performance polling, individual data points (raw data) are stored intermittently on the polling machine. Depending on what polling mechanism you are using, the data could be in either a raw format or in a relational database.

To best keep the data manageable, the raw data should periodically be aggregated, and stored in another database or file to be kept for future reporting. The raw data can be kept for a period of time for backup purposes, but eventually this data should be purged and only the aggregate data is kept. The last step in the process is to produce reports from the aggregate data that will be periodically reviewed for trending or capacity planning purposes.

To best describe this process, here's an example of a company's performance polling system:

- Individual MIB variables are grouped together in a series of polling groups. Each group is polled every 5 minutes and the data is stored in a Sybase database according to the name of the poll group. Every morning at 12:01 a.m., the raw data in Sybase is aggregated into minimum, maximum, and averages for each hour and stored in another Sybase database (the user has written SQL programs to accomplish this).

- Every Saturday morning at 1:00 a.m. the individual raw data points are purged from the database for the previous week. On the first day of the month, the hourly min/max/avg data is aggregated into daily min/max/avg data and stored in another database. A series of reports are generated from both the daily and hourly data for review at the Capacity Planning meeting on the first Tuesday of the month. After the reports are produced the data from the hourly database is archived to tape.

For more detailed information on performance monitoring, see the IBM reference book (IBM Red Books) titled *Monitoring Performance In Router Networks*, Document GG24-4157-00.

RMON

As mentioned previously, most Catalyst switches support "mini-RMON," which consists of four basic RMON-1 groups: statistics, history, alarms, and events. For baselining purposes, the *etherStats* group provides a useful range of Layer 2 traffic statistics. You can use the objects in Table 14-3 to get statistics on unicast, multicast, and broadcast traffic as well as a variety of Layer 2 errors. The RMON agent on the switch can be configured to store these samples in the history group. This mechanism enables you to reduce the amount of polling without reducing the sample rate. Using RMON histories can give you more accurate baselines without substantial polling overhead. The more histories you collect, however, the more switch resources you use.

The most powerful part of RMON-1 is the thresholding mechanism provided by the alarm and event groups. RMON thresholding enables you to configure the switch to send an SNMP trap informing you of an anomalous condition. Now that you have identified all your critical ports and used SNMP polling (and maybe RMON histories) to create baselines showing normal traffic activity for those ports, you are ready to set RMON thresholds. Set the thresholds to generate an alarm when there is a large variance from the baseline for that particular port. Then, set the thresholds to notify you when the traffic returns to baseline levels for that port.

The setting of these thresholds is best done using an RMON management package. Properly creating the rows in the alarm and event tables is tedious and complex. Commercial RMON NMS packages such as TrafficDirector incorporate graphical user interfaces (GUIs), which make the setting of RMON thresholds much easier.

Although switches provide only four basic groups of RMON-1, it is important to not forget the rest of RMON-1 and RMON-2. You can get Layer 3 and higher information on your switches using the SPAN port feature and an external RMON probe such as a Cisco SwitchProbe. A SwitchProbe supports RMON-2 and can take a feed from a SPAN port to monitor full RMON data on any given port or a whole VLAN on a particular switch. You can use a SPAN port and a SwitchProbe to capture a packet stream for a particular port (using the packet capture group of RMON-1) and upload the packets for decoding to an RMON management package. You can also use the SPAN port and an external SwitchProbe to give network and application layer statistics on a particular port or VLAN. The SPAN port is SNMP-controllable via the SPAN group in the CISCO-STACK-MIB, so this process is easy to automate. TrafficDirector makes use of these features with its "roving agent" feature.

There are caveats to spanning a whole VLAN. Even if you use a 100-Mbps probe, the entire packet stream from one VLAN or even one 100-Mbps full-duplex port may exceed the bandwidth of the SPAN port. Use care to see that you are not overloading the SPAN port. If the SPAN port is running at full bandwidth continuously, chances are you are losing data.

RMON Memory Constraints

It is important to remember that the primary function of a switch is to switch frames—not to act as a large multiport RMON probe. Therefore, as you are setting up histories and thresholds on multiple ports for every condition imaginable, keep in mind that you are stealing resources the switch could otherwise use for its primary purpose—forwarding network traffic. Also remember the critical port rule: Only poll and set thresholds on the ports which you identified as critical.

RMON memory usage is constant across all switch platforms relating to statistics, histories, alarms, and events. RMON uses what is called a "bucket" to store histories and statistics on the RMON agent (which is the switch in this case). The bucket size is defined on the RMON probe (SwitchProbe) or RMON application (TrafficDirector), and then sent to the switch to be set.

Catalyst 5000 Family

Around 450 KB of code space will be added to the NMP image to support mini-RMON (four RMON groups: statistics, history, alarms, and events). The dynamic memory requirement for RMON varies because it depends on the run-time configuration. Table 14-3 explains the run-time RMON memory usage information for each mini-RMON group.

Table 14-3   *Run-Time RMON Memory Usage*

RMON Group Definition	DRAM Space Used	Notes
Statistics	140 bytes per switched Ethernet/Fast Ethernet port	Per port.
History	3.6 KB for 50 buckets	Each additional bucket uses 56 bytes.
Alarm and Event	2.6 KB per alarm and its corresponding event entries	Per alarm per port.

There is a single pool of DRAM for dynamic allocation. Every feature/process draws from this pool. In Catalyst 5000, Release 3.1 and later, use the **show version** command to see the amount of used and free DRAM. Use the preceding formulas to determine the RMON memory requirements. Saving the RMON-related configuration takes approximately the following memory:

- 10 KB NVRAM of space if the system total NVRAM size is 128 KB
- 20 KB of NVRAM space if the system total NVRAM size is 256 KB or more
- The CPU impact of using RMON collection and alarms in a Cisco switch can best be described as follows:
- **Statistics group**—Only requires CPU cycles when it's processing an SNMP get request for a port's RMON statistics; very minimal impact otherwise, because *etherStats* are collected in hardware.
- **History and alarm/event groups**—Uses a few CPU cycles for each polling interval per port (that is, for every history snapshot and each alarm threshold that it must evaluate). The impact depends on the polling interval and number of ports. The CPU overhead should be minimal with a Sup2 or Sup3 (assuming less than 150 ports and polling intervals of 30 seconds or more).

Syslog Memory Constraints

Configuring syslog on the Catalyst 5000 series switches consumes 1 KB of memory (supported in software version 2.2 and higher) to save the last syslog messages generated.

VLANs and Community String Indexing

Some standard MIBs assume that a particular SNMP entity contains only one instance of the MIB. Therefore, the standard MIB does not have any index that would enable users to directly access a particular instance of the MIB. In these cases, we provide community string indexing to access each instance of the standard MIB. The syntax is *community string@instance number.*

The Catalyst switch includes one instance of the standard BRIDGE-MIB for each VLAN in the switch, for example. If the read-only community string is "public" and the read-write community string is "private," you could use **public@25** to read the BRIDGE-MIB for VLAN 25 and use **private@33** to read and write the BRIDGE-MIB for VLAN 33. Only using the community string **public** or **private** will result in always accessing the BRIDGE-MIB for VLAN 1 (default behavior).

Traps sent from a MIB indexed by a community string also indicate the instance of the MIB to which it corresponds by using community string indexing. An STP *newRoot* trap from the BRIDGE-MIB for VLAN 25, for example, would have a community string of **public@25** in the trap community field, assuming the read-only community string is **public**.

Also note that community string indexing does not affect access to MIBs that have only one instance. Therefore, **public@25** can be used to access RFC1213-MIB at the same time as the BRIDGE-MIB for VLAN 25 is being accessed.

Another example for the Catalyst switch is the SNMP-REPEATER-MIB. To access this MIB for a particular repeater in the Catalyst switch, use *community string@module number/port number.* If the read-only community string is **public**, for example, you can use **public@3/1** to read the SNMP-REPEATER-MIB for the repeater attached to port 1 on module 3.

To determine the available VLANs on a given Catalyst switch, you must query the *vlanTable* MIB group from the CISCO-STACK-MIB using the VLAN ID as index.

Starting with Cat5*xxx* Release 4.1(1), the newRoot and topologyChange traps defined in the BRIDGE-MIB have the vlanIndex appended in their varBind list. This eliminates the need for SNMP platforms and applications to decode the community string within the trap. Here are two examples of the new traps supported:

```
Received SNMPv1 Trap:
Community: public@2
Enterprise: dot1dBridge
Agent-addr: 172.10.17.31
Enterprise Specific trap.
```

```
Enterprise Specific trap: 2      (This is a topologyChange trap)
Time Ticks: 27654316
vtpVlanIndex.1.2 = 2             (This is the VLAN number)
ifName.97 = 4/2                  (This is the interface index)

Received SNMPv1 Trap:
Community: public@3
Enterprise: dot1dBridge
Agent-addr: 172.10.17.31
Enterprise Specific trap.
Enterprise Specific trap: 1      (This is a newRoot trap)
Time Ticks: 27651818
vtpVlanIndex.1.3 = 3             (This is the VLAN number)
```

For a summary of community string indexing, see the CCO Web site.

SNMP Interface Indexing from ifIndex and ifName

One frustrating issue is trying to decipher which port created a certain trap. Knowing that a trap came from ifIndex 100 does not help pinpoint the source of the trap, but knowing that the trap came from port 1/1 is very useful. We use the IF-MIB to map ifIndex to a port number. If you poll the ifXTable for ifName, you can get a correspondence between ifIndex and the actual port. If you received a trap for ifIndex 17, for example, you could poll ifName to find the port, as shown here:

```
$ snmpwalk robotron ifName

ifMIB.ifMIBObjects.ifXTable.ifXEntry.ifName.1 : DISPLAY STRING- (ascii):  sc0
ifMIB.ifMIBObjects.ifXTable.ifXEntry.ifName.2 : DISPLAY STRING- (ascii):  sl0
ifMIB.ifMIBObjects.ifXTable.ifXEntry.ifName.3 : DISPLAY STRING- (ascii):  1/1
ifMIB.ifMIBObjects.ifXTable.ifXEntry.ifName.4 : DISPLAY STRING- (ascii):  1/2
ifMIB.ifMIBObjects.ifXTable.ifXEntry.ifName.5 : DISPLAY STRING- (ascii):  2/1
ifMIB.ifMIBObjects.ifXTable.ifXEntry.ifName.6 : DISPLAY STRING- (ascii):  2/2
ifMIB.ifMIBObjects.ifXTable.ifXEntry.ifName.7 : DISPLAY STRING- (ascii):  2/3
ifMIB.ifMIBObjects.ifXTable.ifXEntry.ifName.8 : DISPLAY STRING- (ascii):  2/4
ifMIB.ifMIBObjects.ifXTable.ifXEntry.ifName.9 : DISPLAY STRING- (ascii):  2/5
ifMIB.ifMIBObjects.ifXTable.ifXEntry.ifName.10 : DISPLAY STRING- (ascii):  2/6
ifMIB.ifMIBObjects.ifXTable.ifXEntry.ifName.11 : DISPLAY STRING- (ascii):  2/7
ifMIB.ifMIBObjects.ifXTable.ifXEntry.ifName.12 : DISPLAY STRING- (ascii):  2/8
ifMIB.ifMIBObjects.ifXTable.ifXEntry.ifName.13 : DISPLAY STRING- (ascii):  2/9
ifMIB.ifMIBObjects.ifXTable.ifXEntry.ifName.14 : DISPLAY STRING- (ascii):  2/10
ifMIB.ifMIBObjects.ifXTable.ifXEntry.ifName.15 : DISPLAY STRING- (ascii):  2/11
ifMIB.ifMIBObjects.ifXTable.ifXEntry.ifName.16 : DISPLAY STRING- (ascii):  2/12
ifMIB.ifMIBObjects.ifXTable.ifXEntry.ifName.17 : DISPLAY STRING- (ascii):  2/13
ifMIB.ifMIBObjects.ifXTable.ifXEntry.ifName.18 : DISPLAY STRING- (ascii):  2/14
ifMIB.ifMIBObjects.ifXTable.ifXEntry.ifName.19 : DISPLAY STRING- (ascii):  2/15
ifMIB.ifMIBObjects.ifXTable.ifXEntry.ifName.20 : DISPLAY STRING- (ascii):  2/16
```

The output of this indicates that port 2/13 generated the trap.

Setting Up SNMP, SPAN, Syslog, and Traps

Use the **set snmp** commands to set all SNMP parameters: community strings, RMON, and other SNMP traps. Table 14-4 explains these commands.

Table 14-4   *IOS SNMP Configuration Commands*

Command	Description
set snmp ?	Provides the syntax to use to set different parameters.
set snmp trap	Enables the different SNMP traps on the switch.
set port trap	Enables or disables link traps on a port-by-port basis. If you have end stations connected to the switch, you should have link traps for your "critical" ports only.
show snmp	Checks the current configuration of SNMP on the switch.
set span	Sets up the source and destination of the SPAN feature. The SPAN feature can also be configured via SNMP using the objects in the *monitorGrp* in the CISCO-STACK-MIB.
set logging	Configures the switch to send its console messages to a syslog server. We recommend using the set logging level command to set the severity level for all facilities to 4, or the "warning" level.

Details of all these set commands for Release 4.2 can be found on the Cisco Web site.

The common tools for fault management include logging SNMP traps (which include the RMON threshold traps) and syslog messages, and then processing the data and reacting appropriately. Most NMS packages provide a trap daemon that receives and logs SNMP traps, and then provides some mechanism for reacting to that trap. Some typical mechanisms used are pop-up messages and audible alarms on the NMS station or the execution of a paging script. More complex reactions may be to execute an Expect script that collects time-critical data to determine the state of the switch immediately following the occurrence of a fault, or perhaps trigger a packet capture from the appropriate port using an external RMON probe. Several such scenarios are described later in this chapter.

Regarding syslog messages, most (if not all) UNIX systems provide a syslog daemon. Commercial and public domain syslog daemons are also available for Win95 and WinNT systems. These daemons usually log all switch messages into a particular file. Then, a Perl script or some other reporting tool can be used to parse the log file into usable information. Cisco Resource Manager has a Syslog Analyzer, for example, which creates reports from syslog messages based on message severity levels or based on the devices generating the messages.

Most commercial NMS products understand standard basic SNMP traps (such as *linkUp* and *linkDown* traps) and RMON thresholds. But for Cisco-specific traps, you must configure the NMS to format the traps so that they are readable and recognizable. The CCO

Web site contains information on formatting traps for HP OpenView Network Node Manager and Tivoli NetView in the trapd.conf file.

Cisco-specific MIBs can be found in Cisco MIBs, such as those listed in Table 14-5.

Table 14-5   *List of SNMP Traps for Cisco Switches*

MIB Document	Specific Traps
CISCO-STACK-MIB	Module traps: • lerAlarmOn • lerAlarmOff • moduleUp • moduleDown Chassis traps: • chassisAlarmOn • chassisAlarmOff IP permit traps: • IpPermitDeniedTrap
BRIDGE-MIB (RFC 1493)	STP traps
RFC 1157	Authentication trap
CISCO-VTP-MIB	VTP traps: • vtpConfigRevNumberError • vtpConfigDigestError • vtpServerDisabled • vtpMtuTooBig • vtpVlanRingNumberConfigConflict • vtpVersionOneDeviceDetected
CISCO-VLAN-MEMBERSHIP-MIB	VLAN Membership Policy Server (VMPS) traps
SNMP-REPEATER-MIB (RFC 1516)	Repeater traps
IF-MIB (RFC 1573)	LinkUp and LinkDown traps for each port

Switch Resource Status

Switch resource status is information needed to validate the overall health of the switch as it pertains to traffic, system, CPU, and memory utilization.

SNMP MIBS

The following variables are useful in determining the backplane utilization of the switch. The same counters are used when displaying the red traffic level indicators on the front of the supervisor card. However, these variables should not be confused with CPU or memory utilization.

The following information is available at the CCO Web site:

- **SysTraffic**—Traffic meter value—for example, the percentage of bandwidth utilization for the previous polling interval.

- **SysTrafficPeak**—Peak traffic meter value since the last time the port counters were cleared or the system started (see *sysClearPortTime*).

- **SysTrafficPeakTime**—The time (in hundredths of a second) since the peak traffic meter value occurred.

- **SysTrafficMeterTable**—Traffic in the system processor and on internal system buses. Only applies to Catalyst 5000 Supervisory III modules.

CLI (Command-Line Interface)

Use the commands described in this section as an additional method of gathering switch resource data.

show biga—Switch Resource Errors (RsrcErrors)

This indicates supervisor queue drops, similar to input queue drops on routers, and shows traffic destined to supervisors, such as bridge protocol data units (BPDUs). This command applies to supervisor engine 1 and 2. The main field of interest in its output is RsrcErrors:

```
switch 5000 (enable) show biga
BIGA Registers:
    cstat:       00  upad :      FFFF  pctrl :      0000  nist :      0000
    sist :     0018  hica :      0000  hicb  :      0000  hicc :        00
    dctrl:     F5FF  dstat:      0000  dctrl2:        80  npim :      00F8
    thead: 101F196C  ttail: 101F196C  ttmph : 101F196C  tptr : 104347E2
    tdsc : 00000500  tlen :      0000  tqsel :        05
    rhead: 101F1220  rtail: 101F1204  rtmph : 101F123C  rptr : 10586C80
    rdsc : 804D0000  rplen: 101F1234  rtlen : 00000000  rlen :      1600
    fltr :     00FF  fc   :        00  Rev   :        04  CFG  : 02020202
BIGA Driver:
    Initializd:     TRUE  SpurusIntr: 00000000  NPIMShadow:      00F8

BIGA Receive:
    RxDone    :     FALSE
    First RBD : 101EF894  Last  RBD : 101F1478
    SoftRHead : 101F1210  SoftRTail : 101F11F4
    FramesRcvd: 04572393  BytesRcvd : 589914384
    QueuedRBDs: 00000256  RsrcErrors: 00000000

BIGA Transmit:
    First TBD : 101F1494  Last  TBD : 101F1B78
```

```
SoftTHead : 101F19D4  SoftTTail : 101F19D4
Free TBDs : 00000064  No TBDs   : 00000000
AcknowErrs: 00000000  HardErrors: 00000000
QueuedPkts: 00000000  XmittedPkt: 11353833
XmittedByt: 909016542 Panic     : 00000000
Frag<=4Byt: 00000306
```

show inband—Switch Resource Errors (RsrcErrors)

This indicates supervisor queue drops, similar to input queue drops on routers, and shows traffic destined to supervisors, such as BPDUs. This command applies to supervisor engine 3. The main field of interest in its output is RsrcErrors:

```
switch 5000 (enable) show inband
Inband Driver:
DriverPtr: A0559F20   Initializd:     TRUE SpurusIntr: 00000000
   RxDone:       FALSE TxDMAWorking:  FALSE RxRecovPtr: 00000000(-1)
   FPGACntl:     004F  Characteristics:0000 LastISRCause:    04

   Transmit:
    First TBD : A055E7A4(0  )  Last  TBD : A055F784(0  )
    TxHead    : A055F5A4(112)  TxTail    : A055F5A4(112)
    AvailTBDs : 00000128       QueuedPkts: 00000000
    XmittedPkt: 07626990       XmittedByt: 581073462
    PanicEnd  : 00000000       PanicNullP: 00000000
    BufLenErrs: 00000000       Len0Errs  : 00000000
    Frag<=4Byt: 00000162       SpursTxInt: 00000000
    No TBDs   : 00000000       NullMbuf  : 00000000

   Receive:
    First RBD : A0559FA4(0  )  Last  RBD : A055E780(511)
    RxHead    : A055AE44(104)  RxTail    : A055AE20(103)
    AvailRBD  : 00000512       RsrcErrors: 00000824
    PanicNullP: 00000000       PanicFakeI: 00000000
    FramesRcvd: 18507368       BytesRcvd : 1676456769
    RuntsRcvd : 00000000       HugeRcvd  : 00000000

GT64010 IntMask: F00F0000  IntCause: 0330E083
GT64010 TX DMA (CH 1):
    Count:       0000  Src  :      0134B062  Dst  :      4ff10056  NRP  :      0
0000000
    Cntl :       15C0
GT64010 RX DMA (CH 2):
    Count:       0680  Src  :      4FF20000  Dst  :      01c3e580  NRP  :      0
0558590
    Cntl :       55C0

PSI (PCI SAGE/PHOENIX Interface) FPGA:
    Control : 004F  TxCount : 0056
    RxDMACmd: 35C0  RxBufSiz: 0680  MaxPkt  : 0680
    IntCause: 0002  IntMask : 0003
```

show mbuf

This output shows the memory used on the NMP. This data should be collected when your initial baseline is performed. You can trend the memory usage on the switch. The "clusters" and "mbufs" fields represent two areas of working memory. The second line of output in this code shows the total number of clusters and mbufs available to the system. The third line shows how many are free at the moment the output is displayed. The fourth line shows the "low-water" mark since the switch was last booted:

```
switch 5000 (enable) show mbuf
MBSTATS:
          mbufs                  10224   clusters        3932
          free mbufs              9946   clfree          3675
          lowest free mbufs       9935   lowest clfree   3665

MALLOC STATS :
Block Size        Free Blocks
   16             1
   48             2
  112             1
  144             1
  208             1
  240             1
  400             1
  496             4

Largest block available : 7510096
Total Memory available  : 7546400
Total Memory used       : 563952
```

ps −c

This command outputs the CPU utilization of the NMP. The last line of output represents the "idle" time. In this example, the switch CPU is 59% busy (41% idle). In that same line of output, "high" and "low" represent "water marks" since the switch was last booted. "Average" shows the amount of idle time since the last boot. The "CPU-Usage" column totals 100% (+/- rounding errors) and indicates how much of the busy CPU time was used by that process. In this example, the Kernel is using 93% of 59%, which is about 49% of the CPU capacity:

```
switch 5000 (enable) ps -c
CPU usage information:
Name             CPU-Usage    Invokations
---------------  -----------  ------------
Kernel           93%          1
SynDiags         0%           1
SynConfig        0%           1
Earl             1%           1
THREAD           0%           1
Console          0%           1
telnetd          0%           1
cdpd             0%           1
cdpdtimer        0%           1
SptTimer         0%           1
SptBpduRx        0%           1
VtpTimer         0%           1
VtpRx            0%           1
DISL_Rx          0%           1
DISL_Timer       0%           1
sptHelper        0%           1
..etc
..etc
System Idle - Current: 41% High: 51% Low: 8% Average: 47%
```

show log

This command shows the status of uptime as well as exceptions. This example displays the output from a switch crash in addition to the standard logging information. Crashes can be caused by hardware or software problems. A "Vector: 007C", as seen here, is a switch bus timeout and is very likely to be a hardware problem. Make sure all cards are properly seated. If the crash keeps occurring, you can remove modules one at a time until the problem stops. Call the TAC to get the module replaced. For software problems (Vector != 007C), call the TAC as well:

```
switch 5000 show log
Network Management Processor (ACTIVE NMP) Log:
  Reset count:    100
  Re-boot History:   Mar 19 1998 16:06:10 3, Mar 11 1998 12:03:03 3
                     Mar 10 1998 04:34:52 3, Mar 08 1998 08:38:30 3
                     Mar 08 1998 08:09:51 3, Mar 08 1998 06:28:31 3
                     Mar 08 1998 05:33:23 3, Mar 02 1998 09:02:13 3
                     Feb 20 1998 05:02:35 3, Feb 20 1998 04:55:45 3
  Bootrom Checksum Failures:       0    UART Failures:                0
  Flash Checksum Failures:         0    Flash Program Failures:       0
  Power Supply 1 Failures:        39    Power Supply 2 Failures:      1
  DRAM Failures:                   0

  Exceptions:                      9
    Last Exception occurred on Feb 18 1998 17:14:18 ...
    Software version = 2.3(1)
    Error Msg:
    PID = 0 Co_-_Ô_?
    PC: 1015A3AC, Status: 2009, Vector: 007C
    sp+00: 20091015 A3AC007C 00000000 00000001
    sp+10: 00400000 AAAA0000 107F0008 1025EEC0
    sp+20: 107FFFAC 1017563E 00000000 107FFFE8
    sp+30: 10175EA0 00000000 000006C7 00000000
    sp+40: 00000000 00000000 00000000 00000000
    sp+50: 00000000 00000000 50000200 00000007
    sp+60: 68000000 00000000 00000000 00000000
    sp+70: 00000000 00000000 00000000 00000000
    sp+80: 00000000 00000000 00000000 00000000
    sp+90: 00000000 00000000 00000000 00000000
    sp+A0: 00000000 00000000 00000000 00000000
    sp+B0: 00000000 00000000 00000000 00000000
    sp+C0: 00000000 00000000 00000000 00000000
    sp+D0: 00000000 00000000 00000000 00000000
    sp+E0: 00000000 00000000 00000000 00000000
    sp+F0: 00000000 4937F8E7 00000000 00000000
    D0: 00000003, D1: 00000010, D2: 00000000, D3: 00000001
    D4: 0040B5C1, D5: AAAAF0E7, D6: 00000003, D7: 10800000
    A0: 68000000, A1: 00000079, A2: 50000200, A3: 50000200
    A4: 103FFFFC, A5: 64000000, A6: 107FFFA0, sp: 107FFF80

NVRAM log:

01. 12/29/97,07:05:17:convert_post_SAC_CiscoMIB:Nvram block 0 unconvertable: 2(1)
02. 12/29/97,07:05:17:convert_post_SAC_CiscoMIB:Nvram block 1 unconvertable: 1(0)
03. 12/29/97,07:05:17:convert_post_SAC_CiscoMIB:Nvram block 5 unconvertable: 1(0)
04. 12/29/97,07:05:17: check_block_and_log:Block 59 has been deallocated: (0x500
191D8)
05. 12/29/97,07:05:17: convert_post_SAC_CiscoMIB:Nvram block 61 unconvertable:
 1(0)

Module 2 Log:
```

```
        Reset Count:    2
        Reset History: Thu Mar 19 1998, 16:09:04
                       Wed Mar 11 1998, 12:05:57

    FCP Flash Checksum Failures:    0   DMP Flash Checksum Failures:    0
    FCP Flash Program Failures:     0   DMP Flash Program Failures:     0
    FCP DRAM Failures:              0   DMP DRAM Failures:              0
    FCP SRAM Failures:              0   DMP SRAM Failures:              0
    FCP Exceptions:                 0   DMP Exceptions:                 0
    Path Test Failures:             0

Module 3 Log:
    Reset Count:    2
    Reset History: Thu Mar 19 1998, 16:08:18
                   Wed Mar 11 1998, 12:05:11


Module 4 Log:
    Reset Count:    1
    Reset History: Mon Mar 23 1998, 10:50:06


Module 5 Log:
    Reset Count:    2
    Reset History: Thu Mar 19 1998, 16:08:18
                   Wed Mar 11 1998, 12:05:11
```

Chassis and Environmental Status

Chassis and environmental status information is useful in determining the physical operational and operational state of the switch chassis and power supplies.

SNMP MIBS

The SNMP MIB objects in this list should be polled if the chassisAlarmOn trap is received.

The following information is available at the CCO Web site:

- **chassisPs1Status**—Status of power supply number 1. If the status is not okay, the value of *chassisPs1TestResult* gives more detailed information about the power supply's failure condition(s).

- **chassisPs2Status**—Status of power supply number 2. If the status is not okay, the value of *chassisPs2TestResult* gives more detailed information about the power supply's failure condition(s).

- **chassisFanStatus**—Status of the chassis fan. If the status is not okay, the value of *chassisFanTestResult* gives more detailed information about the fan's failure condition(s).

- **chassisMinorAlarm**—The chassis minor alarm status.

- **chassisMajorAlarm**—The chassis major alarm status.

- **chassisTempAlarm**—The chassis temperature alarm status.

What is a *minor* and *major* chassis alarm? When the system LED status turns to red, a *chassisMajorAlarm* is generated. When the system LED status turns orange, a *chassisMinorAlarm* is generated. The trap generated will be a *chassisAlarmOn* trap. Included with the traps are variables that indicate whether the trap is from a *chassisTempAlarm*, a *chassisMinorAlarm*, or a *chassisMajorAlarm*. Decoding the trap indicates what kind of alarm generated the trap.

The following conditions cause a major alarm:

- Any voltage failure
- Simultaneous temp and fan failure
- 100% power supply failure (2 out of 2, or 1 out of 1)
- EEPROM failure
- NVRAM failure
- MCP communication failure
- NMP status "unknown"

The following conditions cause a minor alarm:

- Temp alarm
- Fan failure
- Partial power-supply failure (1 out of 2)
- Two power supplies of incompatible types

With either a minor or major alarm, the system status LED on the front panel turns red. This information applies to the Catalyst 5000 series switches. Other products that use the CISCO-STACK-MIB have different definitions of major and minor alarms.

CLI

This section contains samples of the output from the CLI commands that provide chassis and environmental status.

show system

The data output by this command can be collected via SNMP as well:

```
switch 5000 (enable) show system
PS1-Status PS2-Status Fan-Status Temp-Alarm Sys-Status Uptime d,h:m:s Logout
---------- ---------- ---------- ---------- ---------- --------------- ----------
ok         none       ok         off        ok          14,21:20:38    20 min

PS1-Type   PS2-Type   Modem   Baud  Traffic Peak Peak-Time
---------- ---------- ------- ----- ------- ---- -------------------------
WS-C5008A  none       disable 9600  0%      0%   Wed Oct 22 1997, 14:17:56
```

```
System Name              System Location        System Contact
......................   ......................  ......................
switch 5000
```

show test

This command output displays hardware status of switch components. You must specify the module from which you want the test results:

```
switch 5000 show test 1
Environmental Status (. = Pass, F = Fail, U = Unknown)
PS (3.3V):    .    PS (12V): .    PS (24V):   .    PS1: .        PS2: .
Temperature: .    Fan:      .

Module 1 : 2-port 100BaseFX MM Supervisor
Network Management Processor (NMP) Status: (. = Pass, F = Fail, U = Unknown)
ROM:  .    Flash-EEPROM: .    Ser-EEPROM: .    NVRAM: .    MCP Comm: .

EARL Status :
        NewLearnTest:          .
        IndexLearnTest:        .
        DontForwardTest:       .
        MonitorTest:           .
        DontLearn:             .
        FlushPacket:           .
        ConditionalLearn:      .
        EarlLearnDiscard:      .
        EarlTrapTest:          .


LCP Diag Status for Module 1  (. = Pass, F = Fail, N = N/A)
CPU       : .    Sprom   : .    Bootcsum : .    Archsum  : N
RAM       : .    LTL     : .    CBL      : .    DPRAM    : .    SAMBA : N
Saints    : .    Pkt Bufs : .   Repeater : N    FLASH    : N

MII Status:
Ports 1  2
-----------
      N  N

SAINT/SAGE Status :
Ports 1  2  3
--------------
      .  .  .

Packet Buffer Status :
Ports 1  2  3
-------------
      .  .  .

Loopback Status [Reported by Module 1] :
Ports  1  2  3
-------------
       .  .  .
```

Module Status

Module status is the current operational status of switch modules and their components.

SNMP MIBS

The SNMP MIBs in this list should be used for polling if the moduleUp or moduleDown trap is received:

The following information is available at the CCO Web site:

- **moduleStatus**—The operational status of the module. If the status is not okay, the value of *moduleTestResult* gives more information about the module's failure condition(s).

- **moduleAction**—This object, when read, returns one of the following results:
    - other(1)—Module permanently enabled
    - enable(3)—Module currently enabled
    - disable(4)—Module currently disabled

  Setting this object to one of the acceptable values results in the following:
    - other(1)—Gives an error
    - reset(2)—Resets the module's control logic
    - enable(3)—If the module status is configurable, enables the module, else gives error
    - disable(4)—If the module status is configurable, disables the module, else gives error

  Setting this object to any other values results in an error.

- **ModuleStandbyStatus**—Status of a redundant module.

CLI

This section contains samples of the output from CLI commands that provide module status.

show module

This output can be collected via SNMP as well:

```
switch 5000 (enable) show module
Mod Module-Name          Ports Module-Type          Model      Serial-Num Status
--- -------------------- ----- -------------------- ---------- ---------- -------
1                        2     100BaseFX MM Supervis WS-X5006   003292389  ok
3                        12    10BaseFL Ethernet     WS-X5011   003140385  ok
4                        12    10BaseFL Ethernet     WS-X5011   003418318  ok
5                        12    100BaseTX Ethernet    WS-X5113   002203857  ok

Mod MAC-Address(es)                            Hw     Fw     Sw
--- ------------------------------------------ ------ ------ ----------------
1   00-60-47-96-f2-00 thru 00-60-47-96-f5-ff  1.4    2.1    2.1(9)
3   00-60-3e-d1-86-e4 thru 00-60-3e-d1-86-ef  1.3    1.2    2.1(9)
```

```
4    00-60-3e-c9-90-54 thru 00-60-3e-c9-90-5f  1.1    1.2    2.1(9)
    5    00-40-0b-d5-0e-10 thru 00-40-0b-d5-0e-1b  1.4    1.2    2.1(9)
```

show test module number

This output shows the status of hardware self tests on the individual modules:

```
switch 5000 (enable) show test 4

Module 4 : 12-port 10/100BaseTX Ethernet

LCP Diag Status for Module 4  (. = Pass, F = Fail, N = N/A)
  CPU         : .    Sprom    : .    Bootcsum : .    Archsum  : N
  RAM         : .    LTL      : .    CBL      : .    DPRAM    : N    SAMBA : .
  Saints      : .    Pkt Bufs : .    Repeater : N    FLASH    : N

  SAINT/SAGE Status :
  Ports 1  2  3  4  5  6  7  8  9  10 11 12
  -----------------------------------------
        .  .  .  .  .  .  .  .  .  .  .  .

  Packet Buffer Status :
  Ports 1  2  3  4  5  6  7  8  9  10 11 12
  -----------------------------------------
        .  .  .  .  .  .  .  .  .  .  .  .

  Loopback Status [Reported by Module 1] :
  Ports 1  2  3  4  5  6  7  8  9  10 11 12
  -----------------------------------------
        .  .  .  .  .  .  .  .  .  .  .  .

  Channel Status :
  Ports 1  2  3  4  5  6  7  8  9  10 11 12
  -----------------------------------------
        .  .  .  .  .  .  .  .  .  .  .  .
```

Spanning-Tree Topology

These **show** commands and MIB variables enable you to determine the status of spanning tree running in the switch. Refer earlier in the chapter to the sections about spanning tree and SNMP community-based indexing.

SNMP MIBs

NOTE   Refer to the "VLANs and Community String Indexing" section for usage.

The SNMP MIBs in this list should be used for polling if the newRoot or topologyChange trap is received.

The following information is available at the CCO Web site:

- **dot1dStpTimeSinceTopologyChange**—The time (in hundredths of a second) since the last time a topology change was detected by the entity.

- **dot1dStpTopChanges**—The total number of topology changes detected by this bridge since the management entity was last reset or initialized.

- **dot1dStpDesignatedRoot**—The bridge identifier of the root of the spanning tree as determined by the Spanning-Tree Protocol as executed by this node. This value is used as the Root Identifier parameter in all configuration bridge protocol data units (PDUs) originated by this node.

- **dot1dStpRootCost**—The cost of the path to the root as seen from this bridge.

- **dot1dStpRootPort**—The port number of the port which offers the lowest-cost path from this bridge to the root bridge.

CLI

show spantree

The data in this output can be collected via SNMP as well:

```
switch 5000 (enable) show spantree1
VLAN 1
Spanning tree enabled

Designated Root               00-60-47-96-f2-00
Designated Root Priority      32768
Designated Root Cost          0
Designated Root Port          1/0
Root Max Age   20 sec    Hello Time 2  sec   Forward Delay 15 sec

Bridge ID MAC ADDR            00-60-47-96-f2-00
Bridge ID Priority            32768
Bridge Max Age 20 sec    Hello Time 2  sec   Forward Delay 15 sec

Port    Vlan Port-State      Cost  Priority Fast-Start
------- ---- -------------   ----- -------- ----------
1/1     1    not-connected   10    32       disabled
1/2     1    not-connected   10    32       disabled
5/8     1    disabled        10    32       disabled
5/9     1    disabled        10    32       disabled
5/10    1    not-connected   10    32       disabled
```

Bridge Forwarding Database (CAM) Information

The following MIB and **show** command information report the contents and status of the switch-forwarding database. Refer to the "Content-Addressable Memory (CAM) Table" section earlier in this chapter for more details.

To determine to which port a given MAC address is attached on a particular Catalyst switch, you must first search the dot1dTpFdbTable (1.3.6.1.2.1.17.4.3) for the MAC address and determine which bridge port is associated with that port using the object dot1dTpFdbPort (1.3.6.1.2.1.17.4.3.1.2). Remember that you may need to use community string indexing if more than one VLAN is associated with this switch.

Then, convert this bridge index to an ifIndex by using the object dot1dBasePortIfIndex (1.3.6.1.2.1.17.1.4.1.2). You can then use the ifName (1.3.6.1.2.1.31.1.1.1.1) object from the IF-MIB (RFC 1573) to get the slot number/port number of the port with which the MAC address is associated.

NOTE   Ethernet transparent bridging is the only media addressed here.

SNMP MIBs

NOTE   Refer to the "VLANs and Community String Index" section for usage information.

The bridge forwarding database or "CAM table" used by the EARL is available via this MIB object:

- **dot1dTpFdbTable**—A table that contains information about unicast entries for which the bridge has forwarding and/or filtering information. This information is used by the transparent bridging function in determining how to propagate a received frame.

CLI

The following contains sample output from the CLI command that provides information about the CAM table.

show cam count dynamic

This command outputs the total number of CAM entries learned by the switch. This data should be collected when your initial baseline is performed to follow the growth of MAC addresses on an individual switch:

```
switch 5000> show cam count dynamic
Total Matching CAM Entries = 200
```

Port Errors

The MIB variables and Telnet output that follows report errors on individual switch interfaces.

SNMP MIBs

The following information is available at the CCO Web site:

- **dot3StatsAlignmentErrors**—A count of frames received on a particular interface that are not an integral number of octets in length and do not pass the FCS check.

  The count represented by an instance of this object is incremented when the alignmentError status is returned by the MAC service to the logical link control (LLC) (or other MAC user). Received frames for which multiple error conditions obtain are, according to the conventions of IEEE 802.3 Layer Management, counted exclusively according to the error status presented to the LLC.

- **dot3StatsFCSErrors**—A count of frames received on a particular interface that are an integral number of octets in length but do not pass the FCS check.

  The count represented by an instance of this object is incremented when the frameCheckError is returned by the MAC service to the LLC (or other MAC user). Received frames for which multiple error conditions obtain are, according to the conventions of IEEE 802.3 Layer Management, counted exclusively according the error status presented to the LLC.

- **dot3StatsSingleCollisionFrames**—A count of successfully transmitted frames on a particular interface for which transmission is inhibited by exactly one collision.

  A frame that is counted by an instance of this object is also counted by the corresponding instance of either the ifOutUcastPkts, ifOutMulticastPkts, or ifOutBroadcastPkts, and is not counted by the corresponding instance of the dot3StatsMultipleCollisionFrames object.

- **dot3StatsMultipleCollisionFrames**—A count of successfully transmitted frames on a particular interface for which transmission is inhibited by more than one collision.

  A frame that is counted by an instance of this object is also counted by the corresponding instance of either the ifOutUcastPkts, ifOutMulticastPkts, or ifOutBroadcastPkts, and is not counted by the corresponding instance of the dot3StatsSingleCollisionFrames object.

- **dot3StatsLateCollisions**—The number of times that a collision is detected on a particular interface later than 512 bit-times into the transmission of a packet.

Five hundred and twelve bit-times correspond to 51.2 microseconds on a 10-Mbps system. A (late) collision included in a count represented by an instance of this object is considered a (generic) collision for purposes of other collision-related statistics.

- **dot3StatsExcessiveCollisions**—A count of frames for which transmission on a particular interface fails because of excessive collisions.

- **dot3StatsCarrierSenseErrors**—The number of times that the carrier-sense condition was lost or never asserted when attempting to transmit a frame on a particular interface.

The count represented by an instance of this object is incremented (at most) once per transmission attempt, even if the carrier-sense condition fluctuates during a transmission attempt.

- **dot3StatsInternalMacReceiveErrors**—A count of frames for which reception on a particular interface fails because of an internal MAC sublayer receive error. A frame is only counted by an instance of this object if it is counted by the corresponding instance of either the dot3StatsFrameTooLongs object, the dot3StatsAlignmentErrors object, or the dot3StatsFCSErrors object.

The precise meaning of the count represented by an instance of this object is implementation specific. In particular, an instance of this object may represent a count of receive errors on a particular interface that are not otherwise counted.

- **dot3StatsInternalMacTransmitErrors**—A count of frames for which transmission on a particular interface fails because of an internal MAC sublayer transmit error. A frame is counted by an instance of this object only if it is not counted by the corresponding instance of the dot3StatsLateCollisions object, the dot3StatsExcessiveCollisions object, or the dot3StatsCarrierSenseErrors object.

The precise meaning of the count represented by instance of this object is implementation specific. In particular, an instance of this object may represent a count of transmission errors on a particular interface that are not otherwise counted.

- **dot3StatsFrameTooLongs**—A count of frames received on a particular interface that exceed the maximum permitted frame size.

The count represented by an instance of this object is incremented when the frameTooLong status is returned by the MAC service to the LLC (or other MAC user). Received frames for which multiple error conditions obtain are, according to the conventions of IEEE 802.3 Layer Management, counted exclusively according to the error status presented to the LLC.

CLI

The following sample output is from the CLI command that provides error counts by port.

show port counters

Displays error counters on ports such as alignment error, FCS error, collision statistics, and so on:

```
switch 5000 (enable) show port counters
Port  Align-Err  FCS-Err   Xmit-Err  Rcv-Err  UnderSize
----- ---------- --------- --------- -------- ---------
1/1        0          0         0        0         0
1/2        0          0         0        0         0
2/7        0          0         0        0         0
2/8      428        159         0        0       718
2/9        0          0         0        0         0

Port  Single-Col Multi-Coll Late-Coll  Excess-Col Carri-Sen Runts    Giants
----- ---------- ---------- ---------- --------- --------- --------- ---------
1/1        0          0         0         0         0         0        0
1/2        0          0         0         0         0         0        0
2/1     4855        479         0         0         0         0        0
2/2      775         94         0         0         0         0        0
2/3       65          6         0         0         0         0        0
2/4       69          9         0         0         0         0        0
2/5      354         36         0         0         0         0        0
2/6        0          0         0         0         0         0        0
2/7      104         14         0         0         0         0        0
2/8        0          0         0         0         0       621        -
```

Port Utilization, Broadcast, Multicast, and Unicast Ratios

A concern for network managers is the rate of broadcast traffic on switched ports. Because broadcast traffic is forwarded to every port on a VLAN, you can set up a "dummy" port as part of a VLAN and capture the broadcast traffic only. Then you can compare the broadcast rate to the theoretical max rate of the line.

SNMP MIBs

The following are the SNMP MIBs; the information can be found on the CCO Web site:

- **dot1dTpPortInFrames**—The number of frames that have been received by this port from its segment. Note that a frame received on the interface corresponding to this port is counted by this object if and only if it is for a protocol being processed by the local function, including bridge management frames.

- **dot1dTpPortOutFrames**—The number of frames that have been transmitted by this port to its segment. Note that a frame transmitted on the interface corresponding to this port is counted by this object if and only if it is for a protocol being processed by the local bridging function, including bridge management frames.

- **ifInMulticastPkts**—The number of packets, delivered by this sublayer to a higher (sub-)layer, which were addressed to a multicast address at this sublayer. For a MAC layer protocol, this includes both group and functional addresses.

- **ifInBroadcastPkts**—The number of packets, delivered by this sublayer to a higher (sub-)layer, which were addressed to a broadcast address at this sublayer.

- **ifOutMulticastPkts**—The total number of packets that higher-level protocols requested be transmitted, and which were addressed to a multicast address at this sublayer, including those that were discarded or not sent. For a MAC layer protocol, this includes both group and functional addresses.

- **ifOutBroadcastPkts**—The total number of packets that higher-level protocols requested be transmitted, and which were addressed to a broadcast address at this sublayer, including those that were discarded or not sent.

- **etherStatsBroadcastPkts**—The total number of good packets received that were directed to the broadcast address. Note that this does not include multicast packets.

- **etherStatsMulticastPkts**—The total number of good packets received that were directed to a multicast address. Note that this number does not include packets directed to the broadcast address.

CLI

The following sample output is from the CLI command that provides MAC-level statistics.

show mac

Displays MAC-level statistics such as received/transmitted frames, received/transmitted multicast packets, and received/transmitted broadcast packets:

```
switch 5000 (enable) show mac

MAC      Rcv-Frms    Xmit-Frms   Rcv-Multi   Xmit-Multi  Rcv-Broad   Xmit-Broad
-------- ----------- ----------- ----------- ----------- ----------- -----------
 1/1             0           0           0           0           0           0
 1/2             0           0           0           0           0           0
 2/1       7564831     3159859       93795     2982015     7375010       47356
 2/2        839319    11317193       97413     2991019        1560     7417591
 2/3         40744    10516768        5631     3096045           6     7419192
 2/4         40989    10523185        6222     3102759           0     7419195
 2/5         87858    10577397        6179     3114275         920     7418557
 2/6             0           0           0           0           0           0
 2/7         53448    10557561        5632     3124050           0     7419181
 2/8       1646786    31124783     1645159    31124783           0           0
 2/9         45666    10610469        4980     3150899         543     7418652
 2/10        44872    10582388        5723     3158925         118     7417517
 2/11     24269744     8525203    24269742     1104787           0     7420184
```

Client Usage (Utilization Accounting)

Some customers look to their switches to provide them with user or application usage information to determine service-level agreement (SLA) adherence and perhaps for user or group billing. It is recommended that you look above OSI Layer 2 for this type of information. The switches should be treated as hubs or MAUs in this situation, and you should look to higher-level protocols (which will travel over the switch) to collect this type of information.

If you are interested in how available a server is to its users, for instance, you should ping the server periodically (but not so frequently that you congest the server) and measure the response time. Assume that the switch is switching at line speeds unless data indicates that the switch is the bottleneck.

This chapter does not cover Cisco Netflow or multilayer switching.

Response-Time Reporting

Response-time reporting is the response measurement between two points in the network to determine delays in the network. Although most NMS can ping from a central workstation, you can also use the CISCO-PING-MIB to request Cisco routers and certain switches to ping specific devices and report on the round-trip time. You can also retrieve all Cisco neighboring devices of Cisco routers and switches by querying the CISCO-CDP-MIB.

MIB Variables for Switched Environments

This section, including Tables 14-6 and 14-7, identifies typical MIB variables of interest for fault and performance management and explains the most common errors encountered.

Table 14-6   *Overall Switch Performance*

MIB File	MIB Objects
CISCO-STACK-MIB	SysTraffic
	SysTrafficPeak
	SysTrafficPeaktime
	SysConfigChangeTime
	ChassisPs1Status
	ChassisPs2Status
	ChassisFanStatus
	ChassisMinorAlarm
	ChassisMajorAlarm
	ChassisTempAlarm
	ModuleStatus
	ModulePortStatus
	ModuleStandbyStatus

Table 14-7   *Trunk Ports and Critical Server Ports*

MIB File	MIB Objects
From the CISCO-STACK-MIB based on portIndex (cross-referenced to ifIndex through the corresponding portIfIndex field for the corresponding table instance).	PortOperStatus
	VlanPortIslOperStatus (trunk ports only)
	PortAdminSpeed
	PortDuplex
	PortSpantreeFastStart

continues

Table 14-7   *Trunk Ports and Critical Server Ports (Continued)*

MIB File	MIB Objects
From the ETHERLIKE-MIB based on ifIndex.	Dot3StatsAlignmentErrors
	Dot3StatsFCSErrors
	dot3StatsSingleCollisionFrames
	dor3StatsMultipleCollisionFrames
	dot3StatsLateCollisions
	dot3StatsExcessiveCollisions
	dot3StatsInternalMacTransmitErrors
	dot3StatsInternalMacReceiveErrors
	dot3StatsDeferredTransmissions
From the BRIDGE-MIB based on ifIndex.	dot1dStpPortStatus
	dot1dStpPortForwardTransitions
	dot1dTpLearnedEntryDiscards
From RFC1213 based on ifIndex. It is recommended to monitor rates rather than absolute values on these counters.	if.ifInDiscards
	if.ifInErrors
	if.ifOutDiscards
	if.ifOutErrors
	if.ifInOctets
	if.ifOutOctets
	if.ifInUcastPkts
	if.ifInNUcastPkts
	if.ifOutUcastPkts
	if.fOutNUcastPkts
	ip.ipInRequests
	ip.ipInDelivers
	ip.ipForwDatagrams

Alignment Errors

Alignment errors are a count of the number of frames received that don't end with an even number of octets and have a bad CRC.

When packets less than 64 bytes in length not ending on a whole byte boundary (for example, a fragments left from a collision) are received, the Catalyst will increment the *runts counter* and the *align-err counter.*

An alignment error is an indication of a cable problem or a faulty transmitter on the network equipment connected at the other end. This count should be zero or very low. When the cable is first connected, some may occur. Also, if there is a hub connected, collisions between other devices on the hub may cause this.

FCS Errors

FCS error count is the number of frames that were transmitted and received with a bad checksum (CRC value) in the Ethernet frame. These frames are dropped and not propagated on to other ports. A small number of these errors is acceptable, but it could also be an indication of bad cables, NICs, and so on.

Runts

Runt frames are too small for an Ethernet segment.

The behavior of runts is as follows:

- With packets less than 64 bytes in length (for example, fragments left from a collision) with a bad CRC, the Catalyst will increment the *runts counter*.

- With packets less than 64 bytes in length not ending on a whole byte boundary (for example, fragments left from a collision), the Catalyst will increment the *runts counter* AND the *align-err counter*.

- No FCS-err is logged with packets less than 64 bytes in length.

- One case when an FCS-err is logged is when a 63-byte packet is received, and 4 bits are added for the alignment error and 4 bits added for the dribble, resulting in an incorrect packet of 64 bytes in length (see Table 14-8).

A small number of these errors is acceptable, but it could also be an indication of bad cables, NICs, and so on. In a shared Ethernet environment, runt frames are almost always caused by collisions. If runt frames occur when collisions are not high or in a switched Ethernet environment, they are the result of underruns or bad software on a network interface card. Attach a protocol analyzer to try to identify the faulty network interface card by determining the source address of the runt frames.

Table 14-8 describes which counters are incremented under certain error situations.

Table 14-8   *Error Conditions Associated with Error Counters*

Packet Size (Bytes)	Errors	Port Counter Incremented
66-1500		
63		Undersize
63	CRC	Runts
63	align	align-err and runts

continues

Table 14-8   *Error Conditions Associated with Error Counters (Continued)*

Packet Size (Bytes)	Errors	Port Counter Incremented
63	dribble	Undersize
63	symbol	Runts
63	CRC/align	align-err and runts
63	CRC/align/dribble	FCS-err
63	CRC/align/dribble/ symbol	FCS-err
63	align/dribble	FCS-err
62	align/dribble	Runts
54	align/dribble	Runts
44	align/dribble	Runts

The error types are defined as follows:

- **align**—Four extra bits inserted before the CRC.
- **CRC**—Incorrect CRC generated.
- **symbol**—At first octet before the CRC, the first nibble of that byte will generate an invalid symbol.
- **dribble**—Four extra bits appended after the CRC.

Other Objects to Monitor

The basic assumption is that a network needs to be monitored after a steady state is reached. When a subsystem (be it module configuration, port configuration, VLAN configuration, or whatever) reaches its configuration and operations steady state, additional thresholds and correlation scenarios may be enabled for that subsystem.

Simple MIB Objects

This section lists the MIB objects that should be monitored and what information each will provide.

MIB-II

For the purpose of port management, the MIB-II objects listed in Table 14-9 need to be monitored.

Table 14-9   *MIB-II Objects*

MIB Object	Description	Reason to Monitor
ifEntry.ifOperStatus	Basic port operating status.	Detect whether a port transitions from the up state to any other state. It is recommended to monitor this condition for trunk ports only.
ifEntry.ifLastChange	Monitor unexpected port configuration changes.	Detect when administrators make port configuration changes. Normal changes should be ignored.
ifEntry.ifInDiscards ifInErrors ifUnknownProtos ifOutDiscards ifOutErrors	Monitor interface errors.	Detect high rates of such errors. ipOutDiscards may indicate router failures to route valid packets, indicating lack of buffers or other router-specific conditions. ipOutNoRoutes indicates rogue applications or security attacks may generate packets which cannot be routed. Report ifOutQLen when such an error occurs.
ipInHdrErrors ipInAddrErrors ipInUnknownProtos ipInDiscards ipOutDiscards ipOutNoRoutes ipReasmReqds ipReasmFails ipFragFails ipFragCreates	Monitor IP traffic errors.	Detect high rates of such errors.
tcpInErrs tcpOutRsts	Monitor TCP traffic errors.	Detect high rates of such errors.
udpInErrors	Monitor UDP traffic errors.	Detect high rates of such errors.
snmpInBadCommunity Names	Monitor security attacks against the SNMP agent.	Detect major rate increase of this object.

continues

Table 14-9 *MIB-II Objects (Continued)*

MIB Object	Description	Reason to Monitor
snmpInBadVersions snmpInASNParseErrs snmpInTooBigs snmpInNoSuchNames snmpInBadValues snmpOutTooBigs	Monitor NMS requests.	Detect whether an NMS generates too many invalid requests, or valid requests that lead to too many invalid responses.
snmpInGenErrs	Monitor SNMP agent behavior.	Detect whether an SNMP reports too many errors.
snmpEnableAuthenTraps	Monitor that traps are sent as configured.	Detect transitions in this object.

CISCO-STACK-MIB

Several MIB objects in the CISCO-STACK MIB need to be monitored to ensure some correctness.

System and Chassis Groups Table 14-10 lists the MIB objects in the system and chassis group that should be monitored.

Table 14-10 *System and Chassis MIB Objects*

MIB Object	Description	Reason to Monitor
sysIpVlan	VLAN associated with the switch IP address.	Detect whether the switch is in a different VLAN than expected. This is useful to detect whether management traffic may be colliding with end-user traffic, if they are supposed to run in different VLANs.
sysClearPortTime	Time in hundredth of a second since port counters were cleared. Writing a zero to this object clears all port counters.	Any discontinuity (except rollover) of this counter indicates the clearing of counters, which must be detected because it will affect other baseline and monitoring activities.
sysEnableChassis Traps	Allows chassisAlarmOn and chassisAlarmOff traps to be generated.	Avoid disabling chassis traps unknowingly.
sysEnableModule Traps	Allows moduleUp and moduleDown traps to be generated.	Avoid disabling chassis traps unknowingly.

Table 14-10   *System and Chassis MIB Objects (Continued)*

MIB Object	Description	Reason to Monitor
sysEnableBridge Traps	Allows newRoot and topologyChange traps to be generated.	Avoid disabling STP traps unknowingly.
sysEnableRepeater Traps	Allows RFC1516 rptrHealth, rptrGroupChange and rptrResetEvent traps to be generated.	Avoid disabling repeater traps unknowingly.
sysEnableIpPermit Traps	Allows ipPermitDeniedTrap traps to be generated.	Avoid disabling IP permit traps unknowingly.
sysEnableConfig Traps	Allows sysConfigChangeTrap traps to be generated.	Detect when switch configuration is modified. Serves a similar purpose as SYS-5-CONFIG× syslog messages. Collect sysConfigChangeTime to attach in notification.
sysConfigChange Time	Time since the switch configuration was last changed.	Detect when this object presents a discontinuity (except rollover) to track configuration changes.
sysEnableEntity Trap	Allows entConfigChange traps to be generated.	Detect when a hardware or software change occurs. This trap may also be used to trigger a new inventory of the device (moduleTable) to determine the difference in configuration.
sysEnableStpxTrap	Allows stpxInconsistencyUpdate (from the CISCO-STP-EXTENSIONS-MIB) traps to be generated.	Detect when an UplinkFast transition from blocking to forwarding occurred. Ensure that the stpxUplinkFastEnabled flag (from the CISCO-STP-EXTENSIONS-MIB) is enabled when testing for this condition.
chassisPs1Status	Status of power-supply 1.	Detect when a problem develops with power-supply 1. When a fault is detected, collect chassisPs1TestResult to further inform operator.
chassisPs2Status	Status of power-supply 2.	Detect when a problem develops with power-supply 2. When a fault is detected, collect chassisPs2TestResult to further inform operator.

continues

Table 14-10   *System and Chassis MIB Objects (Continued)*

MIB Object	Description	Reason to Monitor
chassisFanStatus	Status of chassis fan.	Detect when a problem develops with the chassis fan. When a fault is detected, collect chassisFanTestResult to further inform operator.
chassisMinorAlarm	Chassis minor alarm status.	Detect minor alarms when this object transitions between off and on. Included in the chassisAlarmOn trap.
chassisMajorAlarm	Chassis major alarm status.	Detect major alarms when this object transitions between off and on. Included in the chassisAlarmOn trap.
chassisTempAlarm	Chassis temperature alarm	Detect major alarms when this object transitions between off, on, and critical. Included in the chassisAlarmOn trap.

Module Conditions   Table 14-11 lists the MIB objects for modules (line cards) that should be monitored.

Table 14-11   *Module MIB Objects*

MIB Object	Description	Reason to Monitor
moduleEntry.moduleSerialNumber moduleEntry.moduleSwVersion	Uniquely identifies a module by its serial number and software version	Detect when any of these objects change.
moduleEntry.moduleStatus	Monitor module status.	Detect when this object is not ok(2), assuming *moduleEntry.moduleStandbyStatus* is *active(2)*.
moduleEntry.moduleStandbyStatus	Monitor whether a supervisor module is in active or standby mode.	Detect when a supervisor switchover occurs. A supervisor module is identified by its *moduleEntry.moduleType* being one of a set of valid types. (See MIB for more information.)

Port Conditions   Table 14-12 lists the MIB objects for ports that should be monitored.

Table 14-12   *Port MIB Objects*

MIB Object	Description	Reason to Monitor
portEntry.portDuplex	Indicates whether port is operating in half or full duplex.	Detect when a duplex change occurs. Detect when its value is disagree(3), which indicates a duplex mismatch. Notification may be ignored if transition was part of normal operation.
portEntry.portSpantreeFastStart	Indicates whether port transitions immediately to forwarding state.	Detect when this object transitions from enabled to disabled or vice versa. Notification may be ignored if transition was part of normal operation.
portEntry.portLinkFaultStatus	Monitor gigabit Ethernet ports.	Detect when this object transitions from a noFault status.
moduleEntry.modulePortStatus	Monitor module and port status. (This object offers the capability to verify all ports in the module in a single SNMP query.)	Detect when this object changes. When it changes, sort out whether it applies to the module status or a port status change. If it is a port status change, report which port changed status. Report ifOperStatus and ifAdminStatus using its corresponding portEntry.portIfIndex to index into the ifTable.
portEntry.portOperStatus	Monitor port failures. This function would be performed if the previous condition did not apply to all ports, but rather only to specific ports.	Detect when this object is not ok(2), assuming it is not on a Sup module in standby mode. Report ifOperStatus and ifAdminStatus using portEntry.portIfIndex to index into the ifTable.
portEntry.portLinkFaultStatus	Monitor gigabit links.	Detect when this object is not noFault(1) or transitions to any other state.

Trunk Conditions   Table 14-13 lists the MIB objects for trunks that should be monitored.

Table 14-13   *Trunk MIB Objects*

MIB Object	Description	Reason to Monitor
vlanPortEntry.vlan PortIslAdminStatus	Monitor trunks are configured as trunks.	Detect when a trunk fails to operate.
		For the ports known (assuming predefined port configuration) to be trunk ports between switches as defined by portEntry.portModuleIndex and portEntry.portIndex, read their corresponding portEntry.portIfIndex and use that value to index into the ifTable to verify their ifEntry.ifAdminStatus = up and ifEntry.ifOperStatus = up.
		For those very same ports, use portModuleIndex and portIndex to index into the vlanPortEntry table to verify their vlanPortIslAdminStatus = trunking.

VLAN Conditions   Table 14-14 lists the MIB objects for VLANs that should be monitored.

Table 14-14   *VLAN MIB Objects*

MIB Object	Description	Reason to Monitor
vlanEntry.vlanSpnTreeEnable	Monitor spanning-tree enabling per VLAN.	Detect any change in VLAN spanning-tree configuration.
vlanEntry.vlanPortVlan	Monitor when a port is moved to a different VLAN, for security and traffic-engineering reasons.	Monitor the VLAN membership of each port. Report vlanPortModule and vlanPort in the notification.
vlanEntry.vlanPortIslOperStatus	Monitor trunk ports.	For every port in trunking mode, detect when this object transitions to notTrunking mode, and vice versa. Report vlanPortModule and vlanPort in the notification.
vlanEntry.vlanPortOperStatus	Monitor VLAN status on ports.	Assuming this condition applies to all ports in active mode, detect when this object transitions to another state. Report the corresponding vlanPortModule and vlanPort in the notification.

EtherChannel Conditions   Table 14-15 lists the MIB objects for EtherChannel that should be monitored.

Table 14-15   *EtherChannel MIB Objects*

MIB Object	Description	Reason to Monitor
portChannelEntry.portChanelPorts	Monitor ports assigned to a single EtherChannel.	Detect whether ports are added or removed from an EtherChannel. Report portChannelModuleIndex, portChannelPortIndex, and portChannelIfIndex in the operator notification.
portChannelOperStatus	Monitor status of EtherChannel ports.	Detect status transitions. Report portChannelModuleIndex, portChannelPortIndex, and portChannelIfIndex in the operator notification.
portChannelNeighbourDeviceId portChannelNeighbourPortId	Monitor if the other end of the EtherChannel is modified.	Detect value changes in these objects. Report portChannelModuleIndex, portChannelPortIndex, and portChannelIfIndex in the operator notification.

RSM Conditions   Table 14-16 lists the MIB objects for the RSM that should be monitored.

Table 14-16   *RSM MIB Objects*

MIB Object	Description	Reason to Monitor
moduleIpAddress	Monitor RSM routes.	For wsx5302 and wsx5304 modules (for example, RSM modules), read its moduleIPAddress. Then, use that IP address to read MIB-II information. Apply rules defined earlier for MIB-II.

Miscellaneous Conditions monitored.

Table 14-17 lists general MIB objects that should be

Table 14-17 *Miscellaneous MIB Objects*

MIB Object	Description	Reason to Monitor
tftpHost tftpFile tftpModule	Monitor when new images may be loaded.	For each tftpModule that is configured in the switch, ensure that the correct combination of these three MIB objects is correct (that is, as expected). Notify operator if any inconsistencies are detected.
tftpResult	Monitor tftp transfers.	Detect whether this object is not successful. Inform operator if this object is inProgress. Alert operator for all other values of this object.
brouter scalar objects in the brouter group	Monitor brouter configuration. This group applies to FDDI.	Detect whether any changes of the brouter configuration. Applicable to FDDI interfaces only.
brouterPortEntry.brouterPort BridgeVlan	Monitor brouter port VLAN membership.	Detect when a port is placed in a different VLAN. Applicable to FDDI interfaces only.
mcastRouterEntry.mcastRouter OperStatus mcastEnableCgmp mcastEnableIgmp	Monitor multicast is enabled on router.	Detect whether any port changes status or enabled characteristics.
dnsGrp.dnsenable	Monitor DNS configuration.	Detect whether DNS transitions to a different state. Dump the dnsServerTable with the notification.
dnsServerEntry.dnsServerType	Monitor DNS server entries.	Detect whether any entry transitions to a different type. Generate a critical alert if an entry is removed.
syslogServerEntry.syslogHost Enable	Monitor switch syslog configuration.	Detect whether syslog messages are no longer sent to the correct hosts.
syslogServerEntry	Monitor switch syslog configuration.	Detect whether any entry is removed.

Table 14-17   *Miscellaneous MIB Objects (Continued)*

MIB Object	Description	Reason to Monitor
syslogMessageControlEntry.sys logMessageFacility syslogMessageSeverity	Monitor switch syslog configuration.	Detect whether any facility is logged with a lower severity (meaning more syslog messages) or higher severity (meaning fewer syslog messages).
tacacsGrp.tacacsLogin Authentication tacacsEnableAuthentication tacacsLocalLoginAuthentication tacacsLocalEnableAuthentication tacacsDirectedRequest	Monitor TACACS configuration. Only applicable if TACACS is used in the switch.	Detect any transition changes of these objects, indicating some enabled or disabled TACACS features.
ipPermitEnable	Monitor whether remote Telnet is allowed into the switch.	Detect any transition change, indicating either loss of remote Telnet access, or security hole, if not part of an authorized configuration change.
ipPermitListEntry	Monitor allowed Telnets into the switch.	Detect whether entries are added or removed. Report the ipPermitAddress to the operator.
ipPermitDeniedListEntry	Monitor denied accesses into the switch.	Detect whether entries are added in this table. Report ipPermitDeniedAddress, ipPermitDeniedAccess, and ipPermitDeniedTime to the operator.

Further Correlation   The event-correlation scenarios in this section can be developed for a Catalyst 5000 switch.

Scenario 1—Detect that all modules came up, as expected. This scenario requires knowing how many modules exist in the switch. Otherwise, the number of modules can be extracted from *chassisGrp.chassisNumSlots*.

After a switch restarts (SYS-5: system reset) or a *coldStart* trap is received, verify that all expected modules are back online, through SYS-5: Module x is online *syslog* message, where x is the module index. An alternative means to detect this situation is to process *sysConfigChangeTrap* traps (with *varBind* containing the module index). Correlate the polling and trap to avoid duplicate notifications to the operator. Include in the notification to the operator, the value of the corresponding *moduleEntry*, given the received module index.

An alternative is to monitor *chassisSlotConfig* value to detect whether the value ever changes.

Scenario 2—Sort out minor from major power-supply faults.

Generate a minor or major notification to operator depending on whether a power-supply fault is minor or major (as per the *chassisPs1Status* or *statusPs2Status* MIB objects).

Scenario 3—Correlate chassis alarm traps with MIB object polling for status change.

Correlate any *chassisTempAlarm*, *chassisMinorAlarm*, or *chassisMajorAlarm* status change with a *chassisAlarmOn* trap to ensure that only one notification is sent to the operator for the same problem, depending on the new value of one of these objects. Raise, escalate, or clear the alarm accordingly.

Ensure that the *sysEnableChassisTraps* object is set to enabled for this scenario to be working.

Scenario 4—Monitor supervisory modules.

For all modules whose *moduleType* corresponds to a supervisory module (value = 23, 38 through 42, 57, 78, or 300), perform the following periodic checks. In operator notifications, include *moduleName*, *moduleModel*, *moduleHwVersion*, *moduleFwVersion*, and *moduleSwVersion*.

Monitor their status with *moduleStatus* and generate an alarm corresponding to the severity of the status field. Add the *moduleTestResult* in the operator notification.

Detect whether the supervisory firmware version is correct, by verifying that the *moduleHwVersion*, *moduleFwVersion*, and *moduleSwVersion* fields are what they are supposed to be. If the correlation engine cannot compare strings, the MIB objects *moduleHwHiVersion*, *moduleHwLoVersion*, *moduleFwHiVersion*, *moduleFwLoVersion*, *moduleSwHiVersion*, and *moduleSwLoVersion* are what they are supposed to be.

Detect when a supervisor card goes from active to standby status or vice versa by monitoring the *moduleStandbyStatus* object. Detect also when this object is not *active* or *standby*.

From all supervisory modules installed (as defined by *moduleType*), ensure that one of them is active (*moduleStandbyStatus* is *active*) and all others are in *standby* mode.

Scenario 5—Monitor ports in supervisory cards.

For all modules whose *moduleType* corresponds to a supervisory module (value = 23, 38 through 42, 57, 78, or 300), perform the following periodic checks on the ports whose *portModuleIndex* (in the *portTable*) cross-checks with a supervisory module index (in the *moduleTable*). In operator notifications, include *moduleName* and *moduleModel*, *moduleHwVersion*, *moduleFwVersion*, and *moduleSwVersion*.

Monitor *modulePortStatus* (decode the octet string as specified in the MIB). Report any status change.

Verify that when a module's *moduleStandbyStatus* is *active(2)*, the ports on that module have the correct status if they are used, by checking the *portOperStatus* field in the *portTable*. Note that a future Catalyst 5000 release will make ports active even on standby supervisory cards, which will affect this scenario.

Scenario 6—Monitor port flow control.

For each port in the *portTable*, detect discrepancies between the following:

- portAdminRxFlowControl and portOperRxFlowControl
- portAdminTxFlowControl and portOperTxFlowControl

Scenario 7—Verify links are connected to the correct port on the other switches.

Based on Cisco's CDP MIB:

Verify every port known to be *trunking* (given the predefined *portEntry.portModuleIndex* and *portEntry.portIndex*) on a switch is configured with CDP—for example, *cdpInterfaceEntry.cdpInterfaceEnable* = true where cdpInterface.*cdpInterfaceIfIndex* matches *portEntry.portIfIndex*.

For the same ports identified in the preceding step, verify *cdpCacheEntry* entries with the following:

- cdpCacheEntry.cdpCacheIfIndex = portEntry.portIfIndex (given the pre-defined portEntry.portModuleIndex and portEntry.portIndex)

    and

- cdpCacheEntry.cdpCacheDeviceIndex = 1..N

The corresponding *cdpCacheEntry.cdpCacheDeviceId* and *cdpCacheEntry.cdpCacheDevicePort* are what they are expected to be.

Scenario 8—For each VLAN in this switch, do the following:

- Verify trunk ports expected to be configured in that VLAN exist. If a port exists:
    - Verify they are configured as ISL.
    - Verify the port is configured for static VLAN (assumption in this scenario).
    - Verify STP is enabled on the port.
    - Retrieve its STP state and report differences with previous known state.

- Verify that ports with vlanPortEntry.vlanPortIslOperStatus set to trunking(1) have their corresponding *vlanPortEntry.vlanPortIslAdminStatus* set to *on(1)* or *noNegotiate(5)*.

For each port in the preceding step, do the following:

- Verify their vlanPortEntry.vlanPortAdminStatus is set to static.

- Search the vlanTable for entries whose vlanEntry.vlanIfIndex matches the predefined module/port for trunks, and verify their vlanEntry.vlanSpantreeEnable = enabled(1).

- Use the corresponding portEntry.portCrossIndex to index into RFC1493.dot1dStpPortEntry (where portEntry.portCrossIndex = RFC1493.dot1dStpPortEntry.dot1dStpPort) to retrieve RFC1493.dot1dStpPortEntry. dot1dStpPortState and report any state change.

Cisco Router Recommendations

This section provides information on network management for Cisco routers. See the CCO Web site for more information on *monitoring the router and network* and their *performance*.

Fault Management

The main objective of fault management is to detect problems and notify users as early as possible so that actions can be taken before any performance degradation occurs. This discussion first examines the functions of fault management, and then focuses on different options for implementation.

The following lists the main functions of fault management:

- Monitoring network status
- Problem detection and notification
- Problem diagnosis and service restoration

Monitoring Network Status

The ability to detect problems quickly in any network is critical. Network operations personnel can rely on a graphical network map to display the operational states of critical network elements such as routers and switches. Most commercial network management can perform discovery of network devices. Each network device is represented by a graphical element on the management platform's console. Different colors on the graphical elements represent the current operational status of network devices. These network-management platforms can also receive and display events generated from network devices.

Network devices can be configured to send notifications to network-management platforms. Upon receiving the notifications, the graphical element representing the network device changes to a different color, depending on the severity of the notification received.

Problem Detection and Notification

There are a few ways to detect faults on a network consisting of Cisco routers and switches. The most common ones are via syslog messages, SNMP/traps, and RMON. Cisco devices are capable of sending syslog messages to a syslog server. Syslog messages are system messages from routers/switches describing different conditions on a device. SNMP traps forwarded by devices are useful to notify faulty conditions, such as if an interface goes up/down.

Not all syslog and trap messages indicate faulty conditions on a device. Some messages are informational messages and do not require any action from the user. The amount of syslog and trap messages sent by a network device can be limited by specific commands on the configuration file.

Syslog Messages

Syslog messages from routers and switches can be directed at single or multiple syslog servers. The devices can be configured to send only certain syslog messages. By limiting the amount of syslog messages to be generated by a device, a user can concentrate on specific aspects of network operations. As an example, the following syslog message will appear when an interface on a router goes down:

```
%LINEPROTO-5-UPDOWN: Line protocol on Interface Ethernet1, changed state to down
```

Syslog messages from routers and switches can be collected from any UNIX-type syslog daemon. These messages can then be viewed and reports can be generated, or actions be taken.

SNMP

Cisco devices configured with SNMP can be polled for various information. In addition, the devices can send traps to a management station when specific conditions occur. By configuring network devices to send SNMP traps, conditions of interest can be detected quickly. A user can quickly determine the operational status of all interfaces in a router via SNMP, for example, without having to input the regular CLI commands. Table 14-18 contains a sample of the information returned via SNMP.

Table 14-18   *Status of Network Interfaces via SNMP*

Index	Description	AdminStatus	OperStatus
1	Ethernet0	Up	Up
2	Ethernet1	Up	Up
3	FastEthernet0	Up	Up
4	Fddi0	Up	Up
5	Tunnel0	Up	Down

The CLI command to display interface status is as follows:

```
gateway> show interface ethernet 0

Ethernet0 is up, line protocol is up  (OperStatus)
Hardware is Lance, address is 0000.0c38.1669 (bia 0000.0c38.1669)
Internet address is 172.16.97.1/24
MTU 1500 bytes, BW 10000 Kbit, DLY 1000 usec, rely 255/255, load 1/255
Encapsulation ARPA, loopback not set, keepalive set (10 sec)
ARP type: ARPA, ARP Timeout 04:00:00
Last input 00:00:00, output 00:00:00, output hang never
```

In addition to standard MIBs, Cisco routers and switches support a variety of MIBs specific to Cisco devices. These specific devices enable you to gather operational data from each device. The following is a partial list of Cisco-specific MIBs:

- **Technology specific**—ISDN, LANE, CIP, DLSW+, Frame Relay, ATM, and so on.

- **Router specific**—Memory pool, chassis, CPU, flash memory, and so on.

- **Switch specific**—VLAN, STACK, VTP, VMPS, CDP, and so on.

Most of the MIB files also define SNMP traps. Each trap definition lists the MIB objects included in the trap PDU and the specific conditions when it is generated. Table 14-19 lists, by category, the SNMP traps defined in router MIB files.

Table 14-19   *List of SNMP Traps for Cisco Routers*

MIB File	Supported Traps
Router Internals	
CISCO-FLASH	ciscoFlashCopyCompletionTrap
	ciscoFlashPartitioningCompletionTrap
	ciscoFlashMiscOpCompletionTrap
	ciscoFlashDeviceChangeTrap
CISCO-ACCESS-ENVMON	caemTemperatureNotification

Table 14-19   *List of SNMP Traps for Cisco Routers (Continued)*

MIB File	Supported Traps
CISCO-ENVMON	ciscoEnvMonShutdownNotification
	ciscoEnvMonVoltageNotification
	ciscoEnvMonTemperatureNotification
	ciscoEnvMonFanNotification
	ciscoEnvMonRedundantSupplyNotification
CISCO-CONFIG-MAN	ciscoConfigManEvent
SNA	
CISCO-RSRB	rsrbPeerStateChangeNotification
CISCO-DLSW	ciscoDlswTrapTConnPartnerReject
	ciscoDlswTrapTConnProtViolation
	ciscoDlswTrapTConnUp
	ciscoDlswTrapTConnDown
	ciscoDlswTrapCircuitUp
	ciscoDlswTrapCircuitDown
CISCO-CHANNEL	cipCardLinkFailure
	cipCardDtrBrdLinkFailure
CISCO-DSPU	newdspuPuStateChangeTrap
	newdspuPuActivationFailureTrap
	newdspuLuStateChangeTrap
	dspuLuActivationFailureTrap
	dspuSapStateChangeTrap
CISCO-CIPCSNA	cipCsnaOpenDuplicateSapFailure
	cipCsnaLlc2ConnectionLimitExceeded
CISCO-BSTUN	bstunPeerStateChangeNotification
CISCO-STUN	stunPeerStateChangeNotification
CISCO-SNA-LLC	llcCcStatusChange
CISCO-SDLLC	convSdllcPeerStateChangeNotification
ISDN	
CISCO-ISDN	demandNbrCallInformation
	demandNbrCallDetails

continues

Table 14-19 *List of SNMP Traps for Cisco Routers (Continued)*

MIB File	Supported Traps
FRAME RELAY	
RFC 1315 (Frame Relay)	frDLCIStatusChange
X.25	
RFC 1382 (X.25)	x25Restart
	x25Reset

RMON

The preceding section showed how SNMP traps can provide alerts to a management station. This reactive approach is useful for informing network operators after a problem has occurred. A more proactive approach, however, would be to inform the operators before a potential problem hits the device. For example, performance will become an issue when CPU utilization on a router hits a high value. The regular approach of polling the router using SNMP to find out its utilization could miss the event depending on the polling interval. By utilizing RMON support on Cisco devices, they can be configured to monitor CPU utilization and only send an alert when a threshold is reached (that is, CPU utilization hits 90).

Figure 14-2 shows how RMON can be used to monitor CPU utilization. The device will sample the value of CPU utilization at predefined intervals. If the value hits Threshold 1, either an event can be generated to inform the user or an entry is logged in the router's retrievable RMON table. Threshold 2 is set to reactivate the monitoring when CPU utilization hits that value. RMON eliminates the regular polling from a management console, and reduces SNMP network traffic.

Figure 14-2 *Setting Thresholds for CPU Utilization Using RMON*

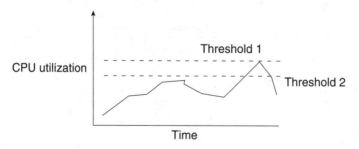

Other statistics that can be monitored using RMON include input/output drops, buffer failures, internal temperatures, number of Frame Relay BECN/FECN packets, and so on.

Problem Diagnosis and Service Restoration

Events observed at the management console need to be diagnosed to determine the severity of a problem and the necessary action to correct the problem. With syslog messages, the severity and description of the problems can be determined quickly because of the message verbosity. Corrective actions can be taken after reviewing the nature of the problem.

System Internals

The syslog messages in Table 14-20 have been identified as being conditions that you may want to monitor. The list is not an exhaustive list; it addresses system-related messages only. It does not address syslog messages for routing protocols and specific network interfaces such as X.25, ISDN, Frame Relay, and so on.

Table 14-20   *Syslog Messages to Monitor*

Syslog Message	Description	Reason to Monitor
%SYS-4-SNMP_HOSTCONFIGSET : SNMP hostConfigSet request. Loading configuration from ... %SYS-4-SNMP_NETCONFIGSET: SNMP netConfigSet request. Loading configuration from ...	These messages indicate the router is loading a new configuration.	These messages may indicate a legitimate condition initiated by a network operator or a router software/ hardware problem that caused the router to reload its configuration.
%IP-4-DUPADDR	This message indicates that the router detected a duplicate IP address.	This condition may seriously affect your network if the duplicate IP address relates to a router or server.
%IPRT-3-NOMEMORY	This message reports a shortage of memory in the router.	Low memory conditions are critical to monitor because they may severely affect router operations.
%SYS-...	These messages are system messages on router internals.	Select the messages of interest to your environment.

Environmental Monitor

Certain models of Cisco routers can perform environmental monitoring to track the voltage and temperature status. Sensors on the card periodically obtain measurements on the chassis and check whether they are within specified ranges. Warning messages are displayed on the console for out-of-range measurements.

The environmental status can be accessed via SNMP from routers supporting the following MIBs: OLD-CISCO-ENV-MIB, CISCO-ENVMON-MIB, or CISCO-ACCESS-ENVMON-MIB. Objects defined on the MIB files can return similar information provided by CLI commands.

In Table 14-21, the voltage readings are obtained from objects defined in the CISCO-ENVMON-MIB. The values returned correspond to those from the IOS CLI *show environmental* command. In addition to providing SNMP objects for monitoring temperature and voltage, CISCO-ENVMON-MIB and CISCO-ACCESS-ENVMON-MIB also have traps defined. These traps are sent to a management console when the measurements are out of the normal range. Refer to the "Fault Management" section earlier in this chapter for additional information regarding supported traps.

Table 14-21   *Voltage Status Table*

Description	Value	Low	High	LastShutdown	State
+12 Voltage	12308	10904	13384	12308	Normal
+5 Voltage	5171	4606	5698	5171	Normal
−12 Voltage	−12073	−10146	−13859	−12073	Normal
+24 Voltage	24247	20377	27646	24247	Normal
2.5 Reference	2490	1250	3714	0	Normal

Table 14-22 lists environment-related syslog messages.

Table 14-22   *Environmental Syslog Messages*

Syslog Message	Description	Reason to Monitor
%ENV-x, %ENVM-x, %CI-3-BLOWER, %CI-1-BLOWSHUT, %CI-2-ENVCRIT, %CI-4-ENVWARN, %SYS-1-OVERTEMP	These messages signal environmental problems with the fan and temperature inside the router.	Any of these messages may be an indication of an imminent router failure.
%CI-3-PSFAIL	These messages signal system problems such as a power-supply failure.	All these messages should be considered critical.

Performance Management

Performance management is a functional area that deals with various aspects of network performance. Performance of a network can be measured by taking a measurement of response time, line utilization, throughput, and so on. A baseline can be established as a comparison for subsequent performance measurements. Performance level can be measured to determine whether it is in line with the metrics defined in service-level agreements. This section briefly discusses several aspects of performance management in general. The main objective is to demonstrate how router performance measurements can be taken and viewed using SNMP.

The tasks involved in performance management are as follows:

1 Establishing a baseline of network performance

2 Defining service-level agreement and metrics

3 Performance monitoring and measurement

4 Setting thresholds and exception reporting

5 Analysis and tuning

Establishing a Baseline of Network Performance

Obtaining a baseline of network performance involves taking samples of network statistics over an extended period of time. The baseline data can be collected using standalone probes attached to a LAN segment or WAN link. The data is used to determine a *normal* traffic pattern in the network. Additional measurements on network performance can be compared against the baseline to determine whether they are within the normal pattern.

Defining Service-Level Agreement and Metrics

SLA involves the task of defining specific performance characteristics expected from the network. The agreement defines certain performance metrics used to measure the actual service level obtained from the network against the stated level of service in the SLA. It is a very common agreement between the provider of a service and a recipient of the service. The metrics for network performance can include response time, availability, and so on.

Performance Monitoring and Measurement

The performance of a network is directly linked to the operational state of devices within the network. Hardware and software components of a network device also affect its performance. Failed hardware components can cause a complete outage in the network. It is critical to monitor the operating environments of network devices such as voltage, temperature, airflow, and ensure they are operating within specifications. Software components such as buffers, memory, and so on can have a significant impact on the protocols running on the device.

CPU Utilization and Memory/Buffers Allocation

A useful performance indicator on a router is its CPU utilization. By measuring CPU utilization over time, a trend can be established to determine traffic patterns. Routers running constantly at high-utilization levels can affect the overall performance of forwarding and processing packets. CLI commands exist on the router to display the CPU utilization and information on running processes. Information returned by the command on CPU load can be accessed using objects defined in the OLD-CISCO-CPU-MIB file. The following displays CPU utilization using the proper CLI command:

```
Router# show processes
CPU utilization for five seconds: 1%/0%; one minute: 1%; five minutes: 1%

PID QTy       PC Runtime (ms)    Invoked   uSecs    Stacks TTY Process
  1 Mwe 6039CCC8    2203448      9944378     221 7392/9000   0 IP-EIGRP Router
  2 Lst 60133594     329612        34288    9613 5760/6000   0 Check heaps
  3 Cwe 6011D820          0            1       0 5648/6000   0 Pool Manager
  4 Mst 6015FAA8          0            2       0 5608/6000   0 Timers
```

CPU utilization can be read using the MIB objects in Table 14-23.

Table 14-23   *MIB Objects in OLD-CISCO-CPU-MIB for Monitoring CPU Utilization*

Objects	Description	OID
busyPer	CPU busy percentage in the last 5 seconds	1.3.6.1.4.1.9.2.1.56
avgBusy1	1-minute moving average of the CPU busy percentage	1.3.6.1.4.1.9.2.1.57
AvgBusy5	5-minute moving average of the CPU busy percentage	1.3.6.1.4.1.9.2.1.58

The amount of main memory left on a router's processor has a significant impact on performance. Buffers are allocated from memory into different memory pools that are used by a protocol. IPX SAP packets, for example, use middle buffers in sending out packets. The following CLI commands are commonly used to monitor the memory and buffer statistics on a router:

- **show memory**
- **show buffers**
- **show interface**

The values collected from CLI commands are accessible via SNMP. Cisco provides the following MIB files for obtaining the equivalent output from CLI commands: CISCO-MEMORY-POOL-MIB, OLD-CISCO-INTERFACES-MIB, and OLD-CISCO-MEMORY-MIB.

The **show memory** command displays memory allocation:

```
Router# show memory

              Head    Total(b)   Used(b)   Free(b)    Lowest(b)   Largest(b)
```

```
Processor  60DB19C0   119858752   1948928   117909824   117765180   117903232
     Fast  60D919C0      131072     69560       61512       61512       61468
```

Memory allocation can be read using the MIB objects in table Table 14-24.

Table 14-24   *MIB Objects in CISCO-MEMORY-POOL-MIB for Monitoring **show memory** Output*

Objects	Description	OID
CiscoMemoryPoolName	A textual name assigned to the memory pool	1.3.6.1.4.1.9.9.48.1.1.1.2
CiscoMemoryPoolUsed	The number of bytes from the memory pool that are currently in use	1.3.6.1.4.1.9.9.48.1.1.1.5
CiscoMemoryPoolFree	Indicates the number of bytes from the memory pool that are currently unused on the managed device	1.3.6.1.4.1.9.9.48.1.1.1.6
CiscoMemoryPoolLargestFree	The largest number of contiguous bytes from the memory pool that are currently unused	1.3.6.1.4.1.9.9.48.1.1.1.7

NOTE   You can use the *freemem* MIB object in the CISCO-MEMORY-MIB for IOS releases prior to 11.1.

The **show buffers** command displays buffer allocation:

```
Router# show buffers
Buffer elements:
     499 in free list (500 max allowed)
     124485689 hits, 0 misses, 0 created

Public buffer pools:
Small buffers, 104 bytes (total 120, permanent 120):
     112 in free list (20 min, 250 max allowed)
     35868550 hits, 0 misses, 0 trims, 0 created
     0 failures (0 no memory)
Middle buffers, 600 bytes (total 90, permanent 90):
     88 in free list (10 min, 200 max allowed)
     37894226 hits, 0 misses, 0 trims, 0 created
     0 failures (0 no memory)
Big buffers, 1524 bytes (total 90, permanent 90):
     90 in free list (5 min, 300 max allowed)
     1161634 hits, 0 misses, 0 trims, 0 created
     0 failures (0 no memory)
Large buffers, 5024 bytes (total 10, permanent 10):
     10 in free list (0 min, 30 max allowed)
     0 hits, 0 misses, 0 trims, 0 created
     0 failures (0 no memory)
Huge buffers, 18024 bytes (total 0, permanent 0):
```

```
0 in free list (0 min, 13 max allowed)
0 hits, 0 misses, 0 trims, 0 created
0 failures (0 no memory)
```

Buffer allocation can be read using the MIB objects in Table 14-25.

Table 14-25   *MIB Objects in OLD-CISCO-MEMORY-MIB for Monitoring **show buffer** Output*

Objects	Description	OID
Buffer Elements		
bufferElFree	Number of free buffer elements	1.3.6.1.4.1.9.2.1.9
bufferElMax	Maximum number of buffer elements	1.3.6.1.4.1.9.2.1.10
bufferElHit	Number of buffer element hits	1.3.6.1.4.1.9.2.1.11
bufferElMiss	Number of buffer element misses	1.3.6.1.4.1.9.2.1.12
bufferElCreate	Number of buffer element creates	1.3.6.1.4.1.9.2.1.13
Small Buffers		
bufferSmSize	The size of small buffers	1.3.6.1.4.1.9.2.1.14
bufferSmTotal	Total number of small buffers	1.3.6.1.4.1.9.2.1.15
bufferSmFree	Number of free small buffers	1.3.6.1.4.1.9.2.1.16
bufferSmMax	Maximum number of small buffers	1.3.6.1.4.1.9.2.1.17
bufferSmHit	Number of small buffer hits	1.3.6.1.4.1.9.2.1.18
bufferSmMiss	Number of small buffer misses	1.3.6.1.4.1.9.2.1.19
bufferSmTrim	Number of small buffer trims	1.3.6.1.4.1.9.2.1.20
bufferSmCreate	Number of small buffer creates	1.3.6.1.4.1.9.2.1.21
Medium Buffers		
bufferMdSize	The size of medium buffers	1.3.6.1.4.1.9.2.1.22
bufferMdTotal	Total number of medium buffers	1.3.6.1.4.1.9.2.1.23
bufferMdFree	Number of free medium buffers	1.3.6.1.4.1.9.2.1.24
bufferMdMax	Maximum number of medium buffers	1.3.6.1.4.1.9.2.1.25
bufferMdHit	Number of medium buffer hits	1.3.6.1.4.1.9.2.1.26
bufferMdMiss	Number of medium buffer misses	1.3.6.1.4.1.9.2.1.27
bufferMdTrim	Number of medium buffer trims	1.3.6.1.4.1.9.2.1.28
bufferMdCreate	Number of medium buffer creates	1.3.6.1.4.1.9.2.1.29
Big Buffers		
bufferBgSize	The size of big buffers	1.3.6.1.4.1.9.2.1.30

Table 14-25 *MIB Objects in OLD-CISCO-MEMORY-MIB for Monitoring **show buffer** Output (Continued)*

Objects	Description	OID
bufferBgTotal	Total number of big buffers	1.3.6.1.4.1.9.2.1.31
bufferBgFree	Number of free big buffers	1.3.6.1.4.1.9.2.1.32
bufferBgMax	Maximum number of big buffers	1.3.6.1.4.1.9.2.1.33
bufferBgHit	Number of big buffer hits	1.3.6.1.4.1.9.2.1.34
bufferBgMiss	Number of big buffer misses	1.3.6.1.4.1.9.2.1.35
bufferBgTrim	Number of big buffer trims	1.3.6.1.4.1.9.2.1.36
bufferBgCreate	Number of big buffer creates	1.3.6.1.4.1.9.2.1.37
Large Buffers		
bufferLgSize	The size of large buffers	1.3.6.1.4.1.9.2.1.38
bufferLgTotal	Total number of large buffers	1.3.6.1.4.1.9.2.1.39
bufferLgFree	Number of free large buffers	1.3.6.1.4.1.9.2.1.40
bufferLgMax	Maximum number of large buffers	1.3.6.1.4.1.9.2.1.41
bufferLgHit	Number of large buffer hits	1.3.6.1.4.1.9.2.1.42
bufferLgMiss	Number of large buffer misses	1.3.6.1.4.1.9.2.1.43
bufferLgTrim	Number of large buffer trims	1.3.6.1.4.1.9.2.1.44
bufferLgCreate	Number of large buffer creates	1.3.6.1.4.1.9.2.1.45
Huge Buffers		
bufferHgSize	The size of huge buffers	1.3.6.1.4.1.9.2.1.62
bufferHgTotal	Total number of huge buffers	1.3.6.1.4.1.9.2.1.63
bufferHgFree	Number of free huge buffers	1.3.6.1.4.1.9.2.1.64
bufferHgMax	Maximum number of huge buffers	1.3.6.1.4.1.9.2.1.65
bufferHgHit	Number of huge buffer hits	1.3.6.1.4.1.9.2.1.66
bufferHgMiss	Number of huge buffer misses	1.3.6.1.4.1.9.2.1.67
bufferHgTrim	Number of huge buffer trims	1.3.6.1.4.1.9.2.1.68
bufferHgCreate	Number of huge buffer creates	1.3.6.1.4.1.9.2.1.69
Buffer Failures		
bufferFail	Number of buffer allocation failures	1.3.6.1.4.1.9.2.1.46
bufferNoMem	Number of buffer create failures due to no free memory	1.3.6.1.4.1.9.2.1.47

The **show interface** command displays interface statistics:

```
Router# show interface

Ethernet0/0 is up, line protocol is up
  Hardware is cxBus Ethernet, address is 0010.f65f.7000 (bia 0010.f65f.7000)
  Internet address is 172.16.97.1/24
  MTU 1500 bytes, BW 10000 Kbit, DLY 1000 usec, rely 255/255, load 1/255
  Encapsulation ARPA, loopback not set, keepalive set (10 sec)
  ARP type: ARPA, ARP Timeout 04:00:00
  Last input 00:00:01, output 00:00:01, output hang never
  Last clearing of "show interface" counters never
  Queueing strategy: fifo
  Output queue 0/40, 0 drops; input queue 0/75, 0 drops
  5 minute input rate 0 bits/sec, 0 packets/sec
  5 minute output rate 0 bits/sec, 0 packets/sec
     12072853 packets input, 1379751443 bytes, 0 no buffer
     Received 1824605 broadcasts, 0 runts, 0 giants
     0 input errors, 0 CRC, 0 frame, 0 overrun, 0 ignored, 0 abort
     0 input packets with dribble condition detected
     11283674 packets output, 1218604416 bytes, 0 underruns
     0 output errors, 24888 collisions, 1 interface resets
     0 babbles, 0 late collision, 0 deferred
     0 lost carrier, 0 no carrier
     0 output buffer failures, 0 output buffers swapped out
```

Interface information can be read using the MIB objects in Table 14-26.

Table 14-26   *MIB Objects in OLD-CISCO-INTERFACES-MIB and RFC1213 for Monitoring **show interface** Output*

Objects	Description	OID
Input Statistics		
cisco.local.lifTable.locIfIn BitsSec	5-minute exponentially decayed moving average of input bits per second	1.3.6.1.4.1.9.2.2.1.1.6
locIfInPktsSec	5-minute exponentially decayed moving average of input packets per second	1.3.6.1.4.1.9.2.2.1.1.7
interfaces.ifTable.ifInErrors	Number of inbound packets that contained errors preventing them from being delivered to a higher-layer protocol	1.3.6.1.2.1.2.2.1.14
interfaces.ifTable.ifOutError	Number of outbound packets that contained errors preventing them from being delivered to a higher-layer protocol	1.3.6.1.2.1.2.2.1.20
ifInNUcastPkts	Number of non-unicast packets delivered to a higher-layer protocol	1.3.6.1.2.1.2.2.1.12

Table 14-26   *MIB Objects in OLD-CISCO-INTERFACES-MIB and RFC1213 for Monitoring **show interface** Output (Continued)*

Objects	Description	OID
locIfInRunts	Number of packets input that were smaller than the allowable physical media permitted	1.3.6.1.4.1.9.2.2.1.1.10
locIfInGiants	Number of input packets that were larger than the physical media permitted	1.3.6.1.4.1.9.2.2.1.1.11
locIfInCRC	Number of input packets that had cyclic redundancy checksum errors	1.3.6.1.4.1.9.2.2.1.1.12
locIfInOverrun	Count of input that arrived too quickly for the hardware to receive	1.3.6.1.4.1.9.2.2.1.1.14
locIfInIgnored	Number of input packets that were just ignored by this interface	1.3.6.1.4.1.9.2.2.1.1.15
locIfInAbort	Number of input packets that were aborted	1.3.6.1.4.1.9.2.2.1.1.16
locIfInputQueueDrops	Number of packets dropped because the input queue was full	1.3.6.1.4.1.9.2.2.1.1.26
Output Statistics		
locIfOutBitsSec	5-minute exponentially decayed moving average of output bits per second	1.3.6.1.4.1.9.2.2.1.1.8
locIfOutPktsSec	5-minute exponentially decayed moving average of output packets per second	1.3.6.1.4.1.9.2.2.1.1.9
ifOutErrors	Number of outbound packets that could not be transmitted because of errors	1.3.6.1.2.1.2.2.1.20
locIfCollisions	Number of output collisions detected on this interface	1.3.6.1.4.1.9.2.2.1.1.25

continues

Table 14-26 *MIB Objects in OLD-CISCO-INTERFACES-MIB and RFC1213 for Monitoring **show interface** Output (Continued)*

Objects	Description	OID
locIfResets	Number of times the interface internally reset	1.3.6.1.4.1.9.2.2.1.1.17
locIfRestarts	Number of times the interface had to be completely restarted	1.3.6.1.4.1.9.2.2.1.1.18
locIfCarTrans	Number of times interface saw the carrier signal transition	1.3.6.1.4.1.9.2.2.1.1.21
locIfOutputQueueDrops	Number of packets dropped because the output queue was full	1.3.6.1.4.1.9.2.2.1.1.27

Another way to look at MIB objects is to sort them by types of interfaces, as shown in Table 14-27.

Table 14-27 *Table of Interface-Related MIB Objects*

Applicability	MIB Objects
All interfaces	cisco.local.lifTable.locIfInbitsSec
	cisco.local.lifTable.locIfOutbitsSec
	mib-2.interfaces.ifTable.ifInErrors
	mib-2.interfaces.ifTable.ifOutErrors
	cisco.local.lifTable.locIfInputQueueDrops
	cisco.local.lifTable.locIfOutputQueueDrops
	cisco.local.lifTable.locIfInIgnored
	cisco.local.lifTable.locIfResets
	cisco.local.lifTable.locIfRestarts
For serial interfaces	cisco.local.lifTable.locIfCRC
	cisco.local.lifTable.locIfAbort
	cisco.local.lifTable.locIfFrame
	cisco.local.lifTable.locIfCarTrans
	cisco.local.lifTable.locIfOverrun

Table 14-27   *Table of Interface-Related MIB Objects (Continued)*

Applicability	MIB Objects
For Ethernet interfaces	cisco.local.lifTable.locIfCollisions
	cisco.local.lifTable.locIfRunts
	cisco.local.lifTable.locIfGiants
	cisco.local.lifTable.locIfFrame
For Token Ring interfaces (from RFC 1231)	dot5StatsLineErrors
	dot5StatsBurstErrors
	dot5StatsACErrors
	dot5StatsAbortTransErrors
	dot5StatsInternalErrors
	dot5StatsFrameCopiedErrors
	dot5StatsTokenErrors
	dot5StatsSoftErrors
	dot5StatsSignalLoss
	dot5StatsFreqErrors
For FDDI interfaces (from RFC 1512)	snmpFddiMACLostCts
	snmpFddiMACErrorCts

The final tasks involved in performance management are setting thresholds, exception reporting, analysis, and tuning.

Network-Based Correlation Scenarios

The chapter concludes with a number of network-based correlation scenarios. The section begins with an overview of scenario information and concludes with several specific scenarios.

Periodic Reachability Test

It is assumed that all network devices are being polled either through ICMP (ping) or SNMP, or both, for basic reachability from the NMS. Whenever a device is not reachable, a DEVICE_DOWN event will be generated by the NMS to the event-correlation engine.

Most NMS support this capability.

Logical Topology Database

It is assumed that the logical (that is, Layer 3) topology of the network is available to the correlation engine to understand the logical subnet connectivity and figure out whether a device is "logically" before or beyond another device from the NMS perspective.

Most NMS support this capability.

Physical Topology Database

Some correlation rules require knowledge of the physical (that is, Layer 2) topology of the network to understand how switches and routers are interconnected within a subnet.

Very few NMSs support this capability.

Baselining

Some event-correlation scenarios require assessing the state difference of managed objects before and after an event occurs. The event-correlation engine must maintain or have access to such state variables and have the capability to collect the new state when needed.

Thresholding also requires setting thresholds at levels representative of a customer's network. Because every network is different and displays different traffic patterns, this chapter cannot provide fixed numeric thresholds. Instead, the most representative MIB objects and events for a more proactive monitoring approach are discussed.

Customization

The event-correlation engine must allow some form of customization to tailor correlation rules for every customer. Defaults should be provided to reflect most situations.

Problems Scenarios

To illustrate the event model as shown in Figure 14-1, the following conditions were identified as being the most critical conditions in a typical network of switches and routers. This study focused essentially on the Catalyst 5000 family and the 7500 router.

Simple thresholding rules involving simple cause-effect situations (such as a Counter exceeding a certain value causing operator notification) are intentionally ignored in this chapter, because they do not require any form of correlation.

Some scenarios present definitions for a *simple correlation* rule and an *advanced correlation* rule to allow for phased-in implementations. The simple correlation rule is provided as the minimal set of functionality to address the problem scenario. The advanced correlation rule presents a more extensive resolution.

Some indication of polling intervals is provided. However, every site should reevaluate these polling intervals based on their traffic patterns and equipment capacity.

Basic Filtering Functions

A few key syslog messages need to be filtered to reduce the number of notifications to network operators. These filters need to suppress identical messages repeated within n seconds.

Selected syslog messages apply to Cisco 7500 routers and are listed in Table 14-28.

Table 14-28   *Filtered Syslog Messages*

Message Type/Description	Message Encoding
Configuration Changes Report	SYS-5-CONFIG
	SYS-5-CONFIG_I
	SYS-5-CONFIG_L
	SYS-5-CONFIG_M
	SYS-5-CONFIG_NV
	SYS-5-CONFIG_NV_M
	These messages apply to 7500 routers and other IOS-based routers. The identifier after the work CONFIG specifies the origin of the configuration change. All these messages are considered identical for event correlation *because* operators are concerned about configuration changes, irrespective of how the changes were applied. They need to be filtered if multiple messages occur within n minutes from the same device.
	Recommendation: $n = 5$ minutes
CPU Hog Report	This message applies to 7500 routers and other IOS-based routers. IOS-based routers generate a SYS-3-CPUHOG syslog message.
	This message repeats itself if the CPU is hogged for a long time. These messages need to be filtered to eliminate duplicates within n minutes from the same router.
	Recommendation: $n = 5$ minutes

The SNMP trap in Table 14-29 should be filtered similarly.

Table 14-29   *Filtered SNMP Trap*

SNMP Trap Type/Description	Message Encoding
snmpAuthenticationFailure	This trap is defined in RFC 1213, MIB.
	This trap indicates an attempt to access an SNMP agent with an invalid community string.
	If no more than three such traps are received within 5 minutes from the same device, the traps should be ignored. Otherwise, a warning notification should be sent to the network operator to alert him of a possible security attack.

Device Restart Conditions #1

Platform: 7500 router.

Objective: Detect when a device reports it is shutting down (as opposed to not reaching it, which is covered in the *Router/Switch Down* scenario).

Symptoms: Cisco IOS logs syslog message before (SYS-5-RELOAD) and after (SYS-5-RESTART) a device restarts.

Correlation Logic: When the SYS-5-RELOAD message is received, the event-correlation engine must wait for a SYS-5- RESTART to arrive within n minutes and cancel the original message. If *no* SYS-5-RESTART message is received within n minutes, the operator should be notified of a critical alert. If the router reports a SYS-5- RESTART message within n minutes, the condition will only be logged as informational, along with the value of the *whyReload* MIB object.

If the router is detected as down, this information will be fed as input into the correlation rule for the router up/down problem, so that the background reachability check will not report it as down again.

Probable Cause: Software error or operator intervention.

Actions/Resolution: Notify operator if router does not issue a SYS-5-RESTART message within n minutes (n = time for router to reload + 1 minute).

Device Restart Conditions #2

Platform: Catalyst 5000.

Objective: Detect when a device reports it is being reset from the console (as opposed to not reaching it, which is covered in the *Router/Switch Down* scenario).

Symptoms: Cisco IOS logs syslog message before the switch is reset from the console (SYS-5:System reset). An SNMP cold start trap and/or the IOS message (SNMP-5:Cold Start Trap) after the device restarts.

Correlation Logic: When the *SYS-5:System reset* message is received, the event-correlation engine must wait for an IOS message *SNMP-5:Cold Start Trap* or a *cold start trap* to arrive within *n* minutes and cancel the original message. If *no SNMP-5:Cold Start Trap* message is received within *n* minutes, the operator should be notified of a critical alert. If the switch reports a *SNMP-5:Cold Start Trap* IOS message or *cold start trap* within *n* minutes, the condition will only be logged as informational.

If the switch is detected as down, this information will be fed as input into the correlation rule for the router/switch up/down problem, so that the background reachability check will not report it as down again.

Probable Cause: Software error or operator intervention.

Actions/Resolution: Notify operator if router does not issue a *SNMP-5:Cold Start Trap* or *cold start trap* message within *n* minutes (*n* = time for switch to reload + 1 minute).

Detect Link Up/Down Conditions

Platforms: 7500 router and other routers with BRI interfaces.

Objective: Knowing when a link is up or down is perceived by customers as being the most important requirement. Added correlation will allow detecting normal link up/down transitions from dialup lines to more serious transitions for other links.

An interface being down can be a critical alert on a router or switch. Access routers with ISDN and ASCII links have their interfaces going up and down many times a day, however, as part of their normal activity, as dialup calls are initiated and torn down. A correlation rule should be applied to sort out the relevant link-down conditions from normal operation.

Symptoms: LINK_3_UPDOWN syslog messages are logged.

Correlation Logic: Two levels of correlation were identified:

- Simple correlation
- Advanced correlation

For simple correlation, if the string BRI is contained in the message, the message should be discarded.

For advanced correlation, if the message does not contain the string BRI, the physical topology database should be queried to determine the type of link, namely whether it is a link between two routers, a router and a switch, or router and an end-user port.

The syslog message should be further processed only if it is a link between two Cisco devices.

Probable Cause: Link was either disconnected or broken.

Actions/Resolution: Notify the network operator, except if the interface is that of an end user or an ASCII or BRI interface.

Spanning-Tree Topology Changes

Platform: Catalyst 5000 only.

Objective: STP reconfiguration can have disastrous effects, such as some parts of the network not being accessible any longer. Upon detection of an STP reconfiguration, the event-correlation engine should ensure that the network is still functional.

Symptoms: If you received any of the following syslog messages:

- SPANTREE-6: "port [dec]/[dec] state in vlan [dec] changed to blocking."
- SPANTREE-6: "port [dec]/[dec] state in vlan [dec] changed to forwarding."

Or any of the following RFC 1493 (Bridge MIB) SNMP traps:

- topologyChange
- newRoot

These traps contain the community string in the format *community@vlanId*, where *vlanId* is the VLAN identifier in which the spanning tree changed. For Catalyst 5000 switch Release 4.1 and higher, these traps will contain the *vtpVlanIndex* and *ifName* varBinds to provide additional information to the application processing these traps.

Correlation Logic: Three types of correlation are possible, depending on the extent the ECS can query the network:

- Simple correlation
- Medium correlation
- Advanced correlation

The simple STP correlation refers to ensuring that every device reporting an STP change through the means referred to earlier is monitored to ensure that it is restored to a valid state. This will be accomplished as follows, based on the Catalyst 5000 MIB.

First of all, the CISCO-STACK-MIB object *sysEnableBridgeTraps* should be verified to be set to enabled(1), or an alert should be raised.

The community field in the *topologyChange* or *newRoot* trap must be read and used to further interrogate the switch the trap came from. This enables you to query the specific VLAN the topology change occurred on.

First, you need to determine whether any ports were a trunk before the STP change. To do so, the list of all trunks per VLAN must be maintained and verified against the list after the

STP change. A trunk port is defined as having its *vlanPortIslOperStatus* MIB object in the *vlanPortTable* of the CISCO-STACK MIB with a value of *trunking(1)*.

Second, you need to determine which trunk ports in this VLAN had a state change by scanning the *vlanPortTable* for those entries with *vlanPortVlan* set to the VLAN ID specified in the trap.

For each of the selected ports, identify the *vlanPortIslOperStatus* MIB object with a value of *trunking(1)*. For each trunk, you need to monitor its status as identified in RFC 1493. This is accomplished as follows.

Read the *vlanPortIslAdminStatus* object in the *vlanPortTable* and ensure it is not set to *off(2)*. Otherwise, generate an alert that the port was disabled.

For each trunk port in the selected VLAN, read the corresponding *vlanPortModule* and *vlanPort* from the *vlanPortTable*. Use these two values of *vlanPortModule* and *vlanPort* to index into the CISCO-STACK-MIB *portTable* to retrieve the corresponding *portIfIndex* value. Use the *portIfIndex* to read the MIB-II *ifOperStatus* to determine whether the interface is still up. If not, generate an alert.

Read the *portCrossIndex* value in the *portTable* in the CISCO-STACK-MIB for the selected entry and use this value to index into the RFC 1493 *dot1dStpPortTable* to verify that the *dot1dStpPortEnable* is set to *enabled(1)*.

Then, use the same *portCrossIndex* value in the *portTable* in the CISCO-STACK-MIB to locate the corresponding entry in the RFC 1493 *dot1dStpPortTable* to verify that *dot1dStpPortState* is either in *blocking(2)* or *forwarding(5)* mode, 2 minutes after the trap is received. Otherwise, send an alert.

Verify also that the ports that were known to be trunks before the trap occurred are still trunks (that is, that all trunks known to be valid trunks are still functioning as trunks). Otherwise, an alert should be generated. Similarly, the situation when a port was known not to be a trunk, but is found to be a trunk while processing the trap, should be reported.

Alerts should also include e-mail summarizing the discrepancies found as a result of this correlation. Whether a separate e-mail is generated for each port discrepancy or all port discrepancies associated with an STP change are accumulated in a single e-mail is implementation dependent.

NOTE   An alternative to processing traps would be to poll the RFC 1493 *dot1dStpTopChanges* MIB object to determine whether it incremented by at least one or decremented (indicating an agent reset) since the last poll.

The next correlation type is a medium correlation. An STP reconfiguration is always limited to a subnet. Assuming the event-correlation engine knows the devices in the subnet prior to the reconfiguration, a simple correlation could ensure that all these devices are still up and running (by performing a reachability test) and that these are still the same devices (by comparing the previously known and the current RFC1213-MIB *sysDescr* string for each device). A logical topology discovery will also be initiated to detect whether any new device was added to the network. An alternative is to rely on switches newly added to the network to generate either trap, so that the ECS can detect them.

Although not 100% perfect, this correlation rule can assist a network operator in narrowing down the scope of the error more quickly.

The final correlation type is an advanced correlation. One way to realize why an STP configuration occurred is to know ahead of time the list of devices involved in each spanning tree in the network. An STP topology can be collected by querying the *dot1Stp* MIB group from the RFC 1493 MIB. CWSI 1.2 and greater can also be used to display a graphical map of the STP tree over the physical topology discovered using CDP. Note that Cisco supports one spanning tree per VLAN. The VLAN ID is reported either in the syslog message or in the community string contained in the SNMP trap. If no VLAN is configured in the network, it is assumed that there is only one VLAN with a VLAN ID of 1. Therefore, the term VLAN in this section is used to represent the subnet if no VLANs are configured.

When any spanning tree in a VLAN reconfigures, the event-correlation engine can then identify which VLAN reconfigured and determine what changed in the spanning tree.

The event correlation listens for RFC 1493 (Bridge MIB) *newRoot* or *topologyChange* SNMP traps to detect when an STP reconfiguration occurs. These traps are always sent by a device whose port changed state as defined in the RFC.

If a *topologyChange* trap is received, the event-correlation engine can easily compile the list of devices involved in the STP reconfiguration.

If the ECS cannot adequately extract the community string from the trap and does not process syslog messages, the event-correlation rule needs to relate the trap to a VLAN by detecting which VLAN had its topology change counter increased by one. For that purpose, the CISCO-STACK *vlanTable* MIB group can be queried to list the VLANs configured in the switch. Using the SNMP community string to address individual VLANs (using *community@vlanId*), the NMS could alternately poll for the RFC 1493 *dot1dStpTopChanges* MIB object, which gives the number of topology changes since the device rebooted or initialized. This method would enable you to isolate which VLAN had a topology change so that further verification could be performed in that VLAN only.

Because STP reconfiguration is automatic, the event-correlation logic needs to determine the following:

- The cause of the topology change
- The correctness of the new STP topology

The event-correlation engine needs to determine whether a node was detected as going down prior to an STP topology change being detected. The event-correlation rule will calculate the difference between the known STP topology prior to the STP reconfiguration and the new STP configuration with the following objectives:

- If a new root was defined, identify whether the previous root device is down, and whether the new root is a new device added to the network.

- If a single topology change occurred, identify whether another node in the STP tree was added (for example, restarted) or removed (for example, is restarting or is not reachable at all) by rediscovering all devices involved in the VLAN.

- If no device was added or removed, it would imply that a redundant link was either removed (for example, a cable was unplugged) or added.

In any of these three situations, the event-correlation engine needs to assess which ports involved in a spanning tree changed from a forwarding state to a blocking state, or from a learning to forwarding state. It also needs to correlate whether any of these ports had their RFC1213-MIB *operStatus* MIB object toggle from *up* to *down*, in an attempt to identify a port failure or disconnection.

The operator will be notified of the actual device and port that caused the topology change. It may be that the event correlation identifies more than one possible failure cause or device, in which case it should report all possible causes or devices to the operator.

The notion of correctness can be very complex, depending on the network characteristics.

The simplest means to determine correctness of an STP configuration is to ensure that every device in the VLAN spanning tree is reachable. Therefore, the correlation rule will trigger a reachability test to all devices known to have been members in the spanning tree prior to the reconfiguration. The correlation rule will also trigger a discovery of the new STP tree to detect whether a new device was added to the spanning tree.

The correlation engine of the device(s) involved in the reconfiguration will notify the network operator and will specify the most likely cause of the STP reconfiguration, namely:

- A device was added to or removed from the subnet.

- A link was added or removed between two devices.

A more difficult test is to detect which interfaces went down or up, and which would therefore have caused the STP reconfiguration, while not reporting interfaces which were known to be down *before* the STP topology change occurred. This correlation rule can be performed through the same mechanisms described earlier. STP discovery must include the ports involved in an STP tree with their *operStatus* and *adminStatus* as defined in the *ifTable* of RFC1213 MIB and compare the values of these MIB objects prior to and after an STP reconfiguration. Another way to detect whether STP reconfiguration occurred because of a down interface is to correlate it to a *linkDown* SNMP trap or *syslog* message received within seconds of a *topologyChange* or *newRoot* SNMP trap or topology change *syslog* message within a VLAN.

An alternative method is to monitor the *dot1dStpPortForwardTransitions* MIB object to detect when this object increments by one.

Probable Cause: A device involved in the spanning tree was removed from service, failed, or was added to the network, or a link was added or removed between two switches.

Actions/Resolution: Notify operator as specified earlier. No automatic action is expected.

Router/Switch Down Problem

Platforms: Catalyst 5000 and 7500 router.

Objective: Detect when a switch or router is down, without reporting the unreachable switches and routers behind it.

Based on knowledge of the topology layout, a correlation engine must identify the most likely failure from a group of unreachable nodes. Assuming Cisco manages Cisco equipment only, end-user devices' status—such as PCs and servers—will not be monitored.

Symptoms: Several devices are not reachable at the same time.

Correlation Logic: A logical (Layer 3) topology database can serve to detect a faulty router from a group of unreachable routers. However, a physical (for example, Layer 2) topology database is needed to detect a faulty switch from a group of unreachable switches.

Every device reported as not reachable within n minutes will be queried for RFC1213-MIB *sysObjectID* MIB object and use Cisco's mapping table.

Then, the event-correlation engine would either perform a simple or advanced correlation. The recommendation is $n = 5$ minutes.

Simple correlation involves using the existing NMS topology database.

This will work best for determining a faulty router from other routers, but will not differentiate between switches (*because* most NMS do not support L2 topology).

Advanced correlation allows determining a faulty switch from multiple switches in a subnet by making use of a physical-connectivity database describing how switches are interconnected. The ECS would need to first use L3 topology to identify which subnet is most likely to have a failure. Then an L2 topology database can be used to identify which switch may have failed.

NOTE	It is best not to connect the NMS workstation directly to a switched network *because* the NMS cannot isolate which switch may be "behind" other switches unless the event-correlation engine can determine which switch the NMS is connected to. This can be accomplished by querying the MAC cache tables in every switch and matching them to the MAC address of the NMS workstation. This can be a very lengthy process *because* there will be potentially thousands of MAC addresses to collect.

Probable Cause: A single router or switch is down.

Actions/Resolution: Notify operator with a single notification identifying the faulty device.

Device Performance Problem

Platform: 7500 router.

Objective: Detect when excessive traffic causes excessive CPU load.

Network managers have only a limited understanding of the traffic flowing through their Cisco switches and routers. Detecting high traffic conditions becomes increasingly important. CPU overload conditions as reported by SYS-3-CPUHOG syslog messages will be monitored and an alert will be generated when excessive conditions are detected—conditions not related to transient traffic flows as reported by NetFlow, which may indicate a temporary overload condition.

Symptoms: The SYS-3-CPUHOG syslog message is logged, indicating a CPU overload condition.

Correlation Logic: Two levels of correlation were identified.

The first type of correlation is simple correlation. The event-correlation engine will trigger traffic statistics collection every 20 seconds for *n* minutes for the *ifInOctets* and *ifOutOctets* from the RFC1213 MIB *ifTable*. If any interface traffic utilization exceeds 40% of the link capacity (*ifSpeed*) for more than 50% of the collection period, the operator will be notified with a reference to the interface(s) having excessive traffic.

If the interface with excessive traffic is the same interface used for ping and SNMP reachability, it is likely that the condition will result in the device not being reachable temporarily, which would report the device as down. The device low-performance condition will be fed as input into the reachability correlation rule so that the operator is not notified twice for the same problem, or that other devices are assumed down/unreachable because this interface is overloaded (see the Router Down problem).

The low-performance condition will be deemed a minor alarm for *n* minutes and not reported to the network operator if it goes away within *n* minutes. The recommendation is *n* = 15 minutes.

If no performance condition exists, the lack of reachability will be treated as a critical alarm *because* the device is probably totally down.

The second type of correlation is advanced correlation. NetFlow can be used to perform more advanced correlation and to avoid reporting transient overloads by verifying which protocols are responsible for the high-performance impact. This is explained as follows.

The IOS command **show ip cache flow** will report a table of IP addresses that are communicating on which port and which device interface. The table columns are labeled *SrcIPaddress*, *DstIPaddress*, *SrcP*, *DstP*, *SrcIf*, and *DstIf*. From this information, you can determine whether CPU overload is due to excessive traffic on a given interface, and whether the traffic is transient (FTP on port 21, for example). If the traffic is identified as transient, the event-correlation engine will ignore the CPUHOP syslog message for 5 minutes for that specific session. If the CPUHOP syslog message is repeated because of the same NetFlow session, over a period of 30 minutes, the operator will be notified as a warning that an unusual NetFlow session is taking place. The IOS command **export ip flow** can also be used for this purpose.

If the CPUHOP syslog message occurs repeatedly for different sessions (such as 10 times per hour), the operator will be notified as an indication that the device is consistently being overloaded and should be looked at further.

Probable Cause: The cause may be due to a transient session (such as FTP) or the router is underpowered for the traffic going through it.

Actions/Resolution: Notify operator if performance problem persists as described earlier.

Environmental Problem #1

Platform: Catalyst 5000 with redundant supervisor module.

Objective: Detect when temperature rises and may cause a device shutdown.

Symptoms: The Catalyst 5000 switch with a redundant supervisor module reports a syslog message: *SYS-0: "Temp high Failure"* or an SNMP trap: CISCO-STACK MIB *chassisAlarmOn* with the varBindList containing *chassisTempAlarm* = on(2), *chassisMinorAlarm* = on(2) or off(1), and *chassisMajorAlarm* = on(2), whenever the temperature exceeds 50° Celsius.

Correlation Logic: If, within 5 minutes, you receive another syslog message: SYS-0: "Temp Critical Recovered" or SYS-2: "Temp high Okay" or the SNMP trap: CISCO-STACK MIB *chassisAlarmOff*, the alert should be cleared from the event-correlation engine.

If none of these messages or an SNMP trap is received, the alert should be fed as input into the Device Up/Down correlation rule reporting that the device is down.

Probable Cause: The air-conditioning in the room failed or the fan failed.

Actions/Resolution: The original error should be reported immediately as a paging notification to the network operator. If the problem clears itself, the operator should be notified again.

Environmental Problem #2

Platform: 7000 router.

Objective: Detect when temperature rises and may cause a device shutdown.

Symptoms: Any of the following syslog messages are received:

- ENV-2-TEMP
- ENV-1-SHUTDOWN
- ENVM-2-TEMP
- ENVM-1-SHUTDOWN

The -TEMP messages will generate a major alarm; the SHUTDOWN messages will generate a critical alarm.

More granularity may be supported if the ECS can decode the actual temperature from the syslog message and apply its own thresholds and alarm severities.

The alarm would eventually have to be cleared manually by the operator.

Correlation Logic: Pass through.

Probable Cause: The air-conditioning in the room failed.

Actions/Resolution: Notify operator.

Summary

This chapter provides Cisco customers with a reference to the various manageable elements of Cisco routers and Catalyst switches. From this chapter, you should have learned the elements of Catalyst switches, how to manage them, and how managing a switch differs from managing a router. The following items were covered:

- An introduction to network management.
- Bridging theory and implementation on Cisco switches, on Cisco routers and those technologies common to both switches and routers.

- An introduction to network-management protocols, Cisco's event model, and a description of Cisco events, namely syslog messages and SNMP traps.

- Keys to a successful network-management strategy.

- The various aspects of switches that require management, and the appropriate techniques to manage those resources.

- The various aspects of routers that require management, and the appropriate techniques to manage those resources.

- Advanced monitoring and correlation scenarios within a single device or across several devices.

- Details on syslog messages and reporting facilities.

- Examples to set RMON thresholds.

CHAPTER 15

Packet Switching Architecture

By Russ White

This chapter will appear in the forthcoming Cisco Press title, Inside Cisco IOS.

A multiprotocol router's primary purpose is, of course, to switch packets from one network segment to another. If the scheduler and memory manager are the router's software infrastructure, then the IOS switching architecture is the router's very foundation. The switching methods and structures that IOS employs essentially dictate how the router performs its primary task. So, as you can imagine, a great deal of effort has been put into designing and refining this important part of IOS.

In spite of all the fanfare, the packet-switching operation itself is fairly straightforward: A packet comes in, and then its destination address is inspected and compared against a list of known destinations. If a match is found, the packet is forwarded out the appropriate interface. Otherwise, it is dropped. Clearly this isn't rocket science. Indeed the problem to be solved isn't so much *how* to switch packets, but how to switch them *quickly*. Switching packets is a data-intensive operation as opposed to a computation-intensive one; speeding up the operation isn't as simple as just using a faster CPU. Other factors such as I/O bus performance and data memory speed can have a big impact on switching performance. The challenge for IOS developers has been to create the highest possible switching performance given the limits of available CPU, I/O bus, and memory technology.

As the size and number of routed networks has grown, IOS developers have had to continuously look for better ways to solve this performance problem. The result has been a continuous redesign and refinement in IOS switching methods. When IOS was first developed, there was only one switching method, known today as process switching. Later releases introduced newer improved methods of switching; some of these methods rely on hardware-specific optimizations, and others use software techniques and work well on many platforms. Today IOS contains switching methods capable of switching several hundred thousand packets per second using routing tables containing hundreds of thousands of routes. These switching methods can operate in the backbone of the Internet.

The following list summarizes the switching methods developed as of Cisco IOS Release 12.0:

- Process switching
- Fast switching
- Autonomous switching
- SSE (silicon switching engine) switching
- Optimum switching
- Distributed fast switching
- Cisco Express Forwarding (CEF)
- Distributed Cisco Express Forwarding

Four of these methods—process switching, fast switching, optimum switching, and Cisco Express Forwarding (CEF)—are covered in detail in this chapter.

It's worth noting that although IP routing examples are used here to illustrate the switching methods, many of these methods also work for other network protocols such as IPX and bridging. The structures used are often independent for each protocol (for example, there is a separate Fast Cache for IP and IPX). The contents of the switching structures are similar, however, and the methods work essentially the same way for each protocol.

Routing 101: Process Switching

Process switching was the first switching method implemented in IOS and contains the fewest number of performance optimizations. Process switching basically uses the brute-force method to switch packets and can consume large amounts of CPU time. It does, however, have the advantage of being platform independent, making it universally available across all Cisco IOS–based products. Process switching also provides some load-balancing capabilities not found in most of the other switching methods. These capabilities are discussed in detail later in this chapter.

To get an understanding of just how process switching works, take a look at the steps required to switch a packet using this method. Figure 15-1 illustrates the process-switched path for an IP packet.

This example begins with the network interface on the router sensing that there is a packet on the wire that needs to be processed. The interface hardware receives the packet, and transfers it into input/output (I/O) memory—Step 1 in Figure 15-1.

Figure 15-1 *The Process Switched Path*

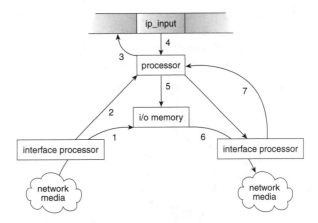

The network interface interrupts the main processor, telling it there is a received packet waiting in I/O memory that needs to be processed. The IOS interrupt software inspects the packet's header information (encapsulation type, network layer header, and so forth), determines that it is an IP packet, and then places the packet on the input queue for the appropriate switching process—Step 2 in Figure 15-1. For IP packets, the switching process is named **ip_input**.

After at least one packet is in the input queue of the **ip_input** process, **ip_input** becomes eligible to run—Step 3 in Figure 15-1.

After the **ip_input** process is running (Step 4 in Figure 15-1), the actual packet-forwarding operation can begin. It is here that all the decisions are made about where to direct the received packet. In this example, **ip_input** looks in the routing table to see whether a route exists to the destination IP address. If one is found, it retrieves the address of the next hop (the next router in the path or the final destination) from the routing table entry. It then looks into the ARP cache to retrieve the information needed to build a new Media Access Control (MAC) header for the next hop. The **ip_input** process builds a new MAC header, writing over the old one in the input packet. Finally, the packet is queued for transmission out the outbound network interface—Step 5 in Figure 15-1.

When the outbound interface hardware senses a packet waiting for output, it dequeues the packet from I/O memory and transmits it on to the network—Step 6 in Figure 15-1. After it has finished transmitting the packet, it interrupts the main processor to indicate that the packet has been transmitted. IOS will then update its outbound packet counters and free the space in I/O memory formerly occupied by the packet. This is the final step in Figure 15-1, Step 7.

Traffic Load Sharing with Process Switching

One of the advantages of process switching is that it supports load sharing on a per-packet basis. Per-packet load sharing provides a relatively simple way to balance link utilization when multiple routes (paths) exist to a destination. When multiple paths exist, process-switched packets are automatically distributed among the available paths based on the routing metric (referred to as the path cost) assigned to each path.

The metric or cost of each path in the routing table is used to calculate a *load share* counter, which is actually used to determine which path to take. To better understand how this works, take a look at Figure 15-2.

Figure 15-2 *Traffic Sharing Across Equal Cost Paths*

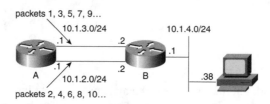

Here, Router A has two paths to the 10.1.4.0/24 network. Given that they are equal-cost paths, the routing table on Router A would look like the following:

```
RouterA#sho ip route 10.1.4.0 255.255.255.0
Routing entry for 10.1.4.0/24
  Known via "static", distance 1, metric 0
  Routing Descriptor Blocks:
    10.1.2.1
    Route metric is 0, traffic share count is 1
  * 10.1.3.1
    Route metric is 0, traffic share count is 1
```

Note the asterisk (*) next to one of the two network paths. This indicates the path that will be used for the next packet switched toward 10.1.4.0/24. The traffic-share count on both paths is 1, meaning packets are switched out each path in a round-robin fashion.

In this example, the very next packet arriving for this network will be routed to next hop 10.1.3.1. The second packet arriving will be routed to next hop 10.1.2.1, the third to 10.1.3.1, and so on (as shown by the packet numbers in Figure 15-2).

Some IP routing protocols, in particular Interior Gateway Protocol (IGRP) and Enhanced IGRP (EIGRP), can install unequal cost paths in the routing table; in cases where path costs differ, the traffic-sharing algorithm changes slightly. If a link is changed in the preceding example, for instance, so that one path has about twice the bandwidth of the other, the network that would result is shown in Figure 15-3.

Figure 15-3 *Traffic Sharing Across Unequal Cost Paths*

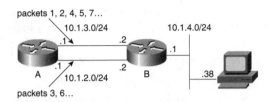

The routing table would look something like the following:

```
RouterA#sho ip route 10.1.4.0 255.255.255.0
Routing entry for 10.1.4.0/24
  Known via "EIGRP", distance 90, metric 284600
  Routing Descriptor Blocks:
    10.1.2.1
    Route metric is 569200, traffic share count is 1
  * 10.1.3.1
    Route metric is 284600, traffic share count is 2
```

Note the traffic-share counts in this **show ip route** output. The lower-cost path through 10.1.3.1 has a traffic-share count of 1; the higher-cost path through 10.1.2.1 has a traffic-share count of 2. Now for each packet switched out the higher-cost path, two packets will be switched out the lower-cost path, as indicated by the packet numbers in the diagram.

NOTE	Although per-packet traffic sharing is very good at balancing traffic load across multiple links, it does have one significant drawback: It can result in packets arriving out of order at the destination. This is especially true if there is a wide variation in latency among the available routes. Out-of-order packet processing can significantly degrade end-station performance.

Disadvantages of Process Switching

As noted before, a key disadvantage of process switching is its speed—or lack thereof. Process switching requires a routing table lookup for every packet; as the size of the routing table grows, so does the time required to perform a lookup (and hence the total switching time). Longer lookup times also increase the main processor utilization, an effect that is multiplied by the incoming packet rate. Although this effect may not be noticeable on very small networks with a few routes, large networks can have hundreds or even thousands of routes. For these networks, routing table size can significantly impact main processor utilization and routing latency (the delay between the time the packet enters and exits the router).

Another major factor that affects process-switching speed is in-memory data transfer time. On some platforms, process switching requires that received packets be copied from I/O memory to another memory area before they can be switched. After the routing process finishes, they must then be copied back to I/O memory before they can be transmitted. Memory data copy operations are very CPU intensive. So, again, on these platforms, process switching can be a very poor performer.

It became quite clear to the early IOS developers that a better switching method would be required if IOS was to be viable in the world of ever-growing routed networks. To understand the solution they devised, take a look at some of the more obvious areas for improvement in the process-switching method.

Looking back at the IP process-switching example, the **ip_input** process needs three key pieces of data to switch the packet:

- **Reachability**—Is this destination reachable? If so, what is the IP network address of the next hop toward this destination? This data is in the routing table (also called forwarding table).

- **Interface**—Which interface should this packet be transmitted on to reach its destination? This data is also stored in the routing table.

- **MAC layer header**—What MAC header needs to be placed on the packet to correctly address the next hop? MAC header data comes from the ARP table for IP or other mapping tables such as the Frame Relay map table.

Because every incoming packet can be different, **ip_input** must look up these key pieces of data anew each time it switches a packet. It has to search through a potentially huge routing table for reachability and interface data and then search another potentially large table for a MAC layer header. Wouldn't it be useful if the **ip_input** process could "remember" the results of these lookups for destinations it has already seen before? If it could keep a smaller table of the reachability/interface/MAC combinations for the most popular destinations, it could significantly reduce the lookup time for most of the incoming packets. Furthermore, because the lookup is the most intensive task, if the smaller table could speed up the task enough, the entire switching operation could possibly be performed by the packet receive interrupt software. That would also remove the need for in-memory data copying, saving even more time. So, how can IOS keep such a smaller lookup table and recognize these performance savings? The answer is called the Fast Cache.

Fast Switching: Caching to the Rescue

The term *cache* in the computer industry usually refers to the concept of storing some frequently used subset of a data set in a local storage area with very fast access properties. A computer may keep a local copy in RAM of frequently accessed parts of a disk file, for example, or a CPU may pre-fetch some instructions into a very fast associative memory area to boost performance. The two key characteristics of such a cache are a relatively small size as compared to the entire data space, and the capability to provide very fast access to any addressable member of its contents.

The IOS developers used these concepts when they created the Fast Cache. The Fast Cache quite simply is a data structure in IOS used to keep a copy of the reachability/interface/MAC-header combinations learned while process-switching packets.

To understand how the Fast Cache can be helpful, consider the example of process switching a packet discussed earlier in this chapter. Now add a step to the switching operation performed by the **ip_input** process. After **ip_input** looks up the next hop, output interface, and MAC-header data for a packet, add a step that saves this information in a special data structure that allows very fast access to any member based on a destination IP address. This structure is the Fast Cache. Over time the **ip_input** process will build a large number of frequently used IP destinations into the cache. Now you'll learn how to put this cache to use in switching packets.

Figure 15-4 *The Fast Switched Path*

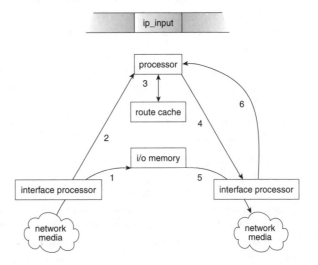

Consider the process-switching method again—only this time the newly built Fast Cache is introduced. Again, the switching process begins with the interface hardware sensing there is a packet on the wire. It receives the packet and transfers it to I/O memory—Step 1 in Figure 15-4.

In Step 2, the interface hardware interrupts the main processor to inform it that there is a received packet waiting in I/O memory. The IOS interrupt software inspects the packet's header information and determines that it is an IP packet. Now, instead of placing the packet in the input queue for **ip_input** as before, the interrupt software consults the Fast Cache directly to determine whether an outbound interface and MAC header have been cached for this destination. Assuming there is a cache entry, the interrupt software reads the MAC header from the entry and writes it into the packet. It also reads a pointer to the appropriate outbound interface from the cache entry. Step 3 in Figure 15-4 illustrates the cache read and MAC rewrite.

The main processor (still within the same interrupt) then notifies the outbound interface hardware that a packet in I/O memory is ready to transmit and dismisses the interrupt so that other processes can continue—Step 4 in Figure 15-4.

The interface hardware dequeues the packet from I/O memory and transmits it in Step 5, and then interrupts the main processor to update its counters and release the I/O memory, Step 6.

The example just described illustrates how the fast-switching method works. Notice that the **ip_input** process never gets involved in switching this packet; in fact, no scheduled process gets involved when a packet is fast switched as long as a cache entry exists. With the introduction of the Fast Cache, IOS can now perform the entire packet-switching operation within the very brief period of an interrupt! Caching has enabled IOS to separate the resource-intensive task of making a routing decision from the relatively easy task of forwarding a packet. Thus, fast switching introduced the concept of "route once, forward many times."

An important implication of the fast-switching process should be noted. As you've seen, Fast Cache entries are built while packets are process switched. Because the process-switching operation builds the cache entries, the first packet sent to any given destination *will always be process switched* even when fast switching is enabled. After the cache entry is built, future packets to that destination can be fast switched.

This method of using the process-switching operation to populate the Fast Cache works well as long as certain assumptions are met: The network must be generally stable with few routes changing and traffic must tend to flow between a particular subset of destinations. These assumptions are true in most cases. In some network environments, however, particularly the Internet backbone, they are not true. In those environments, network conditions can cause an increased number of cache *misses* (an instance where no cache entry matches a packet) and result in a high number of packets being process switched. It's also possible for a certain set of conditions to cause *cache trashing*, where older cache entries are continually overwritten with older cache entries because there just isn't enough room in the cache for all the entries required. Such environments are discussed later in this chapter.

Fast Cache Organization

How does a Fast Cache actually work? How can it provide forwarding data so quickly? For the answer, look at how a typical Fast Cache is organized.

First, to get an idea of exactly what's in the Fast Cache, take a look at the output of the **show ip cache verbose** command:

```
router#sho ip cache verbose
IP routing cache 1 entry, 172 bytes
   124 adds, 123 invalidates, 0 refcounts
Minimum invalidation interval 2 seconds, maximum interval 5 seconds,
   quiet interval 3 seconds, threshold 0 requests
Invalidation rate 0 in last second, 0 in last 3 seconds

Prefix/Length    Age     Interface    Next Hop
10.1.1.16/32-24  1w4d    Ethernet0    10.1.1.16
         14 00403337E5350060474FB47B0800
```

From the output, it's obvious the router keeps the destination prefix, the length of the prefix, the outbound interface, the next hop IP address, and a MAC header—just what you'd expect. All the data necessary to switch a packet to a particular destination is contained in this one entry.

Another characteristic of the cache is not evident from **show** command output. Unlike the master tables used to build them, which are basically just big lists, caches are implemented using special data structures. These special data structures allow any particular member to be retrieved with a minimal amount of searching. With the master tables, the searching time increases proportionately with the size of the table. With the cache data structures, because of the way they are organized, the searching time can be kept small and fairly constant regardless of the total number of entries.

The IP Fast Cache was originally implemented as a data structure called a *hash table*; Figure 15-5 illustrates.

Figure 15-5 *Fast Cache Organization*

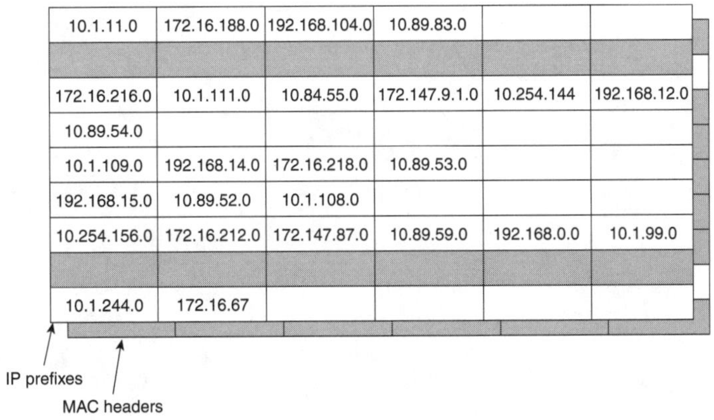

In the hash table, each IP prefix points to a particular place in the table. A particular hash table entry is found by computing some XOR operations on the upper and lower 16 bits of the 32-bit IP address being searched; the result of the calculation points to the desired hash table location, called a *hash bucket*. Each hash bucket contains a cache entry, including a prebuilt MAC header for the next hop.

A hash calculation (or, simply, *hash*) does not always produce a unique hash bucket address for every IP address. The case where more than one IP address points to the same hash location is called a *collision*. When collisions occur, IOS links each of the colliding cache entries together in a list within the bucket up to a maximum of six entries. This way, no more than six entries in the cache need to be searched to find a particular match.

In Cisco IOS Release 10.2, the hash table was replaced with another data structure called a *2-way radix tree* (a form of a binary tree). The MAC headers are still stored as part of the cache in this implementation.

Radix Trees

The *radix tree*, like the hash table, is another special data structure used to improve retrieval time of the member data.

A radix tree gets its name from the way in which data is stored—by its *radix*. In practice, this means that the information is stored in a tree structure based on the binary representation of the key (unique field which uniquely identifies each set of data). For instance, consider the following numbers:

— 10, which is 1010 in binary

— 7, which is 0111 in binary

— 2, which is 0010 in binary

You could store them in a radix tree structure, as shown in Figure 15-6.

Figure 15-6 *A Radix Tree*

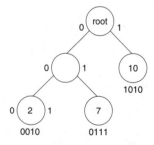

The tree branches are based on the binary digits within the number at any given level. To store, or find, the number 10, for instance, you begin at the root with the first bit in 1010, which is 1.

This first 1 causes you to choose the right branch, which takes you to a node on the tree. You find that this node doesn't have any children, so you compare the number in the node to the number you are searching for to see whether you have a match. In this case, there is a match.

To find or store 7, you would begin at the root of the tree again. The first bit in the binary representation of the number 7 is a 0, so you would take the left branch. You find yourself at a node with children, so you branch based on the second digit in the number, which is 1. This causes you to branch right.

Fast Cache Limitations for IP Routing

There is one major limitation on the way the Fast Cache stores IP prefixes: Overlapping cache entries are not possible. For example, consider building cache entries for the following IP prefixes:

- 172.31.46.0/24
- 172.31.46.128/25
- 172.31.46.129/32

Because the Fast Cache doesn't use the subnet mask, or prefix length, when looking up routing information, there isn't any way to know that the entry for 172.31.46.129 uses a 32-bit prefix, and the 172.31.46.128 entry uses a 25-bit prefix.

A simple way to overcome this limitation is to build a cache entry for each destination host; but this is impractical for several reasons, including the processing required to build this many cache entries and the amount of memory a cache containing all this information would consume.

So how does IOS solve this problem? It builds cache entries according to a simple set of rules:

- If the destination is directly attached, cache with a 32-bit prefix length.
- If there are multiple equal-cost paths for this destination, cache with a 32-bit prefix length.
- If it's a supernet, cache using the prefix length of the supernet.
- If it's a major network with no subnets, cache using the prefix length of the major network.
- If it's a major network with subnets, cache using the longest length prefix in this major network.

So, given the following snippet of an IP routing table from a Cisco router, you could determine what prefix lengths the router would use for various destinations:

```
router#show ip route
....
O    172.31.0.0 [110/11] via 172.25.10.210, 2d01h, Ethernet0
         [110/11] via 172.25.10.215, 2d01h, Ethernet0
```

```
      172.16.0.0/16 is variably subnetted, 2 subnets, 2 masks
D EX   172.16.180.0/25 [170/281600] via 172.25.10.210, 3d20h, Ethernet0
D EX   172.16.180.24/32 [170/281600] via 172.25.10.210, 3d20h, Ethernet0
O      10.0.0.0 [110/11] via 172.25.10.210, 2d01h, Ethernet0
O      192.168.0.0/16 [110/11] via 172.25.10.210, 2d18h, Ethernet0
      172.25.0.0/24 is subnetted, 1 subnet
C      172.25.10.0 [0/0] via connected, Ethernet0
```

The following are some examples:

- Every destination in the 172.31.0.0/16 network will be cached with a 32-bit prefix length because there are two equal-cost paths for this network installed in the routing table.

- Every destination in the 172.16.0.0/16 network will be cached with a 32-bit prefix length because there is a host route within this range.

- Network 10.0.0.0/8 will have one cache entry, because it is a major network route with no subnets, host routes, equal-cost paths, and so on.

- 192.168.0.0/16 will have one cache entry because it is a supernet route with no subnets.

- All destinations within the 172.25.10.0/24 network will be cached using a 32-bit prefix, because this destination is directly connected to the router.

Maintaining the Cache

Any time data is cached, it's important to somehow maintain the cached data so that it doesn't become outdated or out of sync with the master data used to build the cache in the first place. There are two issues to address in this area: cache invalidation and cache aging.

In the case of fast switching, the issue is how to keep the Fast Cache updated so that it contains the same information as the routing table and the ARP cache (or other tables from which the MAC headers are built).

Cache Invalidation

The problem of keeping the route cache synchronized with the routing table is complicated when switching IP packets because of recursion or dependencies within the routing table.

Recursive Routing

Because recursion is such an important concept when considering the operation of route caches, it's helpful to walk through an example of recursive routing. Figure 15-7 provides an example of what recursion looks like in a network.

In Figure 15-7, Router A needs to look up a route for the host 10.1.3.38 and find out what next hop and MAC header to use. When Router A examines its routing table, it finds that this destination is reachable through 10.1.2.2.

This destination isn't directly attached to Router A, so it needs to look into the routing table again to determine how to reach the next hop. Router A looks up the route to 10.1.1.2, and discovers that it is reachable through 10.1.1.2, which is directly connected.

Figure 15-7 *A Recursive Route*

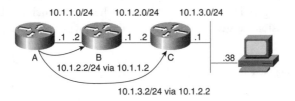

Router A will send all traffic destined to 10.1.3.38 to 10.1.1.2 for further processing.

In fast switching, recursion is resolved when the cache entry is built rather than when the packet is switched. So, the route cache contains the MAC header and outbound interface of the actual next hop toward the destination being cached. This disconnects the cache entry from both the routing table entry and the ARP cache (or other MAC-layer table) entry.

Because recursion is resolved when a cache entry is built, there is no direct correlation between the Fast Cache and the routing table or the ARP cache. So, how can the cache be kept synchronized with the data in the original tables? The best way to solve this problem is to just invalidate, or remove, cache entries when any corresponding data changes in the master tables.

Cache entries can be removed from the Fast Cache, for example, because of the following reasons:

- The ARP cache entry for the next hop changes, is removed, or times out.
- The routing table entry for the prefix changes or is removed.
- The routing table entry for the next hop to this destination changes.

Cache Aging

IOS also ages entries in the Fast Cache periodically; a small portion of the Fast Cache is invalidated every minute to make certain the cache doesn't grow out of bounds, and to resynchronize entries with the routing and ARP tables periodically. When the amount of available memory is greater than 200 KB, the *cache ager* process randomly invalidates

1/20th of the cache entries every minute. If free memory is lower than 200 KB, the cache ager process will start aging entries more aggressively—1/5th of the cache entries are invalidated every minute.

Traffic Load Sharing Considerations with Fast Switching

Unlike process switching, fast switching does not support load sharing on a per-packet basis. This restriction can lead to uneven link utilization in some situations where multiple paths exist between two destinations. The reason for this restriction has to do with the separation of routing and forwarding that occurs when fast switching. To understand this reason and the possible disadvantages, consider the following example illustrated by Figure 15-8.

Figure 15-8 *Load Sharing Using the Fast Cache*

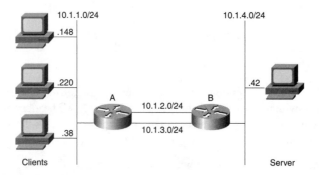

In Figure 15-8, several workstations are connected to a network segment attached to Router A; each workstation communicates with a single server on another network segment attached to Router B. Router A has multiple parallel paths to Router B. Assume for this example that both parallel paths have the same cost. One would like the traffic between the client and server networks to be evenly distributed over those two paths. Now, check out what happens.

Starting with an empty Fast Cache, Router A receives a packet from client 10.1.1.220, destined toward the server, 10.1.4.42. As you've seen, this first packet will be process switched and Router A will build a Fast Cache entry for the 10.1.4.42 destination. Because there are two equal-cost paths to the 10.1.4.42 destination (via Router B), Router A will have to choose one of these when it builds the cache entry. It will use the per-packet load-balancing algorithm described earlier for process switching to make the decision.

Next, Router A receives another client packet destined to server 10.1.4.42. This time the packet is fast switched because there is already an entry in the Fast Cache. Because the transmit interface pointer is built in to the cache entry, Router A switches this second packet through the same path as the first. As you can see, Router A will continue to send all packets destined for the 10.1.4.42 server through this same path until the cache entry either ages out or is invalidated for some reason. If the cache entry does happen to get removed, the other path may be chosen but packets will still only be forwarded out that one path for the 10.1.4.42 server.

If there happened to be multiple servers on the 10.1.4.0/24 network, this same process would apply to each of them. The path cached for each server might vary, but for any given server all packets coming from the clients would take the same path.

Now consider traffic originating from the other direction. Router B will also cache destinations on the client network in the same manner Router A did. In this case, Router B will build two cache entries along one path, and the third along the other path. It could turn out that Router B will choose to send the traffic for two clients along the path not chosen by Router A. This would result in a fairly well distributed traffic load on the parallel paths. It's just as likely that Router B will choose to cache two client entries along the same path that Router A chose for the server traffic, however, resulting in unbalanced utilization of the paths.

This lack of a deterministic load-balancing scheme is an area of concern for many network designers. In response, newer switching methods now support load-balancing schemes that help overcome this problem. One such method, Cisco Express Forwarding, is covered later in this chapter.

Optimum Switching

Optimum switching is essentially fast switching with some caching optimizations. Like fast switching, optimum switching accomplishes the entire task of switching a packet during a single interrupt. The primary difference between optimum and fast switching is in the way the route cache is accessed. The optimum-switching software is also crafted to take advantage of specific processor architectures. The fast-switching code is generic, and is not optimized for any specific processor. Unlike fast switching, optimum switching is only available for the IP protocol.

Earlier in this chapter, you learned that the Fast Cache is accessed using a hash table in earlier releases, and is accessed via a two-way radix tree in later releases. The optimum cache is accessed via a *256-way multiway trie* (mtrie). Figure 15-9 provides an illustration of a 256-way mtrie.

Figure 15-9 *The Optimum Cache*

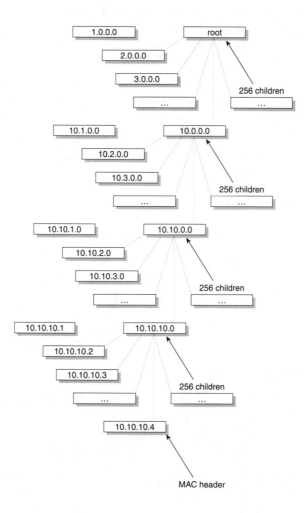

Reachability information is stored as a set of nodes, each with 256 children, and the prebuilt MAC headers are stored in the nodes. Although this provides faster lookups than the Fast Cache's two-way radix tree, it still has the same limitations as the Fast Cache.

Optimum switching is still similar to fast switching in many ways, including the following:

- Cache entries are built when the first packet is process switched toward a destination.
- Cache entries are aged and invalidated as the routing table or other cache information changes.

- Load sharing still occurs based strictly on the destination address.

- The same rules are still used to decide what cache entry to build for each particular destination.

The output of **show ip cache optimum** is very similar to the output of **show ip cache**—the headers are different, accounting for the mtrie data structure, as you can see here:

```
router#sho ip cache optimum
Optimum Route Cache
 1 prefixes, 1 nodes, 0 leaf refcount, 8K bytes
 0 nodes pending, 0 node alloc failures
 8 prefix updates, 4 prefix invalidations

Prefix/Length    Age    Interface    Next Hop
10.1.1.16/32-24  1w4d   Ethernet0    10.1.1.16
```

Cisco Express Forwarding

Cisco Express Forwarding (CEF) is the newest, and fastest, switching method available in IOS. CEF was invented to help overcome the major deficiencies of the fast-switching method. Reviewing the description of fast switching for a moment, the major deficiencies noted were the following:

- Lack of support for overlapping cache entries.

- Any change in the routing table or ARP cache results in the invalidation of large sections of the route cache, because there is little or no correlation between the route cache and the tables the cache is based on.

- The first packet to any given destination must be process switched to build a route cache entry.

- Inefficient load balancing in some situations (primarily in cases where many hosts are transacting with one server).

Most of these deficiencies do not pose a problem in the average enterprise network because routes don't change often and routing tables aren't extremely large. However, there is one environment in which these shortcomings *do* become a problem: the Internet backbone.

Internet backbone routers have extremely large routing tables—around 56,000 routes in early 1999 and still growing. Some Internet backbone routers actually carry more than 100,000 routes. The routing table also changes constantly, causing cache entries to be invalidated frequently. In fact, entries are invalidated often enough to cause a significant portion of traffic through some Internet routers to be process switched. CEF was developed specifically to improve routing performance in these types of environments.

CEF was initially tested in the large-scale network environment of the Internet. Internet service providers were given a series of special IOS software images (nicknamed the *ISP Geeks images*) with CEF to see how it operated under extreme conditions. The technology proved itself capable of handling the Internet backbone workload and was eventually integrated into the Cisco IOS product, becoming the default switching mode in Cisco IOS Release 12.0. It is now the only switching mode available on some platforms—in particular, the Cisco 12000 and the Catalyst 8500.

How CEF Works

Unlike fast switching, which builds a cached subset of the routing table and MAC address tables, CEF builds its own structures that mirror the entire routing and MAC address tables. There are two major structures maintained by CEF. These structures collectively can be considered the CEF "Fast Cache":

- CEF table
- Adjacency table

The CEF Table

The CEF table is a "stripped-down" version of the routing table, implemented as a 256-way mtrie data structure for optimum retrieval performance. The size of the CEF table (and other general information about the table) can be displayed by the command **show ip cef summary**:

```
router#show ip cef summary
IP Distributed CEF with switching (Table Version 96)
    33 routes, 0 reresolve, 0 unresolved (0 old, 0 new)
    33 leaves, 31 nodes, 36256 bytes, 96 inserts, 63 invalidations
    1 load sharing elements, 328 bytes, 2 references
    1 CEF resets, 8 revisions of existing leaves
    refcounts:  8226 leaf, 8192 node

Adjacency Table has 5 adjacencies
```

In a 256-way mtrie structure, each node in the structure can have up to 256 children. In the CEF table, each child, or link, is used to represent a different address in one octet of an IP address, as shown in Figure 15-10.

So, for example, given the IP address 10.10.10.4, one would locate the data by choosing the tenth child off of the root, then the tenth child off of that node, then the tenth child off of that node, and then, finally, the fourth child off of the last node. This final node, or *end node*, contains a pointer to an entry in another table outside the CEF, called the adjacency table. It is the adjacency table that actually contains the MAC header and other information needed to switch the packet.

Figure 15-10   *CEF mtrie and Adjacency Table*

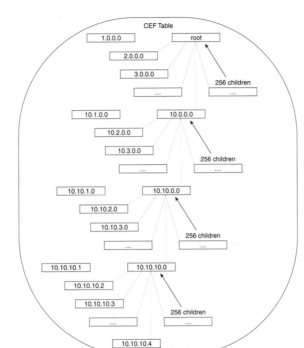

NOTE   An *mtree* data structure stores the actual data within the tree structure itself; for example, in the optimum-switching mtree cache, the MAC header data used for forwarding packets is actually stored inside the mtree. In an mtrie data structure, the tree structure is used to locate the desired data, but the data itself is stored elsewhere.

The Adjacency Table

The adjacency table contains the MAC-layer packet-header data for directly connected next hops. The adjacency table is populated with data from the ARP table, Frame Relay map table, and other tables of this type. The command to display the adjacency table is **show adjacency**:

```
router#show adjacency
Protocol Interface            Address
IP       POS0/0/0             point2point(15)
IP       Serial1/0/0          point2point(5)
IP       FastEthernet6/0/0    17.1.1.2(16)
IP       Ethernet4/0          10.105.1.1(9)
IP       Ethernet4/0          10.105.1.179(5)
Router#
```

There are several types of adjacency entries, as follows:

- **Cached adjacency**—A prebuilt MAC header for the next hop toward this destination.

- **Punt**—Packets destined to this address must be punted up to the next switching path.

- **Host-route**—This destination is a directly connected host.

- **Drop**—Packets destined to this address are dropped.

- **Incomplete**—The MAC-layer header for this destination is incomplete; typically this means the ARP cache entry for this destination is incomplete or otherwise malformed.

- **Glean**—This is a directly attached destination, but there is no prebuilt MAC-layer header; an ARP request needs to be sent so that a MAC-layer header can be built.

The CEF Method and Its Advantages

Like fast switching, CEF switching utilizes cache entries to perform its switching operation entirely during a processor interrupt. A major difference between fast switching and CEF switching, however, is the point at which the cache entries are built. Although fast switching requires that the first packet to any given destination be process switched to build a cache entry, CEF does not. Instead, the CEF table is built directly from the routing table and the adjacency table is built directly from the ARP cache. These CEF structures are built before any packets are switched.

The result of this difference is that for CEF, every packet received for a reachable destination can be forwarded by the IOS interrupt software. It is never necessary to process switch a packet to get a cache entry built. This greatly improves the routing performance on routers that have many routing table entries. With normal fast switching, IOS can be overwhelmed with process-level traffic before the route cache entries are created. With CEF technology, this massive process-level load is eliminated, preventing the IOS from choking on the process-level switching bottleneck when network routes are flapping.

Splitting the reachability/interface data and the MAC-layer header data into two structures also provides an advantage: Because the tables used in switching packets are directly related to their information sources, the cache doesn't need an aging process anymore.

Entries in the CEF structures never age out; any changes in the routing table or the ARP cache can be easily reflected in the CEF structures. Also, with CEF there is no longer any need to invalidate a large number of entries when the routing table or the ARP cache change.

Traffic Load Sharing with CEF

Traffic load sharing with CEF switching can either be per source/destination pair (the default), or per packet. Traffic sharing based on the source/destination pair resolves the problems described in the earlier fast-switching example, where all the traffic destined to the server would take one link because the cache is built on a per-destination basis. How does it do this? Instead of pointing to an entry in the adjacency table, an entry in the CEF table can also point to a *load share* structure, as shown in Figure 15-11.

When the CEF switching method finds a load-share entry, rather than an adjacency table entry, as the result of a CEF table search, it uses the source and destination address to decide which of the entries to use from the load-share table. Each entry in the load-share table then points to an adjacency table entry that contains the MAC header and other information needed to forward the packet.

Figure 15-11 *The Load Share Table in CEF*

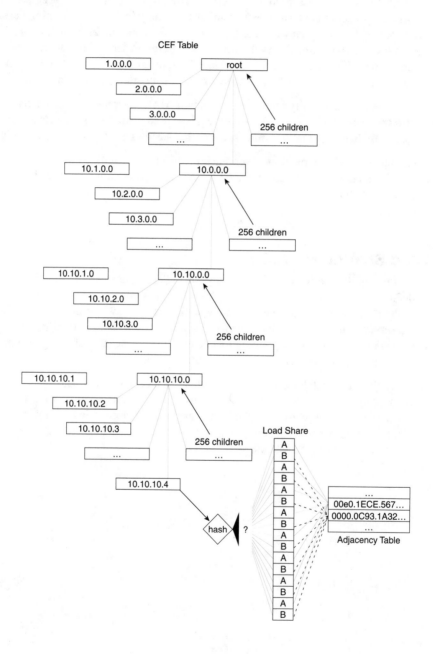

CEF in Review

To help understand how the CEF switching structures fit together, review them briefly within the context of Figure 15-12.

Figure 15-12   *The CEF Tables*

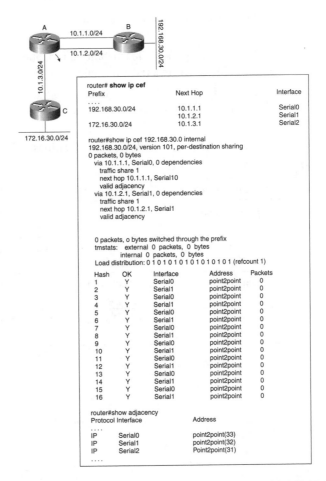

Here, Router A has three tables used to CEF switch packets toward the 192.168.30.0/24 network: the CEF table, the adjacency table, and the load-share table. For switching toward the 172.16.30.0/24 network, only two tables are needed: the CEF table and the adjacency table.

Summary

Cisco routers switch packets through one of several paths; the characteristics of the switching path depend on whether a route cache is used, how that cache is accessed or built, and what context (process or interrupt) the switching actually takes place in:

- Process switching doesn't cache any information, and switches packets in the context of a process.

- Fast switching caches reachability information and the MAC headers needed to forward packets in a radix tree and switches packets during interrupts.

- CEF switching caches reachability information in an mtrie, and the MAC headers needed to forward packets within an adjacency table. CEF switches packets during interrupts.

Table 15-1 summarizes characteristics of various switching methods.

Table 15-1 *Switching Paths in IOS*

Switching Method	Type of Cache	Processing Characteristics
Process switching	None	Packet switching is done by a scheduled process.
Fast switching	Hash table or two-way radix tree and route cache	Packet is switched by the main processor during an interrupt.
Optimum switching	mtrie and fast route cache	Packet is switched by the main processor during an interrupt.
Cisco Express Forwarding (CEF)	mtrie and adjacency table	Packet is switched by the main processor during an interrupt.

CHAPTER 16

EIGRP and OSPF Redistribution

Edited by Anthony Bruno

This case study addresses the issue of integrating Enhanced Interior Gateway Routing Protocol (EIGRP) networks with Open Shortest Path First (OSPF) networks. Cisco supports both the EIGRP and OSPF protocols and provides a way to exchange routing information between EIGRP and OSPF networks. Both are classless protocols that support VLSM and route summarization. This case study provides examples of how to redistribute information between EIGRP and OSPF networks, including the following topics:

- Setting Up EIGRP and OSPF Mutual Redistribution
- Verifying the Redistribution of Routes
- Adding a Route to the Redistribution List

Setting Up EIGRP and OSPF Mutual Redistribution

It is sometimes necessary to accommodate complex network topologies such as independent EIGRP and OSPF clouds that must perform mutual redistribution. For example, when a company acquires another company, one of them may be running OSPF while the other is running EIGRP. Also, the physical topology of a network may not support the two-layer hierarchy of OSPF, requiring redistribution from another routing protocol such as EIGRP. Redistribution is also required when migrating from one routing protocol to another. In this scenario, it is critically important to prevent potential routing loops by filtering routes. Figure 16-1 shows an EIGRP cloud connecting to an OSPF cloud. Router A is in the EIGRP cloud. Router B is running both OSPF and EIGRP; it functions as an OSPF Autonomous System Border (ASBR) between these two network clouds. Router C is an Area Border Router (ABR) in the OSPF cloud. Router C also provides an ASBR function to the external network 170.10.0.0.

Figure 16-1 *Mutual Redistribution Between EIGRP And OSPF Networks*

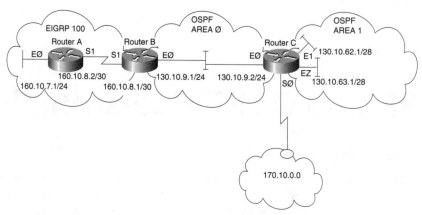

In Figure 16-1, there are no secondary or redundant routers directly connecting the EIGRP and OSPF clouds. In typical networks, however, these paths, or back doors, frequently exist, allowing the potential for feedback loops. You can use route maps and access lists to configure the routes that are advertised and accepted by each router, and thus prevent potential routing loops. With the following commands, OSPF routes will be redistributed into EIGRP:

```
!
router eigrp 100
default-metric 10000 1000 255 1 1500
network 160.10.0.0
redistribute ospf 109 route-map OSPFtoEIGRP
!
route-map OSPFtoEIGRP permit 10
 match ip address 11
 !
access-list 11 permit 130.10.0.0 0.0.255.255
!
```

You must use the **default-metric** command to set the metrics of the redistributed route in EIGRP updates. All routes redistributed into EIGRP will have the following default metric:

```
default-metric bandwidth delay reliability loading mtu
```

Each field value's ranges are listed in Table 16-1.

Table 16-1   *Field Value Ranges for the **default-metric** Command*

Bandwidth (in kbps)	1–4294967295
Delay metric (in 10 microsecond units)	0–4294967295
Reliability metric (where 255 is 100% reliable)	0–255
Effective bandwidth metric, or loading (where 255 is 100% loaded)	0–255
Maximum Transmission Unit (MTU) metric of the path	1–4294967295

Access list 11 in the configuration for Router B allows the redistribution of network 130.10.0.0 into EIGRP. Notice that in this example the OSPF external network 170.10.0.0 is not redistributed into EIGRP. You will see later in the chapter how to add this network to the redistribution list.

Configuration File Examples

This section contains the configurations of Routers A, B, and C in Figure 16-1. The configurations demonstrate how redistribution can be accomplished using route maps on Router B. Access lists are used with the route maps to configure which networks will be redistributed. Router A is configured with EIGRP, and Router C is configured with OSPF.

The configuration for Router A is as follows:

```
!
hostname routerA
!
interface Ethernet0
ip address 160.10.7.1 255.255.255.0
!
interface Serial1
 ip address 160.10.8.2 255.255.255.252
!
router eigrp 100
 network 160.10.0.0
!
```

Router A has a simple configuration that defines two interfaces and the EIGRP process 100. Because no redistribution occurs on Router A, no route maps and redistribution commands are used. Router B will be Router A's EIGRP neighbor.

The configuration for Router B is as follows:

```
!
hostname routerB
!
interface Ethernet0
 ip address 130.10.9.1 255.255.255.0
!
interface Serial1
 ip address 160.10.8.1 255.255.255.252
!
router eigrp 100
 redistribute ospf 109 route-map OSPFtoEIGRP
 network 160.10.0.0
 default-metric 10000 1000 255 1 1500
!
router ospf 109
 redistribute eigrp 100 subnets route-map EIGRPtoOSPF
 network 130.10.9.0 0.0.0.255 area 0
!
access-list 10 permit 160.10.0.0 0.0.255.255
access-list 10 deny   any
access-list 11 permit 130.10.0.0 0.0.255.255
access-list 11 deny   any
!
route-map OSPFtoEIGRP permit 10
```

```
  match ip address 11
 !
route-map EIGRPtoOSPF permit 10
  match ip address 10
  !
```

The Router B configuration uses **route-map OSPFtoEIGRP** with access list 11 to control which networks get redistributed into EIGRP. The **default-metric** command sets the EIGRP metrics of the redistributed routes to 10,000 for bandwidth, 1000 for delay, 255 for reliability, 1 for load, and 1500 bytes for the MTU. In this example, all subnets of network 130.10.0.0 get redistributed into EIGRP. Using **route-map EIGRPtoOSPF** with access list 10 controls which networks get redistributed into OSPF. Redistributed routes appear as external type 2 routes in OSPF by default. In this example, all subnets of network 160.10.0.0 get redistributed into OSPF.

NOTE   When redistributing into OSPF, use the **subnets** keyword. It tells OSPF to redistribute all subnet routes. Without the **subnets** keyword, only networks not subnetted will be redistributed by OSPF.

The configuration for Router C is as follows:

```
!
hostname routerC
!
interface Ethernet0
 ip address 130.10.9.2 255.255.255.0
!
interface Ethernet1
 ip address 130.10.62.1 255.255.255.240
!
interface Ethernet2
 ip address 130.10.63.1 255.255.255.240
!
router ospf 109
 redistribute static metric 1000
 network 130.10.9.0 0.0.0.255 area 0
 network 130.10.62.0 0.0.0.255 area 1
 network 130.10.63.0 0.0.0.255 area 1
 area 1 range 130.10.62.0 255.255.255.0
 area 1 range 130.10.63.0 255.255.255.0
!
ip classless
ip route 170.10.0.0 255.255.0.0 Serial0
!
```

As you can see from Router C's configuration, this router is an OSPF ABR for Area 0 and Area 1. The **area range** command is used to summarize the network subnets from a particular area on an ABR. The **area 1 range 130.10.62.0 255.255.255.0** summarizes the 16 following subnets (assuming that a 255.255.255.240 mask is used on 130.10.62.0) to one route entry. The 130.10.63.0 network is also summarized to 24 bits with the **area 1 range 130.10.63.0 255.255.255.0** command. If Router C had other OSPF neighbor routers with these subnets, they would be summarized at this router before the route is passed along to Area 0.

Router C is also an OSPF ASBR to network 170.10.0.0. Using the **redistribute static metric 1000** command, the static route will be entered into the OSPF database as an external type 2 route with a metric (cost) of 1000.

Verifying the Redistribution of Routes

Take a look at the following routing table for Router A. It shows the two connected networks: 160.10.7.0/24 and 160.10.8.0/30. Notice the EIGRP external (D EX) routes coming from Router B; these are the routes that were redistributed from OSPF. The numbers in brackets are the Administrative distance (170) and the calculated EIGRP metric. By default, all EIGRP external routes have an administrative distance of 170:

```
routerA#show ip ro
Codes: C - connected, S - static, I - IGRP, R - RIP, M - mobile, B - BGP
       D - EIGRP, EX - EIGRP external, O - OSPF, IA - OSPF inter area
       N1 - OSPF NSSA external type 1, N2 - OSPF NSSA external type 2
       E1 - OSPF external type 1, E2 - OSPF external type 2, E - EGP
       i - IS-IS, L1 - IS-IS level-1, L2 - IS-IS level-2, * - candidate default
       U - per-user static route, o - ODR
       T - traffic engineered route

Gateway of last resort is not set

     160.10.0.0/16 is variably subnetted, 2 subnets, 2 masks
C       160.10.8.0/30 is directly connected, Serial1
C       160.10.7.0/24 is directly connected, Ethernet0
     130.10.0.0/16 is variably subnetted, 3 subnets, 2 masks
D EX    130.10.9.0/24 [170/2425856] via 160.10.8.1, 00:02:01, Serial1
D EX    130.10.63.0/24 [170/2425856] via 160.10.8.1, 00:02:01, Serial1
D EX    130.10.62.0/24 [170/2425856] via 160.10.8.1, 00:02:01, Serial1
routerA#
```

Now look at the routing table for Router B. An OSPF external type 2 route (O E2) is coming from Router C; this is the static route that was redistributed into OSPF in Router C. The router also sees OSPF interarea routes (O IA) from Router C. The only EIGRP route present is for 160.10.7.0/24 because 160.10.8.0/30 is directly connected. (The routing table does not show whether the redistribution commands worked; to verify that, you need to look at the EIGRP topology table and the OSPF database.)

```
routerB#show ip ro
Codes: C - connected, S - static, I - IGRP, R - RIP, M - mobile, B - BGP
       D - EIGRP, EX - EIGRP external, O - OSPF, IA - OSPF inter area
       N1 - OSPF NSSA external type 1, N2 - OSPF NSSA external type 2
       E1 - OSPF external type 1, E2 - OSPF external type 2, E - EGP
       i - IS-IS, L1 - IS-IS level-1, L2 - IS-IS level-2, * - candidate default
       U - per-user static route, o - ODR
       T - traffic engineered route

Gateway of last resort is not set

O E2 170.10.0.0/16 [110/1000] via 130.10.9.2, 00:08:36, Ethernet0
     160.10.0.0/16 is variably subnetted, 2 subnets, 2 masks
```

```
C        160.10.8.0/30 is directly connected, Serial1
D        160.10.7.0/24 [90/2297856] via 160.10.8.2, 00:08:37, Serial1
     130.10.0.0/16 is variably subnetted, 3 subnets, 2 masks
C        130.10.9.0/24 is directly connected, Ethernet0
O IA     130.10.63.0/24 [110/11] via 130.10.9.2, 00:08:37, Ethernet0
O IA     130.10.62.0/24 [110/11] via 130.10.9.2, 00:08:37, Ethernet0
routerB#
```

The EIGRP topology table shows the redistributed OSPF routes. These routes will be propagated in the EIGRP cloud. Notice that the OSPF external 170.10.0.0 route does not show in this table:

```
routerB#show ip eigrp topology

IP-EIGRP Topology Table for process 100

Codes: P - Passive, A - Active, U - Update, Q - Query, R - Reply,
       r - Reply status

P 130.10.9.0/24, 1 successors, FD is 512000
        via Redistributed (512000/0)
P 160.10.8.0/30, 1 successors, FD is 2169856
        via Connected, Serial1
P 160.10.7.0/24, 1 successors, FD is 2297856
        via 160.10.8.2 (2297856/128256), Serial1
P 130.10.63.0/24, 1 successors, FD is 512000
        via Redistributed (512000/0)
P 130.10.62.0/24, 1 successors, FD is 512000
        via Redistributed (512000/0)
routerB#
```

The **show ip ospf database** command shows all the link states in the OSPF database for all link-state types. There are two OSPF routers; hence, two router link states. There is one broadcast network (Ethernet) in Area 0; hence, one Net Link State. The two Summary Net Link States come from ABR Router C. There are two externals coming from the local redistribution on Router B (160.10.8.1) and one external from Router C (130.10.63.1):

```
routerB#show ip ospf data

        OSPF Router with ID (160.10.8.1) (Process ID 109)

                Router Link States (Area 0)

Link ID         ADV Router      Age         Seq#          Checksum Link count
130.10.63.1     130.10.63.1     1627        0x80000009 0xF164    1
160.10.8.1      160.10.8.1      1852        0x80000002 0x3A57    1

                Net Link States (Area 0)

Link ID         ADV Router      Age         Seq#          Checksum
130.10.9.2      130.10.63.1     47          0x80000002 0x60F3

                Summary Net Link States (Area 0)

Link ID         ADV Router      Age         Seq#          Checksum
130.10.62.0     130.10.63.1     47          0x80000004 0x168A
130.10.63.0     130.10.63.1     47          0x80000004 0xB94

                Type-5 AS External Link States

Link ID         ADV Router      Age         Seq#          Checksum Tag
```

```
160.10.7.0       160.10.8.1       506      0x80000001 0xC575   0
160.10.8.0       160.10.8.1       527      0x80000001 0xA894   0
170.10.0.0       130.10.63.1      1647     0x80000001 0x88BE   0
routerB#
```

Now look at the routing table in Router C. There is one static entry for 170.10.0.0. The routes coming from the EIGRP cloud show up as OSPF externals (E2). The other networks are directly connected:

```
routerC#show ip ro
Codes: C - connected, S - static, I - IGRP, R - RIP, M - mobile, B - BGP
       D - EIGRP, EX - EIGRP external, O - OSPF, IA - OSPF inter area
       N1 - OSPF NSSA external type 1, N2 - OSPF NSSA external type 2
       E1 - OSPF external type 1, E2 - OSPF external type 2, E - EGP
       i - IS-IS, L1 - IS-IS level-1, L2 - IS-IS level-2, * - candidate default
       U - per-user static route, o - ODR
       T - traffic engineered route

Gateway of last resort is not set

S    170.10.0.0/16 is directly connected, Serial0
     160.10.0.0/16 is variably subnetted, 2 subnets, 2 masks
O E2    160.10.8.0/30 [110/20] via 130.10.9.1, 00:11:03, Ethernet0
O E2    160.10.7.0/24 [110/20] via 130.10.9.1, 00:11:03, Ethernet0
     130.10.0.0/24 is subnetted, 3 subnets
C       130.10.9.0 is directly connected, Ethernet0
C       130.10.62.0 is directly connected, Ethernet1
C       130.10.63.0 is directly connected, Ethernet2
routerC#
```

Notice in the preceding output that there are two subnets from the 160.10.0.0 network. You can use the OSPF **summary-address** command on Router B to further summarize this network. The **summary-address** command is used to summarize external routers on ASBRs; it is not used to summarize interarea routes on ABRs:

```
routerB(config)#router ospf 109
routerB(config-router)# summary-address 160.10.0.0 255.255.0.0
```

Now Router C sees only one network:

```
routerC>show ip ro
Codes: C - connected, S - static, I - IGRP, R - RIP, M - mobile, B - BGP
       D - EIGRP, EX - EIGRP external, O - OSPF, IA - OSPF inter area
       N1 - OSPF NSSA external type 1, N2 - OSPF NSSA external type 2
       E1 - OSPF external type 1, E2 - OSPF external type 2, E - EGP
       i - IS-IS, L1 - IS-IS level-1, L2 - IS-IS level-2, * - candidate default
       U - per-user static route, o - ODR
       T - traffic engineered route

Gateway of last resort is not set

S    170.10.0.0/16 is directly connected, Null0
O E2 160.10.0.0/16 [110/20] via 130.10.9.1, 00:03:04, Ethernet0
     130.10.0.0/24 is subnetted, 3 subnets
C       130.10.9.0 is directly connected, Ethernet0
C       130.10.62.0 is directly connected, Loopback0
C       130.10.63.0 is directly connected, Loopback1
routerC>
```

Adding a Route to the Redistribution List

The 170.10.0.0 network was an external route in OSPF. This network was not redistributed into EIGRP on Router B (see **route-map OSPFtoEIGRP** and **access-list 11** in the configuration of Router B in the earlier "Configuration File Examples" section). Now suppose you want to permit users in the EIGRP cloud to reach the 170.10.0.0 network (see Figure 16-2). This can be accomplished by adding network 170.10.0.0 to access list 11 to permit this route to show up in the EIGRP topology table. The access list should now appear as follows:

```
access-list 11 permit 130.10.0.0 0.0.255.255
access-list 11 permit 170.10.0.0 0.0.255.255
access-list 11 deny any
```

Figure 16-2 *Network 170.10.0.0—External Route to EIGRP*

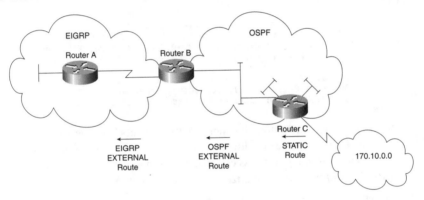

The EIGRP topology table on Router B now shows the new network:

```
routerB#show ip eigrp top
IP-EIGRP Topology Table for process 100

Codes: P - Passive, A - Active, U - Update, Q - Query, R - Reply,
       r - Reply status

P 130.10.9.0/24, 1 successors, FD is 512000
        via Redistributed (512000/0)
P 170.10.0.0/16, 1 successors, FD is 512000
        via Redistributed (512000/0)
P 160.10.8.0/30, 1 successors, FD is 2169856
        via Connected, Serial1
P 160.10.7.0/24, 1 successors, FD is 2297856
        via 160.10.8.2 (2297856/128256), Serial1
P 130.10.63.0/24, 1 successors, FD is 512000
        via Redistributed (512000/0)
P 130.10.62.0/24, 1 successors, FD is 512000
        via Redistributed (512000/0)
```

Now that Router B shows the route in the topology table, you can look at Router A's route table, which now shows the new network:

```
routerA>show ip route
Codes: C - connected, S - static, I - IGRP, R - RIP, M - mobile, B - BGP
       D - EIGRP, EX - EIGRP external, O - OSPF, IA - OSPF inter area
       N1 - OSPF NSSA external type 1, N2 - OSPF NSSA external type 2
       E1 - OSPF external type 1, E2 - OSPF external type 2, E - EGP
       i - IS-IS, L1 - IS-IS level-1, L2 - IS-IS level-2, * - candidate default
       U - per-user static route, o - ODR
       T - traffic engineered route

Gateway of last resort is not set

D EX 170.10.0.0/16 [170/2425856] via 160.10.8.1, 00:01:11, Serial1
        160.10.0.0/16 is variably subnetted, 2 subnets, 2 masks
C          160.10.8.0/30 is directly connected, Serial1
C          160.10.7.0/24 is directly connected, Loopback0
        130.10.0.0/16 is variably subnetted, 3 subnets, 2 masks
D EX       130.10.9.0/24 [170/2425856] via 160.10.8.1, 00:20:47, Serial1
D EX       130.10.63.0/24 [170/2425856] via 160.10.8.1, 00:01:12, Serial1
D EX       130.10.62.0/24 [170/2425856] via 160.10.8.1, 00:01:12, Serial1
routerA>
```

Now that the route is present in the EIGRP cloud, this case study is finished. Route maps and access lists have been used to control the networks to be redistributed between EIGRP and OSPF, and **area-range** and **summary-address** commands have been used to summarize routes in OSPF.

Summary

Because it is possible to find OSPF and EIGRP used together, it is important to use the practices described here to provide functionality for both protocols on an internetwork. You can configure Autonomous System Boundary Routers that run both EIGRP and OSPF and redistribute EIGRP routes into the OSPF and vice versa. Use the **summary** command in OSPF to further summarize redistributed networks. Use route maps and access lists to control the networks to be redistributed. You can also create OSPF areas using Area Border Routers that provide route summarizations.

CHAPTER 17

Configuring EIGRP for Novell and AppleTalk Networks

Edited by Anthony Bruno

In addition to IP, Enhanced IGRP (EIGRP) supports two other network-level protocols: AppleTalk and Novell Internetwork Packet Exchange (IPX). Each of these has protocol-specific, value-added functionality. IPX Novell EIGRP supports incremental Service Advertisement Protocol (SAP) updates, removes the Routing Information Protocol (RIP) limitation of 15 hop counts, and provides optimal path use. A router running AppleTalk EIGRP supports partial, bounded routing updates and provides load sharing and optimal path use.

The case studies provided here discuss the benefits and considerations involved in integrating EIGRP into the following types of networks:

- **Novell IPX**—The existing IPX network is running RIP and SAP.
- **AppleTalk**—The existing AppleTalk network is running the Routing Table Maintenance Protocol (RTMP).

Novell IPX Network

This case study illustrates the integration of EIGRP into a Novell IPX network in two phases: configuring an IPX network and adding EIGRP to the IPX network. The key considerations for integrating EIGRP into an IPX network running RIP and SAP are as follows:

- Route selection
- Redistribution and metric handling
- Redistribution from IPX RIP to EIGRP and vice versa
- Reducing SAP traffic

Configuring a Novell IPX Network

Cisco's implementation of Novell's IPX protocol provides all the functions of a Novell router. In this case study, routers are configured to run Novell IPX (see Figure 17-1).

Figure 17-1 *Configuring a Novell IPX Network*

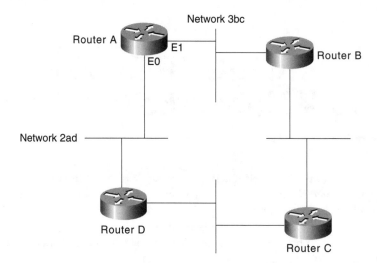

The configuration commands to enable IPX routing for Router A are as follows:

```
ipx routing
interface ethernet 0
 ipx network 2ad
interface ethernet 1
 ipx network 3bc
```

NOTE   In Software Release 9.21 and later, the command to enable Novell IPX routing is **ipx** rather than **novell**.

Adding EIGRP to a Novell IPX Network

EIGRP for a Novell IPX network has the same fast rerouting and partial update capabilities as EIGRP for IP. In addition, EIGRP has several capabilities designed to facilitate the building of large, robust Novell IPX networks.

The first capability is support for incremental SAP updates. Novell IPX RIP routers send out large RIP and SAP updates every 60 seconds. This can consume substantial amounts of bandwidth. EIGRP for IPX sends out SAP updates only when changes occur and sends only changed information.

The second capability that EIGRP adds to IPX networks is the potential to build large networks. IPX RIP networks have a diameter limit of 15 hops. EIGRP networks can have a diameter of 224 hops.

The third capability that EIGRP for Novell IPX provides is optimal path selection. The RIP metric for route determination is based on ticks with hop count used as a tie-breaker. If more than one route has the same value for the tick metric, the route with the least number of hops is preferred. Instead of ticks and hop count, IPX EIGRP uses a combination of these metrics: delay and bandwidth. For an illustration of how IPX EIGRP provides optimal path selection, see Figure 17-2.

Figure 17-2 *EIGRP Novell IPX Optimal Path Utilization*

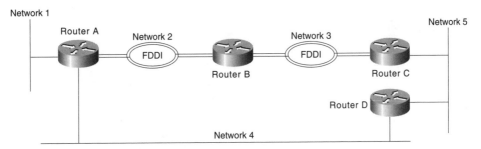

Both Ethernet and FDDI interfaces have a tick value of 1. If configured for Novell RIP, Router A will choose the Ethernet connection via Network 4 to reach Network 5 because Router D is only one hop away from Router A. However, the fastest path to Network 5 is two hops away, via the FDDI rings. With IPX EIGRP configured, Router A will automatically take the optimal path through Routers B and C to reach Network 5.

To add EIGRP to a Novell RIP and SAP network, configure EIGRP on the Cisco router interfaces that connect to other Cisco routers also running EIGRP. Configure RIP and SAP on the interfaces that connect to Novell hosts and to Novell routers that do not support EIGRP.

In Figure 17-3, Routers E, F, and G are running IPX EIGRP. Router E redistributes EIGRP route information via Network AA to Router D.

Figure 17-3 *Adding EIGRP to a Novell IPX Network*

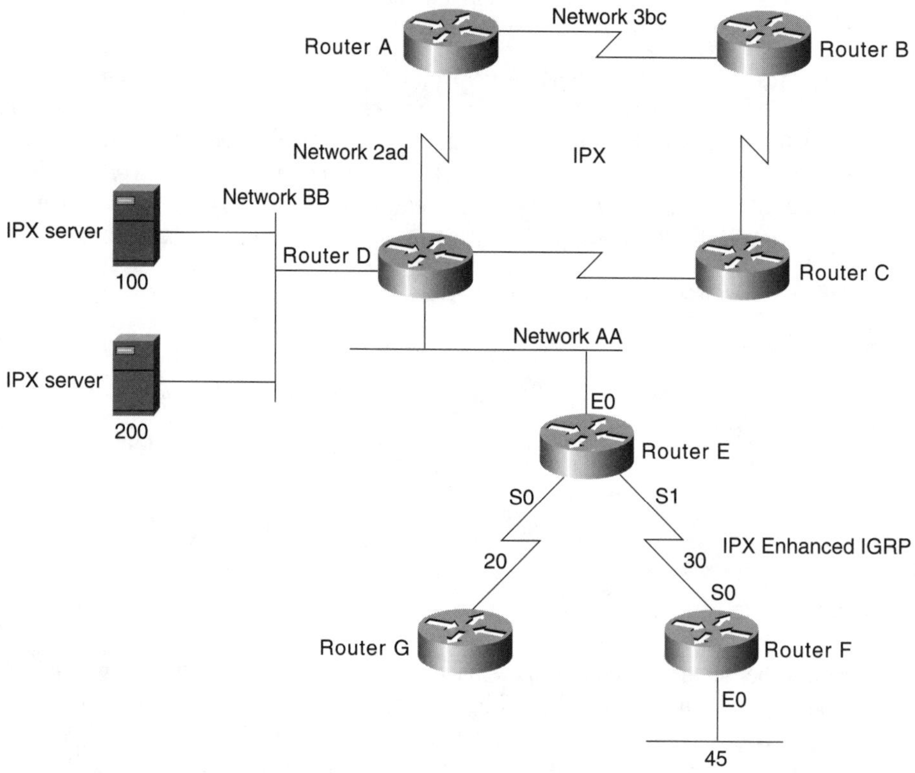

The configuration for Router E is as follows:

```
ipx routing
interface ethernet 0
 ipx network AA
interface serial 0
 ipx network 20
interface serial 1
 ipx network 30
ipx router eigrp 10
 network 20
 network 30
ipx router rip
 no network 20
```

With EIGRP configured, periodic SAP updates are replaced with EIGRP incremental updates when an EIGRP peer is found. Unless RIP is explicitly disabled for an IPX network number, as shown for Network 20, both RIP and EIGRP will be active on the interface associated with that network number. Based on the preceding configuration, and assuming an EIGRP peer on each EIGRP-configured interface, RIP updates are sent on Networks AA and 30, while EIGRP routing updates are sent on Networks 20 and 30. Incremental SAP updates are sent on Network 20 and Network 30, and periodic SAP updates are sent on Network AA.

The configuration for Router F is as follows:

```
ipx routing
interface ethernet 0
 ipx network 45
interface serial 0
 ipx network 30
ipx router eigrp 10
 network 30
 network 45
```

Partial output for a **show ipx route** command on Router E indicates that Network 45 was discovered using EIGRP (E), whereas network BB was discovered via a RIP (R) update:

```
R  Net 3bc
R  Net 2ad
C  Net 20 (HDLC), is directly connected, 66 uses, Serial0
C  Net 30 (HDLC), is directly connected, 73 uses, Serial1
E  Net 45 [2195456/0] via 30.0000.0c00.c47e, age 0:01:23, 1 uses, Serial1
C  Net AA (NOVELL-ETHER), is directly connected, 3 uses, Ethernet0
R  Net BB [1/1] via AA.0000.0c03.8b25,  48 sec, 87 uses, Ethernet0
```

Partial output for a **show ipx route** command on Router F indicates that Networks 20, AA, and BB were discovered using EIGRP (E):

```
E  Net 20 [2681856/0] via 30.0000.0c01.f0ed, age 0:02:57, 1 uses, Serial0
C  Net 30 (HDLC), is directly connected, 47 uses, Serial0
C  Net 45 (NOVELL-ETHER), is directly connected, 45 uses, Ethernet0
E  Net AA [267008000/0] via 30.0000.0c01.f0ed, age 0:02:57, 1 uses, Serial0
E  Net BB [268416000/2] via 30.0000.0c01.f0ed, age 0:02:57, 11 uses, Serial0
```

A **show ipx servers** command on Router E shows that server information was learned via periodic (P) SAP updates:

```
Codes: S - Static, I - Incremental, P - Periodic, H - Holddown
5 Total IPX Servers
Table ordering is based on routing and server info
Type  Name           Net Address        Port   Route  Hops  Itf
P     4 Networkers   100.0000.0000.0001:0666   2/02   2     Et1
P     5 Chicago      100.0000.0000.0001:0234   2/02   2     Et1
P     7 Michigan     100.0000.0000.0001:0123   2/02   2     Et1
P     8 NetTest1     200.0000.0000.0001:0345   2/02   2     Et1
P     8 NetTest      200.0000.0000.0001:0456   2/02   2     Et1
```

A **show ipx servers** command on Router F shows that server information was learned via incremental (I) SAP updates allowed with EIGRP:

```
Codes: S - Static, I - Incremental, P - Periodic, H - Holddown
5 Total IPX Servers
Table ordering is based on routing and server info
Type  Name           Net Address        Port Route         Hops  Itf
I     4 Networkers   100.0000.0000.0001:0666 268416000/03   3     Se0
I     5 Chicago      100.0000.0000.0001:0234 268416000/03   3     Se0
I     7 Michigan     100.0000.0000.0001:0123 268416000/03   3     Se0
I     8 NetTest1     200.0000.0000.0001:0345 268416000/03   3     Se0
I     8 NetTest      200.0000.0000.0001:0456 268416000/03   3     Se0
```

A **show ipx eigrp topology** command on Router E shows that the state of the networks is passive (P) and that each network provides one successor, and it lists the feasible distance (FD) of each successor via a neighbor to the destination. For network 45, for example, the neighbor is located at address 0000.0c00.c47e and the computed/advertised metric for that neighbor to the destination is 2195456/281600:

```
IPX EIGRP Topology Table for process 10
Codes: P - Passive, A - Active, U - Update, Q - Query, R - Reply,
       r - Reply status
P 20, 1 successors, FD is 1
        via Connected, Serial0
P 30, 1 successors, FD is 1
        via Connected, Serial1
P 45, 1 successors, FD is 2195456
        via 30.0000.0c00.c47e (2195456/281600), Serial1
P AA, 1 successors, FD is 266496000
        via Redistributed (266496000/0),
P BB, 1 successors, FD is 267904000
        via Redistributed (267904000/0),
```

The output for a **show ipx eigrp topology** command on Router F lists the following information:

```
IPX EIGRP Topology Table for process 10
Codes: P - Passive, A - Active, U - Update, Q - Query, R - Reply,
       r - Reply status
P 20, 1 successors, FD is 2681856
        via 30.0000.0c01.f0ed (2681856/2169856), Serial0
P 30, 1 successors, FD is 1
        via Connected, Serial0
P 45, 1 successors, FD is 1
        via Connected, Ethernet0
P AA, 1 successors, FD is 267008000
        via 30.0000.0c01.f0ed (267008000/266496000), Serial0
P BB, 1 successors, FD is 268416000
        via 30.0000.0c01.f0ed (268416000/267904000), Serial0
```

Route Selection

IPX EIGRP routes are automatically preferred over RIP routes regardless of metrics unless a RIP route has a hop count less than the external hop count carried in the EIGRP update (for example, a server advertising its own internal network).

Redistribution and Metric Handling

Redistribution is automatic between RIP and EIGRP, and vice versa. Automatic redistribution can be turned off using the **no redistribute** command. Redistribution is not automatic between different EIGRP autonomous systems.

The metric handling for integrating RIP into EIGRP is bandwidth plus delay, left shifted by 8 bits. The metric handling for EIGRP to RIP is the external metric plus 1. An IPX EIGRP router that is redistributing RIP into EIGRP takes the RIP metric associated with each RIP route, increments it, and stores that metric in the EIGRP routing table as the external metric.

In Figure 17-4, a Novell IPX server with an internal network number of 100 advertises this network number using RIP on Network 222. Router A hears this advertisement and installs it in its routing table as being one hop and one tick away. Router A then announces this network to Router B on Network 501 using EIGRP.

Figure 17-4 *IPX Metric Handling Example*

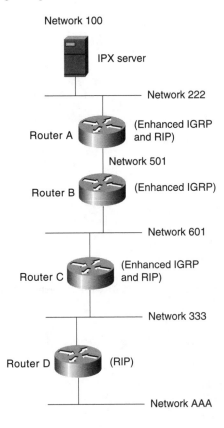

The configuration for Router A is as follows:

```
ipx routing
!
interface ethernet 0
 ipx network 222
!
interface serial 0
 ipx network 501
!
ipx router eigrp 9000
 network 222
 network 501
!
!The following commands turn off IPX RIP on the serial interface:
```

```
!
 ipx router rip
 no network 501
```

The configuration for Router B is as follows:

```
ipx routing
!
interface ethernet 0
 ipx network 601
!
interface serial 0
 ipx network 501
ipx router eigrp 9000
 network 501
 network 601
!
!The following command turns off IPX RIP on this router:
!
no ipx router rip
```

The configuration for Router C is as follows:

```
ipx routing
!
interface ethernet 0
 ipx network 333
!
interface ethernet 1
 ipx network 601
!
ipx router eigrp 9000
 network 333
 network 601
!
!The following commands turn off IPX RIP on ethernet 1:
!
ipx router rip
 no network 601
```

The configuration for Router D is as follows:

```
ipx routing
!
interface ethernet 0
 ipx network 333
!
interface ethernet 1
 ipx network AAA
```

The output from a **show ipx route** command on Router A is as follows:

```
R  Net 100 [1/1] via 222.0260.8c4c.4f22,   59 sec, 1 uses, Ethernet0
C  Net 222 (ARPA), is directly connected, 1252 uses, Ethernet0
E  Net 333 [46277376/0] via 501.0000.0c05.84bc, age 0:04:07, 1 uses, Serial0
C  Net 501 (HDLC), is directly connected, 3908 uses, Serial0
E  Net 601 [46251776/0] via 501.0000.0c05.84bc, age 5:21:38, 1 uses, Serial0
E  Net AAA [268441600/2] via 501.0000.0c05.84bc, age 0:16:23, 1 uses, Serial0
```

The output from a **show ipx route** command on Router B is as follows:

```
E  Net 100 [268416000/2] via 501.0000.0c05.84b4, age 0:07:30, 2 uses, Serial0
E  Net 222 [267008000/0] via 501.0000.0c05.84b4, age 0:07:30, 1 uses, Serial0
```

```
E  Net 333 [307200/0] via 601.0000.0c05.84d3, age 0:07:30, 1 uses, Ethernet0
C  Net 501 (HDLC), is directly connected, 4934 uses, Serial0
C  Net 601 (NOVELL-ETHER), is directly connected, 16304 uses, Ethernet0
E  Net AAA [267929600/2] via 601.0000.0c05.84d3, age 0:14:40, 1 uses, Ethernet0
```

The output from a **show ipx route** command on Router C is as follows:

```
E  Net 100 [268441600/2] via 601.0000.0c05.84bf, age 0:07:33, 1 uses, Ethernet1
E  Net 222 [267033600/0] via 601.0000.0c05.84bf, age 0:07:34, 1 uses, Ethernet1
C  Net 333 (NOVELL-ETHER), is directly connected, 15121 uses, Ethernet0
E  Net 501 [46251776/0] via 601.0000.0c05.84bf, age 0:07:32, 9 uses, Ethernet1
C  Net 601 (NOVELL-ETHER), is directly connected, 1346 uses, Ethernet1
R  Net AAA [1/1] via 333.0000.0c05.8b25,  35 sec, 1 uses, Ethernet0
```

The output from a **show ipx route** command on Router D is as follows:

```
R  Net 100 [8/2] via 333.0000.0c05.84d1,  18 sec, 1 uses, Ethernet0
R  Net 222 [6/1] via 333.0000.0c05.84d1,  18 sec, 1 uses, Ethernet0
R  Net 333 [1/1] via 333.0000.0c05.84d1,  18 sec, 1 uses, Ethernet0
R  Net 501 [3/1] via 333.0000.0c05.84d1,  17 sec, 3 uses, Ethernet0
R  Net 601 [1/1] via 333.0000.0c05.84d1,  18 sec, 1 uses, Ethernet0
C  Net AAA (SNAP), is directly connected, 20 uses, Ethernet1
```

The EIGRP metric is created using the RIP ticks for the delay vector. The hop count is incremented and stored as the external metric. The external delay is also stored. Router B computes the metric to Network 100 given the information received from Router A and installs this in its routing table. In this case, the tick value for Network 100 is 8.

The "2" after the slash in the routing entry for Network 100 is the external metric. This number does not increase again while the route is in the EIGRP autonomous system. Router C computes the metric to Network 100 through Router B and stores it in its routing table. Finally, Router C redistributes this information back into RIP with a hop count of 2 (the external metric) and a tick value derived from the original tick value of the RIP route (1) plus the EIGRP delay through the autonomous system converted to ticks.

Reducing SAP Traffic

Novell IPX RIP routers send out large RIP and SAP updates every 60 seconds regardless of whether a change has occurred. These updates can consume a substantial amount of bandwidth. You can reduce SAP update traffic by configuring EIGRP to do incremental SAP updates. When EIGRP is configured for incremental SAP updates, the updates consist only of information that has changed and the updates are sent out only when a change occurs, thus saving bandwidth.

When you configure EIGRP for incremental SAP updates, you can do the following:

- Retain RIP, in which case only the reliable transport of EIGRP is used for sending incremental SAP updates. (This is the preferred configuration over bandwidth-sensitive connections.)

- Turn off RIP, in which case EIGRP replaces RIP as the routing protocol.

Figure 17-5 shows a bandwidth-sensitive topology in which configuring incremental SAP updates is especially useful. The topology consists of a corporate network that uses a

56-kbps Frame Relay connection to communicate with a remote branch office. The corporate network has several Novell servers, each of which advertises many services. Depending on the number of servers and the number of advertised services, a large portion of the available bandwidth could easily be consumed by SAP updates.

Figure 17-5 *Example of Incremental SAP Updates*

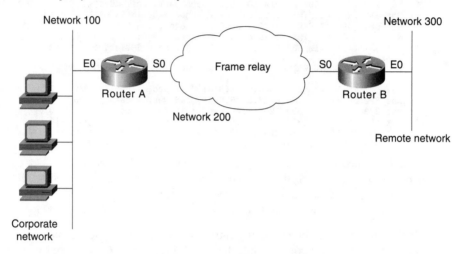

Router A is configured as follows:

```
ipx routing
!
interface ethernet 0
 ipx network 100
!
interface serial 0
 encapsulation frame-relay
!
interface serial 0.1 point-to-point
 ipx network 200
 ipx sap-incremental eigrp 90 rsup-only
 frame-relay interface-dlci 101
!
ipx router eigrp 90
 network 200
```

The **ipx routing** global configuration command enables IPX routing on the router.

The **ipx network** interface configuration command enables IPX routing on Ethernet interface 0 for Network 100.

For serial interface 0, the **encapsulation frame-relay** interface configuration command establishes Frame Relay encapsulation using Cisco's own encapsulation, which is a 4-byte header, with 2 bytes to identify the DLCI and 2 bytes to identify the packet type.

The **interface serial** global configuration command establishes a point-to-point subinterface (0.1). *Subinterfaces* are logical interfaces associated with a physical interface.

Using subinterfaces allows Router A to receive multiple simultaneous connections over a single Frame Relay interface.

The **ipx network** interface configuration command enables IPX routing on subinterface serial interface 0.1 for Network 200.

The **ipx sap-incremental** interface configuration command enables the incremental SAP feature. The required **eigrp** keyword enables EIGRP and its transport mechanism and, in this case, specifies an autonomous system number of 90. Because this command uses the **rsup-only** keyword, the router sends incremental SAP updates on this link.

The **frame-relay interface-dlci** interface configuration command associates data link connection identifier (DLCI) 101 with subinterface serial interface 0.1.

The **ipx router eigrp** global configuration command starts an EIGRP process and assigns to it autonomous system number 90.

The **network** configuration command enables EIGRP for Network 200.

Router B is configured as follows:

```
ipx routing
!
interface ethernet 0
 ipx network 300
!
interface serial 0
 encapsulation frame-relay
 ipx network 200
 ipx sap-incremental eigrp 90 rsup-only
!
ipx router eigrp 90
 network 200
```

The **ipx routing** global configuration command enables IPX routing on the router.

The **ipx network** interface configuration command enables IPX routing on Ethernet interface 0 for Network 300.

On serial interface 0, the **encapsulation frame-relay** interface configuration command establishes Frame Relay encapsulation using Cisco's own encapsulation, which is a 4-byte header, with 2 bytes to identify the DLCI and 2 bytes to identify the packet type.

The **ipx network** interface configuration command enables IPX routing on subinterface serial 0 for Network 200.

The **ipx sap-incremental** interface configuration command enables the incremental SAP feature. The required **eigrp** keyword enables EIGRP and its transport mechanism and, in this case, specifies an autonomous system number of 90. Because this command uses the **rsup-only** keyword, the router sends incremental SAP updates on this link.

The **ipx router eigrp** global configuration command starts an EIGRP process and assigns to it autonomous system number 90.

The **network** configuration command enables EIGRP for network 200.

NOTE	The absence of the **ipx router rip** command means the IPX RIP is still being used for IPX routing, and the use of the **rsup-only** keyword means that the router is sending incremental SAP updates over the Frame Relay link.

AppleTalk Network

This case study illustrates the integration of EIGRP into an existing AppleTalk network in two phases: configuring an AppleTalk network and adding EIGRP to an AppleTalk network. The key considerations for integrating EIGRP into an AppleTalk network are as follows:

- Route selection
- Metric handling
- Redistribution from AppleTalk to EIGRP and vice versa

Configuring an AppleTalk Network

Cisco routers support AppleTalk Phase 1 and AppleTalk Phase 2. For AppleTalk Phase 2, Cisco routers support both extended and nonextended networks. In this case study, Routers A, B, and C are running AppleTalk, as illustrated in Figure 17-6.

Figure 17-6 *Configuring an AppleTalk Network*

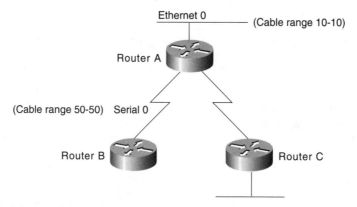

The configuration for Router A is as follows:

```
appletalk routing
interface ethernet 0
 appletalk cable-range 10-10
 appletalk zone casestudy
interface serial 0
 appletalk cable-range 50-50
 appletalk zone casestudy
```

Adding EIGRP to an AppleTalk Network

To add EIGRP to an AppleTalk network, configure EIGRP on the interface that connects to the routers. Do not disable RTMP on the interfaces that connect to AppleTalk hosts or that connect to AppleTalk routers that do not support EIGRP. RTMP is enabled by default when AppleTalk routing is enabled and when an interface is assigned an AppleTalk cable range.

In this case study, Routers D and E are running AppleTalk EIGRP. Routers F and G run both AppleTalk and AppleTalk EIGRP. Router G redistributes the routes from the AppleTalk network to the AppleTalk EIGRP network, and vice versa (see Figure 17-7).

Figure 17-7 *Example of Adding EIGRP to an AppleTalk Network*

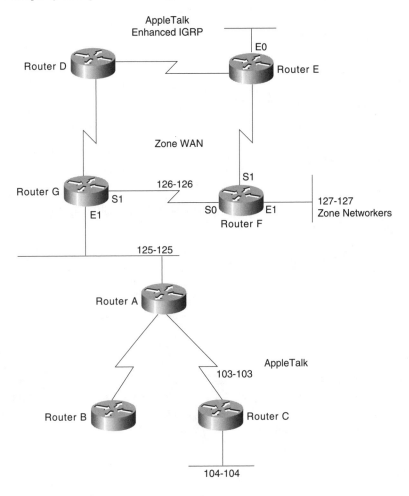

The configuration for Router G is as follows:

```
appletalk routing eigrp 1
interface ethernet 1
 appletalk cable-range 125-125
 appletalk zone Marketing Lab
 appletalk protocol eigrp
interface serial 1
 appletalk cable-range 126-126
 appletalk zone WAN
 appletalk protocol eigrp
 no appletalk protocol rtmp
```

The configuration for Router F is as follows:

```
appletalk routing eigrp 2
interface serial 0
 appletalk cable-range 126-126
 appletalk zone WAN
 appletalk protocol eigrp
 no appletalk protocol rtmp
```

A **show appletalk route** command on Router G shows that the first set of routes is learned from an RTMP update, that the second set of routes is directly connected, and that the last route is learned by AppleTalk EIGRP via serial interface 1:

```
R Net 103-103 [1/G] via 125.220, 0 sec, Ethernet1, zone Marketing Lab
R Net 104-104 [1/G] via 125.220, 1 sec, Ethernet1, zone Marketing Lab
R Net 105-105 [1/G] via 125.220, 1 sec, Ethernet1, zone Marketing Lab
R Net 108-108 [1/G] via 125.220, 1 sec, Ethernet1, zone Marketing Lab
C Net 125-125 directly connected, Ethernet1, zone Marketing Lab
C Net 126-126 directly connected, Serial1, zone Wan
E Net 127-127 [1/G] via 126.201, 114 sec, Serial1, zone Networkers
```

A **show appletalk route** command on Router F shows that routes are learned from AppleTalk EIGRP:

```
E Net 103-103 [2/G] via 126.220, 519 sec, Serial0, zone Marketing Lab
E Net 104-104 [2/G] via 126.220, 520 sec, Serial0, zone Marketing Lab
E Net 105-105 [2/G] via 126.220, 520 sec, Serial0, zone Marketing Lab
E Net 108-108 [2/G] via 126.220, 520 sec, Serial0, zone Marketing Lab
E Net 125-125 [1/G] via 126.220, 520 sec, Serial0, zone Marketing Lab
C Net 126-126 directly connected, Serial0, zone Wan
C Net 127-127 directly connected, Ethernet1, zone Networkers
```

Route Selection

AppleTalk EIGRP routes are automatically preferred over Routing Table Maintenance Protocol (RTMP) routes. Whereas the AppleTalk metric for route determination is based on hop count only, AppleTalk EIGRP uses a combination of these configurable metrics: delay, bandwidth, reliability, and load.

Metric Handling

The formula for converting RTMP metrics to AppleTalk EIGRP metrics is hop count multiplied by 252524800. This is a constant based on the bandwidth for a 9.6-kbps serial line and includes an RTMP factor. An RTMP hop distributed into EIGRP appears as a path slightly worse than an EIGRP-native, 9.6-kbps serial link. The formula for converting EIGRP to RTMP is the value of the EIGRP external metric plus 1.

Redistribution

Redistribution between AppleTalk RTMP and EIGRP and vice versa is automatic by default. Redistribution involves converting the EIGRP metric back into an RTMP hop count metric. In reality, there is no conversion of an EIGRP composite metric into a RTMP metric. Because a hop count is carried in an EIGRP metric tuple as the EIGRP route spreads through the network, 1 is added to the hop count, carried in the EIGRP metric blocks through the network, and put into any RTMP routing tuple generated.

There is no conversion of an EIGRP metric back into an RTMP metric because, in reality, what RTMP uses as a metric (the hop count) is carried along the EIGRP metric all the way through the network. This is true of EIGRP-derived routes and routes propagated through the network that were originally derived from an RTMP route.

Summary

This case study illustrates the integration of EIGRP in Novell and Appletalk networks. To add EIGRP to IPX networks, it is critical to configure RIP and SAP on interfaces connecting to Novell hosts or routers that do not support EIGRP. When adding EIGRP to AppleTalk networks, turn off RTMP on the interfaces configured to support EIGRP.

CHAPTER 18

Designing, Configuring, and Troubleshooting Multiprotocols over ATM

By Himanshu Desai

Introduction

This chapter discusses the methods of transferring legacy protocols over ATM.

Protocols such as IP, IPX, SNA, and so on have long been ported over WAN media such as Frame Relay and SMDS. ATM allows these protocols to be ported over campuses, as well as over WAN connections. Design considerations must be looked at, however, before choosing one method over another. Usually, Multiprotocols over ATM with AAL5 (RFC 1483) is used over WAN connections, and LANE is used over a campus ATM backbone.

This chapter covers these methods separately, using configuration examples. Specific design considerations are noted for each method. The chapter does not discuss the exact implementation of any particular method. The "Design Considerations" sections compare and contrast each method. The "Configuration" and "Troubleshooting" sections support these considerations.

The chapter begins with a discussion of RFC 1483 on PVCs and SVCs, and highlights their merits. RFC 1577 is also covered because it simplifies the operation issues encountered with RFC 1483. However, the section on RFC 1577 does not go into detail regarding deployment of Layer 3 routing protocols. While reading this chapter, you should also consider the issues associated with deploying routing protocols over any one of these methods.

The chapter's primary focus is on how these methods of deploying legacy protocols over ATM differ from each other and in what kind of network it makes sense to use one over another.

The third method of deploying legacy protocols over ATM is LAN Emulation (LANE). This method is used most often in campus backbone networks. The section begins with pointers to design consideration. It is highly encouraged, before deploying LANE in the campus backbone, that you look closely at these design points for scaling the backbone and ease of troubleshooting. Understanding the topology layout and distributing LANE services to different components is critical. Cisco has published an excellent paper on designing LANE networks, called "Campus ATM LANE Design."

The last section covers Multiprotocols over ATM (MPOA), which works in conjunction with LANE. The section briefly describes how MPOA can create cut-through switching over a LANE domain, enhancing the performance of LANE networks and reducing the load of Layer 3 routing when crossing one LANE cloud to another.

The chapter briefly describes each method, including design considerations, configuration examples, and troubleshooting of basic functionality. You can quickly summarize by reading the opening and "Design Consideration" sections for each method to get a basic idea of all methods. To help you after a method has been chosen, the "Configuration" and "Troubleshooting" sections provide additional advice for implementation.

It is highly recommended that you be familiar with the fundamentals of ATM before reading this chapter because it does not discuss basic theory.

Multiprotocols over ATM with AAL5 (RFC 1483)

Multiprotocol encapsulation over ATM AAL5 configuration can be accomplished in two ways.

The first method uses PVCs to configure point-to-point connections between nodes in an ATM cloud. This method requires individual PVCs for every node in a fully meshed ATM cloud.

The second method uses SVCs to connect to every node in the fully meshed ATM cloud.

This section covers PVCs and SVCs. PVCs are permanent virtual circuits, or virtual circuits that are permanently established. PVCs save bandwidth associated with circuit establishment and tear down in situations where certain virtual circuits must exist all the time.

SVCs are switched virtual circuits, or virtual circuits dynamically established on demand and torn down when transmission is complete. SVCs are used in situations where data transmission is sporadic. They are called a "switched virtual connection" in ATM terminology.

Using PVCs

RFC 1483 describes two methods of carrying connectionless network traffic over an ATM cloud:

- **AAL5SNAP**—Allows multiple protocols over a single ATM virtual circuit
- **AAL5MUX**—Allows one protocol per ATM virtual circuit

Protocols supported using these ATM encapsulation methods include IP, IPX, AppleTalk, CLNS, DECnet, VINES, and bridging. This section discusses design considerations, configuration, and troubleshooting of ATM networks using RFC 1483 with Cisco products and AAL5MUX or AAL5SNAP. This includes configuration using both PVCs and SVCs.

Design Considerations

RFC 1483 networks are usually deployed in small scale. This type of network is ideal for campus or WAN backbones, consisting of 5–10 end nodes with a few intermediate switches. Using the three-node network in this example, you need eight VPI/VCI pairs to be configured across the network and three **map** statements for each router to form a fully meshed ATM cloud. As the number of end nodes and protocols to support increases, RFC 1483 does not scale, and it becomes increasingly difficult to manage and troubleshoot. RFC 1483 networks provide an easy transition if you are replacing existing FDDI or other media backbones with an ATM backbone. An RFC 1483 network starting with two router nodes and a couple of intermediate switches can be increased by just moving the end node from the old backbone to the ATM backbone and adding this node to the newly formed cloud using the **map** statement. Although this provides ease of transition, as the ATM backbone becomes larger, it requires substantial maintenance.

NOTE	*VPI* stands for virtual path identifier. It is an 8-bit field in the header of an ATM cell. The VPI, together with the VCI, is used to identify the next destination of a cell as it passes through a series of ATM switches on its way to its destination. ATM switches use the VPI/VCI fields to identify the next VCL that a cell needs to transit on its way to its final destination.
	VCI stands for virtual channel identifier. It is a 16-bit field in the header of an ATM cell. The VCI, together with the VPI, is used to identify the next destination of a cell as it passes through a series of ATM switches on its way to its destination. ATM switches use the VPI/VCI fields to identify the next network VCL that a cell needs to transit on its way to its final destination.

RFC 1483 is a simple concept, easy to configure, and requires less protocol overhead. It is also a stable and approved solution. It does not scale to large networks; however, it requires lots of manual configuration, and does not support ATM to the desktop.

Topology (PVCs)

Figure 18-1 shows an example of ATM topology. The ATM cloud in this topology could easily be one or more ATM switches co-located with routers in a LAN environment or multiple switches in a carrier cloud.

Figure 18-1 *RFC 1483 Topology with PVCs*

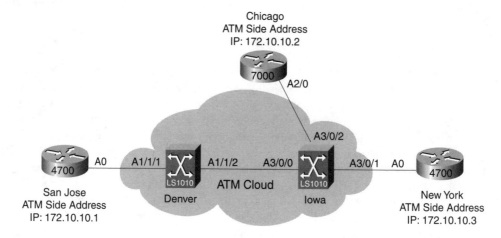

Configuring with PVCs

Configuring PVCs requires manual mapping on all switches to each end node. Although it is cumbersome and difficult to troubleshoot in larger topologies, PVC configuration is generally simpler in smaller topologies.

In the topology described earlier, there are three ATM-enabled routers—San Jose, Chicago, and New York. They are interconnected physically via two ATM switches, Denver and Iowa. You want a fully meshed ATM cloud between the three routers.

You have two ATM PVCs configured on the San Jose router; one for connectivity to Chicago, and one for New York.

The statement **atm pvc 1 0 40 aal5snap** enables you to configure the PVC, where number 1 indicates virtual circuit descriptor (VCD), number 0 indicates virtual path identifier (VPI), and number 40 indicates virtual circuit identifier. Valid VPI values to use when configuring PVC on Cisco devices are 0 to 7. VCI values are 32 to 1023. ATM Forum reserves VCI values of 0 to 31.

The statement **map-group 1483pvc** enables you to apply **map-list 1483pvc** to the ATM interface, which in turn maps remote router IP addresses to the local VPI or VCI using the VCD number. The other two routers are configured similarly. The San Jose router configuration is as follows:

```
interface ATM0
ip address 172.10.10.1 255.255.255.0
atm pvc 1 0 40 aal5snap
atm pvc 2 0 50 aal5snap
map-group 1483pvc
map-list 1483pvc
```

```
ip 172.10.10.2 atm-vc 1 broadcast
ip 172.10.10.3 atm-vc 2 broadcast
```

The configuration of the Chicago router is as follows:

```
interface ATM2/0
ip address 172.10.10.2 255.255.255.0
map-group 1483pvc
atm pvc 1 0 40 aal5snap
atm pvc 2 0 60 aal5snap
map-list 1483pvc
ip 172.10.10.1 atm-vc 1 broadcast
ip 172.10.10.3 atm-vc 2 broadcast
```

The configuration of the New York router is as follows:

```
interface ATM0
ip address 172.10.10.3 255.255.255.0
atm pvc 1 0 60 aal5snap
atm pvc 2 0 50 aal5snap
map-group 1483pvc
map-list 1483pvc
ip 172.10.10.1 atm-vc 2 broadcast
ip 172.10.10.2 atm-vc 1 broadcast
```

The Denver switch configuration shows incoming 0/40 VPI/VCI pairs on interface 1/1/1 coming from the San Jose router and outgoing on interface 1/1/2 with 1/40 as VPI/VCI pairs to the Iowa switch. The configuration is shown from interface 1/1/2's point of view. It also shows another incoming 0/50 VPI/VCI pair on interface 1/1/1 coming from the San Jose router and going out on interface 1/1/2 with 1/50.

The configuration of the Denver LS1010 switch is as follows:

```
interface ATM1/1/2
no keepalive
atm pvc 1 40 interface ATM1/1/1 0 40
atm pvc 1 50 interface ATM1/1/1 0 50
interface ATM1/1/1
```

The Iowa switch configuration shows incoming 1/40 VPI/VCI pairs from the Denver switch and outgoing to interface 3/0/2 with 0/40 VPI/VCI pairs to the Chicago router. This creates end-to-end PVC between the San Jose and Chicago routers. The Iowa switch has another incoming 1/50 VPI/VCI pair from the Denver switch going out to interface 3/0/1 with 0/50 VPI/VCI pairs to the New York router. Also, 0/60 VPI/VCI pairs are coming in from the Chicago router on interface 3/0/2, which is being switched out on interface 3/0/1 with VPI/VCI pairs of 0/60 to the New York router. This forms a fully meshed ATM cloud with all three routers directly connected to each other.

The configuration of the Iowa LS1010 switch is as follows:

```
interface ATM3/0/0
no keepalive
interface ATM3/0/1
no keepalive
atm pvc 0 50 interface ATM3/0/0 1 50
interface ATM3/0/2
no keepalive
atm pvc 0 40 interface ATM3/0/0 1 40
atm pvc 0 60 interface ATM3/0/1 0 60
```

Troubleshooting with PVCs

Planning is the key to successful deployment and stability of RFC 1483 networks.

First, create a VPI/VCI pair table for each and every device you want to connect in the cloud. After that is done, make a configuration template, and start configuring individual routers and switches. Then, execute the subsequent commands to see whether the configuration and the design deployed are working accordingly.

The following command shows that two PVCs are active on the ATM0 interface. These VCs have local significance and show an active connection to the nearest switch. These VC values do not indicate a router-to-router ATM connection. For that, you must go to each device between the two end routers and begin checking the interface status and incoming VPI/VCI pair. The outgoing VPI/VCI pair of the San Jose router should match the incoming VPI/VCI pair of the Denver switch. If it doesn't match, the router continues sending out ATM cells, but the switch drops them because it considers them coming from an unknown VPI/VCI pair:

```
SanJose#show atm vc
Interface  VCD  VPI  VCI  Type  AAL/          Peak    Avg.    Burst   Status
                               Encapsulation  KBPS    KBPS    Cells
ATM0        1    0   40   PVC   AAL5-SNAP     155000  155000  94      Active
ATM0        2    0   50   PVC   AAL5-SNAP     155000  155000  94      Active
```

NOTE   A VC (virtual circuit) is a logical circuit created to ensure reliable communication between two network devices. A virtual circuit is defined by a VPI/VCI pair, and can be either permanent (a PVC) or switched (an SVC).

NOTE   A VCC (virtual channel connection) is a logical connection between two ATM-enabled edge devices. Edge devices can be an ATM-enabled host, router, or switch. VCCs are comprised of many VCs in between, to complete the virtual channel connection.

The following command displays mapping of the layer 3 IP address to the ATM VC address, and it also indicates that broadcast is enabled to go out on the same VC:

```
SanJose#show atm map
Map list 1483pvc : PERMANENT
ip 172.10.10.2 maps to VC 1, broadcast
ip 172.10.10.3 maps to VC 2 , broadcast
```

On the Denver switch, you can see that the interface status is up:

```
Denver#show atm statistics
NUMBER OF INSTALLED CONNECTIONS: (P2P=Point to Point,
P2MP=Point to MultiPoint)
Type    PVCs    SoftPVCs    SVCs    PVPs    SoftPVPs    SVPs    Total
```

```
P2P      11      0        0       0       0        0       11
P2MP     0       0        0       0       0        0       0
TOTAL INSTALLED CONNECTIONS = 11
PER-INTERFACE STATUS SUMMARY AT 10:11:00 UTC Fri Jan 16 1998:
Interface   IF Status  Admin    Auto-Cfg  ILMI Addr    SSCOP   Hello
Name                   Status             Reg State    State   State
ATM1/0/0    DOWN       down     waiting   n/a          Idle    n/a
ATM1/0/1    DOWN       down     waiting   n/a          Idle    n/a
ATM1/0/2    DOWN       down     waiting   n/a          Idle    n/a
ATM1/0/3    DOWN       down     waiting   n/a          Idle    n/a
ATM1/1/0    UP         up       waiting   WaitDevType  Idle    n/a
ATM1/1/1    UP         up       done      UpAndNormal  Idle    n/a
ATM1/1/2    UP         up       done      UpAndNormal  Active  2way_in
ATM1/1/3    DOWN       down     waiting   n/a          Idle    n/a
ATM2/0/0    UP         up       n/a       UpAndNormal  Idle    n/a
ATM3/0/0    DOWN       down     waiting   n/a          Idle    n/a
ATM3/0/1    DOWN       down     waiting   n/a          Idle    n/a
```

The following command displays the incoming VPI/VCI pair 0/40 from the San Jose router on interface ATM 1/1/1 and is going out on ATM 1/1/2 to the Iowa switch:

```
Denver#show atm vc int atm 1/1/1
Interface   VPI  VCI  Type  X-Interface  X-VPI  X-VCI  Status
ATM1/1/1    0    5    PVC   ATM2/0/0     0      47     UP
ATM1/1/1    0    16   PVC   ATM2/0/0     0      48     UP
ATM1/1/1    0    18   PVC   ATM2/0/0     0      49     UP
ATM1/1/1    0    40   PVC   ATM1/1/2     1      40     UP
ATM1/1/1    0    50   PVC   ATM1/1/2     1      50     UP
```

The following command displays the incoming VPI/VCI pair 1/40 from the Denver switch on interface ATM 3/0/0 and is going out on ATM 3/0/0 to the Chicago router:

```
Iowa#show atm vc int atm 3/0/0
Interface   VPI  VCI  Type  X-Interface  X-VPI  X-VCI  Status
ATM3/0/0    0    5    PVC   ATM2/0/0     0      32     UP
ATM3/0/0    0    16   PVC   ATM2/0/0     0      33     UP
ATM3/0/0    0    18   PVC   ATM2/0/0     0      34     UP
ATM3/0/0    1    40   PVC   ATM3/0/2     0      40     UP
ATM3/0/0    1    50   PVC   ATM3/0/1     0      50     UP
```

After checking VPI/VCI pair and mapping statements for each device, you should be able to ping from the San Jose router to the Chicago router:

```
SanJose#ping 172.10.10.2
Type escape sequence to abort.
Sending 5, 100-byte ICMP Echoes to 172.10.10.2, timeout is 2
  seconds:
!!!!!
Success rate is 100 percent (5/5), round-trip min/avg/max = 1/2/4 ms

SanJose#ping 172.10.10.3
Type escape sequence to abort.
Sending 5, 100-byte ICMP Echoes to 172.10.10.3, timeout is 2
  seconds:
!!!!!
Success rate is 100 percent (5/5), round-trip min/avg/max = 1/2/4 ms
```

Using SVCs

This section discusses RFC 1483 using SVCs. It covers configuring routers and switches for SVCs, and some troubleshooting techniques.

Topology (SVCs)

Figure 18-2 presents the topology for this example.

Figure 18-2 *RFC 1483 with SVCs*

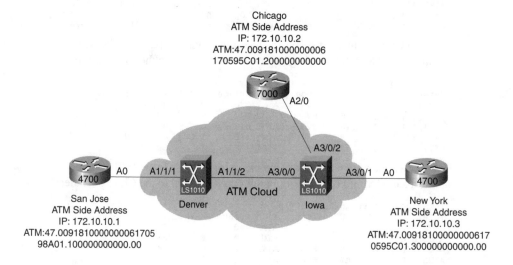

Configuring with SVCs

Multiprotocol encapsulation over ATM AAL5 (RFC 1483) configuration using SVCs is semi-dynamic. It still requires mapping of all ATM NSAP node addresses to protocol addresses. The advantage of this configuration is that it does not require any kind of mapping in the ATM switches that interconnect two or more routers. The configuration is performed dynamically using PNNI protocol.

NOTE   *NSAP* stands for network service access point. It is a network address, as specified by ISO. An NSAP is the point at which OSI network service is made available to a transport layer (Layer 4) entity.

PNNI has two definitions

1   Private Network-Network Interface. This is an ATM Forum specification for distributing topology information between switches and clusters of switches; the information is used to compute paths through the network. The specification is based on well-known link-state routing techniques, and includes a mechanism for automatic configuration in networks in which the address structure reflects the topology.

2   Private Network Node Interface. This is an ATM Forum specification for signaling to establish point-to-point and point-to-multipoint connections across an ATM network. The protocol is based on the ATM Forum's UNI specification with additional mechanisms for source routing, crankback, and alternate routing of call setup requests.

In the illustrated topology in Figure 18-2, there are three ATM-enabled routers—San Jose, Chicago, and New York. They are interconnected physically via two ATM switches, Denver and Iowa. You want a fully meshed ATM cloud between the three routers.

The statement **atm pvc 10 0 5 qsaal** enables you to configure the PVC, providing a channel for sending signaling messages for SVC call setup. The VPI and VCI values must also be configured consistently with the local switch. The standard value of VPI is 0 and VCI is 5. It uses a special kind of ATM adaptation encapsulation called qsaal.

The statement **atm pvc 20 0 16 ilmi** enables you to configure the PVC, providing a channel to send Interim Local Management Interface (ILMI) messages to the ATM switch. The standard value of VPI is 0 and VCI is 16 for ILMI. ILMI has many functions; here, it enables you to register the prefix for the ATM interface address. It sends a trap upon ATM interface restart to the switch, and the switch registers its 13-byte prefix with the router. This 13-byte prefix constitutes a 20-byte ATM interface address.

NOTE   *ILMI* stands for Interim Local Management Interface. It is the specification developed by the ATM Forum for incorporating NETWORK-management capabilities into the ATM UNI.

The statement **atm esi-address 100000000000.00** configures the last seven bytes of the ATM interface address. Using the 13-byte prefix learned via ILMI, and the 7-byte address from the end system identifier (ESI), the router forms an ATM interface address. This address should be unique for each device in the ATM cloud. ESI should be configured so that it can create a unique NSAP address.

NOTE	*ESI* stands for end system identifier. It is an identifier that distinguishes multiple nodes at the same level when the lower-level peer group is partitioned.

The statement **map-group 1483svc** applies **map-list 1483svc** to the ATM interface, which in turn maps remote router IP addresses to their respective NSAP addresses for call setup. You can get remote router NSAP addresses by executing the **show interface ATM x/x** command. The **map** statement maps the Chicago router IP address to the NSAP address.

The configuration of the San Jose router is as follows:

```
interface ATM0
ip address 172.10.10.1 255.255.255.0
atm esi-address 100000000000.00
atm pvc 10 0 5 qsaal
atm pvc 20 0 16 ilmi
map-group 1483svc
map-list 1483svc
ip 172.10.10.2 atm-nsap
   47.00918100000000006170595C01.200000000000.00 broadcast
ip 172.10.10.3 atm-nsap
   47.00918100000000006170595C01.300000000000.00 broadcast
```

The other two routers are configured similarly with appropriate protocols to ATM NSAP addresses. The configuration of the Chicago router is as follows:

```
interface ATM2/0
ip address 172.10.10.2 255.255.255.0
map-group 1483svc
atm esi-address 200000000000.00
atm pvc 10 0 5 qsaal
atm pvc 20 0 16 ilmi
map-list 1483svc
ip 172.10.10.1 atm-nsap
   47.00918100000000006170598A01.100000000000.00 broadcast
ip 172.10.10.3 atm-nsap
   47.00918100000000006170595C01.300000000000.00 broadcast
```

The configuration of the New York router is as follows:

```
interface ATM0
ip address 172.10.10.3 255.255.255.0
atm esi-address 300000000000.00
atm pvc 1 0 5 qsaal
atm pvc 2 0 16 ilmi
map-group 1483svc
map-list 1483svc
ip 172.10.10.1 atm-nsap
   47.00918100000000006170598A01.100000000000.00 broadcast
ip 172.10.10.2 atm-nsap
   47.00918100000000006170595C01.200000000000.00 broadcast
```

The statement **atm address 47.0091.8100.0000.0061.7059.8a01.0061.7059.8a01.00** represents the Denver switch ATM address. This is generated automatically, although

LS1010 switches allow user-defined addresses. Cisco uses the following mechanism to generate unique ATM addresses for the ATM switches:

AFI	CISCO ICD	Assigned by CISCO	ESI Field	Selector Byte
47	00 91	81 00 00 00	MAC Address	00
3 bytes	4 bytes	6 bytes	1 byte	

The statement **atm router pnni** enables PNNI on all NNI interfaces after ILMI has determined the interface type. The statement **node 1 level 56 lowest** configures the switch for a PNNI node with node-index 1 at the lowest level of 56.

NOTE   *NNI* stands for Network-to-Network Interface. It is an ATM Forum standard that defines the interface between two ATM switches that are both located in a private network or are both located in a public network. The interface between a public switch and a private one is defined by the UNI standard.

The San Jose router ATM interface is directly connected to the Denver switch ATM interface 1/1/1. As revealed by the configuration of the ATM interface 1/1/1, you can see that there is no configuration required on it, as well as on ATM interface 1/1/2 that connects to the Iowa switch. The link between the San Jose router and the Denver switch ATM interface 1/1/1 is called User-Network Interface (UNI), and the link between the Denver switch ATM interface 1/1/2 to the Iowa switch ATM interface 3/0/0 is called Network-to-Network Interface (NNI). PNNI runs on the NNI links.

NOTE   *UNI* stands for User-Network Interface. It is an ATM Forum specification that defines an interoperability standard for the interface between ATM-based products (a router or an ATM switch) located in a private network and the ATM switches located within the public carrier networks.

The configuration of the Denver switch is as follows:

```
atm address47.0091.8100.0000.0061.7059.8a01.0061.7059.8a01.00
atm router pnni
node 1 level 56 lowest
redistribute atm-static
interface ATM1/1/1
no keepalive
interface ATM1/1/2
no keepalive
```

The configuration of the Iowa switch is similar to the Denver switch:

```
atm address
    47.0091.8100.0000.0061.7059.5c01.0061.7059.5c01.00
atm router pnni
node 1 level 56 lowest
redistribute atm-static
interface ATM3/0/0
no keepalive
interface ATM3/0/1
no keepalive
interface ATM3/0/2
no keepalive
```

Troubleshooting with SVCs

The configuration of SVCs requires mapping the protocol address to the remote router NSAP address. Routers form this NSAP address by combining the prefix obtained via ILMI from the ATM switch and the preconfigured ESI address. This creates a complete 20-byte ATM NSAP address for the router ATM interface. So, you need to make sure that ILMI is working properly. Some of the following analysis ensures this.

The following command output indicates that it received the prefix 47.009181000000006170598A01 from the ATM switch. It forms the ATM interface NSAP address by adding its ESI address to the prefix, and it registers itself in the switch table for the PNNI to propagate the information. It also tells the peer interface address whether it is a Cisco device:

```
SanJose#show atm ilmi
Interface        ATM0      ILMI VCC:      (0, 16)
ILMI Keepalive:            Disabled
Address Registration:            Enabled
Addr Reg State:      UpAndNormal
Peer IP Addr:            0.0.0.0            Peer IF Name:      ATM1/1/1
Prefix(s):
47.009181000000006170598A01
Addresses Registered:
Local Table :
47.009181000000006170598A01.100000000000.00
Remote Table :
47.009181000000006170598A01.100000000000.00
```

The following command confirms that ILMI between the router and switch is working because you can see that the ATM interface has its associated NSAP address. ILMI also exchanges information regarding the UNI version and whether the router is user side or network side. In this example, the router is running UNI Version 3, and it is user side:

```
SanJose#show int atm 0
ATM0 is up, line protocol is up
Hardware is ATMizer BX-50
Internet address is 172.10.10.1/24
MTU 4470 bytes, sub MTU 4470, BW 156250 Kbit, DLY 100 usec,
   rely 210/255, load 1/255
NSAP address:   47.009181000000006170598A01.100000000000.00
Encapsulation ATM, loopback not set, keepalive set (10 sec)
Encapsulation(s): AAL5 AAL3/4, PVC mode
1024 maximum active VCs, 1024 VCs per VP, 4 current VCCs
VC idle disconnect time: 300 seconds
```

```
Signalling vc = 10, vpi = 0, vci = 5
UNI Version = 3.0, Link Side = user
Last input 00:00:20, output 00:00:01, output hang never
Last clearing of "show interface" counters never
```

The following command displays the ILMI message exchanges between the router and switch. ILMI uses standard SNMP messages. The output shows the NSAP address passed by the switch. It is then registered by the router in the local table and sent for registration in the peer switch table. Some of the parameters, such as UNI version and peer interface name, are also exchanged:

```
SanJose#debug atm ilmi
ILMI Transition : Intf := 1 From Restarting To AwaitRestartAck
    <ilmi_initiate_addreg>
ILMI: REQ_PROCESSING Reqtype = GETNEXT Reqid = 12
    Requestor = ILMI, Transid = 1 (ATM0)
ILMI: Trap Received (ATM0)
ILMI Transition : Intf := 1 From AwaitRestartAck To UpAndNormal
    <ilmi_snmp_callback>
ILMI: REQ_PROCESSING Reqtype = GET Reqid = 13 Requestor =
    ILMI, Transid = 1 (ATM0)
ILMI: REQ_PROCESSING Reqtype = GET Reqid = 14 Requestor =
    ILMI, Transid = 1 (ATM0)
ILMI: REQ_PROCESSING Reqtype = GET Reqid = 15 Requestor =
    ILMI, Transid = 1 (ATM0)
ILMI: VALID_RESP_RCVD Reqtype = GET Reqid = 13 Requestor =
    ILMI, Transid = 1 (ATM0)
ILMI: VALID_RESP_RCVD Reqtype = GET Reqid = 14 Requestor =
    ILMI, Transid = 1 (ATM0)
ILMI: VALID_RESP_RCVD Reqtype = GET Reqid = 15 Requestor =
    ILMI, Transid = 1 (ATM0)
ILMI: Peer UNI Version on 1 = 3
ILMI: TERMINATE Reqtype = GET Reqid = 13 Requestor = ILMI,
    Transid = 1 (ATM0)
ILMI: TERMINATE Reqtype = GET Reqid = 14 Requestor = ILMI,
    Transid = 1 (ATM0)
ILMI: Peer IfName on 1 = ATM1/1/1
ILMI: TERMINATE Reqtype = GET Reqid = 15 Requestor = ILMI,
    Transid = 1 (ATM0)
ILMI: REQ_TIMEOUT Reqtype = GETNEXT Reqid = 12 Requestor =
    ILMI, Transid = 1 (ATM0) ILMI Retry count (before decrement) =
3
ILMI: REQ_PROCESSING Reqtype = GETNEXT Reqid = 12
    Requestor = ILMI, Transid = 1 (ATM0)
ILMI: ERROR_RESP_RCVD (No Such Name) Reqtype = GETNEXT
    Reqid = 12 Requestor = ILMI,
Transid = 1 (ATM0)
ILMI: TERMINATE Reqtype = GETNEXT Reqid = 12 Requestor =
    ILMI, Transid = 1 (ATM0)
ILMI: No request associated with Expired Timer Reqid = 13
ILMI: No request associated with Expired Timer Reqid = 14
ILMI: No request associated with Expired Timer Reqid = 15
ILMI: Trap sent. Waiting for Prefix ATM0
ILMI: No request associated with Expired Timer Reqid = 12
ILMI: Prefix will be Added (If currently not registered):
    4709181000006170598A1
ILMI: Notifying Address Addition 4709181000006170598A1 (ATM0)
ILMI: REQRCVD Reqtype = SET Reqid = 0 Requestor = atmSmap,
    Transid = 1621657796 (ATM0)
ILMI: Notifying Address Addition 4709181000006170598A1 (ATM0)
ILMI: Notifying Address Addition 4709181000006170598A1 (ATM0)
ILMI: REQ_PROCESSING Reqtype = SET Reqid = 16 Requestor =
    atmSmap, Transid = 1621657796
```

```
(ATM0)
ILMI: (Local) Reg. validation attempt for
    470918100006170598A110000000
ILMI: Address added to local table.
ILMI: Register request sent to peer
ILMI: VALID_RESP_RCVD Reqtype = SET Reqid = 16 Requestor =
    atmSmap, Transid = 1621657796 (ATM0)
ILMI: Set confirmed. Updating peer address table
ILMI: TERMINATE Reqtype = SET Reqid = 16 Requestor =
    atmSmap, Transid = 1621657796 (ATM0)
ILMI: No request associated with Expired Timer Reqid = 16
```

The following debug output indicates the switch side ILMI messages. You can see the switch sending its prefix upon receiving the trap. It also validates the address for the end station to be registered in the end system remote table:

```
Denver#debug atm ilmi ATM 1/1/1
ILMI: Querying peer device type. (ATM1/1/1)
ILMI : (ATM1/1/1) From ilmiIntfDeviceTypeComplete To
    ilmiIntfAwaitPortType <ilmi_initiate_portquery>
ILMI: The Maximum # of VPI Bits (ATM1/1/1) is 3
ILMI: The Maximum # of VCI Bits (ATM1/1/1) is 10
ILMI: Response Received and Matched (ATM1/1/1)
The peer UNI Type on (ATM1/1/1) is 2
The Peer UNI Version on (ATM1/1/1) is 2
ILMI: Assigning default device type (ATM1/1/1)
ILMI: My Device type is set to Node (ATM1/1/1)
ILMI: Auto Port determination enabled
ILMI: For Interface (ATM1/1/1)
ILMI: Port Information Complete :
ILMI: Local Information :Device Type = ilmiDeviceTypeNode Port
    Type = ilmiPrivateUNINetworkSide
ILMI: Peer Information :Device Type = ilmiDeviceTypeUser Port
    Type = ilmiUniTypePrivate
MaxVpiBits = 3 MaxVciBits = 10
ILMI: KeepAlive disabled
ILMI : (ATM1/1/1) From ilmiIntfAwaitPortType To
    ilmiIntfPortTypeComplete <ilmi_find_peerPort>
 Restarting Interface (ATM1/1/1)
ILMI : (ATM1/1/1) From ilmiIntfPortTypeComplete To
    AwaitRestartAck <ilmi_process_intfRestart>
ILMI: Response Received and Matched (ATM1/1/1)
ILMI: Errored response <No Such Name> Intf (ATM1/1/1) Function
    Type = ilmiAddressTableCheck
ILMI : (ATM1/1/1) From AwaitRestartAck To UpAndNormal
    <ilmi_process_response>
ILMI: Response Received and Matched (ATM1/1/1)
ILMI: The Neighbor's IfName on Intf (ATM1/1/1) is ATM0
ILMI: The Neighbor's IP on Intf (ATM1/1/1) is 2886339073
 ILMI: Trap Received (ATM1/1/1)
ILMI: Sending Per-Switch prefix
ILMI: Registering prefix with end-system
    47.0091.8100.0000.0061.7059.8a01
ILMI: Response Received and Matched (ATM1/1/1)
ILMI: Validating address
    47.0091.8100.0000.0061.7059.8a01.1000.0000.0000.00
ILMI: Address considered validated (ATM1/1/1)
ILMI: Address added :
    47.0091.8100.0000.0061.7059.8a01.1000.0000.0000.00
    (ATM1/1/1)
ILMI: Sending Per-Switch prefix
ILMI: Registering prefix with end-system
    47.0091.8100.0000.0061.7059.8a01
ILMI: Response Received and Matched (ATM1/1/1)
```

The following debug command displays the output for signaling events occurring on the San Jose router. If the VC to the remote router is not present and if you try to ping it, it will open up the call using the signaling protocol and, once connected, it will start sending data packets. This phenomenon is very fast, but depends on the number of call requests on that device at the time and the number of ATM switches in between:

```
SanJose#debug atm sig-events
ATMAPI: SETUP
ATMSIG: Called len 20
ATMSIG: Calling len 20
ATMSIG(0/-1 0,0 - 0031/00): (vcnum:0) build Setup msg, Null(U0)
    state
ATMSIG(0/-1 0,0 - 0031/00): (vcnum:0) API - from sig-client
    ATM_OWNER_SMAP
ATMSIG(0/-1 0,0 - 0031/00): (vcnum:0) Input event : Req Setup in
    Null(U0)
ATMSIG(0/-1 0,0 - 0031/00): (vcnum:0) Output Setup
    msg(XferAndTx), Null(U0) state
ATMSIG: Output XferSetup
ATMSIG: Called Party Addr:
    47.009181000000006170595C01.200000000000.00
ATMSIG: Calling Party Addr:
    47.009181000000006170598A01.100000000000.00
ATMSIG(0/-1 0,0 - 0031/00): (vcnum:0) Null(U0) -> Call Initiated(U1)
ATMSIG(0/-1 0,0 - 0031/00): (vcnum:0) Input event : Rcvd Call
    Proceeding in Call Initiated(U1)
ATMSIG(0/-1 0,153 - 0031/00): (vcnum:0) Call Initiated(U1) ->
    Outgoing Call Proceeding(U3)
ATMSIG(0/-1 0,153 - 0031/00): (vcnum:0) Input event : Rcvd
    Connect in Outgoing Call Proceeding(U3)
ATMSIG(0/-1 0,153 - 0031/00): (vcnum:114) API - notifying Connect
    event to client ATM0
ATMSIG(0/-1 0,153 - 0031/00): (vcnum:114) Input event : Req
    Connect Ack in Active(U10)
```

The following debug command displays output on the signaling events occurring on the Denver ATM switch when the New York router is trying to call the San Jose router. The Denver switch acts as a transit node for this call:

```
Denver#debug atm sig-events
ATMSIG(1/1/2:0 0 - 161222): Input Event : Rcvd Setup in Null(N0)
ATMSIG(1/1/2:0 0 - 161222):Call Control Rcvd Setup in state : Call
    Initiated(N1)
ATMSIG: Called Party Addr:
    47.009181000000006170598A01.100000000000.00
ATMSIG: Calling Party Addr:
    47.009181000000006170595C01.300000000000.00
ATMSIG(1/1/2:0 215 - 161222): Input Event : Req Call Proceeding in
    Call Initiated(N1)
ATMSIG(1/1/2:0 215 - 161222): Output Call Proc msg, Call
    Initiated(N1) state
ATMSIG(1/1/2:0 215 - 161222): Call Initiated(N1) -> Call Proceeding
    sent (NNI) (N3)
ATMSIG: 1/1/1:0 findSvcBlockByCr, Svc not found, callref = 219
ATMSIG: 1/1/1:0 findSvcBlockByCr, Svc not found, callref = 220
ATMSIG(1/1/1:0 36 - 0220): Input Event : Req Setup in Null(N0)
ATMSIG(1/1/1:0 36 - 0220): Output Setup msg(XferAndTx), Null(N0)
    state
ATMSIG(1/1/1:0 36 - 0220): Null(N0) -> Call Present(N6)
ATMSIG: openTransitConnection, svc 0x60685D68, partnerSvc
    0x606863A0
```

```
ATMSIG(1/1/2:0 215 - 161222): Null(N0) -> Call Proceeding sent
   (NNI) (N3)
ATMSIG(1/1/1:0 36 - 0220): Input Event : Rcvd Call Proceeding in
   Call Present(N6)
ATMSIG(1/1/1:0 36 - 0220): Call Present(N6) -> Incoming Call
   Proceeding(N9)
ATMSIG(1/1/1:0 36 - 0220): Input Event : Rcvd Connect in Incoming
   Call Proceeding(N9)
ATMSIG(1/1/1:0 36 - 0220):Call Control Rcvd Connect in state :
   Incoming Call Proceeding(N9)
ATMSIG(1/1/1:0 36 - 0220): Input Event : Req Connect Ack in
   Incoming Call Proceeding(N9)
ATMSIG(1/1/1:0 36 - 0220): Output Connect Ack msg, Incoming Call
   Proceeding(N9) state
ATMSIG(1/1/1:0 36 - 0220): Incoming Call Proceeding(N9) ->
   Active(N10)
ATMSIG(1/1/2:0 215 - 161222): Input Event : Req Connect in Call
   Proceeding sent (NNI) (N3)
ATMSIG(1/1/2:0 215 - 161222): Output Connect msg(XferAndTx),
   Call Proceeding sent (NNI) (N3) state
ATMSIG(1/1/2:0 215 - 161222): Call Proceeding sent (NNI) (N3) ->
   Active(N10)
ATMSIG: connectTransitPath, svc 0x60685D68, partnerSvc
   0x606863A0
ATMSIG(1/1/1:0 36 - 0220): Incoming Call Proceeding(N9) ->
   Active(N10)
```

The following CLI command, **show atm map**, indicates mapping of protocol address (IP) to ATM address (NSAP). It also indicates that the connections to the remote routers are up, and indicates which VCD value it is using to create a connection through the ATM switch:

```
SanJose#show atm map
Map list 1483svc : PERMANENT
ip 172.10.10.2 maps to NSAP
   47.00918100000000006170595C01.200000000000.00, broadcast,
   connection up, VC 2, ATM0
ip 172.10.10.3 maps to NSAP
   47.00918100000000006170595C01.300000000000.00, broadcast,
   connection up, VC 1, ATM0
```

The following CLI command, **show atm vc**, indicates the status of VCD values used by the router connecting to a remote router, as shown by the preceding command. It also provides corresponding VPI/VCI values associated with that VCD value:

```
SanJose#show atm vc
Interface  VCD  VPI  VCI  Type  AAL/          Peak    Avg     Burst  Status
                                 Encapsulation Kbps    Kbps    Cells
ATM0       1    0    32   SVC   AAL5-SNAP      155000  155000  94     ACTIVE
ATM0       2    0    33   SVC   AAL5-SNAP      155000  155000  94     ACTIVE
```

The following CLI command, **show atm vc***n*, provides detailed output of the associated VCDs for the local router. This assists in troubleshooting connectivity to the remote router because this output can tell you that the local router is transmitting the cells and may not be receiving anything coming in:

```
SanJose#show atm vc 1
ATM0: VCD: 1, VPI: 0, VCI: 32, etype:0x0, AAL5 - LLC/SNAP, Flags:
   0x50
PeakRate: 155000, Average Rate: 155000, Burst Cells: 94,
   VCmode: 0x1
OAM DISABLED, InARP DISABLED
InPkts: 42, OutPkts: 46, InBytes: 3796, OutBytes: 4172
InPRoc: 42, OutPRoc: 12, Broadcasts: 34
```

```
InFast: 0, OutFast: 0, InAS: 0, OutAS: 0
OAM F5 cells sent: 0, OAM cells received: 0
Status: ACTIVE , TTL: 4
interface = ATM0, call remotely initiated, call reference = 2
vcnum = 1, vpi = 0, vci = 32, state = Active
 aal5snap vc, point-to-point call
Retry count: Current = 0, Max = 10
timer currently inactive, timer value = 00:00:00
Remote ATM Nsap address:
    47.009181000000006170595C01.300000000000.00

SanJose#show atm vc 2
ATM0: VCD: 2, VPI: 0, VCI: 33, etype:0x0, AAL5 - LLC/SNAP, Flags:
    0x50
PeakRate: 155000, Average Rate: 155000, Burst Cells: 94,
    VCmode: 0x1
OAM DISABLED, InARP DISABLED
InPkts: 45, OutPkts: 46, InBytes: 4148, OutBytes: 4220
InPRoc: 45, OutPRoc: 12, Broadcasts: 34
InFast: 0, OutFast: 0, InAS: 0, OutAS: 0
OAM F5 cells sent: 0, OAM cells received: 0
Status: ACTIVE , TTL: 4
interface = ATM0, call locally initiated, call reference = 1
vcnum = 2, vpi = 0, vci = 33, state = Active
aal5snap vc, point-to-point call
Retry count: Current = 0, Max = 10
timer currently inactive, timer value = 00:00:00
Remote ATM Nsap address:
    47.009181000000006170595C01.200000000000.00
```

Classical IP over ATM (RFC 1577)

RFC 1577, or "Classical IP and ATMARP over ATM," provides a mechanism to talk dynamically to IP-enabled routers through the ATM cloud. You do not require any kind of IP address–to–ATM address mapping to go from one router to another. It does so by using an ARP mechanism similar to Ethernet ARP.

In the following topology, you have three routers connected to the ATM cloud formed by two ATM switches. These three routers form a LIS, 172.10.x.x. Classical IP over ATM allows them to talk to each other dynamically with minimum configuration.

In the following example, treat the Denver switch as an ARP server and all three routers as clients. Each client connects to the ARP server by using a preconfigured ARP server ATM NSAP address and the ARP server gets the corresponding IP address of all the clients using InARP. The ARP server has an ARP table with IP-to-ATM NSAP address pairs. If any router wants to talk to another router, it sends ARP to the server, asking for another router's ATM NSAP address. After the requesting router receives the NSAP address, it communicates with that router directly over the ATM cloud.

The preceding scenario specifies one LIS group. You can have another set of ATM-enabled routers connected to the same ATM switches, but at Layer 3 they might be in a different LIS. This second LIS is independent of the first LIS. Both LIS groups have their own ARP server and corresponding clients. If the router in one LIS wants to talk to a router in another LIS, it has to go through an IP router that is configured as a member of both LIS groups; that is, it has to do Layer 3 routing even though it might be possible to open a direct VC between the two over the ATM cloud.

Design Considerations

RFC 1577 is very simple and straightforward to implement. Its simplicity comes from ease of configuration and troubleshooting. This kind of network is well suited for 10–15 nodes with one logical IP subnet. It does not scale, however, because of the problems with finding neighbors at the routing protocol level if the VCs are not already established. Usually, a multivendor RFC 1577 environment has a single point of failure because of its centralized ARP server. Cisco supports multiple ARP servers for the same LIS, but it is a proprietary solution.

Topology

Figure 18-3 presents the topology for this example.

Figure 18-3 *Classical IP Over ATM (RFC 1577)*

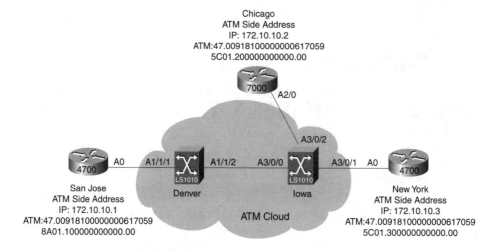

Configuration

The configuration of RFC 1577 requires an ATM ARP server configuration. Cisco routers with an ATM interface or an ATM switch LS1010 can act as an ATM ARP server for RFC 1577. In the following example, the Denver switch is an ARP server.

The CLI command **atm arp-server self** enables the Denver switch CPU card to act as an ARP server for LIS 172.10.x.x.

The configuration of the Denver switch is as follows:

```
interface ATM2/0/0
ip address 172.10.10.4 255.255.255.0
no keepalive
am esi-address 123456789000.00
atm arp-server self
```

The CLI command **atm arp-server nsap**
47.00918100000000006170598A01.123456789000.00 enables the San Jose router ATM
interface to become an ARP client for LIS 172.10.x.x, and also provides it with an NSAP
address of the ARP server for that LIS. It uses this NSAP address to establish a connection
to the ARP server when the ATM interface is administratively enabled. The configuration
of other routers in the same LIS is similar:

The configuration of the San Jose router is as follows:

```
interface ATM0
ip address 172.10.10.1 255.255.255.0
atm esi-address 100000000000.00
atm pvc 10 0 5 qsaal
atm pvc 20 0 16 ilmi
atm arp-server nsap
   47.00918100000000006170598A01.123456789000.00
```

The configuration of the Chicago router is as follows:

```
interface ATM2/0
ip address 172.10.10.2 255.255.255.0
atm esi-address 200000000000.00
atm pvc 10 0 5 qsaal
atm pvc 20 0 16 ilmi
atm arp-server nsap
   47.00918100000000006170598A01.123456789000.00
```

The configuration of the New York router is as follows:

```
interface ATM0
ip address 172.10.10.3 255.255.255.0
atm esi-address 300000000000.00
atm pvc 10 0 5 qsaal
atm pvc 20 0 16 ilmi
atm arp-server nsap
   47.00918100000000006170598A01.123456789000.00
```

Troubleshooting

Classical IP over ATM requires the same MTU size on all ATM clients and ARP servers in
the same LIS. Understanding the client-server interaction eases the problem of
troubleshooting. The **show** and **debug** commands provide insight into the client/server
interaction.

The following CLI command, **show atm map**, reveals that as soon as the client interface is
enabled, it connects to the ARP server via VC 159. The CLI command **debug atm arp** on
the same client reveals that the client is getting an InARP request from the ARP server
(172.10.10.4) to resolve the ATM NSAP address to an IP address and to update its table.

The client responds back with its IP address and the server builds its ARP table. Similarly, any client that is enabled is registered into the ARP table using this process.

```
SanJose#show atm map
Map list ATM0_ATM_ARP : DYNAMIC
arp maps to NSAP
   47.009181000000006170598A01.123456789000.00
, connection up, VC 159, ATM0

SanJose#debug atm arp
ATMARP(ATM0)I: INARP Request VCD#159 from 172.10.10.4
ATMARP(ATM0)O: INARP Response VCD#159 to 172.10.10.4
ATMSM(ATM0): Attaching to VC #159 for type 1 traffic

SanJose#show atm vc
Interface  VCD  VPI  VCI  Type  AAL/         Peak    Avg     Burst  Status
                                Encapsulation Kbps   Kbps    Cells
ATM0       10   0    5    PVC   AAL5-SAAL     155000  155000  94     ACTIVE
ATM0       20   0    16   PVC   AAL5-ILMI     155000  155000  94     ACTIVE
AMT0       159  0    62   PVC   AAL5-SNAP     155000  155000  94     ACTIVE
```

The following CLI command displays the corresponding VC to the ATM ARP server and reveals that the call was locally initiated:

```
SanJose#show atm vc 159
ATM0: VCD: 159, VPI: 0, VCI: 62, etype:0x0, AAL5 - LLC/SNAP,
    Flags: 0xD0
PeakRate: 155000, Average Rate: 155000, Burst Cells: 94,
    VCmode: 0x1
OAM DISABLED, InARP DISABLED
InPkts: 1, OutPkts: 5, InBytes: 52, OutBytes: 376
InPRoc: 1, OutPRoc: 0, Broadcasts: 4
InFast: 0, OutFast: 0, InAS: 0, OutAS: 0
OAM F5 cells sent: 0, OAM cells received: 0
Status: ACTIVE , TTL: 0
interface = ATM0, call locally initiated, call reference = 112
vcnum = 159, vpi = 0, vci = 62, state = Active
aal5snap vc, point-to-point call
Retry count: Current = 0, Max = 10
timer currently inactive, timer value = 00:00:00
Remote ATM Nsap address:
    47.009181000000006170598A01.123456789000.00
```

The following CLI command, **show atm map**, now has one entry with a corresponding IP-NSAP address pair from the ARP server:

```
SanJose#show atm map
Map list ATM0_ATM_ARP : DYNAMIC
arp maps to NSAP
   47.009181000000006170598A01.123456789000.00, connection
   up, VC 159, ATM0
ip 172.10.10.4 maps to NSAP
   47.009181000000006170598A01.123456789000.00, broadcast,
   connection up, VC 159, ATM0
```

The following CLI command **debug atm arp** on the ARP server reveals that as each client comes up, it establishes an ATM connection to the ARP server using a predefined ARP server ATM address. The ARP server sends an InARP request to get the IP address of each client, and the output shows exactly that. You can see from the bold text that the server transmitted the InARP for client 172.10.10.2, receives a reply, and updates its ARP table:

```
Denver#debug atm arp
ARPSERVER (ATM2/0/0): tx InARP REQ on vc 254
ATMARP(ATM2/0/0)O: INARP_REQ to VCD#254 for link 7(IP)
ARPSERVER (ATM2/0/0): tx InARP REQ on vc 255
ATMARP(ATM2/0/0)O: INARP_REQ to VCD#255 for link 7(IP)
ATMARP(ATM2/0/0)I: INARP Reply VCD#254 from 172.10.10.2
ARPSERVER (ATM2/0/0): rx InARP REPLY from 172.10.10.2 (vc
254)
ARPSERVER (ATM2/0/0): New IP address for vcd 254 -- was
0.0.0.0, now 172.10.10.2
ATMARP(ATM2/0/0)I: INARP Reply VCD#255 from 172.10.10.3
ARPSERVER (ATM2/0/0): rx InARP REPLY from 172.10.10.3 (vc
255)
ARPSERVER (ATM2/0/0): New IP address for vcd 255 -- was
0.0.0.0, now 172.10.10.3
ARPSERVER (ATM2/0/0): tx InARP REQ on vc 256
ATMARP(ATM2/0/0)O: INARP_REQ to VCD#256 for link 7(IP)
ARPSERVER (ATM2/0/0): vc 256 wait timer expiry. Retransmitting.
ARPSERVER (ATM2/0/0): tx InARP REQ on vc 256
ATMARP(ATM2/0/0)O: INARP_REQ to VCD#256 for link 7(IP)
ATMARP(ATM2/0/0)I: INARP Reply VCD#256 from 172.10.10.5
ARPSERVER (ATM2/0/0): rx InARP REPLY from 172.10.10.5 (vc
256)
ARPSERVER (ATM2/0/0): New IP address for vcd 256 -- was
0.0.0.0, now 172.10.10.5
ARPSERVER (ATM2/0/0): tx InARP REQ on vc 257
ATMARP(ATM2/0/0)O: INARP_REQ to VCD#257 for link 7(IP)
ARPSERVER (ATM2/0/0): vc 257 wait timer expiry. Retransmitting.
ARPSERVER (ATM2/0/0): tx InARP REQ on vc 257
ATMARP(ATM2/0/0)O: INARP_REQ to VCD#257 for link 7(IP)
ATMARP(ATM2/0/0)I: INARP Reply VCD#257 from 172.10.10.1
ARPSERVER (ATM2/0/0): rx InARP REPLY from 172.10.10.1 (vc 257)
ARPSERVER (ATM2/0/0): New IP address for vcd 257 - was 0.0.0.0, now 172.10.10.1A
```

Until now, you have seen how each client is registered in the ARP table. The following analysis tells how client-client interaction occurs for existing clients, and what happens if the client does not exist.

You are pinging from the San Jose router to the Chicago router (172.10.10.2), but don't know the ATM address of the Chicago router. So, the San Jose router sends an ARP request to the server and receives a response with a corresponding NSAP address:

```
SanJose#ping 172.10.10.2
Type escape sequence to abort.
Sending 5, 100-byte ICMP Echoes to 172.10.10.2, timeout is 2
    seconds:
Success rate is 60 percent (3/5), round-trip min/avg/max = 1/1/1 ms

SanJose#debug atm arp
ATMARP(ATM0): Sending ARP to 172.10.10.2
ATMARP:(ATM0): ARP reply from 172.10.10.2 ->
   47.009181000000006170595C01.200000000000.00
ATMARP(ATM0): Opening VCC to
   47.009181000000006170595C01.200000000000.00..!!!
```

The following output from the ARP server shows that it received the ARP request from 172.10.10.1 for ATM NSAP address of 172.10.10.2. It replies back with the appropriate ATM NSAP address:

```
Denver#debug atm arp
ATMARP:(ATM2/0/0): ARP Request from 172.10.10.1 ->
```

```
     47.009181000000006170598A01.100000000000.00
ATMARP(ATM2/0/0): ARP VCD#0 172.10.10.1 replacing NSAP
ARPSERVER (ATM2/0/0): rx ARP REQ from 172.10.10.1 to
     172.10.10.2 (vc 257)
ARPSERVER (ATM2/0/0): tx ARP REPLY from 172.10.10.2 to
     172.10.10.1 (vc 257)
ATMARP:(ATM2/0/0): ARP Request from 172.10.10.2 ->
     47.009181000000006170595C01.200000000000.00
ATMARP(ATM2/0/0): ARP VCD#0 172.10.10.2 replacing NSAP
ARPSERVER (ATM2/0/0): rx ARP REQ from 172.10.10.2 to
     172.10.10.1 (vc 254)
ARPSERVER (ATM2/0/0): tx ARP REPLY from 172.10.10.1 to
     172.10.10.2 (vc 254)
```

Now, see what happens if you try to ping a nonexistent client in the LIS:

```
SanJose#ping 172.10.10.10
Type escape sequence to abort.
Sending 5, 100-byte ICMP Echoes to 172.10.10.10, timeout is 2
     seconds:
Success rate is 0 percent (0/5)
```

The pinging to the 172.10.10.10 nonexistent client failed. Assuming that you don't know that the client does not exist, you might think the ARP server is down. But the **debug atm arp** command tells you that the server is alive and is sending you an ARP_NAK response, indicating that the client does not exist or at least is not registered with that server:

```
SanJose#debug atm arp
ATMARP(ATM0): Sending ARP to 172.10.10.10
ATMARP(ATM0): ARP_NAK received on VCD#159.
ATMARP(ATM0): Sending ARP to 172.10.10.10
ATMARP(ATM0): ARP_NAK received on VCD#159.
ATMARP(ATM0): Sending ARP to 172.10.10.10
ATMARP(ATM0): ARP_NAK received on VCD#159.
ATMARP(ATM0): Sending ARP to 172.10.10.10
ATMARP(ATM0): ARP_NAK received on VCD#159.
ATMARP(ATM0): Sending ARP to 172.10.10.10
ATMARP(ATM0): ARP_NAK received on VCD#159.
```

The following CLI command, **debug atm arp**, on the ARP server displays the response from the server to the client requesting a nonexistent IP-NSAP ARP resolution:

```
Denver#debug atm arp
ATMARP:(ATM2/0/0): ARP Request from 172.10.10.1 ->
     47.009181000000006170598A01.100000000000.00
ATMARP(ATM2/0/0): ARP Update from VCD#257 172.10.10.1 MAP
     VCD#0
ARPSERVER (ATM2/0/0): rx ARP REQ from 172.10.10.1 to
     172.10.10.10 (vc 257)
ARPSERVER (ATM2/0/0): tx ARP NAK to 172.10.10.1 for
     172.10.10.10 (vc 257)
ATMARP:(ATM2/0/0): ARP Request from 172.10.10.1 ->
     47.009181000000006170598A01.100000000000.00
ATMARP(ATM2/0/0): ARP Update from VCD#257 172.10.10.1 MAP
     VCD#0
ARPSERVER (ATM2/0/0): rx ARP REQ from 172.10.10.1 to
     172.10.10.10 (vc 257)
ARPSERVER (ATM2/0/0): tx ARP NAK to 172.10.10.1 for
     172.10.10.10 (vc 257)
ATMARP:(ATM2/0/0): ARP Request from 172.10.10.1 ->
     47.009181000000006170598A01.100000000000.00
ATMARP(ATM2/0/0): ARP Update from VCD#257 172.10.10.1 MAP
     VCD#0
```

```
ARPSERVER (ATM2/0/0): rx ARP REQ from 172.10.10.1 to
    172.10.10.10 (vc 257)
ARPSERVER (ATM2/0/0): tx ARP NAK to 172.10.10.1 for
    172.10.10.10 (vc 257)
ATMARP:(ATM2/0/0): ARP Request from 172.10.10.1 ->
    47.00918100000000006170598A01.100000000000.00
```

The following CLI command, **show atm map**, shows that the San Jose router can now talk directly to all other routers in the same LIS using ATM SVCs. Now, it does not require the server to provide the end-router's NSAP address. This table will remain in effect as long as the two routers continue to exchange some packets/cells. In this case study, OSPF Hellos are exchanged at regular intervals, keeping the VC up.

Also, it is important to notice that the broadcast packet cannot initiate a VC in the ATM cloud because ATM itself is NBMA media. So, there should be some way for the router to find all its neighbors in the ATM cloud or in the same LIS. To do this, it can either ping each LIS router or manually configure its neighbors:

```
SanJose#show atm map
Map list ATM0_ATM_ARP : DYNAMIC
arp maps to NSAP
    47.00918100000000006170598A01.123456789000.00, connection
    up, VC 159, ATM0
ip 172.10.10.1 maps to NSAP
    47.00918100000000006170598A01.100000000000.00, broadcast,
    connection up, VC 162, ATM0
ip 172.10.10.2 maps to NSAP
    47.00918100000000006170595C01.200000000000.00, broadcast,
    connection up, VC 160, ATM0
ip 172.10.10.3 maps to NSAP
    47.00918100000000006170595C01.300000000000.00, broadcast,
    connection up, VC 163, ATM0
ip 172.10.10.4 maps to NSAP
    47.00918100000000006170598A01.123456789000.00, broadcast,
    connection up, VC 159, ATM0
```

The following CLI command, **show atm arp**, shows the ARP table on the server with all the active-client entries:

```
Denver#show atm arp
Note that a '*' next to an IP address indicates an active call
IP Address ATM2/0/0:      TTL      ATM Address
* 172.10.10.1           19:29      47009181000000006170598a0110000000000000
* 172.10.10.2           12:56      47009181000000006170595c0120000000000000
* 172.10.10.3           19:31      47009181000000006170595c0130000000000000
* 172.10.10.4            9:23      47009181000000006170598a0112345678900000
* 172.10.10.5           16:02      47009181000000006170595c0150000000000000
```

LAN Emulation Introduction

LAN Emulation (LANE) is a method of emulating LAN over an ATM infrastructure. Standards for emulating Ethernet 802.3 and Token Ring 802.5 are defined. Because ATM is connection-oriented in nature, it becomes difficult to support popular multiprotocols, such as IP and IPX, which are connectionless in nature. By having ATM emulate Ethernet, it becomes easier to support Multiprotocols over ATM without creating new protocols. It is also possible to create multiple LANs over the same ATM infrastructure. These ELANs cannot talk to each other directly at Layer 2, but need to be routed. Therefore, such a setup always requires a router running multiple ELANs.

Design Considerations

Designing LANE in a campus environment requires planning and careful allocation of devices to enable LANE services. There is lots of documentation written on this topic. This discussion highlights some of the most common issues associated with LANE design in a campus environment. Finally, LANE design depends on the particular network traffic pattern and how ATM resources are allocated to accommodate that pattern.

One of the most important and heavily utilized components in LANE is its BUS service because all the broadcast packets come to the BUS and are forwarded back to all the LECs in an ELAN. The Cisco Catalyst 5000 LANE card BUS-processing capability is around 120 kbps and the router AIP card capability is around 60 kbps.

NOTE   *BUS* stands for broadcast-and-unknown server. It is a multicast server used in ELANs that is used to flood traffic addressed to an unknown destination, and to forward multicast and broadcast traffic to the appropriate clients.

The other important factor in LANE design is its VC consumption in edge devices and the ATM switch cloud itself. Equation 18-1 provides some insight.

Equation 18–1   *LANE Maximum VC Consumption Equation*

$$\text{Total VCs} = E((2N + 2) + (\tfrac{NX(N-1)}{2})) + W$$

In this equation, the values are as follows:

W   Total number of wiring-closet ATM-LAN switches and routers
E   Total number of ELANs (VLANs)
N   Typical number of wiring closets per ELAN

Using this equation, a LANE cloud with four edge devices and running a single ELAN requires 20 VCs. As the number of ELANs per cloud increases, the VCC requirement increases. This places a burden on the device running LANE services, in case of ELAN failure. It is a recommended practice, therefore, to spread LANE services across different devices.

The last important factor to consider when designing LANE is the call-setup capability of ATM switches that form the ATM cloud. This capability is especially important during a failure scenario—suddenly, for example, all the LECs try to connect to the LANE services through these switches. In such a case, the ATM switches might experience many simultaneous call-setup requests. If they are not configured to successfully handle the load, a negative ripple effect could result.

The call-handling capability of an LS1010 is about 110 calls per second.

Topology

Figure 18-4 presents the topology for this example.

Figure 18-4 *LAN Emulation*

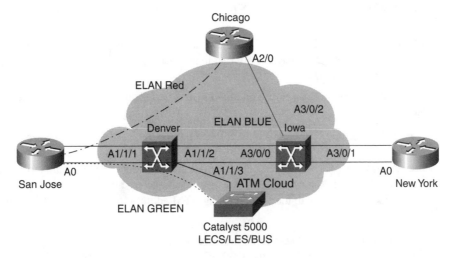

NOTE	LAN Emulation is commonly used in a campus environment. The routers represented here are named for cities, but should be referred to as "Building A, Building B, and Building C."

Configuration

LAN Emulation configuration requires the LECS/LES/BUS to be configured first for its full functionality. These components of LANE can be configured on ATM-enabled routers and catalysts. The difference is in their performance. A Catalyst switch provides better performance than routers for running these services.

NOTE	*LEC* stands for LAN Emulation Client. It is an entity in an end system that performs data forwarding, address resolution, and other control functions for a single ES within a single ELAN. An LEC also provides a standard LAN service interface to any higher-layer entity that interfaces to the LEC. Each LEC is identified by a unique ATM address, and is associated with one or more MAC addresses reachable through that ATM address.

LECS stands for LAN Emulation Configuration Server. It is an entity that assigns individual LANE clients to particular ELANs by directing them to the LES that corresponds to the ELAN. There is logically one LECS per administrative domain, and this serves all ELANs within that domain.

LES stands for LAN Emulation Server. It is an entity that implements the control function for a particular ELAN. There is only one logical LES per ELAN, and it is identified by a unique ATM address.

The configuration in this section on an ATM-enabled Catalyst 5000 enables the LECS/LES/BUS.

The command **lane database ABC** creates a named database for the LANE configuration server. This database contains a different LANE server ATM address and other information. It contains the LANE characteristic information. When some device wants to join a particular LANE in the database with a specific characteristic, it compares the request and, if satisfied, responds with the LANE server ATM address to continue the LEC joining process.

The command **name red server-atm-address 47.009181000000006170598A01.00602FBCC511.01** binds the red LANE with its appropriate ATM address of the LANE server. Similarly, for the blue and green LANE clouds, refer to your configuration manual regarding assignment of ATM addresses to various LANE services on Cisco devices.

The command **lane config database ABC** links the configuration server's database name to the specified major interface and enables the configuration server.

The command **lane auto-config-atm-address** specifies that the configuration server's ATM address be computed by Cisco's automatic method of assigning the addresses to the various LANE services.

The command **lane server-bus ethernet red** enables a LANE server and a LANE BUS for the first emulated LAN. Similarly, for the emulated LANs green and blue on different subinterfaces, this command creates a separate LANE cloud with every separate IP subnet.

The command **lane client ethernet 1 green** enables the green LANE client and binds VLAN1 on the Catalyst 5000 to the ELAN green. With this configuration, VLAN1 and ELAN green comprise one big IP subnet. So, ELAN is actually an extension of VLAN in the ATM-switched network from the Ethernet/token-switched network.

In short, Catalyst 5000 in this example is acting as LECS for one big LANE domain and LES/BUS for ELAN red, green, and blue. It also acts as the LANE client for ELAN green.

The configuration of Catalyst 5000 is as follows:

```
lane database ABC
name red server-atm-address
    47.009181000000006170598A01.00602FBCC511.01
name blue server-atm-address
    47.009181000000006170598A01.00602FBCC511.03
name green server-atm-address
    47.009181000000006170598A01.00602FBCC511.02
!
interface ATM0
atm pvc 1 0 5 qsaal
atm pvc 2 0 16 ilmi
lane config database ABC
lane auto-config-atm-address
!
interface ATM0.1 multipoint
lane server-bus ethernet red
!
interface ATM0.2 multipoint
lane server-bus ethernet green
lane client ethernet 1 green
!
interface ATM0.3 multipoint
lane server-bus ethernet blue
```

In the following configuration of the San Jose router, the ATM interface is acting as a LANE client for three different ELANs, creating three different IP subnets. Therefore, San Jose is a router with a common interface for intra-ELAN routing or connectivity. LEC in the red LANE cannot talk at the ATM layer directly to the LEC in ELAN green. It has to go through the router San Jose and do Layer 3 routing:

```
interface ATM0
atm pvc 10 0 5 qsaal
atm pvc 20 0 16 ilmi
interface ATM0.1 multipoint
ip address 192.10.10.1 255.255.255.0
lane client ethernet red
!
interface ATM0.2 multipoint
ip address 195.10.10.1 255.255.255.0
lane client ethernet green
!
interface ATM0.3 multipoint
ip address 198.10.10.1 255.255.255.0
lane client ethernet blue
```

In the following configuration of the Chicago router, the ATM interface is acting as an LEC for the ELAN red:

```
interface ATM2/0
atm pvc 10 0 5 qsaal
atm pvc 20 0 16 ilmi
interface ATM2/0.1 multipoint
ip address 192.10.10.2 255.255.255.0
lane client ethernet red
```

In the following configuration of the New York router, the ATM interface is acting as an LEC for the ELAN blue:

```
interface ATM0
atm pvc 10 0 5 qsaal
atm pvc 20 0 16 ilmi
!
interface ATM0.1 multipoint
ip address 198.10.10.2 255.255.255.0
lane client ethernet blue
```

In the following configuration of the Denver and Iowa ATM switches, there is no configuration needed on the interfaces if you are running PNNI between them. The command **atm lecs-address-default 47.0091.8100.0000.0061.7059.8a01.0060.2fbc.c513.00 1** provides the LECS address to any directly connected LEC upon initialization. This command is an absolute requirement for LANE to be in operation on all the edge ATM switches directly connected to the routers, or the Catalyst 5000 running LEC, if you are using the automatic configuration option for assigning the LECS address.

The configuration of the Denver switch is as follows:

```
atm lecs-address-default
    47.0091.8100.0000.0061.7059.8a01.0060.2fbc.c513.00 1
atm address
    47.0091.8100.0000.0061.7059.8a01.0061.7059.8a01.00
atm router pnni
node 1 level 56 lowest
redistribute ATM-static
interface ATM1/1/1
no keepalive
interface ATM1/1/2
no keepalive
interface ATM1/1/3
no keepalive
```

The configuration of the Iowa switch is as follows:

```
atm lecs-address-default
    47.0091.8100.0000.0061.7059.8a01.0060.2fbc.c513.00 1
atm address
    47.0091.8100.0000.0061.7059.5c01.0061.7059.5c01.00
atm router pnni
node 1 level 56 lowest
redistribute ATM-static
interface ATM3/0/0
no keepalive
interface ATM3/0/1
no keepalive
interface ATM3/0/2
no keepalive
```

Troubleshooting

Troubleshooting LANE is most complex. Usually, the problem is either LES/BUS performance or connectivity to the LANE. LES/BUS performance is a design issue and involves many factors. But the connectivity problem mostly arises from the LEC being unable to join the particular LANE. The intra-LANE connectivity problem is dependent more on IP routing than on LANE, so you need to look at the LANE LEC client operation and its connection phase. After it is operational in the particular LANE, it should be able to talk directly to other LECs.

To be operational, LEC needs to have all the following VCCs (except Data Direct):

- **Configure Direct**—LEC-to-LECS connect phase
- **Control Direct and Control Distribute**—LEC-to-LES control VCs connection and join phase
- **Multicast Send and Multicast Forward**—LEC-to-BUS connect phase
- **Data Direct**—LEC-to-LEC connect phase

Figure 18-5 illustrates these connections. This section discusses troubleshooting these connections.

Figure 18-5 *Basic Control VCs Required for LANE*

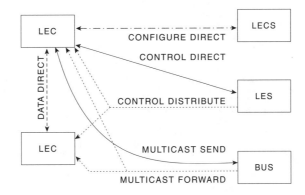

The following analysis examines how the LEC on blue ELAN on the New York router joins the LANE and becomes operational, and how it talks with other LECs on the same ELAN.

NOTE   The mention of color is not actually color, but the name of a logical LAN created by ATM LANE technology. There is a logical LAN between the New York router and the San Jose router.

NOTE   Even though I have named the routers San Jose, New York, Chicago, and so on, these routers are on the same campus. It is like Building A, Building B, or Building C. The names do not indicate actual geographical distances.

For any LEC to join the ELAN, there must be an operational LECS/LES/BUS before it attempts to join the LANE.

The command **show lane brief** on the Catalyst reveals the ELAN blue LES and BUS address, and confirms that they are in operational mode. This is required before any LEC can join the ELAN blue:

```
Catalyst#show lane brief
LE Server ATM0.3 ELAN name: blue Admin: up State: operational
type: ethernet Max Frame Size: 1516
ATM address: 47.009181000000006170598A01.00602FBCC511.03
LECS used: 47.009181000000006170598A01.00602FBCC513.00
connected, vcd 261
control distribute: vcd 159, 2 members, 4022 packets
LE BUS ATM0.3 ELAN name: blue Admin: up State: operational
type: ethernet Max Frame Size: 1516
ATM address: 47.009181000000006170598A01.00602FBCC512.03
data forward: vcd 163, 2 members, 6713 packets, 0 unicasts
```

The command **show lane config** reveals that the LECS configured on Catalyst 5000 is operational and active with its corresponding LECS address. Also, it indicates that it serves three ELANs and that they are all active:

```
Catalyst#show lane config
LE Config Server ATM0 config table: ABC
Admin: up State: operational
LECS Mastership State: active master
list of global LECS addresses (12 seconds to update):
47.009181000000006170598A01.00602FBCC513.00 <-------- me
ATM Address of this LECS:
47.009181000000006170598A01.00602FBCC513.00
vcd  rxCnt  txCnt  callingParty
252  1      1      47.009181000000006170598A01.00602FBCC511.01 LES red 0 active
256  2      2      47.009181000000006170598A01.00602FBCC511.02 LES green 0 active
260  6      6      47.009181000000006170598A01.00602FBCC511.03 LES blue 0 active
cumulative total number of unrecognized packets received so far: 0
cumulative total number of config requests received so far: 100
cumulative total number of config failures so far: 29
cause of last failure: no configuration
culprit for the last failure:
   47.009181000000006170595C01.00000C7A5660.01
```

LEC-to-LECS Connect Phase

This section covers getting an LECS address via ILMI. Cisco LEC can find LECS by using one of three methods:

- Hard-coded ATM address

- Get the LECS via ILMI VPI=0, VCI=16

- Fixed address defined by the ATM Forum (47007900000000000000000000.00A03E000001.00)

The command **debug lane client all** reveals that the LEC on ATM0.1 is trying to get the LECS address from its directly connected switch:

```
NewYork#debug lane client all
LEC ATM0.1: predicate PRED_LEC_NSAP TRUE
LEC ATM0.1: state IDLE event LEC_TIMER_IDLE =>
  REGISTER_ADDR
LEC ATM0.1: action A_POST_LISTEN
LEC ATM0.1: sending LISTEN
LEC ATM0.1: listen on
  47.009181000000006170595C01.00000C5CA980.01
LEC ATM0.1: state REGISTER_ADDR event
  LEC_CTL_ILMI_SET_RSP_POS => POSTING_LISTEN
LEC ATM0.1: received LISTEN
LEC ATM0.1: action A_ACTIVATE_LEC
LEC ATM0.1: predicate PRED_CTL_DIRECT_NSAP FALSE
LEC ATM0.1: predicate PRED_CTL_DIRECT_PVC FALSE
LEC ATM0.1: predicate PRED_LECS_PVC FALSE
LEC ATM0.1: predicate PRED_LECS_NSAP FALSE
LEC ATM0.1: state POSTING_LISTEN event
  LEC_SIG_LISTEN_POS => GET_LECS_ADDR
LEC ATM0.1: action A_ALLOC_LECS_ADDR
LEC ATM0.1: state GET_LECS_ADDR event
  LEC_CTL_ILMI_SET_RSP_POS => GET_LECS_ADDR
LEC ATM0.1: action A_REGISTER_ADDR
```

Configure Direct:

- Bidirectional VCC setup by LEC as part of the LECS connect phase

- Used to obtain LES ATM address

Figure 18-6 illustrates the LEC-to-LECS connect phase.

Figure 18-6 *LEC-to-LECS Connect Phase*

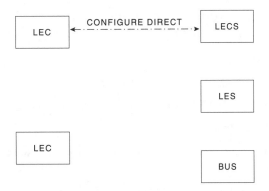

The following output reveals that upon finding the LECS address, an LEC establishes the call to the LECS. This VCC is called Configure Direct VCC. It then sends the configuration request to the LECS on the same VCC with its own information, asking for a corresponding LES address of that ELAN. LECS responds, confirming that the ELAN blue information LEC requested is defined and supplies the LEC with a corresponding LES address of ELAN blue:

```
NewYork#debug lane client all
LEC ATM0.1: action A_SEND_LECS_SETUP
LEC ATM0.1: sending SETUP
LEC ATM0.1: callid 0x60AC611C
LEC ATM0.1: called party
    47.009181000000006170598A01.00602FBCC513.00
LEC ATM0.1: calling_party
    47.009181000000006170595C01.00000C5CA980.01
LEC ATM0.1: state GET_LECS_ADDR event
    LEC_CTL_ILMI_SET_RSP_NEG => LECS_CONNECT
LEC ATM0.1: received CONNECT
LEC ATM0.1: callid 0x60AC611C
LEC ATM0.1: vcd 28
LEC ATM0.1: action A_SEND_CFG_REQ
LEC ATM0.1: sending LANE_CONFIG_REQ on VCD 28
LEC ATM0.1: SRC MAC address 0000.0c5c.a980
LEC ATM0.1: SRC ATM address
    47.009181000000006170595C01.00000C5CA980.01
LEC ATM0.1: LAN Type 1
LEC ATM0.1: Frame size 1
LEC ATM0.1: LAN Name blue
LEC ATM0.1: LAN Name size 4
LEC ATM0.1: state LECS_CONNECT event LEC_SIG_CONNECT
    => GET_LES_ADDR
LEC ATM0.1: received LANE_CONFIG_RSP on VCD 28
LEC ATM0.1: SRC MAC address 0000.0c5c.a980
LEC ATM0.1: SRC ATM address
    47.009181000000006170595C01.00000C5CA980.01
LEC ATM0.1: LAN Type 1
LEC ATM0.1: Frame size 1
LEC ATM0.1: LAN Name blue
LEC ATM0.1: LAN Name size 4
```

LEC-to-LES Control Connections

After the LEC gets the LES address of its ELAN, it establishes the following:

Control Direct:

- Bidirectional point-to-point VCC to the LES for sending control traffic
- Setup by the LEC as part of the initialization process

Control Distribute:

- Unidirectional point-to-multipoint control VCC to the LEC for distributing control traffic.

Figure 18-7 illustrates LEC-to-LES control VCs.

Figure 18-7 *LEC-to-LES Control VCs*

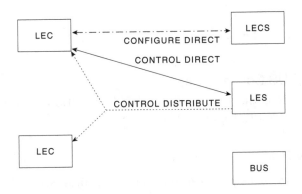

The following debug output reveals that the LEC is setting up the Control Direct VCC to the LES. On this VCC, it sends out the LANE_JOIN_REQ. LES responds back with LECID on the same VCC. At this point, the LES opens the Control Distribute VCC to the LEC and the LEC must accept this VCC to enable LES to distribute the control traffic:

```
NewYork#debug lane client all
LEC ATM0.1: action A_SEND_LES_SETUP
LEC ATM0.1: sending SETUP
LEC ATM0.1: callid 0x60ABEDF4
LEC ATM0.1: called party
    47.009181000000006170598A01.00602FBCC511.03
LEC ATM0.1: calling_party
    47.009181000000006170595C01.00000C5CA980.01
LEC ATM0.1: received CONNECT
LEC ATM0.1: callid 0x60ABEDF4
LEC ATM0.1: vcd 97
LEC ATM0.1: action A_SEND_JOIN_REQ
LEC ATM0.1: sending LANE_JOIN_REQ on VCD 97
LEC ATM0.1: Status 0
LEC ATM0.1: LECID 0
LEC ATM0.1: SRC MAC address 0000.0c5c.a980
LEC ATM0.1: SRC ATM address
    47.009181000000006170595C01.00000C5CA980.01
LEC ATM0.1: LAN Type 1
LEC ATM0.1: Frame size 1
LEC ATM0.1: LAN Name blue
LEC ATM0.1: LAN Name size 4
LEC ATM0.1: received SETUP
LEC ATM0.1: callid 0x60AC726C
LEC ATM0.1: called party
    47.009181000000006170595C01.00000C5CA980.01
LEC ATM0.1: calling_party
    47.009181000000006170598A01.00602FBCC511.03
LEC ATM0.1: sending CONNECT
LEC ATM0.1: callid 0x60AC726C
LEC ATM0.1: vcd 98
LEC ATM0.1: received CONNECT_ACK
LEC ATM0.1: received LANE_JOIN_RSP on VCD 97
LEC ATM0.1: Status 0
LEC ATM0.1: LECID 1
```

```
LEC ATM0.1: SRC MAC address 0000.0c5c.a980
LEC ATM0.1: SRC ATM address
    47.00918100000006170595C01.00000C5CA980.01
LEC ATM0.1: LAN Type 1
LEC ATM0.1: Frame size 1
LEC ATM0.1: LAN Name blue
LEC ATM0.1: LAN Name size 4
```

LEC-to-BUS Connections

After the LEC connects to the LES, it ARPs for the BUS ATM address, and LES responds to it. Upon receiving the BUS ATM address, LEC and BUS establish the following VCCs to each other:

Multicast Send:

- LEC sets up bidirectional point-to-point Multicast Send VCC to the BUS.
- Used for sending broadcast/multicast data to the BUS.

Multicast Forward:

- BUS sets up point-to-multipoint Multicast Forward VCC to the LEC.
- Used for forwarding multicast/broadcast traffic to all the LECs.

Figure 18-8 illustrates LEC-to-BUS VCs.

Figure 18-8   *LEC-to-BUS VCs*

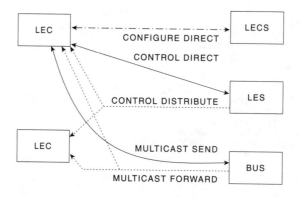

The following **debug** output reveals that the LEC sends out a LANE_ARP_ REQ to the LES on Control Direct VCC to resolve the BUS ATM address. LES responds back on the Control Distribute VCC with the BUS ATM address. LEC then sets up a connection to the bus directly. This VCC is called a *Multicast Send* and is used for forwarding broadcast traffic to other LECs. Also, the BUS sets up the multipoint VCC to the LEC, and this VCC is called *Multicast Forward*. Every time a new client comes up, it adds it to this point-to-multipoint VCC.

This VCC is used by the BUS for forwarding broadcast and multicast traffic to all the LECs in that ELAN.

At this point, the LEC client on the New York router in ELAN blue changes its state to up, and becomes operational and ready to talk with other LECs in the same ELAN:

```
NewYork#debug lane client all
LEC ATM0.1: action A_SEND_BUS_ARP
LEC ATM0.1: sending LANE_ARP_REQ on VCD 97
LEC ATM0.1: SRC MAC address 0000.0c5c.a980
LEC ATM0.1: SRC ATM address
    47.00918100000000006170595C01.00000C5CA980.01
LEC ATM0.1: TARGET MAC address ffff.ffff.ffff
LEC ATM0.1: TARGET ATM address
    00.00000000000000000000000.000000000000.00
LEC ATM0.1: received LANE_ARP_RSP on VCD 98
LEC ATM0.1: SRC MAC address 0000.0c5c.a980
LEC ATM0.1: SRC ATM address
    47.00918100000000006170595C01.00000C5CA980.01
LEC ATM0.1: TARGET MAC address ffff.ffff.ffff
LEC ATM0.1: TARGET ATM address
    47.00918100000000006170598A01.00602FBCC512.03
LEC ATM0.1: action A_SEND_BUS_SETUP
LEC ATM0.1: predicate PRED_MCAST_SEND_NSAP FALSE
LEC ATM0.1: predicate PRED_MCAST_SEND_PVC FALSE
LEC ATM0.1: sending SETUP
LEC ATM0.1: callid 0x60AC7418
LEC ATM0.1: called party
    47.00918100000000006170598A01.00602FBCC512.03
LEC ATM0.1: calling_party
    47.00918100000000006170595C01.00000C5CA980.01
LEC ATM0.1: received CONNECT
LEC ATM0.1: callid 0x60AC7418
LEC ATM0.1: vcd 99
LEC ATM0.1: action A_PROCESS_BUS_CONNECT
LEC ATM0.1: received SETUP
LEC ATM0.1: callid 0x60AC6CA4
LEC ATM0.1: called party
    47.00918100000000006170595C01.00000C5CA980.01
LEC ATM0.1: calling_party
    47.00918100000000006170598A01.00602FBCC512.03
LEC ATM0.1: action A_SEND_BUS_CONNECT
LEC ATM0.1: sending CONNECT
LEC ATM0.1: callid 0x60AC6CA4
LEC ATM0.1: vcd 100
%LANE-5-UPDOWN: ATM0.1 elan blue: LE Client changed state
    to up
LEC ATM0.1: state MCAST_FORWARD_CONN event
    LEC_SIG_SETUP => ACTIVE
LEC ATM0.1: received CONNECT_ACK
LEC ATM0.1: action A_PROCESS_CONNECT_ACK
LEC ATM0.1: state ACTIVE event LEC_SIG_CONNECT_ACK =>
    ACTIVE
```

The command **show lane client** on the New York router shows LEC in an operational state and all the corresponding VCCs it has established to the different LANE services.

The important thing to note here is that if the LEC fails in establishing any one of these VCCs, it will start the join process from the beginning and keep trying until successful.

Therefore, looking at the client's operate state itself, you can determine where the problem lies and perform additional debugging accordingly:

```
NewYork#show lane client
LE Client ATM0.1 ELAN name: blue Admin: up State: operational
Client ID: 1 LEC up for 1 hour 35 minutes 35 seconds
Join Attempt: 1
HW Address: 0000.0c5c.a980 Type: ethernet Max Frame Size: 1516
ATM Address: 47.009181000000006170595C01.00000C5CA980.01

VCD   rxFrames  txFrames  Type        ATM Address
0     0         0         configure   47.009181000000006170598A01.00602FBCC513.00
97    1         2         direct      47.009181000000006170598A01.00602FBCC511.03
98    1         0         distribute  47.009181000000006170598A01.00602FBCC511.03
99    0         95        send        47.009181000000006170598A01.00602FBCC512.03
100   190       0         forward     47.009181000000006170598A01.00602FBCC512.03
```

LEC-to-LEC Connection

After LEC is operational, it can connect to other LECs in the same ELAN; the following analysis shows exactly that.

The following **debug** output reveals that the LEC is sending out a LANE_ARP_REQ for the target LEC it wants to talk on the Control Direct VCC. It receives a response from the LANE_ARP_RSP on the Control Distribute with a corresponding ATM address. It then registers the ATM address in its cache table and sets up the VCC directly to the other LEC; this VCC is called Data Direct VCC:

```
NewYork#debug lane client all
LEC ATM0.1: state ACTIVE event LEC_CTL_READY_IND =>
   ACTIVE
LEC ATM0.1: sending LANE_ARP_REQ on VCD 97
LEC ATM0.1: LECID 2
LEC ATM0.1: SRC MAC address 0000.0c5c.a980
LEC ATM0.1: SRC ATM address 47.009181000000006170595C01.
   00000c5ca980.01
LEC ATM0.1: TARGET MAC address 00e0.1eae.fa38
LEC ATM0.1: TARGET ATM address
   00.000000000000000000000000.000000000000.00
LEC ATM0.1: num of TLVs 0
LEC ATM0.1: received LANE_ARP_REQ on VCD 98
LEC ATM0.1: LECID 2
LEC ATM0.1: SRC MAC address 0000.0c5c.a980
LEC ATM0.1: SRC ATM address 47.009181000000006170595C01.
   00000c5ca980.01
LEC ATM0.1: TARGET MAC address 00e0.1eae.fa38
LEC ATM0.1: TARGET ATM address
   00.000000000000000000000000.000000000000.00
LEC ATM0.1: num of TLVs 0
LEC ATM0.1: action A_SEND_ARP_RSP
LEC ATM0.1: state ACTIVE event LEC_CTL_ARP_REQ => ACTIVE
LEC ATM0.1: received LANE_ARP_RSP on VCD 98
LEC ATM0.1: LECID 2
LEC ATM0.1: SRC MAC address 0000.0c5c.a980
LEC ATM0.1: SRC ATM address 47.009181000000006170595C01.
   00000c5ca980.01
LEC ATM0.1: TARGET MAC address 00e0.1eae.fa38
LEC ATM0.1: TARGET ATM address
   47.009181000000006170598A01.00E01EAEFA38.03
```

```
LEC ATM0.1: num of TLVs 1
LEC ATM0.1: TLV id 0x00A03E2A, len 28, 01 01 47 00 91 81 00 00
   00 00
61 70 59 8A 01 00 E0 1E AE FA
3C 00 00 E0 1E AE FA 38
LEC ATM0.1: action A_PROCESS_ARP_RSP
LEC ATM0.1: lec_process_lane_tlv: msg LANE_ARP_RSP,
   num_tlvs 1
LEC ATM0.1: process_dev_type_tlv:
lec 47.0091810000000006170598A01.00E01EAEFA38.03, tlv
   0x60C90C70
```

Figure 18-9 illustrates LEC-to-LEC Data Direct VC.

Figure 18-9 *LEC-to-LEC Data Direct VC*

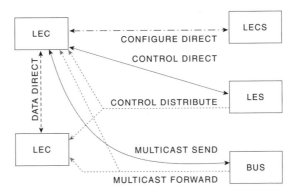

The command **show lane client** shows the Data Direct VCC being established to the remote LEC. Because this LEC creates individual connections to remote LECs, additional Data Direct VCCs appear on this output. This VCC gets removed if there is no activity between the two LECs for a certain amount of time:

```
NewYork#show lane client
LE Client ATM0.1 ELAN name: blue Admin: up State: operational
Client ID: 1 LEC up for 1 hour 35 minutes 35 seconds
Join Attempt: 1
HW Address: 0000.0c5c.a980 Type: ethernet Max Frame Size: 1516
ATM Address: 47.0091810000000006170595C01.00000C5CA980.01
VCD     rxFrames  txFrames  Type        ATM Address
0       0         0         configure   47.0091810000000006170598A01.00602FBCC513.00
97      1         2         direct      47.0091810000000006170598A01.00602FBCC511.03
98      1         0         distribute  47.0091810000000006170598A01.00602FBCC511.03
99      0         95        send        47.0091810000000006170598A01.00602FBCC512.03
100     190       0         forward     47.0091810000000006170598A01.00602FBCC512.03
101     6         4         data        47.0091810000000006170598A01.00E01EAEFA38.03
```

Multiprotocols over ATM (MPOA)

Multiprotocols over ATM works in conjunction with LANE. Intersubnet transfer of data in LANE requires a router, even though two devices in different subnets are connected by a common ATM infrastructure. This creates performance degradation for an ATM-based network. At the same time, it is absolutely necessary to separate ATM infrastructure into small IP layer subnets to keep the large broadcast transmission to its minimum and to where it is required. MPOA provides the facility to create small subnets for the devices, and at the same time provides cut-through connection to the intersubnet devices at the ATM layer if required.

MPOA has two main logical components—Multiprotocol Client (MPC) and Multiprotocol Server (MPS). MPC usually resides in an edge device such as Catalyst switches or ATM-enabled hosts. The main function of MPC is to act as a point of entry and exit for traffic using shortcuts. It caches the shortcut information it gets from its interaction with MPS. MPS usually resides in the router running multiple LECs. Its main function is to provide Layer 3 forwarding information to the MPCs.

Design Considerations

MPOA is well-suited in a large enterprise campus environment with a common ATM backbone connecting different campuses. This common ATM infrastructure can be divided into many logical Layer 3 subnets to reduce the broadcast transmission to its minimum, yet allow intersubnet direct connection as needed, enhancing the overall performance. You can view MPOA as enlarging the scale of the LANE in the campus environment, without creating a bottleneck at the router.

Topology

The following topology has two ELANs—one between the Chicago and San Jose router, and another between the New York and San Jose router. Therefore, if the device behind the Chicago router needs to talk to the device behind the New York router, it goes through the San Jose router because it is running multiple LECs and it needs to do Layer 3 routing. Although it is obvious that the Chicago and New York routers are connected to the same ATM switch, it still must pass through the San Jose router for any intersubnet transmission. This is an inefficient use of the ATM infrastructure and also degrades performance.

NOTE   MPOA is commonly used in a campus environment. The routers represented here are named for cities, but should be referred to as "Building A," "Building B," and "Building C."

Using MPOA in this scenario allows a direct connection from the Chicago router to the New York router, even though they are in different subnets. This can be achieved by enabling MPCs on the Chicago and New York routers, and MPS on the San Jose router.

Figure 18-10 shows the topology for this example.

Figure 18-10 *MPOA Example Topology*

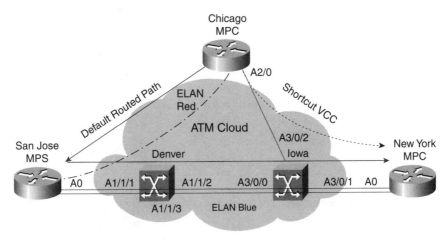

Configuration of MPOA

MPOA configuration works in conjunction with LANE. The following configuration example reveals MPCs and MPS configuration on various ATM-enabled devices.

In the following configuration example, the Chicago router acts as the MPOA client, which is the MPC. The command **mpoa client config name CHI** defines an MPC with a specified name. But the MPC is not functional until it is attached to a specific interface. The command **mpoa client name CHI** starts an MPC process on a specific interface. This command makes MPC fully operational. MPC has acquired an ATM address using a specific algorithm and is ready to accept calls. The command **lane client mpoa client name CHI** associates a LANE client red with the specified MPC CHI. The configuration of the Chicago router is as follows:

```
mpoa client config name CHI
interface Loopback1
ip address 40.1.1.1 255.255.255.0
interface ATM2/0
no ip address
atm pvc 10 0 5 qsaal
atm pvc 20 0 16 ilmi
mpoa client name CHI
!
interface ATM2/0.1 multipoint
ip address 192.10.10.2 255.255.255.0
lane client mpoa client name CHI
lane client ethernet red
```

In the following configuration example, the New York router is acting as an MPOA client for the devices behind it. The configuration of the New York router is as follows:

```
mpoa client config name NY
!
interface Loopback0
ip address 50.1.1.1 255.255.255.0
interface ATM0
no ip address
no ip mroute-cache
atm pvc 10 0 5 qsaal
atm pvc 20 0 16 ilmi
mpoa client name NY
!
interface ATM0.1 multipoint
ip address 198.10.10.2 255.255.255.0
lane client mpoa client name NY
lane client ethernet blue
```

In the following configuration example, the San Jose router is acting as the MPOA server for ELAN red and blue.

The command **mpoa server config name SJ** defines an MPS with the specified name, but the MPS is not functioning until it is attached to specific hardware.

The command **mpoa server name SJ** binds an MPS to a specific major interface. At this point, the MPS can obtain its auto-generated ATM address and an interface through which it can communicate to the neighboring MPOA devices. Only when both an MPS is defined globally and attached to an interface is it considered to be operational.

The command **lane client mpoa server name SJ** associates an LEC with the named MPS. The specified MPS must exist before this command is accepted.

The configuration of the San Jose router is as follows:

```
lane database ABC
name red server-ATM-address
   47.00918100000000061705989A01.00E01EAEFA39.01
name red elan-id 10
name blue server-ATM-address
   47.00918100000000061705989A01.00E01EAEFA39.03
name blue elan-id 30
!
mpoa server config name SJ
!
interface Loopback0
ip address 60.1.1.1 255.255.255.0
interface ATM0
atm pvc 10 0 5 qsaal
atm pvc 20 0 16 ilmi
lane config database ABC
lane auto-config-ATM-address
mpoa server name SJ
!
interface ATM0.1 multipoint
ip address 192.10.10.1 255.255.255.0
lane server-bus ethernet red
lane client mpoa server name SJ
lane client ethernet red
!
interface ATM0.3 multipoint
ip address 198.10.10.1 255.255.255.0
lane server-bus ethernet blue
```

```
lane client mpoa server name SJ
lane client ethernet blue
```

Troubleshooting

MPOA troubleshooting becomes easier when you understand the interaction of its logical components, such as MPCs and MPSs. Figure 18-11 shows the operation of MPOA.

Figure 18-11   *Operation of MPOA*

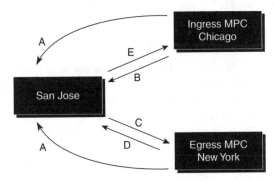

MPOA operation is as follows:

- **MPCs must know their MPSs**—Discovering the MPS
- **MPOA resolution request**—A request from an MPC to resolve a destination protocol address to an ATM address to establish a shortcut SVC with the egress device
- **MPOA cache imposition request**—A request from MPS to an egress MPC, providing the MAC rewrite information for a destination protocol address
- **MPOA cache imposition reply**—Reply from egress MPC, matching a previous egress MPS request
- **MPOA resolution reply**—Reply from MPS, resolving a protocol address to an ATM address

The following troubleshooting analysis uses different **show** and **debug** commands to illustrate the MPC and MPS interaction used to create a shortcut VCC.

The command **show mpoa client** on the Chicago router shows that it does not know any other MPS or MPC.

Discovering the MPS

The following output first shows, there is no MPS being discovered. Then, after initiating the LE_ARP, as shown by the **debug** output, it will get the MPS address. The last of the output reveals the discovered MPS:

```
Chicago#show mpoa client
MPC Name: CHI    Interface: ATM2/0    State: Up
MPC ATM Address:
    47.009181000000006170595C01.006070CA9045.00
Shortcut-Setup Count: 1    Shortcut-Setup Time: 1
LECs bound to CHI: ATM2/0.1
MPS Neighbors of CHI:
ATM Address    MPS-ID    VCD    rxPkts    txPkts
Remote Devices known to CHI:
ATM Address    VCD    rxPkts    txPkts
```

The command **debug lane client mpoa** shows output indicating that the local MPC is getting the MPS ATM address. Every time an LEC_ARP_REQ or an LEC_ARP_RESP is sent from an LEC, a TLV (type, length, value) is included, specifying the ATM address of the MPC associated with the LEC:

```
Chicago#debug lane client mpoa
LEC ATM2/0.1: received lec_process_lane_tlv: msg
    LANE_ARP_REQ, num_tlvs 1
LEC ATM2/0.1: process_dev_type_tlv: lec
    47.009181000000006170598A01.00E01EAEFA38.01,
tlv 0x61039220
LEC ATM2/0.1: type MPOA_MPS, mpc
    00.00000000000000000000000.000000000000.00
mps 47.009181000000006170598A01.00E01EAEFA3C.00 mac
    00e0.1eae.fa38
LEC ATM2/0.1: process_dev_type_tlv: create le_arp for le_mac
    00e0.1eae.fa38
LEC ATM2/0.1: create mpoa_lec
LEC ATM2/0.1: new mpoa_lec 0x611401D4
LEC ATM2/0.1: process_dev_type_tlv: type MPS, tlv-
    >num_mps_mac 1
LEC ATM2/0.1: lec_add_mps: remote lec
    47.009181000000006170598A01.00E01EAEFA38.01
mps 47.009181000000006170598A01.00E01EAEFA3C.00
    num_mps_mac 1,
mac 00e0.1eae.fa38
LEC ATM2/0.1: lec_add_mps: add mac 00e0.1eae.fa38, mps_mac
    0x611407C0
LEC ATM2/0.1: lec_append_mpoa_dev_tlv:
```

NOTE   LE_ARP stands for LAN Emulation Address Resolution Protocol. It is a protocol that provides the ATM address that corresponds to a MAC address.

The command **show mpoa client** now has neighboring MPS and MPC ATM addresses with its associated VCs:

```
Chicago#show mpoa client
MPC Name: CHI    Interface: ATM2/0    State: Up
```

```
MPC ATM Address: 47.009181000000006170595C01.006070CA9045.00
Shortcut-Setup Count: 1      Shortcut-Setup Time: 1
LECs bound to CHI: ATM2/0.1
MPS Neighbors of CHI:
ATM Address                                       MPS-ID  VCD    rxPkts    txPkts
47.009181000000006170598A01.00E01EAEFA3C.00         1     20     1256      836
Remote Devices known to CHI:
ATM Address                                       VCD
47.009181000000006170595C01.00E01EAEFA6D.00        257------MPC on New York Router
```

MPOA Resolution Request and Reply

In the following troubleshooting example, tracing the route 50.1.1.1 from Chicago requires the data packets to flow through the San Jose router because it is running both ELAN red and blue. But, with MPOA enabled, and a common ATM infrastructure to allow the cut-through VCC, CHI MPC will send an MPOA resolution request to resolve the IP address 50.1.1.1 to an ATM address, through which it can reach that network.

MPS San Jose responds to the request with IP-to-ATM address resolution. Upon learning the ATM address through which 50.1.1.1 can be reached, the Chicago router makes a direct VCC through the ATM cloud. This can be confirmed by another trace to 50.1.1.1, which shows that it can be reached via one hop 198.10.10.2 rather than two:

```
Chicago#trace 50.1.1.1
Tracing the route to 50.1.1.1
1 192.10.10.1 0 msec
198.10.10.2 0 msec 0 msec

Chicago#debug mpoa client all
MPOA CLIENT: mpc_trigger_from_lane: mac 00e0.1eae.fa38 on out
    ATM2/0.1
MPOA CLIENT: Is MAC 00e0.1eae.fa38 interesting on i/f: ATM2/0.1
MPOA CLIENT: MAC 00e0.1eae.fa38 interesting
MPOA CLIENT CHI: Ingress Cache entry created for 50.1.1.1
MPOA CLIENT CHI: manage_hw_ingress_cache: msgtype
    QUERY_DATA_FLOW_ACTIVE for ip 50.1.1.1
MPOA CLIENT CHI: ipcache not exist
MPOA CLIENT CHI: mpc_manage_ingress_cache(): called with
MPC_IN_CACHE_UPDATE_ADD for destIp=50.1.1.1
MPOA CLIENT CHI: Ingress Cache- curr state=
    MPC_IN_CACHE_INITIALIZED, event=
MPC_ELIGIBLE_PACKET_RECEIVED, dest IP= 50.1.1.1
MPOA CLIENT CHI: Flow detected for IP=50.1.1.1
MPOA CLIENT CHI: MPOA Resolution process started for 50.1.1.1
MPOA CLIENT CHI: Sending MPOA Resolution req for 50.1.1.1
MPOA CLIENT CHI: Ingress Cache state changed- old=0, new=1, IP
    addr=50.1.1.1
MPOA CLIENT: mpc_count_and_trigger: cache state TRIGGER
MPOA DEBUG: nhrp_parse_packet finished, found 1 CIE's and 2
    TLV's
MPOA CLIENT: received a MPOA_RESOLUTION_REPLY (135)
    packet of size 127 bytes on ATM2/0 vcd 1
MPOA CLIENT CHI: Resol Reply-IP addr 50.1.1.1, mpxp
    addr=47.009181000000006170595C01.00E01EAEFA6D.00,TA
    G=2217672716
MPOA CLIENT CHI: Ingress Cache- curr state=
    MPC_IN_CACHE_TRIGGER, event=
MPC_VALID_RESOL_REPLY_RECVD, dest IP= 50.1.1.1
```

```
MPOA CLIENT CHI: No Active VC-connect to remote MPC
   47.009181000000006170595C01.00E01EAEFA6D.00
MPOA CLIENT CHI: connect to remote MPC
   47.009181000000006170595C01.00E01EAEFA6D.00 called
MPOA CLIENT CHI: SETUP sent to remote MPC
   47.009181000000006170595C01.00E01EAEFA6D.00
MPOA CLIENT CHI: Ingress Cache state changed- old=1, new=4, IP
   addr=50.1.1.1
MPOA DEBUG: nhrp_parse_packet finished, found 1 CIE's and 2
   TLV's

Chicago#trace 50.1.1.1
Tracing the route to 50.1.1.1
1 198.10.10.2 0 msec
```

MPOA Cache Imposition Request and Reply

Upon receiving the MPOA resolution request, MPS San Jose sends out an MPOA cache imposition request, as revealed in the following **debug** output, to the egress MPC. It gets the response back from the egress MPC with DLL (data link layer) information in the form of MPOA cache imposition reply, and MPS will convert this reply into MPOA resolution reply back to originating ingress MPC.

The **show** output reveals that the originating ingress MPC now has cache for destination IP address and it can establish the cut-through Layer 2 switching to the destination egress MPC, avoiding Layer 3 switching in the router:

```
SanJose#debug mpoa server
MPOA SERVER: received a MPOA_RESOLUTION_REQUEST
   (134) packet of size 64 bytes on ATM0 vcd 342
MPOA SERVER SJ: packet came from remote MPC
   47.009181000000006170595C01.006070CA9045.00
MPOA SERVER SJ: process_mpoa_res_req called
MPOA SERVER SJ: mps_next_hop_info activated
MPOA SERVER SJ: next hop interface and next hop ip address are
   NOT known, trying to find them
MPOA SERVER SJ: mps_next_hop_info: next hop interface:
   ATM0.3, next hop ip address: 198.10.10.2
MPOA SERVER SJ: ingress cache entry created for:
   47.009181000000006170595C01.006070CA9045.00, 50.1.1.1
MPOA SERVER SJ: ingress cache entry is not yet valid, started the
   giveup timer (40 secs) on it
MPOA SERVER: next_hop_mpoa_device: returning type MPC for
   198.10.10.2
MPOA SERVER SJ: I am the egress router: starting mpoa cache
   impo req procedures
MPOA SERVER SJ: egress cache entry created for:
   47.009181000000006170595C01.006070CA9045.00, 50.1.1.1
   198.10.10.1 (src)
MPOA SERVER SJ: a NEW cache id (28) is assigned
MPOA SERVER SJ: egress cache entry is not yet valid, started the
   giveup timer (40 secs) on it
MPOA SERVER SJ: MPOA_CACHE_IMPOSITION_REQUEST
   packet sent to remote MPC
   47.009181000000006170595C01.00E01EAEFA6D.00
MPOA SERVER: received a MPOA_CACHE_IMPOSITION_REPLY
   (129) packet of size 127 bytes on ATM0 vcd 327
MPOA SERVER SJ: packet came from remote MPC
   47.009181000000006170595C01.00E01EAEFA6D.00
```

```
MPOA SERVER SJ: process_mpoa_cache_imp_reply called
MPOA SERVER: searching cache entry by new req id 58
MPOA SERVER SJ: egress MPS received a 'proper' mpoa cache
   impo REPLY: validating and starting the holding timer on the
   egress cache entry
MPOA SERVER SJ: snooping on the mpoa cache imposition reply
   packet CIE: cli_addr_tl = 20, cli_nbma_addr =
   47.009181000000006170595C01.00E01EAEFA6D.00
MPOA SERVER SJ: tag value 2217672716 extracted
MPOA SERVER SJ: mps_next_hop_info activated
MPOA SERVER SJ: next hop interface and next hop ip address are
   NOT known, trying to find them
MPOA SERVER SJ: mps_next_hop_info: next hop interface:
   ATM0.3, next hop ip address: 198.10.10.1
MPOA SERVER SJ: converting the packet to a nhrp res reply
MPOA SERVER SJ: process_nhrp_res_reply called
MPOA SERVER SJ: searching cache entry by new req id 57
MPOA SERVER SJ: success: ingress MPS picked up holding time of
   1200 seconds from the 1st CIE
MPOA SERVER SJ: validated and started the holding timer on the
   ingress cache entry
MPOA SERVER SJ: converting the packet to an mpoa res reply
MPOA SERVER SJ: MPOA_RESOLUTION_REPLY packet sent to
   remote MPC
   47.009181000000006170595C01.006070CA9045.00

Chicago#show mpoa client cache
MPC Name: CHI Interface: ATM2/0 State: Up
MPC ATM Address:
   47.009181000000006170595C01.006070CA9045.00
Shortcut-Setup Count: 1 Shortcut-Setup Time: 1
Number of Ingress cache entries: 1
MPC Ingress Cache Information:
Dst IP addr State MPSid VCD Time-left Egress MPC ATM addr
RESOLVE 1 57 19:27
   47.009181000000006170595C01.00E01EAEFA6D.00
Number of Egress cache entries: 1
MPC Egress Cache Information:
Dst IP addr Dst MAC Src MAC MPSid Elan Time-left CacheId
192.10.10.2 0060.70ca.9040 00e0.1eae.fa38 1 10 19:26 29
```

Summary

This chapter covered various methods of deploying Multiprotocols over ATM. You can apply appropriate methods, based on your network requirements and environment, and then use these configuration examples to familiarize yourself with the method(s). Of course, you can also try out some troubleshooting in the lab before deploying a method. After your method is deployed on the production network, keep the following in mind:

- Turning on debugging is not as easy as it seems. It can cause CPU performance problems and should be approached with caution.

- Try to use **show** commands as much as possible before turning on the debugging.

- For RFC 1483 debugging, ILMI does not impose much stress on the CPU, but debugging signaling events can.

- For RFC 1577, debugging on the ARP client side is an excellent way to identify problems. Avoid debugging on the ARP server side.

- LANE debugging is very sensitive on both the LEC and LES/BUS side. Try to use **show** commands to see where the client is stuck to join the ELAN. If you are running multiple LECs on the router/switch, **debug** only the client with the problem.

- Avoid turning on debugging on LES/BUS because they are heavily utilized and can output lots of data, causing troubles for the CPU.

- For MPOA, debugging on the MPC with keepalive debugging off gives the most useful information.

CHAPTER 19

Dial-on-Demand Routing

Edited by Salman Asad

Cisco's dial-on-demand routing (DDR) feature enables you to use existing telephone lines to form a wide area network (WAN). While using existing telephone lines, you can analyze traffic patterns to determine whether the installation of leased lines is appropriate. DDR provides significant cost savings over leased lines for links that are utilized for only a few hours each day or that experience low traffic flow.

DDR over serial lines requires the use of dialing devices that support V.25bis. V.25bis is an International Telecommunication Union Telecommunication (ITU-T) Standardization Sector standard for in-band signaling to bit-synchronous data communications equipment (DCE) devices. A variety of devices support V.25bis, including analog V.32 modems, ISDN terminal adapters, and inverse multiplexers. Cisco's implementation of V.25bis supports devices that use the 1984 version of V.25bis (which requires the use of odd parity), as well as devices that use the 1988 version of V.25bis (which does not use parity).

NOTE   The ITU-T carries out the functions of the former Consultative Committee for International Telegraph and Telephone (CCITT).

This case study describes the use of DDR to connect a worldwide network that consists of a central site located in San Francisco and remote sites located in Tokyo, Singapore, and Hong Kong. The following scenarios and configuration file examples are described:

- Having the Central Site Dial Out:

  Describes the central and remote site configurations for three setups: a central site with one interface per remote site, a single interface for multiple remote sites, and multiple interfaces for multiple remote sites. Includes examples of the usage of rotary groups and access lists.

- Having the Central and Remote Sites Dial In and Dial Out:

  Describes the central and remote site configurations for three setups: central site with one interface per remote site, a single interface for multiple remote sites, and multiple interfaces for multiple remote sites. Also describes the usage of Point-to-Point Protocol (PPP) encapsulation and the Challenge Handshake Authentication Protocol (CHAP).

- Having Remote Sites Dial Out:

  A common configuration is one in which the remote sites place calls to the central site, but the central site does not dial out. In a star topology, it is possible for all the remote routers to have their serial interfaces on the same subnet as the central site serial interface.

- Using DDR as a Backup to Leased Lines:

  Describes the use of DDR as a backup method to leased lines, and provides examples of how to use floating static routes on single and shared interfaces.

- Using Leased Lines and Dial Backup:

  Describes the use of data terminal ready (DTR) dialing and V.25bis dialing with leased lines.

Figure 19-1 shows the topology of the DDR network that is the subject of this case study.

NOTE   All examples and descriptions in this case study refer to features available in Software Release 9.1(9) or later. Some features are available in earlier releases. Features available only in Software Release 9.21 are indicated as such.

Figure 19-1 *DDR Internetwork Topology*

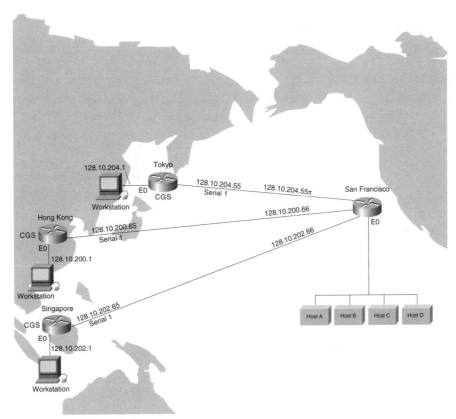

Having the Central Site Dial Out

In this example, the central site calls the remote sites. The cost of initiating a call from the United States to international sites is often lower than if the remote sites initiate the call, and it is expected that remote offices will need to connect to the central site network only periodically. This section provides the following configuration examples in which the central site is configured to dial out:

- Configuring one interface per remote site
- Configuring a single interface for multiple remote sites
- Configuring multiple interfaces for multiple remote sites

Configuring One Interface per Remote Site

For the initial configuration, the San Francisco central site is configured to have one interface per remote site.

Central Site: Dial Out Only

In the following configuration, the central site places the calls with a separate interface configured for each remote site. There is no support for answering calls in this configuration.

```
interface serial 5
description DDR connection to Hong Kong
ip address 128.10.200.66 255.255.255.192
dialer in-band
dialer wait-for-carrier-time 60
dialer string 0118527351625
pulse-time 1
dialer-group 1
!
interface serial 6
description DDR connection to Singapore
ip address 128.10.202.66 255.255.255.192
dialer in-band
dialer wait-for-carrier-time 60
dialer string 011653367085
pulse-time 1
dialer-group 1
!
interface serial 7
description DDR connection to Tokyo
ip address 128.10.204.66 255.255.255.192
dialer in-band
dialer wait-for-carrier-time 60
dialer string 0118127351625
pulse-time 1
dialer-group 1
!
router igrp 1
network 128.10.0.0
redistribute static
! route to Hong Kong
ip route 128.10.200.0 255.255.255.192 128.10.200.65
! route to Singapore
ip route 128.10.202.0 255.255.255.192 128.10.202.65
! route to Tokyo
ip route 128.10.204.0 255.255.255.192 128.10.204.65
access-list 101 deny igrp 0.0.0.0 255.255.255.255 255.255.255.255 0.0.0.0
access-list 101 permit ip 0.0.0.0 255.255.255.255 0.0.0.0 255.255.255.255
dialer-list 1 list 101
```

Interface Configuration

The configuration of the individual interfaces and Internet Protocol (IP) addresses is straightforward. The IP address for each interface is provided. The example uses a 6-bit host portion in IP addresses. The dialer in-band command enables DDR and V.25bis dialing on the interface. V.25bis is a ITU-T standard for in-band signaling to bit-synchronous DCE devices. A variety of devices support V.25bis, ranging from analog V.32 modems to ISDN terminal adapters to inverse multiplexers.

The **dialer wait-for-carrier-time** command is set to 60 seconds. When using V.25bis, the router does not parse any responses it receives from the DCE. Instead, the router depends on the modem's Carrier Detect (CD) signal to indicate that a call has been connected. If the modem's CD signal is not activated before the time allotted with the **dialer wait-for-carrier-time** command, the router assumes that the call has failed and disconnects the line. Because the calls are international, and therefore take longer to connect than local calls, the wait for carrier time is set to 60 seconds. Even for local calls, analog modems can take 20 to 30 seconds to synchronize to each other, including the time to dial and answer.

The **dialer string** command identifies the telephone number of the targeted destination. Because the central site is calling only a single destination, this dialer string is the simplest possible configuration. The **pulse-time** command specifies how long data terminal ready (DTR) is held inactive. When using DDR and V.25bis modems, the router disconnects calls by deactivating DTR. This command is automatically inserted into the configuration when the **dialer in-band** command is entered.

The **dialer-group** command is used to identify each interface with a dialer list set. The **dialer-list** command associates each interface with access lists that determine which packets are "interesting" versus "uninteresting" for an interface. For details on access lists and dialer lists, see the "Access List Configuration" section that follows.

Routing Configuration

The Interior Gateway Routing Protocol (IGRP) is used to route traffic on the network. The first two commands in the routing section of the configuration file are **router igrp** and **network**. These define the IGRP number and the network over which IGRP runs.

The **redistribute** command causes the static route information (defined with the **ip route** commands shown in the configuration example) to be sent to other routers in the same IGRP area. Without this command, other routers connected to the central site will not have routes to the remote routers. The three static routes define the subnets on the Ethernet backbone of the remote routers. DDR tends to use static routes extensively because routing updates are not received when the dialup connection is not active.

Access List Configuration

The last section of the configuration file provides the access lists that DDR uses to classify "interesting" and "uninteresting" packets. Interesting packets are packets that pass the restrictions of the access lists. These packets either initiate a call (if one is not already in progress) or reset the idle timer if a call is in progress. Uninteresting packets are transmitted if the link is active, but dropped if the link is not active. Uninteresting packets do not initiate calls or reset the idle timer. Access list 101 provides the following filters:

- IGRP packets that are sent to the broadcast address (255.255.255.255) do not cause dialing.

- All other IP packets are interesting, so they may cause dialing and reset the idle timer.

Remote Sites: Dial In Only

Except for the IP address and the default route, each of the remote sites is configured identically as an answer-only site. The following example lists Hong Kong's configuration:

```
interface serial 1
description interface to answer calls from San Francisco
ip address 128.10.200.65 255.255.255.192
dialer in-band
!
ip route 0.0.0.0 0.0.0.0 128.10.200.66
```

The answering site will not disconnect the call. It is up to the calling site to disconnect the call when the line is idle. In this case, the answering site is using static routing. The default route points to the serial interface at the central site.

Configuring a Single Interface for Multiple Remote Sites

It is possible to use a single interface to call multiple destinations, such as a site in Hong Kong and a site in Paris, France. Because of the time differences, these sites would never need to be connected at the same time. Therefore, a single interface could be used for both sites without the possibility of contention for the interface and without the cost of dedicating a serial port and modem to each destination.

Central Site: Dial Out Only

In the following configuration, the central site places the calls. A single interface is configured to call multiple remote sites. There is no support for answering calls in this configuration.

```
interface serial 5
description DDR connection to Hong Kong and Singapore
ip address 128.10.200.66 255.255.255.192
ip address 128.10.202.66 255.255.255.192 secondary
dialer in-band
dialer wait-for-carrier-time 60
! map Hong Kong to a phone number
dialer map ip 128.10.200.65 0118527351625
! map Singapore to a phone number
dialer map ip 128.10.202.65 011653367085
pulse-time 1
dialer-group 1
```

```
!
router igrp 1
network 128.10.0.0
passive-interface serial 5
redistribute static
! route to Hong Kong
ip route 128.10.200.0 255.255.255.192 128.10.200.65
! route to Singapore
ip route 128.10.202.0 255.255.255.192 128.10.202.65
!The following access list denies the IGRP broadcast
access-list 101 deny igrp 0.0.0.0 255.255.255.255 255.255.255.255 0.0.0.0
!The following access list permits all the IP packets
access-list 101 permit ip 0.0.0.0 255.255.255.255 0.0.0.0 255.255.255.255
dialer-list 1 list 101
```

Interface Configuration

The configuration of the interface in this example is slightly more complicated than the configuration described in the "Configuring One Interface per Remote Site" section. In addition to the original IP address, there is a secondary IP address configured for serial interface 5 because the Singapore and Hong Kong offices are on different subnets.

The **dialer in-band**, **dialer wait-for-carrier-time**, **pulse-time**, and **dialer-group** commands are used in the same manner as described previously in the "Configuring One Interface per Remote Site" section. However, the previous **dialer string** command has been removed and replaced with two **dialer map** commands.

The first **dialer map** command maps the telephone number for Hong Kong to its next hop address, which is the IP address of the serial port of the router in Hong Kong. The second **dialer map** command maps the telephone number for the Singapore router to the next hop address for Singapore.

Routing Configuration

The IP static routes define the next hops used in the **dialer map** commands. When a packet is received for a host on network 128.10.200.0, it is routed to a next hop address of 128.10.200.65. This route goes out serial interface 5. DDR uses the next hop address to obtain the telephone number of the destination router.

NOTE   The use of the **passive-interface** command states that routing updates are not to be sent out serial interface 5. Because the remote sites are using a default route, there is no need to send routing updates over the wire.

Access List Configuration

The use of **dialer map** commands provides an additional level of filtering. When a packet is received for a host on network 128.10.200.0, it is routed to a next hop address of 128.10.200.65. This route goes out serial interface 5. The packet is compared to the access lists. If the packet is deemed "interesting," the packet's next hop address is compared to the **dialer map** commands defined for that interface. If a match is found, the interface is checked to determine whether it is connected to the telephone number for that next hop address. If the interface is not connected, a call is placed to the telephone number. If the interface is currently connected to that number, the idle timer is reset. If the interface is connected to another number (from another **dialer map** command), the fast-idle timer is started due to contention for the interface. If there is no match of the next hop address to any of the dialer maps and there is no dialer string defined (which matches all next hop addresses), the packet is dropped.

This additional layer of filtering for the next hop address causes problems for broadcast packets such as routing updates. Because a broadcast packet is transmitted with a next hop address of the broadcast address, the check against the **dialer map** commands will fail. If you want broadcast packets transmitted to telephone numbers defined by **dialer map** commands, additional **dialer map** commands must specify the broadcast address as the next hop address with the same telephone number. For example, you might add the following **dialer map** commands:

```
dialer map ip 255.255.255.255 0118527351625
dialer map ip 255.255.255.255 011653367085
```

If the interface is currently connected to one of these telephone numbers, and if it receives an IGRP broadcast packet, that packet will now be transmitted because it matches a **dialer map** command to an already connected telephone number. (If the connection is already established, both "interesting" and "uninteresting" packets are sent.) If a connection is not already established, adding the **dialer map** commands will not cause an IGRP packet sent to the broadcast address to cause dialing because the access lists determine that the IGRP packet is uninteresting.

NOTE   In the configuration example described in the "Configuring a Single Interface for Multiple Remote Sites" section, the **dialer string** command permits broadcast packets to be sent when the link is connected because the dialer string matches all next hop addresses that did not have a dialer map.

Remote Sites: Dial In Only

Except for the IP address and the default route, each of the remote sites is configured identically as an answer-only site. The following example illustrates the Hong Kong configuration:

```
interface serial 1
description interface to answer calls from San Francisco
ip address 128.10.200.65 255.255.255.192
dialer in-band
!
ip route 0.0.0.0 0.0.0.0 128.10.200.66
```

The answering site will not disconnect the call. It is up to the calling site to disconnect the call when the line is idle. A default route is defined back to the central site.

Configuring Multiple Interfaces for Multiple Remote Sites

When using a single interface with dialer maps, contention for the interface can occur. This contention starts a fast-idle timer that causes lines to remain connected for a shorter idle time than usual, allowing other destinations to use the interface. Dialer rotary groups prevent contention by creating a set of interfaces that can be used to dial out. Rather than statically assigning an interface to a destination, dialer rotary groups allow dynamic allocation of interfaces to telephone numbers. Before a call is placed, the rotary group is searched for an interface that is not in use to place the call. It is not until all the interfaces in the rotary group are in use that the fast-idle timer is started.

NOTE   The following configurations appear as they would be entered at the command line. Because of the way dialer rotary groups function, the output from a **write terminal** command on the router may differ slightly from what is shown here.

Central Site: Dial Out Only

The following configuration defines dialer rotary groups on the central site router:

```
interface dialer 1
description rotary group for Hong Kong, Tokyo, and Singapore
ip address 128.10.200.66 255.255.255.192
ip address 128.10.202.66 255.255.255.192 secondary
ip address 128.10.204.66 255.255.255.192 secondary
dialer in-band
dialer wait-for-carrier-time 60
! map Hong Kong to a phone number
dialer map ip 128.10.200.65 0118527351625
! map Singapore to a phone number
dialer map ip 128.10.202.65 011653367085
! map Tokyo to a phone number
dialer map ip 128.10.204.65 0118127351625
pulse-time 1
dialer-group 1
!
interface serial 5
dialer rotary-group 1
!
interface serial 6
dialer rotary-group 1
!
```

```
router igrp 1
network 128.10.0.0
passive-interface dialer 1
redistribute static
!
! route to Hong Kong
ip route 128.10.200.0 255.255.255.192 128.10.200.65
! route to Singapore
ip route 128.10.202.0 255.255.255.192 128.10.202.65
! route to Tokyo
ip route 128.10.204.0 255.255.255.192 128.10.204.65
!
access-list 101 deny igrp 0.0.0.0 255.255.255.255 255.255.255.255 0.0.0.0
access-list 101 permit ip 0.0.0.0 255.255.255.255 0.0.0.0 255.255.255.255
dialer-list 1 list 101
```

Interface Configuration

Specifying a dialer interface is the first step in defining a dialer rotary group. Although a dialer interface is not a physical interface, all the configuration commands that can be specified for a physical interface can be used for a dialer interface. The commands listed under the **interface dialer** command are identical to those used for physical serial interface 5, for example, as described in the "Configuring a Single Interface for Multiple Remote Sites" section. Also, an additional **dialer map** command has been added to map the next hop address for Tokyo to the telephone number.

The **dialer rotary-group** command places physical serial interface 5 and serial interface 6 in the rotary group. Either of these interfaces can be used to dial any of the destinations defined by the **interface dialer** command.

As mentioned earlier, when you look at the configuration on the router using the **write terminal** command, the configuration may look slightly different from your input. For example, the **pulse-time** command associated with the dialer interface will appear with all the serial interfaces that were added with the **dialer rotary-group** command. Certain configuration information associated with the dialer interface is propagated to all the interfaces in the rotary group.

Routing Configuration

The routing section of this configuration has not changed from the example in the "Configuring a Single Interface for Multiple Remote Sites" section. But if you were to examine the routing table for one of the remote networks using the show **ip route** command (for example, **show ip route 128.10.200.0**), you would see that the output interface for packets sent to this subnet is interface dialer 1. The actual physical interface over which the packet will be transmitted is not determined until the DDR steps described in the following paragraph are performed.

Before a packet is sent out the dialer interface, DDR checks to determine whether the packet is "interesting" or "uninteresting." DDR then checks the dialer map. Next, all the physical interfaces in the rotary group are checked to determine whether they are connected to the telephone number. If an appropriate interface is found, the packet is sent out that physical interface. If an interface is not found and the packet is deemed interesting, the rotary group is scanned for an available physical interface. The first available interface found is used to place a call to the telephone number.

NOTE   To use dynamic routing, in which two of the remote sites communicate with each other via the central site, the **no ip split-horizon** command is required and the **passive-interface** command must be removed.

Access List Configuration

This configuration uses the same access lists as the example in the "Configuring a Single Interface for Multiple Remote Sites" section. A default route is defined back to the central site.

Remote Sites: Dial In Only

Except for the IP address and the default route, each of the remote sites is configured identically as an answer-only site. The following example illustrates the Hong Kong configuration:

```
interface serial 1
description interface to answer calls from San Francisco
ip address 128.10.200.65 255.255.255.192
dialer in-band
!
ip route 0.0.0.0 0.0.0.0 128.10.200.66
```

The answering site will not disconnect the call. It is up to the calling site to disconnect the call when the line is idle.

Having the Central and Remote Sites Dial In and Dial Out

It is often more convenient to have the remote sites call the central site as its users require, instead of depending on the central site to poll the remote sites. This section provides the following configuration examples, in which both the central site and the remote sites are placing calls:

- Configuring One Interface per Remote Site
- Configuring a Single Interface for Multiple Remote Sites
- Configuring Multiple Interfaces for Multiple Remote Sites

Configuring One Interface per Remote Site

To support dial-in and dial-out for both the central and remote sites using one interface per remote site, each remote site must call in on the specific central site interface that has the dialer string corresponding to the respective remote site telephone number.

Central Site: Dial In and Dial Out

In the following example, the central San Francisco site is configured to place and answer calls. One interface is configured per remote site.

```
interface serial 5
description DDR connection to Hong Kong
ip address 128.10.200.66 255.255.255.192
dialer in-band
dialer wait-for-carrier-time 60
dialer string 0118527351625
pulse-time 1
dialer-group 1
!
interface serial 6
description DDR connection to Singapore
ip address 128.10.202.66 255.255.255.192
dialer in-band
dialer wait-for-carrier-time 60
            dialer string 011653367085
pulse-time 1
dialer-group 1
!
interface serial 7
description DDR connection to Tokyo
ip address 128.10.204.66 255.255.255.192
dialer in-band
dialer wait-for-carrier-time 60
dialer string 0118127351625
pulse-time 1
dialer-group 1
!
router igrp 1
network 128.10.0.0
redistribute static
!
! route to Hong Kong
ip route 128.10.200.0 255.255.255.192 128.10.200.65
! route to Singapore
ip route 128.10.202.0 255.255.255.192 128.10.202.65
! route to Tokyo
ip route 128.10.204.0 255.255.255.192 128.10.204.65
!
access-list 101 deny igrp 0.0.0.0 255.255.255.255 255.255.255.255 0.0.0.0
access-list 101 permit ip 0.0.0.0 255.255.255.255 0.0.0.0 255.255.255.255
dialer-list 1 list 101
```

Remote Sites: Dial In and Dial Out

All the remote configurations are similar. Each defines a default route back to the central site and a dialer string that contains the telephone number of the central site.

Hong Kong

In the following example, the remote Hong Kong site is configured to place and answer calls. Hong Kong's configuration file contains a dialer string of 14155551212, which should call serial interface 5 in San Francisco.

```
interface serial 1
description DDR connection to San Francisco
ip address 128.10.200.65 255.255.255.192
dialer in-band
dialer wait-for-carrier-time 60
dialer string 14155551212
pulse-time 1
dialer-group 1
!
router igrp 1
network 128.10.0.0
!
ip route 128.10.0.0 255.255.0.0 128.10.200.66
!
access-list 101 deny igrp 0.0.0.0 255.255.255.255 255.255.255.255 0.0.0.0
access-list 101 permit ip 0.0.0.0 255.255.255.255 0.0.0.0 255.255.255.255
dialer-list 1 list 101
```

Singapore

In the following example, the remote Singapore site is configured to place and answer calls. The Singapore configuration file contains a dialer string of 14155551213, which should call serial interface 6 in San Francisco.

```
interface serial 1
description DDR connection to San Francisco
ip address 128.10.202.65 255.255.255.192
dialer in-band
dialer wait-for-carrier-time 60
dialer string 14155551213
pulse-time 1
dialer-group 1
!
router igrp 1
network 128.10.0.0
!
ip route 128.10.0.0 255.255.0.0 128.10.202.66
!
access-list 101 deny igrp 0.0.0.0 255.255.255.255 255.255.255.255 0.0.0.0
access-list 101 permit ip 0.0.0.0 255.255.255.255 0.0.0.0 255.255.255.255
dialer-list 1 list 101
```

Tokyo

In the following example, the remote Tokyo site is configured to place and answer calls. The Tokyo configuration file contains a dialer string of 14155551214, which should call serial interface 7 in San Francisco.

```
interface serial 1
description DDR connection to San Francisco
ip address 128.10.204.65 255.255.255.192
```

continues

```
dialer in-band
dialer wait-for-carrier-time 60
dialer string 14155551214
pulse-time 1
dialer-group 1
router igrp 1
network 128.10.0.0
!
ip route 128.10.0.0 255.255.0.0 128.10.204.66
!
access-list 101 deny igrp 0.0.0.0 255.255.255.255 255.255.255.255 0.0.0.0
access-list 101 permit ip 0.0.0.0 255.255.255.255 0.0.0.0 255.255.255.255
dialer-list 1 list 101
```

Because all incoming calls are assumed to be from the telephone number configured with the **dialer string** command, it is important to configure the central and remote sites correctly. If the Singapore dialer string uses the telephone number that Hong Kong uses to call the central site, for example, packets from the central site intended for Hong Kong would be sent to Singapore whenever Singapore called in because Singapore called in using the Hong Kong interface.

Configuring a Single Interface for Multiple Remote Sites

When multiple sites are calling into a central site, an authentication mechanism must be used unless that central site has one interface dedicated to each incoming call. Without the authentication mechanism, the central site router has no way of identifying the sites to which it is currently connected and cannot ensure that additional calls are not made. Point-to-Point Protocol (PPP) encapsulation with CHAP or Password Authentication Protocol (PAP) provides the mechanism to identify the calling party.

NOTE   A router with a built-in ISDN port may be able to use calling-party identification. Because calling-party identification is not available everywhere, PPP with CHAP provides the identification mechanism. In Software Release 9.21, PPP and Password Authentication Protocol (PAP) can be used in place of CHAP, although PAP is less secure than CHAP. The configuration of PAP would differ slightly from the configuration for CHAP illustrated in this section.

Central Site: Dial In and Dial Out

In the following example, the central San Francisco site is configured to place and answer calls. A single interface is configured for multiple remote sites.

```
hostname SanFrancisco
interface serial 5
description DDR connection to Hong Kong and Singapore
ip address 128.10.200.66 255.255.255.192
ip address 128.10.202.66 255.255.255.192 secondary
encapsulation ppp
```

```
ppp authentication chap
dialer in-band
dialer wait-for-carrier-time 60
dialer map ip 128.10.200.65 name HongKong 0118527351625
dialer map ip 128.10.202.65 name Singapore 011653367085
pulse-time 1
dialer-group 1
!
router igrp 1
network 128.10.0.0
passive-interface serial 5
redistribute static
!
! route to Hong Kong
ip route 128.10.200.0 255.255.255.192 128.10.200.65
! route to Singapore
ip route 128.10.202.0 255.255.255.192 128.10.202.65
access-list 101 deny igrp 0.0.0.0 255.255.255.255 255.255.255.255 0.0.0.0
access-list 101 permit ip 0.0.0.0 255.255.255.255 0.0.0.0 255.255.255.255
dialer-list 1 list 101
!
username HongKong password password1
username Singapore password password2
```

The command **encapsulation ppp** enables PPP encapsulation. The command **ppp authentication chap** enables CHAP authentication. In addition, **username** commands are entered for each of the remote sites that places calls. The **username** command defines the name of the remote router and a password to be associated with that router. When **ppp authentication chap** is configured, authentication must be verified; otherwise, network traffic will not be transmitted.

The **dialer map** command contains the host name of the remote router. This associates the remote router with a next hop address and a telephone number. When a packet is received for a host on network 128.10.200.0, it is routed to a next hop address of 128.10.200.65 via serial interface 5. The packet is compared to the access lists, and then the packet's next hop address is compared to the **dialer map** commands for serial interface 5.

If the packet is "interesting" and a connection to the number in the **dialer map** command is already active on the interface, the idle timer is reset. If a match is found, DDR checks the interface to determine whether it is connected to the telephone number for the next hop address. The comparison to the telephone number is useful only if the router placed the call or if the telephone number was received via calling-party ID on an ISDN router. With CHAP and the name keyword included in the **dialer map** command, both the telephone number and the name for a given next hop address are compared to the names of the routers already connected. In this way, calls to destinations to which connections are already established can be avoided.

Remote Sites: Dial In and Dial Out

In the following configuration examples, the remote sites are configured to place and receive calls to or from a single interface at the central site.

Hong Kong

The following configuration allows Hong Kong to place and receive calls to and from the central site in San Francisco:

```
hostname HongKong
interface serial 1
description DDR connection to SanFrancisco
ip address 128.10.200.65 255.255.255.192
encapsulation ppp
dialer in-band
dialer wait-for-carrier-time 60
dialer string 14155551212
pulse-time 1
dialer-group 1
!
router igrp 1
network 128.10.0.0
!
ip route 128.10.0.0 255.255.0.0 128.10.200.66
!
access-list 101 deny igrp 0.0.0.0 255.255.255.255 255.255.255.255 0.0.0.0
access-list 101 permit ip 0.0.0.0 255.255.255.255 0.0.0.0 255.255.255.255
dialer-list 1 list 101
!
username SanFrancisco password password1
```

Singapore

The following configuration allows Singapore to place and receive calls to and from the central site in San Francisco:

```
hostname Singapore
interface serial 1
description DDR connection to San Francisco
ip address 128.10.202.65 255.255.255.192
encapsulation ppp
dialer in-band
dialer wait-for-carrier-time 60
dialer string 14155551212
pulse-time 1
dialer-group 1
!
router igrp 1
network 128.10.0.0
ip route 128.10.0.0 255.255.0.0 128.10.202.66
!
access-list 101 deny igrp 0.0.0.0 255.255.255.255 255.255.255.255 0.0.0.0
access-list 101 permit ip 0.0.0.0 255.255.255.255 0.0.0.0 255.255.255.255
dialer-list 1 list 101
!
username SanFrancisco password password2
```

Unlike the central site, the remote sites do not contain the **ppp authentication chap** command. This is because only one site, the central site, is calling in to the remote sites. If only one site is calling in, DDR assumes that the call is from the number defined with the **dialer string** command; therefore, the command **ppp authentication chap** is not required.

NOTE   If the remote sites use **dialer map** commands rather than **dialer string**, the **ppp authentication chap** command is required, and the **dialer map** commands require the name keyword. This is because the assumption is made that if the **dialer map** command is used, multiple sites either can be called or can call in.

Also, the remote sites have a username entry for the San Francisco router, and the San Francisco router contains the username passwords for Singapore and Hong Kong.

Configuring Multiple Interfaces for Multiple Remote Sites

The configurations in this section are similar to the examples provided in the earlier "Configuring a Single Interface for Multiple Remote Sites" section. The encapsulation is set to PPP, and CHAP authentication is required.

Central Site: Dial In and Dial Out

The following example configures the central site router to dial in and dial out on multiple interfaces to multiple remote sites:

```
hostname SanFrancisco
interface dialer 1
description rotary group for Hong Kong, Tokyo, and Singapore
ip address 128.10.200.66 255.255.255.192
ip address 128.10.202.66 255.255.255.192 secondary
ip address 128.10.204.66 255.255.255.192 secondary
encapsulation ppp
ppp authentication chap
dialer in-band
dialer wait-for-carrier-time 60
dialer map ip 128.10.200.65 name HongKong 0118527351625
dialer map ip 128.10.202.65 name Singapore 011653367085
dialer map ip 128.10.204.65 name Tokyo 0118127351625
pulse-time 1
dialer-group 1
!
interface serial 5
dialer rotary-group 1
!
interface serial 6
dialer rotary-group 1
!
router igrp 1
network 128.10.0.0
passive-interface dialer 1
redistribute static
! route to Hong Kong
ip route 128.10.200.0 255.255.255.192 128.10.200.65
! route to Singapore
ip route 128.10.202.0 255.255.255.192 128.10.202.65
! route to Tokyo
ip route 128.10.204.0 255.255.255.192 128.10.204.65
```

```
!
access-list 101 deny igrp 0.0.0.0 255.255.255.255 255.255.255.255 0.0.0.0
access-list 101 permit ip 0.0.0.0 255.255.255.255 0.0.0.0 255.255.255.255
dialer-list 1 list 101
!
username HongKong password password1
username Singapore password password2
username Tokyo password password3
```

Remote Sites: Dial In and Dial Out

In the following configuration examples, the remote sites are configured to place and receive calls to or from multiple interfaces at the central site. All the remote sites dial the same telephone number. At the San Francisco site, that single telephone number will connect to either serial interface 5 or serial interface 6. The telephone service provider provides this capability.

Hong Kong

The following configuration allows Hong Kong to place and receive calls to and from the central site in San Francisco:

```
hostname HongKong
interface serial 1
description DDR connection to SanFrancisco
ip address 128.10.200.65 255.255.255.192
encapsulation ppp
dialer in-band
dialer wait-for-carrier-time 60
dialer string 14155551212
pulse-time 1
dialer-group 1
router igrp 1
network 128.10.0.0
ip route 128.10.0.0 255.255.0.0 128.10.200.66
!
access-list 101 deny igrp 0.0.0.0 255.255.255.255 255.255.255.255 0.0.0.0
access-list 101 permit ip 0.0.0.0 255.255.255.255 0.0.0.0 255.255.255.255
dialer-list 1 list 101
!
username SanFrancisco password password1
```

Singapore

The following configuration allows Singapore to place and receive calls to and from the central site in San Francisco:

```
hostname Singapore
interface serial 1
description DDR connection to San Francisco
ip address 128.10.202.65 255.255.255.192
encapsulation ppp
dialer in-band
dialer wait-for-carrier-time 60
dialer string 14155551212
```

```
pulse-time 1
dialer-group 1
router igrp 1
network 128.10.0.0
ip route 128.10.0.0 255.255.0.0 128.10.202.66
!
access-list 101 deny igrp 0.0.0.0 255.255.255.255 255.255.255.255 0.0.0.0
access-list 101 permit ip 0.0.0.0 255.255.255.255 0.0.0.0 255.255.255.255
dialer-list 1 list 101
!
username SanFrancisco password password2
```

Tokyo

The following configuration allows Tokyo to place and receive calls to and from the central site in San Francisco:

```
hostname Tokyo
interface serial 1
description DDR connection to San Francisco
ip address 128.10.204.65 255.255.255.192
encapsulation ppp
dialer in-band
dialer wait-for-carrier-time 60
dialer string 14155551212
pulse-time 1
dialer-group 1
router igrp 1
network 128.10.0.0
ip route 128.10.0.0 255.255.0.0 128.10.204.66
!
access-list 101 deny igrp 0.0.0.0 255.255.255.255 255.255.255.255 0.0.0.0
access-list 101 permit ip 0.0.0.0 255.255.255.255 0.0.0.0 255.255.255.255
dialer-list 1 list 101
!
username SanFrancisco password password3
```

The remote sites do not use the **ppp authentication chap**. This is because only one site, the central site, is calling in to the remote sites. If only one site is calling in, DDR assumes that the call is from the number defined with the **dialer string** command; therefore, the command **ppp authentication chap** is not required. If the remote sites use **dialer map** commands rather than **dialer string**, however, the **ppp authentication chap** command is required, and the **dialer map** commands require the name keyword.

Also, each remote site has a **username SanFrancisco** entry containing the same password that the central San Francisco site uses to identify the remote site.

Having Remote Sites Dial Out

A common configuration is to have the remote sites place calls to the central site, which does not dial out.

Configuring Multiple Interfaces for Multiple Remote Sites

In a star topology, all the remote routers can have their serial interfaces on the same subnet as the central site serial interface (see Figure 19-2).

Figure 19-2 *Remote Sites Dial Out (Star Topology)*

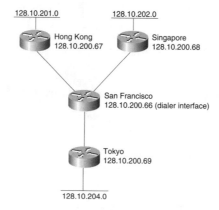

Central Site: Dial In Only

The following example configures the central site router to accept dial-ins on multiple interfaces:

```
hostname SanFrancisco
interface dialer 1
description rotary group for inbound calls
ip address 128.10.200.66 255.255.255.192
encapsulation ppp
ppp authentication chap
dialer in-band
dialer wait-for-carrier-time 60
dialer map ip 128.10.200.67 name HongKong
dialer map ip 128.10.200.68 name Singapore
dialer map ip 128.10.200.69 name Tokyo
pulse-time 1
dialer-group 1
!
interface serial 5
dialer rotary-group 1
!
interface serial 6
dialer rotary-group 1
!
router igrp 1
network 128.10.0.0
passive-interface dialer 1
redistribute static
! route to Hong Kong
ip route 128.10.201.0 255.255.255.192 128.10.200.67
! route to Singapore
ip route 128.10.202.0 255.255.255.192 128.10.200.68
```

```
! route to Tokyo
ip route 128.10.204.0 255.255.255.192 128.10.200.69
!
access-list 101 deny igrp 0.0.0.0 255.255.255.255 255.255.255.255 0.0.0.0
access-list 101 permit ip 0.0.0.0 255.255.255.255 0.0.0.0 255.255.255.255
dialer-list 1 list 101
!
username HongKong password password1
username Singapore password password2
username Tokyo password password3
```

Remote Sites: Dial Out Only

In the following configurations, the remote sites are configured to place calls to multiple interfaces at the central site. The assumption here is that a single telephone number on the central site will get any one of two possible inbound serial interfaces (serial interface 5 or serial interface 6).

Hong Kong

The following configuration allows Hong Kong to place calls to the central site in San Francisco:

```
hostname HongKong
interface ethernet 0
ip address 128.10.201.1 255.255.255.192
interface serial 1
description DDR connection to SanFrancisco
ip address 128.10.200.67 255.255.255.192
encapsulation ppp
dialer in-band
dialer wait-for-carrier-time 60
dialer string 14155551212
pulse-time 1
dialer-group 1
router igrp 1
network 128.10.0.0
ip route 128.10.0.0 255.255.0.0 128.10.200.66
!
access-list 101 deny igrp 0.0.0.0 255.255.255.255 255.255.255.255 0.0.0.0
access-list 101 permit ip 0.0.0.0 255.255.255.255 0.0.0.0 255.255.255.255
dialer-list 1 list 101
!
username SanFrancisco password password1
```

Singapore

The following configuration allows Singapore to place calls to the central site in San Francisco:

```
hostname Singapore
interface ethernet 0
ip address 128.10.202.1 255.255.255.192
interface serial 1
description DDR connection to San Francisco
```

```
ip address 128.10.200.68 255.255.255.192
encapsulation ppp
dialer in-band
dialer wait-for-carrier-time 60
dialer string 14155551212
pulse-time 1
dialer-group 1
router igrp 1
network 128.10.0.0
ip route 128.10.0.0 255.255.0.0 128.10.200.66
!
access-list 101 deny igrp 0.0.0.0 255.255.255.255 255.255.255.255 0.0.0.0
access-list 101 permit ip 0.0.0.0 255.255.255.255 0.0.0.0 255.255.255.255
dialer-list 1 list 101
!
username SanFrancisco password password2
```

Tokyo

The following configuration allows Tokyo to place calls to the central site in San Francisco:

```
hostname Tokyo
interface ethernet 0
ip address 128.10.204.1 255.255.255.192
interface serial 1
description DDR connection to San Francisco
ip address 128.10.200.69 255.255.255.192
encapsulation ppp
dialer in-band
dialer wait-for-carrier-time 60
dialer string 14155551212
pulse-time 1
dialer-group 1
router igrp 1
network 128.10.0.0
ip route 128.10.0.0 255.255.0.0 128.10.200.66
!
access-list 101 deny igrp 0.0.0.0 255.255.255.255 255.255.255.255 0.0.0.0
access-list 101 permit ip 0.0.0.0 255.255.255.255 0.0.0.0 255.255.255.255
dialer-list 1 list 101
!
username SanFrancisco password password3
```

Using DDR as a Backup to Leased Lines

DDR allows you to quickly enable a WAN connection through the use of existing analog telephone lines. Also, DDR provides cost savings because the line is used on an as-needed basis, whereas a leased line is paid for even when the line is not in use. At times, however, a leased line may provide benefits.

Figure 19-3 shows that there can be a point (when a connection needs to be maintained for more than a certain number of hours per day) at which a DDR link no longer has cost savings, and a leased line may be more cost-effective. Additionally, DDR links have a variable cost. It is difficult to predict what a DDR link may cost per month, given that users can initiate traffic at any time.

Figure 19-3 *DDR-to-Leased Line Cutover*

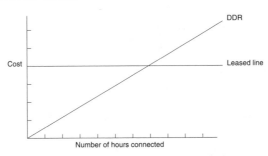

With leased lines, you can still continue to use dialup lines as a backup by using either of the following methods:

- Floating static routes (single and shared interfaces) and DDR
- DTR dialing or V.25bis dialing

Floating Static Routes

Floating static routes are static routes that have an administrative distance greater than the administrative distance of dynamic routes. Administrative distances can be configured on a static route so that the static route is less desirable than a dynamic route. In this manner, the static route is not used when the dynamic route is available. If the dynamic route is lost, however, the static route can take over, and traffic can be sent through this alternative route. If this alternative route is provided by a DDR interface, DDR can be used as a backup mechanism.

Central Site

The following example outlines a configuration of a central site using leased lines for primary connectivity and DDR for backup:

```
interface serial 1
description Leased connection to Hong Kong
ip address 128.10.200.66 255.255.255.192
!
interface serial 2
description leased connection to Singapore
ip address 128.10.202.66 255.255.255.192
!
interface serial 5
description backup DDR connection to Hong Kong
ip address 128.10.200.130 255.255.255.192
dialer in-band
dialer wait-for-carrier-time 60
dialer string 0118527351625
pulse-time 1
```

```
dialer-group 1
!
interface serial 6
description backup DDR connection to Singapore
ip address 128.10.202.130 255.255.255.192
dialer in-band
dialer wait-for-carrier-time 60
dialer string 011653367085
pulse-time 1
dialer-group 1
!
interface serial 7
description DDR connection to Tokyo
ip address 128.10.204.66 255.255.255.192
dialer in-band
dialer wait-for-carrier-time 60
dialer string 0118127351625
pulse-time 1
dialer-group 1
!
router igrp 1
network 128.10.0.0
redistribute static
!
! route to Hong Kong with administrative distance
ip route 128.10.200.0 255.255.255.192 128.10.200.129 150
! route to Singapore with administrative distance
ip route 128.10.202.0 255.255.255.192 128.10.202.129 150
! route to Tokyo
ip route 128.10.204.0 255.255.255.192 128.10.204.65
!
access-list 101 deny igrp 0.0.0.0 255.255.255.255 255.255.255.255 0.0.0.0
access-list 101 permit ip 0.0.0.0 255.255.255.255 0.0.0.0 255.255.255.255
dialer-list 1 list 101
```

Serial interfaces 1 and 2 are used as leased lines to Hong Kong and Singapore. Serial interface 5 backs up serial interface 1; serial interface 6 backs up serial interface 2; and serial interface 7 is used for DDR to Tokyo.

Remote Sites

Each remote site has a leased line as a primary link and a DDR line as a backup. For example:

```
interface serial 0
description leased line from San Francisco
ip address 128.10.200.65 255.255.255.192
!
interface serial 1
description interface to answer backup calls from San Francisco
ip address 128.10.200.129 255.255.255.192
dialer in-band
!
router igrp 1
network 128.10.0.0
! route back to San Francisco with administrative distance
ip route 128.10.0.0 255.255.0.0 128.10.200.130 150
```

The first serial interface is the leased line, whereas the second answers calls from the central site, in case the central site needs to use DDR as a backup method.

Floating Static Routes on Shared Interfaces

The central site configuration requires a large number of serial ports because each primary port has its own backup. For true redundancy, backup is a requirement. In many cases, however, an interface or a set of interfaces can be shared as backup for a set of primary lines. The following configuration shows how to set up a single interface to back up all the primary lines:

```
interface serial 1
description Leased connection to Hong Kong
ip address 128.10.200.66 255.255.255.192
!
interface serial 2
description leased connection to Singapore
ip address 128.10.202.66 255.255.255.192
!
interface serial 5
description backup DDR connection for all destinations except Tokyo
ip address 128.10.200.130 255.255.255.192
ip address 128.10.202.130 255.255.255.192 secondary
dialer in-band
dialer wait-for-carrier-time 60
! map Hong Kong to a phone number
dialer map ip 128.10.200.129 0118527351625
! map Singapore to a phone number
dialer map ip 128.10.202.129 011653367085
pulse-time 1
dialer-group 1
!
interface serial 7
description DDR connection to Tokyo
ip address 128.10.204.66 255.255.255.192
dialer in-band
dialer wait-for-carrier-time 60
dialer string 0118127351625
pulse-time 1
dialer-group 1
!
router igrp 1
network 128.10.0.0
passive-interface serial 5
redistribute static
!
! route to Hong Kong with administrative distance
ip route 128.10.200.0 255.255.255.192 128.10.200.129 150
! route to Singapore with administrative distance
ip route 128.10.202.0 255.255.255.192 128.10.202.129 150
! route to Tokyo
ip route 128.10.204.0 255.255.255.192 128.10.204.65
!
access-list 101 deny igrp 0.0.0.0 255.255.255.255 255.255.255.255 0.0.0.0
access-list 101 permit ip 0.0.0.0 255.255.255.255 0.0.0.0 255.255.255.255
dialer-list 1 list 101
```

Serial interface 5 is the DDR backup interface for all destinations and is configured with multiple IP addresses for routing. The **dialer map** commands map the next hop addresses to the telephone numbers for each of the destinations. If a dynamic route is lost, the floating static route takes over. The next hop address sends the packets to serial interface 5, where the **dialer map** commands place the telephone call.

If two primary lines fail at the same time, there will be contention to use serial interface 5. The fast-idle timer may disconnect the calls. If serial interface 5 were in constant use, one of the primary lines would be disconnected and packets would be dropped. The fact that the backup route is unavailable is not communicated because there is no way to announce that one of the two IP addresses on the interface is unavailable. If you use a dialer rotary group, the contention problem can be avoided.

Using Leased Lines and Dial Backup

This section describes how to use the following two methods for dial backup with leased lines:

- DTR dialing
- V.25bis dialing

DTR Dialing

Since Software Release 8.3, a dial backup capability has been provided. Although it is somewhat more restrictive than floating static routes, dial backup can be used if V.25bis modems are not available or if protocols that do not have support for floating static routes are used.

Central Site

Dial backup requires that the modems place a call when the data terminal ready (DTR) signal is raised. The telephone number is configured into the modem or other DCE device. That number is called when DTR is raised. The call is disconnected when DTR is lowered. The following configuration illustrates how to take advantage of dial backup and DTR dialing:

```
interface serial 1
description Leased connection to Hong Kong
ip address 128.10.200.66 255.255.255.192
backup interface serial 4
backup delay 0 20
!
interface serial 2
description leased connection to Singapore
ip address 128.10.202.66 255.255.255.192
backup interface serial 5
backup delay 0 20
!
interface serial 4
description backup connection for Hong Kong
ip address 128.10.200.67 255.255.255.192
pulse-time 10
!
interface serial 5
description backup connection for Singapore
```

```
ip address 128.10.202.67 255.255.255.192
pulse-time 10
!
interface serial 7
description DDR connection to Tokyo
ip address 128.10.204.66 255.255.255.192
dialer in-band
dialer wait-for-carrier-time 60
dialer string 0118127351625
pulse-time 1
dialer-group 1
!
router igrp 1
network 128.10.0.0
```

This solution requires one serial port per primary line. Because the backup ports are placed on the same subnet as the primary serial port, no static routes are required. The **backup delay** command is used to specify how long to wait after the primary has failed before activating the backup line, and how long to delay before deactivating the backup line after the primary line comes back up. In this case, the primary link will be active for 20 seconds before disabling the backup line. This delay allows for flapping in the primary link when it returns to functioning.

Remote Sites

For the remote sites, the floating static route is not needed. The IP address of the backup interface must be on the same subnet as the primary interface. The following example illustrates the Hong Kong router configuration. Serial interface 0 is the leased line, whereas serial interface 1 answers calls as a backup method:

```
interface serial 0
description leased line from San Francisco
ip address 128.10.200.65 255.255.255.192
!
interface serial 1
description interface to answer backup calls from San Francisco
ip address 128.10.200.68 255.255.255.192
!
router igrp 1
network 128.10.0.0
```

V.25bis Dialing

V.25bis dialing can be preferable to DTR dialing when multiple telephone numbers are required. Using DTR dialing, most devices will call only a single number. With V.25bis, the router can attempt to call several numbers if the first number does not answer. The following configuration illustrates V.25bis dialing:

```
interface serial 1
description Leased connection to Hong Kong
ip address 128.10.200.66 255.255.255.192
backup interface serial 4
backup delay 0 20
!
```

```
interface serial 2
description leased connection to Singapore
ip address 128.10.202.66 255.255.255.192
backup interface serial 5
backup delay 0 20
!
interface serial 4
description backup connection for Hong Kong
ip address 128.10.200.67 255.255.255.192
dialer in-band
dialer wait-for-carrier-time 60
dialer map IP 128.10.200.68 0118527351625
dialer map IP 128.10.200.68 0118527351872
dialer-group 1
pulse-time 1
!
interface serial 5
description backup connection for Singapore
ip address 128.10.202.67 255.255.255.192
dialer in-band
dialer wait-for-carrier-time 60
dialer string 011653367085
dialer-group 1
pulse-time 1
!
interface serial 7
description DDR connection to Tokyo
ip address 128.10.204.66 255.255.255.192
dialer in-band
dialer wait-for-carrier-time 60
dialer string 0118127351625
pulse-time 1
dialer-group 1
!
router igrp 1
network 128.10.0.0
redistribute static
!
! route to Hong Kong
ip route 128.10.200.0 255.255.255.192 128.10.200.68
! route to Singapore
ip route 128.10.202.0 255.255.255.192 128.10.202.68
! route to Tokyo
ip route 128.10.204.0 255.255.255.192 128.10.204.65
!
dialer-list 1 protocol IP PERMIT
```

Multiple telephone numbers are configured for serial interface 4. The two **dialer map** commands have the same next hop address. The software first attempts to call the telephone number specified in the first **dialer map** command. If this number fails—that is, if no connection is made before the wait-for-carrier timer expires—the second number is dialed. Each of the other backup interfaces uses a dialer string for the backup telephone number. When using V.25bis with dial backup, the **dialer-list protocol** command shown in the preceding example should be used. The dialer list states that all IP traffic is interesting and will, therefore, cause dialing. Routing updates are included. When a serial line is used as a backup, it is normally the state of the primary link, not the fast-idle timer, that determines when to disconnect the call.

Chat Scripts

In the following example, the configuration is shown on the sanjose router. Chat script called dial is used to dial the modem connected to rtp router. Chat script called login is used to log in to rtp router. The dialer string 555555 is the number of the modem connected to rtp router, and the IP address 10.20.30.1 is the address of rtp router.

```
chat-script dial ABORT ERROR "" "AT Z" OK "ATDT \T" TIMEOUT 60 CONNECT \c
chat-script login ABORT invalid TIMEOUT 30  name: sasad word: sraza ">"
        "slip default"

interface async 10
dialer in-band
dialer map ip 10.20.30.1 modem-script dial system-script login 5555555
```

Writing and Implementing Chat Scripts

In the following configuration example, a random line will be used when there is traffic. When there is traffic, the dialer code will try to locate a script that matches both the modem script sanjose and the system script rtp. If the dialer code cannot locate the modem script and the system script, a "no matching chat script found" message would be sent to the user.

```
interface dialer 1
! sanjose rotaries are defined in dialer rotary-group 1
dialer rotary-group 1
! Use sanjose generic script
dialer map ip 10.10.10.10 modem-script sanjose system-script rtp 5555555
```

In the following chat script, " " means expect anything and \r means send a return.

```
" " \r "name:" "your_name" "ord":" "your_password" ">" "slip default"
```

In the following configuration, chat scripts are defined for lines connected to Best Data and US Robotics modems separately:

```
! Lines one through five have Best Data modems connected to them
line 1 5
modem chat-script bestdata.*
! Lines six through nine have US Robotics modems connected to them
line 6 9
modem chat-script usrobotics.*
```

Chat Scripts and Dialer Mapping

In the following configuration, a dialing chat script and a login chat script is shown. The **dialer in-band** command makes asynchronous interface 0 a DDR interface and the **dialer map** command dials 5555555 after the specified dialing and the login scripts are located.

```
chat-script dial ABORT ERROR "" "AT Z" OK "ATDT \T" TIMEOUT 60 CONNECT \c
chat-script login ABORT invalid TIMEOUT 30  name: sasad word: sraza ">"
            "slip default"

interface async 0
dialer in-band
dialer map ip 10.10.10.10 modem-script dial system-script login 5555555
```

When a packet is received for the destination IP address 10.10.10.10, the first thing that happens is that the modem script called dial is located. The following line shows what is done with each expect-send pair in the modem script called dial:

ABORT ERROR: If the text "ERROR" is found end the script execution.

" " "AT Z": Send an **"AT Z"** command to the modem without expecting anything else. The quotation marks are used to allow a space in the send string.

```
OK "ATDT \T:  Wait for "OK." Send "ATDT 5555555."

TIMEOUT 60:  Wait up to 60 seconds for next expect string.
Time could  be changed depending on the different kind of modems.

 CONNECT \c:  Expect "connect," but do not send anything else.
\c  means effectively nothing.
Quotes " " would have been nothing followed by a carriage return.
```

After the modem script is executed successfully, the second step is to execute the login script. The following code shows what is done with each expect-send pair in the system script called login:

```
ABORT invalid: If the message "invalid username or password" is displayed
 end the script execution.

TIMEOUT 30:  Wait up to 15 seconds.

name: sasad:  Try to look for "name:" and send "sasad.".

word: sraza:  Wait for "word:" and send the password which is sraza.

 ">" "slip default":  Wait for the ts prompt and put the line into
 slip mode with its default address.
```

Summary

As this case study indicates, dial-on-demand routing (DDR) can be used in many ways both for primary access and backup access. Sites can place calls, receive calls, and both place and receive calls. Additionally, using dialer rotary groups provides increased flexibility. This chapter also briefly explained the use and implementation of chat scripts.

CHAPTER 20

Scaling Dial-on-Demand Routing

Edited by Salman Asad

This case study describes the design of an access network that allows a large number of remote sites to communicate with an existing central-site network. The remote sites consist of local-area networks (LANs) that support several workstations. The workstations run transaction-processing software that accesses a database located at the central site. The following objectives guided the design of the access portion of the network:

- The existing network could not be modified to accommodate access by the remote sites.
- The central site must be able to connect to any remote site at any time, and any remote site must be able to connect to the central site at any time.
- When choosing between alternative technologies, choose the most cost-effective technology.
- The design must be flexible enough to accommodate additional remote sites in the future.

Network Design Considerations

The following considerations influenced the design of this network:

- Traffic patterns
- Media selection
- Application protocol requirements

Traffic Patterns

An analysis of the anticipated traffic indicated that each remote site would call the central site an average of four times an hour throughout the business day. This type of traffic pattern means that cost savings can be realized at the central site by providing one telephone line for every 2.5 remote sites (for a total of 48 telephone lines). To spread the calls evenly among the 48 lines, the remote sites connect through a hunt group. The hunt group provides an additional benefit in that all the remote routers dial the same telephone number to access the central site, which makes the configurations of the remote site routers easier to maintain.

To complete a transaction initiated by a remote site, the central site sometimes needs to call that remote site shortly after it has disconnected from the central site. To make this possible, the access network must converge rapidly. The central site also calls the remote sites periodically to update the transaction-processing software on the remote workstations.

Media Selection

The designers chose asynchronous dialup technology through the Public Switched Telephone Network (PSTN) for the following reasons:

- *Availability*—PSTN is available at all the remote sites. Potential alternatives, such as Frame Relay and Integrated Digital Services Network (ISDN), were not available at some of the remote sites.

- *Bandwidth*—The transaction-processing software causes a small amount of data to be transferred between the remote sites and the central site. For this type of low-bandwidth application, the bandwidth provided by asynchronous dialup is acceptable. Occasionally, the central site dials the remote sites to maintain the transaction-processing software on the remote clients. This activity will occur at night (in the absence of transaction-processing activity), so the bandwidth provided by asynchronous dialup is adequate.

- *Cost*—Given the low-bandwidth requirement, the cost of installing and operating Frame Relay or ISDN equipment could not be justified.

NOTE   Although the network described in this case study uses asynchronous dialup technology over the PSTN, most of the concepts, such as routing strategy and addressing, also apply when scaling other circuit-switched technologies (such as ISDN).

Application Protocol Requirements

The remote workstations run transaction-processing software that uses the Transmission Control Protocol/Internet Protocol (TCP/IP) to connect to a database located at the central site. The remote workstations have no need to run any other network layer protocol. Given this requirement, the most cost-effective choice of router for the remote site is a router that provides an Ethernet interface and an asynchronous interface, and that supports the Routing Information Protocol (RIP).

The Hardware Solution

A Cisco AS5100 is installed at the central site to provide 48 asynchronous interfaces. The Cisco AS5100 consists of three access server cards based on the Cisco 2511 access server, making the Cisco AS5100 equivalent to three Cisco 2511 access servers. Each access server card provides 16 asynchronous lines. Each asynchronous line is equipped with a built-in U.S. Robotics Courier modem.

NOTE	For the purposes of this case study, the three Cisco AS5100 access server cards are referred to as the central-site access routers.

Each remote site is equipped with a Cisco 1020 router. The Cisco 1020 provides a single asynchronous interface and an Ethernet interface for connecting to the remote-site LAN. The Cisco 1020 runs a limited set of protocols, including TCP/IP and RIP. U.S. Robotics Sportster modems provide connectivity at the remote sites. Using the same brand of modem throughout the access network simplifies chat scripts and modem definition, and makes the network more manageable.

A Cisco 4500 controls routing between the new access portion of the network and the backbone. In particular, the Cisco 4500 ensures that when hosts on the other side of the backbone need to connect to a remote site, the connection is made through the optimum central-site access router. Figure 20-1 shows the topology of the access portion of the network.

Figure 20-1 *Remote Access Topology*

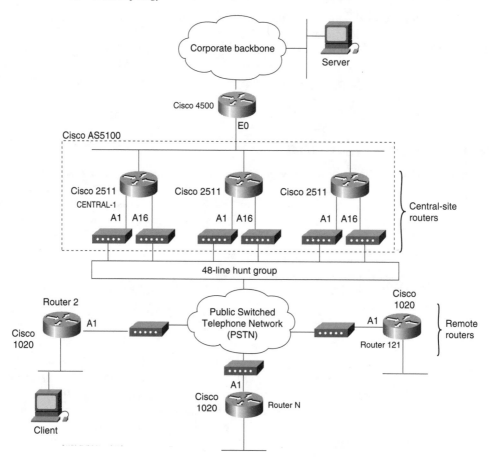

The Software Solution

The configuration of the central-site access routers and the remote-site routers must provide the following:

- Authentication
- Network layer addressing
- Routing strategy

Authentication

Traffic between the remote sites and the central site includes confidential information. For that reason, authentication is a primary concern. Sites can authenticate themselves in two ways:

- *Point-to-Point Protocol (PPP) authentication*—Either the Password Authentication Protocol (PAP) or the Challenge Handshake Authentication Protocol (CHAP) can be used.

- *Login authentication*—With login authentication, the router prompts for a host name and password when a remote router dials in. The remote router logs in and starts PPP.

In either case, the database of usernames and passwords can be stored locally or on an extended Terminal Access Controller Access Control System (TACACS+) server. TACACS+ provides centralized password management for all the central-site access routers and detailed accounting information about connections to and from the remote sites.

For the purposes of this network design, login authentication is used because it allows the remote sites to announce their IP addresses to the central-site access routers, as described in the following section, titled "Network Layer Addressing." Alternatively, PPP could be started automatically if TACACS+ were used to support per-user IP address assignment.

Network Layer Addressing

Network layer addressing is accomplished through two strategies:

- Subnet address assignment
- Next-hop address

Subnet Address Assignment

The remote routers and the central-site access routers have no need to connect to the Internet, so they use RFC 1597 addresses. The Class B address 172.16.0.0 is used for the entire access portion of the network, and Class C equivalent addresses are assigned to the remote routers. Each subnet gets one Class C equivalent (172.16.x.0 with a mask of 255.255.255.0), which makes addressing easy to manage. Network 172.16.1.0 is reserved for numbering the dialer cloud later if needed. (The *dialer cloud* is defined as the subnet to which all the asynchronous interfaces are attached.)

Initially, the dialer cloud is unnumbered. If, in the future, the dialer cloud were to be numbered, the following questions must be considered:

- Can the dialer cloud use the same subnet mask as the remote sites? If not, variable-length subnet mask (VLSM) support will be required. (RIP does not support VLSM.)

- Would the use of multiple subnetted Class C addresses cause discontiguous subnets at the remote sites? If so, discontiguous subnet support will be required. (RIP does not support discontiguous subnets.)

In this network, these issues are not a problem. A mask of 255.255.255.0 can be used everywhere, so there are no VLSM concerns. All subnets are from the same major Class B network, so there are no discontiguous subnet concerns. Table 20-1 summarizes the addressing for the access portion of the network.

Table 20-1   *Addressing Summary*

Site	Subnet	Mask
Central access site[*]	172.16.1.0	255.255.255.0
Router2	172.16.2.0	255.255.255.0
Router3	172.16.3.0	255.255.255.0
...	...	...
Router121	172.16.121.0	255.255.255.0

[*]   Can be used for numbering the dialer cloud.

Next-Hop Address

To facilitate an accurate routing table and successful IP Control Protocol (IPCP) address negotiation, all next-hop IP addressing must be accurate at all times. To accomplish this, the remote sites need to know the IP address that they will dial in to, and the central site needs to know the IP address of the remote site that has dialed in.

All central-site access routers use the same IP address on all their asynchronous interfaces. This is accomplished by configuring the Dialer20 interface for IP unnumbered off of a loopback interface. The IP address of the loopback interface is the same on all the central-site access routers. This way, the remote router can be configured with the IP address of the router to which it connects, regardless of which router the remote router dials in to.

The remote router needs to announce its IP address to the central-site router when the remote router connects. This is accomplished by having the remote router start PPP on the central site using the exec command **ppp 172.16.x.1**. To support this, each central-site access router is configured with the **async dynamic address** interface configuration command.

NOTE   The Autoselect feature allows the router to start an appropriate process, such as PPP, automatically when it receives a starting character from the router that has logged in. To use Autoselect, a mechanism for supporting dynamic IP address assignment would be required, such as per-user address support in TACACS+.

Routing Strategy

The development of the routing strategy for this network is based on the following two requirements:

- When a particular remote site is not dialed in to the central site, that remote site must be reachable through any central-site access router by means of a static route configured in each central-site access router.

- When a particular remote site router is logged in to a central-site access router, that remote site must be reachable through that central-site access router by means of the dynamic route that has been established for that connection and propagated to the backbone.

To meet these requirements, the central-site access routes advertise the major network route of the remote sites to the Cisco 4500. All routes to the remote sites are equal cost through all the central-site access routers. Each central-site access router is configured to have a static route to each remote site. To allow the Cisco 4500 to use all the central-site access routers for connecting to the remote sites, the **no ip route-cache** interface configuration command is configured on Ethernet interface 0 of the Cisco 4500, disabling fast switching of IP to the subnet shared with the central-site access routers. This causes the Cisco 4500 to alternate between the three access routers when initiating outbound calls. This strategy increases network reliability for those cases when one of the access routers goes down.

When a remote router logs in, it announces its IP address and sends a RIP flash. The RIP flash causes a dynamic route to the remote site to be installed immediately in the routing table of the central-site access router. The dynamic route overrides the static route for the duration of the connection.

Next, the central-site access router redistributes the RIP route into Open Shortest Path First (OSPF) and sends the route to all its OSPF neighbors, including the Cisco 4500, which installs it in its routing table. The Cisco 4500 now has a major network route to all the remote sites, plus a dynamic route to the specific remote site that has logged in. If a central-site host needs to communicate with a particular remote site that is currently logged in, it does so through the dynamic route.

When the remote site logs out, the dynamic route must be removed from the Cisco 4500, and the static route to the remote site must be restored on the central-site access router to which the remote router logged in.

If a central-site host requires communication with a remote site that is not logged in, it will use the major network route defined in the Cisco 4500. A central-site access router, selected in round-robin fashion, is used to initiate the call to the remote site via the static route defined for it in the configuration for the selected access router. As in the case of a remote site that calls the central site, after the connection is made, the remote-site router sends a RIP flash that causes a dynamic route to the remote site to be installed immediately in the routing table of the central-site access router. This dynamic route is redistributed into OSPF and is installed in the routing table of the Cisco 4500. Figure 20-2 uses a state diagram to summarize the routing strategy.

Figure 20-2 *Routing Strategy State Diagram*

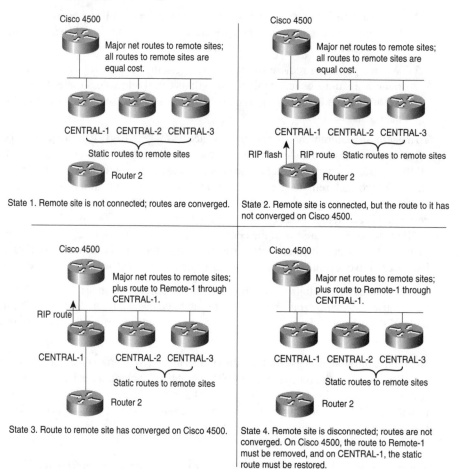

State 1. Remote site is not connected; routes are converged.

State 2. Remote site is connected, but the route to it has not converged on Cisco 4500.

State 3. Route to remote site has converged on Cisco 4500.

State 4. Remote site is disconnected; routes are not converged. On Cisco 4500, the route to Remote-1 must be removed, and on CENTRAL-1, the static route must be restored.

The following convergence issues pertain to the state diagram shown in Figure 20-2:

- During the time between State 2 and State 3, a host at the central site might initiate a call to the remote site. Until State 3, at which time the routes converge on the Cisco 4500, any central-site access router that dials the remote site will fail with a busy signal. In practice, only one call fails: By the time a second connection attempt is made, the routes will have converged in State 3, the dynamic route will be available for use, and there will be no need to make another call.

- When the remote site disconnects, at minimum 120 seconds will elapse before the static route is restored to the routing table of the central-site access router on which the remote site logged in. First, up to 35 seconds might elapse before RIP determines that the remote site has disconnected and is no longer sending RIP updates. Sixty seconds later, the central-site access router scans its routing table and restores one of the two static routes for the remote site, and 60 seconds after that, it scans its routing table again and restores the second of the two static routes. (For information about why there are two static routes for each remote site, see the section titled "Static Routing Configuration" later in this chapter.)

NOTE   Fast install of static routes is a new feature in Cisco IOS Release 11.1 that quickly converges back to the static route when a remote site disconnects.

If, before convergence occurs, the Cisco 4500 directs a call through CENTRAL-1 to Router 2, the call will fail and must be retried. IP fast switching is turned off on the Cisco 4500, the Cisco 4500 (which is using equal-cost paths to each of the central-site access routers) will send the next packet through CENTRAL-2 or CENTRAL-3 (which still have a static route for Router 2) and the call will go through.

NOTE   When developing the routing strategy for this network, the designers considered the use of snapshot routing, which reduces connection cost by limiting the exchange of routing protocol updates. For snapshot routing to work, each remote site must connect to the same access router every time it dials in to the central site. In this design, the remote routers connect to the central-site access routers through a hunt group, so there is no way to control to which central-site access router a remote router will connect for any particular connection. Therefore, snapshot routing cannot be used for this design.

Configuring the Central-Site Access Routers

This section describes how the configuration of the central-site access routers implements authentication, network layer addressing, and the routing strategy. The configuration for each central-site access router is the same with the following exceptions:

- The IP address specified for loopback interface 0
- The IP address specified for Ethernet interface 0
- The name of the router as specified by the **hostname** global configuration command

This discussion is divided among the following topics:

- Username configuration for the remote sites
- Dialup configuration for the remote sites
- Loopback interface configuration
- Asynchronous line configuration
- Dialer interface configuration
- OSPF routing configuration
- RIP routing configuration
- Static routing configuration
- Security issues
- Configuration file size

For the complete configuration, see the section titled "CENTRAL-1 Configuration" later in this chapter.

Username Configuration for the Remote Sites

The configuration of each central-site access router includes the following **username** global configuration commands:

```
username Router2 password 7 071C2D4359
...
username Router121 password 7 0448070918
```

Each remote router can dial in to any of the three central-site access routers, so there is a **username** global configuration command for each remote router. When a remote router logs in, it specifies a name (for example, Router2) and a password (for example, outthere) that must match the values specified by a **username** command. Each remote site uses a chat script to log in and specify its host name (which must match a value specified by the **username** command) and password. (For information about the chat script that the remote sites use, see the section titled "Chat Script Configuration for Dialing the Central Site" later in this chapter.)

Dialup Configuration for the Remote Sites

The configuration of each central-site access router includes the following **chat-script** global configuration commands:

```
chat-script CALL1020 ABORT ERROR ABORT BUSY TIMEOUT 30 "" "ATDT\T" "CONNECT" \c
chat-script REM TIMEOUT 40 "name:" "CENTRAL" "word:" "secret"
chat-script USRV32BIS "" "AT&F1S0=1&D2" "OK" ""
!
interface dialer 20
dialer map ip 172.16.2.1 name Router2 modem-script CALL1020 system-script REM
5551234
...
dialer map ip 172.16.121.1 name Router2 modem-script CALL1020 system-script REM
5555678
!
line 1 16
script reset USRV32BIS
```

The three **chat-script** global configuration commands establish three scripts named CALL1020, REM, and USRV32BIS. CALL1020 and REM are invoked by the **dialer map** commands to dial and log in to the remote sites, respectively. The **script reset** command specifies that the USRV32BIS script is to be run whenever an asynchronous line is reset, to ensure that the central-site modems are always configured correctly.

Loopback Interface Configuration

The configuration of each central-site access router includes the commands for configuring loopback interfaces. The IP address for loopback interface 0 is unique for each access router and, to satisfy the rules by which OSPF selects the router ID, must be the highest loopback IP address on the router. The IP address for loopback interface 1 is the same for each central-site access router. The commands are as follows:

```
interface loopback 0
ip address 172.16.254.3 255.255.255.255
...
interface loopback 1
ip address 172.16.1.1 255.255.255.0
```

The goal is for all three access routers to appear to have the same IP address during IPCP negotiation with the remote sites. (*IPCP* is the part of PPP that brings up and configures IP support.) This goal is accomplished by creating a loopback interface, assigning to it the same IP address on each central-site access router, and running the **ip unnumbered** interface configuration command using the loopback interface address. The problem with this strategy is that OSPF takes its router ID from the IP address of a loopback interface, if one is configured, which would mean that all three access routers would have the same OSPF router ID.

The solution is to create loopback interface 0 and assign to it a unique IP address (which results in a unique OSPF router ID for each router). The configuration then creates loopback interface 1 and assigns to it the same IP address on each router. Loopback interface 1 allows the **ip unnumbered** command to be applied to dialer rotary group 20 later in the configuration.

Asynchronous Line Configuration

The configuration of each central-site access router includes the following commands for configuring each asynchronous interface:

```
interface async 1
ip unnumbered loopback 1
async dynamic address
async dynamic routing
async mode interactive
dialer in-band
dialer rotary-group 20
```

For each of the 16 asynchronous interfaces provided by the access router, the configuration uses the **ip unnumbered** interface configuration command to specify that the asynchronous interface is to use the IP address of loopback interface 1 as the source address for any IP packets that the asynchronous interface generates. The IP address of loopback interface 1 is also used to determine which routing processes are sending updates over the asynchronous interface.

The **async dynamic address** interface configuration command enables dynamic addressing on the asynchronous interface. This command is required to allow each remote router to specify its IP address when it logs in. The **async dynamic routing** interface configuration command allows the interface to run a routing protocol, in this case RIP.

The **async mode interactive** interface configuration command allows a remote router to dial in and access the exec command interface, which allows the remote router to start PPP and specify its IP address.

The **dialer in-band** interface configuration command allows chat scripts to be used on the asynchronous interface. The chat scripts allow the access router to dial the remote sites. The **dialer rotary-group** interface configuration command assigns each asynchronous interface to dialer rotary group 20.

Dialer Interface Configuration

The configuration of each central-site access router includes the following commands for configuring dialer rotary group 20:

```
interface dialer 20
ip unnumbered loopback 1
encapsulation ppp
dialer in-band
dialer idle-timeout 60
dialer map ip 172.16.2.1 name Router2 modem-script CALL1020 system-script REM
5551234
...
dialer map ip 172.16.121.1 name Router121 modem-script CALL1020 system-script REM
5555678
dialer-group 3
dialer-list 3 list 101
access-list 101 deny udp 0.0.0.0 255.255.255.255 0.0.0.0 255.255.255.255 eq 520
access-list 101 permit ip 0.0.0.0 255.255.255.255 0.0.0.0 255.255.255.255
```

The **interface dialer** global configuration command defines dialer rotary group 20. Any interface configuration commands applied to a dialer rotary group apply to the physical interfaces that are its members. When the router's configuration includes multiple destinations, any of the interfaces in the dialer rotary group can be used to place outgoing calls.

The **ip unnumbered** interface configuration command specifies that the IP address of loopback interface 1 is to be used as the source address for any IP packets that dialer rotary group 20 might generate. The **dialer idle-timeout** interface configuration command causes a disconnect if 60 seconds elapses without any interesting traffic.

The configuration includes a **dialer map** interface configuration command for each remote router that the central-site access router might dial. The **ip** keyword specifies that the dialer map is to be used for IP packets, the IP address is the next-hop address of the destination that is to be called, and the **name** keyword specifies the host name of the remote router that is to be called. The **modem-script** keyword specifies that the CALL1020 chat script is to be used, and the **system-script** keyword specifies that the REM chat script is to be used. The last value specified by the **dialer map** command is the telephone number for the remote router. The **dialer map** commands do not specify the **broadcast** keyword, so RIP updates are not sent to the remote sites.

For the Dialer20 interface, the **dialer-group** interface configuration command defines *interesting* packets to be those packets defined by the corresponding **dial-list** command. Interesting packets cause a call to be made or cause a call to be maintained. In this case, access list 101 defines RIP as uninteresting. (RIP uses User Datagram Protocol [UDP] port 520.) All other packets are defined as interesting.

OSPF Routing Configuration

Each central-site access router uses the following commands to configure OSPF. These commands limit the routes that are redistributed into OSPF to the major Class B static route and any dynamic subnet routes that may exist for currently connected remote sites. Limiting the routes that are redistributed into OSPF significantly simplifies the routing table on the Cisco 4500.

```
router ospf 110
redistribute static subnets route-map STATIC-TO-OSPF
redistribute rip subnets route-map RIP-TO-OSPF
passive-interface async 1
...
passive-interface async 16
network 172.19.0.0 0.0.255.255 area 0
distance 210
!
route-map RIP-TO-OSPF PERMIT
match ip address 20
!
access-list 20 permit 172.16.0.0 0.0.255.0
!
route-map STATIC-TO-OSPF PERMIT
match ip address 21
!
access-list 21 permit 172.16.0.0
```

The **router ospf** global configuration command enables an OSPF routing process and assigns to it a process ID of 110.

The first **redistribute** router configuration command causes static IP routes to be redistributed into OSPF. The **subnets** keyword specifies that subnets are to be redistributed, and the **route-map** keyword specifies that only those routes that successfully pass through the route map named STATIC-TO-OSPF are to be redistributed. The STATIC-TO-OSPF route map permits the redistribution of routes that match access list 21. Access list 21 permits only major network 172.16.0.0.

The second **redistribute** router configuration command causes RIP routes to be redistributed into OSPF. The **subnets** keyword specifies that subnets are to be redistributed, and the **route-map** keyword specifies that only those routes that successfully pass through the route map named RIP-TO-OSPF are to be redistributed. The RIP-TO-OSPF route map permits the redistribution of routes that match access list 20. Access list 20 permits only routes that start with 172.16 and end with .0 (the third octet is wild). In effect, the RIP-TO-OSPF route map allows only subnets that match 172.16.x.0.

For each asynchronous interface, there is a **passive-interface** router configuration command, which means that OSPF routing information is neither sent nor received through the asynchronous interfaces. The **distance** router configuration command assigns the OSPF routing process an administrative distance of 210. This allows the central-site access routers to prefer their static routes (with an administrative distance of 200) over routes learned by OSPF.

NOTE   When a remote site logs in and a dynamic route is established for it, the other access routers retain their static routes for that remote site. When a remote site logs out, the other access routers do not need to update their routing tables—their routing tables still contain the static routes necessary for dialing out to the remote site.

RIP Routing Configuration

Each access router uses the following commands to configure RIP:

```
router rip
 timers basic 30 35 0 1
 network 172.16.0.0
 distribute-list 10 out Dialer20
 !
 access-list 10 deny 0.0.0.0 255.255.255.255
```

The **timers basic** router configuration adjusts the RIP update, invalid, holddown, and flush timers. The command specifies that RIP updates are to be sent every 30 seconds, that a route is to be declared invalid if an update for the route is not received within 35 seconds after the previous update, that the time during which better routes are to be suppressed is 0 seconds, and that 1 second must pass before an invalid route is removed from the routing table. These timer adjustments produce the fastest possible convergence when a remote site logs out.

The **network** router configuration command specifies that network 172.16.0.0 is to participate in the RIP routing process. There is no need to propagate RIP routes to the Cisco 1020s, so the **distribute-list out** router configuration command specifies that access list 10 is to be used to control the advertisement of networks in updates. Access list 10 prevents RIP routes from being sent to the remote site.

Static Routing Configuration

The configuration of each central-site access router includes the following commands for configuring static routes to the remote sites:

```
ip route 172.16.0.0 255.255.0.0 Dialer20
```

The first **ip route** global configuration command creates a static route for major network 172.16.0.0 and assigns it to the dialer interface 20. The route, when distributed into OSPF, tells the Cisco 4500 that this central-site access router can get to the remote sites. If the access router goes down, the Cisco 4500 learns that the route is not longer available and removes it from its routing table. This route is redistributed into OSPF by the STATIC-TO-OSPF filter. The first **ip route** command is followed by pairs of static routes, one pair for each remote site:

```
ip route 172.16.2.0 255.255.255.0 172.16.2.1 200
ip route 172.16.2.1 255.255.255.255 Dialer20
...
ip route 172.16.121.0 255.255.255.0 172.16.121.1 200
ip route 172.16.121.1 255.255.255.255 Dialer20
```

In unnumbered IP environments, two static routes are required for each remote site:

- One static route points to the next hop on the dialer map. Note that the **200** makes this route a floating static route, but that it is lower than OSPF routes (which are set to 210 by the **distance** command, earlier in the configuration). This means that a RIP route triggered by a connection to a remote site (whether the connection is initiated by the remote site or the central site) will override the static route. An OSPF update initiated by a remote site that dials in will not override a static route that points to the next-hop address on the dialer map.

- One static route that defines the interface at which the next hop can be found (in this case, dialer interface 20). This static route is required for unnumbered interfaces. Note there is no need to make this a floating static route.

Security Issues

The configuration for each central-site access router includes the **login** line configuration command for each asynchronous line and specifies the **local** keyword. This command causes the access router to match the username and password specified by the **username** global configuration command against the username and password that the remote site specifies when it logs in. This security method is required to allow the remote sites to log in and specify their IP addresses.

Configuration File Size

As the number of remote sites increases, the size of the configuration file for each central-site access router might increase to a size at which it can no longer be stored in NVRAM. There are two ways to alleviate this problem:

- Compress the configuration file using the **service compress-config** global configuration command.

- Have the central-site access routers boot using configuration files stored on a Trivial File Transfer Protocol (TFTP) server.

Configuring the Remote-Site Routers

With the exception of the host name and the IP address of the Ethernet interface of each remote site router, the configuration of each remote site router is the same. The discussion of the configuration is divided among the following topics:

- Chat script configuration for dialing the central site
- Configuring the asynchronous interface
- Using the **site** command
- Static routing configuration

For the complete configuration, see the section titled "Router2 Configuration" later in this chapter.

Chat Script Configuration for Dialing the Central Site

The configuration of each remote router includes the following **chat-script** global configuration commands:

```
chat-script CENTRALDIAL "" "ATDT 5551111" "CONNECT" "" "name:" "Router2" "word:"
"outthere" ">" "ppp 172.16.2.1"
```

The **chat-script** command defines a chat script named CENTRALDIAL that is used to place calls to the central site. The CENTRALDIAL chat script specifies the telephone number (555-1111) of the central site and the expect-send sequences that guide the modem through the dialup process. A key feature of the chat script is that when the remote router receives the string ">" (the prompt indicating that the remote site router has successfully logged in to a central-site access router), the remote router sends the exec command **ppp 172.16.2.1**, which informs the central-site access router of the remote router's IP address.

Configuring the Asynchronous Interface

The configuration of each remote router includes the following commands that configure the asynchronous interface:

```
interface async 1
speed 38400
modem-type usr-sport-v32
dialer rotary-group 1
!
modem-def usr-sport-v32 "USR Sportster v.32bis" 38400  "" "AT&F1" "OK"
```

The **speed** line configuration command sets the baud rate to 38400 bits per second for both sending and receiving. The **modem-type** command specifies the initialization string sent to the modem when the interface is reset or when a **clear interface async** command is issued. The initialization string is defined by the **modem-def** command for **usr-sport-v32**. The **dialer rotary-group** interface configuration command assigns asynchronous interface 1 to dialer rotary group 1.

Using the site Command

The configuration of each remote router includes the following **site** configuration commands:

```
site CENTRAL
dial-on demand
encapsulation ppp
ip address 172.16.1.1 255.255.255.0
routing rip broadcast
dialgroup 1
session-timeout 5
system-script CENTRALDIAL
password secret
max-ports 1
```

The **site** global configuration command defines a remote location that the router can dial in to or that can dial in to this router, or both, and names it CENTRAL. The name is used to authenticate the central site when it dials in.

The **dial-on** site configuration command uses the **demand** keyword to specify that the central site is to be dialed and a connection established only when packets are queued for the central site. The **encapsulation** site configuration command specifies that when the router establishes a connection with the central site, it is to use PPP encapsulation.

The **ip address** interface configuration command associates IP address 172.16.1.1 with the central site. Note that IP address 172.16.1.1 is the address of the dialer 20 interface on each of the central-site access routers. The **routing rip** interface configuration command and the **broadcast** keyword specify that when the router is connected to the central site, IP routing updates are to be broadcast, but any incoming IP routing updates are to be ignored.

The **dialgroup** command specifies that dial group 1 is to be used when connecting to the central site. Earlier in the configuration, the **dialer rotary-group** command assigned asynchronous interface 1 to group 1.

The **session-timeout** site configuration command specifies that if a period of five minutes elapses during which there is no input or output traffic, the router is to close the connection. The **system-script** site configuration command specifies that the CENTRALDIAL chat script is to be used to dial the central site. The **password** site configuration command specifies that when a central-site access router logs in, its password must be the string "*secret.*"

Static Routing Configuration

The configuration of each remote router includes the following **ip route** global configuration commands:

```
ip route 150.10.0.0 172.16.1.1 1
ip route 172.18.0.0 172.16.1.1 1
ip route 172.19.0.0 172.16.1.1 1
ip route 172.21.0.0 172.16.1.1 1
ip route 172.22.0.0 172.16.1.1 1
```

The **ip route** commands establish static IP routes for networks located at the central site, all reachable through a next-hop address of 172.16.1.1, which is the IP address shared by all the access routers at the central site. All **ip route** commands specify an administrative distance of 1, which is the default.

The Complete Configurations

This section contains the complete configurations for CENTRAL-1 and Router2.

CENTRAL-1 Configuration

The complete configuration for CENTRAL-1 follows. Those portions of the configuration that must be unique to each central-site access router are highlighted in bold.

```
!
version 10.2
service timestamps debug datetime
service timestamps log datetime
service udp-small-servers
service tcp-small-servers
!
hostname CENTRAL-1
!
enable-password as5100
!
username Router2 password 7 071C2D4359
...
username Router121 password 7 0448070918
```

```
!
chat-script CALL1020 ABORT ERROR ABORT BUSY TIMEOUT 30 "" "ATDT\T" "CONNECT" \c
chat-script REM TIMEOUT 40 "name:" "CENTRAL" "word:" "secret"
chat-script USRV32BIS "" "AT&F1S0=1&D2" "OK" ""
!
interface loopback 0
ip address 172.16.254.3 255.255.255.255
!
interface loopback 1
ip address 172.16.1.1 255.255.255.0
!
interface ethernet 0
ip address 172.19.1.8 255.255.0.0
!
interface serial 0
no ip address
shutdown
!
interface async 1
ip unnumbered loopback 1
encapsulation ppp
async dynamic address
async dynamic routing
async mode interactive
dialer in-band
dialer idle-timeout 60
dialer rotary-group 20
...
interface async 16
ip unnumbered loopback 1
encapsulation ppp
async dynamic address
async dynamic routing
async mode interactive
dialer in-band
dialer idle-timeout 60
dialer rotary-group 20
!
interface dialer 20
ip unnumbered loopback 1
encapsulation ppp
dialer in-band
dialer idle-timeout 60
dialer fast-idle 60
dialer map ip 172.16.2.1 name Router2 modem-script CALL1020 system-script REM
5551234
...
dialer map ip 172.16.121.1 name Router121 modem-script CALL1020 system-script REM
5555678
dialer-group 3
!
router ospf 110
redistribute static subnets route-map STATIC-TO-OSPF
redistribute rip subnets route-map RIP-TO-OSPF
passive-interface async 1
...
passive-interface async 16
network 172.19.0.0 0.0.255.255 area 0
distance 210
!
router rip
timers basic 30 35 0 1
network 172.16.0.0
distribute-list 10 out Dialer20
```

```
!
ip default-gateway 172.19.1.10
!
ip route 172.16.0.0 255.255.0.0 Dialer20
ip route 172.16.2.0 255.255.255.0 172.16.2.1 200
ip route 172.16.2.1 255.255.255.255 Dialer20
...
ip route 172.16.121.0 255.255.255.0 172.16.121.1 200
ip route 172.16.121.1 255.255.255.255 Dialer20

access-list 10 deny 0.0.0.0 255.255.255.255
access-list 20 permit 172.16.0.0 0.0.255.0
access-list 21 permit 172.16.0.0
access-list 101 deny udp 0.0.0.0 255.255.255.255 0.0.0.0 255.255.255.255 eq 520
access-list 101 permit ip 0.0.0.0 255.255.255.255 0.0.0.0 255.255.255.255

route-map RIP-TO-OSPF PERMIT
match ip address 20
!
route-map STATIC-TO-OSPF PERMIT
match ip address 21
!
snmp-server community public RO
snmp-server community private RW
dialer-list 3 list 101
!
line con 0
line 1 16
login local
modem inout
script reset USRV32BIS
transport input all
rxspeed 38400
txspeed 38400
flowcontrol hardware
line aux 0
transport input all
line vty 0 4
exec-timeout 20 0
password cisco
login
!
end
```

Router2 Configuration

The complete configuration for Router2 follows. Those portions of the configuration that must be unique to each remote site router are highlighted in bold.

```
version 1.1(2)
!
hostname Router2
!
enable-password cisco-a
!
chat-script CENTRALDIAL "" "ATDT 5551111" "CONNECT" "" "name:" "Router2" "word:"
"outthere" ">" "ppp 172.16.2.1"
!
interface ethernet 0
ip address 172.16.2.1 255.255.255.0
!
```

```
interface async 1
speed 38400
modem-type usr-sport-v32
dialer rotary-group 1
!
site CENTRAL
dial-on demand
encapsulation ppp
ip address 172.16.1.1 255.255.255.0
routing rip broadcast
dialgroup 1
session-timeout 5
system-script CENTRALDIAL
password secret
max-ports 1
!
modem-def usr-sport-v32 "USR Sportster v.32bis" 38400  "" "AT&F1" "OK"
!
ip route 150.10.0.0 172.16.1.1 1
ip route 172.18.0.0 172.16.1.1 1
ip route 172.19.0.0 172.16.1.1 1
ip route 172.21.0.0 172.16.1.1 1
ip route 172.22.0.0 172.16.1.1 1
```

Dial Enterprise Networks

Scalability and design issues must be considered when building dial enterprise networks. As the number of company employees increases, the number of remote users needing to dial in increases. A scalable dial solution is needed as the demand for dial-in ports grows. For a fast-growing enterprise to grow from a demand of 50 modems to 200 modems in less than one year is very common. Always keep a number of dial-in ports in storage to accommodate company growth and occasional increases in access demand. In the early stages of a fast-growing company that has 50 modems installed for 3,000 registered remote users, only 20 to 30 modems might be active at any given time. One year later, however, 200 modems might be installed to support 8,000 registered token cardholders.

Always keep in mind that during special company occasions, demand for remote access can also increase significantly. During such situations, dial-in lines are heavily stressed throughout the day and evening by remote users using laptops to access e-mail and share files. This behavior is indicative of remote users working away from their home areas. Network administrators need to prepare for these remote access bursts, which cause significant increases for remote-access demand. Also, at certain times of the day you might see that the dial-in lines are stressed out depending on the nature of the business. Users in remote offices or other locations often dial in to central sites to download or upload files and check e-mail. These users often dial in to the corporate network from a remote-office LAN using ISDN or from another location, such as a hotel room, using a modem.

Several different types of remote enterprise users dial in to enterprise networks:

- Remote users using workstations to dial in from a small remote office or a home office, making ISDN connections with terminal adapters or PC Cards through the public telephone network, which rules out the need for a modem.

- Remote users such as sales people who are not in a steady location, usually dial in to the network with a laptop and modem through the public telephone network, and primarily access the network to check e-mail or transfer a few files.

- Users who primarily work in the company office, occasionally dial in to the enterprise network with a mobile or stationary workstation and modem, and primarily access the network to check e-mail or transfer a few files.

Remote-office LANs typically dial in to other networks using ISDN, which provides a larger bandwidth that cannot be attained over analog telephone connections. Remote offices that use Frame Relay to access other networks require a dedicated link. In certain scenarios, connections initiated by remote offices or mobile users are brought up on an as-needed basis, which results in cost savings for the company. In dial-on-demand scenarios, users are not connected for long periods of time. The number of remote nodes requiring access is relatively low, and the completion time for the dial-in task is short. When using dial-on-demand routing for IP-only configurations, static routes are commonly used for remote dial-in. For IPX networking, snapshot routing is often used to minimize configuration complexity.

Central sites typically do not dial out to the remote LANs or remote mobile users. Instead, remote LANs or remote mobile users dial in to the central site and it is a one-way communication. A field office might use ISDN to dial in to a central site's intranet. Also, for example, a remote LAN in a warehouse comprised of five employees might use ISDN to log in to a remote network server to download or upload information. In very rare cases, the central-site access server is required to dial out to a remote site while receiving incoming calls when the central-site Cisco AS5300 initiates a connection with a Cisco 1604 at remote office. After a connection is established, the remote site's file runs a batch-processing application with the central-site mainframe. While files are being transferred between remote site X and the central site, remote site Y is successfully dialing in to the central site. Dial-out analog and digital calls are commonly made to remote ISDN routers, such as the Cisco 1604. The dial-out calls are not made from a central-site router to a remote PC, but rather from a remote PC in to the central site. In some cases, central sites call remote sites on demand to deliver e-mail. Callback is enabled on dial-in scenarios only. Always keep in mind that MMP and VPDN are dial-in–only solutions.

Dial ISP Networks

Scalability and design issues must also be considered when building dial ISP networks. As the number of ISP customers increases, the number of remote users needing to dial in increases. A scalable dial solution is needed as the demand for dial-in ports grows. You must consider scalability and call-density issues when designing a large-scale dial-in point of presence (POP). Because access servers have physical limitations, such as how many dial-in users can be supported on one device, you should consider the conditions and recommendations of different access servers. Many small- and medium-size ISPs configure one or two access servers to provide dial-in access for their customers. Many of these dial-in customers use individual remote PCs that are not connected to LANs. Using the Windows 95 dialup software, remote clients initiate analog or digital connections using modems or home-office ISDN BRI terminal adapters.

There are three types of single-user dial-in scenarios for service providers:

- ISPs can configure a single Cisco access server such as AS52/53/5800 to receive analog calls at the POP from remote PCs connected to the modems. For smaller solutions, the point of presence at the ISP central site could also be a Cisco 2511 access server connected to external modems. In this scenario the remote client PCs dial in with analog modems over traditional T1 lines. ISDN calls do not transmit across these older types of channelized lines. The configuration assumes that the client can dial in and connect to the router in either terminal emulation mode (text only) or PPP packet mode.

- ISPs can configure a single Cisco access server such as AS52/53/5800 to receive digital multilink calls from remote PCs connected to terminal adapters. The point of presence at the ISP's central site can be any Cisco router that supports ISDN PRI, such as the Cisco 4700-M loaded with a channelized T1 PRI network module.

- ISPs can also configure a single Cisco access server such as AS52/53/5800 to receive calls from a mixture of remote PCs connected to terminal adapters and modems. Because the Internet has grown exponentially and there is a significant increase in demand for Internet access, large points of presence are required by many telcos and ISPs. Internet access configurations can be set up to enable users dialing in with individual computers to make mixed ISDN multilink or modem connections using a stack of universal access servers running MultiChassis MultiLink PPP (MMP). The incoming ISDN calls carry information about whether they are data or voice, using the bearer capability information element in the call setup packet. After the call enters the access server, it is routed either to the serial configuration or to the modems and group asynchronous configuration.

Summary

This case study shows that it is possible to scale dial-on-demand routing to accommodate large dialup networks. If, in the future, the number of remote sites exceeds the capacity of the 48 asynchronous interfaces, additional routers can be installed without modifying the routing strategy. Although this case study focuses on asynchronous media, many of the techniques can be applied to other dialup technologies, such as ISDN. This chapter also discusses the design aspects of enterprise and ISP dial networks.

CHAPTER 21

Using ISDN Effectively in Multiprotocol Networks

Edited by Salman Asad

As telephone companies make Integrated Services Digital Network (ISDN) services available, ISDN is becoming an increasingly popular way to connect remote sites. This case study covers the following ISDN scenarios:

- **Configuring DDR over ISDN**—This telecommuting scenario describes the configuration of home sites that use ISDN to connect to a central company network and shows you how to use calling line identification numbers to prevent unauthorized access to the central network.

- **Configuring Snapshot Routing over ISDN**—Snapshot routing provides cost-effective access to a central company network from branch or home offices. Snapshot routing is used to upgrade the telecommuting network and control routing updates in Novell IPX networks.

- **Configuring AppleTalk over ISDN**—This scenario shows you how to control AppleTalk packets that might otherwise trigger unnecessary ISDN connections.

- **Configuring IPX over ISDN**—This scenario shows you how to configure IPX as a Layer 3 protocol for ISDN.

Configuring DDR over ISDN

In the United States, many companies today regard telecommuting as a way to solve space problems, conform to the Clean Air Act, and make employees more productive. In Europe, companies are looking for solutions that allow central offices to connect to remote sites. In the past, analog modems provided the necessary connectivity over serial lines, but they are not fast enough for LAN-to-LAN connections or for remote use of graphics programs, such as computer-aided design (CAD) tools. ISDN provides the needed additional bandwidth without requiring a leased line.

An ISDN Basic Rate Interface (BRI) provides two 64-kbps B channels for voice or data, and one 16-kbps D channel for signaling. Voice and data information is carried over the B channels digitally. In the United States, an ISDN Primary Rate Interface (PRI) provides 23 64-kbps B channels for voice and data over a T1 connection, and one 64-kbps D channel for signaling. In Europe, a PRI provides 30 B channels for voice and data, and one D channel for signaling over an E1 connection.

Figure 21-1 shows the network that will be discussed in this case study. The ISDN network uses multiple central-office ISDN switches.

Figure 21-1 *ISDN Network Example*

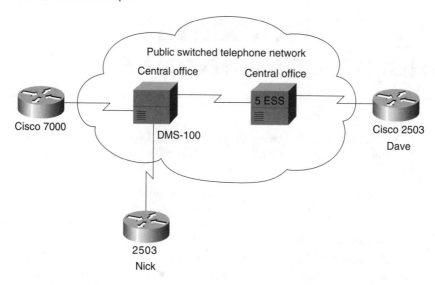

In this case study, the remote sites (homes) use Cisco 2503 routers, which provide one BRI, an Ethernet interface, and two high-speed serial interfaces. At the central company site, a Cisco 7000 series router equipped with a channelized T1 card answers the calls. The channelized T1 card provides a PRI.

Currently, in many parts of the United States, telephone companies have not deployed Signaling System 7, which means that calls between certain central offices must be placed at 56 kbps. This restriction does not apply to all parts of the United States or to other countries, but it does apply to some of the sample ISDN networks described in this chapter.

Native ISDN Interfaces

If you are using an external ISDN terminal adapter, also known as an ISDN modem, you can use the configuration examples provided in Chapter 19, "Dial-on-Demand Routing." Although an ISDN modem provides ISDN connectivity and enables you to use existing serial interfaces, it is not always the optimal solution because of the investment in an external unit and in additional cabling. Also, using V.25bis does not give the router full access to certain information available in an ISDN network, such as the speed of the call or the number of the calling party.

The native ISDN interface on the Cisco 2503 router allows the router to be directly connected to an ISDN NT1 device. In many countries, the NT1 is provided by the telephone company. In the United States, however, the NT1 is customer-owned equipment. By directly connecting to the ISDN network, the router has more direct control over ISDN parameters and has access to ISDN information.

Configuring an ISDN Interface

Configuring a native ISDN interface is similar to configuring a serial interface using DDR routing, as described in Chapter 19. There are, however, two major differences:

- The **dialer in-band** command is not required with ISDN. PRI and BRI interfaces are assumed by the router to be a DDR interface.

- The individual B channels cannot be configured separately, unless you are using the dialer profile feature of the Cisco IOS. The B channels of a BRI appear to be a dialer rotary group with two members. In the United States, the B channels of a PRI appear to be a dialer rotary group with 23 members, and in Europe, the B channels of a PRI appear to be a dialer rotary group with 30 members. Because the PRI or BRI is a dialer rotary group, all configuration commands associated with a PRI or BRI apply to all B channels.

The following sections describe the configurations of the central-site and home-site routers. In this case study, both the central site and the home sites can place calls. The central site uses a Cisco 7000 router that connects to a NorTel DMS-100 central-office ISDN switch. One remote-site router (nick-isdn) connects to the same central-office switch that the central-site router uses. Connections from the other remote-site router (dave-isdn) pass through two central-office switches to reach the central-site router.

Central Site

Two remote-site users, Dave and Nick, dial from their homes in to the central-site router that is configured as follows. Part of the configuration of the central-site router is specific to the DMS-100 switch, whereas other commands apply to any type of ISDN central-office switch.

```
hostname central-isdn
!
username dave-isdn password 7 130318111D
username nick-isdn password 7 08274D02A02
isdn switch-type primary-dms100
!
interface ethernet 0
ip address 11.108.40.53 255.255.255.0
no mop enabled
!
controller t1 1/0
framing esf
linecode b8zs
pri-group timeslots 2-6
!
interface serial 1/0:23
ip address 11.108.90.53 255.255.255.0
encapsulation ppp
```

```
dialer idle-timeout 300
dialer map ip 11.108.90.1 name dave-isdn speed 56 914085553680
dialer map ip 11.108.90.7 name nick-isdn 8376
dialer-group 1
ppp authentication chap
!
router igrp 10
network 11.108.0.0
redistribute static
!
! route to nick-isdn
ip route 11.108.137.0 255.255.255.0 11.108.90.7
! route to dave-isdn
ip route 11.108.147.0 255.255.255.0 11.108.90.1
!
!NTP
access-list 101 deny udp 0.0.0.0 255.255.255.255 0.0.0.0 255.255.255.255 eq 123
!SNMP
access-list 101 deny udp 0.0.0.0 255.255.255.255 0.0.0.0 255.255.255.255 eq 161
access-list 101 permit ip 0.0.0.0 255.255.255.255 0.0.0.0 255.255.255.255
!
dialer-list 1 list 101
```

The configuration begins by establishing the host name of the router. The **username** commands establish the names of the routers allowed to dial up this router. The names correspond to the host names of Dave's router and Nick's router. The **isdn switch-type** command specifies that the central-site router connects to a NorTel DMS-100 switch. The host name, usernames, and ISDN switch type vary from router to router.

Controller Configuration

The **controller** command uses **t1** to specify a T1 controller interface. The "1" indicates that the controller card is located in backplane slot number 1. The "0" indicates port 0.

The **framing** command selects the frame type for the T1 data line. In this case, the **framing** command uses the **esf** keyword to indicate the extended super frame (ESF) frame type. The service provider determines which framing type, either sf, esf, or crc4, is required for your T1/E1 circuit.

The **linecode** command defines the line-code type for the T1 data line. In this case, the **linecode** command uses the **b8zs** keyword to indicate that the line-code type is bipolar 8 zero substitution (B8ZS). The service provider determines which line-code type, either alternate mark inversion (AMI) or B8ZS, is required for your T1/E1 circuit.

The **pri-group** controller configuration command specifies an ISDN PRI on a channelized T1 card in a Cisco 7000 series router. The **timeslots** keyword establishes the B channels. In this example, only five B channels (channels 2 through 6) are in use on this controller.

Interface Configuration

The **ip address** command establishes the IP address of the interface, and the **encapsulation ppp** command establishes the Point-to-Point Protocol (PPP) as the encapsulation method. PPP supports Challenge Handshake Authentication Protocol (CHAP) and Password Authentication Protocol (PAP) as authentication mechanisms for identifying the caller and providing a level of security. The **dialer idle-timeout** command sets the idle timeout to five minutes.

The **dialer map** commands establish the remote sites that the router can call. Because Dave's router connects to a central-office switch that does not use Signaling System 7, the **dialer map** command for calling Dave's router uses the **speed** keyword, which is valid for native ISDN interfaces only. The native ISDN interface on the Cisco 2503 operates at either 64 or 56 kbps. If the calling party and the called party use the same ISDN switch, they can communicate at 64 kbps. Otherwise, they must communicate at 56 kbps.

Because Nick's ISDN line connects to the same central office as the line that the central-site router uses, the telephone number in the **dialer map** command for connecting to Nick's router does not have to include the three-digit prefix. Note that because the central-site router uses lines that are part of a Centrex, the outgoing telephone numbers start with 9 if they are not four-digit numbers.

The **dialer-group** command associates the BRI with dialer access group 1. The **ppp authentication chap** command enables CHAP authentication.

Routing Configuration

In the routing section of the configuration, the **router igrp** command enables the Interior Gateway Routing Protocol (IGRP) and sets the autonomous system number to 10. The **network** command assigns the network number. The **redistribute** command sends the static route information (defined with the **ip route** commands) to other routers in the same IGRP area. Without this command, other routers connected to the central site would not have routes to the remote routers.

DDR tends to use static routes extensively because routing updates are not received when the dialup connection is not active. The first two **ip route** commands create the static routes that define the subnets that Dave and Nick use.

NOTE   The IGRP commands are the same on all central-site routers, except that the static routes correspond to the home sites calling in to each central-site router.

Access List Configuration

DDR uses access lists to determine whether a packet is *interesting* or *uninteresting*. Interesting packets cause a call to be placed if a call is not active, or cause a call that has already been placed to be maintained as active. The first extended **access-list** command states that IGRP updates are uninteresting. The second extended **access-list** command states that Network Time Protocol (NTP) packets are uninteresting. The third extended **access-list** command specifies that Simple Network Management Protocol (SNMP) packets are uninteresting, and the final extended **access-list** command states that all other IP packets are interesting. The **dialer-list** command assigns the set of access lists to dialer access group 1.

Home Site

The configurations of the home-site routers are similar, but Nick's configuration is simpler because his router connects to the same central-office switch as the central-site router.

Nick

The configuration for the router at Nick's home is as follows:

```
hostname nick-isdn
!
username central-isdn password 7 050D130C2A5
isdn switch-type basic-dms100
!
interface ethernet 0
ip address 11.108.137.1 255.255.255.0
no mop enabled
!
interface bri 0
ip address 11.108.90.7 255.255.255.0
encapsulation ppp
no ip route-cache
isdn spid1 415555837601 5558376
isdn spid2 415555837802 5558378
dialer idle-timeout 300
dialer map ip 11.108.90.53 name central-isdn 8362
dialer map ip 11.108.90.53 name central-isdn 8370
dialer-group 1
ppp authentication chap
!
ip route 11.108.0.0 255.255.0.0 11.108.90.53
!
access-list 101 deny udp 0.0.0.0 255.255.255.255 0.0.0.0 255.255.255.255 eq 177
access-list 101 permit ip 0.0.0.0 255.255.255.255 0.0.0.0 255.255.255.255
!
dialer-list 1 list 101
```

As with the central-site router, the **isdn switch-type** command specifies that the switch is an NT DMS-100 switch. Because Nick's router connects to the DMS-100, service profile identifiers (SPIDs) are required for the BRI. PPP and CHAP are configured, along with a **username** command for the central-site router. The configuration for Nick's router differs from that of the central site with regard to the **dialer map** commands and the routing section. Two **dialer map** commands point to the same next-hop address. If the attempt to call the first number fails, the second number will be used to connect to the next-hop address.

The **isdn spid1** and **isdn spid2** commands represent SPIDs. SPIDs are used when a BRI connects to a NorTel DMS-100 switch or to a National ISDN-1 switch. SPIDs are assigned by the service provider to associate a SPID number with a telephone number. Other switch types do not require SPIDs. Your service provider can tell you whether SPIDs are required for your switch. In this example, SPID 1 identifies 415 as the area code, 555 as the exchange, 8376 as the station ID, and 01 as the terminal identifier. The SPID format required by your service provider may differ from the examples shown in this case study.

Dave

The configuration for Dave's router is similar to the configuration for Nick's router, except that Dave's router is not in the same Centrex as the central company site. The configuration for Dave's router is as follows:

```
hostname dave-isdn
!
username central-isdn password 7 08274341
isdn switch-type basic-5ess
!
interface ethernet 0
ip address 11.108.147.1 255.255.255.0
no mop enabled
!
interface bri 0
ip address 11.108.90.1 255.255.255.0
encapsulation ppp
no ip route-cache
bandwidth 56
dialer map ip 11.108.90.53 name central-isdn speed 56 14155558370
dialer-group 1
ppp authentication chap
!
ip route 11.108.0.0 255.255.0.0 11.108.90.53
!
dialer-list 1 list 101
```

Dave's configuration is different from Nick's configuration because Dave's router connects to an AT&T 5ESS central-office ISDN switch that does not run Signaling System 7. The **isdn switch-type** command specifies a basic rate AT&T switch, which does not require Dave's router configuration to use the **isdn spid1** and **isdn spid2** commands that the DMS-100 switch requires. The **bandwidth** interface configuration command tells routing protocols that the line operates at 56 kbps. The **dialer map** command uses the **speed** keyword so that when Dave's router dials up the central-site router, it sets the line speed to 56 kbps. This setting is necessary when the connection traverses a switch that does not run Signaling System 7.

Configuring Calling Line Identification Numbers

Because Nick is in the same Centrex as the central company routers, the central router can use the calling line identification (CLID) number received from the ISDN switch to identify Nick. With CLID, the configuration for Nick does not require CHAP or PAP; however, Nick needs to modify his configuration to include CLID. Nick's new configuration and a sample of the central-site changed configuration are shown in the following sections.

NOTE   CLID is not available in all parts of the United States and other countries. Some countries do not require Centrex for CLID.

Central Site

Here is the central-site PRI interface configuration modified for CLID:

```
controller t1 1/0
framing esf
linecode b8zs
pri-group timeslots 2-6
!
interface serial 1/0:23
ip address 11.108.90.53 255.255.255.0
dialer idle-timeout 300
dialer map ip 11.108.90.7 name 5558376 8376
dialer-group 1
```

The **name** keyword in the **dialer map** command specifies the actual string that calling line identification returns. This string differs from the number called: The number called is a four-digit Centrex number, and the number returned is the full seven digits.

Home Site

As with the central site, the major difference in Nick's configuration is the use of the **name** keyword with the **dialer map** command that specifies the actual number being returned as the calling line number.

```
interface bri 0
ip address 11.108.90.7 255.255.255.0
no ip route-cache
isdn spid1 415555837601 5558376
isdn spid2 415555837802 5558378
dialer idle-timeout 300
dialer map ip 11.108.90.53 name 5558362 8362
dialer map ip 11.108.90.53 name 5558370 8370
dialer-group 1
```

NOTE	If the **debug isdn-q931** EXEC command is enabled, the decode for an incoming call setup can be seen and the CLID number will be shown.

Configuring Callback

Because Dave is located several miles from the central office, calls to the central-office router are metered and billed to Dave's telephone number. The callback feature (introduced in Cisco IOS 11.0) allows Dave's router to place a call to the central-site router, requesting that the central-site router call Dave's router. Then, the central-site router disconnects the call and places a return call to Dave's router. With callback configured, Dave's telephone bill is reduced because actual data transfers occur when the central-office router calls back. The following commands configure callback on Dave's router:

```
interface bri 0
ppp callback request
dialer hold-queue 100 timeout 20
```

The **ppp callback** command with the **request** keyword specifies that when the interface places a call, it is to request callback. The **dialer hold-queue** interface configuration command specifies that up to 100 packets can be held in a queue until the central-site router returns the call. If the central-site router does not return the call within 20 seconds plus the length of the enable timeout configured on the central-site router, the packets are dropped. The following commands configure callback on the central office router:

```
map-class dialer class1
dialer callback-server username
interface serial 1/0:23
dialer map ip 11.108.90.1 name dave-isdn speed 56 class class1 914085553680
ppp callback accept
dialer callback-secure
dialer enable-timeout 1
dialer hold-queue
```

The **map-class** command establishes a quality of service (QoS) parameter to be associated with a static map. The **dialer** keyword specifies that the map is a dialer map. The **class1** parameter is a user-defined value that creates a map class to which subsequent encapsulation-specific commands apply.

The **dialer map** interface configuration command has been modified to include the **class** keyword and the name of the class, as specified in the **map-class** command. The **name** keyword is required so that, when Dave's router dials in, the interface can locate this dialer map statement and obtain the dial string for calling back Dave's router.

The **ppp callback** command with the **accept** keyword allows the interface to accept and honor callback requests that come into the interface. (Callback depends on PPP authentication, using PAP or CHAP.)

The **dialer callback-server** command allows the interface to return calls when callback is successfully negotiated. The **username** keyword specifies that the interface is to locate the dial string for making the return call by looking up the authenticated host name in a **dialer map** command.

The **dialer callback-secure** command specifies that the router is to disconnect the initial call, and to call back only if it has a **dialer map** command with a defined class for the remote router. If the **dialer callback-secure** command is not present, the central router will not drop the connection if it does not have a **dialer map** command with a defined class. The **dialer enable-timeout** interface configuration command specifies that the interface is to wait one second after disconnecting the initial call before making the return call.

Configuring Snapshot Routing over ISDN

Snapshot routing is an easy way to reduce connection time in ISDN networks by suppressing the transfer of routing updates for a configurable period of time. Snapshot routing is best suited for networks whose data-transfer connections typically last longer than five minutes and that are running the following distance vector protocols:

- Routing Information Protocol (RIP) and Integrated Gateway Routing Protocol (IGRP) for IP
- Routing Table Maintenance Protocol (RTMP) for AppleTalk
- Routing Information Protocol (RIP) and Service Advertisement Protocol (SAP) for Novell Internet Packet Exchange (IPX)
- Routing Table Protocol (RTP) for Banyan VINES

The goal of snapshot routing is to allow routing protocols to exchange updates as they normally would. Because Enhanced IGRP and link-state routing protocols, such as Novell Link Services Protocol (NLSP), Open Shortest Path First (OSPF), and Intermediate System-to-Intermediate System (IS-IS) depend on the frequent sending of hello messages to neighboring routers to discover and maintain routes, they are incompatible with snapshot routing.

NOTE   This case study applies snapshot routing to an ISDN network; other similar media, however, such as dedicated leased lines, can benefit from the reduction of periodic updates that snapshot routing provides.

Before snapshot routing became available in Cisco Internetwork Operating System (IOS) Software Release 10.2, ISDN interfaces were configured using static routes. Static routes, such as the routes defined by the **ip route** commands in the "Central Site" section earlier in this chapter, prevent bandwidth from being consumed by routing updates, but they are difficult to maintain as the network grows.

Snapshot routing supports dynamic routes by allowing routing updates to occur during an active period and reduces connection cost by suppressing routing updates during a quiet period, which can be up to 65 days long. During the quiet period, the routing tables on the routers at both ends of a link are frozen. Figure 21-2 shows the relationship of active and quiet periods over time.

Figure 21-2 *Active Periods and Frozen Periods Over Time*

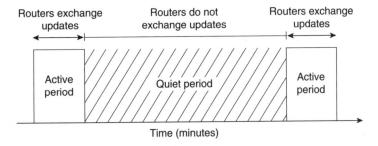

During the active period, the routers at each end of the connection exchange the routing updates that are normal for their configured routing protocols. They continue to exchange routing updates until the active period ends. When the active period ends, each router freezes its routing tables, stops sending routing updates, and enters the quiet period. Each router remains in the quiet period until a configurable timer expires, at which time one of the routers initiates a connection to send and receive routing updates.

To ensure that routing tables are updated, the active period must be long enough for several routing updates to come through the link. An active period that is too short might allow only one routing update to cross the link. If that update is lost due to noise on the line, the router on the other end would age out a valid route or would not learn about a new valid route. To make sure that updates occur, the active period must be at least five minutes long (that is, three times longer than the routing protocols' update intervals). Because the routing protocols update their routing tables during the active period as they normally would, there is no need to adjust any routing protocol timers.

If the line is not available when the router transitions from the quiet period to the active period, it enters a retry period. During the retry period, the router continually attempts to connect until it enters an active period, as shown in Figure 21-3.

Figure 21-3   *The Router Continually Attempts to Connect During the Retry Period*

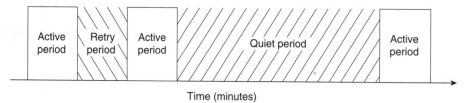

Table 21-1 shows the minimum and maximum lengths of each period.

Table 21-1   *Snapshot Routing Periods*

Period	Configurable	Minimum Length	Maximum Length
Active	Yes	5 minutes	100 minutes
Quiet	Yes	5 minutes	65 days
Retry	No	8 minutes	8 minutes

By default, snapshot routing allows routing updates to be exchanged over connections established to transfer user data. This means that, if necessary, snapshot routing forces the connection to last as long as the active period. If you do not want the routers to exchange updates during connections established to transfer user data, use the **suppress-statechange-updates** keyword.

Upgrading the Telecommuting Network

Snapshot routing is well suited to the hub-and-spoke topology of the telecommuting network described in the "Configuring DDR over ISDN" section at the beginning of this chapter. Snapshot routing is designed for a client/server relationship. The client routers, such as the home sites, determine the frequency at which the routers exchange updates by setting the length of the quiet period, and the server router accepts incoming snapshot connections from several client routers.

NOTE   Snapshot routing is not recommended for meshed topologies. In meshed topologies, configuring static routes is more efficient than configuring snapshot routing.

Central Site Modified for Snapshot Routing

The following is the configuration of the central-site router after modification for snapshot routing:

```
hostname central-isdn
!
username dave-isdn password 7 130318111D
username nick-isdn password 7 08274D02A02
isdn switch-type primary-dms100
!
interface ethernet 0
ip address 11.108.40.53 255.255.255.0
no mop enabled
!
controller t1 1/0
framing esf
linecode b8zs
pri-group timeslots 2-6
ip address 11.108.90.53 255.255.255.0
encapsulation ppp
dialer idle-timeout 300
dialer map ip 11.108.90.1 name dave-isdn speed 56 914085553680
dialer map ip 11.108.90.7 name nick-isdn 8376
dialer-group 1
isdn spid1 415555836201 5558362
isdn spid2 415555837002 5558370
snapshot server 5
ppp authentication chap
!
router igrp 10
network 11.108.0.0
redistribute static
!
! route to nick-isdn
ip route 11.108.137.0 255.255.255.0 11.108.90.7
! route to dave-isdn
ip route 11.108.147.0 255.255.255.0 11.108.90.1
!
access-list 101 deny igrp 0.0.0.0 255.255.255.255 0.0.0.0 255.255.255.255
!NTP
access-list 101 deny udp 0.0.0.0 255.255.255.255 0.0.0.0 255.255.255.255 eq 123
!SNMP
access-list 101 deny udp 0.0.0.0 255.255.255.255 0.0.0.0 255.255.255.255 eq 161
access-list 101 permit ip 0.0.0.0 255.255.255.255 0.0.0.0 255.255.255.255
!
dialer-list 1 list 101
```

The **ip route** commands that configured static routes for the home sites have been removed
from the configuration. The **snapshot server** command enables snapshot routing. The "5"
sets the length of the active period to five minutes.

NOTE   Snapshot routing must be configured on rotary interfaces, which are established by the
dialer rotary-group command. ISDN interfaces are rotary interfaces by definition, so you
do not need to use the **dialer rotary-group** command in ISDN configurations.

Home Site Modified for Snapshot Routing

The following is the configuration of Dave's home-site router after modification for
snapshot routing:

```
hostname dave-isdn
!
username central-isdn password 7 08274341
isdn switch-type basic-5ess
!
interface ethernet 0
ip address 11.108.147.1 255.255.255.0
no mop enabled
!
interface bri 0
ip address 11.108.90.1 255.255.255.0
encapsulation ppp
no ip route-cache
bandwidth 56
dialer map snapshot 1 name central-isdn 14155558370
dialer map ip 11.108.90.53 name central-isdn speed 56 14155558370
dialer-group 1
snapshot client 5 43200 suppress-statechange-updates dialer
ppp authentication chap
!
dialer-list 1 list 101
```

The **ip route** commands that configured static routes for the home sites have been removed from the configuration. The **dialer map snapshot** command establishes a map (whose sequence number is 1) that the router uses to connect to the central-site router for the exchange of routing updates. The **name** keyword specifies the name of the remote router associated with the dial string. Because the **ppp authentication** interface configuration command enables CHAP authentication, when this router dials the central router, it receives the host name of the central router and compares it with the name specified by the **name** keyword.

The **snapshot client** command sets the length of the active period to five minutes (a value that must match the value set in the snapshot server's configuration) and sets the length of the quiet period to 43,200 seconds (12 hours). The **suppress-statechange-updates** keyword prevents the routers from exchanging updates during connections established to transfer user data. The **dialer** keyword allows the client router to dial up the server router in the absence of regular traffic, and is required when you use the **suppress-statechange-update** keyword.

Snapshot and Novell IPX Networks

This section describes a Novell IPX network for which snapshot routing has been configured. Client routers at branch offices use DDR to connect to a central router over ISDN. At the central office, NetWare servers use the Novell IPX protocol to provide services to NetWare clients on each branch office network. Some client-to-server connections are required during a limited period of the day. Figure 21-4 illustrates the network.

Figure 21-4   *Topology of the Novell IPX Network*

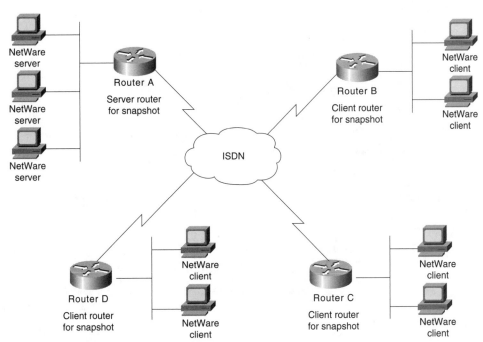

In this topology, the client routers are responsible for updating their routing tables by connecting to the server router when the quiet period expires. The client routers also retrieve update information if a reload occurs.

NOTE   Snapshot routing works with Novell 3.x and 4.x networks. However, Novell 4.x includes a time-synchronization protocol that causes Novell 4.x time servers to send an update every 10 minutes. To prevent the time server from generating update packets that would cause unwanted connections, you should load a NetWare Loadable Module (NLM) named TIMESYNC.NLM, which enables you to increase the update interval for these packets to several days. A similar problem is caused by Novell's efforts to synchronize NDS replicas. NetWare 4.1 includes two NLMs, DSFILTER.NLM and PINGFILT.NLM, which work together to control NDS synchronization updates. You should use these two modules to make sure that NDS synchronization traffic is sent to specified servers only at the specified times.

Server Router Configuration

The following is the complete configuration for the server router:

```
hostname RouterA
!
username RouterB password 7 120D0A031D
username RouterC password 7 111D161118
username RouterD password 7 43E7528384
isdn switch-type vn3
!
ipx routing

interface Ethernet 0
ip address 192.104.155.99 255.255.255.0
ipx network 300
!
interface bri 0
ip address 1.0.0.1 255.0.0.0
encapsulation ppp
ipx network 10
no ipx route-cache
ipx update-time 20
ipx watchdog-spoof
dialer idle-timeout 60
dialer wait-for-carrier-time 12
dialer map ipx 10.0000.0000.0002 name RouterB broadcast 041389082
dialer map ipx 10.0000.0000.0003 name RouterC broadcast 041389081
dialer map ipx 10.0000.0000.0004 name RouterD broadcast 041389083
!
dialer-group 1
snapshot server 10
ppp authentication chap
!
access-list 901 deny 0 FFFFFFF 0 FFFFFFFF 457
access-list 901 deny 1 10.0000.0000.0001 0 10.ffff.ffff.ffff 453
access-list 901 deny 4 10.0000.0000.0001 0 10.ffff.ffff.ffff 452
access-list 901 deny 4 FFFFFFF 0 FFFFFFFF 456
access-list 901 permit -1
!
dialer-list 1 list 901
```

The configuration begins with the host name used for CHAP authentication. The usernames correspond to the host names of Router B, Router C, and Router D. The **isdn switch-type** command specifies that the router connects to a French VN3 ISDN BRI switch.

Interface Configuration

The **dialer idle-timeout** command specifies 60 seconds as the amount of idle time that must elapse before the router disconnects the line. The **dialer wait-for-carrier-time** command sets the wait-for-carrier time to 60 seconds.

The first **dialer map** command sets the next-hop address of Router B to 10.0000.0000.0002. When Router B dials up the server router (Router A), the server router uses the next-hop address to transmit packets to Router B. The **broadcast** keyword sets 041389082 as the address to which IPX broadcasts are to be forwarded. The second and third **dialer map** commands set similar values for Router C and Router D.

The **snapshot server** command sets the length of the active period to 10 minutes. The **ppp authentication** command sets CHAP as the authentication protocol.

Access List Configuration

Access lists are used to determine whether an outgoing packet is interesting or uninteresting. Uninteresting packets are dropped, and interesting packets cause a call to be placed if a call is not active, or cause a call that has already been placed to be maintained as active. The access lists defined by this configuration are extended Novell IPX access lists. The first **access-list** command defines any packets intended for the Novell serialization socket as uninteresting. The second **access-list** command defines RIP packets as uninteresting. The third **access-list** command defines SAP packets as uninteresting. The fourth **access-list** command defines Novell diagnostic packets generated by the Autodiscovery feature as uninteresting, and the final **access-list** command states that all other packets are interesting. The **dialer-list** global configuration command assigns access list 901 to dialer access group 1, which is associated with BRI 0 by the **dialer-group** interface configuration command.

Client Router Configuration

The configurations for the client routers are the same except for the commands that configure the router's host name, the username that it uses when it dials up Router A, and the router's network numbers. The following is the configuration for Router B:

```
hostname RouterB
!
username RouterA password 7 105A060D0A
ipx routing
isdn switch-type vn3
isdn tei first-call
!
interface ethernet 0
ip address 192.104.155.100 255.255.255.0
ipx network 301
!
interface bri 0
no ip address
encapsulation ppp
ipx network 10
no ipx route-cache
ipx update-time 20
ipx watchdog-spoof
dialer idle-timeout 60
dialer wait-for-carrier-time 12
dialer map snapshot 1 name RouterA 46148412
dialer map ipx 10.0000.0000.0001 name RouterA broadcast 46148412
dialer-group 1
snapshot client 10 86400 dialer
ppp authentication chap
!
access-list 901 deny 0 FFFFFFFF 0 FFFFFFFF 457
access-list 901 deny 1 10.0000.0000.0002 0 10.ffff.ffff.ffff 453
```

```
access-list 901 deny 4 10.0000.0000.0002 0 10.ffff.ffff.ffff 452
access-list 901 deny 4 FFFFFFFF 0 FFFFFFFF 456
access-list 901 permit 0
!
dialer-list 1 list 901
```

The configuration begins with the host name used for CHAP authentication. The usernames correspond to the host names of Router B, Router C, and Router D. The **isdn switch-type** command specifies that the router connects to a French VN3 ISDN BRI switch.

The **isdn tei** global configuration command uses the **first-call** keyword to specify that ISDN terminal *endpoint identifier* (TEI) negotiation is to occur when Router A places or receives its first ISDN call. (The default is for TEI negotiation to occur when the router is powered on.)

Interface Configuration

The **dialer wait-for-carrier** interface configuration command specifies 12 seconds as the number of seconds that the interface will wait for the carrier to come up when it places a call.

The **snapshot client** interface configuration command sets the length of the active period to 10 minutes (a value that must match the value set in the snapshot server's configuration), and sets the length of the quiet period to 86,400 seconds (24 hours). Because the **suppress-statechange-updates** keyword is not used, the routers can exchange updates during connections established to transfer user data. The **dialer** keyword allows the client router to dial up the server router in the absence of regular traffic.

Configuring AppleTalk over ISDN

To run AppleTalk over an ISDN network effectively, you need to prevent Name Binding Protocol (NBP) packets and RTMP updates from triggering unnecessary connections over ISDN connections.

Figure 21-5 shows a sample AppleTalk network that uses ISDN to connect two networks located in different cities. Users on the district-office network occasionally need access to servers located on the main-office network and vice versa. In this scenario, both routers dial up each other when user data from one part of the network needs to reach the other part of the network.

Figure 21-5 *An AppleTalk Network over ISDN*

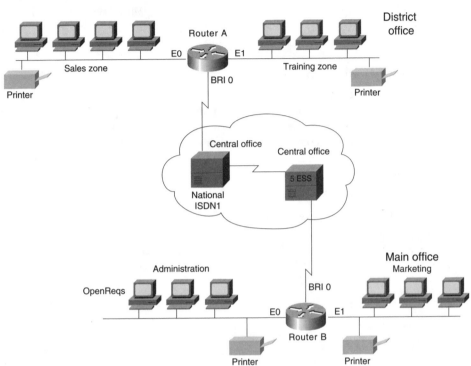

Users of hosts connected to the main-office network do not need to access the Training zone, so when configuring Router A, one goal is to prevent NBP packets generated by the Training zone from triggering an ISDN connection with the main-office network. Another configuration goal for both routers is to prevent NBP packets generated by the printers on each network from triggering an ISDN connection.

To control the forwarding of NBP packets, use AppleTalk-style access lists. AppleTalk-style access lists enable you to control the flow of NBP packets based on the type of the entity that originated the packet, the name of the entity that originated the packet, and the zone of the entity that originated the packet.

NOTE	The capability to control the forwarding of NBP packets was introduced in Cisco IOS Software Release 11.0.

Both routers also need to control RTMP packets. To control RTMP packets, configure static AppleTalk cable ranges and node numbers, and use the **no appletalk send rtmps** command on the ISDN BRI or PRI interface that connects two AppleTalk networks.

Router A Configuration

As shown in Figure 21-5, Router A is located in the district office. The district-office network consists of two zones: Sales and Training. On Router A, an AppleTalk-style access list is assigned to BRI 0 to prevent the forwarding of NBP packets that come from printers and NBP packets that come from the Training zone. If the router were to allow the forwarding of these packets, they would trigger an unnecessary ISDN connection to the main-office network.

```
hostname RouterA
!
username RouterB password 7 125D063D2E
appletalk routing
appletalk static cable-range 20-20 to 15.43 zone Administration
appletalk static cable-range 25-25 to 15.43 zone Marketing
isdn switch-type basic-ni1
!
interface ethernet 0
appletalk cable-range 5-5 5.128
appletalk zone Sales
!
interface ethernet 1
appletalk cable-range 10-10 10.26
appletalk zone Service
!
interface bri 0
appletalk static cable-range 15-15 15.42
appletalk zone PhoneZone
no appletalk send-rtmps
encapsulation ppp
ppp authentication chap
dialer idle-timeout 240
bandwidth 56
dialer map appletalk 15.43 name RouterA speed 56 912065553240
dialer-group 1
isdn spid1 602555463101 5554631
!
access-list 601 deny nbp 1 type LaserWriter
access-list 601 deny nbp 2 zone Training
access-list 601 permit nbp 3 zone Sales
access-list 601 deny other-nbps
access-list 601 permit other-access
!
dialer-list 1 list 601
```

The **hostname** command establishes the host name of Router A. The **username** command establishes the name of the router allowed to dial up Router A. The name corresponds to the host name of Router B. The **password** keyword indicates that the **username** command specifies a password. The "7" indicates that the password is encrypted using a Cisco-defined encryption algorithm. The **appletalk routing** command enables AppleTalk routing.

The **appletalk static cable-range** commands create static AppleTalk routes to the zones in the main office network. Static AppleTalk routes are required because the **no appletalk send-rtmps** command prevents the exchange of RTMP updates between the two networks. Without static routes, zones for the main office would not appear when users open the Chooser on hosts connected to the district-office network. The **isdn switch-type** command specifies that Router A connects to a National ISDN-1 switch.

Interface Configuration

The **appletalk cable-range** commands for each Ethernet interface establish the network number for the cable segment to which the interface connects and the node number of the interface. For each interface, the **appletalk zone** command establishes the zone name for the network connected to the interface. None of the interface configurations specifies an AppleTalk routing protocol, so the interfaces use the default routing protocol, RTMP.

The **no appletalk send-rtmps** interface configuration command prevents Router A from sending RTMP updates out on interface BRI 0. To compensate for the lack of RTMP exchange, you must configure static AppleTalk routes (using the **appletalk static cable-range** command).

The **encapsulation ppp** command specifies PPP encapsulation, and the **ppp authentication chap** command enables CHAP authentication. The **dialer idle-timeout** command sets the idle timeout to 240 seconds (four minutes). The **bandwidth** command tells routing protocols that the line operates at 56 kbps.

The **dialer map** command establishes the remote site that Router A is to call. In this case, the **dialer map** command establishes 15.43 as the next-hop address. The **name** keyword specifies the name of the remote router associated with the dial string. The **speed** keyword specifies that Router A is to set the line's rate to 56 kbps, which is required when the connection traverses a switch that does not support Signaling System 7. The **dialer-group** command associates the interface BRI 0 with dialer access group 1.

The **isdn spid1** commands represent SPIDs and are required by National ISDN-1 switches. Service providers assign SPIDs to associate a SPID number with a telephone number. Your service provider can tell you whether SPIDs are required for your switch. In this example, SPID 1 identifies 602 as the area code, 555 as the exchange, 4631 as the station ID, and 01 as the terminal identifier.

Access List Configuration

The first **access-list nbp** command defines access list 601 and prevents the forwarding of NBP packets generated by any LaserWriter printer on the district-office network. The second **access-list nbp** command prevents the forwarding of NBP packets generated by the Training zone. The third **access-list nbp** command allows the forwarding of NBP packets generated by the Sales zone.

The **access-list other-nbps** global configuration command prevents the forwarding of all other NBP packets that have not been explicitly permitted or denied by previous **access-list nbp** global configuration commands.

The **access-list other-access** command permits all other access checks that would otherwise be denied because they are not explicitly permitted by an **access-list** command. The **dialer-list** command assigns the access list 601 to dialer access group 1, which is associated with BRI 0.

Router B Configuration

As shown in Figure 21-5, Router B is located in the main office. The main-office network consists of two zones: Marketing and Administration. With the exception of the OpenReqs server in the Administration zone, users of hosts connected to the district-office network do not need to access servers located in the Administration zone. Like the district-office network, each zone in the main-office network has its own printer, so there is no need for Router B to forward NBP packets that the printers originate. The access list for Router B prevents NBP packets that come from printers and NBP packets that come from all servers in the Administration zone (except OpenReqs) from triggering an ISDN connection to the district-office network.

```
hostname RouterB
!
username RouterA password 7 343E821D4A
appletalk routing
appletalk static cable-range 5-5 to 15.42 zone Sales
appletalk static cable-range 10-10 to 15.42 zone Training
isdn switch-type basic-5ess
!
interface ethernet 0
appletalk cable-range 20-20 20.5
appletalk zone Administration
!
interface ethernet 1
appletalk cable-range 25-25 25.36
appletalk zone Marketing
!
interface bri 0
appletalk static cable-range 15-15 15.43
appletalk zone PhoneZone
no appletalk send-rtmps
encapsulation ppp
ppp authentication chap
dialer idle-timeout 240
bandwidth 56
dialer map appletalk 15.42 name RouterB speed 56 917075553287
dialer-group 1
!
access-list 601 deny nbp 1 type LaserWriter
access-list 601 permit nbp 2 object OpenReqs
access-list 601 permit nbp 3 zone Marketing
access-list 601 deny other-nbps
access-list 601 permit other-access
dialer-list 1 list 601
```

The configuration for Router B is similar to the configuration for Router A, with the following differences:

- The **isdn switch-type** command specifies that Router B connects to an AT&T 5ESS central-office ISDN switch. This type of switch does not use SPID numbers, so the **isdn spid1** command is not used.

- The first **access-list nbp** command defines access list 601 and prevents the forwarding of NBP packets generated by the LaserWriter printers connected to the main-office network. The second **access-list nbp** command allows the forwarding of packets generated by the server OpenReqs. The third **access-list nbp** command configurations allows the forwarding of packets generated by the Marketing zone.

Configuring IPX over ISDN

Configuring ISDN when using IPX as a Layer 3 protocol can be achieved by using the configuration examples in this section. Explanations of the network diagram and the configuration commands used are also contained in this section.

Example Network Scenario for Configuring IPX over ISDN

In the following network, the internal IPX address, IPX network, and IPX address on the BRI of the router have been defined, respectively. Also, the SPID numbers on the BRI have been defined.

Figure 21-6 *Configuring IPX over ISDN Sample Network*

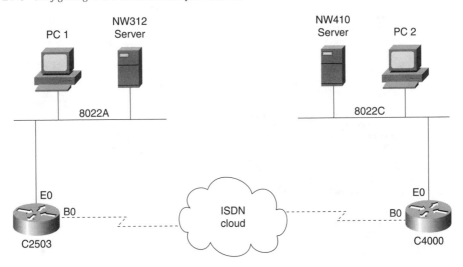

The following information applies to the network diagramed in Figure 21-6:

NW312 internal IPX address	2EE67FE3.0000.0000.0001
PC1/NW312 IPX network	8022A
NW410 internal IPX address	301586E0.0000.0000.0001
PC2/NW410 IPX network	8022C
C2503 interface B0 IPX address	8022B.0000.0c09.509f
C2503 ISDN phone numbers	4085554321
	4085559876
C2503 ISDN SPIDs	408555432101 5554321
	408555987601 5559876
C4000 interface B0 IPX address	8022B.0000.0c02.e649
C4000 ISDN phone numbers	4155551234
	4155556789
C4000 ISDN SPIDs	415555123401 5551234
	415555678901 5556789

Configuration for the C2503 Router

The following shows the configuration for the C2503 router for configuring IPX over ISDN. The configuration includes line numbers that will be referred to in the explanation section after the configuration:

```
 1   C2503#wr t
 2   #####
 3   Current configuration:
 4   !
 5   version 10.2
 6   !
 7   hostname C2503
 8   !
 9   enable password test
10   !
11   username C4000 password cisco
12   ipx routing 0000.0c09.509f
13   ipx gns-response-delay 1000
14   isdn switch-type basic-dms100
15   !
16   interface Ethernet0
17   ipx network 8022A
18   ipx encapsulation SAP
19   !
20   interface Serial0
21   no ip address
22   shutdown
23   !
24   interface Serial1
25   no ip address
26   shutdown
```

```
27  !
28  interface BRI0
29  encapsulation ppp
30  bandwidth 56
31  ipx network 8022B
32  no ipx route-cache
33  ipx watchdog-spoof
34  dialer idle-timeout 300
35  dialer map ipx 8022B.0000.0c02.e649 name C4000 speed 56 broadcast 14155551234
36  dialer map ipx 8022B.0000.0c02.e649 name C4000 speed 56 broadcast 14155556789
37  dialer hold-queue 5
38  dialer load-threshold 100
39  dialer-group 1
40  isdn spid1 408555432101 5554321
41  isdn spid2 408555987601 5559876
42  ppp authentication chap
43  !
44  access-list 900 deny -1 FFFFFFFF 0 FFFFFFFF 452
45  access-list 900 deny -1 FFFFFFFF 0 FFFFFFFF 453
46  access-list 900 deny -1 FFFFFFFF 0 FFFFFFFF 457
47  access-list 900 permit -1
48  ipx route 8022C 8022B.0000.0c02.e649
49  ipx route 301586E0 8022B.0000.0c02.e649
50  !
51  ipx sap 4 NW410 301586E0.0000.0000.0001 451 2
52  !
53  !
54  dialer-list 1 list 900
55  !
56  line con 0
57  line aux 0
58  line vty 0 4
59  password test
60  login
61  !
62  end
```

Explanation of the C2503 Configuration

This section contains an explanation of the C2503 router configuration by referring to the line numbers.

Lines 1–11

```
C2503#wr t
######
Current configuration:
!
version 10.2
!
hostname C2503
!
enable password test
!
username C4000 password cisco
```

The username C4000 is the hostname of the remote router and is used by the **dialer map** command. The username is case-sensitive and must match the remote router's host name exactly.

The password, which is used by the CHAP authentication process, is case-sensitive and must match the corresponding entry on the remote router exactly.

NOTE   To avoid confusion, the unencrypted form of the password **cisco** is shown in this sample configuration. In the actual configuration, the password would appear in its encrypted form: 7 13061E010803, where 7 denotes the encryption type and 13061E010803 is the encrypted form of the password **cisco**. When entering or making changes to the **username** command, always type the password in its unencrypted form and do not enter the encryption type (7), which is set automatically.

Line 12

```
ipx routing 0000.0c09.509f
```

This command enables IPX routing. The router will choose a MAC address from one of its interfaces to associate with the process, so you do not need to specify it with the command. Just enter the command **ipx routing**.

Line 13

```
ipx gns-response-delay 1000
```

The static SAP command that follows will advertise the remote server, even when the ISDN link is not active. Therefore, it may be necessary to increase the period of time before the router replies to a workstation's Get Nearest Server (GNS) request to ensure that the local file server can respond first.

Line 14

```
isdn switch-type basic-dms100
```

The ISDN switch type must match your carrier's equipment. If you change the switch type, you must reload the router for the new switch type to take effect.

Lines 16–17

```
interface Ethernet0
ipx network 8022A
```

8022A is the network number of the local network. To determine this number, type **config** at the local server's console prompt and match the router=92's interface network number to the LAN protocol network number. You do not need to include the leading zeros displayed for the LAN protocol network number with this command.

Line 18

```
ipx encapsulation SAP
```

This command sets the Ethernet frame type of the interface to match that of the local file server. To determine the server=92s frame type, type **config** at the local server's console prompt, and match the router's interface IPX encapsulation to the frame type specified.

NOTE	The Cisco supported frame types are as follows:

Novell Frame Type	*Cisco Encapsulation*
Novell Ethernet_II	arpa
Novell Ethernet_802.3	novell-ether
IEEE 802.2	sap
IEEE 802.2 SNAP	snap

Lines 20–29

```
interface Serial0
no ip address
shutdown
!
interface Serial1
no ip address
shutdown
!
interface BRI0
encapsulation ppp
```

PPP encapsulation is recommended over HDLC to allow use of CHAP authentication.

Line 30

```
bandwidth 56
```

The default bandwidth setting for a BRI interface is 64 kbps. If you configure your **dialer map** statements with the speed 56 option, you should include the bandwidth statement.

NOTE	This command does not control the speed of your ISDN line. It is used to set the correct reference point for the BRI port's show interface statistics, for the **dialer load-threshold** command, and for IGRP/EIGRP routing metrics.

Line 31

```
ipx network 8022B
```

8022B is the IPX network number of the ISDN segment for both routers. This network number should be unique to your network.

Line 32

```
no ipx route-cache
```

IPX route cache must be turned off when IPX watchdog spoofing is enabled.

Line 33

```
ipx watchdog-spoof
```

This command enables the router to reply to the local server's watchdog packets on behalf of the remote client. Without it, the server's watchdog packets would be seen as interesting packets and would activate the ISDN link.

Line 34

```
dialer idle-timeout 300
```

This command sets the number of seconds the ISDN connection will remain open if no interesting traffic is being routed. The timer is reset each time an interesting packet is forwarded.

Lines 35–36

```
dialer map ipx 8022B.0000.0c02.e649 name C4000 speed 56 broadcast 14155551234
dialer map ipx 8022B.0000.0c02.e649 name C4000 speed 56 broadcast 14155556789
```

The **dialer map** command is used with CHAP authentication to place the initial call to the remote router when interesting traffic is forwarded to the BRI interface. After the connection is active, the **dialer idle-timeout** command determines how long it will remain active. A **dialer map** statement is required for each ISDN phone number to be called. Be aware, however, that two **dialer map** statements pointing to the same location might activate both B channels when the use of only one channel might be desired.

The parameters for this command are as follows:

- **8022B.0000.0c02.e649**—The IPX address of the remote router's BRI interface. To determine this address, type **show ipx interface B 0** at the remote router's console prompt.

- **name C4000**—The host name of the remote router. The name is case-sensitive and should match the name configured for the **username** command shown earlier.

- **speed 56**—Sets the dialer speed to 56 kbps for ISDN circuits that are not 64 kbps end-to-end, and should be included in both routers' **dialer map** statements. (Most installations in North America must be configured for 56 kbps.)
- **broadcast**—Allows the forwarding of broadcast packets. Use of the **broadcast** parameter does not make broadcast packets interesting, however. Unless broadcast packets are specified as interesting packets by the **dialer-list** command, they will only be forwarded when the ISDN link is active.
- **14155551234 14155556789**—The remote router's ISDN telephone numbers.

Line 37

```
dialer hold-queue 5
```

This command allows interesting packets to be queued until the ISDN connection is established. It is especially useful when a NetWare login is used to activate the connection to prevent the workstation from timing out. In this example, five interesting packets will be queued.

Line 38

```
dialer load-threshold 100
```

This command is used to configure bandwidth on demand by setting the maximum load before the dialer places another call through the second B channel. The load is the calculated weighted average load value for the interface, where 1 is unloaded and 255 is fully loaded. The actual load value you should configure depends on the characteristics of your particular network. In this example, the second B channel will be activated when the load reaches 39% of maximum utilization, which is 100 divided by 255.

Line 39

```
dialer-group 1
```

The **dialer-group 1** command enables the dialer list 1 on the BRI interface, which determines which packets will be interesting to activate the ISDN connection.

Lines 40–41

```
isdn spid1 408555432101 5554321
isdn spid2 408555987601 5559876
```

The **isdn spid** commands are used if your carrier assigns SPIDs to your ISDN lines.

Line 42

```
ppp authentication chap
```

This command enables CHAP authentication.

Lines 44–47

```
access-list 900 deny -1 FFFFFFFF 0 FFFFFFFF 452
access-list 900 deny -1 FFFFFFFF 0 FFFFFFFF 453
access-list 900 deny -1 FFFFFFFF 0 FFFFFFFF 457
access-list 900 permit -1
```

This access list determines which IPX packets will be interesting and activate the ISDN link. The access list you should create depends on your particular network design.

The command parameters for this example are as follows:

- **access-list 900 deny -1 -1 0 -1 452**—This will determine all SAP packets to be uninteresting.

- **access-list 900 deny -1 -1 0 -1 453**—This will determine all RIP packets to be uninteresting.

- **access-list 900 deny -1 -1 0 -1 457**—This will determine all security packets to be uninteresting.

- **access-list 900 permit -1**—This will determine all other packets to be interesting.

Line 48

```
ipx route 8022C 8022B.0000.0c02.e649
```

This command creates a static route to the remote router's Ethernet network via the remote router's BRI interface. This is necessary because dynamic routes are removed when the ISDN link is down.

The command parameters for this example are as follows:

- **8022C**—The external IPX network number of the remote network. To determine this number, type **config** at the remote server's console prompt and match the network number to the LAN protocol statement.

- **8022B.0000.0c02.e649**—The IPX address of the remote router's BRI interface. To determine this address, type **show ipx interface B 0** at the remote router's console prompt.

Line 49

```
ipx route 301586E0 8022B.0000.0c02.e649
```

This **ipx route** command creates a static route to the remote server via the remote router's BRI interface. This is required because dynamic routes are lost when the ISDN link is down.

The command parameters for this example are as follows:

- **301586E0**—The network portion of the remote server's internal IPX address. To determine this address, type **show ipx servers** at the remote router's console prompt.
- **8022B.0000.0c02.e649**—The IPX address of the remote router's BRI interface. To determine this address, type **show ipx interface B 0** at the remote router=92's console prompt.

Line 51

```
ipx sap 4 NW410 301586E0.0000.0000.0001 451 2
```

This command creates a static SAP entry for the remote server, which the local router will advertise even when the ISDN link is not active.

The command parameters for this example are as follows:

- **4**—SAP type (server).
- **NW410**—Name of SAP service.
- **301586E0.0000.0000.0001**—Internal IPX network and host address of remote server. To determine this address, type **show ipx servers** at the remote router's console prompt.
- **451**—Socket (port) number of remote server, which is determined by the command **show ipx servers** on the remote router.
- **2**—RIP hop count to the remote server.

Line 54

```
dialer-list 1 list 900
```

This command points to access list 900, which determines which IPX packets will be interesting.

Lines 56–62

```
line con 0
line aux 0
line vty 0 4
password test
login
!
end
```

These lines are self explanatory.

Configuration for the C4000 Router

The following shows the configuration for the C4000 router for configuring IPX over ISDN. For an explanation of the commands, see the section titled "Explanation of the C2503 Configuration," earlier in this chapter. (Note that this explanation is in the context of the C2503 configuration, but the general command descriptions still apply):

```
 1  C4000#wr t
 2  ######
 3  Current configuration:
 4  !
 5  version 10.2
 6  !
 7  hostname C4000
 8  !
 9  enable password test
10  !
11  username C2503 password cisco
12  ipx routing 0000.0c02.e649
13  ipx gns-response-delay 1000
14  isdn switch-type basic-dms100
15  !
16  interface Ethernet0
17  ipx network 8022C
18  ipx encapsulation SAP
19  !
20  interface Serial0
21  no ip address
22  shutdown
23  !
24  interface Serial1
25  no ip address
26  shutdown
27  !
28  interface BRI0
29  encapsulation ppp
30  bandwidth 56
31  ipx network 8022B
32  no ipx route-cache
33  ipx watchdog-spoof
34  dialer idle-timeout 300
35  dialer map ipx 8022B.0000.0c09.509f name C2503 speed 56 broadcast 14085554321
36  dialer map ipx 8022B.0000.0c09.509f name C2503 speed 56 broadcast 14085559876
37  dialer hold-queue 5
38  dialer load-threshold 100
39  dialer-group 1
40  isdn spid1 415555123401 5551234
41  isdn spid2 415555678901 5556789
42  ppp authentication chap
43  !
44  access-list 900 deny -1 FFFFFFFF 0 FFFFFFFF 452
45  access-list 900 deny -1 FFFFFFFF 0 FFFFFFFF 453
46  access-list 900 deny -1 FFFFFFFF 0 FFFFFFFF 457
47  access-list 900 permit -1
48  ipx route 8022A 8022B.0000.0c09.509f
49  ipx route 2EE67FE3 8022B.0000.0c09.509f
50  !
51  ipx sap 4 NW312 2EE67FE3.0000.0000.0001 451 2
```

```
52  !
53  !
54  dialer-list 1 list 900
55  !
56  line con 0
57  line aux 0
58  line vty 0 4
59  password test
60  login
61  !
62  end
```

Summary

When you configure ISDN, controlling packets that trigger unnecessary connections is a major concern. In the past, one way to control routing update packets was to configure static routes. Snapshot routing and NBP-packet filtering provide new ways to control routing updates. Snapshot routing enables you to configure the network so that routed protocols update their routing tables dynamically without triggering frequent and costly ISDN connections. Snapshot routing is ideally suited for relatively stable networks in which a single router is a central point through which routing updates flow. Configuring ISDN in an IPX environment was also covered in this chapter.

CHAPTER 22

Increasing Security in IP Networks

Edited by Thomas M. Thomas II

It is summertime in the not too distant future; the children are out of school, and as highways and airports fill with vacationers off to holiday destinations, unexplained power outages hit sections of the United States. Airliners begin mysteriously disappearing from and reappearing on air traffic control systems, causing panic in many airports.

Rumors of the new "Rosebud" virus fill Internet chat rooms. Even as the chat rooms are announcing the virus' presence, system administrators are trying to cope with this new Melissa-like virus. The virus, in addition to infecting e-mail, also attaches itself to Web browsers, speeding its spread as it begins denial of service activities against communication and e-commerce via the Internet. The Internet mysteriously slows to a crawl.

Parts of the 911 service begin to fail in major U.S. cities, as supervisors at the Department of Defense discover that their e-mail and telephone services are disrupted. Officers aboard a U.S. Navy cruiser find that their computer systems have been attacked.

As these disturbing and mysterious incidents mount, global stock markets drop precipitously, and panic surges across the globe. The fabric that bound the globe and nations together begins to unravel and rebel against its creators…and you were afraid of Y2K.

Much of the preceding scenario occurred in 1997 when 35 hackers hired by the U.S. National Security Agency (NSA) launched simulated attacks on the U.S. electronic infrastructure.

"Eligible Receiver," as the exercise was called, achieved root-level access to 36 of the Department of Defense's 40,000 networks. The simulated attack also "turned off" sections of the U.S. power grid; "shut down" parts of the 911 network in Washington, D.C. and other cities; and gained access to systems aboard a Navy cruiser at sea.

Although "Eligible Receiver" took place in the United States, which has about 40% of the world's computers, the threat of cyber-terrorism and cyber-warfare is global.

Consider the following:

- During the Gulf War, Dutch hackers stole information about U.S. troop movements from U.S. Defense Department computers and tried to sell it to the Iraqis, who thought it was a hoax and turned it down.

- In 1997 and 1998, an Israeli youth calling himself "The Analyzer" allegedly hacked into Pentagon computers with help from California teenagers. Ehud Tenebaum, 20, was charged in Jerusalem in February 1999 with conspiracy and harming computer systems.

- In February 1999, unidentified hackers seized control of a British military communication satellite and demanded money in return for control of the satellite. The report was vehemently denied by the British military, of course.

- In January 1999, President Clinton announced a $1.46 billion initiative to deal with U.S. government computer security—a 40% increase over fiscal 1998 spending. Of particular concern is the Pentagon, the military stronghold of the world's most powerful nation, a.k.a. "The Holy Grail of Hackers."

It is clear that governmental sites are just part of the targets available to those conducting cyber-warfare. Experience tells us that in many cases it is far easier and profitable to attack corporate networks. In such a high-stakes environment, only premier expertise is acceptable. Trial-and-error networking is not an option when it comes to securing your network. A single vulnerability could compromise the network's data—the corporate lifeblood—into unfriendly hands. Whether the threat is a corporate competitor in search of trade secrets, a teenage hacker joyriding on your network, or a disgruntled employee seeking revenge, the end result is network downtime, compromised trade secrets, and, invariably, unnecessary expenses and loss of potential revenue.

Overview of Cisco Security and Network Assessment

For these reasons, Cisco offers network security consulting services to provide highly specialized, unmatched expertise largely gained from years of experience in military and classified backgrounds.

Instead of concentrating on policy-intensive exercises and reviews, Cisco security consulting teams focus on the bits and bytes of the network—where the security vulnerabilities are, how to fix them, and, in especially trying times, how to get a hacker off the network. The Cisco network security consulting teams offer two primary services:

- Security Posture Assessments (SPA)
- Incident Control and Recovery (ICR)

Cisco security engineers provide Security Posture Assessments (SPAs). These assessments include comprehensive security analysis of large-scale, distributed client networks, externally from the perspective of an outside hacker, and internally from the perspective of a disgruntled employee or contractor. Security vulnerability information is compiled, analyzed, and concisely presented to the client with operational-level recommendations about how to better secure the corporate network and help enable it to reach its full business potential.

Intrusion control and recovery services, which are short-notice deployments to client sites to terminate ongoing attacks to the client network, are available on a limited basis to qualified clients as well.

Security Posture Assessment

Before an organization can take the necessary steps to improve its network security, it needs to conduct a thorough review of its existing vulnerabilities. By providing a security-oriented "snapshot in time" and by taking the unique perspective of quantifying the current level of network security, Cisco Security Posture Assessment (SPA) services can help an organization effectively and objectively understand the security state of the network and identify areas to improve.

When conducting an SPA, Cisco network security experts examine a client's internal and external connectivity to determine the following:

- The effectiveness of current safeguards

- The extent of any network-level vulnerabilities present

- The organization's ability to detect and respond to attack

The SPA is substantially more comprehensive than a simple penetration test because the Cisco security teams produce a thorough data set of security vulnerabilities and potential means of gaining unauthorized access for the entire network, as opposed to testing only several points of entry. One phase of the SPA externally probes the network from the perspective of an Internet or dial-in hacker, whereas the second phase probes from an internal position on the network, much like a disgruntled employee or an internal contractor might, as shown in Figure 22-1.

Cisco security engineers then validate and confirm the presence of each specific detected vulnerability, performing extensive, nondestructive network penetrations to more effectively determine the level of unauthorized network access that may be achieved.

Figure 22-1 *Security Assessment Wheel*

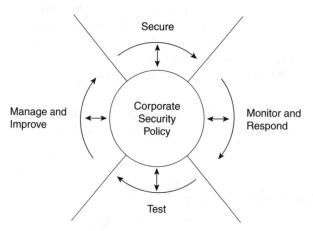

Specifically, the Cisco SPA process includes the following:

- Network mapping and target analysis to determine network topology, correlate the network's electronic Internet presence with information collected from public and corporate records, and provide insight into the probability of a successful attack.

- Host and service discovery to determine how many hosts are on the network and which network services each host is currently running.

- Vulnerability analysis to determine all potential vulnerabilities that exist for each network service running on each identified host. This phase also includes additional analysis—not only to confirm the presence of these vulnerabilities on specific systems by exploiting identified potential vulnerabilities, but also to conduct secondary exploitation to determine what additional vulnerabilities could be exploited when the first-level vulnerabilities are leveraged appropriately.

- Vulnerability measurement and data collection to identify methods of entry into a corporate network through exploitation of network vulnerabilities using specialized SPA tools.

- Data analysis and security design review to compare test results with current operational requirements to identify critical deficiencies.

- Recommendations and reporting to identify optimum safeguards, and present findings and specific recommendations for each system for use by corporate management, system administrators, and users.

Cisco security engineers present the data in a detailed report and a briefing, addressing security vulnerabilities to both corporate executives and network engineers in a timely and strictly confidential manner. In addition to recommending specific security improvements, the SPA process also gives clients metrics to characterize the security status of their networks and systems. This data can establish a corporate network's security-posture baseline or measure incremental improvement and trends from previous assessments.

To maintain a secure state for an ever-changing network, Cisco recommends that organizations conduct an SPA on a periodic basis as a critical component of an ongoing corporate information-protection program. In addition, Cisco clients have found security-posture assessments helpful before and after major network changes, such as a network merger resulting from a corporate acquisition or an implementation of an e-commerce Web site. These periodic reviews help migrate the security risks that such network changes invariably create.

Incident Control and Recovery Service

Although organizations are frequently unaware of actual security breaches, they sometimes recognize that an incident has occurred or is ongoing. In these circumstances, an organization needs to not only terminate the activity but also know the time, source, type, and extent of the attack. And the organization needs to know this information immediately because network downtime and the compromise of corporate information almost always directly affect the bottom line.

Cisco Incident Control and Recovery (ICR) service assists clients who have been subjected to such network attacks. Cisco network security engineers are deployed to the customer site within hours of the client's initial request for assistance. Once on site, the ICR team coordinates closely with network administrators and security staff to match the client's operational priorities with appropriate ICR services, which may include the following:

- Isolating compromised hosts and networks to contain suspicious activity and prevent further compromise
- Reconfiguring network resources to get the client back online securely
- Confirming whether a security incident has occurred
- Identifying the time(s), source(s), and means of intrusion
- Identifying affected resources and quantifying loss
- Assisting in data recovery
- Performing an SPA to identify other vulnerabilities
- Recommending security solutions to prevent future security incidents

Cisco professionals have extensive experience in providing ICR services and have developed specialized tools for forensics analysis, damage assessment, and intrusion containment. This service is offered on a limited basis and is subject to personnel availability.

More information about Cisco network security consulting services and the entire range of Cisco security products, services, and technologies may be found at www.cisco.com/security.

Cyber-Warfare: Is It Happening?

Cyber-warfare is occurring all around you, as announced by the media, so network security must be an integral part of the design of every aspect of your network. The threats are there, as evidenced by some of the more recent articles and stories:

"Urgent Care Needed, Stat"
Internet Week, March 1, 1999.

"Cyber-Vigilantes Hunt Down Hackers"
Network World, January 12, 1999, www.nwfusion.com.

"Large Companies Now See Outside Security Threat"
Computerworld, August 17, 1998.

"Cyberweapons: Information Warfare"
Radio Free Europe/Radio Liberty, July 28, 1998, www.rferl.org.

"Security Breach"
Computerworld, June 15, 1998, www.computerworld.com.

"Attacks Spur Intrusion-Detection Efforts"
Internet Week, May 28, 1998.

NOTE   Now, what do you think? As you can see, cyber-warfare is happening every day and night. Is your network protected? Would you know whether your network was under attack?

This situation is going to become increasingly common as e-commerce grows. The Internet is the world's first truly global resource, linking the *people* of the world together in a virtual community. As with every large community, there will be people who want to take advantage of the situation in whatever manner possible.

Network security has probably been one of the least considered aspects of network operation and design. As enterprise networks evolve and connect to the Internet, it has become an increasingly larger concern for many of them. Is this concern justified? A resounding "yes," and the concerns are probably late in coming. Consider recent FBI statistics that estimate businesses in the United States alone lost an estimated $10 billion from computer break-ins in 1997. That number is larger than the gross national product of many nations. When considered this way, you can easily see why people have dedicated their lives to computer theft. Are these security breaches occurring in your network, as well? Although it might not be happening in your network yet, it is occurring elsewhere. As discussed previously, the media are responding and reporting on the increase in cyber-warfare. Likewise, many of the world's top companies are also reporting on security threats and breaches.

What Are the Threats?

Consider the following excerpts from Cisco's home page (http://www.cisco.com) regarding their recent announcements on the subject of security. These announcements are even more important than those previously mentioned because Cisco, as the world's largest supplier of networking equipment, has already recognized this threat and is responding to it.

The campus infrastructure is vulnerable to threats from any number of intruders. These intruders are varied and are difficult to detect. The following list describes some of the commonly acknowledged types of intruders:

- Hostile current employees—This group may be the most difficult to detect and prevent because of trust relationships between personnel and their employers
- Hostile former employees
- Employees or users initiating unintentional activities
- Employees who mismanage the environment
- Spies

What Is the Purpose of Cyber-Warfare?

The purposes of cyber-warfare are as varied as the cyber-thieves themselves; and it seems that every single thief has a different reason for doing it. For example, some of the threats you will face will come from the following:

- Thrill seekers
- Hostile employees or former employees
- Enemies, such as spies or thieves
- Those looking for peer recognition
- Those wanting to make a statement or to be heard
- Radical and fringe groups

These people can be out to gain or achieve any number of things. The most common reasons/purposes of these cyber-thieves are as follows:

- Profit or theft
- Revenge, anarchy, spite

- Ignorance, boredom, curiosity
- Espionage (industrial or national)
- Challenge or sport

Network Vulnerabilities

The campus network infrastructure is vulnerable to multiple security threats:

- Insufficient physical security
- Accessing device console and Telnet ports
- Accessing sensitive internal networks
- Misrouting via spoofed routing updates
- Accessing device configurations via SNMP community strings

Vulnerabilities in Cisco CHAP Authentication

Challenge Handshake Authentication Protocol (CHAP) is a security feature that prevents unauthorized access; it is supported on lines using PPP encapsulation. CHAP does not itself prevent unauthorized access; it merely identifies the remote end. The router or access server then determines whether that user is allowed access.

A serious security vulnerability (bug ID CSCdi91594) exists in PPP CHAP authentication in all "classic" Cisco IOS software versions. The vulnerability permits attackers with appropriate skills and knowledge to completely circumvent CHAP authentication. Other PPP authentication methods are not affected.

TCP Loopback Denial of Service Attack (land.c) and Cisco Devices

Somebody has released a program, known as land.c, that can be used to launch denial of service (DoS) attacks against various TCP implementations. The program sends a TCP SYN packet (a connection initiation), giving the target host's address as both source and destination, using the same port on the target host as both source and destination.

"Smurfing" Denial of Service Attacks

The "smurf" attack, named after its exploit program, is the most recent in the category of network-level attacks against hosts. A perpetrator sends a large amount of ICMP echo (ping) traffic at broadcast addresses, all of which has a spoofed source address of a victim. If the routing device delivering traffic to those broadcast addresses performs an IP broadcast to the Layer 2 broadcast function, most hosts on that IP network will take the ICMP echo request and reply to it with an echo reply each, multiplying the traffic by the number of hosts responding. On a multiaccess broadcast network, there could potentially be hundreds of machines replying to each packet.

UDP Diagnostic Port Denial of Service Attacks

What is a UDP diagnostic port attack? A sender transmits a volume of requests for UDP diagnostic services on the router, which causes all CPU resources to be consumed by servicing the phony requests. There is a potential denial of service attack at Internet service providers (ISPs) that targets network devices.

Cisco IOS Password Encryption

A non-Cisco source has recently released a new program to decrypt user passwords (and other passwords) in Cisco configuration files. The program will not decrypt passwords set with the enable secret command.

The unexpected concern that this program has caused among Cisco customers has led us to suspect that many customers are relying on Cisco password encryption for more security than it was designed to provide. This chapter explains the security model behind Cisco password encryption and the security limitations of that encryption.

Assessing the Need for Security

As more users access the Internet, and as companies expand their networks, the challenge to provide security for internal networks becomes increasingly difficult. Companies must determine which areas of their internal networks they must protect, learn how to restrict user access to these areas, and determine which types of network services they should filter to prevent potential security breaches.

It should now be obvious that security must be a consideration at all levels of your network. Complacency is also something you should try to avoid when considering security. The rapidly advancing sophistication of technology means that your security measures are limited in the length of time they will be effective.

Network security is a broad topic that can be addressed at the data link, or media, level (where packet snooping and encryption problems can occur); at the network, or protocol, layer (the point at which Internet Protocol [IP] packets and routing updates are controlled); and at the application layer (where, for example, host-level bugs become issues).

Cisco Systems provides several network, or protocol, layer features to increase security on IP networks. These features include controls to restrict access to routers and communication servers by way of console port, Telnet, Simple Network Management

Protocol (SNMP) Terminal Access Controller Access Control System (TACACS), vendor token cards, and access lists. Firewall architecture setup is also discussed in this chapter.

NOTE   Although this case study addresses network layer security issues, which are the most relevant in the context of an Internet connection, ignoring host-level security, even with network layer filtering in place, can be dangerous. For host-level security measures, refer to your application's documentation and the recommended reading list at the end of this case study.

Security Policy

Security policies are the paperwork of cyber-warfare. Security policies can be viewed as the nitty-gritty details of your network's security procedures. The following is a quote from RFC 2196, the Site Security Handbook:

"A security policy is a formal statement of the rules by which people who are given access to an organization's technology and information assets must abide."

You must be aware that a security policy needs to cover both the internal and external security. As has been shown, the threats come from both directions, requiring you to address all threats to achieve proper protection of your network.

Security policies provide many benefits, and are worth the time and effort needed to develop them. The following is a list of common reasons to develop a security policy:

- Provides a process to audit existing network security.
- Helps determine which tools and procedures are needed for the organization.
- Helps communicate consensus among a group of key decision-makers, and define responsibilities of users and administrators.
- Enables global security implementation and enforcement: Computer security is now an enterprise-wide issue and computing sites are expected to conform to the network security policy.
- Creates a basis for legal action, if necessary.

Many companies have implemented security policies as a part of their network security program. Security policies provide an accessible set of standards that can be used to weigh actions and also provide a procedure for responding to an attack so that all your users are both educated and accountable.

Figure 22-2 is from the WarRoom survey and provides some insight into how important Fortune 1000 companies feel a security policy is. For more information on the WarRoom Survey, visit http://www.warroomresearch.com/ResearchCollabor/SurveyResults.htm.

Figure 22-2 *WarRoom Survey Results Demonstrate that a Majority of Companies Surveyed Have Experienced Security Threats in the Past Year*

More than 200 Fortune 1000 companies
were asked if they had detected attempts
from outsiders to gain computer access
in the past 12 months

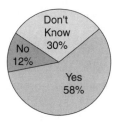

If they answered yes, how many
successful accesses were there?

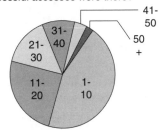

The *Site Security Handbook* (RFC 2196) is a good reference for developing network security policies. According to the *Site Security Handbook*, a security policy is essentially a document that summarizes how corporate computing and network resources will be used and protected.

Key characteristics of a good security policy are as follows:

- Capable of being implemented both technically and organizationally
- Enforceable with security tools, where appropriate; and with sanctions, where actual prevention is not technically feasible
- Define the areas of responsibility for the users, administrators, and management
- Flexible and maintainable to adapt to changing environments
- Balance the maximum possible level of network security while being as transparent as possible to the users
- Use and access policies
- Use incident-handling procedures and notification process

How Do I Create a Network Security Policy?

As with many things in networking, the answer to this question is, it depends. When you begin to create a security policy, you should first gather data about security procedures that you already have in place (such as how often users change their login passwords, and the SNMP read/write community string). You must also find out when these security measures were last changed. You can also hire outside security specialists to assist you in evaluating your existing security procedures and policies. Perhaps you have never considered any of this, and instead you begin to build a security policy from the ground up. As you can see, the creation (and evolution) of a security policy does depend on your situation; however, the following items (as the minimum) should be included in any policy:

- Perform a risk assessment and a cost-benefit analysis
- Identify the network assets you are trying to protect
- Identify who you are trying to protect your resources from
- Determine the costs of network security measures
- Design and implement measures that will protect your assets in a cost-effective manner
- Review the process continuously and make improvements each time a weakness is found
- Gather current procedures, both documented and undocumented, which are being done, such as changing passwords every other month, and so on

It is important to remember that a security policy is *not* a static document. Instead, it is continually growing, changing, and evolving as required. Proactively designing and implementing a network security policy is just as important as designing and implementing a well-thought-out network. After you develop your security policy, document it.

NOTE   A security policy is not *the* solution to your security concerns. Rather, it provides you with a framework in which to build security into your network. When combined with the other aspects discussed in this case study, a security policy provides comprehensive and robust security.

Document and Audit Your Security Policy

Do not, of course, write down all the network passwords under your keyboard. Instead, as you go through the process of identifying and designing your network security, document your findings and the security actions taken. A written, living security document is vital to the proper implementation of your overall network security strategy. It will also help those who come after you to understand why the network security was implemented and designed in that way (perhaps it'll even be a learning tool for future network engineers). This document should *not* be publicly accessible.

Ensure that your security policy has provisions that require regular and comprehensive audits. These audits can be used as a means to continually test your policy and overall network security against new vulnerabilities and attacks.

Understanding Cisco's Approach to Network Security

Another issue in shared networking is preventing data from falling into the wrong hands. Anyone who has a promiscuous mode driver and application can capture network frames and decode the contents. In shared networking, traffic from any port on a hub is sent to all ports on that hub because the ports are all part of the same collision domain.

Security measures keep people honest in the same way that locks do. This case study discusses specific actions that you can take to improve the security of your network. Before going into those specifics, however, this section reviews basic concepts that should be remembered when you are planning network security.

Know Your Enemy

This statement refers specifically to cyber-thieves who are either *attackers* or *intruders*. Consider who might want to circumvent your security measures and identify their motivations. Determine what they might want to do and the damage that they could cause to your network. For example, does your organization deal in money, electronic commerce, or sensitive data? Any of these can be of value to a thief.

Security measures can never make it impossible for a user to perform unauthorized tasks with a computer system. They can only make performing unauthorized tasks harder. The goal is to make sure that the network security controls are beyond the attacker's ability or motivation.

Count the Cost

Security measures usually reduce convenience, especially for sophisticated users. Security can delay work, and create expensive administrative and educational overhead. It can use significant computing resources and require dedicated hardware. Just as in anything in life, nothing worth having is free; you must work for the results you want to receive.

When you design your security measures, understand their costs, and weigh those costs against the potential benefits. To do that, you must understand the costs of the measures themselves and the likelihood of security breaches. If you incur security costs out of proportion to the actual dangers, you have done yourself a disservice. Very few organizations can actually justify having the extreme security measures found within the Department of Defenses (DOD) network, for example. Yes, it is effective, but at what cost?

Identify Your Assumptions

Every security system has underlying assumptions. You might assume that your network is not tapped, for example, or that attackers know less than you do, that they are using standard software, or that a locked room is safe. All these assumptions are most likely incorrect and could cause holes in your security policy. Be sure to examine and justify your assumptions. Any hidden assumption is a potential security hole.

A nice rule of thumb here is to be painfully honest concerning your network security requirements and remember that incomplete or not duly considered assumptions can cause disastrous consequences. When identifying and justifying your assumptions, you might encounter a network concern that has nothing to do with security, so this is truly a double-edged sword.

Control and Limit Your Secrets

Most security is based on and required by secrets. Passwords and encryption keys SNMP community strings, for example are secrets. Too often, though, the secrets are not all that secret. The most important part of keeping secrets is knowing the areas you need to protect. What knowledge would enable someone to circumvent your system? You should jealously guard that knowledge and assume that your adversaries know everything else. The more secrets you have, the harder it will be to keep all of them. Security systems should be designed so that only a limited number of secrets need to be kept.

Always Remember Human Factors

Many security procedures fail because their designers do not consider how users will react to them. Because they can be difficult to remember, for example, automatically generated "nonsense" passwords are often found written on the undersides of keyboards. For convenience, a "secure" door that leads to the system's only tape drive is sometimes propped open. For expediency, unauthorized modems are often connected to a network to avoid onerous dial-in security measures.

If your security measures interfere too much with the essential use of the system or network, those measures will be resisted and perhaps circumvented by resourceful users. To get compliance, you must make sure that users can get their work done, and you must sell your security measures to users. Users must understand and accept the need for security. Communication with users is essential here because if users understand the business reasons behind your security measures, they will be more open to accepting them. No matter how hard you try, there will be users who will still try to *get around* your security.

Any user can compromise system security, at least to some degree. Passwords, for instance, can often be found just by calling legitimate users on the telephone, claiming to be a system administrator, and asking for them. If your users understand security issues, and if they understand the reasons for your security measures, they are far less likely to make an intruder's job easier.

At a minimum, users should be taught never to release passwords or other secrets over unsecured telephone lines (especially cellular telephones) or electronic mail (e-mail). Users should be wary of questions asked by people who call them on the telephone. Some companies have implemented formalized network security training for their employees; that is, employees are not allowed access to the Internet until they have completed a formal training program. This is helpful in raising awareness in a user community and it should be reinforced with a written security policy for your organization that is accessible to every user. One last point to make is that you should never violate your own security procedures, no matter how tempting!

Know Your Weaknesses

Every security system has vulnerabilities and identifying them is no place for egos, but rather honesty and directness. It is sometimes very helpful to get another set of eyes to assist you in reviewing the network for weaknesses.

You should be able to understand your system's weak points and know how they could be exploited. You should also know the areas that present the largest danger, and prevent access to them immediately. Understanding the weak points in your network is the first step toward turning them into secure areas.

Limit the Scope of Access

You should create appropriate barriers inside your network so that if intruders access one part of the network, they do not automatically have access to the rest of the network.

As with many things, the security of a network is only as good as the weakest security level (link) of any single device in the system. Having a layered approach to security will certainly slow down an intruder and allow their detection. Having a nice big lock is good, but if that lock is your only line of defense, you might want to consider adding motion sensors, a dog, outside lights, a home security system, and nosy neighbors! A rather simplistic analogy, but my point is that it is always harder to be a criminal when there are many barriers to overcome.

Understand Your Environment

Understanding how your system normally functions, knowing what is expected and what is unexpected, and being familiar with how devices are usually used will help you to detect security problems. Noticing unusual events can help you to catch intruders before they can damage the system. Auditing tools can help you to detect those unusual events.

Auditing tools are very useful, although you will also want to ensure that there are methods for you to receive alarms when there is an attempt to violate or bypass the security measures in place. The thought here is that it is better to know what is happening *before* you lose something than having to go back and audit the crime; an ounce of prevention!

Limit Your Trust

You should know exactly which software or hardware you rely on, and your security system should not have to rely on the assumption that all software is bug-free. Learn from history by not reliving it, and remember to question everything!

Remember Physical Security

Physical access to a workstation, server, switch, firewall, or router usually gives a sufficiently sophisticated user total control over that device. Physical access to a network link usually enables a person to tap that link, jam it, or inject traffic into it. It makes no sense to install complicated software security measures when access to the hardware is not controlled.

Security Is Pervasive

Almost any change you make in your system might have security effects. This is especially true when new services are created. Network engineers, system administrators, programmers, and users should consider the security implications of every change they make. Understanding the security implications of a change is something that takes practice. It requires lateral thinking and a willingness to explore every way in which a service could potentially be manipulated. Intelligent changes are good and can be judged accordingly; however, quick or ill-considered changes can often result in severe security problems.

Controlling Access to Cisco Routers

It is important to control access to your Cisco routers. You can control access to the router using the following methods:

- Console Access
- Telnet Access
- Simple Network Management Protocol (SNMP) Access

You can secure access to a router through the use of the router's IOS. For each method, you can permit nonprivileged access and privileged access for a user (or group of users):

- **Nonprivileged access**—Allows users to monitor the router, but not to configure the router. Read-only access.

- **Privileged access**—Allows the user to fully configure the router. Read-write access.

For console port and Telnet access, you can set up two types of passwords. The first type of password, the login password, allows the user nonprivileged access to the router. After accessing the router, the user can enter privileged mode by entering the **enable** command and the proper password. Privileged mode provides the user with full configuration capabilities.

SNMP access allows you to set up different SNMP community strings for both nonprivileged and privileged access. Nonprivileged access allows users on a host to send the router SNMP get-request and SNMP get-next-request messages. These messages are used for gathering statistics from the router. Privileged access allows users on a host to send the router SNMP set-request messages to make changes to the router's configurations and operational state.

Console Access

A *console* is a terminal attached directly to the router via the console port. Security is applied to the console by asking users to authenticate themselves via passwords. By default, no passwords are associated with console access.

Assigning a Nonprivileged Mode Password

You configure a password for nonprivileged mode by entering the following commands in the router's configuration file. Passwords are case-sensitive. In this example, the password is **1forAll**:

```
line console 0
login
password 1forAll
```

When you log in to the router, the router login prompt is as follows:

```
User Access Verification
Password:
```

You must enter the password **1forAll** to gain nonprivileged access to the router. The router response is as follows:

```
router>
```

Nonprivileged mode is signified on the router by the > prompt. At this point, you can enter a variety of commands to view statistics on the router, but you cannot change the configuration of the router.

TIP   Never use **cisco** or other obvious derivatives, such as **pancho**, for a Cisco router password. These will be the first passwords intruders will try if they recognize the Cisco login prompt.

Assigning a Privileged Mode Password

Configure a password for privileged mode by entering the following commands in the router's configuration file. In this example, the password is **san-fran**:

```
enable-password san-fran
```

To access privileged mode, enter the following command:

```
router> enable
Password:
```

Enter the password **san-fran** to gain privileged access to the router. The router responds as follows:

```
router#
```

Privileged mode is signified by the # prompt. In privileged mode, you can enter all commands to view statistics and configure the router.

TIP   Another way to set the enable password is by using the **enable secret** command. The **enable secret** command overrides the **enable-password** command and automatically encrypts the enable password when viewing the router configuration.

Telnet Access

You can access both nonprivileged and privileged mode on the router via Telnet. As with the console port, Telnet security is provided when users are prompted by the router to authenticate themselves via passwords. In fact, many of the same concepts described in the "Console Access" section earlier in this chapter apply to Telnet access. You must enter a password to go from nonprivileged mode to privileged mode, and you can encrypt passwords and specify timeouts for each Telnet session.

Assigning a Nonprivileged Mode Password

Each Telnet port on the router is known as a virtual terminal. The router has a maximum of five virtual terminal (VTY) ports, allowing five concurrent Telnet sessions. (The communication server provides more VTY ports.) On the router, the virtual terminal ports are numbered from 0 through 4. You can set up nonprivileged passwords for Telnet access via the virtual terminal ports with the following configuration commands. In this example, virtual terminal ports 0 through 4 use the password **marin**:

```
line vty 0 4
login
password marin
```

When a user telnets to a router IP address, the router provides a prompt similar to the following:

```
% telnet router
Trying ...
Connected to router.
Escape character is '^]'.
User Access Verification
Password:
```

If the user enters the correct nonprivileged password, the following prompt appears:

```
router>
```

Assigning a Privileged Mode Password

The user now has nonprivileged access to the router and can enter privileged mode by entering the **enable** command, as described in the "Privileged Mode Password" section earlier in this chapter.

Simple Network Management Protocol (SNMP) Access

SNMP is another method you can use to access your routers. With SNMP, you can gather statistics or configure the router. Gather statistics with get-request and get-next-request messages, and configure routers with set-request messages. Each of these SNMP messages has a community string that is a clear text password sent in every packet between a management station and the router (which contains an SNMP agent). The SNMP community string is used to authenticate messages sent between the manager and agent. Only when the manager sends a message with the correct community string will the agent respond.

The SNMP agent on the router allows you to configure different community strings for nonprivileged and privileged access. You configure community strings on the router via the configuration command **snmp-server community** *string* [**ro** | **rw**] [*access-list*]. The following sections explore the various ways to use this command.

Unfortunately, SNMP community strings are sent on the network in clear text ASCII. Therefore, anyone who has the ability to capture a packet on the network can discover the community string. This may allow unauthorized users to query or modify routers via SNMP. For this reason, using the **no snmp-server trap-authentication** command may prevent intruders from using trap messages (sent between SNMP managers and agents) to discover community strings.

The Internet community, recognizing this problem, greatly enhanced the security of SNMP version 2 (SNMPv2) as described in RFC 1446. SNMPv2 uses an algorithm called MD5 to authenticate communications between an SNMP server and agent. MD5 verifies the integrity of the communications, authenticates the origin, and checks for timeliness. Further, SNMPv2 can use the data encryption standard (DES) for encrypting information.

Assigning a Nonprivileged Mode Password

Use the **ro** keyword of the **snmp-server community** command to provide nonprivileged access to your routers via SNMP. The following configuration command sets the agent in the router to allow only SNMP get-request and get-next-request messages sent with the community string public:

```
snmp-server community public ro
```

You can also specify a list of IP addresses allowed to send messages to the router using the *access-list* option with the **snmp-server community** command. In the following configuration example, only hosts 1.1.1.1 and 2.2.2.2 are allowed nonprivileged mode SNMP access to the router:

```
access-list 1 permit 1.1.1.1
access-list 1 permit 2.2.2.2
snmp-server community public ro 1
```

Assigning a Privileged Mode Password

Use the **rw** keyword of the **snmp-server community** command to provide privileged access to your routers via SNMP. The following configuration command sets the agent in the router to allow only SNMP set-request messages sent with the community string private:

```
snmp-server community private rw
```

You can also specify a list of IP addresses allowed to send messages to the router by using the *access-list* option of the **snmp-server community** command. In the following configuration example, only hosts 5.5.5.5 and 6.6.6.6 are allowed privileged mode SNMP access to the router:

```
access-list 1 permit 5.5.5.5
access-list 1 permit 6.6.6.6
snmp-server community private rw 1
```

Additional Techniques to Secure a Router

These additional techniques can be used on an "as needed" basis to further protect access to your routers.

Session Timeouts

Setting the login and enable passwords may not provide enough security in some cases. The timeout for an unattended console (by default, 10 minutes) provides an additional security measure. If the console is left unattended in privileged mode, any user can modify the router's configuration. You can change the login timeout via the command **exec-timeout** *mm ss,* where *mm* is minutes and *ss* is seconds. The following commands change the timeout to 1 minute and 30 seconds:

```
line console 0
exec-timeout 1 30
```

Password Encryption

All passwords on the router are visible via the **write terminal** and **show configuration** privileged mode commands. If you have access to privileged mode on the router, you can view all passwords in clear text by default.

There is a way to hide clear text passwords. The command **service password-encryption** stores passwords in an encrypted manner so that anyone performing a **write terminal** and **show configuration** will not be able to determine the clear text password. If you forget the password, however, regaining access to the router requires you to have physical access to the router.

NOTE   Although encryption is helpful, it can be compromised and therefore should not be your only network security strategy.

Restricting Telnet Access to Particular IP Addresses

If you want to allow only certain IP addresses to use Telnet to access the router, you must use the **access-class** command. The command **access-class** *nn in* defines an access list (from 1 through 99) that allows access to the virtual terminal lines on the router. The following configuration commands allow incoming Telnet access to the router only from hosts on network 192.85.55.0:

```
access-list 12 permit 192.85.55.0 0.0.0.255
line vty 0 4
access-class 12 in
```

Restricting Telnet Access TCP Ports

It is possible to access Cisco products via Telnet to specified TCP ports. The type of Telnet access varies, depending on the following Cisco software releases:

- Software Release 9.1 (11.4) and earlier, and 9.21 (3.1) and earlier
- Software Release 9.1 (11.5), 9.21 (3.2), and 10.0 and later

Earlier Software Releases

For Software Release 9.1 (11.4) and earlier, and Software Release 9.21 (3.1) and earlier, it is possible, by default, to establish TCP connections to Cisco products via the TCP ports listed in Table 22-1.

Table 22-1   *TCP Port Telnet Access to Cisco Products (Earlier Releases)*

TCP Port Number	Access Method
7	Echo
9	Discard
23	Telnet (to virtual terminal VTY ports in rotary fashion)
79	Finger
1993	SNMP over TCP
2001 through 2999	Telnet to auxiliary (AUX) port, terminal (TTY) ports, and virtual terminal (VTY) ports
3001 through 3999	Telnet to rotary ports (access via these ports is possible only if the rotaries have been explicitly configured first with the **rotary** command)
4001 through 4999	Telnet (stream mode) mirror of 2000 range
5001 through 5999	Telnet (stream mode) mirror of 3000 range (access via these ports is possible only if the rotaries have been explicitly configured first)
6001 through 6999	Telnet (binary mode) mirror of 2000 range
7001 through 7999	Telnet (binary mode) mirror of 3000 range (access via these ports is possible only if the rotaries have been explicitly configured first)
8001 through 8999	Xremote (communication servers only)
9001 through 9999	Reverse Xremote (communication servers only)
10001 through 19999	Reverse Xremote rotary (communication servers only; access via these ports is possible only if the ports have been explicitly configured first)

NOTE   Because Cisco routers have no TTY lines, configuring access (on communication servers) to terminal ports 2002, 2003, 2004, and greater could potentially provide access (on routers) to virtual terminal lines 2002, 2003, 2004, and greater. To provide access to TTY ports only, you can create access lists to prevent access to VTYs.

Also, when configuring rotary groups, keep in mind that access through any available port in the rotary group is possible (unless access lists are defined). Cisco recommends that if you are using firewalls that allow in-bound TCP connections to high-number ports, remember to apply appropriate in-bound access lists to Cisco products.

The following example illustrates an access list denying all in-bound Telnet access to the auxiliary port and allowing Telnet access to the router only from IP address 192.32.6.7:

```
access-class 51 deny 0.0.0.0 255.255.255.255
access-class 52 permit 192.32.6.7
line aux 0
access-class 51 in
line vty 0 4
access-class 52 in
```

To disable connections to the echo and discard ports, you must disable these services completely with the **no service tcp-small-servers** command.

NOTE   If the **ip alias** command is enabled on Cisco products, TCP connections to any destination port are considered valid connections. You may want to disable the **ip alias** command.

You might want to create access lists to prevent access to Cisco products via these TCP ports. For information on how to create access lists for routers, see the section titled "Configuring the Firewall Router," later in this chapter. For information on how to create access lists for communication servers, see the section titled "Configuring the Firewall Communication Server," later in this chapter.

Software Releases 9.1 (11.5), 9.21 (3.2), and 10.0 and Later

With Software Release 9.1 (11.5), 9.21 (3.2), and any version of Software Release 10, the following enhancements have been implemented:

- Direct access to virtual terminal lines (VTYs) through the 2000, 4000, and 6000 port ranges has been disabled. If you want to keep access open, you can set up one-to-one mapping of VTY-to-rotary ports.
- Connections to echo and discard ports (7 and 9) can be disabled with the **no service tcp-small-servers** command.
- All Cisco products allow connections to IP alias devices only on destination port 23.

For later releases, a Cisco router accepts TCP connections on the ports listed in Table 22-2 by default.

Table 22-2   *TCP Port Telnet Access to Cisco Products (Later Releases)*

TCP Port Number	Access Method
7	Echo
9	Discard
23	Telnet
79	Finger
1993	SNMP over TCP
2001	Auxiliary (AUX) port
4001	Auxiliary (AUX) port (stream)
6001	Auxiliary (AUX) port (binary)

Access via port 23 can be restricted by creating an access list and assigning it to virtual terminal lines. Access via port 79 can be disabled with the **no service finger** command. Access via port 1993 can be controlled with SNMP access lists. Access via ports 2001, 4001, and 6001 can be controlled with an access list placed on the auxiliary port.

Access Control Lists

Access lists are just that: lists. Just like any other list that you can create, access control lists (ACLs) are just a set of criteria. The criteria can be either rather simplistic or extremely advanced, with everything in between. The criteria could begin, for example, with a list of those IP addresses permitted to telnet to a router's VTY port. Access control lists can be used for many other things as well, including the following:

1 Filter either incoming or outgoing traffic

2 Organize your queuing strategy

3 Determine what types of traffic will activate your dial-on-demand routing (DDR) circuits

4 Filter routing updates sent to or from the router

This criteria list may eventually be used to filter traffic in or out of the router, in addition to the items as shown in the preceding list. Regardless of the filtering criteria defined within an access control list, if not used correctly, the list has no function or might even function incorrectly.

Operation

Access-list definitions provide a set of criteria applied to each packet processed by the router. The router decides whether to forward or block each packet, based on whether that packet matches the access list criteria.

Typical access list criteria include packet source addresses, packet destination addresses, or upper-layer protocol of the packet. Each protocol has its own specific set of criteria, however, that can be further defined using port numbers.

For a given access list, you can define each criteria in a separate access list statement. These statements specify whether to block or forward packets that match the criteria listed. An access list, then, is the sum of individual statements that all share the same identifying name or number.

TIP   Each additional access list statement that you enter is appended to the end of the access list statements. Also, you cannot delete individual statements after they have been created. You can delete only an entire access list.

Each packet is compared against each line of the list (the criteria). When a match is found, the packet is either permitted or denied, depending on the criteria. Each line of an access list can either permit or deny traffic.

At the end of every access list is an implied *"deny all traffic"* criteria statement. Therefore, if a packet does not match any of your criteria statements, the packet will be blocked. This is the default behavior of an access list in a Cisco router. It is important to remember that the access list by itself denies all traffic if it has not been permitted.

The overall behavior of an access list can be easily compared to an if-then situation. Each line of the access list is a separate criteria. The "if" portion of the line is the criteria; the "then" portion is either a permit or deny statement. For example:

> if <criteria #1> then <permit | deny>
> if <criteria #2> then <permit | deny>
> .
> .
> .
> deny all traffic

The order of access list statements is also important. When the router is deciding whether to forward or block a packet, the Cisco IOS software tests the packet against each criteria statement in the order in which the statements were created. After a match is found, no more criteria statements are checked. This is known as *top-down processing*.

Top-down processing is one of the simpler concepts found in Cisco routers, if you follow the rules. When designing your ACL, keep these concepts in mind:

- Specific items, such as individual IP addresses, are put at the top of the list.

- Generalized items, such as subnet numbers, should reside in the middle.

- Open-ended items such as networks, would go at the end.

If you create a criteria statement that explicitly permits all traffic, no statements added later will ever be checked. If you need additional statements, you must delete the access list and retype it with the new entries.

NOTE	When entering or modifying access lists, it is strongly suggested that you do not modify or alter them on-the-fly. You can either design them on a TFTP server, in a word processor, or on paper. The use of access lists requires the router processor to work more because each entry in the list must be checked until a match is found.

You should also not save the changes to the router configuration until you are sure that the desired security is adequately working. This gives you a quick and easy backout plan in case of errors.

Applying Access Lists to the Router

Table 22-3 shows the different methods of applying access lists within a router's configuration.

Table 22-3   *Access List Application Commands*

Command	Where Applies	Purpose
ip access-group	Router interface	Restricts packets flowing either in or out of the router
access-class	VTY lines	Restricts Telnet access in or out of the router
distribute-list	Routing protocol	Restricts routing updates in or out

You can apply only one access list to an interface for a given protocol. With most protocols, you can apply access lists to interfaces as either inbound or outbound. If the access list is inbound, when the router receives a packet, the Cisco IOS software checks the access list's criteria statements for a match. If the packet is permitted, the software continues to process the packet. If the packet is denied, the software discards the packet.

If the access list is outbound, after receiving and routing a packet to the outbound interface, the software checks the access list's criteria statements for a match. If the packet is permitted, the software transmits the packet. If the packet is denied, the software discards the packet.

To understand basic ACL operation, you must realize that the direction in which the ACL is applied is all a matter of perspective. Figure 22-3 shows the router's perspective.

Figure 22-3 *ACL Direction Is Based On the Router's Perspective*

WARNING   For most protocols, if you define an inbound access list for traffic filtering, you should include explicit access list criteria statements to permit routing updates. If you do not, you might effectively lose communication from the interface when routing updates are blocked by the implicit deny all traffic statement at the end of the access list.

Remember that access lists, regardless of how you actually use them, are configured *inside* a router. As long as you can temporarily see things from the router's perspective, you can differentiate between the terms *inbound* and *outbound*.

Wildcard Mask

Both standard and extended IP access lists use a wildcard mask. Like an IP address, a *wildcard mask* is a 32-bit quantity written in dotted-decimal format. Address bits corresponding to wildcard mask bits set to 1 are ignored in comparisons; address bits corresponding to wildcard mask bits set to 0 are used in comparisons.

An alternative way to think of the wildcard mask is as follows:

- If a 0 bit appears in the mask, the corresponding bit location in the access list address and the same location in the packet address must match; either bit must be both 0 or both 1.

- If a 1 bit appears in the mask, the bit location in the packet will match, regardless of whether it is 0 or 1; and the bit location in the access list address is ignored. For this reason, 1 bits in the mask are sometimes called "don't care" bits.

An access list can contain an indefinite number of actual and wildcard addresses. A wildcard address has a nonzero address mask and therefore potentially matches more than one actual address. Remember that the order of the access list statements is important because the access list is not processed further after a match has been found.

NOTE	An important benefit of the wildcard masks is that the router can quickly process packets against ACL entries, and thus reduce the amount of time and CPU cycles the router uses.

In simplistic terms, the wildcard mask is the exact opposite of the subnet mask. This allows the router to quickly check and see whether only one IP address is referenced or whether a range is referenced. Consider this example: You have an IP address of 172.19.1.1 with a subnet mask of 255.255.255.255 or (/32). This causes you to mask the entire subnet; and for an ACL wildcard mask to reference it as well, a wildcard mask of 0.0.0.0 would be used. Therefore, you can see that the wildcard mask is the exact opposite of the subnet.

Take a look at another more complex example of how wildcard masking works. You have a network of 172.19.0.0 and it has been subnetted with a /28 mask. Therefore, you have the following subnets available for use:

> 172.19.0.16/28
> 172.19.0.32/28
> 172.19.0.48/28

To permit one specific subnet in an ACL, you would need the exact opposite of the subnet mask for the wildcard mask, which can be determined as follows:

> 255.255.255.255
> 255.255.255.240—subnet mask
> ----------------
> 0 . 0 . 0 . 15—wildcard mask

Standard Access Control Lists

Standard access control lists can be very powerful and can block an entire range of source addresses. Standard access lists permit or deny packets, based only on the source IP address of the packet. The access list number range for defining standard access lists is 1 to 99. Standard access lists are easier to configure than their more flexible counterparts, extended access lists.

Standard Access List Configuration

The following is the syntax for a standard access list:

```
Router (config)#
access-list access-list-number {permit ¦ deny} source source-mask
```

This configuration command will enable you to determine how the access list is implemented:

- Sets the parameters for this access list
- Standard IP access lists are numbered from 1 to 99

The following command syntax will activate the list on the desired interface; only one access list is allowed on an interface:

```
Router (config-if)#
ip access-group access-list-number {in | out}
```

Table 22-4 explains the elements of these two commands.

Table 22-4   *Access List Option Definitions*

access-list Command	Description
access-list-number	Identifies the list to which the entry belongs; for standard access lists, this is a number from 1 to 99.
permit ǀ deny	Indicates whether this entry allows or blocks traffic from the specified address.
source	Identifies source IP address.
source-mask	Identifies which bits in the address field are matched. It has a 1 in positions indicating "don't care" bits and a 0 in any position that is strictly followed.

ip access-group Command	Description
access-list-number	Indicates the number of the access list to be linked to this interface.
in ǀ out	Selects whether the access list is applied to the incoming or outgoing interface. If in or out is not specified, out is the default.

NOTE   To remove an access list, first enter the **no access-group** command with all of its set parameters, and then enter the **no access-list** command with all the access list parameters.

Standard Access List Example

The following access list allows only traffic from the 10.10.0.0 source network to be forwarded. Non-10.10.0.0 network traffic is blocked:

```
access-list 1 permit 10.10.0.0 0.0.255.255
! Don't forget the implicit deny all at the end of every access list.
! It is not visible in the list: access-list 1 deny 0.0.0.0 255.255.255.255
interface ethernet 0
ip access-group 1 out
interface ethernet 1
ip access-group 1 out
```

Extended Access Control Lists

Standard access lists offer quick configuration and low overhead by limiting traffic based on the source address within a network. Extended access lists provide a higher degree of control by enabling filtering based on the session layer protocol, destination address, and application port number. These features make it possible to limit traffic based on the uses of the network. Figure 22-4 shows how the router's IOS will process an extended access control list.

Figure 22-4 *Extended Access Control List Processing Tree*

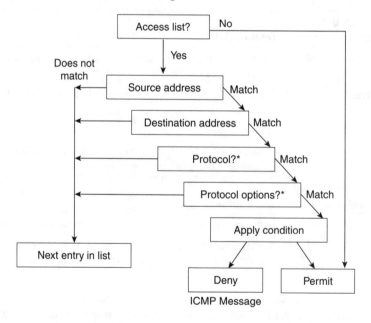

Every condition tested must match for the line of the access list to match, and the permit or deny condition to be applied. As soon as one parameter or condition fails, the next line in the access list is compared.

Extended Access List Configuration

Extended ACLs are much more configurable and precise than standard ACLs, as shown in the following and in Table 22-5.

```
access-list access-list-number {permit|deny} protocol source source-mask
    destination destination-mask [operator operand] [established]
```

Table 22-5   *Extended Access List Option Definitions*

access-list Command	Description
access-list-number	Identifies the list to which the entry belongs; for standard access lists, this is a number from 100 to 199.
**permit	deny**	Indicates whether this entry allows or blocks traffic from the specified address.
protocol	**ip**, **tcp**, **udp**, **icmp**, **gre**, **igrp**.
source and *destination*	Identifies source and destination IP address.
source-mask and *destination-mask*	Which bits in the address field are matched. A 1 indicates a "don't care" bit position; a 0 in any position indicates a match bit position.
operator and *operand*	**lt**, **gt**, **eq**, **neq** (less than, greater than, equal, not equal) and a port number.
established	Allows traffic to pass if packet is a response to traffic initiated by a directly connected network/subnet.

ip access-group Command	Description
access-list-number	Indicates the number of the access list to be linked to this interface.
**in	out**	Selects whether the access list is applied to the incoming or outgoing interface. If in or out is not specified, out is the default.

Extended Access List Example

The following is an extended access list example:

```
access-list 100 permit icmp 10.251.3.48 255.255.255.248 66.34.40.45 0.0.0.0
access-list 100 permit tcp 10.251.3.48 255.255.255.248 66.34.40.45 0.0.0.0
established
access-list 100 permit tcp 10.251.3.48 255.255.255.248 66.34.40.45 0.0.0.0  eq 21
access-list 100 permit tcp 10.251.3.48 255.255.255.248 66.34.40.45 0.0.0.0  eq 161
access-list 100 permit tcp 10.251.3.48 255.255.255.248 66.34.40.45 0.0.0.0  eq 162
access-list 100 deny ip 10.251.3.48 255.255.255.248 0.0.0.0 255.255.255.255
access-list 100 permit ip any any
```

A pseudo-configuration of the preceding statements follows:

```
If source is net and equal to 10.251.3.48
Then allow full icmp access to destination 66.34.40.45
Else if source is net and equal to 10.152.3.48
Then allow TCP access to the port 21, 161 and 162
Else if source is net and not equal to 10.251.3.48
    Then allow open access
End if a.k.a. DENY ALL TRAFFIC
```

Reflexive Access Control Lists

Reflexive access control lists are a new type of ACL with the following characteristics:

- Filter IP traffic so that TCP or UDP "session" traffic is only permitted through the firewall if the session originated from *within* the internal network.

- Reflexive access lists provide a level of security against spoofing and certain denial-of-service attacks.

- There is *no* implicit *"deny all traffic"* statement after reflexive ACLs because they are nested.

- They are temporary permit entries. An entry is created when a new IP session begins (for example, outbound packet) and removed when it ends.

- Not applied directly to an interface, but are *"nested"* within a named extended ACL applied to an interface.

- A pair of named extended ACLs is needed (inbound and outbound).

- To define a reflexive access list, you use an entry in an extended named IP access list. This entry must use the **reflect** keyword. Then, another extended access list, named IP access list, is needed with the **evaluate** keyword.

Reflexive Access Control List Example

For this example, use the following analogy:

A security guard records traffic information (IP address, protocol, and port number) leaving a site and creates a temporary permit entry for the returning traffic through the use of the **reflect** keyword.

Returning traffic is checked against the temporary entry through the use of the **evaluate** keyword. If it matches the temporary entry, it is allowed in. If it does not match, the extended ACL entries are used to evaluate the traffic.

To define reflexive access lists, perform the following tasks, starting in global configuration mode:

1 For an external interface, specify the outbound access list; for an internal interface, specify the inbound access list. (Performing this task also causes you to enter the access list configuration mode.) Use the following command to perform this task:

   ip access-list extended *name*

2 Define the reflexive access list using the reflexive permit entry. Repeat this step for each IP upper-layer protocol; for example, you can define reflexive filtering for TCP sessions and also for UDP sessions. You can use the same name for multiple protocols. This command is also known as "nesting." To perform this task, use the following command:

```
permit protocol any any reflect name [timeout seconds]
```

Reflexive access lists are most commonly used with one of two basic network topologies. Determining which of these topologies is most like your own can help you decide whether to use reflexive access lists with an internal interface or with an external interface. Figure 22-5 shows the common topologies.

Figure 22-5 *Common Reflexive Access Control List Topologies*

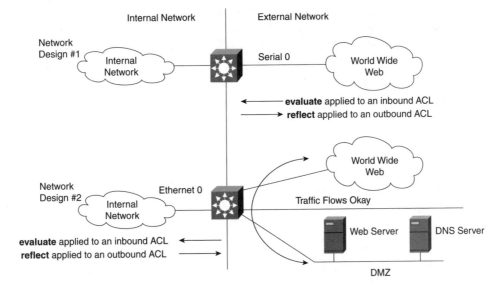

External Interface

The first topology is shown as Network Design #1. In this simple topology, reflexive access lists are configured for the external interface Serial 0. This prevents IP traffic from entering the router and the internal network, unless the traffic is part of a session already established from within the internal network.

Internal Interface

The second topology is shown as Network Design #2. In this topology, reflexive access lists are configured for the internal interface Ethernet 0. This allows external traffic to access the services in the Demilitarized Zone (DMZ), such as DNS services, but prevents IP traffic from entering your internal network—unless the traffic is part of a session already established from within the internal network.

Configuring a Reflexive Access Control List

Reflexive ACLs allow for more granular security by allowing the router to remember what it has seen and allow only the corresponding response packets from the destination through the filtering mechanism. A data packet is accepted as a valid response packet if, and only if, it is from the host and port where the outbound packet was sent to, and is destined for the host and port that originated the outbound packet.

The information taken from the data packet to generate the reflexive ACL entry is the source IP address and port, the destination IP address and port, and the protocol type. If the protocol type is either TCP or UDP, the port information must match exactly. If the protocol type is ICMP, match an echo reply to an echo request (ping response to ping request). For any other protocol, there is no port information to match.

You do not explicitly configure reflexive ACLs. They are generated automatically in response to a packet matching an ACL entry that contains the **reflect** clause. Figure 22-6 shows the proper steps used to configure a reflexive ACL.

Figure 22-6 *Configuring a Reflexive Access Control List*

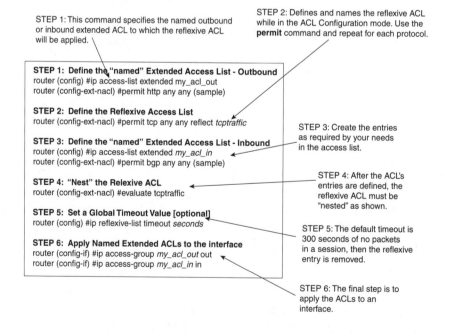

Reflexive Access Control List Configuration Example

The following ACL entry has been applied to an interface in the outbound direction:

```
ip access-list extended outbound-data
! any permit/deny clauses as needed.
permit udp any any reflect check-udp-data
! any other permit/deny clauses as needed may include other reflect clauses.
```

The following ACL entry has been applied to an interface in the inbound direction:

```
ip access-list extended inbound-data
! any permit/deny clauses as needed.
evaluate check-udp-data
! any other permit/deny clauses as needed. May include other evaluate clauses.
```

The outbound packet will be evaluated by the **reflect** entry only if no other match occurs first. If the packet matches the protocol specified in the **reflect** entry, a temporary entry is created in the specified reflect ACL and the packet is forwarded out on the interface. The temporary entry specifies criteria that permits inbound traffic only for the same session.

If a corresponding entry already exists, the outbound packet belongs to a session in progress and no other entry needs to be created. The only action is to reset the activity timer.

When a data packet is checked against the ACL *outbound-data*, if it is a UDP packet, the information from the packet, source IP address and port, and destination IP address and port are taken from the packet and a permit clause for it is created in the IP access list named check-udp-data. Only one ACL entry per session or flow is created.

NOTE   If an outbound data packet matches any other **permit** or **deny** clause within the outbound-data access control list, the **reflect** clause is not reached, and a reflexive entry will not be created.

When a data packet is checked against the ACL inbound-data, if the router reaches the **evaluate** clause, the packet is then evaluated against the ACL check-udp-data. If the packet matches, it is then permitted. If there is no match, the ACL inbound-data continues to be evaluated.

NOTE   If an inbound data packet matches any other **permit** or **deny** clause within the inbound-data extended ACL, the **evaluate** clause is never reached, and the reflexive entry will not be checked.

When the router that has an access list in place receives a packet, the packet and the access list are compared. The router evaluates the packet against the extended access control list.

If the packet matches a normal extended access list entry before the nested reflexive access list, it is evaluated against the reflexive statements. If it does not match, however, the packet goes through the reflexive statements.

If the packet matches a reflexive permit entry, a temporary entry is created and the packet is handled according to this match criteria. The temporary entry stays active until the session ends.

For TCP sessions, the entry is removed five seconds after two set FIN bits are detected, or immediately after matching a TCP packet with the RST bit set. Alternatively, the temporary entry is removed after no packets of the session have been detected for a configurable length of time, which is the timeout period.

NOTE   Two set FIN bits in a session indicate that the session is about to end; the five-second window allows the session to close gracefully. A set RST bit indicates an abrupt session close.

For UDP and other protocols, the end of the session is determined differently than for TCP. Because other protocols are considered to be connectionless (sessionless) services, no session tracking information is embedded in packets. Therefore, the end of a session is considered to be when no packets of the session have been detected for a configurable length of time.

It is possible to view the process used by the router to process reflexive access control list entries, as shown in Figure 22-7. Remember to keep the following key concepts in mind while reviewing the figure:

- As with all ACLs, the order of their entry is extremely critical to their operation, as shown in Figure 22-7.

- If the packet matches an entry prior to the reflexive evaluate entry, it will not be evaluated against the reflexive ACL permit statements, and no temporary entry will be created.

- A temporary reflexive ACL is created only if a corresponding entry is not already in existence.

Figure 22-7 *Reflexive ACL Operation*

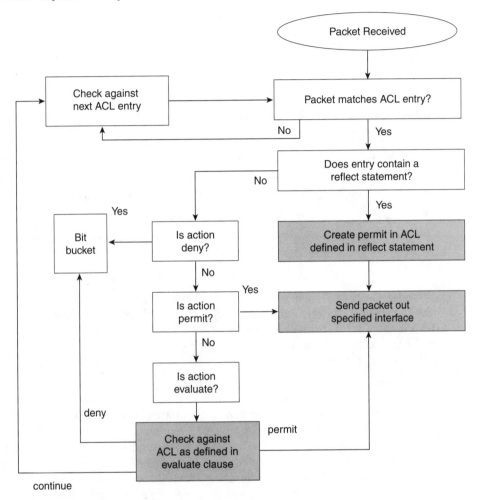

Golden Rules of Reflexive ACL Implementation

The following dos and don'ts of reflexive ACL implementation are extremely important to properly design reflexive ACLs. They should be considered when designing your implementation with a campus network.

Do:

- Define with extended named IP access lists only.

- Provide an increased level of security against spoofing and certain denial-of-service attacks.

Don't:

- Define reflexive access lists with numbered or standard-named IP access lists or with other protocol access lists.

- Use them with applications that use changing port numbers such as FTP in active mode.

Dynamic Access Lists (Lock-and-Key Security)

To authorize remote access to local services, a common security solution is to create access lists, as discussed previously. Standard and static extended access lists have the following limitations:

- They can create the opportunity for break-ins by network hackers.

- They are difficult to manage in a large network.

- They require the router to do excess processing, depending on entries in the access list.

- They do not offer a challenge mechanism to authenticate individual users.

An improved security solution is the lock-and-key access feature, which is available only with IP-extended access lists. Lock-and-key access enables you to set up dynamic access lists that grant access per user to a specific source/destination host through a user-authentication process. You can allow user access through a firewall dynamically, without compromising security restrictions.

WARNING   Enhancements to the **access-list** command are backward-compatible; migrating from releases prior to Cisco IOS Release 11.1 converts your access lists automatically. However, releases prior to Cisco IOS Release 11.1 are not upwardly compatible with these enhancements. Therefore, if you save an access list with these images and then use software prior to Cisco IOS Release 11.1, the resulting access list will not be interpreted correctly. *This could cause severe security problems.* Save your old configuration files before booting these images.

In Cisco IOS Release 11.1 software, lock-and-key access is dependent on Telnet. Standard Telnet is the required application on the host platform that activates the authentication process.

Implementation Considerations of Lock-and-Key Access

Because lock-and-key access introduces a potential pathway through your network firewall, you need to evaluate the following serious considerations:

- Primary consideration is dynamic access. Another host, spoofing your authenticated address, might gain access behind the firewall. With dynamic access, there is the possibility that an unauthorized host, spoofing your authenticated address, can gain access behind the firewall. Lock-and-key access does not cause the address-spoofing problem. The problem is identified here only as a concern to the user.

- Performance is affected in the following two situations:

  — Each dynamic access list forces an access list to rebuild on the silicon switching engine (SSE). This causes the SSE switching path to slow down momentarily.

  — Dynamic access lists require the idle timeout facility (even if the timeout is left to default) and therefore cannot be SSE switched. These entries must be handled in the protocol fast-switching path.

- Pay close attention to the border router configurations. Remote users create access list entries on the border router. The access list will grow and shrink dynamically. Entries are dynamically removed from the list after either the idle-timeout or max-timeout period expires. Large access lists degrade packet-switching performance.

WARNING   Lock-and-key access allows an external event to place an opening in the firewall. After this opening exists, the router is susceptible to source-address spoofing. To prevent this, you need to provide encryption support using IP encryption with authentication or encryption. This issue is discussed further in this section. Spoofing is a problem with all existing access lists. Lock-and-key access does not address this problem.

Two examples of when you might use lock-and-key access are as follows:

- When you want a remote host to be able to access a host in your network via the Internet. Lock-and-key access limits access beyond your firewall on an individual host or net basis.

- When you want a subset of hosts on a network to access a host on a remote network protected by a firewall. With lock-and-key access, you can enable only a desired set of hosts to gain access by having them authenticate through a TACACS+ server.

The following process describes the lock-and-key access operation:

1 A user opens a Telnet session to a border router configured for lock-and-key access.

2 The Cisco IOS software receives the Telnet packet and performs a user-authentication process. The user must pass authentication before access is allowed. The authentication process can be done by the router or a central access server such as a TACACS+ or a RADIUS server.

> **Tip**   It is highly recommended that you use the TACACS+ server for
> your authentication-query process. TACACS+ provides
> authentication, authorization, and accounting services. It also
> provides protocol support, protocol specification, and a
> centralized security database.

3 When the user passes authentication, the software creates a temporary entry in the
dynamic access list. The temporary entry inherits the attributes of the main dynamic
access list. You can limit the range of networks to which the user is given temporary
access.

4 The user exchanges data through the firewall and then logs out.

5 The software deletes the temporary access list entry when a configured timeout is
reached, or when the system administrator manually clears it. The timeout can either
be an idle timeout or an absolute timeout.

TIP   When the user terminates a session, the temporary access list entry remains until a
configured timeout is reached or until it is cleared by the system administrator.

To configure lock-and-key access, perform the following tasks, beginning in global
configuration mode:

1 Configure a dynamic access list, which serves as a template and placeholder for
temporary access list entries. You configure the dynamic access list with the following
command:

```
access-list access-list-number
 [dynamic dynamic-name [timeout minutes]] {deny | permit}
 protocol source source-wildcard destination destination-wildcard
 [precedence precedence] [tos tos] [established] [log]
```

2 Configure an interface. To do so, use the following command:

```
interface type number
```

3 In interface configuration mode, apply the access list to the interface with the
following command:

```
ip access-group access-list-number
```

4 In global configuration mode, define one or more virtual terminal (VTY) ports. If you
specify multiple VTY ports, they must all be configured identically because the
software hunts for available VTY ports on a round-robin basis. If you do not want to

configure all your VTY ports for lock-and-key access, you can specify a group of VTY ports for lock-and-key support only. You define virtual terminal (VTY) port(s) with the following command:

```
line VTY line-number [ending-line-number]
```

5 Configure user authentication. Additional information on how you might design this type of authentication is discussed in the section that follows. To configure user authentication, use one of the following commands:

```
login tacacs username name password secret
password password login local
```

6 Enable the creation of temporary access list entries. If the **host** argument is *not* specified, all hosts on the entire network are allowed to set up a temporary access list entry. The dynamic access list contains the network mask to enable the new network connection. To enable the creation of temporary access list entries, use the following command:

```
autocommand access-enable [host] [timeout minutes]
```

Configuring User Authentication

There are three possible methods to configure an authentication-query process (see step 5 in the preceding task list), which are as follows:

- Use a network access server such as TACACS+ server. This method requires additional configuration steps on the TACACS+ server, but allows for stricter authentication queries and more sophisticated tracking capabilities:

  ```
  Router(config)# login tacacs
  ```

- Use the **username** command. This method is more effective because authentication is determined on a user basis. The syntax for this command is as follows:

  ```
  Router# username name password password.
  ```

- Use the **password** and **login** commands. This method is less effective because the password is configured for the port, not for the user. Therefore, any user who knows the password can authenticate successfully. The syntax for these commands is as follows:

  ```
  Router# password password
  Router# login local
  ```

Dynamic Access List Golden Rules

Follow these guidelines when you configure dynamic access lists:

- Assign attributes to the dynamic access list in the same way you assign attributes for a static access list. The temporary access list entries inherit the attributes assigned to this list.

- Configure Telnet only, so the user must use the authentication-query process. Telnet access must be allowed to enable user authentication.

- Define either an idle timeout (with the **access-enable** command in the **autocommand** command) or an absolute timeout value (with the **timeout** keyword in the **access-list** command). Otherwise, the temporary access list entry will remain, even after the user has terminated his session.

- Configure the idle timeout value to be less than the absolute timeout value.

- Configure the idle timeout to be equal to the WAN idle timeout.

- Do *not* create more than one dynamic access list for any one access list. The software refers only to the first dynamic access list defined.

- Do *not* assign the same dynamic name on another access list. Doing so instructs the software to reuse the existing list. All named entries must be globally unique within the configuration.

- If the router executes the **autocommand** command, configure all virtual terminal (VTY) ports with the same **autocommand** command. Omitting an **autocommand** command on a VTY port allows a random host to gain EXEC mode access to the router and does not create a temporary access list entry in the dynamic access list.

When you create dynamic access lists, remember the following:

- The only values replaced in the temporary entry are the source or destination address, depending on whether the access list was in the input access list or output access list. All other attributes such as port are inherited from the main dynamic access list.

- Each addition to the dynamic list is always put at the beginning of the dynamic list. You cannot specify the order of temporary access list entries.

- Temporary access list entries are never written to NVRAM.

User authentication is successful when the following router events occur:

- The user connects via the virtual terminal port on the router.

- The router executes the configured **autocommand** command for the **access-enable** command.

- A temporary access list entry is created and the Telnet session is terminated, and the specified host has placed a temporary access list entry and has access inside the firewall.

You can verify that this operation is successful on the router by either asking the user to test the connection or by using the **show-access-lists** command to view dynamic access lists.

The following sample display illustrates what the end user might see after successfully completing the authentication process. Notice that the connection was closed immediately after the password was entered and authenticated. The temporary access list entry has already been created, and the host that initiated the Telnet session has access inside the firewall:

```
Router# telnet corporate
Trying 172.21.52.1 ...
Connected to corporate.abc.com.
Escape character is '^]'.
User Access Verification
Password:
Connection closed by foreign host.
```

Deleting a Dynamic Access List

If it becomes necessary to delete a dynamic access list, enter the following command (in privileged EXEC mode) for the process:

clear access-template [*access-list-number* | *name*]
[*dynamic-name*] [*source*] [*destination*]

You can display temporary access list entries when they are in use. After a temporary access list entry is cleared by you, or by the absolute or idle timeout parameter, it can no longer be displayed. The number of matches displayed indicates the number of times the access list entry was hit.

Dynamic Access List Configuration Example

The following example shows how to configure lock-and-key access. In this example, login is on the TACACS+ server, so no **autocommand** command appears in this configuration. Lock-and-key access is configured on the BRI0 interface. Four VTY ports are defined with the password **cisco**:

```
aaa authentication login default tacacs+ enable
aaa accounting exec stop-only tacacs+
aaa accounting network stop-only tacacs+
enable password ciscotac
!
isdn switch-type basic-dms100
!
interface ethernet0
ip address 172.18.23.9 255.255.255.0
!
!
interface BRI0
 ip address 172.18.21.1 255.255.255.0
 encapsulation ppp
 dialer idle-timeout 3600
 dialer wait-for-carrier-time 100
 dialer map ip 172.18.21.2 name diana
 dialer-group 1
 isdn spid1 2036333715291
 isdn spid2 2036339371566
 ppp authentication chap
 ip access-group 102 in
!
access-list 102 dynamic testlist timeout 5 permit ip any any
access-list 102 permit tcp any host 172.18.21.2 eq 23
```

```
!
ip route 172.18.250.0 255.255.255.0 172.18.21.2
priority-list 1 interface BRI0 high
tacacs-server host 172.18.23.21
tacacs-server host 172.18.23.14
tacacs-server key test1
tftp-server rom alias all
!
dialer-list 1 protocol ip permit
!
line con 0
 password cisco
line aux 0
line VTY 0 4
password cisco
!
```

Terminal Access Controller Access Control System

Nonprivileged and privileged mode passwords are global, and apply to every user accessing the router from either the console port or from a Telnet session. As an alternative, the Terminal Access Controller Access Control System (TACACS) provides a way to validate every user on an individual basis before he or she can gain access to the router or communication server. TACACS was derived from the United States Department of Defense and is described in RFC 1492. TACACS is used by Cisco to allow finer control over who can access the router in nonprivileged and privileged mode.

With TACACS enabled, the router prompts the user for a username and a password. Then, the router queries a TACACS server to determine whether the user provided the correct password. A TACACS server typically runs on a UNIX workstation. Public domain TACACS servers can be obtained via anonymous FTP to ftp.cisco.com in the /pub directory. Use the /pub/README file to find the filename. A fully supported TACACS server is bundled with CiscoWorks Version 3.

The configuration command **tacacs-server host** specifies the UNIX host running a TACACS server that will validate requests sent by the router. You can enter the **tacacs-server host** command several times to specify multiple TACACS server hosts for a router.

Nonprivileged Access

If all servers are unavailable, you may be locked out of the router. In that event, the configuration command **tacacs-server last-resort [password | succeed]** enables you to determine whether to allow a user to log in to the router with no password (**succeed** keyword) or to force the user to supply the standard login password (**password** keyword).

The following commands specify a TACACS server and allow a login to succeed if the server is down or unreachable:

```
tacacs-server host 129.140.1.1
tacacs-server last-resort succeed
```

To force users who access the router via Telnet to authenticate themselves using TACACS, enter the following configuration commands:

```
line vty 0 4
login tacacs
```

Privileged Access

This method of password checking can also be applied to the privileged mode password with the **enable use-tacacs** command. If all servers are unavailable, you may be locked out of the router. In that event, the configuration command **enable last-resort [succeed | password]** enables you to determine whether to allow a user to log in to the router with no password (**succeed** keyword) or to force the user to supply the enable password (**password** keyword). There are significant risks to using the **succeed** keyword. If you use the **enable use-tacacs** command, you must also specify the **tacacs-server authenticate enable** command.

The **tacacs-server extended** command enables a Cisco device to run in extended TACACS mode. The UNIX system must be running the extended TACACS daemon, which can be obtained via anonymous FTP to ftp.cisco.com. The filename is xtacacsd.shar. This daemon allows communication servers and other equipment to talk to the UNIX system and update an audit trail with information on port usage, accounting data, or any other information the device can send.

The command **username** *user* **password [0 | 7]** *password* enables you to store and maintain a list of users and their passwords on a Cisco device rather than on a TACACS server. The number 0 stores the password in clear text in the configuration file. The number 7 stores the password in an encrypted format. If you do not have a TACACS server and still want to authenticate users on an individual basis, you can set up users with the following configuration commands:

```
username steve password 7 steve-pass
username allan password 7 allan-pass
```

The two users, Steve and Allan, will be authenticated via passwords stored in encrypted format.

Token Card Access

When using TACACS service on routers and communications servers, you can also add support for physical card key devices, or token cards. The TACACS server code can be modified to provide support for this without requiring changes in the setup and configuration of the routers and communication servers. This modified code is not directly available from Cisco.

The token card system relies on a physical card that must be in your possession to provide authentication. By using the appropriate hooks in the TACACS server code, third-party companies can offer these enhanced TACACS servers to customers. One such product is the Enigma Logic SafeWord security software system. Other card-key systems, such as Security Dynamics SmartCard, can be added to TACACS as well.

Further Cisco Security Measures

This chapter covered many of the more major and well-known security features available to you. A variety of techniques should not be forgotten, however, when you are designing a comprehensive security solution. This section covers those techniques.

Controlling Access to Network Servers that Contain Configuration Files

If a router regularly downloads configuration files from a Trivial File Transfer Protocol (TFTP) or Maintenance Operations Protocol (MOP) server, anyone who can access the server can modify the router configuration files stored on the server.

Communication servers can be configured to accept incoming local-area transport (LAT) connections. Protocol translators and their translating router brethren can accept X.29 connections. These different types of access should be considered when creating a firewall architecture.

Using Banners to Set Up Unauthorized Use Notifications

It is also wise to use the **banner** EXEC global configuration command to provide messages and unauthorized use notifications, which will be displayed on all new connections. On the communication server, for example, you can enter the following message:

```
banner exec ^C
If you have problems with the dial-in lines, please send mail to
helpdesk@CorporationX.com. If you get the message "% Your
account is expiring," please send mail with name and voice
mailbox to helpdesk@CorporationX.com, and someone will contact
you to renew your account. Unauthorized use of these resources is
prohibited.
```

It is also wise to use the **motd banner** EXEC global configuration command to provide messages and unauthorized-use notifications, which will be displayed on all new connections. On any network equipment, for example, you could enter the following message:

```
OSPF_Router (config)# motd banner
***************************************************************************
*                    ! ! ! ! ! ! ! WARNING ! ! ! ! ! ! ! !                *
*   THIS SYSTEM IS OWNED BY <company name>.  UNAUTHORIZED ACCESS AND USE OF *
*       THIS SYSTEM IS NOT PERMITTED BY <company name> AND IS STRICTLY     *
*         PROHIBITED BY <company name> SECURITY POLICIES, REGULATIONS,     *
*                        STATE AND FEDERAL LAWS.                           *
*                                                                         *
*       UNAUTHORIZED USERS ARE SUBJECT TO CRIMINAL AND CIVIL PENALTIES     *
*           AS WELL AS COMPANY-INITIATED DISCIPLINARY PROCEEDINGS.         *
***************************************************************************
```

A message-of-the-day banner like the preceding one in your network equipment is very effective. It covers all the possible consequences, and even states that there will be consequences based on their actions.

Securing Nonstandard Services

A number of nonstandard services are available from the Internet and provide value-added services when connecting to the outside world. In the case of a connection to the Internet, these services can be very elaborate and complex. Examples of these services are World Wide Web (WWW), Wide Area Information Service (WAIS), Gopher, and Mosaic. Most of these systems are concerned with providing a wealth of information to the user in some organized fashion, and enabling structured browsing and searching.

Most of these systems have their own defined protocol. Some, such as Mosaic, use several different protocols to obtain the information in question. Use caution when designing access lists applicable to each of these services. In many cases, the access lists will become interrelated as these services become interrelated.

Privilege-Level Security

This feature was introduced by Cisco in Release 10.3 and allows for the establishment of 16 levels of access within the router. Default privilege levels are 1 = user and 15 = privileged.

Privilege levels can be used in a variety of ways within a router:

- Established for both commands and incoming terminal lines.
- Specialized enable passwords can be linked to privilege levels.
- Assigned to specialized EXEC and configure commands to control access.

Privilege-Level Command Modes

You can implement the following command modes by using privilege levels (all of the following are global configuration commands except **EXEC**):

configuration	line	hub	route-map
controller	map-class	interface	router
EXEC	map-list	ipx-router	

Privilege-Level Configuration Example

To associate a privilege level with a specific command, you need to configure the router as follows:

```
Router(config)#privilege exec level 6 ping
Router(config)#privilege exec level 6 clear
```

The preceding two commands, if applied to a router's VTY port (the ones you telnet to), allow anyone accessing the router using just the **vty** command to perform extended pings and a variety of clear commands (that is, **counters**, **interface**, **router**, and so forth).

To establish a specific enable password for a privilege level, you enter the following:

```
Router(config)# enable password level level # password
```

To associate a privilege level with a terminal line, you enter the following:

```
Router(config)# line vty 0 4
Router(config-line)# privilege level level #
```

Network Data Encryption

To safeguard your network data, Cisco provides network data encryption and router authentication services. This section briefly discusses how this is done and how it can benefit your network. Further discussion on the proper techniques and process involved in deploying this feature in your network is beyond the scope of this book. At the end of this section, additional resources are identified, in case you want to read more information on this subject.

Network data encryption is provided at the IP packet level. IP packet encryption prevents eavesdroppers from reading the data being transmitted. When IP packet encryption is used, IP packets can be seen during transmission, but the IP packet contents (payload) cannot be read. Specifically, the IP header and upper-layer protocol (TCP or UDP) headers are not encrypted, but all payload data within the TCP or UDP packet will be encrypted and therefore not readable during transmission.

The actual encryption and decryption of IP packets occurs only at routers that you configure for network data encryption with router authentication. Such routers are considered to be *peer encrypting routers* (or just *peer routers*). Intermediate hops do not participate in encryption/decryption.

Typically, when an IP packet is initially generated at a host, it is unencrypted (clear text). This occurs on a secured (internal) portion of your network. Then, when the transmitted IP packet passes through an encrypting router, the router determines whether the packet should be encrypted. If the packet is encrypted, the encrypted packet will travel through the unsecured network portion (usually an external network such as the Internet) until it reaches the remote peer encrypting router. At this point, the encrypted IP packet is decrypted and forwarded to the destination host as clear text.

NOTE It is important to remember that by requiring the routers to encrypt data, you are adding overhead to the routers' processing loads. You will want to test this first to ensure that the routers in your network can handle the added load.

Router authentication enables peer-encrypting routers to positively identify the source of incoming encrypted data. This means that attackers cannot forge transmitted data or tamper with transmitted data without detection. Router authentication occurs between peer routers each time a new *encrypted session* is established. An encrypted session is established each time an encrypting router receives an IP packet that should be encrypted (unless an encrypted session is already occurring at that time).

TIP The use of data encryption is applied to your data only after it leaves the router because that is the device applying the encryption. This is important to mention because the data will travel from the host to the router in an unsecured format.

To provide IP packet encryption with router authentication, Cisco implements the following standards: Digital Signature Standard (DSS), the Diffie-Hellman (DH) public key algorithm, and Data Encryption Standard (DES). DSS is used in router authentication. The DH algorithm and DES standards are used to initiate and conduct encrypted communication sessions between participating routers.

Case Study #1:   Routing Protocol Authentication

This case study has been taken from *OSPF Network Design Solutions*, the definitive Cisco Press book on OSPF by Thomas M. Thomas II. The information has been updated here to more accurately reflect the content and relevance of this chapter. If you are interested in the case study in its entirety, refer to *OSPF Network Design Solutions*.

OSPF Neighbor Router Authentication

OSPF incorporates a minimal amount of security already within its design. That sounds contradictory: How can a protocol be designed with security, yet still be minimal? Simply put, when OSPF was designed, the necessary fields required for security were included in the design of OSPF's packets. The security included within OSPF protects only its LSAs, but thus protects and maintains the integrity of your network's routing tables. OSPF security is minimal because it does not protect the data flowing across the network, it only protects the way OSPF routers know to route it. This security was designed to protect only the integrity of the OSPF routing domain. You can prevent any OSPF router from receiving fraudulent route updates by configuring this type of security, known as *neighbor router authentication*.

This section describes neighbor router authentication as part of a total security plan: what neighbor router authentication is, how it works, and why you should use it to increase your overall network security. Important topics regarding this issue include the following:

- Benefits of OSPF Neighbor Authentication
- Conditions for Deploying OSPF Neighbor Authentication
- How Neighbor Authentication Works

You can deploy this type of security several different ways within your OSPF network. The first way is by assigning the same OSPF key networkwide. The second is to assign a different key for every link within the network.

NOTE   This section refers to neighbor router authentication as "neighbor authentication." Neighbor router authentication is also sometimes called "route authentication."

Benefits of OSPF Neighbor Authentication

When configured, neighbor authentication occurs whenever routing updates are exchanged between neighboring OSPF routers. This authentication ensures that a router receives reliable routing information from a trusted source.

Without neighbor authentication, unauthorized or deliberately malicious routing updates could compromise the security of your network traffic. A security compromise could occur if an unfriendly party diverts or analyzes your network traffic.

An unauthorized router could send a fictitious routing update to convince your router to send traffic to an incorrect destination, for example. This diverted traffic could be analyzed to learn confidential information about your organization, or merely used to disrupt your organization's capability to effectively communicate using the network. Neighbor authentication prevents any such fraudulent route updates from being received by your router.

Conditions for Deploying OSPF Neighbor Authentication

You should configure any router for OSPF neighbor authentication if that router meets any of these conditions:

- It is conceivable that the router might receive a false route update.
- If the router were to receive a false route update, your network might be compromised.
- You deem it necessary as part of your network security plan.

Remember that if you configure a router for neighbor authentication, you also need to configure the neighbor router for neighbor authentication.

How Neighbor Authentication Works

When neighbor authentication has been configured on a router, the router authenticates the source of each routing update packet that it receives. This is accomplished by the exchange of an authenticating key (sometimes referred to as a password) known to both the sending and the receiving router.

NOTE	Plain text authentication is not recommended for use as part of your security strategy. Its primary use is to avoid accidental changes to the routing infrastructure. Using MD5 authentication, however, is a recommended security practice.

Two types of neighbor authentication are used: plain text authentication and message digest algorithm version 5 (MD5) authentication. Both forms work in the same way, with the exception being that MD5 sends a "message digest" rather than the authenticating key itself. The message digest is created using the key and a message, but the key itself is not sent, preventing it from being read while it is being transmitted. Plain text authentication sends the authenticating key itself over the wire.

TIP	As with all keys, passwords, and other security secrets, it is imperative that you closely guard the authenticating keys used in neighbor authentication. The security benefits of this feature are reliant on your keeping all authenticating keys confident. Also, when performing router-management tasks via Simple Network Management Protocol (SNMP), do not ignore the risk associated with sending keys using nonencrypted SNMP.

Plain Text Authentication

Each participating neighbor router must share an authenticating key. This key is specified at each router during configuration. Multiple keys can be specified with OSPF; each key must then be identified by a key number. You can have a different key for each WAN interface on a router running OSPF, for example. The caveat is that the neighbor router off each interface must have a matching key configured on the receiving interface, as shown in Figure 22-8.

Figure 22-8 *OSPF Plain Text Authentication*

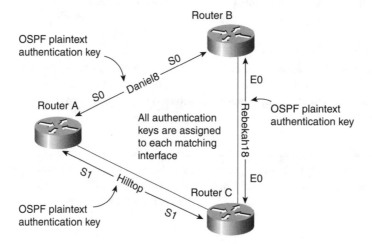

In general, when a routing update is sent, the following authentication sequence occurs:

1 A router sends a routing update with an authentication key within an LSA.

2 The receiving (neighbor) router checks the received key against the same key stored in its own memory.

3 If the two keys match, the receiving router accepts the routing update packet. If the two keys do not match, the routing update packet is rejected.

MD5 Authentication

MD5 authentication works similarly to plain text authentication, except that the key is never sent over the wire. Instead, the router uses the MD5 algorithm to produce a "message digest" of the key (also called a "hash"). The message digest is then sent rather than the key itself. This ensures that nobody can eavesdrop on the line and learn keys during transmission.

Troubleshooting OSPF and Authentication

There are times when it is very difficult to troubleshoot an OSPF implementation. Although there are many different tools available for the network engineer to use, this author has found a new tool that shows a great deal of promise in making this difficult task much easier.

In Figure 22-9, you can see that OSPF authentication was purposefully misconfigured.

Figure 22-9 *Visual Protocols OSPF Troubleshooting Program—Visual Decoder*

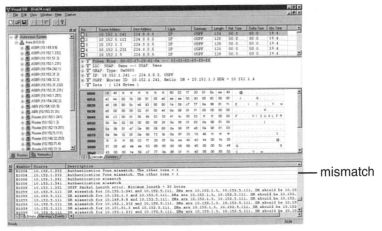

— mismatch

The first message "Authentication type mismatch. The other type = 1" refers to the fact that one router was configured OSPF with MD5, but not the other. This resulted in a mismatch on the type of authentication being used by the OSPF process.

The second message "Authentication mismatch" refers to the fact that the two routers in question also have different passwords in them, resulting in a mismatch on the authentication passwords.

Visual Protocols has several other very interesting tools similar to this that are worth taking a look at. For more information on helpful programs of this nature, see the following Web sites: http://www.netcerts.com and http://www.visualprotocols.com.

Case Study #2:   Designing Your Firewall Architecture

This case study has been taken from *OSPF Network Design Solutions*, the definitive Cisco Press book on OSPF by Thomas M. Thomas II. The information has been updated here to more accurately reflect the content and relevance of this chapter. If you are interested in the case study in its entirety, refer to *OSPF Network Design Solutions*.

This case study discusses the deployment of Cisco PIX firewall within a network. Router firewall architecture is a network structure that exists between you and the outside world (the Internet, for example), designed to protect your network from intruders (that is, cyber-thieves). In most circumstances, intruders are represented by the global Internet and the thousands of remote networks it interconnects. Typically, a network firewall consists of several different machines, as shown in Figure 22-10.

Figure 22-10 *Typical Firewall Router Deployment*

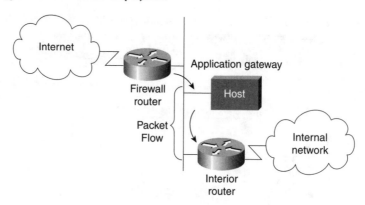

In this network architecture, the router connected to the Internet (exterior router) forces all incoming traffic to go to the application gateway. The router connected to the internal network (interior router) accepts only packets from the application gateway.

The application gateway institutes per-application and per-user policies. In effect, the gateway controls the delivery of network-based services both into and from the internal network. Only certain users might be allowed to communicate with the Internet, for example, or only certain applications are permitted to establish connections between an interior and exterior host.

The route and packet filters should be set up to reflect the same policies. If the only application permitted is electronic mail, only electronic mail packets should be allowed through the interior router. This protects the application gateway and avoids overwhelming it with packets that it would otherwise discard.

Controlling Traffic Flow

This section uses the scenario illustrated in Figure 22-11 to describe the use of access lists to restrict traffic to and from a firewall router and a firewall communication server. Notice the added communication server to the network architecture; it services dial-in users.

Figure 22-11   *Controlling Traffic Flow with the Firewall Router*

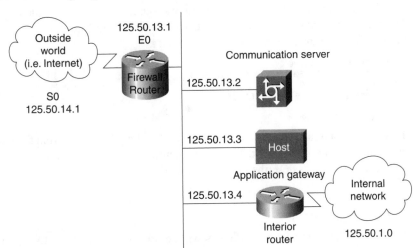

In this case study, the firewall router allows incoming new connections to one or more communication servers or hosts. Having a designated router act as a firewall is desirable because it clearly identifies the router's purpose as the external gateway, and avoids encumbering other routers with this task. In the event that the internal network needs to isolate itself, the firewall router provides the point of isolation so that the rest of the internal network structure is not affected.

Connections to the hosts are restricted to incoming FTP requests and e-mail services, as described in the "Defining Access Lists" section, later in this case study. The incoming Telnet or modem connections to the communication server are screened by the communication server running TACACS username authentication, as described in the "Configuring the Firewall Communications Server" section, later in this casestudy.

TIP	Connections from one communication server modem line to another outgoing modem line (or to the outside world) should be disallowed to prevent unauthorized users from using your resources to launch an attack on the outside world. Because intruders have already passed the communication server TACACS authentication at this point, they are likely to have someone's password. It is an excellent idea to keep TACACS passwords and host passwords distinct from one another.

Configuring the Firewall Router

In the firewall router configuration that follows, subnet 152.50.13.0 of the Class B 152.50.0.0 network is the firewall subnet, and subnet 152.50.14.0 provides the connection to the worldwide Internet via a service provider:

```
interface ethernet 0
  ip address 125.50.13.1 255.255.255.0
interface serial 0
  ip address 125.50.14.1 255.255.255.0
router ospf 500
  network 125.50.0.0
```

This simple configuration provides *no security* and allows all traffic from the outside world on to all parts of your network. To provide security on the firewall router, use access lists and access groups, as described in the next section.

Defining Firewall Access Lists

Access lists define the actual traffic that will be permitted or denied into the internal network, and an access group applies an access list definition to a specific router interface. Access lists can be used to do one of the following:

- Deny connections known to be a security risk and then permit all other connections
- Permit those connections considered acceptable and deny all the rest

For a router firewall implementation, the latter is the more secure method, and that will be how you will be using your access lists.

In this case study, incoming e-mail and news are permitted for a few hosts, but FTP, Telnet, and rlogin services are permitted only to hosts on the firewall subnet. IP-*extended* access lists (range 100–199) and Transmission Control Protocol (TCP) or User Datagram Protocol (UDP) port numbers are used to filter traffic. When a connection is to be established for e-mail, Telnet, FTP, and so forth, the connection will attempt to open a service on a specified port number. Therefore, you can filter out selected types of connections by denying packets attempting to use that service.

Remember, an access list is invoked after a routing decision has been made but *before* the packet is sent out on an interface. The best place to define an access list is on a preferred host, using your favorite text editor (such as Notepad). You can create a file that contains the **access-list** commands, and cut and paste directly into the router while in configuration mode.

It is advisable to remove any instances of an old access list before loading a new or altered version. Access lists can be removed with the following command while in configuration mode:

```
no access-list 101
```

The **access-list** command can now be used to permit any packets returning to machines from already established connections. With the **established** keyword, a match occurs if the TCP datagram has the acknowledgment (ACK) or reset (RST) bits set:

```
access-list 101 permit tcp 0.0.0.0 255.255.255.255 0.0.0.0
    255.255.255.255 established
```

If any firewall routers share a common network with an outside provider, you might want to allow access from those hosts to your network. In this case study, the outside provider has a serial port that uses the firewall router Class B address (125.50.14.2) as a source address, so your access list statement to permit them access would be as follows:

```
access-list 101 permit ip 125.50.14.2 0.0.0.0 0.0.0.0
    255.255.255.255
```

The following example illustrates how to deny traffic from a user attempting to spoof any of your internal addresses from the outside world:

```
access-list 101 deny ip 125.50.0.0 0.0.255.255 0.0.0.0
    255.255.255.255
```

The following access list examples are designed based on many of the well-known port numbers found within the TCP/IP protocol stack. For a list of some of the more common well-known port numbers, refer to Table 22-6, referred to later in the case study.

NOTE	Port 111 is only a directory service. If you can guess the ports on which the actual data services are provided, you can access them. Most RPC services do not have fixed port numbers. You should find the ports on which these services can be found, and block them. Unfortunately, because ports can be bound anywhere, Cisco recommends blocking all UDP ports except DNS, where practical. Cisco recommends that you filter the finger TCP service at port 79 to prevent outsiders from learning about internal user directories and the names of hosts from which users log in.

The following two **access-list** commands will allow Domain Name System (DNS, port 53) and Network Time Protocol (NTP, port 123) requests and replies based on their TCP/IP port address:

```
access-list 101 permit udp 0.0.0.0 255.255.255.255
    0.0.0.0 255.255.255.255 eq 53
access-list 101 permit udp 0.0.0.0 255.255.255.255

    0.0.0.0 255.255.255.255 eq 123
```

The following command denies the Network File Server (NFS) User Datagram Protocol (UDP, port 2049) port:

```
access-list 101 deny udp 0.0.0.0 255.255.255.255

    0.0.0.0 255.255.255.255 eq 2049
```

The following commands deny OpenWindows on ports 2001 and 2002 and deny X11 on ports 6001 and 6002. This protects the first two screens on any host. If you have any machine that uses more than the first two screens, be sure to block the appropriate ports.

```
access-list 101 deny tcp 0.0.0.0 255.255.255.255
    0.0.0.0 255.255.255.255 eq 6001
access-list 101 deny tcp 0.0.0.0 255.255.255.255
    0.0.0.0 255.255.255.255 eq 6002
access-list 101 deny tcp 0.0.0.0 255.255.255.255
    0.0.0.0 255.255.255.255 eq 2001
access-list 101 deny tcp 0.0.0.0 255.255.255.255

    0.0.0.0 255.255.255.255 eq 2002
```

The following command permits Telnet access from anyone to the communication server (125.50.13.2):

```
access-list 101 permit tcp 0.0.0.0 255.255.255.255

    125.50.13.2 0.0.0.0 eq 23
```

The following commands permit FTP access from anyone to the host 125.50.13.100 on subnet 125.50.13.0:

```
access-list 101 permit tcp 0.0.0.0 255.255.255.255
    125.50.13.100 0.0.0.0 eq 21
access-list 101 permit tcp 0.0.0.0 255.255.255.255

    125.50.13.100 0.0.0.0 eq 20
```

For the following examples, network 125.50.1.0 is on the internal network, as shown in Figure 22-11.

The following **access-list** commands permit TCP and UDP connections for port numbers greater than 1023 to a very limited set of hosts. Make sure no communication servers or protocol translators are in this list.

```
access-list 101 permit tcp 0.0.0.0 255.255.255.255
    125.50.13.100 0.0.0.0 gt 1023
access-list 101 permit tcp 0.0.0.0 255.255.255.255
    125.50.1.100 0.0.0.0 gt 1023
access-list 101 permit tcp 0.0.0.0 255.255.255.255
    125.50.1.101 0.0.0.0 gt 1023
access-list 101 permit udp 0.0.0.0 255.255.255.255
    125.50.13.100 0.0.0.0 gt 1023
access-list 101 permit udp 0.0.0.0 255.255.255.255
    125.50.1.100 0.0.0.0 gt 1023
access-list 101 permit udp 0.0.0.0 255.255.255.255

    125.50.1.101 0.0.0.0 gt 1023
```

The following **access-list** commands permit DNS access to the DNS server(s) listed by the Network Information Center (NIC):

```
access-list 101 permit tcp 0.0.0.0 255.255.255.255
    125.50.13.100 0.0.0.0 eq 53
access-list 101 permit tcp 0.0.0.0 255.255.255.255

    125.50.1.100 0.0.0.0 eq 53
```

The following commands permit incoming Simple Mail Transfer Protocol (SMTP) e-mail to only a few machines:

```
access-list 101 permit tcp 0.0.0.0 255.255.255.255
    125.50.13.100 0.0.0.0 eq 25
access-list 101 permit tcp 0.0.0.0 255.255.255.255
    125.50.1.100 0.0.0.0 eq 25
```

The following commands allow internal Network News Transfer Protocol (NNTP) servers to receive NNTP connections from a list of authorized peers:

```
access-list 101 permit tcp 56.1.0.18 0.0.0.0
    125.50.1.100 0.0.0.0 eq 119
access-list 101 permit tcp 182.12.18.32 0.0.0.0
    125.50.1.100 0.0.0.0 eq 119
```

The following command permits Internet Control Message Protocol (ICMP) for error-message feedback:

```
access-list 101 permit icmp 0.0.0.0 255.255.255.255
    0.0.0.0 255.255.255.255
```

Every access list has an implicit deny all (that is, everything not mentioned in the access list) statement at the end of the list to ensure that attributes not *expressly permitted* will be denied. When put together without descriptions of each line's function, the completed access list will look as follows:

```
access-list 101 permit udp 0.0.0.0 255.255.255.255 0.0.0.0
    255.255.255.255 eq 123
access-list 101 deny udp 0.0.0.0 255.255.255.255 0.0.0.0 255.255.255.255 eq 2049
access-list 101 deny tcp 0.0.0.0 255.255.255.255 0.0.0.0 255.255.255.255 eq 6001
access-list 101 deny tcp 0.0.0.0 255.255.255.255 0.0.0.0 255.255.255.255 eq 6002
access-list 101 deny tcp 0.0.0.0 255.255.255.255 0.0.0.0 255.255.255.255 eq 2001
access-list 101 deny tcp 0.0.0.0 255.255.255.255 0.0.0.0 255.255.255.255 eq 2002
access-list 101 permit tcp 0.0.0.0 255.255.255.255 125.50.13.2 0.0.0.0 eq 23
access-list 101 permit tcp 0.0.0.0 255.255.255.255 125.50.13.100 0.0.0.0 eq 21
access-list 101 permit tcp 0.0.0.0 255.255.255.255 125.50.13.100 0.0.0.0 eq 20
access-list 101 permit tcp 0.0.0.0 255.255.255.255 125.50.13.100 0.0.0.0 gt 1023
access-list 101 permit tcp 0.0.0.0 255.255.255.255 125.50.1.100 0.0.0.0 gt 1023
access-list 101 permit tcp 0.0.0.0 255.255.255.255 125.50.1.101 0.0.0.0 gt 1023
access-list 101 permit udp 0.0.0.0 255.255.255.255 125.50.13.100 0.0.0.0 gt 1023
access-list 101 permit udp 0.0.0.0 255.255.255.255 125.50.1.100 0.0.0.0 gt 1023
access-list 101 permit udp 0.0.0.0 255.255.255.255 125.50.1.101 0.0.0.0 gt 1023
access-list 101 permit tcp 0.0.0.0 255.255.255.255 125.50.13.100 0.0.0.0 eq 53
access-list 101 permit tcp 0.0.0.0 255.255.255.255 125.50.1.100 0.0.0.0 eq 53
access-list 101 permit tcp 0.0.0.0 255.255.255.255 125.50.13.100 0.0.0.0 eq 25
access-list 101 permit tcp 0.0.0.0 255.255.255.255 125.50.1.100 0.0.0.0 eq 25
access-list 101 permit tcp 56.1.0.18 0.0.0.0 125.50.1.100 0.0.0.0 eq 119
access-list 101 permit tcp 182.12.18.32 0.0.0.0
    125.50.1.100 0.0.0.0 eq 119
access-list 101 permit icmp 0.0.0.0 255.255.255.255
    0.0.0.0 255.255.255.255
```

Applying Access Lists to Interfaces

After this access list has been loaded onto the router and stored into nonvolatile random-access memory (NVRAM), assign it to the appropriate interface. In this case study, traffic coming from the outside world via the serial 0 interface of the firewall router is filtered (via access list 101) before it is placed on the subnet 125.50.13.0 (Ethernet 0). Therefore, the

access-group command, which assigns an access list to filter incoming connections, must be assigned to Ethernet 0, as follows:

```
interface ethernet 0
ip access-group 101 in
```

To control outgoing access to the Internet from the network, define an access list and apply it to the outgoing packets on serial 0 interface of the firewall router. To do this, returning packets from hosts using Telnet or FTP must be allowed to access the firewall subnetwork 125.50.13.0.

Configuring the Firewall Communication Server

In this case study, the firewall communication server has a single inbound modem on line 2:

```
interface Ethernet0
ip address 125.50.13.2 255.255.255.0
!
access-list 10 deny 125.50.14.0 0.0.0.255
access-list 10 permit 125.50.0.0 0.0.255.255
!
access-list 11 deny 125.50.13.2 0.0.0.0
access-list 11 permit 125.50.0.0 0.0.255.255
!
line 2
login tacacs
location FireWallCS#2
!
access-class 10 in
access-class 11 out
!
modem answer-timeout 60
modem InOut
telnet transparent
terminal-type dialup
flowcontrol hardware
stopbits 1
rxspeed 38400
txspeed 38400
!
tacacs-server host 125.50.1.100
tacacs-server host 125.50.1.101
tacacs-server extended
!
line vty 0 15
login tacacs
```

Defining the Communication Server's Access Lists

In this example, the network number is used to permit or deny access; therefore, standard IP access list numbers (range 1 through 99) are used. For incoming connections to modem lines, only packets from hosts on the internal Class B network and packets from those hosts on the firewall subnetwork are permitted:

```
access-list 10 deny 125.50.14.0 0.0.0.255
access-list 10 permit 125.50.0.0 0.0.255.255
```

Outgoing connections are allowed only to internal network hosts and to the communication server. This prevents a modem line in the outside world from calling out on a second modem line:

```
access-list 11 deny 125.50.13.2 0.0.0.0
access-list 11 permit 125.50.0.0 0.0.255.255
```

Applying Access Lists to Lines

Apply an access list to an asynchronous line with the **access-class** command. In this case study, the restrictions from access list 10 are applied to incoming connections on line 2. The restrictions from access list 11 are applied to outgoing connections on line 2:

```
access-class 10 in
access-class 11 out
```

Spoofing and Inbound Access Lists

In Software Release 9.21, Cisco introduced the capability to assign input access lists to an interface. This enables a network administrator to filter packets before they enter the router, instead of as they leave the router. In most cases, input access lists and output access lists accomplish the same functionality. Some people consider input access lists more intuitive, however, and these lists can be used to prevent some types of IP address "spoofing"; output access lists will not provide sufficient security.

Figure 22-12 illustrates a cyber-thief host "spoofing," or illegally claiming to be an address that it is not. Someone in the outside world is claiming to originate traffic from network 125.50.13.0. Although the IP address is spoofed, the router interface to the outside world assumes that the packet is coming from 125.50.13.0. If the input access list on the router allows traffic coming from 125.50.13.0, it will accept the illegal packet.

Figure 22-12 *Spoofing Example*

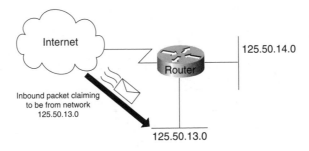

To avoid this spoofing situation, an input access list should be applied to the router interface to the outside world. This access list would not allow any packets with addresses from the internal networks of which the router is aware (13.0 and 14.0).

TIP

If you have several internal networks connected to the firewall router, and the router is using output filters, traffic between internal networks will see a reduction in performance created by the access list filters. If input filters are used only on the interface going from the router to the outside world, internal networks will not see any reduction in performance.

If an address uses source routing, it can send and receive traffic through the firewall router. For this reason, you should always disable source routing on the firewall router with the **no ip source-route** command.

Well-Known Port Assignments

Every application that intends to receive data from a TCP/IP network calls the TCP/IP service to acquire a *port*, a 16-bit number unique to that application on that particular host. Any well-formed incoming datagram with that port number in its TCP or UDP header is delivered to that application. Fragmented datagrams contain port information in the first datagram fragment only (fragment 0). By convention, any transmitting application also owns a port number on its host, and it supplies that port number in the destination port field of the datagrams it sends. The port numbers are divided into three ranges, as follows:

- Well-known ports range from 0–1023

- Registered ports range from 1024–49151

- Dynamic and/or private ports range from 49152–65535

Well-known ports are controlled and assigned by the IANA, and on most systems can only be used by system (or root) processes or by programs executed by privileged users. Ports are used in the TCP (RFC 793) to name the ends of logical connections that carry long-term conversations. For providing services to unknown callers, a service contact port is defined. This list specifies the port used by the server process as its contact port. The contact port is sometimes called the "well-known port." Table 22-6 lists some well-known port numbers.

Table 22-6   *Port Number Assignments*

Port #	Port Type	Protocol
0	TCP & UDP	reserved
1-4	TCP & UDP	unassigned
5	TCP & UDP	Remote Job Entry
7	TCP & UDP	Echo
9	TCP & UDP	Discard
11	TCP & UDP	Active Users
13	TCP & UDP	Daytime
15	TCP & UDP	Who is up or Netstat

Table 22-6   *Port Number Assignments (Continued)*

Port #	Port Type	Protocol
17	TCP & UDP	Quote of the Day
19	TCP & UDP	Character Generator
20	TCP & UDP	File Transfer (Default Data)
21	TCP & UDP	File Transfer (Control)
23	TCP & UDP	Telnet
25	TCP & UDP	Simple Mail Transfer Protocol (SMTP)
37	TCP & UDP	Time
39	TCP & UDP	Resource Location Protocol
42	TCP & UDP	Host Name Server
43	TCP & UDP	Who Is
49	TCP & UDP	Terminal Access Controller Access Control System (TACACS)
53	TCP & UDP	Domain Name Server
67	TCP & UDP	Bootstrap Protocol Server
68	TCP & UDP	Bootstrap Protocol Client
69	TCP & UDP	Trivial File Transfer Protocol
70	TCP & UDP	Gopher
75	TCP & UDP	any private dial-out service
77	TCP & UDP	any private RJE service
79	TCP & UDP	Finger
80	TCP & UDP	Hypertext Transfer Protocol (HTTP)
87	TCP	Link—commonly used by intruders
88	TCP & UDP	Kerberos
89	TCP & UDP	Open Shortest Path First
95	TCP	SUPDUP Protocol
101	TCP	NIC Host Name Server
102	TCP	ISO-TSAP
103	TCP	X400
104	TCP	X400-SND
107	TCP & UDP	Remote Telnet Service

continues

Table 22-6   *Port Number Assignments (Continued)*

Port #	Port Type	Protocol
109	TCP	Post Office Protocol v2
110	TCP	Post Office Protocol v3
111	TCP & UDP	SUN Remote Procedure Call
113	TCP & UDP	Authentication Service
117	TCP & UDP	UUCP Path Service
119	TCP & UDP	USENET Network News Transfer Protocol
123	TCP & UDP	Network Time Protocol (NTP)
133-136	TCP & UDP	unassigned
137	UDP	NetBIOS Name Service
137	TCP	unassigned
138	UDP	NetBIOS Datagram Service
138	TCP	unassigned
139	UDP	NetBIOS Session Service
144	TCP	NeWS
161	TCP & UDP	Simple Network Management Protocol Q/R
162	TCP & UDP	SNMP Event Traps
177	UDP	X Display Manager Control Protocol
179	TCP & UDP	Border Gateway Protocol (BGP)
194	TCP & UDP	Internet Relay Chat
195	UDP	DNSIX security protocol auditing
389	TCP & UDP	Lightweight Directory Access Protocol
434	UDP	Mobile IP Registration
512	TCP	UNIX rexec (Control)
513	TCP & UDP	UNIX rlogin
514	TCP & UDP	UNIX rsh and rcp, Remote Commands
514	TCP	System Logging
515	TCP	UNIX Line Printer Remote Spooling
517	TCP & UDP	Two User Interaction—talk
518	TCP & UDP	ntalk
520	UDP	Routing Information Protocol

Table 22-6   *Port Number Assignments (Continued)*

Port #	Port Type	Protocol
525	UDP	Time Server
540	TCP	UNIX-to-UNIX copy program daemon
543	TCP	Kerberos login
544	TCP	Kerberos shell
1993	TCP	SNMP over TCP
2000	TCP & UDP	Open Windows
2001		auxiliary (AUX) port
2049	UDP	Network File System (NFS)
4001		auxiliary (AUX) port (stream)
6000	TCP & UDP	X11 (X Windows)

Bibliography and Recommended Reading

This section contains a list of publications that provide network security information.

Books and Periodicals

Cheswick, B., and S. Bellovin. 1994. *Firewalls and Internet Security.* Reading, MA: Addison-Wesley.

Comer, D. E., and D. L. Stevens. 1991-1993. *Internetworking with TCP/IP. Volumes I-III.* Englewood Cliffs, NJ: Prentice Hall.

Curry, D. 1992. *UNIX System Security—A Guide for Users and System Administrators.*

Garfinkel and Spafford. 1996. *Practical UNIX and Internet Security.* Cambridge, MA: O'Reilly & Associates.

Quarterman, J., and S. Carl-Mitchell. 1994. *The Internet Connection.* Reading, MA: Addison-Wesley.

Ranum, M. J. *Thinking about Firewalls.* Santa Clara, CA: Trusted Information Systems, Inc.

Stoll, C. 1995. *The Cuckoo's Egg.* New York, NY: Doubleday.

Thomas, Thomas M. II. 1998. *OSPF Network Design Solutions.* Indianapolis, IN: Cisco Press.

Treese, G. W., and A. Wolman. *X through the Firewall and Other Application Relays.*

Requests For Comments (RFCs)

RFC 1118. "The Hitchhiker's Guide to the Internet." September 1989.

RFC 1175. "A Bibliography of Internetworking Information." August 1990.

RFC 1244. "Site Security Handbook." July 1991.

RFC 1340. "Assigned Numbers." July 1992.

RFC 1446. "Security Protocols for SNMPv2." April 1993.

RFC 1463. "FYI on Introducing the Internet—A Short Bibliography of Introductory Internetworking Readings for the Network Novice." May 1993.

RFC 1492. "An Access Control Protocol, Sometimes Called TACACS." July 1993.

Internet Directories

Documents at gopher.nist.gov.

The "Computer Underground Digest" in the /pub/cud directory at ftp.eff.org.

Documents in the /dist/internet_security directory at research.att.com.

Summary

This security chapter provided an overview of internal and external security threats and how to develop a security policy to address them. It also covered how to implement a security policy on Cisco equipment using various access lists and other methods. Finally, the chapter provided two case studies on security implementation.

CHAPTER 23

Using HSRP for Fault-Tolerant IP Routing

This case study examines Cisco's Hot Standby Routing Protocol (HSRP), which provides automatic router backup when you configure it on Cisco routers that run the Internet Protocol (IP) over Ethernet, Fiber Distributed Date Interface (FDDI), and Token Ring local-area networks (LANs). HSRP is compatible with Novell's Internetwork Packet Exchange (IPX), AppleTalk, and Banyan VINES, and it is compatible with DECnet and Xerox Network Systems (XNS) in certain configurations.

NOTE   Banyan VINES serverless clients do not respond well to topology changes (regardless of whether HSRP is configured). This case study describes the effect of topology changes in networks that include Banyan VINES serverless clients.

For IP, HSRP allows one router to automatically assume the function of the second router if the second router fails. HSRP is particularly useful when the users on one subnet require continuous access to resources in the network.

Consider the network shown in Figure 23-1. Router A is responsible for handling packets between the Tokyo segment and the Paris segment, and Router B is responsible for handling packets between the Tokyo segment and the New York segment. If the connection between Router A and Router C goes down or if either router becomes unavailable, fast converging routing protocols, such as the Enhanced Interior Gateway Routing Protocol (EIGRP) and Open Shortest Path First (OSPF) can respond within seconds so that Router B is prepared to transfer packets that would otherwise have gone through Router A.

Figure 23-1 *A Typical WAN*

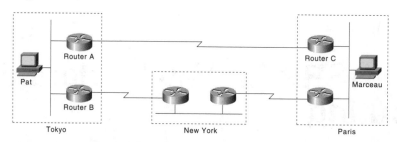

However, in spite of fast convergence, if the connection between Router A and Router C goes down, or if either router becomes unavailable, the user Pat on the Tokyo segment might not be able to communicate with the user Marceau even after the routing protocol has converged. That's because IP hosts, such as Pat's workstation, usually do not participate in routing protocols. Instead, they are configured statically with the address of a single router, such as Router A. Until someone manually modifies the configuration of Pat's host to use the address of Router B instead of Router A, Pat cannot communicate with Marceau.

Some IP hosts use proxy Address Resolution Protocol (ARP) to select a router. If Pat's workstation were running proxy ARP, it would send an ARP request for the IP address of Marceau's workstation. Router A would reply on behalf of Marceau's workstation and would give to Pat's workstation its own media access control (MAC) address (instead of the IP address of Marceau's workstation). With proxy ARP, Pat's workstation behaves as if Marceau's workstation were connected to the same segment of the network as Pat's workstation. If Router A fails, Pat's workstation will continue to send packets destined for Marceau's workstation to the MAC address of Router A even though those packets have nowhere to go and are lost. Pat either waits for ARP to acquire the MAC address of Router B by sending another ARP request or reboots the workstation to force it to send an ARP request. In either case, for a significant period of time, Pat cannot communicate with Marceau—even though the routing protocol has converged, and Router B is prepared to transfer packets that would otherwise go through Router A.

Some IP hosts use the Routing Information Protocol (RIP) to discover routers. The drawback of using RIP is that it is slow to adapt to changes in the topology. If Pat's workstation is configured to use RIP, 3 to 10 minutes might elapse before RIP makes another router available.

Some newer IP hosts use the ICMP Router Discovery Protocol (IRDP) to find a new router when a route becomes unavailable. A host that runs IRDP listens for hello multicast messages from its configured router and uses an alternate router when it no longer receives those hello messages. If Pat's workstation were running IRDP, it would detect that Router A is no longer sending hello messages and would start sending its packets to Router B.

For IP hosts that do not support IRDP, Cisco's HSRP provides a way to keep communicating when a router becomes unavailable. HSRP allows two or more HSRP-configured routers to use the MAC address and IP network address of a virtual router. The virtual router does not physically exist; instead, it represents the common target for routers that are configured to provide backup to each other. Figure 23-2 shows the Tokyo segment of the WAN as it might be configured for HSRP. Each actual router is configured with the MAC address and the IP network address of the virtual router.

Figure 23-2 *HSRP Addressing on the Tokyo Segment*

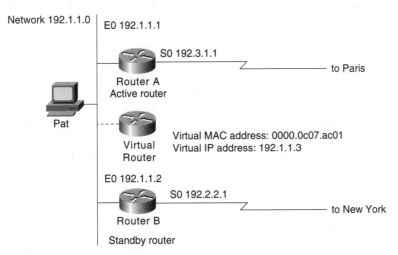

In Figure 23-2, the MAC address of the virtual router is 0000.0c07.ac01. When you configure HSRP, the router automatically selects one of the virtual MAC addresses from a range of addresses in the Cisco IOS software that is within the range of Cisco's MAC address block. Ethernet and FDDI LANs use one of the preassigned MAC addresses as a virtual MAC address. Token Ring LANs use a functional address as a virtual MAC address.

In Figure 23-2, instead of configuring the hosts on network 192.1.1.0 with the IP address of Router A, they are configured with the IP address of the virtual router as their default router. When Pat's workstation sends packets to Marceau's workstation on the Paris segment, it sends them to the MAC address of the virtual router.

In Figure 23-2, Router A is configured as the active router. It is configured with the IP address and MAC address of the virtual router and sends any packets addressed to the virtual router out interface 1 to the Paris segment. As the standby router, Router B is also configured with the IP address and MAC address of the virtual router. If for any reason Router A stops transferring packets, the routing protocol converges, and Router B assumes the duties of Router A and becomes the active router. That is, Router B now responds to the virtual IP address and the virtual MAC address. Pat's workstation continues to use the IP address of the virtual router to address packets destined for Marceau's workstation, which Router B receives and sends to the Paris segment via the New York segment. Until Router A resumes operation, HSRP allows Router B to provide uninterrupted service to the users on the Tokyo segment that need to communicate with users on the Paris segment. While it is the active router, Router B continues to perform its normal function: handling packets between the Tokyo segment and the New York segment.

HSRP also works when the hosts are configured for proxy ARP. When the active HSRP router receives an ARP request for a host that is not on the local LAN, the router replies with the MAC address of the virtual router. If the active router becomes unavailable or its connection to the remote LAN goes down, the router that becomes the active router receives packets addressed to the virtual router and transfers them accordingly.

NOTE   You can configure HSRP on any Cisco router that is running Cisco Internetwork Operating System (Cisco IOS) Software Release 10.0 or later. If you configure HSRP for one Cisco router on a Token Ring LAN, all Cisco routers on that LAN must run Cisco IOS Software Release 10.0 or later. Cisco IOS Software Releases 10.2(9), 10.3(6), and 11.0(2) allow standby IP addresses to respond to ping requests. Cisco Software Release 11.0(3)(1) provides improved support for the use of secondary IP addresses with HSRP.

Understanding How HSRP Works

HSRP uses a priority scheme to determine which HSRP-configured router is to be the default active router. To configure a router as the active router, you assign it a priority that is higher than the priority of all the other HSRP-configured routers. The default priority is 100, so if you configure just one router to have a higher priority, that router will be the default active router.

HSRP works by the exchange of multicast messages that advertise priority among HSRP-configured routers. When the active router fails to send a hello message within a configurable period of time, the standby router with the highest priority becomes the active router. The transition of packet-forwarding functions between routers is completely transparent to all hosts on the network.

HSRP-configured routers exchange three types of multicast messages:

- **Hello**—The hello message conveys to other HSRP routers the router's HSRP priority and state information. By default, an HSRP router sends hello messages every three seconds.

- **Coup**—When a standby router assumes the function of the active router, it sends a coup message.

- **Resign**—A router that is the active router sends this message when it is about to shut down or when a router that has a higher priority sends a hello message.

At any time, HSRP-configured routers are in one of the following states:

- **Active**—The router is performing packet-transfer functions.
- **Standby**—The router is prepared to assume packet-transfer functions if the active router fails.
- **Speaking and listening**—The router is sending and receiving hello messages.
- **Listening**—The router is receiving hello messages.

NOTE   When configured on AGS, AGS+, and Cisco 7000 series routers, HSRP takes advantage of special hardware features that are not available on other Cisco routers. This means that HSRP operates in a slightly different way on these routers. For an example, see the "Using HSRP with Routed Protocols" section later in this chapter.

Configuring HSRP

Figure 23-3 shows the topology of an IP network in which two routers are configured for HSRP.

Figure 23-3   *Example of a Network Configured for HSRP*

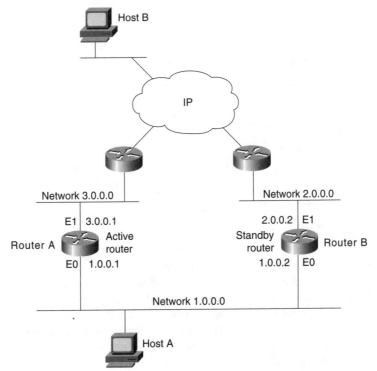

All hosts on the network are configured to use the IP address of the virtual router (in this case, 1.0.0.3) as the default gateway. The command for configuring the default gateway depends on the host's operating system, TCP/IP implementation, and configuration.

NOTE   The configurations shown in this case study use the EIGRP routing protocol. HSRP can be used with any routing protocol supported by the Cisco IOS software. Some configurations that use HSRP still require a routing protocol to converge when a topology change occurs. The standby router becomes active, but connectivity does not occur until the protocol converges.

The following is the configuration for Router A:

```
hostname RouterA
!
interface ethernet 0
ip address 1.0.0.1 255.0.0.0
standby 1 ip 1.0.0.3
standby 1 preempt
standby 1 priority 110
standby 1 authentication denmark
standby 1 timers 5 15
!
interface ethernet 1
ip address 3.0.0.1 255.0.0.0
!
router eigrp 1
network 1.0.0.0
network 3.0.0.0
The following is the configuration for Router B:
hostname RouterB
!
interface ethernet 0
ip address 1.0.0.2 255.0.0.0
standby 1 ip 1.0.0.3
standby 1 preempt
standby 1 authentication denmark
standby 1 timers 5 15
!
interface ethernet 1
ip address 2.0.0.2 255.0.0.0
!
router eigrp 1
network 1.0.0.0
network 2.0.0.0
```

The **standby ip** interface configuration command enables HSRP and establishes 1.0.0.3 as the IP address of the virtual router. The configurations of both routers include this command so that both routers share the same virtual IP address. The 1 establishes Hot Standby group 1. (If you do not specify a group number, the default is group 0.) The configuration for at least one of the routers in the Hot Standby group must specify the IP address of the virtual router; specifying the IP address of the virtual router is optional for other routers in the same Hot Standby group.

The **standby preempt** interface configuration command allows the router to become the active router when its priority is higher than all other HSRP-configured routers in this Hot Standby group. The configurations of both routers include this command so that each router can be the standby router for the other router. The 1 indicates that this command applies to Hot Standby group 1. If you do not use the **standby preempt** command in the configuration for a router, that router cannot become the active router.

The **standby priority** interface configuration command sets the router's HSRP priority to 110, which is higher than the default priority of 100. Only the configuration of Router A includes this command, which makes Router A the default active router. The 1 indicates that this command applies to Hot Standby group 1.

The **standby authentication** interface configuration command establishes an authentication string whose value is an unencrypted eight-character string that is incorporated in each HSRP multicast message. This command is optional. If you choose to use it, each HSRP-configured router in the group should use the same string so that each router can authenticate the source of the HSRP messages that it receives. The "1" indicates that this command applies to Hot Standby group 1.

The **standby timers** interface configuration command sets the interval in seconds between hello messages (called the *hello time*) to five seconds and sets the duration in seconds that a router waits before it declares the active router to be down (called the *hold time*) to eight seconds. (The defaults are three and 10 seconds, respectively.) If you decide to modify the default values, you must configure each router to use the same hello time and hold time. The "1" indicates that this command applies to Hot Standby group 1.

NOTE   There can be up to 255 Hot Standby groups on any Ethernet or FDDI LAN. There can be no more than three Hot Standby groups on any Token Ring LAN.

Configuring Multiple Hot Standby Groups

Multigroup HSRP (MHSRP) is an extension of HSRP that allows a single router interface to belong to more than one Hot Standby group. MHSRP requires the use of Cisco IOS Software Release 10.3 or later and is supported only on routers that have special hardware that allows them to associate an Ethernet interface with multiple unicast Media Access Control (MAC) addresses. These routers are the AGS and AGS+ routers and any router in the Cisco 7000 series. The special hardware allows you to configure a single interface in an AGS, AGS+, Cisco 7000, or Cisco 7500 series router so that the router is the backup router for more than one Hot Standby group, as shown in Figure 23-4.

In Figure 23-4, the Ethernet interface 0 of Router A belongs to group 1. Ethernet interface 0 of Router B belongs to groups 1, 2, and 3. The Ethernet interface 0 of Router C belongs to group 2, and the Ethernet interface 0 of Router D belongs to group 3. When you establish groups, you might want to align them along departmental organizations. In this case, group 1 might support the Engineering Department, group 2 might support the Manufacturing Department, and group 3 might support the Finance Department.

Figure 23-4 *Example of Hot Standby Groups*

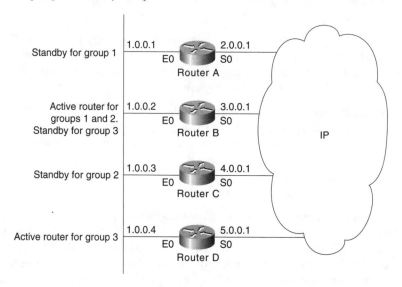

Router B is configured as the active router for groups 1 and 2 and as the standby router for group 3. Router D is configured as the active router for group 3. If Router D fails for any reason, Router B will assume the packet-transfer functions of Router D and will maintain the ability of users in the Finance Department to access data on other subnets. The following is the configuration for Router A:

```
hostname RouterA
!
interface ethernet 0
ip address 1.0.0.1 255.0.0.0
standby 1 ip 1.0.0.5
standby authentication sclara
!
interface serial 0
ip address 2.0.0.1 255.0.0.0
!
router eigrp 1
network 1.0.0.0
network 2.0.0.0
```

The following is the configuration for Router B, which must be an AGS, AGS+, Cisco 7000, or Cisco 7500 series router:

```
hostname RouterB
!
interface ethernet 0
ip address 1.0.0.2 255.0 0.0
```

```
standby 1 ip 1.0.0.5
standby 1 priority 110
standby 1 preempt
standby 1 authentication sclara
standby 2 ip 1.0.0.6
standby 2 priority 110
standby 2 preempt
standby 2 authentication mtview
standby 3 ip 1.0.0.7
standby 3 preempt
standby 3 authentication svale
!
interface serial 0
ip address 3.0.0.1 255.0.0.0
!
router eigrp 1
network 1.0.0.0
network 3.0.0.0
```

The following is the configuration for Router C:

```
hostname RouterC
!
interface ethernet 0
ip address 1.0.0.3 255.0 0.0
standby 2 ip 1.0.0.6
standby 2 preempt
standby 2 authentication mtview
!
interface serial 0
ip address 4.0.0.1 255.0.0.0
!
router eigrp 1
network 1.0.0.0
network 4.0.0.0
```

The following is the configuration for Router D:

```
hostname RouterD
!
interface ethernet 0
ip address 1.0.0.4 255.0 0.0
standby 3 ip 1.0.0.7
standby 3 priority 110
standby 3 preempt
standby 3 authentication svale
!
interface serial 0
ip address 5.0.0.1 255.0.0.0
!
router eigrp 1
network 1.0.0.0
network 5.0.0.0
```

Interface Tracking

For both HSRP and MHSRP, you can use the tracking feature to adjust the Hot Standby priority of a router based on whether certain of the router's interfaces are available. When a tracked interface becomes unavailable, the HSRP priority of the router is decreased. You can use tracking to automatically reduce the likelihood that a router that already has an unavailable key interface will become the active router. To configure tracking, use the

standby track interface configuration command. Figure 23-5 shows a network for which tracking is configured.

Figure 23-5 *A Network with Tracking Configured*

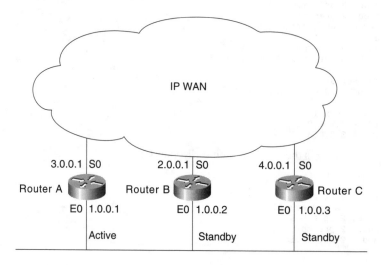

In Figure 23-5, Router A is configured as the active router. Router B and Router C are configured as standby routers for Router A. The following is the configuration for Router A:

```
hostname RouterA
!
interface ethernet 0
ip address 1.0.0.1 255.0.0.0
standby 1 ip 1.0.0.4
standby 1 preempt
standby 1 priority 110
standby authentication microdot
!
interface serial 0
ip address 2.0.0.1 255.0.0.0
!
router eigrp 1
network 1.0.0.0
network 2.0.0.0
```

The **standby ip** interface configuration command enables HSRP and establishes 1.0.0.4 as the IP address of the virtual router. The 1 establishes Hot Standby group 1. The **standby preempt** interface configuration command allows Router A to become the active router when its priority is higher than all other HSRP-configured routers in the Hot Standby group.

The *standby priority interface configuration command* sets the router's HSRP priority to 110, which is highest priority assigned to the three routers in this example. Because Router A has the highest priority, it is the active router under normal operation. The following is the configuration for Router B:

```
hostname RouterB
!
interface ethernet 0
ip address 1.0.0.2 255.0 0.0
standby 1 ip 1.0.0.4
standby 1 preempt
standby 1 priority 105
standby track serial 0
standby 1 authentication microdot

interface serial 0
ip address 3.0.0.1 255.0.0.0
!
router eigrp 1
network 1.0.0.0
network 3.0.0.0
```

The **standby preempt** interface configuration command allows Router B to become the active router immediately if its priority is highest, even before the current active router fails. The **standby priority** interface configuration command specifies a priority of 105 (lower than the priority of Router A and higher than the priority of Router C), so Router B is a standby router.

The **standby track** interface configuration command causes Ethernet interface 0 to track serial interface 0. If serial interface 0 becomes unavailable, the priority of Router B is reduced by 10 (the default). The following is the configuration for Router C:

```
hostname RouterC
!
interface ethernet 0
ip address 1.0.0.3 255.0 0.0
standby 1 ip 1.0.0.4
standby 1 preempt
standby 1 priority
standby track serial 0
standby 1 authentication microdot
!
interface serial 0
ip address 4.0.0.1 255.0.0.0
!
router eigrp 1
network 1.0.0.0
network 4.0.0.0
```

The **standby preempt** interface configuration command allows Router C to become the active router if its priority is highest when the active router fails. The **standby priority** interface configuration command does not specify a priority, so its priority is 100 (the default).

If Router A becomes unavailable and if serial interface 0 on Router B is available, Router B (with its priority of 105) will become the active router. However, if serial interface 0 on Router B becomes unavailable before Router A becomes unavailable, the HSRP priority of Router B will be reduced from 105 to 95. If Router A then becomes unavailable, Router C (whose priority is 100) will become the active router.

Load Sharing

You can use HSRP or MHSRP when you configure load sharing. In Figure 23-6, half of the workstations on the LAN are configured for Router A, and half of the workstations are configured for Router B.

Figure 23-6 *Load Sharing Example*

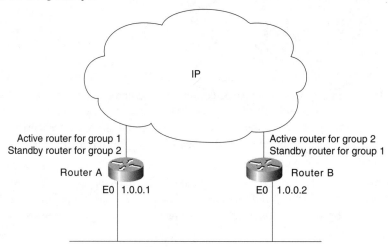

The following is a partial configuration for Router A:

```
hostname RouterA
!
interface ethernet 0
ip address 1.0.0.1 255.0.0.0
standby 1 ip 1.0.0.3
standby 1 priority 110
standby 1 preempt
standby 2 ip 1.0.0.4
standby 2 preempt
```

The following is a partial configuration for Router B:

```
hostname RouterB
!
interface ethernet 0
ip address 1.0.0.2 255.0.0.0
standby 1 ip 1.0.0.3
standby 1 preempt
standby 2 ip 1.0.0.4
standby 2 priority 110
standby 2 preempt
```

Together, the configuration files for Router A and Router B establish two Hot Standby groups. For group 1, Router A is the default active router, and Router B is the standby router. For group 2, Router B is the default active router, and Router A is the standby router. During normal operation, the two routers share the IP traffic load. When either router becomes unavailable, the other router becomes active and assumes the packet-transfer functions of the router that is unavailable. The **standby preempt** interface configuration commands are necessary so that if a router goes down and then comes back up, preemption occurs and restores load sharing.

Using HSRP with Routed Protocols

This section describes the interaction between HSRP and the following routed protocols:

- AppleTalk, Banyan VINES, and Novell IPX
- DECnet and XNS

AppleTalk, Banyan VINES, and Novell IPX

You can configure HSRP in networks that, in addition to IP, run AppleTalk, Banyan VINES, and Novell IPX. AppleTalk and Novell IPX continue to function when the standby router becomes the active router, but they take time to adapt to topology changes. In general, AppleTalk hosts discover a new active router in less than 30 seconds. Novell 4.*x* hosts discover a new active router in 10 seconds, on average. Novell 2.*x* or Novell 3.*x* hosts might require more time to adapt.

NOTE   Regardless of whether HSRP is configured, Banyan VINES does not respond well to topology changes. When HSRP is configured, the effect of a topology change varies, depending on the type of router that becomes the active router.

When the active router becomes unavailable, or its connection to the network goes down, all Banyan VINES sessions that rely on that router stop and must be reinitiated. If an AGS, AGS+, or Cisco 7000 series router becomes the active router, Banyan VINES traffic flowing through that router is not affected as it changes from standby to active. That is because these routers have special hardware that allows them to have more than one MAC address at the same time. If the router that becomes the active router is *not* an AGS, AGS+, or Cisco 7000 series router, Banyan VINES traffic flowing through that router pauses and resumes after no more than 90 seconds while the router changes from standby to active.

Regardless of which type of router becomes the active router, any Banyan VINES serverless clients that obtained their network-layer address from the unavailable router might need to reboot to obtain another network-layer address.

DECnet and XNS

DECnet and XNS are compatible with HSRP and MHSRP over Ethernet, FDDI, and Token Ring on the Cisco 7000 and Cisco 7500 routers. Some constraints apply when HSRP and MHSRP are configured on other routers, such as the Cisco 2500, Cisco 3000, Cisco 4000, and Cisco 4500 series routers, which do not have the hardware required to support multiple MAC addresses. Table 23-1 identifies the supported and unsupported combinations.

Table 23-1   *HSRP and MHSRP Compatibility with DECnet and XNS*

Protocol Combination per Interface	Cisco 2500	Cisco 3000	Cisco 4000	Cisco 4500	Cisco 7000	Cisco 7500
MHSRP with or without DECnet or XNS	No	No	No	No	Yes	Yes
HSRP without DECnet or XNS	Yes	Yes	Yes	Yes	Yes	Yes
HSRP with DECnet or XNS	No	No	No	No	Yes	Yes

Summary

HSRP and MHSRP provide fault-tolerant routing of IP packets for networks that require nonstop access by hosts on all segments to resources on all segments. To provide fault tolerance, HSRP and MHSRP require a routing protocol that converges rapidly, such as EIGRP. A fast-converging protocol ensures that router state changes propagate fast enough to make the transition from standby to active mode transparent to network users.

PART III

Appendixes

Subnetting an IP Address Space

This appendix provides a partial listing of a Class B area intended to be divided into approximately 500 Open Shortest Path First (OSPF) areas. For the purposes of this example, the network is assumed to be a Class B network with the address 150.100.0.0.

NOTE	Although a 500-area OSPF network is unrealistic, using an address space like this can help illustrate the general methodology employed to subnet an OSPF address space.

Only the address space for 2 of 512 areas is shown in Table A-1. These areas are defined with the base address 150.100.2.0. Illustrating the entire address space for 150.100.0.0 would require hundreds of additional pages of addressing information. Each area would require the equivalent number of entries for each of the example areas illustrated here.

Table A-1 illustrates the assignment of 255 IP addresses that have been split between two OSPF areas. Table A-1 also illustrates the boundaries of the subnets and of the two OSPF areas shown (area 8 and area 17).

For the purposes of this discussion, consider a network that requires point-to-point serial links in each area to be assigned a subnet mask that allows two hosts per subnet. All other subnets are to be allowed 14 hosts per subnet. The use of bitwise subnetting and variable-length subnet masks (VLSMs) permits you to customize your address space by facilitating the division of address spaces into smaller groupings than is allowed when subnetting along octet boundaries. The address layout shown in Table A-1 illustrates a structured approach to assigning addresses that uses VLSM. Table A-1 presents two subnet masks: 255.255.255.240 and 255.255.255.252. The first mask creates subnet address spaces that are four bits wide; the second mask creates subnet address spaces that are two bits wide.

Because of the careful assignment of addresses, each area can be summarized with a single **area** router configuration command (used to define address range). The first set of addresses starting with 150.100.2.0*xxxxxxx* (last octet represented here in binary) can be summarized into the backbone with the following command:

```
area 8 range 150.100.2.0 255.255.255.128
```

This command assigns all addresses from 150.100.2.0 to 150.100.2.127 to area 8. Similarly, the addresses from 150.100.2.128 to 150.100.2.255 for the second area can be summarized as follows:

```
area 17 range 150.100.2.128 255.255.255.128
```

This command assigns all addresses from 150.100.2.128 to 150.100.2.255 to area 17.

Allocation of subnets allows you to decide where to draw the line between the subnet and host (using a subnet mask) within each area. Note that in this example there are only seven bits remaining to use because of the creation of the artificial area mask. The nine bits to the left of the area mask are actually part of the subnet portion of the address. By keeping these nine bits the same for all addresses in a given area, route summarization is easily achieved at area border routers, as illustrated by the scheme used in Table A-1.

Table A-1 lists individual subnets, valid IP addresses, subnet identifiers, and broadcast addresses. This method of assigning addresses for the VLSM portion of the address space guarantees that there is no address overlap. If the requirement had been different, any number of the larger subnets might be chosen and divided into smaller ranges with fewer hosts, or combined into several ranges to create subnets with more hosts.

The design approach used in this appendix allows the area mask boundary and subnet masks to be assigned to any point in the address space, which provides significant design flexibility. A change in the specification of the area mask boundary or subnet masks may be required if a network outgrows its initial address space design. In Table A-1, the area mask boundary is to the right of the most significant bit of the last octet of the address, as shown in Figure A-1.

Figure A-1   *Breakdown of the Addresses Assigned by the Example*

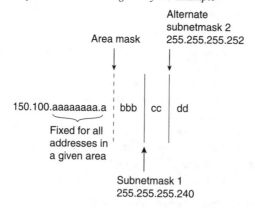

With a subnet mask of 255.255.255.240, the *a* and *b* bits together represent the subnet portion of the address, whereas the *c* and *d* bits together provide four-bit host identifiers. With a subnet mask of 255.255.255.252 (a typical subnet mask for point-to-point serial lines), the *a*, *b*, and *c* bits together represent the subnet portion of the address, and the *d* bits provide two-bit host identifiers. As mentioned earlier, the purpose of the area mask is to keep all of the *a* bits constant in a given OSPF area (independent of the subnet mask) so that route summarization is easy to apply.

The following steps outline the process used to allocate addresses:

Step 1   Determine the number of areas required for your OSPF network. A value of 500 is used for this example.

Step 2   Create an artificial *area mask boundary* in your address space. This example uses nine bits of subnet addressing space to identify the areas uniquely. Because $2^9 = 512$, nine bits of subnet meet our requirement of 500 areas.

Step 3   Determine the number of subnets required in each area and the maximum number of hosts required per subnet. This allows you to determine the placement of the subnet mask(s). In Table A-1, the requirement is for seven subnets with 14 hosts each and four subnets with two hosts each.

Table A-1   *Partial Example of Subnet Address Assignment Using VLSM*

IP Address (Decimal)	Subnet Portion of Last Octet (Binary)	Host Portion of Last Octet (Binary)	Subnet Number	Subnet Mask	Notes
150.100.2.0	0000	0000	150.100.2.0	255.255.255.240	Subnet identifier; area boundary; area 8 starts
150.100.2.1	0000	0001	150.100.2.0	255.255.255.240	
150.100.2.2	0000	0010	150.100.2.0	255.255.255.240	
150.100.2.3	0000	0011	150.100.2.0	255.255.255.240	
150.100.2.4	0000	0100	150.100.2.0	255.255.255.240	
150.100.2.5	0000	0101	150.100.2.0	255.255.255.240	
150.100.2.6	0000	0110	150.100.2.0	255.255.255.240	
150.100.2.7	0000	0111	150.100.2.0	255.255.255.240	
150.100.2.8	0000	1000	150.100.2.0	255.255.255.240	
150.100.2.9	0000	1001	150.100.2.0	255.255.255.240	
150.100.2.10	0000	1010	150.100.2.0	255.255.255.240	
150.100.2.11	0000	1011	150.100.2.0	255.255.255.240	

continues

Table A-1   *Partial Example of Subnet Address Assignment Using VLSM (Continued)*

IP Address (Decimal)	Subnet Portion of Last Octet (Binary)	Host Portion of Last Octet (Binary)	Subnet Number	Subnet Mask	Notes
150.100.2.12	0000	1100	150.100.2.0	255.255.255.240	
150.100.2.13	0000	1101	150.100.2.0	255.255.255.240	
150.100.2.14	0000	1110	150.100.2.0	255.255.255.240	
150.100.2.15	0000	1111	150.100.2.0	255.255.255.240	Subnet broadcast
150.100.2.16	0001	0000	150.100.2.16	255.255.255.240	Subnet identifier
150.100.2.17	0001	0001	150.100.2.16	255.255.255.240	
150.100.2.18	0001	0010	150.100.2.16	255.255.255.240	
150.100.2.19	0001	0011	150.100.2.16	255.255.255.240	
150.100.2.20	0001	0100	150.100.2.16	255.255.255.240	
150.100.2.21	0001	0101	150.100.2.16	255.255.255.240	
150.100.2.22	0001	0110	150.100.2.16	255.255.255.240	
150.100.2.23	0001	0111	150.100.2.16	255.255.255.240	
150.100.2.24	0001	1000	150.100.2.16	255.255.255.240	
150.100.2.25	0001	1001	150.100.2.16	255.255.255.240	
150.100.2.26	0001	1010	150.100.2.16	255.255.255.240	
150.100.2.27	0001	1011	150.100.2.16	255.255.255.240	
150.100.2.28	0001	1100	150.100.2.16	255.255.255.240	
150.100.2.29	0001	1101	150.100.2.16	255.255.255.240	
150.100.2.30	0001	1110	150.100.2.16	255.255.255.240	
150.100.2.31	0001	1111	150.100.2.16	255.255.255.240	Subnet broadcast
150.100.2.32	0010	0000	150.100.2.32	255.255.255.240	Subnet identifier
150.100.2.33	0010	0001	150.100.2.32	255.255.255.240	
150.100.2.34	0010	0010	150.100.2.32	255.255.255.240	
150.100.2.35	0010	0011	150.100.2.32	255.255.255.240	
150.100.2.36	0010	0100	150.100.2.32	255.255.255.240	
150.100.2.37	0010	0101	150.100.2.32	255.255.255.240	

Table A-1   *Partial Example of Subnet Address Assignment Using VLSM (Continued)*

IP Address (Decimal)	Subnet Portion of Last Octet (Binary)	Host Portion of Last Octet (Binary)	Subnet Number	Subnet Mask	Notes
150.100.2.38	0010	0110	150.100.2.32	255.255.255.240	
150.100.2.39	0010	0111	150.100.2.32	255.255.255.240	
150.100.2.40	0010	1000	150.100.2.32	255.255.255.240	
150.100.2.41	0010	1001	150.100.2.32	255.255.255.240	
150.100.2.42	0010	1010	150.100.2.32	255.255.255.240	
150.100.2.43	0010	1011	150.100.2.32	255.255.255.240	
150.100.2.44	0010	1100	150.100.2.32	255.255.255.240	
150.100.2.45	0010	1101	150.100.2.32	255.255.255.240	
150.100.2.46	0010	1110	150.100.2.32	255.255.255.240	
150.100.2.47	0010	1111	150.100.2.32	255.255.255.240	Subnet broadcast
150.100.2.48	0011	0000	150.100.2.48	255.255.255.240	Subnet identifier
150.100.2.49	0011	0001	150.100.2.48	255.255.255.240	
150.100.2.50	0011	0010	150.100.2.48	255.255.255.240	
150.100.2.51	0011	0011	150.100.2.48	255.255.255.240	
150.100.2.52	0011	0100	150.100.2.48	255.255.255.240	
150.100.2.53	0011	0101	150.100.2.48	255.255.255.240	
150.100.2.54	0011	0110	150.100.2.48	255.255.255.240	
150.100.2.55	0011	0111	150.100.2.48	255.255.255.240	
150.100.2.56	0011	1000	150.100.2.48	255.255.255.240	
150.100.2.57	0011	1001	150.100.2.48	255.255.255.240	
150.100.2.58	0011	1010	150.100.2.48	255.255.255.240	
150.100.2.59	0011	1011	150.100.2.48	255.255.255.240	
150.100.2.60	0011	1100	150.100.2.48	255.255.255.240	
150.100.2.61	0011	1101	150.100.2.48	255.255.255.240	
150.100.2.62	0011	1110	150.100.2.48	255.255.255.240	

continues

Table A-1 *Partial Example of Subnet Address Assignment Using VLSM (Continued)*

IP Address (Decimal)	Subnet Portion of Last Octet (Binary)	Host Portion of Last Octet (Binary)	Subnet Number	Subnet Mask	Notes
150.100.2.63	0011	1111	150.100.2.48	255.255.255.240	Subnet broadcast
150.100.2.64	010000	00	150.100.2.64	255.255.255.252	Subnet identifier
150.100.2.65	010000	01	150.100.2.64	255.255.255.252	
150.100.2.66	010000	10	150.100.2.64	255.255.255.252	
150.100.2.67	010000	11	150.100.2.64	255.255.255.252	Subnet broadcast
150.100.2.68	010001	00	150.100.2.68	255.255.255.252	Subnet identifier
150.100.2.69	010001	01	150.100.2.68	255.255.255.252	
150.100.2.70	010001	10	150.100.2.68	255.255.255.252	
150.100.2.71	010001	11	150.100.2.68	255.255.255.252	Subnet broadcast
150.100.2.72	010010	00	150.100.2.72	255.255.255.252	Subnet identifier
150.100.2.73	010010	01	150.100.2.72	255.255.255.252	
150.100.2.74	010010	10	150.100.2.72	255.255.255.252	
150.100.2.75	010010	11	150.100.2.72	255.255.255.252	Subnet broadcast
150.100.2.76	010011	00	150.100.2.76	255.255.255.252	Subnet identifier
150.100.2.77	010011	01	150.100.2.76	255.255.255.252	
150.100.2.78	010011	10	150.100.2.76	255.255.255.252	
150.100.2.79	010011	11	150.100.2.76	255.255.255.252	Subnet broadcast
150.100.2.80	0101	0000	150.100.2.80	255.255.255.240	Subnet identifier
150.100.2.81	0101	0001	150.100.2.80	255.255.255.240	
150.100.2.82	0101	0010	150.100.2.80	255.255.255.240	
150.100.2.83	0101	0011	150.100.2.80	255.255.255.240	

Table A-1   *Partial Example of Subnet Address Assignment Using VLSM (Continued)*

IP Address (Decimal)	Subnet Portion of Last Octet (Binary)	Host Portion of Last Octet (Binary)	Subnet Number	Subnet Mask	Notes
150.100.2.84	0101	0100	150.100.2.80	255.255.255.240	
150.100.2.85	0101	0101	150.100.2.80	255.255.255.240	
150.100.2.86	0101	0110	150.100.2.80	255.255.255.240	
150.100.2.87	0101	0111	150.100.2.80	255.255.255.240	
150.100.2.88	0101	1000	150.100.2.80	255.255.255.240	
150.100.2.89	0101	1001	150.100.2.80	255.255.255.240	
150.100.2.90	0101	1010	150.100.2.80	255.255.255.240	
150.100.2.91	0101	1011	150.100.2.80	255.255.255.240	
150.100.2.92	0101	1100	150.100.2.80	255.255.255.240	
150.100.2.93	0101	1101	150.100.2.80	255.255.255.240	
150.100.2.94	0101	1110	150.100.2.80	255.255.255.240	
150.100.2.95	0101	1111	150.100.2.80	255.255.255.240	Subnet broadcast
150.100.2.96	0110	0000	150.100.2.96	255.255.255.240	Subnet identifier
150.100.2.97	0110	0001	150.100.2.96	255.255.255.240	
150.100.2.98	0110	0010	150.100.2.96	255.255.255.240	
150.100.2.99	0110	0011	150.100.2.96	255.255.255.240	
150.100.2.100	0110	0100	150.100.2.96	255.255.255.240	
150.100.2.101	0110	0101	150.100.2.96	255.255.255.240	
150.100.2.102	0110	0110	150.100.2.96	255.255.255.240	
150.100.2.103	0110	0111	150.100.2.96	255.255.255.240	
150.100.2.104	0110	1000	150.100.2.96	255.255.255.240	
150.100.2.105	0110	1001	150.100.2.96	255.255.255.240	
150.100.2.106	0110	1010	150.100.2.96	255.255.255.240	
150.100.2.107	0110	1011	150.100.2.96	255.255.255.240	
150.100.2.108	0110	1100	150.100.2.96	255.255.255.240	

continues

Table A-1 *Partial Example of Subnet Address Assignment Using VLSM (Continued)*

IP Address (Decimal)	Subnet Portion of Last Octet (Binary)	Host Portion of Last Octet (Binary)	Subnet Number	Subnet Mask	Notes
150.100.2.109	0110	1101	150.100.2.96	255.255.255.240	
150.100.2.110	0110	1110	150.100.2.96	255.255.255.240	
150.100.2.111	0110	1111	150.100.2.96	255.255.255.240	Subnet broadcast
150.100.2.112	0111	0000	150.100.2.112	255.255.255.240	Subnet identifier
150.100.2.113	0111	0001	150.100.2.112	255.255.255.240	
150.100.2.114	0111	0010	150.100.2.112	255.255.255.240	
150.100.2.115	0111	0011	150.100.2.112	255.255.255.240	
150.100.2.116	0111	0100	150.100.2.112	255.255.255.240	
150.100.2.117	0111	0101	150.100.2.112	255.255.255.240	
150.100.2.118	0111	0110	150.100.2.112	255.255.255.240	
150.100.2.119	0111	0111	150.100.2.112	255.255.255.240	
150.100.2.120	0111	1000	150.100.2.112	255.255.255.240	
150.100.2.121	0111	1001	150.100.2.112	255.255.255.240	
150.100.2.122	0111	1010	150.100.2.112	255.255.255.240	
150.100.2.123	0111	1011	150.100.2.112	255.255.255.240	
150.100.2.124	0111	1100	150.100.2.112	255.255.255.240	
150.100.2.125	0111	1101	150.100.2.112	255.255.255.240	
150.100.2.126	0111	1110	150.100.2.112	255.255.255.240	
150.100.2.127	0111	1111	150.100.2.112	255.255.255.240	Subnet broadcast; area boundary; area 8 ends
150.100.2.128	1000	0000	150.100.2.128	255.255.255.240	Subnet identifier; area boundary; area 17 starts
150.100.2.129	1000	0001	150.100.2.128	255.255.255.240	

Table A-1 *Partial Example of Subnet Address Assignment Using VLSM (Continued)*

IP Address (Decimal)	Subnet Portion of Last Octet (Binary)	Host Portion of Last Octet (Binary)	Subnet Number	Subnet Mask	Notes
150.100.2.130	1000	0010	150.100.2.128	255.255.255.240	
150.100.2.131	1000	0011	150.100.2.128	255.255.255.240	
150.100.2.132	1000	0100	150.100.2.128	255.255.255.240	
150.100.2.133	1000	0101	150.100.2.128	255.255.255.240	
150.100.2.134	1000	0110	150.100.2.128	255.255.255.240	
150.100.2.135	1000	0111	150.100.2.128	255.255.255.240	
150.100.2.136	1000	1000	150.100.2.128	255.255.255.240	
150.100.2.137	1000	1001	150.100.2.128	255.255.255.240	
150.100.2.138	1000	1010	150.100.2.128	255.255.255.240	
150.100.2.139	1000	1011	150.100.2.128	255.255.255.240	
150.100.2.140	1000	1100	150.100.2.128	255.255.255.240	
150.100.2.141	1000	1101	150.100.2.128	255.255.255.240	
150.100.2.142	1000	1110	150.100.2.128	255.255.255.240	
150.100.2.143	1000	1111	150.100.2.128	255.255.255.240	Subnet broadcast
150.100.2.144	1001	0000	150.100.2.144	255.255.255.240	Subnet identifier
150.100.2.145	1001	0001	150.100.2.144	255.255.255.240	
150.100.2.146	1001	0010	150.100.2.144	255.255.255.240	
150.100.2.147	1001	0011	150.100.2.144	255.255.255.240	
150.100.2.148	1001	0100	150.100.2.144	255.255.255.240	
150.100.2.149	1001	0101	150.100.2.144	255.255.255.240	
150.100.2.150	1001	0110	150.100.2.144	255.255.255.240	
150.100.2.151	1001	0111	150.100.2.144	255.255.255.240	
150.100.2.152	1001	1000	150.100.2.144	255.255.255.240	
150.100.2.153	1001	1001	150.100.2.144	255.255.255.240	
150.100.2.154	1001	1010	150.100.2.144	255.255.255.240	

continues

Table A-1   *Partial Example of Subnet Address Assignment Using VLSM (Continued)*

IP Address (Decimal)	Subnet Portion of Last Octet (Binary)	Host Portion of Last Octet (Binary)	Subnet Number	Subnet Mask	Notes
150.100.2.155	1001	1011	150.100.2.144	255.255.255.240	
150.100.2.156	1001	1100	150.100.2.144	255.255.255.240	
150.100.2.157	1001	1101	150.100.2.144	255.255.255.240	
150.100.2.158	1001	1110	150.100.2.144	255.255.255.240	
150.100.2.159	1001	1111	150.100.2.144	255.255.255.240	Subnet broadcast
150.100.2.160	1010	0000	150.100.2.160	255.255.255.240	Subnet identifier
150.100.2.161	1010	0001	150.100.2.160	255.255.255.240	
150.100.2.162	1010	0010	150.100.2.160	255.255.255.240	
150.100.2.163	1010	0011	150.100.2.160	255.255.255.240	
150.100.2.164	1010	0100	150.100.2.160	255.255.255.240	
150.100.2.165	1010	0101	150.100.2.160	255.255.255.240	
150.100.2.166	1010	0110	150.100.2.160	255.255.255.240	
150.100.2.167	1010	0111	150.100.2.160	255.255.255.240	
150.100.2.168	1010	1000	150.100.2.160	255.255.255.240	
150.100.2.169	1010	1001	150.100.2.160	255.255.255.240	
150.100.2.170	1010	1010	150.100.2.160	255.255.255.240	
150.100.2.171	1010	1011	150.100.2.160	255.255.255.240	
150.100.2.172	1010	1100	150.100.2.160	255.255.255.240	
150.100.2.173	1010	1101	150.100.2.160	255.255.255.240	
150.100.2.174	1010	1110	150.100.2.160	255.255.255.240	
150.100.2.175	1010	1111	150.100.2.160	255.255.255.240	Subnet broadcast
150.100.2.176	101100	00	150.100.2.176	255.255.255.252	Subnet identifier
150.100.2.177	101100	01	150.100.2.176	255.255.255.252	
150.100.2.178	101100	10	150.100.2.176	255.255.255.252	
150.100.2.179	101100	11	150.100.2.176	255.255.255.252	Subnet broadcast

Table A-1   *Partial Example of Subnet Address Assignment Using VLSM (Continued)*

IP Address (Decimal)	Subnet Portion of Last Octet (Binary)	Host Portion of Last Octet (Binary)	Subnet Number	Subnet Mask	Notes
150.100.2.180	101101	00	150.100.2.180	255.255.255.252	Subnet identifier
150.100.2.181	101101	01	150.100.2.180	255.255.255.252	
150.100.2.182	101101	10	150.100.2.180	255.255.255.252	
150.100.2.183	101101	11	150.100.2.180	255.255.255.252	Subnet broadcast
150.100.2.184	101110	00	150.100.2.184	255.255.255.252	Subnet identifier
150.100.2.185	101110	01	150.100.2.184	255.255.255.252	
150.100.2.186	101110	10	150.100.2.184	255.255.255.252	
150.100.2.187	101110	11	150.100.2.184	255.255.255.252	Subnet broadcast
150.100.2.188	101111	00	150.100.2.188	255.255.255.252	Subnet identifier
150.100.2.189	101111	01	150.100.2.188	255.255.255.252	
150.100.2.190	101111	10	150.100.2.188	255.255.255.252	
150.100.2.191	101111	11	150.100.2.188	255.255.255.252	Subnet broadcast
150.100.2.192	1100	0000	150.100.2.192	255.255.255.240	Subnet identifier
150.100.2.193	1100	0001	150.100.2.192	255.255.255.240	
150.100.2.194	1100	0010	150.100.2.192	255.255.255.240	
150.100.2.195	1100	0011	150.100.2.192	255.255.255.240	
150.100.2.196	1100	0100	150.100.2.192	255.255.255.240	
150.100.2.197	1100	0101	150.100.2.192	255.255.255.240	
150.100.2.198	1100	0110	150.100.2.192	255.255.255.240	
150.100.2.199	1100	0111	150.100.2.192	255.255.255.240	
150.100.2.200	1100	1000	150.100.2.192	255.255.255.240	
150.100.2.201	1100	1001	150.100.2.192	255.255.255.240	

continues

Table A-1   *Partial Example of Subnet Address Assignment Using VLSM (Continued)*

IP Address (Decimal)	Subnet Portion of Last Octet (Binary)	Host Portion of Last Octet (Binary)	Subnet Number	Subnet Mask	Notes
150.100.2.202	1100	1010	150.100.2.192	255.255.255.240	
150.100.2.203	1100	1011	150.100.2.192	255.255.255.240	
150.100.2.204	1100	1100	150.100.2.192	255.255.255.240	
150.100.2.205	1100	1101	150.100.2.192	255.255.255.240	
150.100.2.206	1100	1110	150.100.2.192	255.255.255.240	
150.100.2.207	1100	1111	150.100.2.192	255.255.255.240	Subnet broadcast
150.100.2.208	1101	0000	150.100.2.208	255.255.255.240	Subnet identifier
150.100.2.209	1101	0001	150.100.2.208	255.255.255.240	
150.100.2.210	1101	0010	150.100.2.208	255.255.255.240	
150.100.2.211	1101	0011	150.100.2.208	255.255.255.240	
150.100.2.212	1101	0100	150.100.2.208	255.255.255.240	
150.100.2.213	1101	0101	150.100.2.208	255.255.255.240	
150.100.2.214	1101	0110	150.100.2.208	255.255.255.240	
150.100.2.215	1101	0111	150.100.2.208	255.255.255.240	
150.100.2.216	1101	1000	150.100.2.208	255.255.255.240	
150.100.2.217	1101	1001	150.100.2.208	255.255.255.240	
150.100.2.218	1101	1010	150.100.2.208	255.255.255.240	
150.100.2.219	1101	1011	150.100.2.208	255.255.255.240	
150.100.2.220	1101	1100	150.100.2.208	255.255.255.240	
150.100.2.221	1101	1101	150.100.2.208	255.255.255.240	
150.100.2.222	1101	1110	150.100.2.208	255.255.255.240	
150.100.2.223	1101	1111	150.100.2.208	255.255.255.240	Subnet broadcast
150.100.2.224	1110	0000	150.100.2.224	255.255.255.240	Subnet identifier
150.100.2.225	1110	0001	150.100.2.224	255.255.255.240	
150.100.2.226	1110	0010	150.100.2.224	255.255.255.240	
150.100.2.227	1110	0011	150.100.2.224	255.255.255.240	

Table A-1   *Partial Example of Subnet Address Assignment Using VLSM (Continued)*

IP Address (Decimal)	Subnet Portion of Last Octet (Binary)	Host Portion of Last Octet (Binary)	Subnet Number	Subnet Mask	Notes
150.100.2.228	1110	0100	150.100.2.224	255.255.255.240	
150.100.2.229	1110	0101	150.100.2.224	255.255.255.240	
150.100.2.230	1110	0110	150.100.2.224	255.255.255.240	
150.100.2.231	1110	0111	150.100.2.224	255.255.255.240	
150.100.2.232	1110	1000	150.100.2.224	255.255.255.240	
150.100.2.233	1110	1001	150.100.2.224	255.255.255.240	
150.100.2.234	1110	1010	150.100.2.224	255.255.255.240	
150.100.2.235	1110	1011	150.100.2.224	255.255.255.240	
150.100.2.236	1110	1100	150.100.2.224	255.255.255.240	
150.100.2.237	1110	1101	150.100.2.224	255.255.255.240	
150.100.2.238	1110	1110	150.100.2.224	255.255.255.240	
150.100.2.239	1110	1111	150.100.2.224	255.255.255.240	Subnet broadcast
150.100.2.240	1111	0000	150.100.2.240	255.255.255.240	Subnet identifier
150.100.2.241	1111	0001	150.100.2.240	255.255.255.240	
150.100.2.242	1111	0010	150.100.2.240	255.255.255.240	
150.100.2.243	1111	0011	150.100.2.240	255.255.255.240	
150.100.2.244	1111	0100	150.100.2.240	255.255.255.240	
150.100.2.245	1111	0101	150.100.2.240	255.255.255.240	
150.100.2.246	1111	0110	150.100.2.240	255.255.255.240	
150.100.2.247	1111	0111	150.100.2.240	255.255.255.240	
150.100.2.248	1111	1000	150.100.2.240	255.255.255.240	
150.100.2.249	1111	1001	150.100.2.240	255.255.255.240	
150.100.2.250	1111	1010	150.100.2.240	255.255.255.240	
150.100.2.251	1111	1011	150.100.2.240	255.255.255.240	
150.100.2.252	1111	1100	150.100.2.240	255.255.255.240	
150.100.2.253	1111	1101	150.100.2.240	255.255.255.240	

continues

Table A-1   *Partial Example of Subnet Address Assignment Using VLSM (Continued)*

IP Address (Decimal)	Subnet Portion of Last Octet (Binary)	Host Portion of Last Octet (Binary)	Subnet Number	Subnet Mask	Notes
150.100.2.254	1111	1110	150.100.2.240	255.255.255.240	
150.100.2.255	1111	1111	150.100.2.240	255.255.255.240	Subnet broadcast; area boundary; area 17 ends

IBM Serial Link Implementation

The following discussions clarify some common misconceptions and points of confusion associated with half-duplex, full-duplex, and multipoint connections.

Comparing Half Duplex and Full Duplex

Half-duplex and full-duplex serial links can often be confusing. One reason for the confusion is that there are several different contexts in which these two terms are used. These contexts include asynchronous line implementations, IBM Systems Network Architecture (SNA)-specific implementations, and data communications equipment (DCE) implementations. Each is addressed in the discussions that follow.

Asynchronous Line Definitions

Duplex, as seen on asynchronous communication lines (and in terminal emulation software parameters), implies *full duplex* as it applies to the echoing of transmitted characters by a host back to a terminal. This is also referred to as *echoplex* mode. In this context, half-duplex mode involves no character echo. Some common misconfigurations of terminals and hosts follow:

- Full duplex specified on a terminal when the host is set for half duplex results in typing blind at the terminal.

- Half duplex specified on a terminal when the host is set for full duplex results in double characters on the terminal. This is because the terminal displays entered characters if the terminal's configuration indicates that the host will not echo characters.

NOTE   This interpretation of duplex does not apply in a router context.

IBM SNA-Specific Definitions

IBM's master glossary for VTAM, NCP, and NetView terms defines *duplex*, *full duplex*, and *half duplex* as follows:

- *Duplex*—In data communications, pertaining to a simultaneous two-way independent transmission in both directions; synonymous with full duplex; contrast with half duplex.

- *Half duplex*—In data communications, pertaining to an alternate, one-way-at-a-time, independent transmission; contrast with duplex.

These definitions can be applied in two contexts that are the main source of duplex definition confusion:

- First, there is *full-duplex* and *half-duplex data transfer.* This typically applies to the capability or inability of data terminal equipment (DTE) to support simultaneous, two-way data flow. SNA PU 4 devices (front-end processors such as 3705, 3720, 3725, and 3745 devices) are capable of full-duplex data transfer. Each such device employs a separate data and control path into the control program's transmit and receive buffers.

- Some PU 2.1 devices are also capable of *full duplex data mode*, which is negotiable in the XID-3 format frame—unless the NCP PU definition statement DATMODE=FULL is specified. If FULL is specified, full-duplex mode is forced. PU 2s and PU 1s operate in *half-duplex data mode*.

DCE Definitions

Finally, there is *full duplex* and *half duplex* as they apply to the communication facility, or DCE. This is where most of the technological advancement has been achieved with respect to half and full duplex. DCE installations primarily consist of channel service units (CSUs), data service units (DSUs), or modem devices, and a communications line. The modem can be synchronous or asynchronous and can be analog or digital. The communications line can be two-wire or four-wire and can be leased or switched (that is, dial-up).

Older modems are capable of transmitting or receiving only at a given time. When a DTE wants to transmit data using an older modem, the DTE asserts the Request To Send (RTS) signal to the modem. If the modem *is not* in receive mode, the modem enables its carrier signal in preparation for transmitting data and asserts Clear To Send (CTS). If the modem *is* in receive mode, its Data Carrier Detect (DCD) signal (that is, the carrier signal from the remote modem) is in the active state. The modem does not activate the CTS signal, and the DTE does not transmit, because DCD is in the active state.

Contemporary modems are capable of transmitting and receiving simultaneously over two-wire or four-wire and leased or switched lines. One method uses multiple carrier signals at different frequencies so that the local modem's transmit and receive signals, as well as the remote modem's transmit and receive signals, each have their own carrier frequency.

DTE equipment in an SDLC environment have configuration options that specify which mode of operation is supported by DCE equipment. The default parameters for most PU 2 devices are set for half duplex, although they can also support full-duplex operation. If the facility is capable of full duplex, RTS can be asserted at all times. If the facility supports half duplex or is operating in a *multipoint* environment using modem-sharing devices (as opposed to multipoint provided by a Postal Telephone and Telegraph [PTT] or by a telephone company), RTS must be asserted only when transmitting. A full-duplex-capable communication facility that connects a PU 4 to a PU 2 device or to a PU 1 device (with each PU device specifying full-duplex DCE capability) experiences improved response time because of reduced turnaround delays.

Older PU 2 and PU 1 devices cannot be configured for full-duplex DCE mode. Also, because older PU 2 and PU 1 devices can only support half-duplex data transfer, transmit and receive data cannot be on the line at the same time (in contrast to a PU 4-to-PU 4 full-duplex exchange).

Understanding Multipoint Connections

Multipoint operation is a method of sharing a communication facility with multiple locations. The telephone company or PTT communications authorities offer two-wire and four-wire multipoint configurations for analog service (modem attachment) or four-wire for digital service (CSU/DSU attachment). Most implementations are master-polling, multiple-slave drop implementations. The master connects to only one drop at a time. The switching takes place at a designated local exchange in proximity to the master DTE site. Some service providers offer analog multipoint services that support two-way simultaneous communication, which allows DTEs to be configured for permanent RTS.

Modem-sharing devices and line-sharing devices also provide multipoint capability. These implementations allow a single point-to-point link to be shared by multiple devices. Some of these devices have configurable ports for DTE or DCE operation, which allow for configurations that can accommodate multiple sites (called *cascaded configurations*). The main restriction of these devices is that when RTS is active, other users are locked out. You cannot configure DTEs for permanent RTS, and you must accept the turnaround delays associated with this mode of operation.

SNA Host Configuration for SRB Networks

When designing source-route bridging (SRB) networks featuring routers and IBM Systems Network Architecture (SNA) entities, you must carefully consider the configuration of SNA nodes as well as routing nodes. This appendix provides examples that focus on three specific SNA devices:

- Front-end processors (FEPs)
- Virtual Telecommunications Access Method (VTAM)-switched major nodes
- 3174 cluster controllers

Figure C-1 illustrates a typical environment. Tables C-1 through C-6 present the definition parameters for the devices shown in Figure C-1.

Figure C-1 *Typical SNA Host Environment*

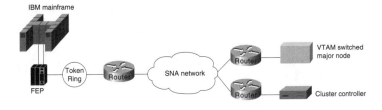

FEP Configuration

The parameters listed in Tables C-1 through C-6 illustrate input to the Network Control Program (NCP) system generation process that runs in the host processor using the Network Definition Facility (NDF). The NDF is part of the ACF/NCP/System Support Program utility. The output produced by the generation process is a *load module* that runs in an FEP. Its typical size can be slightly under 1 MB to more than 3 MB. The ACF/NCP/System Support Program utility is also used for loading and dumping an FEP.

The following tables outline relevant parameters for generating Token Ring resources.

Table C-1   *BUILD Definition Parameters*

Parameter	Example, Parameter Value, or Range	Parameter Description and Implementation Notes
LOCALTO	1.5	Local ring acknowledgment timer (seconds).
REMOTTO	2.5	Remote ring acknowledgment timer (seconds).
MAXSESS	5000	Maximum amount of sessions for all attached resources.
MXRLINE	None	Maximum number of NTRI physical connections (Version 5.2.1 and earlier only).
MXVLINE	None	Maximum number of NTRI logical connections (Version 5.2.1 and earlier only).
T2TIMER	(*localt2*, *remott2*, *N3*)	(Version 5.R4 and later only.) Parameters specify a receiver acknowledgment/timer (T2) for local and remote Token Rings, whether from peripheral or subarea nodes. Acceptable values: *localt2* range is 0 to 2.0 seconds; *remott2* range is 0 to 2.0 seconds; *N3* range is 1 to 127 (default is 2). The values for *localt2* and *remott2* should be 10.0 percent of the value of the adjacent station's T1 timer. *N3* specifies the maximum number of I-frames received without sending an acknowledgment for subarea connections.

The LUDRPOOL definition shown in Table C-2 specifies the number of peripheral resources required for the correct amount of control block storage to be reserved for new connections.

Table C-2   *LUDRPOOL Definition Parameters*

Parameter	Example, Parameter Value, or Range	Parameter Description and Implementation Notes
NUMTYP2	None	Maximum is 16,000.
NUMILU	None	Required for LU Type 2.1 devices (independent LUs).

The GROUP definition shown in Table C-3 specifies group definition parameters.

Table C-3   *GROUP Definition Parameters*

Parameter	Example, Parameter Value, or Range	Parameter Description and Implementation Notes
AUTOGEN	Number	Specifies the number of LINE/PU pairs for this group.
COMPOWN	Y	Twin FEP backup-capable resource.
COMPSWP	Y	TIC portswap-capable (hot backup).
COMPTAD	Y	TIC capable of IPL loading FEP.
DIAL	YES or NO	Applies to ECLTYPE parameter specifications.
		YES required for (LOGICAL,PERIPHERAL); NO required for all other combinations indicated in ECLTYPE specification.
ECLTYPE	(PHYSICAL,ANY)	Allows PU 4 and PU 2 devices to attach.
	(PHYSICAL, PERIPHERAL)	Allows PU 2 devices only.
	(PHYSICAL, SUBAREA)	Allows PU 4 devices only.
	(LOGICAL, PERIPHERAL)	Defines devices attaching as PU 2.
	(LOGICAL, SUBAREA)	Defines devices attaching as PU 4.
LNCTL	SDLC	Required for NCP processing compatibility.
PHYPORT	None	Required for ECLTYPE LOGICAL only; links this to a ECLTYPE PHYSICAL.
TIMER	error, ras, stap, or lstap	Entry points for NTRI timer routines.

The LINE definition shown in Table C-4 specifies line definition parameters.

Table C-4   *LINE Definition Parameters*

Parameter	Example, Parameter Value, or Range	Parameter Description and Implementation Notes
ADAPTER	TIC1	4 MB Token Ring interface.
	TIC2	4 or 16 MB Token Ring interface.
ADDRESS	1088 to1095	Range of valid addresses for TICs; only one specified per LINE definition.
BEACTO	52	Time in seconds the ring can beacon before TIC considers it down; maximum is 600.
LOCADD	4000*abbbbbbb*	Locally administered TIC address, where *a* is any value from 0 to 7, and *b* is any integer value from 0 to 9.
LOCALTO	1.5	V5R4; same as in BUILD (see Table C-1), but only for PU 4 (LOGICAL, SUBAREA) devices; allows granularity for individual TICs for SUBAREA connections.
REMOTTO	2.5	V5R4 parameter; same as LOCALTO; see BUILD parameters in Table C-1.
T2TIMER	*localt2, remott2, N3*	V5.4 parameter; see BUILD parameters in Table C-1; can be defined in LINE definition only if a subarea node was defined in GROUP definition.
MAXTSL	2044 to 16732	Specifies maximum data in bytes that NTRI can transmit; TIC1 maximum is 2044; TIC2 maximum at TRSPEED16 is 16732.
PORTADD	Number	For association of physical to logical ECLTYPEs; matches physical or logical ECLTYPE specification.
RETRIES	*m, t, n, ml*	Where *m* = number of retries for remote ring sessions, *t* = pause between retry sequence, *n* = number of retry sequences, and *ml* = number of retries in a sequence for local ring sessions.
TRSPEED	4 or 16	TIC speed.

Table C-5 specifies physical unit (PU) definition parameters.

Table C-5   *FEP Physical Unit (PU) Definition Parameters*

Parameter	Example, Parameter Value, or Range	Parameter Description and Implementation Notes
ADDR	*aa*4000*bcccccc*	Destination service access point (DSAP) and MAC address for the PU of the Token Ring device in the FEP, where *aa* = the DSAP and is a nonzero hexadecimal multiple of 4; *b* = 0 to 7; *c* = 0 to 9; enter 4000 as shown; only specified if ECLTYPE defined in GROUP definition is one of the following: (LOG,SUB), (PHY,SUB), (PHY,ANY).
PUTYPE	1, 2, or 4	Depends on ECLTYPE: • For NTRI LOGICAL resources, only PUTYPE=2 is valid; for NTRI PHYSICAL resources, only PUTYPE=1 is valid • For NTRI PHYSICAL/SUBAREA LINES and PHYSICAL PERIPHERAL LINES, only PUTYPE=1 is valid. For NTRI LOGICAL PERIPHERAL LINES, only PUTYPE=2 is valid.
XID	YES or NO	Defines the capability of a PU to receive and respond to an XID while in normal disconnected mode; for NTRI LOGICAL LINES, only YES is valid; for NTRI PHYSICAL LINES, only NO is valid.

Table C-6 specifies logical unit (LU) definition parameters.

Table C-6   *FEP Logical Unit (LU) Definition Parameter*

Parameter	Example, Parameter Value, or Range	Parameter Description and Implementation Notes
LOCADDR	0	Specify this response only.

VTAM-Switched Major Node Definitions

Devices that are attached to Token Ring and communicate with an IBM host application must be defined via the VTAM access method associated with the host. These devices are seen as dial-in resources from the host side and are defined in a configuration component named *Switched Major Node*. Some common definitions used in network configurations are outlined in Table C-7 through Table C-9

Table C-7 *VBUILD Definition Parameter*

Parameter	Example, Parameter Value, or Range	Parameter Description and Implementation Notes
TYPE	SWNET	Specifies a type of resource for VTAM; SWNET indicates switched major node type.

Table C-8 *VTAM PU Definition Parameters*

Parameter	Example, Parameter Value, or Range	Parameter Description and Implementation Notes
IDBLK	017	Typical values: • 017 = 3X74 • 05D = PC-base VTAM PU • 0E2 = Cisco SDLLC (registered with IBM)
IDNUM	*xxxxx*	Unique number identifying a device.
MAXOUT	1 to 7	Number of I-frames sent before acknowledgment is required.
MAXDATA	265	Indicates maximum number of bytes a PU 2 device can receive; ignored for PU 2.1, as this value is negotiable. Default for 3174 is 521.
PUTYPE	2	Only valid value.
XID	YES or NO	YES should be used for PU 2.1 devices. NO should be specified for any other device.

Table C-9 *VTAM LU Definition Parameter*

Parameter	Example, Parameter Value, or Range	Parameter Description and Implementation Notes
LOCADDR	2 through FF	Logical unit (LU) addresses attached to a PU.

3174 Cluster Controller Configuration Example

The following configuration was taken from a 3174-13R cluster controller serial number 45362 connected to a Token Ring. These entries were used with a specific 3174 running on a 4 Mbps Token Ring. The configuration of this 3174-13R involved three specific configuration screens. Tables C-10 through C-12 list the configuration line numbers, entries used, and descriptions of the configuration line. When applicable, extended descriptions are included for configuration entries that are relevant to the requirements of the routed network.

| NOTE | Of particular interest when configuring 3174 devices for a router-based SRB environment are configuration line items 106, 107, and 384 in configuration screen 2 (refer to Table C-11). These specify the required addresses and relevant Token Ring type for the cluster controller. |

Table C-10   *3174-13R Screen 1 Configuration Details*

Configuration Line Number	Sample Value	Parameter Description and Implementation Notes
98		Online test password.
99	TKNRNG	Description field.
100	13R	Model number.
101	7	Host attachment type.

Table C-11   *3174-13R Screen 2 Configuration Details*

Configuration Line Number	Sample Value	Parameter Description and Implementation Notes
106	4000 2222 4444 04	The first 12 hexadecimal digits form the source MAC address of the cluster controller (4000 2222 4444); the last two digits are the source SAP (SSAP) for LLC2 (0x04 = SNA).
107	4000 0037 4501 04	The first 12 hexadecimal digits form the destination MAC address of the FEP (4000 0037 4501); the last two digits are the DSAP for LLC2 (0x04 for SNA).
108	0045362	Serial number of the cluster controller.
110	0	MLT storage support.
116	0	Individual port assignment.
121	01	Keyboard language.
123	0	Country extended code page support.
125	00000000	Miscellaneous options (A).

continues

Table C-11   *3174-13R Screen 2 Configuration Details (Continued)*

Configuration Line Number	Sample Value	Parameter Description and Implementation Notes
126	00000000	Miscellaneous options (B).
127	0 0	RTM definition.
132	0000	Alternate base keyboard selection.
136	0000	Standard keyboard layout.
137	0000	Modified keyboard layout.
138	0	Standard keypad layout.
141	A	Magnetic character set.
165	0	Compressed program symbols.
166	A	Attribute select keypad.
168	0	Additional extension; mode key definition.
173	0000	DFT options.
175	000000	DFT password.
179	000	Local format storage.
213	0	Between bracket printer sharing.
215	45362	PU identification.
222	0	Support for command retry.
382	0521	Maximum ring I-frame size; range of values is 265 to 2057.
383	2	Maximum number of I-frames 3174 will transmit before awaiting an acknowledgment (transmit window size).
384	0	Ring speed of the Token Ring network: • 0 = 4 Mbps • 1 = 16 Mbps normal token release • 2 = 16 Mbps early token release

Table C-12   *3174-13R Screen 3 Configuration Details*

Configuration Line Number	Sample Value	Parameter Description and Implementation Notes
500	0	CSCM unique.
501	TOSFNID	Network identifier.
503	TOSFCTLR	LU name.

SNA end stations implement Logical Link Control type 2 (LLC2) when attached to a local-area network (LAN). LLC2 implements the following:

- Timers
- Sequencing
- Error recovery
- Windowing
- Guaranteed delivery
- Guaranteed connection

Figure C-2 illustrates how the T1 reply timer and error recovery operates for a 3174. Assume that the link between the two routers just failed. The following sequence characterizes the error recovery process illustrated in Figure C-2:

1 The 3174 sends a data frame and starts its T1 timer.

2 The T1 timer expires after 1.6 seconds.

3 The 3174 goes into error recovery.

4 The 3174 sends an LLC request (a receiver ready with the poll bit on), which requests the 3745 to immediately acknowledge this frame.

5 The 3174 starts its T1 timer.

6 The T1 timer expires after 1.6 seconds.

This operation is retried a total of seven times. The total elapsed time to disconnect the session is calculated as follows:

- The first attempt plus seven retries multiplied by 1.6 seconds:

    = 8 × 1.6 seconds

    = 12.8 seconds

Figure C-2 *T1 Timer and Error Recovery Process for 3174*

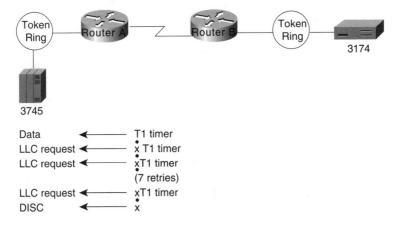

SNA Host Configuration for SDLC Networks

This appendix outlines router implementation information related to the following topics:

- Front-end processor (FEP) configuration for SDLC links
- 3174 SDLC configuration worksheet example

Table D-1 outlines 3x74 SDLC point-to-point connection support for AGS+, MGS, and CGS DCE appliques.

Table D-1   *3x74 SDLC Point-to-Point Connection Support for AGS+, MGS, and CGS DCE Appliques*

Controller Type	RS-232 DCE	RS-232 NRZI/DCE
3274 1st Generation		
• 3274-1C	Supported	Supported
3274 2nd Generation		
• 3274-21C	Not tested	Supported
3274 3rd Generation		
• 3274-31C	Supported	Not tested
• 3274-51C	Supported	Not tested
3274 4th Generation		
3274-41C	Need to tie DSR and DTR together on CU side, break DSR to router	Not tested
3274-61C	Same as 3274-41C	Supported
Telex 274	Supported	Not tested
Telex 1274	Supported	Not tested
DCA/IRMA 3274 emulation for DOS workstations	Not tested	Supported
DEC SNA gateway	Not tested	Supported
RS 6000 multiprotocol adapter	Not tested	Supported

continues

Table D-1   *3x74 SDLC Point-to-Point Connection Support for AGS+, MGS, and CGS DCE Appliques (Continued)*

Controller Type	RS-232 DCE	RS-232 NRZI/DCE
3174 Subsystem CUs		
• 3174-01R	Not tested	3174 ties pin 11 low (-11VDC), which forces the applique into DTE mode (DCE mode is set when pin 11 is set high)
• 3174-03R	Same as 3174-01R	Same as 3174-01R
• 3174-51R	Same as 3174-01R	Same as 3174-01R
3174 Establishment CUs		
• 3174-11R	Not tested	Supported
• 3174-13R	Same as 3174-11R	Not tested
• 3174-61R	Same as 3174-11R	Not tested
• 3174-91R	Same as 3174-11R	Supported
• Telex 1174	Supported	Not tested

FEP Configuration for SDLC Links

Table D-2 through Table D-5 present relevant parameter definitions for an FEP configured to operate within a router-based environment. These parameters are configured as part of the system generation process associated with the Network Control Program (NCP) on an IBM host.

Table D-2   *FEP SDLC Configuration Sample GROUP Parameter Listing and Definitions*

Parameter	Sample Value	Description and Implementation Notes
LNCTL	SDLC	Line control parameter that specifies link protocol.
REPLYTO	2	T1 timer; this timer specifies the reply timeout value for LINEs in this GROUP.

Table D-3   *FEP SDLC Configuration Sample LINE Parameter Listing and Definitions*

Parameter	Sample Value	Description and Implementation Notes
ADDRESS	(001,HALF)	The value 001 is the physical LINE interface address of the FEP. The second parameter specifies whether half- or full-duplex data transfer within the FEP is used. It also affects the DUPLEX parameter: If FULL is specified here, DUPLEX defaults to FULL, and attempts to modify this characteristic are ignored.
DUPLEX	HALF	This parameter specifies whether the communication line and modem constitute a half-duplex or full-duplex facility. If HALF is specified, the RTS modem signal is activated only when sending data. If FULL is specified, RTS always remains active. Refer to the ADDRESS parameter in this table.
NRZI	YES	Encoding for this line; options are NRZ or NRZI.
RETRIES	(6,5,3)	Number of retries when REPLYTO expires. Entry options are *m*, *t*, and *n*, where *m* = number of retries, *t* = pause in seconds between retry cycles, and *n* = number of retry cycles to repeat. This example would retry six times—pausing the value of the REPLYTO between each RETRY (two seconds, per Table D-2), pausing five seconds, and repeating this sequence three times for a total of 63 seconds. At the end of this period, the session is terminated.
PAUSE	2	The delay time in milliseconds between poll cycles. The cycle extends from the time NCP polls the first entry in the service order table to the moment polling next begins at the same entry. During this pause, any data available to send to the end station is sent. If end stations have data to send when polled, and the time to send the data extends beyond the PAUSE parameter, the next poll cycle begins immediately.

Table D-4   *FEP SDLC Configuration Sample PU Parameter Listing and Definitions*

Parameter	Sample Value	Description and Implementation Notes
ADDR	C1	SDLC address of secondary end station.
MAXDATA	265	Maximum amount of data in bytes (including headers) that the UP can receive in one data transfer; that is, one entire PIU or a PIU segment.
MAXOUT	7	Maximum number of unacknowledged frames that NCP can have outstanding before requesting a response from the end station.
PASSLIM	7	Maximum number of consecutive PIU or PIU segments that NCP sends at one time to the end station represented by this PU definition.
PUTYPE	2	Specifies PU type; PU type 2 and 2.1 are both specified as PUTYPE=2.

Table D-5   *FEP SDLC Configuration Sample LU Parameter Listing and Definitions*

Parameter	Sample Value	Description and Implementation Notes
LOCADDR	2	LU address of devices connected to the end station PU.

3174 SDLC Configuration Worksheet

Table D-6 through Table D-8 present a configuration taken from an SDLC-connected 3174-91R cluster controller. The configuration of this 3174-91R involved three specific configuration screens. Table D-6 through Table D-8 list the configuration line numbers, entries used, and descriptions of the configuration lines for each screen. Where applicable, extended descriptions are included for configuration entries that are relevant to the requirements of the routed network.

Table D-6   *3174-91R Screen 1 Configuration Details*

Configuration Line Number	Sample Value	Parameter Description and Implementation Notes
98		Online test password
99	TKNRNG	Description field
100	91R	Model number
101	2	Host attachment type: • 2 = SDLC • 5 = SNA (channel-attached) • 7 = Token Ring network

NOTE   Configuration line items 104, 313, 317, and 340 in Configuration screen 2 (refer to Table D-7) are of particular interest when configuring 3174 devices for a router-based SDLC environment. These lines specify the required SDLC address and relevant SDLC options for the cluster controller.

Table D-7 *3174-91R Screen 2 Configuration Details*

Configuration Line Number	Sample Value	Parameter Description and Implementation Notes
104	C2	Specifies the cluster controller SDLC address. It is the same address that you configure on the router's serial line interface. It also represents the PU address of the controller. In multipoint environments, multiple SDLC addresses may be specified on a single serial interface.
108	0045448	Serial number of the cluster controller
110	0	MLT storage support
116	0	Individual port assignment
121	01	Keyboard language
123	0	Country extended code page support
125	00000000	Miscellaneous options (A)
126	00000000	Miscellaneous options (B)
127	00	RTM definition
132	0000	Alternate base keyboard selection
136	0000	Standard keyboard layout
137	0000	Modified keyboard layout
138	0	Standard keypad layout
141	A	Magnetic character set
150	0	Token Ring network gateway controller
165	0	Compressed program symbols
166	A	Attribute select keypad
168	0	Additional extension; mode key definition
173	0000	DFT options
175	000000	DFT password
179	000	Local format storage
213	0	Between-bracket printer sharing
215	45448	PU identification
220	0	Alert function
310	0	Connect dataset to line operation

continues

Table D-7   *3174-91R Screen 2 Configuration Details (Continued)*

Configuration Line Number	Sample Value	Parameter Description and Implementation Notes
313	0	NRZ = 0; NRZI = 1
317	0	Telecommunications facility: • 0 = Nonswitched • 1 = Switched (dial-up)
318	0	Full/half speed transmission; 0 = full speed, 1 = half speed. Controls speed of modem; can be used in areas where line conditions are poor.
340	0	RTS control options: • 0 = Controlled RTS (for LSD/MSD operation) • 1 = Permanent RTS (improves performance) • 2 = BSC (not valid for SDLC operation)
365	0	X.21 switched-host DTE connection
370	0	Maximum inbound I-frame size: • 0 = 265 bytes • 1 = 521 bytes (recommended for better performance)

Table D-8   *3174-91R Screen 3 Configuration Details*

Configuration Line Number	Sample Value	Parameter Description and Implementation Notes
500	0	Central Site Change Management (CSCM) unique
501	xxxxxxxx	Network identifier
503	xxxxxxxx	LU name (for CSCM)

Broadcasts in Switched LAN Networks

To communicate with all or part of the network, protocols use broadcast and multicast datagrams at Layer 2 of the Open Systems Interconnection (OSI) model. This obviously supposes a medium that supports broadcasting (such as Ethernet, for instance). When a node needs to communicate with every station of the network, it sends a datagram to the MAC address FF-FF-FF-FF-FF-FF (a *broadcast*), which is an address to which the network interface card (NIC) of every host must listen to. Routers, operating at Layer 3 of the OSI model, typically do not forward such broadcasts. They limit them to the segment they originated from. When a host needs to communicate with part of the network, it sends a datagram to a specific MAC address, with the leading bit of the vendor ID set to 1 (01-00-0C-CC-CC-CC, for example). This is known as a *multicast*. NICs respond to that multicast when they are configured to listen to that particular address. Today, a wide range of applications make extensive use of IP multicasting to maximize the bandwidth utilization: Instead of sending *n* streams of *x* megabytes, where *n* would be the number of receivers, only one stream of *x* megabytes is needed. The next section takes a closer look at IP multicasting.

IP Multicasting

A whole range of IP addresses (a class) has been reserved for the purpose of multicasting: 224.0.0.0 to 239.255.255.255. Using a predetermined formula, it is possible to map such a Class D IP address to a Layer 2 multicast MAC address. A block of MAC addresses has been reserved to allow Class D IP addresses to get translated into Layer 2 MAC addresses: 01-00-5E-xx-xx-xx. The mapping is obtained by placing the low-order 23 bits of the Class D IP address into the low-order 23 bits of the reserved Layer 2 multicast address block. For example, the IP address 236.123.1.2 would map to the MAC address 01-00-5E-7B-01-02.

All LAN stations that support IP multicast know how to achieve this transformation and can therefore easily send any IP multicast over any IEEE 802–based LAN. Because there are more addresses in the Class D space (2^{28}) than in IETF's OUI (the vendor field) at the MAC layer (2^{23}), multiple group addresses map to each IEEE 802 address. Some well-known groups have been assigned to specific uses, the most famous ones probably being 224.0.0.1 (all systems on this subnet) and 224.0.0.2 (all routers on this subnet). Other groups are 224.0.0.4 (all DVMRP routers), 224.0.0.6 (OSPF-designated routers), 224.0.0.9 (RIP v2), and 224.0.0.10 (EIGRP routers).

Because switches work like bridges, they must propagate all broadcast, multicast, and unknown unicast traffic, a procedure known as *flooding*. The accumulation of broadcast and multicast traffic from each device in the network is referred to as *broadcast radiation*. Note, however, that flooding is constrained to a VLAN. For example, if a station talks on port x that is part of VLAN z, and this station is trying to reach a destination MAC address that has not yet been learned by the switch, the frame will be sent to all ports of that VLAN except the port on which the frame was received. That is why a VLAN is sometimes referred to as a *broadcast domain*. Because the NIC must interrupt the CPU to process each broadcast, broadcast radiation affects the performance of hosts in the network. The majority of recent NICs can filter unwanted multicasts, and therefore do not need to forward them to the processor. Not all NICs can achieve this, however, and in that case multicasts have to be processed in a fashion similar to broadcasts. Most often, the host does not benefit from processing this broadcast or multicast—that is, the host is not the destination being sought. It doesn't care about the service being advertised, or it already knows about the service. High levels of broadcast radiation can noticeably degrade host performance. Multicast-capable routers do not need to be directly addressed, because their interfaces have to operate promiscuously and receive all multicast IP traffic.

Cisco developed two features to dramatically reduce the flooding of multicast frames: CGMP and IGMP snooping. A CGMP conversation takes place between a Cisco switch and a Cisco router. The router informs the switch about the MAC addresses that have requested to join a multicast group (stations ask routers to join groups via IGMP packets). The switch in turn performs a forwarding table lookup to identify the ports on which these stations reside, and it can then limit the transmission of multicast packets to these stations only by creating static entries. The second feature, IGMP snooping, achieves the same goal but does not involve a router anymore. However, the switch needs to have enough intelligence to be able to parse IP packets and identify IGMP queries.

IP is not the only protocol to use multicasting. The following sections describe how the common desktop protocols—IP, Novell, and AppleTalk—use broadcast and multicast packets to locate hosts and advertise services, and how broadcast and multicast traffic affects the CPU performance of hosts on the network.

Using Broadcasts with IP Networks

There are three sources of broadcasts and multicasts in IP networks:

- *Workstations*—An IP workstation broadcasts an Address Resolution Protocol (ARP) request every time it needs to locate a new IP address on the local network. For example, the command **telnet cio.cisco.com** translates into an IP address through a Domain Name System (DNS) search, and then an ARP request is broadcast to find the actual station. Generally, IP workstations cache 10 to 100 addresses for about 2 hours.

The ARP rate for a typical workstation might be about 50 addresses every 2 hours or 0.007 ARPs per second. Therefore, 2,000 IP end stations produce about 14 ARPs per second.

- **Routers**—An IP router is any router or workstation that runs a routing protocol. A broadcast-intensive routing protocol is RIP, for example. Some administrators configure all workstations to run RIP as a redundancy and reachability policy. Every 30 seconds, RIP uses broadcasts to retransmit the entire RIP routing table to other RIP routers. If 2,000 workstations were configured to run RIP, and if 50 packets were required to retransmit the routing table, the workstations would generate 3,333 broadcasts per second. Most network administrators configure a small number of routers, usually 5 to 10, to run RIP. For a routing table that requires 50 packets to hold it, 10 RIP routers would generate about 16 broadcasts per second. More generally, the more routers there are, the worse the problem is. Fortunately, alternatives to the systematic RIP broadcast mechanism exist (RIP v2 and so on). Many other routing protocols use IP multicast to exchange information (OSPF, EIGRP), but the quantity of traffic they generate is much smaller than protocols such as RIP once the routing information has converged.

- **Multicast applications**—IP multicast applications can adversely affect the performance of large flat-switched networks. Although multicasting is an efficient way to send a stream of multimedia (video data) to many users on a shared-media hub, it affects every user on a switched network, because of the flooding procedure. A particular packet video application can generate a multi-megabyte (MB) stream of multicast data that, in a switched network, would be sent to every segment, resulting in severe congestion.

Figure E-1 shows the results of tests that Cisco conducted on the effect of broadcast radiation on a Sun SPARCstation 2 with a standard built-in Ethernet card. The SPARCstation was running SunOS version 4.1.3 without IP multicast filtering enabled. If IP multicast filtering had been disabled, multicast packets would have affected CPU performance.

Figure E-1 *Effect of Broadcast Radiation on Hosts in IP Networks*

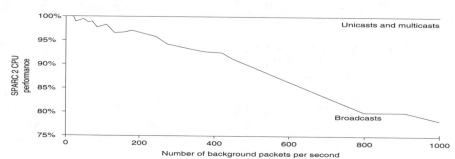

As indicated by the results shown in Figure E-1, an IP workstation can be effectively shut down by broadcasts flooding the network. Although extreme, broadcast peaks of thousands of broadcasts per second have been observed during "broadcast storms." Testing in a controlled environment with a range of broadcasts and multicasts on the network shows measurable system degradation with as few as 100 broadcasts or multicasts per second. Table E-1 shows the average and peak number of broadcasts and multicasts for IP networks ranging from 100 to 10,000 hosts per network.

Table E-1 *Average Number of Broadcasts and Multicasts for IP Networks*

Number of Hosts	Average Percentage of CPU Loss per Host
100	.14
1,000	.96
10,000	9.15

Although the numbers in Table E-1 might appear low, they represent an average, well-designed IP network that is not running RIP. When broadcast and multicast traffic peak due to storm behavior, peak CPU loss can be orders of magnitude greater than average. During either a broadcast or unicast storm due to a Layer 2 loop, powerful end systems can be rendered unusable. Broadcast storms can be caused by a device requesting information from a network that has grown too large. So many responses are sent to the original request that the device cannot process them, or the first request triggers similar requests from other devices that effectively block normal traffic flow on the network.

Do not infer from this, however, that considering multicast is a bad thing to do. Proper use of multicasting results in a much more efficient use of the available bandwidth. Instead of sending *n* streams of *m* MB to *n* receivers, for example, only *one* stream of *m* MB will have to be sent to a single multicast group. Constraining broadcast and multicast traffic to where it belongs is part of the process of building efficient switched networks. Several techniques are available today on Cisco multilayer switches; the Cisco Group Membership Protocol (CGMP) prevents the flooding of multicast traffic to all ports thanks to an interaction that takes place between the switch and a Cisco router. The router informs the switch about the MAC addresses that have requested to join a particular group. This way the switch knows (from its forwarding table) which ports are interested in that multicast stream. Also, the Internet Group Membership Protocol snooping (IGMP snooping) for Layer 3–capable switches removes the need for an external router, giving the switch the intelligence to examine the contents of IGMP packets (used by hosts and routers to exchange group membership information).

Using Broadcasts with Novell Networks

Many PC-based LANs still use Novell's Network Operating System (NOS) and NetWare servers. Novell technology poses the following unique scaling problems:

- NetWare servers use broadcast packets to identify themselves and to advertise their services and routes to other networks via a protocol known as Service Advertisement Protocol (SAP).

- NetWare clients use broadcasts to find NetWare servers—via Get Nearest Server requests (GNS), for example.

- Version 4.0 of Novell's SNMP-based network-management applications, such as NetExplorer, periodically broadcast packets to discover changes in the network.

An idle network with a single server with one shared volume and no print services generates one broadcast packet every four seconds. A large LAN with high-end servers might have up to 150 users per PC server. If the LAN has 900 users with a reasonably even distribution, it would have six or seven servers. In an idle state with multiple shared volumes and printers, this might average out to four broadcasts per second, uniformly distributed. In a busy network with route and service requests made frequently, the rate would peak at 15 to 20 broadcasts per second.

Figure E-2 shows the results of tests that Cisco conducted on the effect of broadcast radiation on the performance of an 80386 CPU running at 25 MHz. Performance was measured with the Norton Utilities System Information utility. Background traffic was generated with a Network General Sniffer and consisted of a broadcast destination packet and a multicast destination packet, with data of all zeros. CPU performance was measurably affected by as few as 30 broadcast or multicast packets per second. Multicast packets had a slightly worse effect than broadcast packets. Even though this test was performed using legacy technology, it still clearly shows the impact that broadcast radiation can have on devices in the network.

Figure E-2   *Effect of Broadcast Radiation on Hosts in Novell Networks*

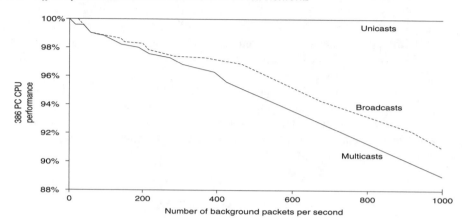

Table E-2 shows the average and peak number of broadcasts and multicasts for Novell networks ranging from 100 to 10,000 hosts per network.

Table E-2   *Average Number of Broadcasts and Multicasts for Novell Networks*

Number of Hosts	Average Percentage of CPU Loss per Host
100	.12
1,000	.22
10,000	3.15

The results listed in Table E-2 represent multihour average operation. Peak traffic load and CPU loss per workstation can be orders of magnitude greater than with average traffic loads. A common scenario is that at 9 a.m. on Monday, everyone starts their computers. Normally, in circumstances with an average level of utilization or demand, the network can handle a reasonable number of stations. In circumstances in which everyone requires service at once (a demand peak), however, the available network capacity can support a much lower number of stations. In determining network-capacity requirements, peak demand levels and duration can be more important than average serviceability requirements.

Using Broadcasts with AppleTalk Networks

AppleTalk uses multicasting extensively to advertise services, request services, and resolve addresses. On startup, an AppleTalk host transmits a series of at least 20 packets aimed at resolving its network address (a Layer 3 AppleTalk node number) and obtaining local "zone" information. Except for the first packet, which is addressed to itself, these functions are resolved through AppleTalk multicasts.

In terms of overall network traffic, the AppleTalk Chooser is particularly broadcast-intensive. The Chooser is the software interface that enables the user to select shared network services. It uses AppleTalk multicasts to find file servers, printers, and other services. When the user opens the Chooser and selects a type of service (for example, a printer), the Chooser transmits 45 multicasts at a rate of one packet per second. If left open, the Chooser sends a five-packet burst with a progressively longer delay. If left open for several minutes, the Chooser reaches its maximum delay and transmits a five-packet burst every 270 seconds. By itself, this does not pose a problem, but in a large network, these packets add to the total amount of broadcast radiation that each host must interpret and then discard.

Other AppleTalk protocols, such as the Name Binding Protocol, which is used to bind a client to a server, and the Router Discovery Protocol, a RIP implementation transmitted by all routers and listened to by each station, are broadcast-intensive. The system in it called AutoRemounter (part of the Macintosh operating system) is also broadcast-intensive.

NOTE	The AppleTalk stack is more efficient than the Novell stack because the AppleTalk stack discards non-AppleTalk broadcasts earlier than the Novell stack discards non-Novell broadcasts.

Figure E-3 shows the results of tests that Cisco conducted on the effect of broadcast radiation on the performance of a Power Macintosh 8100 and a Macintosh IIci. Both CPUs were measurably affected by as few as 15 broadcast or multicast frames per second. Once again, although this test was performed on fairly old technology, the results demonstrate the impact of broadcast traffic.

Figure E-3   *Effect of Broadcast Radiation on Hosts in AppleTalk Networks*

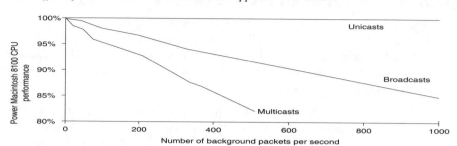

Table E-3 shows the average and peak number of broadcasts and multicasts for AppleTalk networks ranging from 100 to 10,000 hosts per network.

Table E-3   *Average Number of Broadcasts and Multicasts for AppleTalk Networks*

Number of Hosts	Average Percentage of CPU Loss per Host	Peak Percentage of CPU Loss per Host
100	.28	6.00
1,000	2.10	58.00
10,000	16.94	100.00

Slow LocalTalk-to-Ethernet connection devices are a major problem in large-scale AppleTalk networks. These devices fail in large AppleTalk networks because they have limited ARP caches and can process only a few broadcasts per second. Major broadcast storms arise when these devices lose their capability to receive Routing Table Maintenance Protocol (RTMP) updates. After this occurs, these devices send ARP requests for all known devices, thereby accelerating the network degradation because they cause their neighbor devices to fail and send their own ARP requests.

Using Broadcasts with Multiprotocol Networks

The following can be said about the interaction of AppleTalk, IPX, and IP:

- AppleTalk stacks ignore any other Layer 3 protocol.
- AppleTalk and IP broadcast and multicast packets affect the operation of IP and IPX stacks. AppleTalk and IP packets enter the stack and then are discarded, which consumes CPU resources.

Reducing SAP Traffic in Novell IPX Networks

One of the limiting factors in the operation of large Novell Internetwork Packet Exchange (IPX) networks is the amount of bandwidth consumed by the large, periodic Service Advertisement Protocol (SAP) updates. Novell servers periodically send clients information about the services they provide by broadcasting this information onto their connected local-area network (LAN) or wide-area network (WAN) interfaces. Routers are required to propagate SAP updates through an IPX network so that all clients can see the service messages. It is possible to reduce SAP traffic on Novell IPX networks by the following means:

- *Filtering SAP updates through access lists.* SAP updates can be filtered by prohibiting routers from advertising services from specified Novell servers.

- *Configuring Cisco routers on Novell IPX networks to run Enhanced IGRP.* Although filters provide a means of *eliminating* the advertisements of specified services, Enhanced IGRP provides *incremental* SAP updates for a finer granularity of control. Complete SAP updates are sent periodically on each interface only until an IPX Enhanced IGRP neighbor is found. Thereafter, SAP updates are sent only when there are *changes* to the SAP table. In this way, bandwidth is conserved, and the advertisement of services is reduced without being eliminated.

  Incremental SAP updates are automatic on serial interfaces and can be configured on LAN media. Enhanced IGRP also provides partial routing updates and fast convergence for IPX networks. Administrators may choose to run only the partial SAP updates or to run both the reliable SAP protocol and the partial routing update portion of Enhanced IGRP.

- *Configuring Cisco routers on Novell IPX networks to send incremental SAP updates.* With Software Release 10.0, the incremental SAP updates just described can be configured for Cisco routers on Novell IPX networks, *without* the requirement of running the routing update feature of Enhanced IGRP (only the partial SAP updates are enabled). This feature is supported on all interface types. Again, SAP updates are sent only when changes occur on a network. Only the changes to SAP tables are sent as updates.

To illustrate how to reduce SAP traffic, this case study is organized into two parts:

- Configuring access lists to filter SAP updates
- Configuring incremental SAP updates

The work for this case study is illustrated in Figure F-1. The following portions of a large-scale Novell IPX network spanning a Frame Relay WAN are examined:

- Router A connects from the Frame Relay network to the central site with three Novell servers.

- Router B connects from the Frame Relay network to a remote site with one Novell client and one Novell server.

- Router C connects from the Frame Relay network to a remote site with two Novell clients.

Figure F-1   *Large-Scale Novell IPX Internetwork*

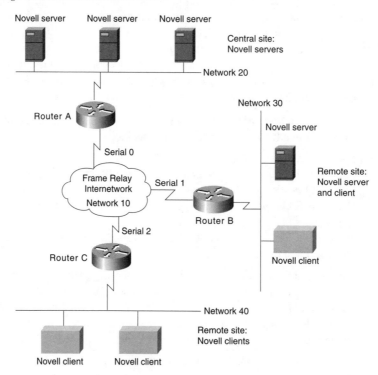

Configuring Access Lists to Filter SAP Updates

Access lists can control which routers send or receive SAP updates and which routers do not send or receive SAP updates. SAP access lists can be defined to filter SAP updates based on the source network address of a SAP entry, the type of SAP entry (file server, print server, and so forth), and the name of the SAP server. A SAP access list is made up of entries in the following format:

```
access-list n [deny |permit] network[.node] [service-type[server-name]]
```

where n is between 1000–1099. A network number of –1 indicates any network, and a service type of 0 indicates any service. For example, the following access list accepts print server SAP entries from server PRINTER_1, all file servers, and any other SAP entries from network 123 except those from a server called UNTRUSTED; all other SAP entries are to be ignored:

```
access-list 1000 permit -1 47 PRINTER_1
access-list 1000 permit -1 4
access-list 1000 deny 123 0 UNTRUSTED
access-list 1000 permit 123
```

When checking the entries in a SAP update, each statement in the access list is processed in order, and if there is no match for a SAP entry, it is not accepted. Thus, to block server UNTRUSTED, the **deny** statement must be placed before the **permit** statement for all other devices on network 123.

Two techniques can be used with filtering. Either the SAP entries that are required can be permitted and the rest denied, or the unwanted SAP entries can be denied and the rest permitted. In general, the first method is preferred because it avoids new and unexpected services being propagated throughout the network.

The most common form of SAP filtering is to limit which services are available across a WAN. For example, it does not, in general, make sense for clients in one location to be able to access print servers in another location, because printing is a local operation. In this case study, only file servers are permitted to be visible across the WAN.

Central Site

Router A connects to the central site. The following access lists configured on Router A permit everything except print servers from being announced out the serial interface:

```
access-list 1000 deny -1 47
access-list 1000 permit -1
!
interface serial 0
ipx network 10
ipx output-sap-filter 1000
```

To permit only IPX file servers and to deny all other IPX servers, use the following configuration:

```
access-list 1000 permit -1 4
!
interface serial 0
ipx network 10
ipx out-sap-filter 1000
```

Remote Sites

This section provides information on the configuration of the routers at the remote sites:

- Router B connected to an IPX server and client
- Router C connected to two IPX clients

IPX Server and Client

For Router B, the following access lists permit everything except print servers from being announced out the serial interface:

```
access-list 1000 deny -1 47
access-list 1000 permit -1
!
interface serial 1
ipx network 10
ipx output-sap-filter 1000
```

To permit only IPX file servers and to deny all other IPX servers, use the following configuration:

```
access-list 1000 permit -1 4
!
interface serial 1
ipx network 10
ipx out-sap-filter 1000
```

IPX Clients

Router C does not require an access list configuration because the remote site does not have any servers. Only Novell servers generate SAP updates.

Configuring Incremental SAP Updates

Incremental SAP updates allow any-to-any connectivity with reduced network SAP overhead. Instead of eliminating the receipt of SAP updates entirely, all necessary IPX services can be broadcast to remote sites only as changes to the SAP tables occur.

Central Site

To configure Enhanced IGRP encapsulated SAP updates to be sent only on an incremental basis, use the following configuration. Although the defined Enhanced IGRP autonomous system number is 999, Enhanced IGRP routing (and routing updates) are not performed because of the **rsup-only** keyword used with the **ipx sap-incremental** command. The **rsup-only** keyword indicates a reliable SAP update.

```
interface ethernet 0
ipx network 20
!
interface serial 0
ipx network 10
ipx sap-incremental eigrp 999 rsup-only
!
ipx router eigrp 999
network 10
```

To configure both incremental SAP and Enhanced IGRP routing, simply configure Enhanced IGRP with the following commands:

```
interface ethernet 0
ipx network 20
!
interface serial 0
ipx network 10
!
ipx router eigrp 999
network 10
```

Remote Sites

This section provides information on the configuration of the routers at the remote sites:

- Router B connected to an IPX server and client
- Router C connected to two IPX clients

IPX Server and Client

To configure Enhanced IGRP encapsulated SAP updates to be sent only on a incremental basis, use the following configuration for Router B. Although the defined Enhanced IGRP autonomous system number is 999, Enhanced IGRP routing is not performed because of the **rsup-only** keyword used with the **ipx sap-incremental** command.

```
interface ethernet 1
ipx network 30
!
interface serial 1
ipx network 10
ipx sap-incremental eigrp 999 rsup-only
```

```
!
ipx router eigrp 999
network 10
```

To configure both incremental SAP and Enhanced IGRP routing, simply configure Enhanced IGRP with the following commands:

```
interface ethernet 1
ipx network 30
!
interface serial 1
ipx network 10
!
ipx router eigrp 999
network 10
```

IPX Clients

To configure Enhanced IGRP encapsulated SAP updates to be sent only on an incremental basis, use the following configuration for Router C:

```
interface ethernet 2
ipx network 40
!
interface serial 2
ipx network 10
ipx sap-incremental eigrp 999 rsup-only
!
ipx router eigrp 999
network 10
```

Even though there are no servers, these configuration commands are required to support the incremental SAP updates being advertised from the central site and other remote sites to Router C.

Summary

This case study illustrates two methods of reducing SAP traffic on Novell IPX networks: the use of access lists to eliminate the advertisements of specified services, and the use of the incremental SAP feature to exchange SAP changes as they occur. This technique eliminates periodic SAP updates.

Packet Voice Primer

Overview

The telephone is the most pervasive of all technology instruments, particularly in business. Every day, businesses make literally thousands of calls, and although the cost of an individual call is often low, the accumulated cost to business is significant.

For many companies, a portion of that cost is avoidable. Traditional public voice telephony is a complex tapestry of tariffs and subsidies, often resulting in situations where calling from "A" to "B" costs a fraction of the rate from "B" to "A." Companies have long relied on private, leased-line networks to bypass public telephone charges, but rates applied to leased lines are also often high. Many have looked for alternative strategies.

In today's networking, there are several attractive alternatives to both conventional public telephony and leased lines. Among the most interesting are networking technologies based on a different kind of voice transmission called *packet voice*. Packet voice appears to a network as "data"; therefore, it can be transported over networks normally reserved for data, where costs are often far less.

Packet voice uses less transmission bandwidth than conventional voice, so more can be carried on a given connection. Where telephony requires as much as 64,000 bits per second (bps), packet voice often needs less than 10,000. For many companies, there is sufficient reserve capacity on national and international data networks to transport considerable voice traffic, making voice essentially "free."

Even where new transport capacity must be added or purchased to support packet voice, the benefits may justify the cost. Public telephone networks often impose distance-based tariffs and added charges to subsidize residential calling. The use of data networks for voice transport, where such use is not contrary to law, can eliminate these costs. Even where there are no tariff-based economies, packet voice can be 20 times or more bandwidth-efficient than traditional 64 kbps digital voice transport.

Like all good things, packet voice has a price. Although network designers are familiar with quality of service (QoS) requirements for specialized data applications such as online transaction processing, packet voice often has more stringent QoS requirements. If the network is not properly conditioned to meet these requirements, the quality of the speech may be impacted. This is particularly true if voice is carried on public data networks such as the Internet, where voice users have few options for securing end-to-end QoS.

Despite QoS concerns, packet voice is exploding in popularity because the potential savings are so large. Even in the United States, where telecommunications costs are low by international standards, corporations can achieve a packet voice cost per minute of one-half to one-third the levels of telephony—even of virtual private networks (VPNs). Companies with high voice calling costs owe it to themselves to consider all the packet voice options.

Unfortunately for potential packet voice users, there are few tutorials on packet voice concepts, and benefits are targeted at business-level consumers of telephone services. Therefore, in this appendix, Cisco Systems remedies that condition with a "no-nonsense" exploration of packet voice technology.

Introduction

All packet voice systems follow a common model, as shown in Figure G-1. The packet voice transport network, which may be IP-based, Frame Relay, or Asynchronous Transfer Mode (ATM), forms the traditional "cloud." At the edges of this network are devices or components that can be called "voice agents." The mission of these devices is to change the voice information from its traditional telephony form to a form suitable for packet transmission. The network then forwards the packet data to a voice agent serving the destination or called party.

This voice agent connection model shows that two issues in packet voice networking must be explored to ensure that packet voice services will meet user needs. The first issue is that of voice coding—how voice information is transformed into packets, and how the packets are used to re-create the voice. Another issue is the signaling associated with identifying whom the calling party is trying to call and where the called party is in the network. The sections that follow explore these issues further.

Figure G-1   *Packet Voice Model*

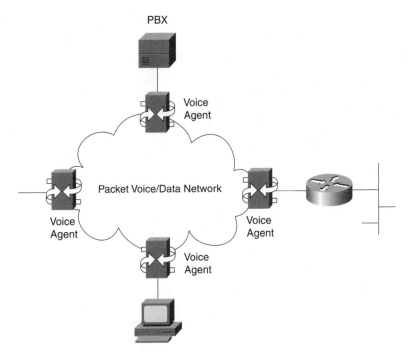

Voice Coding

Human speech, and in fact everything we hear, is naturally in analog form, and early telephone systems were likewise. Analog signals are often depicted as smooth "sine waves," but voice and other signals contain many frequencies and have more complex structures.

Although humans are well equipped for analog communications, analog transmission is not particularly efficient. When analog signals become weak because of transmission loss, it's hard to separate the complex analog structure from the structure of random transmission noise. Amplifying analog signals also amplifies noise, and eventually analog connections become too noisy to use.

Digital signals, having only "1-bit" and "0-bit" states, are more easily separated from noise and can be amplified without corruption. Over time, it became obvious that digital coding was more immune to noise corruption on long-distance connections, and the world's communications systems converted to a digital transmission format called Pulse Code Modulation (PCM).

PCM converts voice into digital form by sampling the voice signals 8000 times per second and converting each sample into a code. The sampling rate of 8000 times per second (125 microseconds between samples) was chosen because virtually all of human speech intelligence is carried at frequencies below 4000 Hz (4 kHz). Sampling the voice waveforms every 125 microseconds is sufficient to detect frequencies below 4 kHz.

After the waveform is sampled, the samples are converted into digital form, with a code representing the amplitude of the waveform at the time the sample was taken. Standard telephone PCM uses 8 bits for the code and therefore consumes 64,000 bps per call. Another telephone voice standard called Adaptive Differential PCM (ADPCM) codes voice into 4-bit values and so consumes only 32,000 bps. ADPCM is often used on long-distance connections.

In traditional telephony applications, PCM or ADPCM is used on synchronous digital channels, which means that a constant stream of bits is generated at the specified rate, whether there is conversation or not. There are, in fact, hundreds of brief silent periods in the average call, and each of them wastes bandwidth and money. On standard telephone connections, there is no alternative to this waste.

There is an alternative if packet voice transport is used. In packet voice applications, speech is transported as data packets, and these packets are generated only when there is actual speech to transport. The elimination of wasted bandwidth during periods of silence will, by itself, reduce the effective bandwidth required for speech transport by one-third or more.

Voice Coding Standards

Other strategies can reduce bandwidth requirements even further. The International Telephony Union (ITU) has defined a series of standards for voice coding, including the 64 and 32 kbps PCM and ADPCM already briefly discussed. Anyone considering packet voice transmission should be aware of the characteristics of each of the voice coding strategies these standards cover.

The first of these standards is the "fixed-sampling" standards, belonging to the G.711 family. These standards use the 8000-samples-per-second strategy for voice coding described earlier. For each sample, the voice coder stores the amplitude of the voice signal at that point. The result of the sampling is a rough, block-like representation of the original voice signal, as Figure G-2 shows. The samples can be used (by smoothing) to reconstruct the analog voice signal at the other end of the call.

Figure G-2 *Pulse Code Modulation*

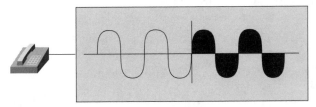

The problem with the sampling strategies is that to reduce the bandwidth utilized for transport of the digital speech, it is necessary to code the voice signals into fewer bits. Using 8 bits for a sample allows recognizing 256 different levels of amplitude. To reduce bandwidth to 32 kbps, only 4 bits (64 values) are used, and the bit value represents the change from the prior value (the "differential" in ADPCM means this). ADPCM can be taken to 16 kbps by using only 2 bits (4 values), but each time the number of different voice amplitude values is reduced, the block representation of voice created is more unlike the original signal, and voice quality is degraded.

A second group of standards provides better voice compression and at the same time better quality. In these standards, the voice coding uses a special algorithm—called linear predictive code (LPC)—that models the way human speech actually works. Because LPC can take advantage of an understanding of the speech process, it can be much more efficient without sacrificing voice quality. Most LPC devices take as input the 64 kbps PCM discussed earlier for two reasons:

- This form of voice is the standard output of digital PBXs and telephone switches.

- PCM coding chips are inexpensive because of their broad usage in telephone networks.

Both LPC and PCM/ADPCM coding of voice information are standardized by the ITU in its G-series recommendations. The most popular voice coding standards for telephony and packet voice include the following:

- G.711, which describes the 64 kbps PCM voice coding technique outlined earlier. G.711-encoded voice is already in the correct format for digital voice delivery in the public phone network or through PBXs.

- G.726, which describes ADPCM coding at 40, 32, 24, and 16 kbps. ADPCM voice may also be interchanged between packet voice and public phone or PBX networks, providing the latter has ADPCM capability.

- G.728, which describes code-excited linear-predictive (CELP) voice compression, requiring only 16 kbps of bandwidth. CELP voice coding must be transcoded to a public telephony format for delivery to or through telephone networks.

- G.729, which describes adaptive CELP compression that enables voice to be coded into 8-kbps streams. There are two forms of this standard, and both provide speech quality as good as that of 32-kbps ADPCM.

- G.723.1, which describes a coded representation that can be used for compressing speech or other audio signal components of multimedia services at a very low bit rate as part of the overall H.324 family of standards. This coder has two bit rates associated with it—5.3 and 6.3 kbps. The higher bit rate has greater quality; the lower bit rate gives good quality and provides system designers with additional flexibility.

Compression Quality

One might wonder why compressed voice isn't just a standard concept; why not compress? The answer is that compression can only approximate the analog waveform. Although the approximation may be very good for some standards, such as G.729, other standards will suffer somewhat from the compression approximation distortion, particularly if the voice is coded to digital form, recoded to analog, and then coded back to digital again. This practice of "tandem coding" should be avoided wherever possible in any compressed voice system.

The voice quality of a compression strategy has been measured by survey—the Mean Opinion Score (MOS) is the most common measurement. On the MOS scale, where 0 is poor quality and 5 is high, standard PCM has a quality of about 4.4. G.726 ADPCM is rated at 4.2 for the 32-kbps version.

G.728 CELP coding achieves a rating of 4.2, and G.729 a score of 4.2. As these figures show, modern linear-predictive model voice coders often have better quality ratings than the older, sampling-based coders.

Delay

Another factor—delay—may have a greater impact on compressed voice. Compressing voice for packet transport induces a delay; Table G-1 shows the average delay associated with each of the popular coding standards described earlier. As shown in the table, the delay associated with voice code/decode can be as high as 25 ms for two CS-ACELP voice samples (an initial 5 ms for a look ahead plus 20 ms for the two 10-byte frames). This delay of itself does not affect speech quality, although it may induce a need for "echo cancellation" so that an objectionable ringing or reverberation effect is not created. Most voice compression devices for packet voice include some form of echo cancellation. But other delay sources in the network may add to this base coding delay to induce an end-to-end delay sufficient to interfere with speech.

Table G-1   *Average Delay Associated with Each of the Popular Coding Standards*

Compression Method	MOS Score	Delay (ms)
PCM (G.711)	4.4	0.75
32K ADPCM (G.726)	4.2	1
16K LD-CELP (G.728)	4.2	3-5
8K CS-ACELP (G729)	4.2	10
8K CS-ACELP (G.729a)	4.2	10
6.3 MPMLG (G.723.1)	3.98	30
5.3K ACLEP (G.723.1)	3.5	30

There are two sources of delay in both traditional telephone voice networks and packet voice networks: propagation delay and handling delay. The former is caused by the limitation of the speed of light in fiber or microwave networks or of electrons in copper networks. The latter is caused by handling of the voice by devices along the route.

Light travels 186,000 miles per second in a vacuum, and electrons travel about 100,000 miles per second in copper. A microwave or fiber network halfway around the world would span about 13,000 miles and induce a one-way delay of about 70 milliseconds. This level of delay is barely perceptible and never a problem.

Handling delays may impact traditional voice networks. Each T1/E1/J1 frame requires 125 microseconds to assemble in a switch and route to the destination line, assuming that each frame is being sent at its native speed (1.544 or 2.048 Mbps). This "serialization delay" accumulates as the frames are handled through the voice network; the total serialization delay can grow to 20 or more milliseconds on transcontinental links. When added to propagation delay, serialization delay can create a one-way delay approaching 100 ms, which is perceptible to most listeners although still not objectionable.

It is with handling delay where packet voice and traditional voice networks begin to differ. Handling delays in data networks can be considerable, particularly when networks become congested and traffic must be queued for transmission on busy trunk lines. The Internet sometimes experiences end-to-end delays approaching 1 second on international routes. Where delays of this magnitude are possible, conversations may depend on a formal structure of "you-talk, I-talk" to ensure that both parties don't take advantage of a delay-induced "silent" period to begin talking at the same time.

The reason why delay in data networking can be a voice quality problem is that voice information has a characteristic "timing." A particular syllable of a word is uttered with an interval of time between it and the following syllable. This tiny pause is as much a part of speech as the verbalized parts, and its timing must be preserved. In traditional voice networks, the voice channel is a synchronized bit stream that preserves timing of all speech elements precisely. In data networks, variable delay can be inserted by congestion or handling and can corrupt speech.

It should be clear from these comments that delay is a problem in two ways: Delay in an absolute sense can interfere with the byplay of human conversation, the rhythm of inquiry and reply; delay variations (called "jitter") can create unexpected pauses between utterances that may impact the intelligibility of the speech itself. As the more serious problem, it is the problem that packet voice networks must address.

Eliminating delay jitter in a network with variable handling and congestion delay is a matter of holdback. Voice applications measure the average delay of a network, and hold back at the destination voice agent enough compressed voice data to equal the average delay jitter. This feature ensures that voice packets are released to be converted to real analog voice at a constant rate, regardless of the variation in network delay. Holdback creates greater absolute delay, of course, and networks with a significant delay jitter will therefore have a total delay large enough to be perceptible to the parties of the conversation.

When holdback buffering is used to control delay jitter, it is often necessary to provide a time stamp on each voice packet to ensure that it is released to the listener with the same timing relative to other voice elements that were found in the input voice signal. In IP transport of voice, for example, this time stamp is provided by the Real-Time Protocol (RTP).

Anything in the network that impacts delay also impacts voice performance, and this fact is critical to the design of packet voice networks. In packet voice applications it is normally better to risk a lost or corrupted voice packet, for example, than to introduce an error recovery strategy that would increase delay jitter. This is why packet voice protocols are almost never provided with any form of error recovery.

In summary, packet voice coding improves network economics in two ways: first by reducing the bandwidth consumed by voice traffic, and second by eliminating silent periods. To take advantage of these benefits, the underlying transport network must be able to support small-bandwidth traffic streams and also to interleave other traffic into silent periods in the voice calls to recover the idle bandwidth that packet voice transport produces. The facilities provided to ensure these capabilities vary depending on the type of network.

Packet Voice Transport Options and Issues

From the preceding section on voice compression, it is clear that "tandem codings," delay, and loss of timing synchronization are the most serious problems in packet voice networks.

Although all packet voice networks must address these issues, the sensitivity of the packet voice network options to each issue is different, and packet voice application design must consider the transport technology before deciding how to deal with specific delay or loss concerns.

Packet voice can be transported over any of the following wide-area network connection types:

- Circuit-switched leased-line networks. These networks are often based on T1/E1/J1 trunks leased from carriers, providing fixed synchronous bandwidth.

- ATM constant-bit-rate or circuit emulation connections. These connections emulate circuit-switched network connections and are sometimes called ATM Class A services.

- ATM connections based on what in ATM are called variable bit rate (VBR), available bit rate (ABR), or unspecified bit rate (UBR) classes of service.

- Frame Relay networks, both those provided by public service providers and those built by corporations as private networks.

- Public packet (X.25) networks, which provide public data services in many international applications and also are used as national data networks in Europe and the Pacific Rim.

- Public IP networks, including the Internet.

- Private corporate data networks of all types.

These many choices, fortunately, can be grouped into broad classes for voice application consideration.

Synchronous Circuit-Switched Networks

The synchronous circuit-switched technologies, such as leased-line networks and constant bit rate (CBR) ATM, provide the same transport network features that standard telephone networks employ and therefore pose no special risk in speech quality or delay. If the "cloud" in Figure G-1 is made up of such a network, voice is transported in the normal telephony manner, and no special voice agent features are required in the network except to complete calls across it as telephone networks or PBX networks would.

Most national and international private networks are based on circuit-switched network technology, and voice traffic travels over these networks on fixed-bandwidth timeslots. This method of transmission, although equivalent to that used in public telephony, wastes bandwidth for the reasons noted earlier. If packet voice coding is used on circuit-switched connections, the only savings that can be achieved are the savings associated with a lower bit rate (8 kbps for G.729, for example), and these savings depend on the network's support for allocating less than 64 kbps timeslots, called subrate multiplexing.

In ATM networks, it is particularly important to ensure that CBR services can support connections of 32, 16, or 8 kbps. Many ATM networks provide these types of connections only at 64 kbps, because the standards promulgated in 1997 by the ATM Forum for voice over ATM specify G.711 coding, so attempts to save money by compressing voice to a lower bandwidth would be wasted.

Frame/Cell Networks

Frame/cell networks, using Frame Relay or the VBR forms of ATM, transport voice in compressed, coded form. For these networks, a voice agent is necessary to code the voice into cells or frames for transport and to decode these cells or frames at the destination. The voice agent must also understand any telephone signaling used by the voice source and destination to receive the called party's number and deliver call progress signals. Finally, the voice agent may need to understand the signaling or addressing needed within the frame/cell network cloud to reach the various destination voice agents. This capability is important when translating between a traditional voice network and a frame/cell network.

In Frame Relay or ATM networks, the network delay and delay jitter are often controlled by the switches themselves, if each of the switches and endpoints is synchronized to a common traceable source or PRS in the network. Normally, the delay jitter in such networks is so low that the timing of output voice packets closely approximates that of the input speech, and no special time-stamping of the voice packets is required to ensure correct output timing. Exceptions do exist for networks that aren't synchronized to a common reference source. The practice of adding a time stamp in an ATM cell is called Synchronous Residual Time Stamp (SRTS) and is a method of passing timing information from end to end.

Some ATM and Frame Relay switches and multiplexers provide VBR ATM voice coding, making the products essentially voice agents. Because standards for Frame Relay and ATM voice are still evolving, buyers should be certain that this support is available, and also ensure that the capabilities of the switches match application requirements. If there is no native voice interface capability for a frame or cell network, an external voice compression product can be used. All the benefits of ATM or Frame Relay networks in controlling delay jitter and overall network delay will be available to such an external product.

Connectionless Data Networks

With connectionless data networks such as internal IP intranets and the Internet, the same voice coding and addressing issues apply as stated for the frame/cell networks. With this type of network, however, there is normally no network-guaranteed level of delay or delay jitter, and it may be necessary to take special steps to ensure that the delay "budget" for the network is kept low. For example, high-level protocols such as Transmission Control

Protocol (TCP) provide flow control and error recovery that combine to create significant delay jitter. For this reason, TCP is not used as the Layer 3 protocol.

Instead, voice traffic is carried within IP's User Datagram Protocol (UDP); unfortunately no time stamp is provided to control output timing, and even small amounts of delay jitter can interfere with speech comprehension. To prevent this problem, the H.323 standard calls for transport of voice over IP using the RTP that resides on top of UDP. RTP provides time-stamp services and also (via a Real-Time Control Protocol, or RTCP) allows for the establishment of point-to-multipoint voice connections. This multipoint voice is a feature rarely available with other packet voice transport options.

An increasing number of networks today are being offered with guaranteed service levels. Such networks are typically using a protocol called Resource Reservation Protocol (RSVP). RSVP is a signaling protocol that can be used to signal the packet switches and routers to reserve resources to reduce the delay and delay jitter that would result from resource competition.

X.25 Packet Networks

Public data networks based on X.25 packet transport have built-in error recovery at Level 2 and built-in flow control at Level 3 that cannot be defeated. These networks also normally operate at very high levels of utilization and therefore experience congestion regularly. For these reasons, packet voice over these networks is rarely able to meet user quality expectations. Except where cost concerns are critical, these networks should not be considered for voice transport.

Private Data Networks

Private data networks can be judged based on whether they conform to the basic connectionless model of IP (Novell SPX/IPX, OSI connectionless, IEEE 802.2 bridging, and so forth) or the connection-oriented model of X.25 (IBM SNA, DEC LAT, and so forth). Because connectionless networks normally offer users the option to bypass error recovery and flow control, they can be used as transport mechanisms for packet voice if the other delay sources (especially congestion delay) can be contained. Virtually all connection-oriented private data network protocols dictate the use of both flow control and error recovery and probably are not suitable for voice transport.

In all the network types suitable for voice transport, the obvious question is whether the "suitable" network would justify packet voice use. This depends on the economics of the packet voice network versus the public phone network and on the sensitivity of the voice applications to be supported to whatever quality limits the packet voice network may generate.

In most packet voice applications, delay plays the deciding role in voice quality. With LPC voice coding like that provided in G.729, packet voice quality in a low-delay environment equals the standard toll-quality voice experienced in public telephony. Maintaining the low delay is the critical problem.

Frame Relay and ATM networks are designed to deliver the lowest practicable transport delay; special delay-management measures are rarely required here, except where the user's voice agent attaches to the network. Utilization on these connections should be maintained below 70% to ensure that delay is manageable; 50% and lower is even better. Often this means selecting an access line speed higher than would normally be selected for data-only applications.

In connectionless networks such as IP, delay can be managed in a variety of ways. As mentioned earlier, RSVP can be used to signal many vendors' routers to induce special enhancements in their products to selectively prioritize certain types of traffic, thus ensuring that packet voice is less subject to congestion. These enhancements are very useful in limiting congestion-induced delay and improving speech quality.

Another option with connectionless networks is to ensure that network resources are sufficient to carry traffic without special prioritization and at low delay levels. In general, utilization levels above 70% result in sharp increases in congestion delay for small increases in traffic, so high-utilization networks are more likely to experience speech quality problems. Network economy depends in large part on securing high levels of utilization, however, so router-based delay-management strategies are preferable.

Which strategy is best for packet voice transport? Usually it is one that a business already has in use to transport data; but all forms of public frame and cell networking should be examined and compared for price and service quality. An issue often compelling is the pricing policies of public services. In many countries, public data services such as Frame Relay are priced without a distance-sensitive component. Therefore, for long-haul connections, these services may be significantly more economical than voice telephony or leased lines, both of which are usually priced based partly on the distance between connection points.

Public network tariffs may also subsidize residential services by pricing business calls and international calls higher. These subsidies create an artificial economy for any form of packet voice, and despite the fact that the value is created by pricing policy and not network technology, the savings are just as real. National administrations may view attempts to evade these higher rates as contrary to public policy, however, and networks that do this may be illegal in some countries. Issues relating to the legality of packet voice must be examined on a country-by-country basis, but a general set of guidelines is provided in a later section of this document.

Signaling: Making the Voice Connection

In many ways the questions of how voice is coded and how voice quality is ensured are the easy parts of packet voice. A useful packet voice application like the one shown in Figure G-1 requires callers in one area to be able to connect to a voice agent that serves them using their standard dialing mechanism and to place calls to at least a selected set of users who are accessible on other voice agents.

There are two basic models of voice connection and signaling in packet voice applications, as shown in Figure G-3.

- **The transport model**—In this model, two voice agents are connected by a trunk through the transport network cloud. All the calls placed by the first voice agent must be completed on the second, so all voice traffic originated on one agent is just trunked to the other. This model is often used for point-to-point applications of voice over the Internet. It can be related to the "tie-line" model of a PBX network, where connection and switching intelligence lies entirely with the PBXs.

- **The translate model**—In this model, any number of voice agents can be connected via a network cloud that understands signaling and addressing requests. The voice agents map native phone numbers to ATM, Frame Relay, or IP addresses via a directory or dial plan that shows which voice addresses (phone numbers, extensions) can be reached at which voice agents. The dial plan is used by an originating voice agent to identify the voice agent that "owns" the called party, and a connection is selected to that voice agent when a call is placed. This model effectively makes the network cloud a virtual voice switch or tandem switch.

Figure G-3 *Connectivity/Signaling Models*

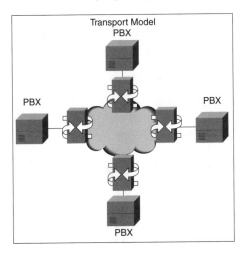
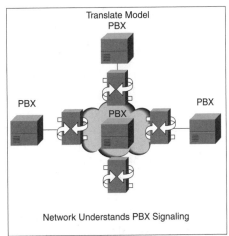

Figure G-3 shows that there are two very different signaling relationships in a packet voice network. One type of signaling, called external signaling, takes place between the voice agent and the voice devices that the agent serves. Because these voice devices are built to participate in ordinary voice networks, this external signaling follows telephone standards. The other type of signaling takes place between the voice agents themselves over the transport network cloud. This internal signaling takes place via the standards of the transport network or of the voice agents themselves.

External Signaling

Voice agents must be interconnected to the voice source and destination in a manner consistent with normal phone system operations, or packet voice will not appear to work the same as traditional telephony. The following four options for external signaling are commonly supported in packet voice systems:

- Standard dual-tone multifrequency (DTMF) or pulse analog signaling of the type used on telephone instruments or small telephone key systems. This type of signaling is appropriate for packet voice applications where standard phone instruments are to be plugged into the voice agent directly using the telephone jack type appropriate to the national administration.

- Analog tie-line signaling, also called E&M signaling, used most often on four-wire analog trunks.

- Digital in-band signaling, called channel-associated signaling (CAS) and used on T1/E1 digital trunks. Standards for CAS vary among the major world geographies (North America and the ITU, for example). With CAS, signaling information travels on the same paths as voice information.

- Digital out-of-band signaling, called common-channel signaling or CCS, in which all signaling for a multiconnection digital trunk (T1/E1/J1) is combined onto one or more common channels, separate from the voice information. This type is normally employed by PBXs (examples are DPNSS and QSIG). ISDN's D channel is also a CCS channel.

Another form of signaling is used in conjunction with public phone networks. Signaling System 7 (SS7) is an internal protocol to such networks, operating out of band between network elements to connect calls and request special services such as 800 numbers or free phone number decoding. Future packet voice products may support SS7 as an external signaling protocol.

When a packet voice network operating with a translate model of service understands signaling protocols at the voice agent and connects calls across the packet transport network based on signaled numbers, the packet voice network is acting as a tandem switch in the voice network. This capability may be an additional source of savings to voice network builders, because tandem switches are expensive.

Tandem switches and the source switches (PBXs, for example) combine to create the numbering plan or dialing plan for a network. This plan associates specific stations with specific dialed numbers, and it must be complete and consistent for the network to function properly. It is important that any translate model packet voice network have adequate facilities for managing its part of the dial plan and ensuring that it is consistent with the numbering plan of the voice networks it serves.

Internal Signaling

Internal signaling, as previously noted, must provide two features: connection control and call progress or status information. Connection control signaling is used to create relationships or paths between voice agents to permit packet voice to flow. Call progress or status information is exchanged by voice agents to signal the state of the call—ringing, busy, and so forth.

In the transport model of packet voice networking, internal signaling is used primarily to avoid maintaining a permanent connection across the transport network to support every possible call between the voice agents. Therefore, internal connection signaling in the transport model is associated with connection-oriented networks that allocate fixed bandwidth resources. For packet voice applications on connectionless networks, there is no need to have a connection created; the two voice agents just address datagrams to each other when traffic is presented.

In the translate model of packet voice networks, connection signaling may be necessary to route a packet flow to the proper voice agent after the identity of that agent is known via a dial-plan function. The multiplicity of connections possible in networks with a large variety of voice agents might well make it impossible for each voice agent to create a connection to each partner for every possible call.

The individual transport network options such as ATM, Frame Relay, and IP all have their own signaling standards; ATM's is Q.931, and Frame Relay packet voice signaling is described in FRF.11. These differing standards could require users to adopt special packet voice agents for each transport network.

The accepted model for internal signaling, both connection and call progress, for IP packet voice networks is the H.323 standard. Although H.323 is popularly viewed as a packet video standard, it actually defines a set of multimedia communications standards between users. In fact, only voice services are required for H.323 participation; video and data support are optional.

H.323 defines a complete multimedia network, from devices to protocols. Linking all the entities within H.323 is H.245, which is defined to negotiate facilities among participants and H.323 network elements. A scaled-down version of ISDN's Q.931 call protocol is used to provide for connection setup.

In H.323 terms, the voice agents are terminals, although the common usage of this concept suggests a single user. H.323 also defines a gatekeeper function that performs the address translations and lookups required for the translate model of packet voice.

If the "cloud" network in a packet voice application is actually made up of several different kinds of transport networks, H.323 defines a gateway function between networks that performs the packet data format translation and signaling translation required for proper communications across the network boundary. The most common use of this gateway is the conversion of videoconferencing from H.320 to H.323 format, permitting packet video users to communicate with traditional room- or cart-based video systems that rely on the circuit-switched form of video.

The H.323 standard may be overlaid on specialized standards for each transport network option. With connectionless IP networks, the RTP protocol and RTCP control protocol are used and in turn carried on UDP. In Frame Relay, FRF.11 describes a standard mechanism for signaling.

These lower-level standards can be used without H.323, of course. Although H.323 is not required for packet voice applications, there are significant benefits to having H.323 compatibility. H.323 makes any form of voice compression other than the G.711 PCM method optional, however, so there is no assurance that H.323-compatible packet voice systems will provide optimum voice coding.

The best model for a packet voice application depends on the nature of the users of the application. Where a packet voice connection is being used as a kind of tie line between two private or public telephone populations, the transport model and a proprietary system of voice coding and signaling are adequate if the needs of the applications are met with the compression system used and the network transport resources available.

Where multiple populations of voice users are to be supported, meaning that there could be many voice agents on the packet voice transport cloud, the translate model probably provides better economy and flexibility. If there is a chance that these voice agents will be provided and supported by different organizations, it is critical that the entire system be based on H.323 to ensure that the voice agents and directory functions (terminals, gatekeepers, and gateways, in H.323 terms) can interoperate. In this situation, however, the buyer should be sure that the H.323 components support additional voice coding standards if these are required to secure the levels of voice quality and network economy the applications dictate.

Public network services based on H.323 are becoming available and will probably continue to grow in popularity. Selecting from among these services or from among public transport network alternatives for packet voice applications is a matter of securing suitable performance (that is, speech quality) at the lowest cost.

In private applications, H.323 conformance can be mandated during the packet video equipment-purchase process; if equipment from several vendors is to be used, however, it may be necessary to undertake conformance or interoperability testing. As is often the case with international standards, H.323 provides many "optional" areas of support, including some of the most efficient methods of voice coding. Equipment may be conforming to the standards and may not provide support for all the options; such equipment interoperates only in the minimal mode supported as mandatory in H.323.

Often prospective packet voice users have multilayered networks available—IP over Frame Relay or ATM, for example. In this type of network, it may be possible to transport packet voice at any or all of these levels, and selecting the best level to use may be an issue. Among factors to be considered are the following:

- The scope of the various network layers must be considered first. Frame Relay networking may be available from site to site, for example, but not within sites or to locations served by private transmission resources such as fiber or microwave. IP, because it is ubiquitous, may be capable of supporting voice users at any location.

- Where scope of both layer options is suitable for the application, it is generally better to transport voice at the lowest protocol layer possible—Frame Relay or ATM rather than IP. Overhead is lower for these low protocol layers, and the QoS connection is often more readily controlled.

Applying Packet Voice

Packet voice networks can be used in two broad contexts: differentiated by geography or by the types of users to be served. The economics and technology of the network may be unaffected by these factors, but there may be legal constraints in some areas for some combinations of these two contexts, and network users or operators should be aware of them.

Telecommunications is regulated within countries by "national administrations" or arms of the governments, based on local regulations. In some countries, such as the United States, there may be multiple levels of regulatory authority. In all cases, treaties define the international connection rules, rates, and so forth. It is important for any business planning to use or build a packet voice network to ensure itself that it is operating in conformance to all laws and regulations in all the areas the network serves. This normally requires some direct research, but the current state of the regulations can be summarized as follows:

- Within a national administration or telephony jurisdiction, it is almost always proper for a business to employ packet voice to support its own voice calling among its own sites.

- In such applications, it is normally expected that some of the calls transported on the packet voice network will have originated in the public phone network. Such "outside" calling over packet voice is uniformly tolerated in a regulatory sense, on the basis that the calls are from employees, customers, or suppliers and represent the company's business.

- When a packet voice connection is made between national administrations to support the activities of a single company—to connect two or more company locations in multiple countries—the application is uniformly tolerated in a regulatory sense.

- In such a situation, an outside call placed from a public phone network in one country and terminated in a company site within another country via packet voice may be a technical violation of national monopolies or treaties on long-distance service. Where such a call is between company employees or between employees and suppliers or customers, such a technical violation is unlikely to attract official notice, however.

- When a packet voice network is used to connect public calls within a company, the packet voice provider is technically providing a local or national telephone service and is subject to regulation as such.

- When a packet voice network is used to connect public calls between countries, the packet voice provider is subject to the national regulations in the countries involved and also to any treaty provisions for international calling to which any of the countries served are signatories.

Therefore, it is safe to say that companies could employ packet voice networking for any applications where traditional leased-line, PBX-to-PBX networking could be legally employed. In fact, a good model for deploying packet voice without additional concerns on regulatory matters is to duplicate an existing PBX trunk network or tie-line network using packet voice facilities.

Summary

The public telephone network of today is in many ways unchanged from the networks of the early 1980s. During this period, there have been great advances in data network technology that have both improved network economics and improved control over network quality of service. It is those advances that have spawned today's market interest in packet voice.

Packet voice transport using advanced compression algorithms such as the ACELP-based G.729 can transport as much as 16 times the voice traffic per unit of network bandwidth as the PCM-based networks used in public telephony. Users with existing data networks can often interleave their voice traffic with data at little or no additional transport cost and little or no impact on application performance. Users with circuit-switched T1/E1/J1 voice networks, with packet voice transmission, can often free up enough bandwidth from existing voice trunks to carry their entire data load.

Much of the attention focused on packet voice networking has been aimed at issues of tariff arbitrage—taking advantage of distance-insensitive Frame Relay pricing or avoiding international voice tariffs. Although these forms of cost avoidance can often produce savings for as long as the tariff differences last, it is the fundamental efficiency of packet voice transport that makes it an increasingly attractive technology to businesses.

Not every network or every user will be able to take advantage of packet voice transmission to reduce telephone costs. Some data networks have insufficient residual capacity for even highly compressed voice, and augmenting these networks with additional public carrier services may be costly. It is interesting to note, however, that packet voice will never be more costly than traditional circuit-switched voice. Most often, it is far less costly and worthy of considerable planning attention, both for now and for the future.

The information in this chapter is from the CCO Web site at www.cisco.com.

References and Recommended Reading

Books and Periodicals

Apple Computer, Inc. *AppleTalk Network System Overview*. Reading, Massachusetts: Addison-Wesley Publishing Company, Inc.; 1989.

Apple Computer, Inc. *Planning and Managing AppleTalk Networks*. Reading, Massachusetts: Addison-Wesley Publishing Company, Inc.; 1991.

Black, U. *Data Networks: Concepts, Theory and Practice*. Englewood Cliffs, New Jersey: Prentice Hall; 1989.

Black, U. *Physical Level Interfaces and Protocols*. Los Alamitos, California: IEEE Computer Society Press; 1988.

Case, J.D., J.R. Davins, M.S. Fedor, and M.L. Schoffstall. "Network Management and the Design of SNMP." *ConneXions: The Interoperability Report,* Vol. 3: March 1989.

Case, J.D., J.R. Davins, M.S. Fedor, and M.L. Schoffstall. "Introduction to the Simple Gateway Monitoring Protocol." *IEEE Network:* March 1988.

Clark, W. "SNA Internetworking." *ConneXions: The Interoperability Report*, Vol. 6, No. 3: March 1992.

Coltun, R. "OSPF: An Internet Routing Protocol." *ConneXions: The Interoperability Report*, Vol. 3, No. 8: August 1989.

Comer, D.E. *Internetworking with TCP/IP: Principles, Protocols, and Architecture*, Vol. I, 2nd ed. Englewood Cliffs, New Jersey: Prentice Hall; 1991.

Davidson, J. *An Introduction to TCP/IP*. New York, New York: Springer-Verlag; 1992.

Ferrari, D. *Computer Systems Performance Evaluation*. Englewood Cliffs, New Jersey: Prentice Hall; 1978.

Garcia-Luna-Aceves, J.J. "Loop-Free Routing Using Diffusing Computations." *IEEE/ACM Transactions on Networking*, Vol. 1, No. 1, 1993.

Green, J.K. *Telecommunications*, 2nd ed. Homewood, Illinois: Business One Irwin; 1992.

Hagans, R. "Components of OSI: ES-IS Routing." *ConneXions: The Interoperability Report*, Vol. 3, No. 8: August 1989.

Hares, S. "Components of OSI: Inter-Domain Routing Protocol (IDRP)." *ConneXions: The Interoperability Report*, Vol. 6, No. 5: May 1992.

Jones, N.E.H. and D. Kosiur. *Macworld Networking Handbook*. San Mateo, California: IDG Books Worldwide, Inc.; 1992.

Joyce, S.T. and J.Q. Walker II. "Advanced Peer-to-Peer Networking (APPN): An Overview." *ConneXions: The Interoperability Report*, Vol. 6, No. 10: October 1992.

Kousky, K. "Bridging the Network Gap." *LAN Technology*, Vol. 6, No. 1: January 1990.

LaQuey, Tracy. *The Internet Companion: A Beginner's Guide to Global Networking*, Reading, Massachusetts: Addison-Wesley Publishing Company, Inc.; 1994.

Leinwand, A. and K. Fang. *Network Management: A Practical Perspective*. Reading, Massachusetts: Addison-Wesley Publishing Company, Inc.; 1993.

Lippis, N. "The Internetwork Decade." *Data Communications*, Vol. 20, No. 14: October 1991.

McNamara, J.E. *Local Area Networks*. Digital Press, Educational Services, Digital Equipment Corporation, 12 Crosby Drive, Bedford, MA 01730.

Malamud, C. *Analyzing DECnet/OSI Phase V*. New York, New York: Van Nostrand Reinhold; 1991.

Malamud, C. *Analyzing Novell Networks*. New York, New York: Van Nostrand Reinhold; 1991.

Malamud, C. *Analyzing Sun Networks*. New York, New York: Van Nostrand Reinhold; 1991.

Martin, J. *SNA: IBM's Networking Solution*. Englewood Cliffs, New Jersey: Prentice Hall; 1987.

Martin, J., with K.K. Chapman and the ARBEN Group, Inc. *Local Area Networks. Architectures and Implementations*. Englewood Cliffs, New Jersey: Prentice Hall; 1989.

Medin, M. "The Great IGP Debate—Part Two: The Open Shortest Path First (OSPF) Routing Protocol." *ConneXions: The Interoperability Report*, Vol. 5, No. 10: October 1991.

Meijer, A. *Systems Network Architecture: A tutorial*. New York, New York: John Wiley & Sons, Inc.; 1987.

Miller, M.A. *LAN Protocol Handbook*. San Mateo, California: M&T Books; 1990.

Miller, M.A. *LAN Troubleshooting Handbook*. San Mateo, California: M&T Books; 1989.

O'Reilly, T. and G. Todino. *Managing UUCP and Usenet*, 10th ed. Sebastopol, California: O'Reilly & Associates, Inc.; 1992.

Perlman, R. *Interconnections: Bridges and Routers*. Reading, Massachusetts: Addison-Wesley Publishing Company, Inc.; 1992.

Perlman, R. and R. Callon. "The Great IGP Debate—Part One: IS-IS and Integrated Routing." *ConneXions: The Interoperability Report*, Vol. 5, No. 10: October 1991.

Rose, M.T. *The Open Book: A Practical Perspective on OSI*. Englewood Cliffs, New Jersey: Prentice Hall; 1990.

Rose, M.T. *The Simple Book: An Introduction to Management of TCP/IP-based Internets*. Englewood Cliffs, New Jersey: Prentice Hall; 1991.

Ross, F.E. "FDDI—A Tutorial." *IEEE Communications Magazine*, Vol. 24, No. 5: May 1986.

Schlar, S.K. *Inside X.25: A Manager's Guide*. New York, New York: McGraw-Hill, Inc.; 1990.

Schwartz, M. *Telecommunications Networks: Protocols, Modeling, and Analysis*. Reading, Massachusetts: Addison-Wesley Publishing Company, Inc.; 1987.

Sherman, K. *Data Communications: A User's Guide*. Englewood Cliffs, New Jersey: Prentice Hall; 1990.

Sidhu, G.S., R.F. Andrews, and A.B. Oppenheimer. *Inside AppleTalk*, 2nd ed. Reading, Massachusetts: Addison-Wesley Publishing Company, Inc.; 1990.

Spragins, J.D. et al. *Telecommunications Protocols and Design*. Reading, Massachusetts: Addison-Wesley Publishing Company, Inc.; 1991.

Stallings, W. *Data and Computer Communications*. New York, New York: Macmillan Publishing Company; 1991.

Stallings, W. *Handbook of Computer-Communications Standards*, Vols. 1–3. Carmel, Indiana: Howard W. Sams, Inc.; 1990.

Stallings, W. *Local Networks*, 3rd ed. New York, New York: Macmillan Publishing Company; 1990.

Sunshine, C.A. (ed.). *Computer Network Architectures and Protocols*, 2nd ed. New York, New York: Plenum Press; 1989.

Tannenbaum, A.S. *Computer Networks*, 2nd ed. Englewood Cliffs, New Jersey: Prentice Hall; 1988.

Terplan, K. *Communication Networks Management*. Englewood Cliffs, New Jersey: Prentice Hall; 1992.

Tsuchiya, P. "Components of OSI: IS-IS Intra-Domain Routing." *ConneXions: The Interoperability Report*, Vol. 3, No. 8: August 1989.

Tsuchiya, P. "Components of OSI: Routing (An Overview)." *ConneXions: The Interoperability Report*, Vol. 3, No. 8: August 1989.

Zimmerman, H. "OSI Reference Model—The ISO Model of Architecture for Open Systems Interconnection." *IEEE Transactions on Communications* COM-28, No. 4: April 1980.

Technical Publications and Standards

Advanced Micro Devices. *The Supernet Family for FDDI*. Technical Manual Number 09779A. Sunnyvale, California; 1989.

——— *The Supernet Family for FDDI*. 1989 Data Book Number 09734C. Sunnyvale, California; 1989.

American National Standards Institute X3T9.5 Committee. *FDDI Station Management (SMT)*. Rev. 6.1; March 15, 1990.

——— Revised Text of ISO/DIS 8802/2 for the Second DIS Ballot, "Information Processing Systems—Local Area Networks." Part 2: Logical Link Control. 1987-01-14.

——— T1.606. Integrated Services Digital Network (ISDN)—Architectural Framework and Service Description for Frame-Relaying Bearer Service. 1990.

——— T1.617. Integrated Services Digital Network (ISDN)—Signaling Specification for Frame Relay Bearer Service for Digital Subscriber Signaling System Number 1 (DSS1). 1991.

——— T1.618. Integrated Services Digital Network (ISDN)—Core Aspects of Frame Protocol for Use with Frame Relay Bearer Service. 1991.

ATM Data Exchange Interface (DXI) Specification, Version 1.0. Document ATM_FORUM/93-590R1; August 4,1993.

Banyan Systems, Inc. *VINES Protocol Definition*. DA254-00, Rev. 1.0. Westboro, Massachusetts; February 1990.

Bellcore. *Generic System Requirements in Support of a Switched Multi-Megabit Data Service*. Technical Advisory, TA-TSY-000772; October 1989.

——— *Local Access System Generic Requirements, Objectives, and Interface Support of Switched Multi-Megabit Data Service*. Technical Advisory TA-TSY-000773, Issue 1; December 1985.

——— *Switched Multi-Megabit Data Service (SMDS) Operations Technology Network Element Generic Requirements*. Technical Advisory TA-TSY-000774.

Chapman, J.T. and M. Halabi. *HSSI: High-Speed Serial Interface Design Specification.* Menlo Park, California and Santa Clara, California: Cisco Systems and T3Plus Networking, Inc.; 1990.

Consultative Committee for International Telegraph and Telephone. *CCITT Data Communications Networks—Services and Facilities, Terminal Equipment and Interfaces, Recommendations X.1–X.29.* Yellow Book, Vol. VIII, Fascicle VIII.2; 1980.

——— *CCITT Data Communications Networks—Interfaces, Recommendations X.20– X.32.* Red Book, Vol. VIII, Fascicle VIII.3; 1984.

DDN Protocol Handbook. Four volumes; 1989.

Defense Communications Agency. *Defense Data Network X.25 Host Interface Specification.* Order number AD A137 427; December 1983.

Digital Equipment Corporation. *DECnet/OSI Phase V: Making the Transition from Phase IV.* EK-PVTRN-BR; 1989.

——— *DECserver 200 Local Area Transport (LAT) Network Concepts.* AA-LD84A-TK; June 1988.

——— *DIGITAL Network Architecture (Phase V).* EK-DNAPV-GD-001; September 1987.

Digital Equipment Corporation, Intel Corporation, Xerox Corporation. *The Ethernet, A Local-Area Network, Data Link Layer and Physical Layer Specifications.* Ver. 2.0; November 1982.

Feinler, E.J., et al. *DDN Protocol Handbook*, Vols. 1–4, NIC 50004, 50005, 50006, 50007. Defense Communications Agency. Alexandria, Virginia; December 1985.

Garcia-Luna-Aceves, J.J. "A Unified Approach to Loop-Free Routing Using Distance Vectors or Link States." ACM 089791-332-9/89/0009/0212, pp. 212–223; September 1989.

Hemrick, C. and L. Lang. "Introduction to Switched Multi-megabit Data Service (SMDS), an Early Broadband Service." *Proceedings of the XIII International Switching Symposium* (ISS 90), May 27–June 1, 1990.

Hewlett-Packard Company. X.25: The PSN Connection; An Explanation of Recommendation X.25. 5958-3402; October 1985.

IEEE 802.2—*Local Area Networks Standard, 802.2 Logical Link Control.* ANSI/IEEE Standard; October 1985.

IEEE 802.3—*Local Area Networks Standard, 802.3 Carrier Sense Multiple Access.* ANSI/ IEEE Standard; October 1985.

IEEE 802.5—*Local Area Networks Standard, 802.5 Token Ring Access Method.* ANSI/ IEEE Standard; October 1985.

IEEE 802.6—*Local & Metropolitan Area Networks Standard, 802.6 Distributed Queue Dual Bus (DQDB) Subnetwork of a Metropolitan Area Network (MAN)*. ANSI/IEEE Standard; December 1990.

International Business Machines Corporation. ACF/NCP/VS network control program, system support programs: general information. GC30-3058.

———— *Advanced Communications Function for VTAM (ACF/VTAM), general information: introduction. GS27-0462.*

———— *Advanced Communications Function for VTAM, general information: concepts. GS27-0463.*

———— *Dictionary of Computing. SC20-1699-7; 1987.*

———— *Local Area Network Technical Reference. SC30-3883.*

———— *Network Problem Determination Application: general information. GC34-2010.*

———— *Synchronous Data Link Control: general information. GA27-3093.*

———— *Systems Network Architecture: concepts and products. GC30-3072.*

———— *Systems Network Architecture: technical overview. GC30-3073-1; 1985.*

———— *Token-Ring Network Architecture Reference. SC30-3374.*

———— *Token-Ring Problem Determination Guide. SX27-3710-04; 1990.*

International Organization for Standardization. *Information Processing System—Open System Interconnection; Specification of Abstract Syntax Notation One (ASN.1)*. International Standard 8824; December 1987.

McGraw-Hill/Data Communications. *McGraw-Hill's Compilation of Data Communications Standards*. Edition III; 1986.

National Security Agency. *Blacker Interface Control Document*. March 21, 1989.

Novell, Inc. IPX Router Specification, Version 1.10. Part Number 107-000029-001. October 16, 1992.

———— NetWare Link Services Protocol (NLSP) Specification, Revision 0.9. Part Number 100-001708-001. March 1993.

StrataCom. *Frame Relay Specification with Extensions*. 001-208966, Rev.1.0; September 18, 1990.

Xerox Corporation. *Internet Transport Protocols*. XNSS 029101; January 1991.

Overview of IP Multicast

This overview is intended to provide background information for Chapter 13, "PIM Sparse Mode." The information in this appendix is from the CCO Web site.

The Advantages of Multicast

Any form of network communication involving the transmission of information to multiple recipients can benefit from the bandwidth efficiency of multicast technology. Examples of applications involving one-to-many or many-to-many communications include video and audio broadcasts, videoconferencing/collaboration, dissemination of stock quotes and news feeds, database replication, software downloads, and Web site caching.

To understand the efficiency of multicasting, consider a video server offering a single channel of content, as shown in Figure I-1. For full-motion, full-screen viewing, a video stream requires approximately 1.5 Mbps of server-to-client bandwidth. In a unicast environment, the server must send a separate video stream to the network for each client (this consumes $1.5 \times n$ Mbps of link bandwidth, where n = number of client viewers). With a 10-Mbps Ethernet interface on the server, it takes only six or seven server-to-client streams to completely saturate the network interface. Even with a highly intelligent Gigabit Ethernet interface on a high-performance server, the practical limit would be from 250 to 300 1.5-Mbps video streams. Therefore, the server interface capacity can be a significant bottleneck, limiting the number of unicast video streams per video server. Replicated unicast transmissions consume a lot of bandwidth within the network, which is another significant limitation. If the path between server and client traverses h3 router hops and h2 switch hops, the "multi-unicast" video would consume $1.5 \times n \times$ h3 Mbps of router bandwidth, plus $1.5 \times n \times$ h2 Mbps of switch bandwidth. With 100 clients separated from the server by two router hops and two switch hops, as shown in Figure I-1, a single multi-unicast channel would consume 300 Mbps of router bandwidth and 300 Mbps of switch bandwidth. Even if the video stream bandwidth is scaled back to 100 kbps (which provides acceptable quality in smaller windows on the screen), the multi-unicast would consume 20 Mbps of both router and switch bandwidth.

Figure I-1 *Video Transmission in Unicast and Multicast Networks*

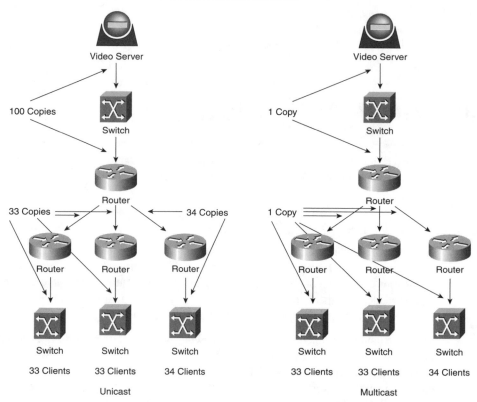

In a multicast environment, the video server needs to transmit a single video stream for each multicast group, regardless of the number of clients that will view it. The video stream is then replicated as required by the network's multicast routers and switches to allow an arbitrary number of clients to subscribe to the multicast address and receive the broadcast. In the router network, replication occurs only at branches of the distribution tree, so essentially all the replication occurs at the last switch hop. In the multicast scenario, only 1.5 Mbps of server-to-network bandwidth is utilized, leaving the remainder free for other uses or additional channels of video content. Within the network, the multicast transmission offers similar efficiency, consuming only 1/nth of the bandwidth of the multi-unicast solution (for example, 3 Mbps of router and switch bandwidth in Figure I-1).

Obviously, where there are large numbers of recipients of a replicated transmission, multicast technology makes a tremendous difference in both server load and network load, even in a simple network with a small number of router and switch hops. Additional features of multicast are beneficial in specific applications such as financial services. Multicast transmissions are delivered nearly simultaneously to all members of the recipient group. The variability in delivery time is limited to differences in end-to-end network delay among the range of server-to-client paths. In a unicast scenario, the server sequences through transmission of multiple copies of the data, so variability in delivery time is immense, especially for large transmissions or large distribution lists. Another unique feature of multicast is that the server does not know the unicast network address of any particular recipient of the transmission—all recipients share the same multicast network address and therefore can join a multicast group while maintaining anonymity.

Primer on Multicast Technology

Multicast transmission technology is available at both the data link layer (Layer 2) and the network layer (Layer 3). For example, Ethernet, Fiber Distributed Data Interface (FDDI), and SMDS all support unicast, multicast, and broadcast MAC layer addresses. Therefore, an individual computer on these networks can simultaneously listen to a unicast address, multiple multicast addresses, and the broadcast address. Token Ring also supports the concept of multicasting, but uses a different technique to address receiver groups.

If the scope of a multicast application is limited to a single physical or logical LAN, multicasting over the data link layer is sufficient. Most multipoint applications are of interest, however, only if their reach can be extended to a distributed campus or even a wide-area environment consisting of many different networking technologies, including Ethernet, FDDI, Token Ring, Frame Relay, and ATM. For these extended environments, multicast must also be implemented at Layer 3. Multicast transmission at Layer 3 involves several special mechanisms:

- Addressing
- Dynamic Registration
- Multicast Forwarding
- Multicast Routing

Addressing

There must be a Layer 3 address that is used to communicate with a group of receivers rather than a single receiver. In addition, there must be a way of mapping this address onto Layer 2 multicast addresses of the underlying physical networks. For IP networks, Class D addresses have been set aside for multicast addressing. A Class D address consists of 1110 as the higher-order bits in the first octet, followed by an unstructured 28-bit group address. For mapping IP multicast addresses to Ethernet addresses, the lower 23 bits of the Class D address are mapped into a block of Ethernet addresses that have been reserved for multicast. With this mapping scheme, each Ethernet multicast address corresponds to 32 IP multicast addresses. This means that a host receiving multicasts may need to filter out unwanted multicast packets being forwarded to other groups with the same MAC layer multicast address. Ethernet multicast addresses have a "01" in the first byte of the destination address to allow the network interface to easily discriminate between multicast and unicast packets.

Dynamic Registration

There must be a mechanism that informs the network that the computer is a member of a particular group. Without this information, the network would be forced to flood rather than multicast the transmissions for each group. For IP networks, the Internet Group Multicast Protocol (IGMP) is an IP datagram protocol between routers and hosts that allows group membership lists to be dynamically maintained. The host sends an IGMP "report," or join, to the router to join the group. Periodically, the router sends a "query" to learn which hosts are still part of a group. If a host wants to continue its group membership, it responds to the query with a report. If the host sends no report, the router prunes the group list to minimize unnecessary transmissions. With IGMP V2, a host may send a "leave" message to inform the router that it no longer is participating in a multicast group. This allows the router to prune the group list before the next query is scheduled, minimizing the time period in which wasted transmissions are forwarded to the network.

Multicast Forwarding

Most IP multicast applications are based on UDP, which uses "best-effort delivery" and lacks the congestion-avoidance windowing mechanism of TCP. As a result, multicast packets may be dropped more often than unicast TCP packets. Because it is not practical for real-time applications to request retransmissions, audio and video broadcasts may suffer degradation because of packet drops. Prior to the deployment of quality of service (QoS), the best way to minimize lost packets in frame-based networks was to provision adequate bandwidth, especially at the edge of the network. The reliability of multicast transmissions will be improved when the Reservation Protocol (RSVP), the Real-Time Transport Protocol (RTP), and 802.1p or other Layer 2 priority mechanisms make it possible to deliver end-to-end QoS over a Layer 2/Layer 3 network.

Multicast Routing

The network must be able to build packet distribution trees that specify a unique forwarding path between the subnet of the source and each subnet containing members of the multicast group. A primary goal of distribution tree construction is to ensure that at most, one copy of each packet is forwarded on each branch of the tree. This is accomplished by constructing a spanning tree rooted at the designated multicast router of the sending host, providing connectivity to the designated multicast routers of each receiving host. For IP multicast, the IETF has offered several multicast routing protocols for consideration. These include the Distance Vector Multicast Routing Protocol (DVMRP), Multicast extensions to OSPF (MOSPF), Protocol-Independent Multicast (PIM), and Core-Based Trees (CBT).

Multicast routing protocols build distribution trees by examining a unicast reachability protocol's routing table. Some protocols use the unicast forwarding table, including PIM and CBT. Alternatively, other protocols use their own private unicast reachability routing tables. DVMRP uses its own distance vector routing protocol to determine how to build source-based distribution trees. Similarly, MOSPF uses its own link-state database to build source-based distribution trees.

Multicast routing protocols fall into two categories: Dense mode (DM) and Sparse mode (SM). DM protocols assume that almost all routers in the network will need to distribute multicast traffic for each multicast group (for example, almost all hosts on the network belong to each multicast group). Accordingly, DM protocols build distribution trees by initially flooding the entire network and then pruning back the small number of paths without receivers. SM protocols assume that relatively few routers in the network will be involved in each multicast. The hosts belonging to the group are widely dispersed, as might be the case for most multicasts in the Internet. Therefore, SM protocols begin with an empty distribution tree and add branches only as the result of explicit requests to join the distribution. The DM protocols—MOSPF, DVMRP, and PIM-DM—are most appropriate in LAN environments with densely clustered receivers and the bandwidth to tolerate flooding; the SM protocols—CBT and PIM-SM—are generally more appropriate in WAN environments. PIM is also capable of functioning in Sparse-Dense mode by adjusting its behavior to match the characteristics of each receiver group.

Multicast Process

Figure I-2 illustrates the following process, whereby a client receives a video multicast from the server:

1 The client sends an IGMP join message to its designated multicast router. The destination MAC address maps to the Class D address of the group being joined rather than being the MAC address of the router. The body of the IGMP datagram also includes the Class D group address.

2 The router logs the join message, and uses PIM or another multicast routing protocol to add this segment to the multicast distribution tree.

3 IP multicast traffic transmitted from the server is now distributed via the designated router to the client's subnet. The destination MAC address corresponds to the Class D address of group.

4 The switch receives the multicast packet and examines its forwarding table. If no entry exists for the MAC address, the packet will be flooded to all ports within the broadcast domain. If an entry does exist in the switch table, the packet will be forwarded only to the designated ports.

5 With IGMP V2, the client can cease group membership by sending an IGMP leave to the router. With IGMP V1, the client remains a member of the group until it fails to send a join message in response to a query from the router. Multicast routers also periodically send an IGMP query to the "all multicast hosts" group or to a specific multicast group on the subnet to determine which groups are still active within the subnet. Each host delays its response to a query by a small random period and will then respond only if no other host in the group has already reported. This mechanism prevents many hosts from congesting the network with simultaneous reports.

Figure I-2   *Multicast Process*

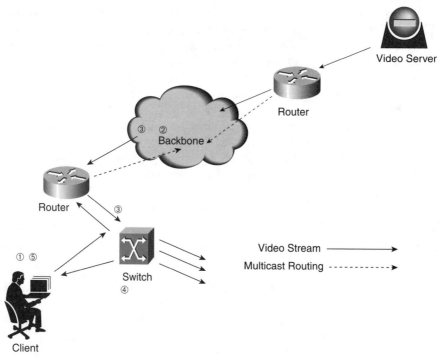

Planning for IP Multicast in Enterprise Network

Support for IP multicast requires multicast-enabling server and clients systems, and at least a portion of the network infrastructure of routers as well as the Layer 3 and Layer 2 switches that interconnect them. IP Multicast lends itself readily to a staged implementation beginning in isolated subnets and then expanding to encompass the entire campus- and wide-area network. Requirements are as follows:

- Server and client hosts must have an IP protocol stack supporting multicast, as specified in Internet RFC 1112. Full support of this RFC (Level 2 support) allows hosts to both send and receive multicast data. TCP/IP stacks supporting Windows Sockets V1.1 and V2.0 are multicast-enabled.

- Servers and clients must have applications, such as audio broadcast, video broadcast, or videoconferencing, that support IP multicast. The applications may have special requirements for system resources, such as processor speed, memory size, and in some cases, recommended NIC cards or graphics accelerator cards.

- Network interface cards (NICs) on all receiving hosts must be configured to monitor multicast packets in addition to the usual unicasts and broadcasts. Depending on the network infrastructure, receiving hosts may also benefit from having intelligent NIC cards that can filter out multicasts to unwanted groups, preventing the host CPU from unnecessary interruption.

- A high-performance routed backbone with a switched connection from the backbone to both the sender and receiver hosts provides a highly scalable LAN infrastructure for multicast. (The ultimate in scalability would be attained with an end-to-end Layer 2/Layer 3 switched network from sender to receiver.) The switched infrastructure is desirable because it can provide enough bandwidth to allow unicast and multimedia applications to coexist within the subnet, without the need for special priority or bandwidth-reservation mechanisms. With dedicated bandwidth to each desktop, switching vastly reduces (or with full duplex, entirely eliminates) Ethernet collisions that can disrupt real-time multimedia traffic. A shared media network may prove adequate for low-bandwidth audio applications or for limited pilot projects.

- All switches are not equally well-suited for multicast. The most appropriate switches have a switch architecture that allows multicast traffic to be forwarded to a large number of attached group members without unduly loading the switch fabric. This allows the switch to provide support for the growing number of new multicast applications without impacting other traffic. Layer 2 switches also need some degree of multicast-awareness to avoid flooding multicasts to all switch ports. Multicast control in Layer 2 switches can be accomplished in the following ways:

  — VLANs can de defined to correspond to the boundaries of the multicast group. This is a simple approach; however, it doesn't support dynamic changes to group membership and adds to the administrative burden of unicast VLANs.

  — Layer 2 switches can snoop IGMP queries and reports to learn the port mappings of multicast group members. This allows the switch to dynamically track group membership. But snooping every multicast data and control packet consumes a lot of switch-processing capacity, and therefore can degrade forwarding performance and increase latency.

  — Taking advantage of the Generic Attribute Registration Protocol (IEEE 802.1p) will allow the end system to communicate directly with the switch to join a 802.1p group corresponding to a multicast group. This shifts much of the responsibility for multicast group configuration from Layer 3 to Layer 2, which may be most appropriate in large, flat-switched networks.

— The traditional role of the router as a control point in the network can be maintained by defining a multicast router-to-switch protocol, such as the Cisco Group Multicast Protocol (CGMP), which allows the router to configure the switch's multicast forwarding table to correspond to the current group membership.

- Widespread deployment of multicast in intranets or over the wide area obviously involves traversing multiple subnet boundaries and router hops. Intermediate routers and Layer 3 switches between senders and receivers must be IP multicast-enabled. At a minimum, the ingress and egress routers to the backbone should be multicast routers. If the intervening backbone routers lack support for IP multicast, IP tunneling (encapsulating multicast packets within unicast packets) may be used as an interim measure to link multicast routers. Although most recent releases of router software include support for IP multicast, an industry-standard multicast routing protocol supported by all vendors is not yet available, making interoperability an issue in multivendor router backbones. The choice of multicast routing protocol among DVMRP, MOSPF, PIM, and CBT should be based on the characteristics of the multicast application being deployed, as well as the "density" and geographic location of receiving hosts (see the discussion of multicast routing protocols in the section titled "Overview of Multicast Technology").

Enterprise-Wide Multicast: Microsoft NetShow and the Microsoft Multicast Network

Microsoft NetShow is a comprehensive solution for provisioning unidirectional unicast (one-to-one) and multicast (one-to-many) multimedia services within enterprise networks or over the Internet. It incorporates components for content creation, encoding, and storage; as well as client/server applications for delivery of multimedia over local- or wide-area networks. NetShow V2.1 is currently shipping, with V3.0 in early beta release since January 1998. The NetShow V3.0 client application will be bundled with Microsoft Windows 98, which is currently in beta release. In addition, NetShow V3.0 client applications will be available for UNIX and MacOS. A companion application, Microsoft NetMeeting, provides a solution for the many-to-many multimedia application— videoconferencing and white-board collaboration.

NetShow includes a universal player that accesses content in Microsoft's Advanced Streaming Format (ASF) as well as content in other popular multimedia file formats, including WAV, AVI, QuickTime, RealAudio, and RealVideo. NetShow includes support in software for a wide range of compression/decompression schemes (codecs), enabling content authors to choose the best algorithm to match their applications and available network bandwidth. Codec software is autodownloaded to the client, as required to allow transparent decompression of all forms of content. High-quality streaming multimedia is supported in bandwidths ranging from 3 kbps (for mono-quality audio) to 8 Mbps (for broadcast-quality video with Microsoft NetShow Theater Server and hardware-supported MPEG). Live content can be archived to disk for subsequent on-demand viewing. NetShow native support for network protocols includes both unicast over TCP, multicast over UDP, and IGMP V2 support in the next release of the NetShow client. NetShow over HTTP allows viewing Internet-resident NetShow content without special configuration of firewalls on the viewer network.

NetShow is tightly integrated with other Microsoft applications, including NT Site Server and Microsoft Office. The integration with Site Server facilitates the creation of commercial Web sites incorporating embedded advertising and audio/video content. PowerPoint integration enables the creation of presentations with synchronized audio or video tracks.

The Microsoft campus network in Redmond, Washington, supports multicast of NetShow content to more than 30,000 desktops. Standard multimedia programming includes three radio stations and an MSNBC television channel feed. Additional channels are available on an ad hoc basis to carry live coverage of corporate events and corporate communications. The latter content is archived on disk for convenient on-demand viewing. Microsoft plans to extend multicast video coverage of corporate events to all Microsoft sites in North America. Microsoft reports that recent uses of the NetShow network have resulted in single-day savings of millions of dollars. By multicasting a major company meeting, the company avoided the costs of renting a facility and transporting more than 5000 employees from the campus. Microsoft also realized significant productivity savings because many workers took advantage of the on-demand viewing option to minimize disruption of their work schedules. Another less tangible benefit of the multicast network is the improvement in the quality of corporate communications because all employees can now be included in important corporate messages for a very low incremental cost.

For economical use of disk storage space and to conserve network resources, bandwidth of video transmissions is optimized at 110 kbps. NetShow servers for stored content are located in the central computer center with approximately 2000 other servers. Live NetShow content is served from the Microsoft Studios campus site. The backbone for multicast traffic consists of a mesh of Cisco 7500 series site routers running PIM and CGMP, interconnected over the ATM LANE campus backbone network. One of the five emulated LANs in the backbone is dedicated to multicast traffic. Multicast packet replication at the branches of the PIM distribution tree is performed by the ATM switches using the point-to-multipoint, hardware-assisted Broadcast and Unknown Server (BUS). Physical connectivity of the site ATM switches is via the Microsoft private SONET infrastructure. Each office or desktop has a dedicated switched 10-Mbps Ethernet connection provided by CGMP-enabled Cisco Catalyst 5000 or Catalyst 5500 switches in the wiring closets. Catalyst 5000 and 5500 switches are trunked together, using Cisco Fast EtherChannel technology to increase bandwidth between the switches.

INDEX

Numerics

A

B

C

D

I

O

P

W

X

CCIE Professional Development

Cisco LAN Switching

Kennedy Clark, CCIE; Kevin Hamilton, CCIE

1-57870-094-9 • AVAILABLE NOW

This volume provides an in-depth analysis of Cisco LAN switching technologies, architectures, and deployments, including unique coverage of Catalyst network design essentials. Network designs and configuration examples are incorporated throughout to demonstrate the principles and enable easy translation of the material into practice in production networks.

Advanced IP Network Design

Alvaro Retana, CCIE; Don Slice, CCIE; and Russ White, CCIE

1-57870-097-3 • AVAILABLE NOW

Network engineers and managers can use these case studies, which highlight various network design goals, to explore issues including protocol choice, network stability, and growth. This book also includes theoretical discussion on advanced design topics.

Large-Scale IP Network Solutions

Khalid Raza, CCIE; and Mark Turner

1-57870-084-1 • AVAILABLE NOW

Network engineers can find solutions as their IP networks grow in size and complexity. Examine all the major IP protocols in-depth and learn about scalability, migration planning, network management, and security for large-scale networks.

Routing TCP/IP, Volume I

Jeff Doyle, CCIE

1-57870-041-8 • AVAILABLE NOW

This book takes the reader from a basic understanding of routers and routing protocols through a detailed examination of each of the IP interior routing protocols. Learn techniques for designing networks that maximize the efficiency of the protocol being used. Exercises and review questions provide core study for the CCIE Routing and Switching exam.

Cisco Press   www.ciscopress.com

Cisco Press Solutions

Enhanced IP Services for Cisco Networks
Donald C. Lee, CCIE

1-57870-106-6 • AVAILABLE NOW

This is a guide to improving your network's capabilities by understanding the new enabling and advanced Cisco IOS services that build more scalable, intelligent, and secure networks. Learn the technical details necessary to deploy Quality of Service, VPN technologies, IPsec, the IOS firewall and IOS Intrusion Detection. These services will allow you to extend the network to new frontiers securely, protect your network from attacks, and increase the sophistication of network services.

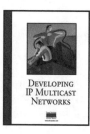

Developing IP Multicast Networks, Volume I
Beau Williamson, CCIE

1-57870-077-9 • AVAILABLE NOW

This book provides a solid foundation of IP multicast concepts and explains how to design and deploy the networks that will support appplications such as audio and video conferencing, distance-learning, and data replication. Includes an in-depth discussion of the PIM protocol used in Cisco routers and detailed coverage of the rules that control the creation and maintenance of Cisco mroute state entries.

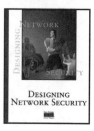

Designing Network Security
Merike Kaeo

1-57870-043-4 • AVAILABLE NOW

Designing Network Security is a practical guide designed to help you understand the fundamentals of securing your corporate infrastructure. This book takes a comprehensive look at underlying security technologies, the process of creating a security policy, and the practical requirements necessary to implement a corporate security policy.

Cisco Press

www.ciscopress.com

Hey, you've got enough worries.

Don't let IT training be one of them.

Get on the fast track to IT training at InformIT,
your total Information Technology training network.

 | **www.informit.com** |

■ Hundreds of timely articles on dozens of topics ■ Discounts on IT books from all our publishing partners, including Cisco Press ■ Free, unabridged books from the InformIT Free Library ■ "Expert Q&A"—our live, online chat with IT experts ■ Faster, easier certification and training from our Web- or classroom-based training programs ■ Current IT news ■ Software downloads ■ Career-enhancing resources

Cisco Press Solutions

EIGRP Network Design Solutions

Ivan Pepelnjak, CCIE

1-57870-165-1 • AVAILABLE NOW

EIGRP Network Design Solutions uses case studies and real-world configuration examples to help you gain an in-depth understanding of the issues involved in designing, deploying, and managing EIGRP-based networks. This book details proper designs that can be used to build large and scalable EIGRP-based networks and documents possible ways each EIGRP feature can be used in network design, implmentation, troubleshooting, and monitoring.

Top-Down Network Design

Priscilla Oppenheimer

1-57870-069-8 • AVAILABLE NOW

Building reliable, secure, and manageable networks is every network professional's goal. This practical guide teaches you a systematic method for network design that can be applied to campus LANs, remote-access networks, WAN links, and large-scale internetworks. Learn how to analyze business and technical requirements, examine traffic flow and Quality of Service requirements, and select protocols and technologies based on performance goals.

Cisco IOS Releases: The Complete Reference

Mack M. Coulibaly

1-57870-179-1 • AVAILABLE NOW

Cisco IOS Releases: The Complete Reference is the first comprehensive guide to the more than three dozen types of Cisco IOS releases being used today on enterprise and service provider networks. It details the release process and its numbering and naming conventions, as well as when, where, and how to use the various releases. A complete map of Cisco IOS software releases and their relationships to one another, in addition to insights into decoding information contained within the software, make this book an indispensable resource for any network professional.

Cisco Press

www.ciscopress.com

Cisco Press

Committed to being your long-term learning resource while you grow as a Cisco Networking Professional

Help Cisco Press **stay connected** to the issues and challenges you face on a daily basis by registering your product and filling out our brief survey. Complete and mail this form, or better yet ...

Register online and enter to win a FREE book!

Jump to **www.ciscopress.com/register** and register your product online. Each complete entry will be eligible for our monthly drawing to win a FREE book of the winner's choice from the Cisco Press library.

May we contact you via e-mail with information about **new releases, special promotions**, and **customer benefits**?

❏ Yes   ❏ No

E-mail address _____

Name _____

Address _____

City _____ State/Province _____

Country_____ Zip/Post code _____

Where did you buy this product?

❏ Bookstore   ❏ Computer store/Electronics store   ❏ Direct from Cisco Systems
❏ Online retailer   ❏ Direct from Cisco Press   ❏ Office supply store
❏ Mail order   ❏ Class/Seminar   ❏ Discount store
❏ Other_____

When did you buy this product? _____ **Month** _____ **Year**

What price did you pay for this product?

❏ Full retail price   ❏ Discounted price   ❏ Gift

Was this purchase reimbursed as a company expense?

❏ Yes   ❏ No

How did you learn about this product?

❏ Friend   ❏ Store personnel   ❏ In-store ad   ❏ cisco.com
❏ Cisco Press catalog   ❏ Postcard in the mail   ❏ Saw it on the shelf ❏ ciscopress.com
❏ Other catalog   ❏ Magazine ad   ❏ Article or review
❏ School   ❏ Professional organization ❏ Used other products
❏ Other_____

What will this product be used for?

❏ Business use   ❏ School/Education
❏ Certification training ❏ Professional development/Career growth
❏ Other_____

How many years have you been employed in a computer-related industry?

❏ less than 2 years   ❏ 2–5 years   ❏ more than 5 years

Have you purchased a Cisco Press product before?

❏ Yes   ❏ No

CISCO SYSTEMS

Cisco Press

ciscopress.com

How many computer technology books do you own?
❏ 1 ❏ 2–7 ❏ more than 7

Which best describes your job function? (check all that apply)
❏ Corporate Management ❏ Systems Engineering ❏ IS Management ❏ Cisco Networking
❏ Network Design ❏ Network Support ❏ Webmaster   Academy Program
❏ Marketing/Sales ❏ Consultant ❏ Student   Instuctor
❏ Professor/Teacher ❏ Other _____

Do you hold any computer certifications? (check all that apply)
❏ MCSE ❏ CCNA ❏ CCDA
❏ CCNP ❏ CCDP ❏ CCIE ❏ Other _____

Are you currently pursuing a certification? (check all that apply)
❏ MCSE ❏ CCNA ❏ CCDA
❏ CCNP ❏ CCDP ❏ CCIE ❏ Other _____

On what topics would you like to see more coverage?
_____
_____

Do you have any additional comments or suggestions?
_____
_____

Thank you for completing this survey and registration. Please fold here, seal, and mail to Cisco Press.

CCIE Fundamentals: Network Design & Case Studies, Second Edition   1-57870-167-8